The Modern RPG IV Language
Third Edition

Robert Cozzi, Jr.

MC PRESS

Third Edition
First Printing—March 2003

First edition published May 1996 by Midrange Computing. Based on *The Modern RPG Language with Structured Programming* © 1987 by Robert Cozzi, Jr.

MC Press Online, LP
125 N. Woodland
Double Oak, TX 75077
www.mcpressonline.com

V5R2

To my family, for their support and dedication,
and to my two first-borns; Officer Chrissy and little Jaden.

ACKNOWLEDGMENTS

Several people, without whom this book may never have been finished, gave me their time, effort, and encouragement.

First and foremost, my girls, Christine Anne, Theresa Anne, Anne Katherine, and Jacqueline Caroline, for whom I have reason to live, work, and play.

To my mother and father, thank you for your spirit and support. To Alan and John, thanks for helping in my search for the unknown. A special thanks to my sister Carole; thank you for helping out at all the right moments.

Several individuals helped put this book together. I am forever in their debt. In previous editions, Jon Paris and George Farr have been an invaluable source of information and support. In this edition, Jon Paris provided the path that allowed me to interface RPG IV with the C language. This capability makes RPG IV as powerful as any other language.

In addition, I'd like to thank *you*, the RPG programmer. Since 1988, this book has been the best-selling RPG book ever printed. While I strive to achieve better quality with each new edition, your feedback and support has been the reason I have been so encouraged to maintain and improve this book. Thank you for your continued support.

Finally, a warm thanks to Sensi Ben Wasman, a good friend and teacher who helped me learn balance and who pushed me to start writing the original edition of this book.

Contents

PREFACE

In 1974, at the request of my father who had a friend in the computer industry since the early 1960s, I signed up for an introduction-to-computer-programming course. The first semester of the course was spent discussing the financial benefits of being in the computer industry over other types of business. I debated with the instructor quite often, arguing that money isn't everything and that becoming an astronaut was what I really wanted to do.

Needless to say, the instructor felt I was unqualified to attend the second semester (this was high school after all). However, after six months of negotiating with the instructor (I think my mother called him), I attended the course during the second semester of the next school year.

In that course, I was exposed to the syntax of COBOL. It looked simple, similar to English, but then again, maybe not.

I spent hours, days, even weeks carefully drawing flowcharts and diagrams as well as keypunching COBOL statements into 80-column punch cards on an IBM 029 keypunch machine. It wasn't the best way to do homework, but it was the only way we had.

Even back then, everyone was required to backup their programs. The only way for a student to backup a program (since no disk space was allocated for student use) was to use the *duplicator* to punch a second set of 80-column punch cards. Carrying all that paper meant toting your homework around in a wheelbarrow. (I think COBOL programs, punched onto 80-column cards, are what started deforestation.) Imagine the frustration I had the day I spilled my 1000-line COBOL program made up of those 80-column cards!

In college, in late 1976, I signed up for two computer-language classes, "FORTRAN IV with WATFOR and WATFIV," and "RPG with RPG II for S/370 and S/3." The FORTRAN class was the most interesting—scientific formulas, mathematical expression, subprograms, and brevity—a pleasant change from COBOL. On the other hand, I considered the RPG class to be an "it's-a-language-so-I'll-take-it" experience. After all, by knowing FORTRAN and COBOL, I was set for life.

Shortly after classes began, I took a job as a Computer Operator working with the IBM System/32. I was awed that, unlike my college courses, businesses could actually run programs without compiling them each time. "What power!" I thought naively. Because the

IBM System/32 used RPG as its primary language, I figured that RPG must be *the* greatest language to use for business programs. I began reading the System/32 RPG II reference manual.

From my FORTRAN and COBOL background, I quickly recognized the perform subroutine (EXSR) operation and used it for all of the assignments in my college course. When I turned in one of my assignments, it included a single "main-line" calculation—the EXSR operation—and the remainder of the program was written with subroutines and the now passé RPG cycle. My self-indulged modular programming style seemed to baffle the instructor. As he pointed to the EXSR operation, the instructor's first question was, "What's that?" followed by, "Why did you use it?"

That day I learned that people who are authorities or who are perceived to be authorities on various subjects often know far less than we think they do. If someone is considered an authority or expert, it simply means they are a person who:

a) Has practiced the subject or profession long enough for others in the profession to notice.

b) Is willing to act as a cornerstone for building and sharing knowledge on the subject.

It doesn't mean they know everything about the subject.

Textbooks contain the knowledge of an individual or group of individuals (authors) on a specific subject. Textbooks can assist in the act of gathering knowledge by presenting the collective knowledge of others. The art of learning is up to you.

THE EVOLUTION OF RPG

In 1960, someone had the inspiration to develop a computer programming language that would replace the manually wired jumper boards of an IBM 1400 business machine. The jumper boards were position-oriented. The designers of this new language used these wired jumper boards as an element in designing the language. The resulted was the *Report Program Generator* (RPG) language.

In 1964, RPG was upgraded to a more usable language. This improvement coincided with the announcement of the IBM 360 model 20. While RPG did a fine job of handling 80-column cards, it couldn't handle tape or disk processing, not to mention display devices—which were just being introduced.

The RPG cycle (the processes during which an RPG program automatically reads a record and performs certain routines) was at the heart of file processing. Unlike other high-level languages, RPG didn't require extensive file declarations for opening and closing files, nor did it require a complex list of instructions to simply print data. The RPG cycle handled these tasks automatically.

In 1969, RPG II, along with a new mini-computer called the IBM System/3, was announced. RPG II had all the features of the original RPG, plus disk processing. In the 1970s limited support for workstation devices (i.e., dumb terminals) was added for System/3 workstation display devices and the newly available System/34 computer.

In 1978, RPG III was announced for a new mini-computer, the IBM System/38. The System/38 was a replacement for the IBM System/3, and was built in case the U.S. Government broke IBM into separate companies. The System/38 would have been the flagship system for the new mid-sized computer system company. Of course the antitrust suit ended and, as we all know, IBM stayed as one company.

The System/38 was the most advanced general-purpose computer of its day. It was the first with a built-in relational database management system. RPG III added a host of new functions beyond RPG and RPG II, among them a nearly complete set of structured programming operations (e.g., IF-THEN-ELSE, DO). With these new features, the benefit of the RPG cycle grew thin. Today, the RPG cycle exists more for compatibility with older systems. The use of the cycle typically is avoided because of structured and modular programming practices.

In 1985, RPG III was enhanced to include support for and/or logic within IF and DO operations. This support greatly enhanced program readability and greatly decreased programmer frustration levels and RPG II became a well entrenched, mainstream programming language.

In 1988, the IBM AS/400 was announced and with it a new compiler called the *AS/400 RPG/400 compiler*. That RPG/400 compiler supports four versions of the RPG language:

1. System/38-compatible RPG III.
2. System/36-compatible RPG II.
3. SAA RPG Level 1.
4. AS/400-compatible RPG III.

By late 1989, IBM quietly dropped the SAA concept, including SAA RPG.

In 1995, IBM introduced the first significant update to the RPG language in over 15 years—RPG IV. RPG IV marked the first time the RPG specifications have changed significantly. RPG IV has eliminated virtually all the limitations of previous versions of RPG. With RPG IV, IBM has added natural expressions, long field names, more data types, including native date and time data type fields, and subprocedures. In addition, the RPG programmer now has a choice which type of syntax they prefer. The traditional fixed-format syntax with Factor 1, Factor 2, and a Result field and operation code, or a new syntax that is similar to, but still slightly different from many other programming languages, such as PL/I and C.

The latest version of RPG is, by far, the best ever. It is easier to learn and offers a rich set of functions for day-to-day, general-purpose business applications.

WHO SHOULD READ THIS BOOK

This text provides the person who has some programming experience with a high-level language, such as PL/I, COBOL, FORTRAN, or any version of RPG, with a comprehensive explanation of the modern RPG IV language.The concepts and terminology are directed at persons with moderate to advanced exposure to the information-technology world.

WHICH VERSION OF RPG IS COVERED

The RPG language described in this text is the same language implemented by the IBM Corporation on IBM computers running the OS/400 operating system (such as the AS/400 and eServer iSeries). The language syntax illustrated is that of RPG IV compatible with OS/400 Version 5, Release 2 and earlier along with any confirmed and planned enhancements beyond that release known at the time of this printing. A subset of this language is also available on other operating systems.

This text discusses only RPG IV implementations of the RPG language. The RPG cycle is no longer considered a productive method for programming. The modern RPG programmer avoids using the RPG cycle. In its place, structured programming constructs are used. Therefore the RPG Cycle, while still included for completeness, is covered only briefly in Chapter 3.

The example code in this book illustrates certain techniques such as how to specify an array in RPG IV. The example segments of source code are not intended to be compiled, but are to illustrate how readers can write similar routines for their own programs.

If you have questions or comments about RPG IV, please visit my RPG IV Web site at: www.rpgiv.com. You'll find example source code, articles, and other information about the RPG IV language.

NAMES ARE IMPORTANT

There has been much confusion in the OS/400 world regarding the proper name of the RPG programming language. This is primarily due to many IBM support personnel as well as the trade press mistakenly reporting the name of RPG III as RPG/400. There is not now, nor has there ever been, a programming language named "RPG/400."

The current AS/400 and iSeries RPG compile package offered by the IBM Corporation is named *ILE RPG/400*. This package contains several compilers for many different RPG languages, including:

- System/36-compatible RPG II.
- System/38-compatible RPG III.
- AS/400 and iSeries RPG III. There is no "RPG/400" language per se (only AS/400 RPG III).
- AS/400 and iSeries RPG IV. This compiler targets the native *integrated programming language environment* (ILE). There is no "ILE RPG" language, only an ILE-targeted RPG IV compiler.

Chapter 1

INTRODUCTION

RPG is both a position-oriented and free-format language. This means that certain information, such as control codes and field names, must be placed into specific positions of the RPG program statements. Failure to fulfill this obligation results in an error message. The free-format component of RPG IV is supported in the procedure area (known as the *calculation specifications*) and to a lesser extent in data definition.

In a free-form procedure language such as COBOL, the value of one variable (or "field") can be copied to another by specifying the following statement:

```
MOVE  FIELDA  TO  FIELDB
```

Most high-level languages use the MOVE instruction to copy data. There is no documentation as to how this tradition started, but it's taken for granted now. The preceding COBOL statement copies each character from the memory location of the first field, FIELDA, to the memory location of the second field, FIELDB.

The same program statement written in C or C++ might look like this:

```
strcpy(fieldb,fielda);
```

In traditional RPG programs, the same program statement looks like this:

```
*... ... 1 ... ... 2 ... ... 3 ... ... 4 ... ... 5 ... ... 6
   C                    MOVE      FieldA        FieldB
```

Using free-format RPG IV commands, the same program statement could look like this:

```
*... ... 1 ... ... 2 ... ... 3 ... ... 4 ... ... 5 ... ... 6
   C                    Eval      FieldB = FieldA
```

The two forms of RPG IV statements shown above are referred to as *fixed format* and *free format*. The field being copied (FIELDA) is referred to as the *source field*. The field that receives the data is referred to as the *target* or *result field*.

The MOVE and EVAL instructions appear in positions 26 through 35. These positions contain the program instruction or *operation code*. The operation code is commonly referred to as *operation* or *opcode*.

The letter "C" must appear in position 6 of RPG "Calculation" statements. Different letters are used to identify the various types of program statements (or *specifications*). The available specifications are:

- Header specification.
- File specifications.
- Definition specifications.
- Input specifications.
- Calculation specifications.
- Output specifications.
- Procedure specifications.

Ordinarily, an editor is available that provides prompting for "fill-in-the-blank" coding of the different RPG specifications. Consequently, programmers need not be concerned with remembering specific positions. However, a thorough knowledge of the various specification types and their layout will greatly improve programmer efficiency.

Another example of the position-oriented structure of RPG follows. Suppose three account totals need to be accumulated. In a free-format procedure language such as PL/I, the program statements look like the source code shown in Figure 1.1.

```
IF ACCT = '01' THEN
               TOTAL1 = TOTAL1 + AMOUNT;
ELSE IF ACCT = '02' THEN
               TOTAL2 = TOTAL2 + AMOUNT;
ELSE IF ACCT = '03' THEN
               TOTAL3 = TOTAL3 + AMOUNT;
```

Figure 1.1: PL/I example.

In traditional RPG, the equivalent program looks like the code shown in Figure 1.2.

```
*... ... 1 ... ... 2 ... ... 3 ... ... 4 ... ... 5 ... ... 6
    C               IF        Acct = '01'
    C               ADD       AMOUNT        TOTAL1
    C               ELSE
    C               IF        Acct = '02'
    C               ADD       AMOUNT        TOTAL2
    C               ELSE
    C               IF        Acct = '03'
    C               ADD       AMOUNT        TOTAL3

    C               ENDIF
    C               ENDIF
    C               ENDIF
```

Figure 1.2: RPG code example.

In this example, the IF operation is used to compare the field ACCT to three numbers, and then the value of the field AMOUNT is added to one of three total fields.

RPG requires an associated ENDIF operation for each IF operation. This is because IF operations are treated as an IF THEN DO structure. This allows several statements to be conditioned and performed for each IF operation. As a by-product, the program's complexity is reduced. However, when IF statements are nested too deeply (usually more than three levels deep) the program's readability is reduced. Readability can be improved greatly, however, through the use of an in-line case structure. RPG support two forms of in-line case. The first is the SELECT-WHEN operations. The source code shown in Figure 1.2—rewritten using the SELECT-WHEN operations—is illustrated in Figure 1.3a.

```
*... ... 1 ... ... 2 ... ... 3 ... ... 4 ... ... 5 ... ... 6
    C                   Select
    C                   When        Acct = '01'
    C                   Add         Amount          Total1
    C                   When        Acct = '02'
    C                   Add         Amount          Total2
    C                   When        Acct = '03'
    C                   Add         Amount          Total3
    C                   EndSL
```

Figure 1.3a: An RPG code example using the SELECT-WHEN operations.

The second form of in-line case is the IF statement itself. However, later versions of RPG include a new ELSEIF operation that eliminates the need for multiple ENDIF statements. The source code shown in Figure 1.2—rewritten using the SELECT-WHEN operations—is illustrated in Figure 1.3b.

```
*... ... 1 ... ... 2 ... ... 3 ... ... 4 ... ... 5 ... ... 6
    C                   IF          Acct = '01'
    C                   Add         Amount          Total1
    C                   elseif      Acct = '02'
    C                   Add         Amount          Total2
    C                   elseif      Acct = '03'
    C                   Add         Amount          Total3
    C                   EndIf
```

Figure 1.3b: An RPG code example using the IF/ELSEIF in-line case.

The primary difference between these three examples is readability. The SELECT-WHEN requires only one ENDSL statement for the entire case group. The IF/ELSEIF style also requires only one ENDxx statement. The SELECT-WHEN operations are available on all versions of RPG whereas the IF/ELSEIF option (Figure 1.3b) is only available on later releases of RPG.

POSITION-ORIENTED PROGRAM SPECIFICATIONS

To simplify writing RPG programs, various preprinted specification forms are available. These forms allow an application program to be written while making certain the correct positions are used. The source statements that make up an application program are transferred to the computer for compilation. This process, known as *desk coding*, was very popular before the onslaught of desktop personal computers, with their full-screen editors, as well as the full-screen editor available with the OS/400 operating system.

Very little desk coding is done any longer. Programmers usually write *pseudocode* (a free-format, English-like, logic-based language that is not compiled). The pseudocode is translated, by hand, into a high-level language. Pseudocode strongly resembles PL/I. When translating pseudocode into a high-level language, such as RPG, a full-screen editor or integrated development environment (IDE) is used to provide a more productive environment with fewer typing errors. This can result in fewer errors being placed into the source program.

Several full-screen editors are available to the RPG programmer, including CodeStudio, a GUI Microsoft Windows-based IDE for RPG and DDS; SEU, the source editor that comes with OS/400; and the GUI-based IDE offered by IBM. These source-code editors provide prompts that allow RPG program statements to be written easily. The editors correctly format the program statement to match the RPG specification.

A programmer with experience writing RPG programs using 80-position cards on an IBM 029 or 129 keypunch machine will appreciate using an online, full-screen editor or IDE that checks the syntax of statements as they are entered. A novice programmer typically makes a few mistakes anyway and will benefit from the assistance of these RPG editors offer.

A BRIEF LANGUAGE

One of the first things anyone should learn about RPG is that it is a brief language. Only a few statements are needed to read a record, change the data in that record, and then update the record. With other languages, such as COBOL, dozens of lines of code are required to perform this process.

Languages such as the C language are often thought to be brief. Actually, RPG is the briefest of all higher-level languages. For example, to read a file containing orders, multiply the quantity ordered by the price, and update the file with the new information, only four RPG statements are required. See Figure 1.4.

```
*... ... 1 ... ... 2 ... ... 3 ... ... 4 ... ... 5 ... ... 6 ... ... 7
0010 FORDERS    UPE  E               DISK
0020 C                      Eval     AmtDue = QtyOrd * Price
0030 OORDRCD    D    N1P
0040 O                          AmtDue
```

Figure 1.4: Read a file, calculate price, and update file.

On line 10 of the example shown in Figure 1.4, the file ORDERS is defined as the primary file (indicated with the letter "P" in position 18). The file is declared as an update file (indicated with the letter "U" in position 17). The records that are read are modified on line 20 by multiplying the quantity ordered by the price, giving the amount due. Each record is automatically updated (i.e., rewritten with the new value) on lines 30 and 40 by the RPG cycle. (Line 30 contains the name of the record format for the file ORDERS; line 40 contains the name of the fields that are updated.)

As demonstrated in Figure 1.4, RPG can be one of the fastest programming languages with which to write. Once a programmer has learned the essentials, and adding in the benefit of prompting source code using an IDE or editor, the RPG language can be the easiest language to use and the most productive for general-purpose business applications.

SPECIFICATION TYPES

RPG programs consist of statement specifications. Specifications provide the layout of each area of the RPG program. For example, the calculation specification defines where each component of a calculation statement belongs. The most common specifications include those listed in Table 1.1.

Table 1.1: RPG IV Specifications		
Specification Type	**Identification**	**Common Name**
Control	H in position 6	Header spec or H-spec
File	F in position 6	File specs or F-specs
Definition	D in position 6	Definition specs or D-specs
Input	I in position 6	Input specs or I-specs
Calculation	C in position 6	Calc specs or C-specs
Output	O in position 6	Output specs or O-specs
Procedure	P in position 6	P-specs

Although no single specification is required by every program, when more than one type is used (as is normally the case in RPG programs), the specifications must appear in a specific sequence. The exception is the procedure specification. The procedure specification defines the beginning and end of a subprocedure—a kind of subroutine or subprogram in RPG. Table 1.2 lists all the RPG specifications and the correct sequence.

The calculation specification and the alternate calculation specification can be intermixed without regard for one another. The RPG compiler determines which calculation specification is being used by inspecting the operation code. Table 1.3 lists descriptions of each RPG IV specification. For more information on each specification form, see chapter 2.

Table 1.2: RPG Specification Sequence
Header specification
File specifications
Definition specification
Input specifications
Calculation specifications
Alternate calculation specification
Output specifications
Procedure specification
**FTRANS
File translation table
**ALTSEQ
Alternate collating sequence
**CTDATA
Compile-time array data
End-procedure specification

Table 1.3: Specification Description	
Position 6	**Description**
H	Header specification. This specification is used to establish the default behavior of the program. For example, the format of date and time variables and of compiler options is specified here. In addition, the compiler's parameters and options may be specified on the Header specification.
F	File specification. This specification is used to define each input and output device file to the program. The type of device on which the file is or will be located (e.g., DISK, PRINTER, or WORKSTN) and the type of access that is required (e.g., input, output, update, or delete) are among the items defined by the F specification.
D	Definition specification. This specification is used to declare the data used in the program. Data structures, stand-alone fields, arrays, tables, named constants, and pointer variables are among the items declared with the Definition specification.
I	Input specification. This specification describes input file record formats—input field locations.
C	Calculation specification. This specification describes the calculations (computations) that are to be performed. The order in which, and the conditions under which, the calculations are to be performed is also specified here. This is where the actual work of the program is performed.
O	Output specification. This specification describes the output file record formats, output field locations, and printer-file control (i.e., spacing and skipping).
P	Procedure specification. This specification is used to declare a subprocedure within an RPG source program. A subprocedure is used to create functions (similar to built-in functions) or bound procedures.

RPG COMPONENTS

Every RPG program is made up of components. Each component is defined through one or more RPG specification. A description of some of the components follows.

- **Files**. The names of files that will be accessed by the RPG program.

- **Input**. The information read and processed by the program.

- **Fields, Arrays, Data Structures, and Named Constants**. The names of the variables—referred to as "fields" in the RPG language—and constants, that are used to store, compare, and process information within the program.

- **Labels**. The names assigned with BEGSR, ENDSR, KLIST, PLIST, EXCEPT, and TAG identifiers. They are used to label subroutines, access data files, declare parameter and key lists, control output, and act as the target of a GOTO, respectively.

- **Calculations**. The computations (e.g., math, field manipulation, decisions, and array searching) performed on the information within the program.

- **Output**. The results of the program. The processed data is written to a printer, written or rewritten (updated) to a data file, or presented to a user through a workstation device.

- **Procedures**. The portions of code that are called to perform a specific task and often to return a value to the caller.

RPG LIMITATIONS

Like all high-level languages, RPG has a set of restrictions. RPG IV has fewer limitations than previous versions of RPG. The features listed in Table 1.4 document any significant RPG language restrictions, along with several previous limitations that have been removed in RPG IV. These are marked "No limit."

Table 1.4: RPG IV Limitations

Feature	Limit
AN/OR (positions 7 to 8 of Calc spec)	No limit
Array elements	32,767 per array/table
Arrays and tables	No limit
Compile-time array or table length	100 positions
Data structure length	65,535 positions for named data structures 9,999,999 for unnamed data structures
Data structure occurrences	32,767 per data structure
Edit word length	Literal: 24 positions Named Const: 115 positions
Field length	Char: 65,535 positions; Numeric: (31, 30)
Field name	4,096 characters
Files (open files per program)	No limit (actually 32767)
File key length	2,000 positions
Lines per page (program-described)	Minimum of 2; maximum of 255
Lines per page (externally described)	Minimum of 1; maximum of 255
Matched fields (combined length)	256 positions
Named constants	Char: 1024 positions; Numeric: (31, 30)
Nested IF, DOxxx, SELECT, FOR groups	100 levels
Parameters	255 program to program; 399 to procedures
Primary files	1 per program
Printer files	No limit (8 standard overflow indicators available)
Program Status Data Structure	1 per program
Record address files (ADDROUT)	1 per program
Record format length	99,999 positions (system limit is)
Spacing and skipping printed output	0 to 255 lines
Subroutines	32,767 per program

NAMING CONVENTIONS

As with other computer languages, RPG has standard naming conventions. Table 1.5 lists the criteria for each named component of an RPG program. Unless otherwise noted, all names must be unique. For example, the name of a data structure cannot be the same as that of an array.

Table 1.5: Naming Conventions	
Name	Naming Convention
All Names	The first character must be A to Z (or a to z), @, #, or $. Subsequent characters can be A to Z (or a to z), @, #, $, 0 to 9, or the underscore (_) character. Letter case is not significant. If @, #, or $ is used as the first character of a name, at least one other character must be specified. No embedded blanks or periods are allowed. Array names can be suffixed with an array index. All names are global to all areas of the RPG IV program unless modules or subprocedures are used. When modules or subprocedures are used, names can be declared local to a module.
File	A file name cannot be the same as a (record) format name.
Format	A (record) format name must be 1 to 10 characters in length. Format names cannot be the same as that of a file name.
Field	A field name must be 1 to 4096 characters in length. Field names may be the same as a data structure or data structure subfield name, but not both.
Structure	A structure name, referred to as a data structure in RPG, can be the same as that of an input file's field name. It can be manipulated the same as any other variable, and can be specified as a parameter of a CALLx operation.
Qualified Name	A qualified name is a data structure subfield name qualified to (i.e., attached to) its parent data structure name. Qualified names are created by specifying the data structure name followed by a period, followed by the data structure subfield name. For example: MyDS.CustName Qualified names are created when the QUALIFIED or LIKEDS keywords are used to declare a data structure.
Array Index	An array index name must represent a numeric field that contains zero decimal places or it can be an expression. The array index can be a field of type packed, signed, integer, or binary. Although binary and integer are the most efficient, packed decimal is most commonly used. Array indexes are identified using parentheses. For example, MyArray(x) indicates that array index x is used with the array name MyArray.
Label	A label is the target of a branch or GOTO operation. A label is defined with either the TAG or ENDSR operation.
Named Constant	A named constant is used to assign a name to a literal value. This name can be used repeatedly throughout the program.

DATA TYPES

RPG supports a wide variety of *data types* such as character, numeric, packed decimal, pointer, date, and time. Data types are used to declare field and array element attributes. This attribute is specified in the data-type position of the definition specification or it is inferred by the compiler when a variable is defined on the calculation specification. Table 1.6 lists the available data types supported by RPG.

Table 1.6: Data Types			
Field Data Type	**Data Type**	**Size/Extent**	**Description**
Character	A or blank	1 to 65,535	Character.
Date	D	6, 8, or 10 bytes	Date. See also: Time, Timestamp.
Float	F	4 or 8 bytes	Double precision floating point.
Graphic (DBCS)	G	32,766	Double-byte character set — Graphic Data or UCS-2.
Integer[1]	I	1, 2, 4, or 8 bytes	Integer. See also: Unsigned Integer 3i0=1 byte, 5i0=2 bytes, 10i0=4 bytes, 20i0=8 bytes.
Left Signed[2]	L	1 to 31	Signed numeric with sign on left side.
Indicator	N	1	Named indicator variable.
Packed	P	1 to 31	Packed decimal.
Pointer	*	16 bytes	Pointer. See also: PROCPTR keyword in Chapter 2.
Right Signed	R	1 to 31	Signed numeric with sign on right side.
RPG Binary	B	2 or 4	RPG "Binary": four or nine digits of accuracy.
Signed	S or blank	1 to 31	Signed numeric with integrated sign.
Time	T	8	Time. See also: Date, Timestamp.
Timestamp	Z	26	Date/Timestamp. See also: Date, Time.
Unsigned Integer	U	1, 2, 4, or 8 bytes	Unsigned integer. See also: Integer.

[1] The INTEGER and UNSIGNED INTEGER data types can be used in place of the binary fields.

[2] Left- and right-signed numeric data-types are typically not used in RPG III and RPG IV.

INDICATORS

Indicators are logical variables or *switches* that are either on or off; that is, they contain a value of 1 or 0. Indicators are used to control program logic, program termination, output, signal conditions, and to communicate with device files.

For example, when an indicator is used to condition the ADD operation, the indicator is tested before the ADD operation is performed. If the indicator test is true, the ADD operation is performed. If the indicator test is false, the ADD operation is bypassed and the program goes to the next statement. Figure 1.5 shows an example.

```
.....CSRnØ1Factor1+++++++OpCode(ex)Factor2+++++++Result++++++++Len++DcHiLoEq....
     C     AREA          COMP       '14Ø1'                                38
     C  38               ADD        1ØØ            COST
     C     SALES         SUB        COST           PROFIT
```

Figure 1.5: Example of indicator usage.

Logically, this program is illustrated as shown in Figure 1.6.

```
        Clear Indicator(38)
        If AREA = '14Ø1' Set On Indicator(38)

Test1:  If Indicator(38) is OFF, Goto EndTest1;

        Add 1ØØ to COST;

EndTest1:
        Subtract COST from SALES giving PROFIT;
```

Figure 1.6: Logic of the program code shown in Figure 1.5.

In early versions of RPG (RPG and RPG II), structured programming constructs did not exist. Consequently, the indicator usage proliferated. However, the modern RPG programmer avoids the use of indicators except where it is impossible to ignore them (such as in accessing files). In place of indicators, structured operations are used to control program logic. Today, the use of the numeric indicators is all but eliminated.

Indicatorless RPG Code

The example code shown in Figure 1.5, if rewritten with structured RPG operations, would appear as shown in Figure 1.7.

```
.....CSRnØ1Factor1+++++++OpCode(ex)Factor2+++++++Result++++++++Len++DcHiLoEq
     C                   IF         Area = '14Ø1'
     C                   Add        100            Cost
     C                   EndIF
     C                   Eval       Profit = Sales - Cost
```

Figure 1.7: Rewriting code without indicators.

In pseudocode, the program (Figure 1.7) is illustrated by Figure 1.8.

```
        If AREA = '14Ø1' Then
                Add 1ØØ to COST;
        EndIf
        Subtract COST from SALES giving PROFIT;
```

Figure 1.8: Pseudocode for Figure 1.7.

Notice how concise and readable the program becomes when structured operations are used properly. A side effect of the use of structured operations is that programs tend to run more efficiently than they do when indicators control the logic. This is a by-product of the OS/400 RPG compilers and not inherent of compilers in general. Table 1.7 lists definitions of the various types of indicators supported by RPG.

Table 1.7: Indicator Definitions	
Indicator	**Description**
1P	First Page Indicator. This indicator is set on as part of the "first time through" routine and is set off just prior to the first detail time routine. It is traditionally used to print a forms alignment character.
01 to 99	General Purpose Indicators. Used for various tasks.
H1 to H9	Halt Indicators. These indicators are used to signal a severe error. When a halt indicator is set on and the program ends, an "abnormal termination" message is issued.
KA to KY	Function Key Indicators. These indicators correspond to 24 function keys on most keyboards. KA to KN represent keys F1 to F14 respectively. KP to KY represent keys F15 to F24 respectively. Avoid the use of these indicators. If possible, use the Attention Identification Byte. See Table 1.8.

Table 1.7: Indicator Definitions, *continued*	
Indicator	**Description**
L1 to L9	Level-Break Indicators. These indicators are used in conjunction with the RPG cycle. They are set on when the value of their corresponding input field changes when a record is read via the RPG cycle.
L0	Level Zero Indicator. This indicator is, by definition, always on and, therefore, never tested at runtime. It is occasionally used during the "total-time" phase of the RPG cycle.
LR	Last Record Indicator. When this indicator is set on, and the end of program is caused by the return operation or the end of cycle, the program terminates, and its storage is released. If LR is off and the program ends, the program's storage is saved, and the program is still considered to be active. If the program is actually a module or a larger program, certain resources are not released.
M1 to M9	Match Field Identifiers. These identifiers are not indicators. They are flags used to control the sequencing of primary/secondary file processing, and to signal a matching record condition (which sets on the MR indicator). Matching record processing is part of the RPG cycle.
MR	Matching Record Indicator. This indicator is set on when all the match fields of a secondary file match all the match fields of the primary file. This function is part of the RPG cycle.
OA to OG, and OV	Overflow Indicators. These indicators are normally associated with a specific printer file. They are set on when printed output reaches the designated overflow line (normally line 60 for a 66-line form or line 80 for an 88-line form).
RT	Return Indicator. When this indicator is set on, the RPG program returns to its caller, but remains active (provided that indicator LR is off). This occurs after the ending calculation specification is reached (i.e., the end of this RPG cycle) or the RETURN operation is performed.
U1 to U8	External User Indicators. These indicators, or switches, are used to communicate between the RPG program and the external operating environment. They can be used to condition the opening of a file or to control calculations.
User-defined	Named indicators. These indicators are programmer specified names that have a data-type of N (named indicator). They may be used similar to any of the original 99 indicators and, along with the INDDS (indicator data structure) may overlay those original indicators when communicating with a device file.

INDICATOR USAGE

Indicators were used extensively in early RPG programming to control program logic, identify input, condition output, detect errors, and signal certain "events." Due to support for structured programming constructs, extensive use of indicators is no longer an endorsed programming practice. However, many hundreds of thousands, or perhaps even millions, of

RPG application programs have been written. This represents nearly 1 billion lines of RPG code. A large percentage of that code was written prior to structured constructs being added to RPG. These programs have to be maintained. When maintaining these applications, try to convert as much of the application as possible to structured programming. Often, this can be accomplished without affecting the program's overall design.

Nowadays, a typical application program uses fewer than four indicators, unless communicating with a device file necessitates using more. The recommendations for each of the four indicators follow:

- **"Trash" Indicator.** The "trash" indicator is used for just about anything. For example, it can be used to condition the ENDDO statement of a DO...ENDDO loop construct or to indicate the result of various operations such as LOOKUP, COMP, SCAN, TEST, MULT, and DIV.

- **Error Indicator.** The error indicator is used to signal error conditions such as record locking, device file time-out, or other errors.

- **File Status Indicator.** The file status indicator is used to signal various file conditions such as record not found, end of file, or beginning of file. In some cases, such as with small programs, the indicator used as the file indicator also can be used as the error indicator.

- **Program Termination Indicator.** Normally, the last record indicator (LR) or the return indicator (RT) is used as the program termination indicator. LR signals that the program should terminate upon reaching the end of calculation specifications or when the return (RETURN) operation is performed. RT, when used independently, signals that the program should end, but remain active in memory at the completion of the calculation specifications.

When communicating with a workstation, printer, or telecommunications *device file*, the number of indicators being used can increase. This is primarily due to limitations in the technology being used for device-file definition. Also, each function key (i.e., special keys on every keyboard that normally cause an immediate reaction by the program) can result in the use of an additional indicator.

FUNCTION KEY ATTENTION IDENTIFICATION BYTE

An alternative to assigning function-key response indicators is being used more frequently in RPG applications. This method avoids indicator assignment and uses the function key *attention identification byte* (located in position 369 of the workstation information data structure) to identify which function key has been pressed. Table 1.8 illustrates how this byte can be interpreted.

Table 1.8: Attention Identification Byte			
Function Key	Value in Hex	Function Key	Value in Hex
F1	X'31'	F17	X'B5'
F2	X'32'	F18	X'B6'
F3	X'33'	F19	X'B7'
F4	X'34'	F20	X'B8'
F5	X'35'	F21	X'B9'
F6	X'36'	F22	X'BA'
F7	X'37'	F23	X'BB'
F8	X'38'	F24	X'BC'
F9	X'39'	CLEAR	X'BD'
F10	X'3A'	ENTER	X'F1'
F11	X'3B'	HELP	X'F3'
F12	X'3C'	Roll Down	X'F4'
F13	X'B1'	Roll Up	X'F5'
F14	X'B2'	Print	X'F6'
F15	X'B3'	Rec'd Bksp	X'F8'
F16	X'B4'	Auto Enter	X'3F'

Figure 1.9 illustrates the use of the attention identification byte (also referred to as the "scan code") in RPG.

```
.....FFilename++IPEASFRlen+LKlen+AIDevice+.Functions++++++++++++++++++++++++++++
     FDSPFILE    CF   E               WORKSTN INFDS(wsds)

.....DName+++++++++++ETDsFrom+++To/L+++IDc.Functions++++++++++++++++++++++++++++
     D WSDS              DS
     D  Fkey                   369     369A

     D  F3                C                       Const(X'33')

.....CSRnØ1Factor1+++++++OpCode(ex)Factor2+++++++Result++++++++Len++DcHiLoEq....
     C                    Dow       FKey   F3
     C                    EXFMT     ShowData

     C                    If        FKey = F3
     C                    Eval      *INLR = *ON
     C                    leave
     C                    endIf
     C* ... program continues...
     C                    endDo
```

Figure 1.9: Example of the attention-identification byte.

INDICATOR CLASSIFICATION

Depending on the type of RPG specifications being used, indicators have various definitions. A list of the indicator classifications and definitions follows.

Overflow Indicator. An indicator that is specified as an overflow indicator (i.e., the OFLIND keyword on the file specification for a printer device file) is set on automatically when the overflow line for a printer file is printed. The overflow line is identified by the FORMOFL keyword on the file specification.

Record-Identifying Indicator. The record-identifying indicator is an indicator specified for the record identification position of the input record specification. RPG automatically sets on a record-identifying indicator when a record is read that matches the record type for the record-identifying indicator.

Level-Break and Control-Level Indicator. An indicator that is specified in positions 63 and 64 of the input specification is called a level-break indicator. In addition, an indicator specified in positions 7 and 8 of the calculation specification is called a control-level indicator. A special set of nine indicators is reserved for level breaks; they are L1 through L9.

A control-level or level-break indicator is set on automatically by the RPG cycle when the cycle reads a record and the value of the field that is associated with the level-break indicator changes. If the RPG cycle is avoided—as is normally the case with new application programs—and the READ and CHAIN op codes are used to access data files, level-break indicators are not changed and become less useful.

Field Record-Relation Indicator. An indicator specified in positions 67 to 68 of the input specifications is called a field-record relation indicator. A field-record relation indicator associates an input field with a specific input record format. For example, when a file contains several record-identifying indicators, the fields within the record are associated with the record format containing the record-identifying indicator. RPG initializes the field only when its corresponding record-identifying indicator is on.

Field Indicator. An indicator specified in positions 69 and 70, 71 and 72, and 73 and 74 of the input specification is called a field indicator. A field indicator is set on or off automatically by RPG when a record is read. A numeric field can be assigned all three field indicators, and a character field can be assigned only one indicator (the "blank or zero" indicator in positions 72 and 73). The field indicator in positions 69 and 70 is set on if the numeric field to which it is assigned is greater than zero. The field indicator in positions 71 and 72 is set on if the numeric field to which it is assigned is less than zero. The field indicator in positions 73 and 74 is set on if the numeric field to which it is assigned is equal to zero or if the character field to which it is assigned is blank.

Controlling and Conditioning Indicator. An indicator specified in positions 10 and 11 of the calculation specification is called a controlling or conditioning indicator. It controls the logic flow of the calculation specifications. For example, indicator 38 can be used to control when an amount is added to a total field. In structured programming, conditioning indicators are not a viable programming tool and, therefore, should be avoided. Specifying the letter N prior to the indicator, in position 9, can reverse the test condition for the indicator.

Resulting Indicator. An indicator specified in positions 71 and 72, 73 and 74, or 75 and 76 of the calculation specification is called a resulting indicator. The purpose of a resulting indicator is to signal various conditions as the result of a calculation operation. For example, the CHAIN operation is used to access a database record. When the CHAIN operation doesn't find a record, the resulting indicator specified in positions 71 and 72 is set on. In RPG III and RPG IV, resulting indicators are set off before the operation is performed. (See chapter 5 for a description of the resulting indicators for each operation.)

First Page Indicator. The single first page indicator, 1P, is set on at the beginning of the RPG program, and it is then set off by the cycle just prior to the first detail cycle.

Last Record Indicator. The last record indicator, LR, is used in old-style RPG to signal that the RPG cycle has read the last record from a primary or secondary input file that has the end-of-file indication on the file specification. This indicates that the program will end after the current cycle is completed. In modern RPG III and RPG IV, the LR indicator is used to cause program termination (i.e., to return to its calling program). Normally, the LR indicator is explicitly set on in the program by a MOVE or SETON operation.

Matching Record Indicator. The matching record indicator, MR, is set on by the RPG cycle when all matching fields of a secondary file match all the matching fields in the primary file. Match fields are identified by specifying the match field identifiers M1 to M9 in positions 65 to 66 of the input specification.

Indicator Variables. Indicator variables allow the RPG programmer to refer to an indicator as if it were a data variable. Indicators are addressed using the convention *INxx where xx is the indicator being addressed. For example, *IN01 is indicator 01 and *INOF is the overflow indicator OF.

Indicator Array. The indicator array is a 99-element array of the 99 general-purpose indicators. The indicator array is addressed like any other array or array element, with the convention *IN(xx) where xx is the indicator being addressed. For example, *IN(38) addresses indicator 38. If no array index is used, the reference is to the entire 99-element array. For example, *IN refers to the entire indicator array.

Named Indicators. The RPG data-type, *named indicator* allows a variable to be declared that can be used like any other indicator. Typically, this kind of variable is used as the return value for procedures or as the storage location for numeric indicators

INDICATORS TO AVOID

The modern RPG programmer avoids using level-break indicators L1 to L9, the matching record indicator MR, conditioning indicators (of any kind), and the default function key indicators KA to KY.

Level-Break Indicators. Level-break indicators (L1 to L9) are of no use when the RPG cycle is avoided and, therefore, aren't used in most RPG applications being written.

Matching Record Indicator. The matching record (MR) indicator and match field identifiers (M1 to M9; remember, M1 to M9 are not indicators) also are of no use in cycleless programming. System functions outside of high-level languages, as well as more sophisticated functions, perform the equivalent of matching record indicators. The *data manipulation language* (DML) *structured query language* (SQL) provides support for organizing data such that matching-record processing is no longer necessary.

On certain computer systems, a DML other than SQL might be available. For example, on the IBM AS/400, a programmer has four options: SQL, a system command called Open Query File (OPNQRYF), an interactive query utility, and the database SORT utility.

Conditioning Indicators. Conditioning indicators have been replaced with structured operations. Conditioning indicators tend to make programs more difficult to read and more difficult to maintain. Avoid using conditioning indicators. In their place, use the IF*xx*, SELECT/WHEN, CAS*xx*, DO, DOW*xx*, and DOU*xx* op codes. Doing so results in programs that are easier to read and easier to maintain.

Default Function Key Indicators. Default function key indicators (KA to KY) are a carryover from the System/32/34/36 RPG II compiler. It is not reasonable to use these indicators in new applications because K*n* indicators bind the requested function to the function key. For example, for years F7 evoked the EXIT function. Today, however, F3 evokes the EXIT function.

Another reason to avoid using K*n* indicators is that not all function keys support them. The ROLLUP, ROLLDOWN, HELP, HOME, and PRINT keys are a few examples. Using function key indicators to control the process of an application is not recommended in this text. Instead, programming by function is encouraged.

CONSTANTS AND LITERAL VALUES

Constants are verbatim values placed in the program. It's often advantageous—for example, when you compare the balance due for an account to zero—to specify a value as a literal or constant.

The length of literal values can be as long as is permitted by the specification position where they are being used. When a literal value is assigned a name, it is referred to as a *named constant* and is often shortened to the simpler *constant*. However, the length of a character constant cannot exceed 1,024 characters; numeric constants cannot exceed 33 characters (31 digits plus the decimal notation and sign); and hexadecimal literal values cannot exceed 2,051 positions (2,048 hexadecimal characters plus the leading capital letter X and two apostrophes). There are three types of constants:

- Figurative constants.
- Named constants.
- Literal values.

Figurative constants represent compiler-defined values. Named constants and literal values, however, can be one of the following:

- Character literal value.
- Numeric literal value.
- Hexadecimal literal value.

Character literal values must be enclosed in apostrophes. For example:

```
'This is a literal value'
```

Numeric literal values are not enclosed in apostrophes, and may contain decimal notation and a sign. If a sign is specified, it must appear to the left of the numeric value. For example:

```
-3.1415962
```

When the actual literal value includes an apostrophe, as in the literal **O'clock**, two consecutive apostrophes must be specified and the entire literal must be enclosed in apostrophes. For example, the literal value **O'clock** would be specified as **'O''clock'**. By doubling the apostrophe **O''clock** and enclosing the literal value in apostrophes, the resulting value specified in the program should be **'O''clock'**.

Numeric constants referenced for their numeric value can contain a decimal notation character. In the United States, the period (.) is used; in other countries the comma (,) is used for decimal notation. The DECFMT keyword, specified on the header specification, is used to specify the decimal notation character.

The sign for all numeric constants can precede the constant. For example -12 is a valid negative numeric constant, and +12 is a valid positive numeric constant. The plus sign (+) for positive numeric values (i.e., unary plus) is implicit and, therefore, seldom specified.

Hexadecimal literal values begin with a capital letter X and must be enclosed in apostrophes. There must be an even number of hexadecimal characters enclosed in apostrophes. The hexadecimal characters can be A, B, C, D, E, F; or a, b, c, d, e, f; or 0, 1, 2, 3, 4, 5, 6, 7, 8, 9. For example:

```
X'1Face2Face'
```

The examples listed in Table 1.9 illustrate several valid and invalid literal values.

Table 1.9: Examples of Literal Values		
Literal Value	Status	Description
123456.78	Valid	Eight-digit numeral with two decimal positions.
-55555	Valid	Five-digit negative numeral.
'O''clock'	Valid	Seven-position character constant O'clock.
'1'	Valid	One-position character constant 1.
'Banyan'	Valid	Six-position character constant Banyan.
X'F100B1'	Valid	Hexadecimal literal.
O'Clock	Invalid	Missing apostrophes. Should be 'O''clock'.
100.00-	Invalid	Invalid sign. Should be -100.00.
Deforestation	Invalid	Missing apostrophes. Should be 'Deforestation'.
32,767.00	Invalid	Thousands notation is not allowed in numeric literal values.

Figurative Constants

Figurative constants are special, built-in names that have a predefined value associated with them. For example, *BLANKS can be used in place of quoted blanks and *ZEROS can be used in place of zeros. All figurative constant names begin with an asterisk (*).

Figurative constants can be specified in factor 1 and factor 2 of calculation specifications. The value that a figurative constant represents is implied and equal to that of the complementary field. For example, if *ZEROS is used with a seven-digit numeric field, its implied value is 0000000. If *ZEROS is used with a five-position character field, its implied value is '00000'. The implied value is unique to the program statement using the figurative constant. A description of each figurative constant is listed in Table 1.10.

Figurative Value	Type of Value	Description
	Table 1.10: Figurative Constants	
*ALL'...'	Figurative Constant	Repeating pattern. Automatically adjusts to the size of the field to which it is being compared or moved. For example: *ALL'abcd' moves 'abcdabcd', etc., to the result field for the length of the result field.
*ALLX'...'	Figurative Constant	Repeating hexadecimal pattern. Automatically adjusts to the size of the field to which it is being compared or moved. For example: *ALLX'00' moves binary zeros to the result field for the length of the result field.
*ALLG'SO...SI'	Figurative Constant	Repeating graphic character set (DBCS) pattern. Automatically adjusts to the size of the corresponding DBCS field.
*ALLU'XXXXYYYY'	Figurative Constant	Repeating USC-2 pattern. Repeats the USC-2 literal, automatically adjusting the length to match that of the field to which it is being compared or moved.
*BLANK *BLANKS	Figurative Constant	Blanks. Automatically adjusts to the size of the field to which it is being compared or moved.
*HIVAL	Figurative Constant	Represents the highest possible valid value for the data type to which it is being compared or moved.
*LOVAL	Figurative Constant	Represents the lowest possible valid value for the data type to which it is being compared or moved.
*NULL	Figurative Constant	Use to set or compare pointer data types to "no value." Currently, RPG supports *NULL with the pointer data type.
*OFF	Figurative Constant	Logical off ('0'). Functionally similar to *ALL'0'. Typically, *OFF is used with the IFxx and MOVE operations to test or set the status of an indicator.
*ON	Figurative Constant	Logical on ('1'). Functionally similar to *ALL'1'. Typically, *ON is used with the IFxx and MOVE operations to test or set the status of an indicator.
*OMIT	Figurative Constant	Use this value on the result field of a parameter for a CALLB operation or a parameter of a CALLP operation to indicate that the parameter is omitted from the parameter list. To test for a *OMIT value, compare the parameter's address to *NULL.
*ZERO *ZEROS	Figurative Constant	Use to represent a repeating pattern of zeros. Can be used with any data type except pointer, date, time, and timestamp variables.

Named Constants

Named constants are programmer-defined literal values with a unique name assigned to them. The name allows long literal values to be used in places like factor 1 and factor 2 of the calculation specification (where only 14 positions are available) or when a value is used repeatedly throughout the program. The value represented by a named constant cannot be changed when the program is run; the value is constant. The name assigned to the constant is specified on the definition specification. The definition type (positions 24 and 25) must contain the letter C. The constant's value is specified by the CONST keyword in the function/keyword area of the definition specification.

Named constants allow a name to be assigned to literal character values and numeric values. Character named constants up to 1,024 characters and numeric named constants of up to 33 positions (31 digits, a sign, and a decimal point) are supported. Named constants can be specified in factor 1 and factor 2 of calculation specifications as an output field or as an output constant. Named constants also can be used on several definition specification keywords, including INZ, DIM, and OCCURS.

Named constants are not restricted to the length of the location where the constant is used. For example, a named constant representing a 1,024-character literal can be used in factor 1 or factor 2 of the calculation specifications.

In the example featured in Figure 1.10, six named constants are defined. Line 1 defines the MESSAGE named constant. Line 2 defines the named constant NEGNUMBER (negative number), which includes a negative sign and decimal notation. Line 3 defines a simple seven-digit numeral with two decimal places. Line 4 defines a hexadecimal value named REVERSEIMG (reverse image). Line 5 defines the named constant LONGNUMBER (long number), which contains decimal notation. And, lines 7 to 9 define the long named constant LONGMSG (long message).

```
.....DName+++++++++++ETDsFrom+++To/L+++IDc.Functions+++++++++++++++++++++++++++++++
0001 D Message          C                    Const('This is a short one')
0002 D NegNumber        C                    Const(-99999.99)
0003 D Short#           C                    Const(38)
0004 D ReverseImg       C                    Const(X'21')
0005 D LongNumber       C                    Const(123456789012345.1234567890123-
0006 D                                       45)
0007 D LongMsg          C                    Const('This is a long named const-
0008 D                                       ant. It spans several lines. It +
0009 D                                          has quotes, and it''s very long.')
0010 D Value            S            7P 2
0011 D BigNumber        S           30P15
```

Figure 1.10: Examples of named constants (part 1 of 2).

```
.....CSRn01Factor1+++++++OpCode(ex)Factor2+++++++Result++++++++Len++DcHiLoEq....
0012 C                    Z-ADD     NegNumber      VALUE
0013 C                    Z-ADD     LONGNumber     BigNumber
0014 C      Message       DSPLY
     *                .
     *   The program continues...

.....OFormat++++DAddn01n02n03Except++++SpbSpaSkbSka
0015 OQPrint     E                          1

.....O..............n01n02n03Field+++++++++YB?End++PConstant/Editword+++++++++++
0016 O                       short#      J    +2 '$'
0017 O                                        +2 LongMsg
```

Figure 1.10: Examples of named constants (part 2 of 2).

In the preceding example, the Z-ADD operation is used to move the named constant NEGNUMBER to the field VALUE (line 12). The named constant LONG# is moved to the field BIGNUMBER, which is a 30-position numeric field with 15 decimal digits (line 13). The named constant MESSAGE is used as factor 1 of the DSPLY (display) operation (line 14). The named constant SHORT# is used as output with numeric editing (line 16). And the named constant LONGMSG is used as an output constant (line 17).

Reserved Names

Reserved field names are predefined fields that contain specific data such as the date. Some reserved fields begin with an asterisk and some do not. Reserved fields cannot be modified. Table 1.11 lists descriptions of each reserved field name.

Table 1.11: Reserved Field Names	
Reserved Field	Description
PAGE	Page number. This four-digit numeric field is used as a page counter. It is incremented each time it is output.
PAGEn	Additional page counters. These four-digit numeric fields are used as additional page counters. PAGEn, where n can be 1 to 7, offers seven additional page counters for a total of eight available page counters.
UDATE[1]	Session date. This numeric field is initialized to the run date when the program is started.
UDAY	Session day. This two-digit numeric field contains the day of the month.
UMONTH	Session month. This two-digit numeric field contains the month.
UYEAR	Session year. This two-digit numeric field contains the year.

[1] Also see *DATE, *MONTH, *DAY, and *YEAR reserved words in Table 1.12.

Reserved Words

There are a number of reserved words in RPG. These reserved words are referred to as *special names*. All special names begin with a unique symbol (such as an asterisk or percent sign). The exceptions to this are the UDATE, UDAY, UMONTH, and UYEAR fields. The PAGE field, however, while technically a reserved word, can be declared with an alternative length and manipulated like any other field. There are many different classifications of reserved words in RPG, including:

- **Reserved Fields.** Special field names containing a specific value. Typically, these values can be changed at runtime.
- **Figurative Constants.** Special field names whose value is constant or is established at pre-runtime. The content of these fields cannot be changed.
- **Control Values.** Special values that control operation function or output specification results.
- **Routines.** Special routines within the RPG cycle.
- **Built-in Functions.** Special routines that provide additional string, math, and expression functions.

Each of these types of reserved words is defined in Table 1.12.

Table 1.12: Reserved Words

Reserved Field	Description
*DATE	Used to retrieve the session date. This date value represents the date with eight positions. For example, if the date format is *MDY, *DATE will contain mmddccyy, where cc=century, yy=year, mm=month, and dd=day. The format of this date is based on the format specified in the header specification for the program
*MONTH	Used to retrieve the session month. This date value represents the month in mm format, where mm=month.
*YEAR	Used to retrieve the session century and year. This date value represents the year in ccyy format, where cc=century and yy=year.
*DAY	Used to retrieve the session day. This date value represents the day of the month in dd format, where dd=day of the month.

OPERATION CODE ARGUMENTS

Operation arguments are used in factor 1 or factor 2 of an operation. They are normally associated with a specific operation and are typically used to identify a specific reserved name or function.

Table 1.13: Operation Code Arguments

Control Value	Operation Code	Description
*ENTRY	PLIST	The *ENTRY parameter list identifies the parameter list used to pass parameters into and return parameters from the program.
*INZSR	BEGSR	The *INZSR subroutine, if specified in the program, is called by the RPG cycle before 1P output.
*LIKE	DEFINE	The *LIKE DEFINE op code is used to define a new field, based on the attributes of another field. The types of fields that can be defined with *LIKE DEFINE are character and packed decimal.
*LOCK	IN	The *LOCK IN op code is used to read a data area and then to place an object lock on that data area.
	OUT	The *LOCK OUT op code is used to write a data area and retain the object lock.
*LDA	DEFINE	The *DTAARA DEFINE *LDA op code is used to assign a variable to receive the contents of the local data area.

Table 1.13: Operation Code Arguments, *continued*

Control Value	Operation Code	Description
*PDA	DEFINE	The *DTAARA DEFINE *PDA op code is used to assign a variable to receive the program initialization parameters.
*DTAARA	DEFINE	The *DTAARA DEFINE op code is used to declare the entry in factor 2 as a data area. An optional field name can be specified in the result field. If factor 2 is not specified, the field name in the result field is used as the data-area name.
	IN	The IN *DTAARA operation is used to read all data areas defined in the program. If *LOCK IN *DTAARA is specified, all data areas defined in the program are read and an object lock is placed on each one.
	OUT	The OUT *DTAARA operation is used to write (i.e., output) all data areas defined in the program. If *LOCK OUT *DTAARA is specified, all data areas are written and any object locks are retained.
*PSSR	BEGSR	The *PSSR subroutine, if specified in the program, is called by the RPG exception/error handling routine whenever an unmonitored error occurs.
*END	SETLL	The *END SETLL operation positions the file cursor for a database file to the end of the database file.
*START	SETLL	The *START SETLL operation positions the file cursor to the beginning of the file.

OUTPUT CONTROL VALUES

Output control values are used by the output specifications to perform certain repetitive tasks. For example, specifying *PLACE replicates all the output up to the *PLACE, which is very useful in printing multi-up address labels or cards.

Table 1.14: Output Control Values

Control Field	Description
*ALL	Output all fields. This control field causes all fields from an externally defined file to be output. It is used on output specifications controlled by an EXCEPT op code.
*PLACE	This control field replicates output specifications, within the specific output line up to the position of the *PLACE. The replicated output is positioned at the end position specified for the *PLACE.
	*PLACE is used in label printing programs to print 2-, 3-, and 4-up labels. It was created primarily to automate printed output from 80-position, card-based programs. It is virtually worthless today considering the online source editors available.

SUBROUTINE RETURN POINTS

RPG subroutines normally return to the point in the RPG program at which they were called. There are certain conditions, however, when the return point must be controlled from within the subroutine. This kind of control is often needed when handling an error or exception event in the RPG program. Table 1.15 lists subroutine return points supported by the RPG IV language.

Table 1.15: *PSSR and INFSR Return Points	
Routine	**Description**
*CANCL	Cancel the program.
*DETC	Return to detail-time calculations.
*DETL	Return to detail-time lines (i.e., detail output).
*GETIN	Return to the next "get in" cycle.
*NEXT	Return to the statement following the one in which the error occurred.
*OFL	Return to the overflow output-time portion of the cycle.
*TOTC	Return to total-time calculations.
*TOTL	Return to total-time lines (i.e., total-time output).
Blanks	If the *PSSR or INFSR subroutines were called by the EXSR or CASxx operation, control returns to the statement following the EXSR or CASxx operation. If the RPG exception/error handler called the subroutine, the following applies: • If the error status code is 1121 to 1126, control returns to the operation where the error occurred. • Any other error status code causes an exception to be issued and the requester is notified (i.e., a message is sent to the user).

DIRECTIVES

Directives are controls that are placed into a source program. Two types of directives exist: *compiler directives* and *preprocessor directives*. All directives begin in position 7 of the RPG statement.

Compiler directives control various functions of the compile process, such as page printing and inclusion of external source code.

Preprocessors analyze and run directives. A preprocessor is a program that reads the RPG source code and performs some work, possibly altering the RPG source code, before calling the RPG compiler. The RPG compiler and SQL preprocessor directives provide functions to alter the RPG program listing and to include the SQL database manager. Table 1.16 lists these directives. Figure 1.11 illustrates the use of several RPG compiler directives as well as SQL preprocessor directives.

Table 1.16: Preprocessor/Compiler Directives	
Directive	Description
/COPY [[library/]file,]member	Causes the compiler to include source code contained in a separate source member. Any RPG source code can be included using the /COPY directive, including another /COPY directive.
/COPY 'ifs-file/folder-name'	Same function as /COPY except supports including source code from the integrated hierarchical file system (IFS). The IFS file name must be enclosed in single quotes.
/INCLUDE [[library/]file,]member	Same function as /COPY except avoids being processed by the SQL preprocessor.
/INCLUDE 'ifs-title/folder-name'	Same function as /INCLUDE except supports including source code from the integrated hierarchical file system (IFS). The IFS file name must be enclosed in single quotes.
/EJECT	Causes the compiler to skip to the top of the next page when the compiled program is printed.
/TITLE TEXT	Causes the compiler to print the text on the top of each page of the printed compiler list. Subsequent /TITLE directives override previous /TITLE.
/SPACE [n]	Causes the compiler to print n blank lines. If no n value is specified, 1 is assumed. Up to 255 can be specified. This directive is a legacy feature. Previous versions of RPG didn't allow blank lines to be embedded in the actual source itself. This directive allowed blank lines to be printed on compiler listings. This directive has been deprecated with the support in RPG for blank lines.
/EXEC SQL [SQL statement]	This SQL preprocessor directive starts an SQL statement. The SQL statement can begin on this line or on a subsequent line.
+ continued-SQL statement	This SQL preprocessor directive indicates the continuation of the SQL statement that began with /EXEC SQL.
/END-EXEC	This SQL preprocessor directive ends the SQL statement that followed the previous /EXEC SQL.

```
/TITLE Example RPG Source with Directives
.....FFilename++IPEASFRlen+LKlen+AIDevice+.Functions+++++++++++++++++++++++++++++
     FQPRINT    O   F  132         PRINTER OFLIND(*INOV)
.....DName+++++++++++++ETDsFrom+++To/L+++IDc.Functions+++++++++++++++++++++++++++++
     D PhoneEdit       C                    Const('Ø(    )&   -     ')
      /SPACE 2
     D KeyValue        S              5P Ø Inz(94Ø4)
     D HostVars        DS
     D   CustNum                      5S Ø
     D   CustName                    3ØA
     D   PhoneNum                    1ØS Ø

.....CSRnØ1Factor1+++++++OpCode(ex)Factor2+++++++Result++++++++Len++DcHiLoEq....
     C/SQL EXEC
     C+        SELECT custnbr,custnam,phone FROM CUSTMAST
     C+          WHERE custnbr = :KEYVALUE
     C+          INTO :HOSTVARS
     C/END-EXEC
     C                    TIME              TIME            6 Ø
     C                    Z-ADD   *DATE     DATE            9 Ø
     C                    EXCEPT
     C                    MOVE    *ON       *INLR
     C/EJECT
.....OFormat++++DAddnØ1nØ2nØ3Except++++SpbSpaSkbSka
     OQPRINT    E                          1

.....O..............nØ1nØ2nØ3Field+++++++++YB?End++PConstant/Editword++++++++++
     O                                        +Ø 'Customer:'
     O                    CustNum    Z        +2
     OQPRINT    E                          1
     O                                        +Ø 'Name:'
     O                    CustName   Z        +2
     OQPRINT    E                          1
     O                                        +Ø 'Phone:'
     O                    PhoneNum            +2 PhoneEdit
     OQPRINT    E                          1
     O                                        +Ø 'Date/Time:'
     O                    DATE       Y        +2
     O                    TIME                +2 'Ø  :  :  '
```

Figure 1.11: Example of RPG directives.

With the exception of the /COPY compiler directive, most compiler directives offer little additional function. The /COPY compiler directive allows external source members to be included at compile time.

Conditional Compiler Preprocessor Source Directives

To condition the inclusion of source, RPG IV supports several compiler directives. These directives are interpreted prior to compiling. They control which sections of source are included when the source is compiled. Compiler directives must be specified starting in position 7 of the RPG source statement. Directives that require a parameter must be followed by one or more blanks and then the parameter. Table 1.17 lists the directives.

Table 1.17: Conditional Preprocessor Source Directives

Preprocessor Directive	Description
/DEFINE identifier	Defines an identifier. An identifier is similar to a variable in a program, except it is not available to the program. Subsequent directives that determine if the identifier has been defined use the identifier. The DEFINE parameter of the CRTBNDRPG and CRTRPGMOD commands also allows an identifier to be defined to the preprocessor.
/UNDEFINE	Removes an identifier. The identifier no longer exists and causes a subsequent /IF DEFINED for that identifier to fail.
/IF DEFINED(identifier)	Returns a true condition if the identifier has previously been defined with a /DEFINE directive. If the condition is true, the source following the directive is included.
/IF NOT DEFINED(identifier)	Returns a true condition if the identifier is not defined. If the condition is true, the source following the directive is included.
/ELSEIF DEFINED(identifier)	Returns true if the identifier has previously been defined. Use this directive to test for an identifier within another /IF or /ELSEIF directive. If the condition is true, the source following the directive is included.
/ELSEIF NOT DEFINED(identifier)	Returns true if the identifier is not defined. Use this directive to test for an identifier within another /IF or /ELSEIF directive. If the condition is true, the source following the directive is included.
/ELSE	Unconditionally includes the source code that follows the directive. Functions as the "else" condition for a corresponding /IF or /ELSEIF directive.
/EOF	Causes the compiler to stop processing the source code following this statement. Use this directive in conjunction with /IF to cause termination of source that is being included with the /COPY directive.
/ENDIF	Ends the previous /IF or /ELSEIF directive.

Chapter 2

SPECIFICATION FORMATS

A somewhat rigid language, RPG is not a completely free-form language like PL/I, COBOL, C, or Java. RPG requires a different statement format for each area of the program. These formats are known as *RPG specification* forms. When writing RPG programs, a general knowledge of each type of specification format is necessary. A specification format guides the programmer in writing specific areas of the RPG program. Most other languages—such as PL/I, COBOL, and C—require only one specification; RPG requires several.

SPECIFICATION TYPES

This chapter describes each RPG specification format type. While chapter 1 introduces the various RPG specification forms, Table 2.1 lists a summary of the RPG IV specifications. RPG source programs can contain any number of specifications. When more than one specification form is used, they must appear in the order listed in Table 2.2.

Table 2.1: RPG IV Specification Types		
Specification Type	Identification	Common or Alternate Name
Control	"H" in column 6	Header spec or H-spec
File description	"F" in column 6	File-spec or F-spec
Definition	"D" in column 6	D-spec
Input	"I" in column 6	Input specs or I-spec
Calculation	"C" in column 6	Calc spec or C-spec
Output	"O" in column 6	Output spec or O-spec
Procedure	"P" in column 6	Procedure spec or P-spec

Table 2.2: RPG Specification Sequence
Header specification
File specifications
Definition specification
Input specifications
Calculation specifications
Output specifications
Procedure specification
Definition specification
Calculation specifications
Procedure specification
**
File translation table
**
Alternate collating sequence
**
Compile-time array data

If the specifications do not appear in this order, the RPG compiler generates a severe error and the program is not created. As listed in Table 2.2, after the final specification, additional information about tables, array, collating sequencing, and file translation can be included in the program. Double asterisks in columns 1 and 2 indicate the beginning of a file translation table, alternate collating sequence table, or compile-time table and array data. Compile-time table and array data is used frequently in RPG. Alternate collating sequence and file translation tables are normally not used.

HEADER (CONTROL) SPECIFICATION

The control specification, more commonly referred to as the header specification, is used to control various options and features of the source program. Keywords are used to set default formats, assign names, and establish the currency symbol. Figure 2.1 illustrates the header specification ruler and Table 2.3 defines the layout by column.

In addition, the parameters needed to compile the RPG IV source can be specified in the header specification. When a compiler parameter is specified, it must use the RPG IV keyword syntax. Specifically, each parameter argument must be separated with a colon. Because compiler options vary from operating system release to release, therefore only compiler keywords that are fundamental to the RPG syntax are illustrated here.

```
.....H.Functions++++++++++++++++++++++++++++++++++++++++++++++++++++++++++++++++++++++
```

Figure 2.1: Header (control) specification ruler.

	Table 2.3: Header (Control) Specification Summary		
Column	Title	Value	Description
6	Form type	H	Identifies the statement as a header (control) specification.
7	Comment	Blank	Normal Header specification.
		*	Comment.
7 - 80	Keyword functions	Header keyword	Optional keywords that control module/program settings. See header keywords in Table 2.4.

Table 2.4: Header (Control) Specification Keyword Summary

Keyword	Parameters	Description
ATLSEQ	*NONE *SRC *EXT	Alternate collating sequence. Identifies where the collating sequence is specified. A value of *SRC, or just the keyword, indicates it is specified near the end of the source program with the **ALTSEQ identifier. The *EXT indicates the collating sequence is specified when the program is compiled. If the keyword is not specified, no collating sequence is used. This is the same as specifying ALTSQ(*NONE).
ALWNULL (compiler directive)	*NO *INPUTONLY *USRCTL	Allow Null. This keyword allows the use of database file records that contain fields with the null indicator property. *NO – Null capable fields are not supported. A runtime error is generated if the program reads a database record containing a null. *INPUTONLY – Null capable fields are allowed. They can be read into the program but not written to or updated in the database file. *USRCTL – Full null capable field support is allowed. Null capable fields can be read, modified, and written to the database.
BNDDIR	Binding directory names	Specify the binding directories needed by this source member during the bind phase of the compile process. Binding directory names are OS/400 objects and may be qualified or unqualified. All binding directory names must be enclosed in apostrophes. If more than one binding directory name is required, separate the names with a colon : symbol.
COPYNEST	1 to 2048 32	Controls the maximum number of /COPY nests that can occur for this source.
COPYRIGHT	'Text'	Copyright notice to be stored in the compiled program object. Up to 255 characters can be specified.
CURSYM	'Symbol'	Any quoted character or symbol can be specified, except the following: * 0 , (comma) . (period) - C R or a blank.
DATEDIT	Format [separator]	This value sets the default format for numeric fields that are edited with the Y edit code, and sets the date format for *DATE and UDATE. Valid entries are: *MDY, *YMD, and *DMY. The separator can be any character. The default separator is the slash (/). Use an & (ampersand) when blanks are needed as the separator.

Table 2.4: Header (Control) Specification Keyword Summary, *continued*

Keyword	Parameters	Description
DATFMT	Format [separator]	Specifies the default format to be used for date fields and literals used in the program. If this keyword is not specified, the *ISO format (ccyy-mm-dd) is used. Any of the following date formats can be specified:

Date Format	Description	Format
*MDY	Month Day Year	mm/dd/yy
*DMY	Day Month Year	dd/mm/yy
*YMD	Year Month Day	yy/mm/dd
*JUL	Julian	yy/ddd
*ISO	ISO standard	ccyy-mm-dd
*USA	USA standard	mm/dd/ccyy
*EUR	Europe standard	dd.mm.ccyy
*JIS	Japan standard	ccyy-mm-dd

The optional separator can be any of the following: / - , . &. The default separator is the / (slash). Use an & (ampersand) when blanks are needed as the separator. Only *MDY, *YMD, *DMY, and *JUL support separators.

Keyword	Parameters	Description
DEBUG	*NO	Controls output of the DUMP operation.
	*YES	
DECEDIT	'symbol'	Controls the symbol used to edit numeric values in the program. Valid entries are:
	*JOBRUN	'.' Decimal point is the period (.123) ',' Decimal point is the comma (,123) '0.' Decimal point is the period (0.123) '0,' Decimal point is the comma (0,123) If *JOBRUN is specified, the external job attribute DECFMT is used as the DECEDIT control.
DECPREC	31 | 30	Controls the default precision for numeric expressions. Originally, RPG supported 30-digit numeric values. For compatibility with the SQL language, 31 digits are supported.

Table 2.4: Header (Control) Specification Keyword Summary, *continued*

Keyword	Parameters	Description
DFTACTGRP (compiler directive)	*YES *NO	This indicates that the program is to run in the default activation group on the AS/400. When a program runs in the default activation group, it is running in a restricted environment. Advanced RPG features are not supported in the default activation group. *YES – Run in the default activation group. *NO – Run in an ILE activation group.
DFTNAME	program name	The default name for the program. Used to name the program when no name is specified on the CRTBNDRPG or CRTRPGMOD commands. Traditionally, this keyword is not used in RPG programs.
EXPROPTS	*MAXDIGITS *RESDECPOS	Controls the default operation extender for the EVAL and EVALR operations. *MAXDIGITS indicates that the M operation extender is used. *RESDECPOS indicates that the R operation extender is used for EVAL and EVALR operations. Use the individual operation extenders to override a specific EVAL or EVALR operation.
EXTBININT	*NO *YES	Convert externally described data that is in binary format (i.e., the "B" data-type) to the integer data-type. If *NO is specified, or the keyword is not specified, no conversion is performed. If the keyword is specified (optional with *YES), externally described binary fields are converted to integer data-types. This allows the full range of integer values (32768) to be stored in the field. Only externally described fields whose attributes are binary, with zero decimal positions, are converted.
FIXNBR	*NOZONED *ZONED *INPUTPACKED *NOINPUTPACKED	Controls correcting decimal data errors that can occur when a database record is read. *ZONED generates internal code that fixes zoned (signed) decimal fields during an input operation. *INPUTPACKED generates internal code that translates invalid packed decimal data to zero during an input operation.
FLTDIV	*NO *YES	FLTDIV and FLTDIV(*YES) causes mathematical expressions containing divide operations to be performed using floating point division. If FLTDIV(*NO) is specified or the keyword is not specified, divide operations are performed using packed decimal.

Table 2.4: Header (Control) Specification Keyword Summary, *continued*

Keyword	Parameters	Description
FORMSALIGN	*NO *YES	This option causes a message to be sent to the computer operator immediately after the first line of output is printed. There are system functions that perform a similar task and do it much better.
FTRANS	*NONE *SRC	Identifies whether or not file translation will occur. The translation table must be specified near the bottom of the source program with the **FTRANS identifier.
GENLVL	10 0 to 20	The GENLVL keyword controls the highest accepted error severity for the source member to compile; generating an object. The default is 10, and is sufficient for most source compiles. In some situations, GENLVL(20) might need to be specified.
INDENT	*NONE Indent-character	When an indent value is specified, the printed compiler listing indents any Calculation specifications containing structured operations codes. This can provide a more readable compiler listing. Any two characters may be specified for the indent character. Traditionally, only one character the vertical bar | is used, for example: INDENT('|').
INTPREC	10 20	Intermediate results use integer data-types, 4-byte integers when INTPREC(10) is specified, or 8-byte integers when INTPREC(20) is specified. If, however, an expression contains an 8-byte integer, an 8-byte integer intermediate result is always used.
NOMAIN		Use this keyword in source files that contain only procedures and no mainline RPG calculations. Source files that contain this keyword must be compiled with the CRTRPGMOD command. Source files that contain the NOMAIN keyword cannot be compiled directly into a program object.
OPENOPT	*NOINZOFL *INZOFL	The Open Options keyword indicates whether the overflow indicators should be switched to *OFF when the print file is opened. Use this keyword when a print file is closed and then reopened within the same instances of the program.
OPTION	*NODEBUGIO *SRCSTMT	Use the OPTION keyword to control how the debug code is generated for the compiled source member. Normally RPG generates debug code for all areas of the language. In practice, however, it may be more productive to prevent some of the debug from being generated. OPTION(*NODEBUGIO) causes the debug code to not be generated for FILE input/output operations. OPTION(*SRCSTMT) causes the compiler to generate debug statement numbers that match that of the RPG source.
THREAD	*SERIALIZE	Access to the procedures in the compiled RPG module is serialized. This option is used for a program that runs in a multi-thread environment, such as when it is called by a Java application.

Keyword	Parameters	Description
TIMFMT	Format [separator]	Specifies the default format for time field and literals used in the program. If this keyword is not specified, the *ISO format (hh.mm.ss 24-hour clock) is used.

Time Format	Format	Description
*HMS	hh:mm:ss	U.S. Standard
*ISO	hh.mm.ss	ISO standard
*USA	hh:mm AM | PM	U.S.A 12-hour format
*EUR	hh.mm.ss	European standard
*JIS	hh:mm:ss	Japanese standard

Keyword	Parameters	Description
		The optional separator can be any of the following characters: , . &. The default separator is the : (colon). Use an & (ampersand) when blanks are needed as the separator. Only the *HMS format supports separators.
TRUNCNBR	*YES

*NO | This keyword allows traditional RPG operation codes, such as Z-ADD, MOVE, MULT, and DIV, to generate an error when high-order truncation occurs. Traditionally, this is not generated.

This support allows the traditional operation codes to generate errors similar to the EVAL and EVALR operations, which don't support high-order truncation. |

Table 2.4: Header (Control) Specification Keyword Summary, *continued*

FILE SPECIFICATION

The file specification is used to declare each file used by the program (except for SQL tables and views, which are accessed through SQL statements). Each file must have its own file specification. Additional information about the file is optionally specified with one or more file keywords.

The two basic file types in RPG are program-described files and externally described files. With program-described files, input and output fields are explicitly defined in the source. With externally described files, the input and output field definitions are inserted into the program by the compiler. Most applications written today use externally described files. Figure 2.2 illustrates the format of the file specification. Table 2.5 lists the file description specifications and Table 2.6 lists the file keywords.

```
.....FFileName++IFEASFRlen+LKeylnKFDevice+.Functions++++++++++++++++++++++++++++
```

Figure 2.2: File specification ruler.

Table 2.5: File Description Specification Summary

Column	Title	Values	Description
6	Form type	F	Identifies the statement as a file description specification.
7 - 16	File name	Blanks	The statement is a file continuation.
		File name	The name of a file to be used by this program.
17	File type	I	The file is opened for input processing.
		O	The file is opened for output processing.
		U	The file is opened for update (read, change, delete) processing.
		C	The file is opened for combined (read, write) processing. Valid for WORKSTN files only.
18	File designation	Blank	The file is an output file. Blank is the only valid entry for output files.
		P	The file is the *primary file*. There can be only one primary file in an RPG program.
		S	The file is a *secondary file*. There can be 0, 1, or more than one secondary file in an RPG program.
		R	The file is a record address (ADDROUT) file.
		T	The file is a pre-runtime table. The file is "read into" the array specified on the extension specifications when the program is called.
		F	The file is a full-procedural file. The file is processed only through procedural RPG file operations, such as READ and WRITE in the calculation specifications. The RPG cycle does nothing more than automatically open and close the file.
19	End of file	Blank	If all files contain a blank entry in this column, then all records in all files are processed before the RPG cycle sets on the LR indicator.
		E	When all the records from this file have been processed, the RPG cycle sets on the LR indicator. If more than one file uses this option, all records from each file containing the end-of-file indication are processed before the RPG cycle sets on the LR indicator.
			The end-of-file indication applies only to files specified as primary or secondary. It does not apply to full procedural files.

Table 2.5: File Description Specification Summary, *continued*

Column	Title	Values	Description
20	File addition	Blanks	For input and update files (file type I or U), no records can be added (i.e., written) to the file. The compiler generates an error if WRITE or EXCEPT with ADD operations are used.
		A	For input and update files (file type I or U) the WRITE and EXCEPT with ADD operations are allowed. This allows new records to be added to the file.
			For output files, the entry in this column is ignored.
21	Sequence	Blank or A	The sequence for matching record fields is ascending order.
		D	The sequence for matching record fields is descending order.
22	Format	F	The file is program described. Input specifications are used to define the record format for this file.
		E	The file is externally described. The RPG compiler imports the record format for the file.
23 - 27	Record length	Blank	Valid when the file is an externally described file. The compiler imports the record length when it is unspecified.
		1 to 32,766	The length used by RPG for the file. The actual record length may be different from this value; RPG pads or truncates the record as required.
28	Mode of processing	Blank	The mode of processing is controlled by the entries in the file designation and the record address type.
		L	The mode of processing is sequential within limits; meaning the file is an ADDROUT file.
29 - 33	Length of key fields	Blanks	The key is established outside the RPG program or the file is not keyed.
		1 to 2,000	The length of the key for a program-described file.

Table 2.5: File Description Specification Summary, *continued*

Column	Title	Values	Description
34	Record address type	Blank	The file processing (access) is sequential or by relative record number.
		A	The key to the file is a character value (for program-described files only).
		P	The key to the file is a packed decimal value (for program-described files only).
		G	Graphic keys (DBCS keyed database file).
		K	Keyed file (for externally described files only).
		D	The key to the file is a date value.
		F	The key to the file is a floating-point value.
		T	The key to the file is a time value.
		Z	The key to the file is a timestamp value.
35	File organization	Blank	The file is not keyed (for program-described files). For externally described files, this entry must be blank.
		I	The program-described file is "indexed"; in other words, it's a keyed file.
		T	The program-described file is a record address file (ADDROUT) file containing relative record numbers to be used for sequencing file input.
36 - 42	Device type	DISK	The file is a database (disk) file.
		PRINTER	The file is a printer file and can be written to.
		WORKSTN	The file is an interactive workstation.
		SEQ	The file is a sequential file that is processed by READ, WRITE, OPEN, and CLOSE operations.
		SPECIAL	The file is processed using a special device "driver." A device driver is a program (such as another RPG program) that handles the input and output requests from this program. The name of the device driver program is specified with the PGMNAME keyword.
43			Not used.
44	File keywords	Blank	Normal file processing.
		Keyword	File keywords. *See* Table 2.6 for a list of valid keywords.

Table 2.6: File Description Keyword Summary

Keyword	Parameters	Description
BLOCK	*YES	Record blocking is performed if the proper conditions are met for the operating system. Use type keyword option to override the default selected by the RPG compiler.
	*NO	No record blocking is performed on the file.
COMMIT	*Commit status*	Activates commitment control and the COMMIT and ROLBK operations in the program. Valid options are '1' and '0'. An indicator or other character field can be specified. The commit status field value is tested when the file is open.
DATFMT	Format separator	Sets the default date format for the fields in the file. This includes the keyfields (if any). The separator is used to edit the date on output operations and when date literals are moved to, or compared with, date fields in this file.
DEVID	Device ID	Device ID being processed. The field name specified for this keyword is automatically defined as a 10-position character field. Typically, this keyword is not used in RPG IV.
EXTIND	*INU*x*	Controls the file open. The file is automatically opened when the program is called and the corresponding UPSI indicator is ON. The file is not open if the indicator is OFF when the program is called. Valid range for *x* is 1 to 8. *See* also USROPN keyword.
EXTFILE	Runtime file name	Identifies the name of the file to be open at runtime. This may be a different file name from that specified in columns 7 to 16. If the EXTFILE keyword is not specified, the file name specified in columns 7 to 16 is used at runtime.

The runtime file name may be a literal or a field name. If a field name is used then its value must be specified before the file is open. This can be accomplished through several methods, including but not limited to:
- A value from entry parameter
- An initial value
- A USROPN keyword. This allows the file name to be specified on a controlled basis, before the file is opened.

The syntax for the file name is as follows:

{LIBRARY/}FILE

The file name may be a qualified or unqualified file name, and if a field is specified, the file name must be left justified within that field, and must be specified in uppercase letters.

The library name is optional, and if not specified, the library list (*LIBL) is used. The only special value that may be used for the library name is *LIBL.

Note that when EXTFILE is used, any overrides applied to the file name specified in columns 7 to 16 of the File specification are ignored. Overrides applied to the file name specified in EXTFILE keyword are processed like normal. |

Table 2.6: File Description Keyword Summary, *continued*

Keyword	Parameters	Description
EXTMBR	Runtime member name	Identifies the name of the member to be open at runtime.
		The member name must be in the correct case. For example, the keyword EXTMBR(mbrname) uses the variable mbrname. If that variable contains the name 'custmast', the member will not be found. Instead, the member name should have been specified in all upper case as follows: 'CUSTMAST'.
FORMLEN	Page size	Specify the number of lines per page for the PRINTER device file. The valid range is 1 to 255 lines. *See* FORMOFL and OFLIND keywords.
FORMOFL	Overflow line	Specify the line number that triggers the overflow indicator. The value specified for this keyword must be less than or equal to the value specified for the FORMLEN keyword. *See* FORMLEN and OFLIND keywords.
IGNORE	Format1 [: format2...]	The record format name(s) specified for the externally described file is not imported into the program by the compiler. Multiple names can be specified, separated by a colon.
INCLUDE	Format1 [: format 2...]	The record format names specified for the externally described file are imported into the program by the compiler. When an INCLUDE keyword is specified, only format names that appear in the INCLUDE keyword are imported; all other formats are ignored. A colon separates multiple names.
INDDS	Data structure	The name of a data structure that is associated with the PRINTER or WORKSTN device file. The positions in this data structure correspond to the standard 99 numeric RPG indicators. For example, position 1 of the data structure corresponds to indicator *IN01 as used by the device file. This data structure is always 99 positions in length.
		Use this data structure to assign more readable named indicator variables to the traditional 99 numeric indicators.
INFDS	Data structure	The name of a data structure that is associated with the file description specification. The data structure receives status and error information about the file.
INFSR	Subroutine	The name of the RPG subroutine that is called when an exception/error occurs on the file being declared.
KEYLOC	Key position	The location (record position) of the key for the file being declared. Valid range is 1 to 32,766, but must not exceed the record length for the file, minus the key length. This entry is ignored for programs running on the IBM AS/400.
MAXDEV	*ONLY	A single device file can be allocated to the program.
	*FILE	The maximum number of devices that can be allocated to the program is retrieved from the WORKSTN device file when the file is open.

Table 2.6: File Description Keyword Summary, *continued*

Keyword	Parameters	Description
OFLIND	*INxx	Overflow indicator is set on when the line specified by the FORMOFL keyword is printed. Valid entries for program-described PRINTER files are *INOA to *INOG, and *INOV as well as any valid numeric indicator. For externally described printer files, indicators *IN01 to *IN99 are supported. *See* FORMOFL and FORMLEN keywords.
PASS	*NOIND	This keyword and its required entry of *NOIND indicates that no indicators are transferred to the program through the internal file buffer. Instead, the program contains input and output fields (identified as *INxx, where xx is the indicator being passed) to pass the indicators.
PGMNAME	Program	For SPECIAL device files, this name identifies the program that is called to perform file input/output processing when a READ, WRITE, UPDATE, etc., operation is used on the file. *See* SPECIAL device files.

PLIST	Parameter-list	For SPECIAL device files, this keyword identifies a *parameter-list* containing optional parameters that are passed to the device driver named in the PGMNAME keyword.
		
		The parameters from the parameter list are added (by the compiler) to the following parameter list:
		
		OPTION CHAR(1) /* Operation */
		         O = Open the file
		         C = Close the file
		         R = Read from the file
		         W = Write to the file
		         D = Delete the current record
		         U = Update the current record
		
		Status CHAR(1) /* Return code */
		         0 = Normal completion
		         1 = End or beginning of file
		         2 = Exception/error occurred
		
		Error ZONED(5,0) /* Error code */
		         Returned to the *RECORD subfield of the INFDS data structure for the file.
		
		Area CHAR(*) /* Data from, or for, the record */
		         The data for the record is placed into this parameter and returned to the input record format of the SPECIAL device file. The actual length of this parameter, as passed to the program, is equal to the file length specified for the SPECIAL device file.
		
		RPG automatically generates this parameter list in the program that contains the SPECIAL device file. In the program being used as the SPECIAL device file's I/O routine, however, this parameter list must be specified.

Table 2.6: File Description Keyword Summary, *continued*

Keyword	Parameters	Description
PREFIX	Prefix [: replace count]	For externally described files, the *prefix* is used to automatically re-name all fields in the file. The prefix is appended to the front of the field name for each field in the file's record format. If the prefix needs to contain special characters, such as the period, it must be specified in all uppercase letters and enclosed in quotes. The *replace count* controls whether or not the first replace-count characters of each field name are trimmed from the field name before the automatic rename occurs. For example, if all the fields in the file begin with CST (as in CSTNAM, CSTNBR, CSTADR), the PREFIX keyword's replace count can be used to remove the leading three characters from each field. In this case, a PREFIX keyword specified as: PREFIX(CM_ : 3) would rename the above fields, as follows: CM_NAM, CM_NBR, CM_ADR The total length of a renamed field name cannot exceed the maximum length for an RPG IV field name.
PRTCTL	Data struct [:*compat]	Specify the name of the data structure that will be used as the printer-control data structure. The printer spacing, skipping, and over-flow information are stored in this data structure. The optional param-eter *COMPAT causes the data structure to be compatible with RPG III. *See* PRTCTL data structure.

Standard PRTCTL data structure:

```
.....DName++++++++++++ETDSFrom+++To/L+++IDc
      D PrtCtl              DS
      D  SpaceB                          3A
      D  SpaceA                          3A
      D  SkipB                           3A
      D  SkipA                           3A
      D  CurLine                         3S 0
```

*PRTCTL data structure with *COMPAT:*

```
.....DName++++++++++++ETDSFrom+++To/L+++IDc
      D PRTCTL_RG3          DS
      D  SPCBFR                          1A
      D  SPCAFT                          1A
      D  SKPBFR                          2A
      D  SKPAFT                          2A
      D  CURLIN                          3S 0
```

Note that there is no entry for total number of pages. Since writing to the printed page is serial in nature, there is no way to automatically determine the page count without first printing all pages.

Table 2.6: File Description Keyword Summary, *continued*

Keyword	Parameters	Description
RAFDATA	Filename	Names the *input file* or *update file* that is associated with this record address file. The filename that appears in the parentheses of this keyword is controlled with this file.
RECNO	Recnum-field	For database files that use relative record-number processing, or for output files that are referenced by a random WRITE calculation or are used with ADD on the output specifications, specify the name of the field that is to contain the relative record number of the file. Typically, this keyword is not used in RPG IV.
RENAME	External-name : new-name	The externally described file's *external-name* record format is renamed to the *new-name*.
SAVEDS	Data struct	The name of a data structure is saved before each input operation to a WORKSTN device file. Typically, this keyword isn't used in RPG IV.
SAVEIND	Saved-indicator-count	Number of indicators to save. Typically, this keyword isn't used in RPG IV.
SFILE	Format : relno	The name of the subfile detail record *format* that is being used in this program. The *relno* parameter is a field name that is used as the subfile's relative record number. You set the value in this field for a CHAIN or WRITE operation to the subfile. RPG sets this field when you perform a READC (read changed subfile record) or a CHAIN (random get) operation.
SLN	Starting-line	Starting line number. The *starting-line* field is used to control the line number to which WORKSTN display device files send their output. RPG automatically defines the field as a two-position numeric field with zero decimal places. Note: The DDS keyword SLNO(*VAR) must also be specified in the DDS for the workstation file.
TIMFMT	Format separator	Sets the default time *format* for time data-type fields in the file. This includes the keyfields for the file. The *separator* identifies the symbol to be used when the field is output or when a time literal is moved to, or compared with, the time fields in this file.
USROPN		User-controlled open. Causes the program to avoid automatically opening this file when the program is called for the first time. When this keyword is used, the file must be opened through some other method, such as with the OPEN operation or by an external file management command.

DEFINITION SPECIFICATION

The definition specification is used to define data to the program. This includes fields, arrays, tables, data structures, data structure subfields, procedure parameter lists, and prototypes. The base properties (attributes) of each data item are specified on the definition specification. In addition to the base properties, the definition specification supports keyword properties. These keyword properties extend the definition of the item.

The definition specification can be specified within the mainline procedure and subprocedures of a program. The four layouts for the definition specification are illustrated in Figures 2.3 through 2.6. Figure 2.3 is the most common definition specification layout in use. Figure 2.5 is used for special reserved locations within the program status data structure (PSDS), and within a file's I/O feedback data structure. Figure 2.6 is often used when converting previous versions of RPG to the RPG IV language. Table 2.7 lists the definition specifications.

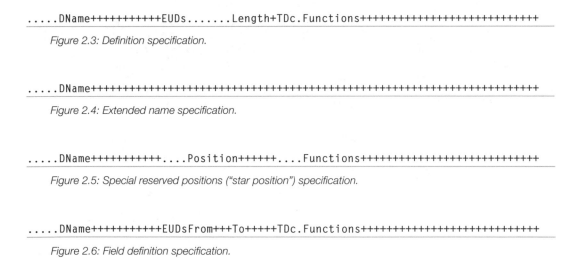

```
.....DName+++++++++++EUDs.......Length+TDc.Functions++++++++++++++++++++++++++++
```
Figure 2.3: Definition specification.

```
.....DName+++++++++++++++++++++++++++++++++++++++++++++++++++++++++++++++++++++++
```
Figure 2.4: Extended name specification.

```
.....DName+++++++++++....Position++++++....Functions++++++++++++++++++++++++++++
```
Figure 2.5: Special reserved positions ("star position") specification.

```
.....DName+++++++++++EUDsFrom+++To+++++TDc.Functions++++++++++++++++++++++++++++
```
Figure 2.6: Field definition specification.

Table 2.7: Definition Specification Summary

Column	Title	Values	Description
7 - 21	Name	Name	The RPG name assigned to the item being defined. The name can be up to 15 positions in length. The name does not have to be left justified within these positions. It can be located in any positions (i.e., it can "float") within the *name location*.
22	Externally described	Blank	The item is not externally described.
		E	The item is externally described. A data structure can be externally described when the EXTNAME keyword is specified. A data structure subfield can be externally described when the EXTFLD keyword is specified.
23	Data area	Blank	The data structure is not a data area.
		U	The data structure is also a data area. The data area name is identified by the DTAARA keyword.
24 - 25	Data set type	Blank	The item is a data structure subfield.
		DS	The item is a data structure.
		S	The item is a stand-alone field.
		C	The Item is a constant.
		PI	The item is a procedure interface definition.
		PR	The item is a procedure prototype.
26 - 32	Starting location	Blank	Length notation is used.
	From/To Notation	1 to 65535	Starting location (within the data structure) of the data structure subfield being declared.
33 - 39	Ending Location or Length	Blank	The item's length is based on the following: • For a data structure, the length is determined by the sum of the length of its subfields. • For a data structure subfield, the length is based on either the length of the external field definition (for externally described data structures) or the field specified for the LIKE keyword (for program-described data structures). If the subfield is not externally defined or based on another field through the LIKE keyword, then a length entry is required. • For constants, this entry must be blank.
	From/To Notation	1 to 65535	If a starting location is specified, this value represents the ending location of the data structure subfield. If no starting location is specified, then positions 33 to 39 are considered to be the field's length.
	Length notation	1 to 65535	The length of the item being defined.
		-65,534 to +65,534	The relative length of the field, whose attributes are based on another field, through the LIKE keyword.

Table 2.7: Definition Specification Summary, *continued*

Column	Title	Values	Description
40	Data type	Blank	The data-type is implied by other item properties.
		A	(CHARACTER) character field. Default for fields with no decimal positions.
		B	(NUMERIC) binary field.
		C	The UCS-2 (Unicode) character set can encode the characters for many written languages. The field is a character field. Each character of the field occupies two bytes in the field itself.
		D	(DATE) date field.
		F	(NUMERIC) floating-point numeric.
		G	(GRAPHIC) double-byte character set field.
		I	(NUMERIC) integer field.
		N	(CHARACTER) named indicator field.
		O	(OBJECT) instantiation of a class object.
		P	(NUMERIC) packed decimal field.
		S	(NUMERIC) zoned decimal. Default for fields with decimal positions of 0 to 30.
		T	(TIME) time field.
		U	(NUMERIC) unsigned integer field.
		Z	(TIMESTAMP) timestamp field.
		*	(POINTER) pointer data-type.
41 - 42	Decimal positions	Blank	The field is non-numeric.
		0 to 30	The field is numeric.
43			Not used.
44 to 80	Functions	Blank	No additional properties are specified.
		Keyword	Additional properties for the item are specified. *See* Table 2.11 (Definition Specification Keyword Summary) for more information.

Extended Name Definition

The definition specification provides a unique syntax to support long names. The default name location, positions 7 through 21, provides support for 15-position names. Under most situations, names are usually less than 15 positions.

In order to support item names longer than 15 positions, the definition specification supports the ellipse (...) that consists of three consecutive periods or dots that can be used to indicate that the name is a long name. The ellipse indicates that the name and definition are continued onto the next source line. Table 2.8 lists the layout of the extended name definition specification.

Table 2.8: Definition Specification Extended Name Summary			
Column	Title	Values	Description
7 - 80	Name	Extended name...	The RPG name assigned to the item being defined. If more space is needed, a second line can be inserted into the source code. The name on this line is continued onto the next line using the ellipse (three dots...).The name can be up to 4,096 positions in length.
			Names must begin in positions 7 to 21 of the definition specification.

Extended item names can be used in expressions throughout the RPG IV source member. The example shown in Figure 2.7 illustrates three extended name declarations.

```
.....DName++++++++++++++++++++++++++++++++++++++++++++++++++++++++++++++++++++++
.....DName++++++++++++EUDS.......Length+TDc.Functions++++++++++++++++++++++++++++
0010 D Very_Long_Field_Name_with_continuation...
0020 D                    S              35A
0030 D This_is_another_very...
0040 D long_field_name_continued_over...
0050 D four_source_lines...
0060 D                    S               7P 2
0070 D A_medium_length_field...
0080 D finishing_here   S              35A
```

Figure 2.7: Extended name declarations.

Lines 10 and 20 declare a 35-position character field.

Lines 30 through 60 define a packed field with a length of 7 and 2 decimal positions.

Lines 70 and 80 define another 35-position character field.

Special PSDS Data Structure Subfields Positions

These special values are used in place of From and To positions. They represent built-in positions that contain special values. They are part of the PSDS. The PSDS is used to store both runtime and error-specific information. Many of these fields are set when the program starts; others are set when an error occurs. The definition specification shown in Figure 2.5 is the basis for this type of definition specification. Note that, although the function area is documented as part of this specification, no keywords are available to extend the properties of these fields. See Table 2.9.

Table 2.9: Definition Specification Special PSDS Data Structure Subfields Summary

Column	Title	Values	Description
7 - 21	Name	Name	The RPG name assigned to the special position value. The special position value is identified by the entry in positions 26 to 39.
26 - 39	Special position	*FILE	Name of the file being processed.
		*OPCODE	The RPG operation being performed when an exception/error occurred.
		*PARMS	Number of parameters passed to the program.
		*ROUTINE	Name of the RPG routine (through the RPG cycle) that was being performed when an exception/error occurred.
		*RECORD	Name of the record format being processed when an exception/error occurred.
		*PROC	Name of the program or procedure being run.
		*STATUS	Program status (error code).
44 - 80	Functions	Keywords	Not used.

Special INFDS Data Structure Subfields

Special values represent built-in positions that contain common values. They are part of the file information input/output feedback data structure (INFDS). The INFDS is used to store information about a file being processed. Each file declared in the program can have its own INFDS. The definition specification shown in Figure 2.5 is the basis for this type of definition specification. Note that, although the function area is documented as part of this specification, no keywords are available to extend the properties of these fields. See Table 2.10.

Table 2.10: Definition Specification Special INFDS Data Structure Subfields Summary

Column	Title	Values	Description
26 - 39	Special position	*FILE	File being processed; the external name for the opened file.
		*INP	A two-digit numeric field containing the DBCS indicator. A value of 0 indicates that a non-DBCS keyboard is being used. A value of 10 indicates that a Katakana or DBCS keyboard is being used.
			This value applies to WORKSTN device files only.
		*OUT	A two-digit numeric field containing the output DBCS indicator. A value of 0 indicates that a non-DBCS output device is being used. A value of 10 indicates that a Katakana or DBCS output is being used.
			This value applies to WORKSTN device files only.
		*OPCODE	A six-position field containing the RPG operation being performed when an exception/error occurs. The sixth position of this field contains one of the following status flags:
			F The operation was performed on a file name. R The operation was performed on a record format. I The operation was an implicit file name.
			For example, the CHAIN operation appears as CHAINR (Chain to a Record Format).
			Note that operation names that appear in this location are RPG III operation names and not RPG IV operation names. This is for compatibility with RPG III compilers. See *The Modern RPG Language*, 4th Edition by Robert Cozzi, Jr., Midrange Computing, 1996, for a description of RPG III operations.
		*MODE	A two-digit numeric field that indicates the type of session. A value of 0 indicates a non-DBCS session. A value of 10 indicates that this is a DBCS session.
			This value applies to WORKSTN device files only.

Table 2.10: Definition Specification Special INFDS Data Structure Subfields Summary, *cont.*

Column	Title	Values	Description
26 - 39 *continued*	Special position	*RECORD	For externally described files, this 8-byte character field contains the name of the record format being processed when an exception/error occurred. For program-described files, the record-identifying indicator of the record just processed is placed, left-adjusted, into the field.
		*ROUTINE	An eight-position character field containing the name of the RPG cycle routine running when an exception/error occurred. This field will contain one of the following routines:
			*INIT=program initialization *DETL=detail-time output *GETIN=get-in *TOTC=total-time calculations *TOTL=total-time output *DETC=detail calculations *OFL=overflow output *TERM=program termination.
		*SIZE	If the exception error occurs during another program—as is normally the case when a SPECIAL file is being processed—this field will contain the first eight characters of that program name.
		*STATUS	A four-digit numeric field containing the number of characters that can be sent to the display device in its current mode.
			File status (error code).
44 - 80			Not used.

Definition Specification Keywords

Table 2.11 summarizes the definition specification keywords.

Keyword	Parameters	Description
Table 2.11: Definition Specification Keyword Summary.		

ALIGN		Forces data structure subfield alignment on either a 2-, 4-, 8-, or 16-byte boundary. Use this keyword on the data structure definition (not subfield definition).
		
		Only the following subfields are aligned:
		    Pointer fields
		    Length notation fields without overlay

ALT	*Array name*	The name of an alternate table or array name. This keyword is valid for definitions of arrays or tables.
ALTSEQ	*NONE	Turns off alternate collating sequence for the specified field.
ASCEND		The array or table data is in ascending sequence.
BASED	Pointer variable	Identifies a pointer variable that holds the address (memory location) of variable being defined. The variable being defined can access the data stored at the memory address contained in the pointer variable. No storage is allocated for a based variable.
CCSID	0 to 65535 *DFT	Identifies the CCSID for double-byte character set data (G data-type) and UCS-2 data (C data-type) fields.
CLASS	*JAVA : class-name	Used with the O (object) data-type to declare an instance of a Java language class.
CONST	*Literal value*	A quoted character string, an expression, or a numeric value can be specified. The length of a constant value can be up to 1024 positions. For procedure parameters, the value being passed is constant; that is, it is considered read-only and is not changed by the called procedure. CONST parameters can be any value, including literal values or expressions.
CTDATA		Identifies the table or array as a compile-time data table or array. The data for the table or array is stored near the bottom of the source module and is identified by the **CTDATA *array/table* identifier.
DATFMT	Format [separator]	Specifies the format to use for the date field being defined. If this keyword is not specified, the date format is based on the DATFMT keyword specified on the header specification. The separator can be any valid separator character.

Table 2.11: Definition Specification Keyword Summary, *continued*

Keyword	Parameters	Description
DESCEND		The table or array data is in descending sequence.
DIM	*Elements*	Identifies the number of elements in the table or array. Up to 32767 elements are allowed per table or array.
	Occurrences	When DIM is used with a data structure, the data structure's occurrences are specified as array elements. The data structures occurrences may be referred to using traditional array syntax. For example, myDS(7) refers to the 7 occurrence of the data structure named MYDS.
		If a subfield of a data structure is also a data structure, and that subfield data structure contains the dim keyword, the qualified name syntax must be used to access the occurrences, for example:
		myDs(7).subfield(3)
		This accesses the third occurrence of the subfield in the seventh occurrence of the higher level data structure. This is referred to as complex data structures.
DTAARA	[Data area name] *VAR : *data-area-name*	Associates a variable (data structure, data area data structure, or field) with the data area name. If the data area name is not specified, the name of the variable is issued as the data area name.
		The data area name must be unquoted. If a field name is needed, it must be specified as the second parameter of the DTAARA keyword.
		When the data area name is to be specified within a field, it must be specified as the second parameter. In addition, the first parameter must contain the value *VAR. The data structure name can be qualified to a library name or *LIBL, or it can be unqualified. The data structure and library name must be specified in all uppercase characters.
EXPORT	'Export name'	The variable (field or data structure) is available to other program modules linked (i.e., bound) into this module. Those other modules can use the IMPORT keyword to access the data for this variable.
		The *export name* value is the name used to export the variable. This is the name that is referred to when importing the variable.
		This provides an alternative to parameters when calling procedures. *See* IMPORT.
EXTFLD	External field name	The external field name is renamed to the name specified in the name entry of this line. The EXTFLD keyword is functionally equivalent to the DDS RENAME keyword. If the PREFIX keyword is used, the prefix value is not applied to a field with the EXTFLD keyword.

Table 2.11: Definition Specification Keyword Summary, *continued*

Keyword	Parameters	Description
EXTFMT	External format code	Identifies the external data-type (format) of data loaded into pre-runtime arrays and tables.
		Valid format codes include the following:
		Format Description
		B RPG binary.
		C UCS-2 format data.
		I Signed integer.
		L Zoned numeric with left-side sign.
		R Zoned numeric with right-side sign.
		P Packed decimal.
		S Zoned numeric.
		U Unsigned integer.
		F Floating point
EXTNAME	File name { : format { : field selection }}	For externally described data structures, the name of the file and, optionally, the format name used to generate the data structure format.
		The third parameter is optional and indicates which fields from the record format are included. If no field selection is specified, only the input fields are included. The valid choices for the field selection parameter include the following:
		*ALL – All fields are included.
		*INPUT – Only the input fields are included.
		*OUTPUT – Only the output fields are included.
		*KEY – Only the key fields from the file are included.
		Note that if the file containing the record format includes the PREFIX keyword, then the subfields will also include that prefix.

Table 2.11: Definition Specification Keyword Summary, *continued*

Keyword	Parameters	Description
EXTPGM	*'External program name'*	The name of the program being prototyped.
		The external program name is the name of the program that is being prototyped. If no name is specified, the name in positions 7 to 21 is used as the name of the program.
EXTPROC	*'External procedure name'*	The name of the procedure being prototyped. A quoted character literal, a named constant, or a procedure pointer can be specified as the external program name.
		If neither EXTPROC nor EXTPGM is specified, the name of the prototype (positions 7 to 21) is used as the procedure name.
		See PROCPTR *keyword.*
	*JAVA : class-name : method	Used to declare a prototype to evoke a method in a Java class object.
	*CL : procedure-name	Used to declare a prototype that receives a return value that uses the CL language parameter standards. Also used when declaring an RPG procedure that is to be called by CL.
	*Cwiden : procedure-name	Used to prototype a procedure written in the C language. Causes parameters passed by value to be widened to the standard C language conventions.
	*Cnowiden : procedure-name	Used to prototype a procedure written in the C language that includes the following C directive: #pragma argument(*procedure-name,nowiden*)
FROMFILE	File name	The name of the database file whose data will be used to load the pre-runtime array or table.
IMPORT	*'External name'*	The memory for the variable (field or data structure) is allocated in another program module. The data can be accessed from this program module.
		The definition of the variable should match that of the variable defined with the EXPORT keyword in the other program module.

Table 2.11: Definition Specification Keyword Summary, *continued*

Keyword	Parameters	Description
INZ	*Initial value* *EXTDFT *USER *SYS *JOB *LIKEDS	The initial value for the variable. The value must be a quoted character string, a numeric literal, a named constant, or an expression that can be analyzed at compile time. The *EXTDFT option can be used for fields specified for an externally described data structure. Specify INZ(*EXTDFT), on the data structure header, to initialize all subfields to the value specified for the DFT keyword in the DDS for the file. Specify INZ(*EXTDFT) on the individual subfield to initialize the subfield itself. INZ(*SYS) and INZ(*JOB) initialize date, time, or time-stamp variables to the current system or job value, respectively. *USER initializes a character field to the user profile ID for the job running the program. *LIKEDS initializes the fields of a data structure that was previously defined using the LIKEDS keyword. The initial values used are the same as those in the data structure specified on the LIKEDS keyword.
LIKE	*Referenced variable*	Use this keyword to assign the attribute of the based-on variable to the new variable. Only the size, decimal positions (if any), and data-type are inherited. The initial value is not. If the based-on variable is the name of a procedure prototype, the new field inherits the same properties as the prototype's return value. If the based-on variable is an array, only the properties of the based-on array's elements are inherited. To also inherit the number of elements from the original array, specify the DIM keyword with the %ELEM built-in function, as follows:
LIKEDS	Data structure name	Declares a new data structure with the same format as its based-on data structure. All the fields from the original data structure are included in the new data structure. In addition, data structures that include the LIKEDS keyword, also automatically include the QUALIFIED keyword, and thus must only be refered to using the qualified data structure syntax of ds.subfield. When the LIKEDS keyword is used, the initial values for the subfields of the new data structure do not inherit the original data structure's initialization. Therefore in order to initialize the new data structure to match the based-on data structure, the INZ(*LIKEDS) keyword option must also be used.

Table 2.11: Definition Specification Keyword Summary, *continued*		
Keyword	Parameters	Description
LIKEREC	Record : field selection	Declares a data structure whose subfields have the same names and attributes of those specified in the record format name specified on the first parameter.
		The second parameter is optional and indicates which fields from the record format are included. If no second parameter is specified, then all fields are included. The valid choices for the second parameter include the following:
		*ALL – All fields are included.
		*INPUT – Only the input fields are included.
		*OUTPUT – Only the output fields are included.
		*KEY – Only the key fields from the file are included.
		Note that if the file containing the record format includes the PREFIX keyword, then the subfields will also include that prefix.
NOOPT		Prohibits optimization of the variable. Functionally similar to the VOLITILE keyword in the C language, it ensures that the content of the variable is the most current assigned value.
		When calling an older version of RPG using a program prototype, specify the NOOPT keyword for each parameter. Older versions of RPG are implicitly defined with NOOPT. This ensures that parameters are passed correctly.
		In addition, any variables used in the *PSSR or other error routines should also include NOOPT in their definition.
OCCURS	*Occurrences*	The number of occurrences for the multiple occurrence data structure. For named data structures, the maximum occurrences is 32767. For unnamed data structures, the maximum is 9999999.
OPDESC		Operational descriptors are passed with the parameters. Use this keyword on the procedure prototype and the procedure interface statements.
OPTIONS	[*opt1* : *opt2* : *opt3* : *opt4* : *opt5*]	Parameter passing options. On a prototype or parameter list, use the OPTIONS keyword on any of the parameters that require special consideration.
	*NOPASS	The parameter is optional. It doesn't have to be specified when the procedure is called by the CALLP operation or as a function. All subsequent parameters for this prototype must also contain OPTIONS(*NOPASS).

Table 2.11: Definition Specification Keyword Summary, *continued*

Keyword	Parameters	Description
OPTIONS *continued*	*OMIT	The *OMIT option is allowed for the parameter. Use *OMIT in place of a parameter value when the procedure is called.
	*RIGHTADJ	For CONST or VALUE parameters the value specified for the parameter is passed right-justified.
	*STRING	The value is converted into a null-terminated string and then a pointer reference to that string is passed to the called procedure. This is valid for parameter of type pointer.
	*VARSIZE	The character, array, or graphic parameter value can be shorter than the length defined in the prototype for the parameter. If *VARSIZE is not specified, the value passed must be at least the length of the parameter length.
		The CEEDOD API can be used to retrieve the length of the parameters passed, provided the OPDESC keyword is also specified for the prototype. Optionally, by specifying that the parameter is VARYING, the %LEN built-in function can be used to retrieve the length of the character value passed as the parameter. *See* CONST.
OVERLAY	*Subfield* [: *nStart* | *NEXT]	The subfield being defined is located at *nStart* of the overlaid *subfield* or data structure name.
		If *NEXT is specified, the field appears in the data structure in the next available position within the overlaid variable.
PACKEVEN		Causes a packed decimal field to be packed with an even number of digits. The decimal precision will be an even number of digits, such as, 2, 4, 6, 8, and so on.
		If this keyword is not specified, the field is packed with an odd number of digits, such as: 3, 5, 7, 9, 11, and so on.
		Use this keyword only when using from and to notation.
PERRCD	*Entries per record*	The number of elements per record for a compile-time or pre-runtime array. The default value for this keyword is 1.

Table 2.11: Definition Specification Keyword Summary, *continued*

Keyword	Parameters	Description
PREFIX	*Prefix* [: *replace count*]	For externally described files, the prefix is used to automatically re-name all fields in the file. The prefix is appended to the front of the field name for each field in the file's record format. If the prefix value is enclosed in quotes, the value must be in all uppercase letters. The PREFIX value cannot contain a period.
		The replace-count controls whether or not the first replace-count characters of each field name are trimmed from the field name before the automatic rename occurs. For example, if all the fields in the file begin with cst, as in cstnam, cstnbr, and cstadr, the prefix keyword's replace-count can be used to remove the leading three characters from each field.
		In this case, a prefix keyword specified as
		prefix('cm_' : 3) will rename the above fields, as follows:
		cm_nam, cm_nbr, cm_adr
PROCPTR		This keyword is used to indicate that a field of type pointer (*) is being declared as a procedure pointer.
QUALIFIED		This keyword causes the data structure to be required to be referred to using the qualified data structure syntax. Traditionally, data structure subfields can be specified individually. When the QUALIFIED keyword is used, subfields must be referred to using the qualified syntax as follows:
		myDS.subfield
		Subfields of qualified data structures may not be referred to by their names alone. This allows two different data structures to contain a subfield with the same name.
		Note that the QUALIFIED keyword is implied when when LIKEDS and LIKEREC keywords are used to declare the data structure.
STATIC		The data item is stored in static storage. Items stored in static storage are retained until the program is terminated. All global data items are static. Data items within a subprocedure are, by default, stored in automatic storage. Automatic storage is initialized each time a subprocedure is called and released when the subprocedure ends.
		Because subprocedures can be called recursively, consideration should be given as to whether a data item should be left in automatic storage, as each invocation of a procedure allocates its own copy of all automatic data items.

Table 2.11: Definition Specification Keyword Summary, *continued*		
Keyword	**Parameters**	**Description**
TIMFMT	Format [: separator]	Specifies the format for time fields. If this keyword is not specified, the *ISO format (hh.mm.ss 24 hour clock) is used.
		The separator can be any separator and defaults to the slash (/).
TOFILE	File name	Identifies the output file for a pre-runtime array or table. The data from the array is written to this file when the program ends. The file must be defined on the file description specifications as a combined file, and must have a file designation of T (table).
VALUE		For procedure prototype parameters. Causes the parameter to be passed "by value" instead of the system-wide default of "by reference." The system makes a copy of the parameter value and passes a reference to that copy to the called procedure.
VARYING		The character field (data-type A) is a variable length field. The length of the field is the maximum length that can be accessed for the field. Use the %LEN built-in function to set and retrieve the length of variable length fields. The actual length of a VARYING field is stored as a two-byte binary (10i0) value. That value is hidden from the RPG program and is stored in the first type bytes of the storage allocated for the field. The physical length of the field is two bytes longer than that declared length.

INPUT SPECIFICATION

Input specifications are used to describe program-described file formats; rename externally described file fields; and assign match field, level-break, and field-to-record relation indicators.

Program-described files require that their formats be defined through input specifications. These specifications are known as *record identifying entries*. They contain identifying codes that allow a record format to be associated with an indicator. For example, if position 6 of the database file record contains the letter H, and position 12 contains the number 1, then indicator 20 is set on.

Externally described files don't require input specifications. The RPG compiler generates the equivalent of input specifications based on the external definition of the file. However, each file format can be associated with a record-identifying indicator by specifying the format name and a record-identifying indicator.

Additionally, externally described files can have their fields renamed by specifying the external field name in the External Field positions of the input specification, and the new name in the Field Name position of the input specification. The PREFIX keyword is also used to change all field names to contain a prefix character set. See the PREFIX keyword in Table 2.6 for more information.

Because there are both program-described and externally described files, there are five different layouts for the input specification. Figures 2.8 through 2.12 illustrate the layouts of the various types of input specifications.

```
.....INAME++++++NS1OINPos1+NCVPos2+NCVPos3+NCV................................
```

Figure 2.8: Program-described file input specification ruler.

```
.....I.........AND..INPos1+NCVPos2+NCVPos3+NCV................................
```

Figure 2.9: Program-described file continuation input specification ruler.

```
.....I.....................Fmt+/TFRom+To+++D+Field+++++++++L1M1FRPLMNZB......
```

Figure 2.10: Program-described field input specification ruler.

```
.....IName++++++....IN........................................................
```

Figure 2.11: Externally described file format input specification ruler.

```
.....I.............ExternName.................Field+++++++++L1M1..PLMNZB......
```

Figure 2.12: Externally described field input specification ruler.

INPUT SPECIFICATION SUMMARY

The following sections summarize program-described and externally described files and file-field descriptions.

Program-Described Files

Program-described files are seldom used with the modern RPG language. Typically, when this type of file exists in a program, the program has been converted from an older system or it is some kind of system utility. See Table 2.12.

Table 2.12: Input Specification Program-Described Files Summary

Column	Title	Values	Description
6	Form type	I	Identifies the statement as an input specification.
7 - 16	File name	Blank	The name of the file (as it appears on a corresponding file specification). The file must be defined as an input, output, update, or combined file on the file specification.
16 - 18	Format entry continuation		The record-identifying entries are continued from the previous statement.
		AND	The AND indicates that both the preceding line's and this line's record-identifying codes must be satisfied in order to set on the record-identifying indicator.
		OR	The record-identifying entries are continued from the previous statement. The OR indicates that the preceding line's or this line's record-identifying codes must be satisfied in order to set on the record-identifying indicator.
17 - 18	Sequencing	Any letters	Alphabetic characters indicate that no special record sequencing is required. Typically, the letters NS are used to indicate *no sequence*. This type of entry must appear prior to records that have a required sequence (i.e., a numeric entry in these positions).
		01 to 99	Special record sequencing is requested, if the sequence is required. Use the sequence number and sequence option entries to control the sequencing.
19	Sequence number	Blank	A blank is required when sequencing contains no entry or when sequencing contains characters.
		1	One record of this type, per sequence, is required. More than one record of this type, per sequence, generates an error.
		N	One record of this type, per sequence, is required or more records of this type, per sequences, are allowed.
20	Option	Blank	A blank is required when no sequencing is specified. If sequencing is specified, then a record of this type is required in the sequence.
		O	Valid for sequenced files only, an entry of O indicates that this sequence entry is optional.

Table 2.12: Input Specification Program-Described Files Summary, *continued*

Column	Title	Values	Description
21 - 22	Record-identify-ing indicator	Indicator	Any valid indicator except overflow (OA to OF, OV), first page (1P), or RPG II function key (KA to KY) can be specified as a record-identifying indicator.
			When a record of the type specified is read, the indicator is set on.
		**	Two asterisks indicate that the statements that follow are *look-ahead fields*. Look-ahead fields are used for viewing the information in the next record in the file when processing a file using the RPG cycle. For example, if a file contains 100 re-cords and the RPG cycle just processed the 39th record, the look-ahead field allows the contents of the 40th record to be interrogated before that record is actually retrieved. Look-ahead fields function with input files only. With other types of files, such as update and combined files, look-ahead fields contain the same data as the record just read.
			When the end of file is reached, the data in the look-ahead fields is set to *HIVAL for all field types, except character fields, which are set to 9s.
23 - 46	Record type identifying codes	Position and character value	Up to three record-identifying codes can be specified for each record-identifying entry. If more than three re-cord-identifying codes are required, specify an AND/OR entry in Format Entry Continuation positions.
23 - 27	Position	Blank	No record-identifying code is specified.
		1 to 32,766	Position within the record of the value specified for the re-cord-identifying value.
28	Not	Blank	The character specified for the record-identifying value must exist in the record at the position specified.
		N	The character specified for the record-identifying value must not exist in the record at the position specified.
29	Comparison type	Blank	No record-identifying code is specified.
		C	The character specified for the record-identifying value is a character, and the full value is used for the record-identifying code comparison.
		Z	The upper 4 bits of the character specified for the re-cord-identifying value are used as the record-identifying code comparison. This allows comparisons for numeric values of positive or negative value, for example.
		D	The lower 4 bits of the character specified for the record identifying-value are used for the record-identifying code.

Column	Title	Values	Description
30	Record-identifying value	Any character	The character used as the record-identifying value.
31 - 38	Record identifying code #2		Same structure as columns 23 to 30.
39 - 46	Record identifying code #3		Same structure as columns 23 to 30.
47 - 80			Not used.

Table 2.12: Input Specification Program-Described Files Summary, *continued*

Program-Described File Field Descriptions

Table 2.13 summarizes the input specification program-described file field descriptions.

Table 2.13: Input Specification Program-Described File Field Description Summary

Column	Title	Values	Description
6	Form type	I	Identifies this statement as an input specification.
7 - 30			Not used.
31 - 34	Date/time format	Blank	For date and time fields only; the format specified on the DATFMT or TIMFMT keyword of the file's file specification is used as the format for the date or time value. For non-date and non-time fields, this entry must be blank.
		Format	Any valid date or time format is supported For date fields, the following formats are supported:

Format	Description	Sep	Format
*MDY	Month Day Year	Yes	mm/dd/yy
*DMY	Day Month Year	Yes	dd/mm/yy
*YMD	Year Month Day	Yes	yy/mm/dd
*JUL	Julian	Yes	yy/ddd
*ISO	ISO standard	No	ccyy-mm-dd
*USA	USA standard	No	mm/dd/ccyy
*EUR	European standard	No	dd.mm.ccyy
*JIS	Japan standard	No	ccyy-mm-dd

Table 2.13: Input Specification Program-Described File Field Description Summary, *cont.*

Column	Title	Values	Description
		Format *continued*	For time fields,the following formats are supported:

Format	Description	Sep	Format
*HMS	Standard	Yes	hh:mm:ss
*ISO	ISO standard	No	hh.mm.ss
*USA	USA standard	No	hh:mm AM
*EUR	European standard	No	hh.mm.ss
*JIS	Japan standard	No	hh:mm:ss

Column	Title	Values	Description
35	Date/time separator	Separator	Any valid date or time separator. Separators are valid only for those date and time formats that support separators. For date formats, the following separator characters can be specified: / , . - & For time formats, the following separator characters can be specified: : , . &
36	Data type	Blank	If the decimal positions are also blank, then the field is a character field. If the decimal positions contain a number value, then the field is a zoned decimal field.
		A	(CHARACTER) character field.
		B	(NUMERIC) binary field.
		C	(CHARACTER) UCS-2 field.
		D	(DATE) date field.
		F	(NUMERIC) floating point.
		G	(GRAPHIC) double-byte character set (DBCS) field.
		I	(NUMERIC) integer field.
		L	(NUMERIC) The field being defined is zoned decimal with a PRECEDING sign value.
		N	(CHARACTER) named indicator.
		P	(NUMERIC) packed decimal field.
		R	(NUMERIC) The field being defined is zoned decimal with trailing sign value.
		S	(NUMERIC) zoned decimal.
		T	(TIME) time field.
		U	(NUMERIC) unsigned integer field.
		Z	(TIMESTAMP) timestamp field.
34 - 38	Start position of field	1 to 32767	The starting position within the file's record of the field.
39 - 46	Ending position of field	1 to 32767	The ending position within the file's record of the field. Start positions and end positions are collectively referred to as the From and To positions.

Table 2.13: Input Specification Program-Described File Field Description Summary, *cont.*

Column	Title	Values	Description
47 - 48	Decimal positions	Blank	The field's data-type is non-numeric, unless one of the following applies: the field is an array or array element, in which case the data-type is specified by the array definition; the field is of type I (signed integer) or U (unsigned integer), in which case the field is numeric.
		0 to 30	The number of decimal positions for the numeric field.
49 - 62	Field name	Name	The name of the field being defined. In addition to a symbolic name, an array name, array element, data structure name, indicator variable, indicator array element, or PAGE*n* can be specified.
63 - 64	Control field	Blanks	The field is not a control field.
		L1 to L9	The field is a control field. When a record is read by the RPG cycle, if the contents of the field change, the level-break indicator is set on. If more than one field contains the same level-break indicator, the indicator is set on when any of the fields change.
			When a specific level-break indicator is set on, all low-level break indicators are also set on. For example, if indicator L4 is set on, L3, L2, and L1 are also set on.
65 - 66	Match field	Blanks	The field is not a matched field.
		M1 to M9	The field is a matched field and has a corresponding matched field in another file.
67 - 68	Field record relation	Blank	No field/record relationship exists.
		Record-identifying indicator	The indicator that associates this field with a specific record-identifying entry code and indicator for this file.
69 - 70	Field status indicator (PLUS)	Blank	No indicator is set on.
		Indicator	The indicator is set on when a record is read and the content of this field is greater than zero.
71 - 72	Field status indicator (MINUS)	Blank	No indicator is set on.
		Indicator	The indicator is set on when a record is read and the content of this field is less than zero.
73 - 74	Field status indicator (Blank/Zero)	Blank	No indicator is set on.
		Indicator	The indicator is set on when a record is read and the content of this field is equal to zero (for numeric fields) or blanks (for character fields).

Externally Described Files

Externally described files are the rule when writing new applications with the modern RPG language. External definitions allow the programmer to avoid specifying lengthy record-format descriptions and to easily take advantage of modern operations.

None of the following specifications are required for externally described files. The compiler automatically generates the necessary input specifications to support this type of file. See Table 2.14.

Column	Title	Values	Description
	Table 2.14: Input Specification Externally Described Files Summary		
Column	**Title**	**Values**	**Description**
6	Form type	I	Identifies this statement as an input specification.
7 - 16	Record format name	Name	The name of a record format from an externally described file.
17 - 20			Not used.
21 - 22	Record-identifying indicator		Any valid indicator except overflow (OA to OF, OV), first page (1P), or RPG II function key (KA to KY) can be specified as a record-identifying indicator.
			When a record of the type specified is read, the indicator is set on.
			Note: The look-ahead field codes (**) are supported by externally described data, but the look-ahead field entries must be program described.
23 - 80			Not used.

Externally Described Field Descriptions

Externally described files need no input specifications. The RPG compiler automatically generates record format(s) from the external definition. Externally described files can, however, rename their external field names and assigned level-break, match field, and field indicators. See Table 2.15.

Table 2.15: Input Specifications Externally Described Field Description Summary

Column	Title	Values	Description
6	Form type	I	Identifies this statement as an input specification.
7 - 20			Not used.
21 - 30	External field name	Blank	The name of the externally described field is used as the name of the field in the program and is referred to as the *internal name*.
		Name	Name of the externally described file's field being renamed to the name specified in the field name positions.
31 - 48			Not used.
49 - 62	Field name	Name	The name used to access the data in the file's record. If the external field name is blank, the field name specified here is also the external name being referenced.
63 - 64	Control field	Blanks	The field is not a control field.
		L1 to L9	The field is a control field. When a record is read by the RPG cycle, if the contents of the field change, the level-break indicator is set on. If more than one field contains the same level-break indicator, the indicator is set on when any of the fields change.
			When a specific level-break indicator is set on, all low-level break indicators are also set on. For example, if indicator L4 is set on, L3, L2, and L1 are also set on.
65 - 66	Match field	Blanks	The field is not a matched field.
		M1 to M9	The field is a matched field and has a corresponding matched field in another file.
67 - 68	Field record relation	Blank	No field/record relationship exists.
		Record-identifying indicator	The indicator that associates this field with a specific record-identifying entry code and indicator for this file.
69 - 70	Field status indicator (PLUS)	Blank	No indicator is set on.
		Indicator	The indicator is set on when a record is read and the content of this field is greater than zero.
71 - 72	Field status indicator (MINUS)	Blank	No indicator is set on.
		Indicator	The indicator is set on when a record is read and the content of this field is less than zero.
73 - 74	Field status Indicator (Blank/Zero)	Blank	No indicator is set on.
		Indicator	The indicator is set on when a record is read and the content of this field is equal to zero (for numeric fields) or blanks (for character fields).
75 - 80			Not used.

CALCULATION SPECIFICATION

Calculation specifications are used to write the program instructions that are run when the program is called. The majority of an RPG program is made up of calculation specifications and definition specifications. All operations, including but not limited to, file processing, computations, and data manipulation, are performed with calculation specifications.

There are two formats for calculation specifications: the *standard calculation specification* and the *alternate calculation specification*. The standard calculation specification is used for most operations (i.e., program instructions). Although the alternate calculation specification is used by fewer operations, these operations control the program logic and most data manipulation. Consequently, RPG programs consist mostly of alternate calculation specifications.

There is no order or priority to either specification. The standard calculation specification can be intermixed with the alternate calculation specification. The layout of the two formats is designed to allow this transparency. Figures 2.13 and 2.14 illustrate the calculation specifications.

```
.....CSRnØ1Factor1+++++++OpCode(ex)Factor2+++++++Result++++++++Len++DcHiLoEq....
```

Figure 2.13: Standard calculation specification.

```
.....CSRnØ1..............OpCode(ex)Extended-factor2++++++++++++++++++++++++++++++
```

Figure 2.14: Alternate calculation specification with extended factor 2.

Calculation Specification Summary

Table 2.16 summarizes the calculation specifications.

Table 2.16: Calculation Specification Summary			
Column	Title	Values	Description
6	Form type	C	Identifies this statement as a calculation specification.
7	Control code	*	The statement is ignored (it is a comment).
		/	The statement contains either a compiler directive, such as /COPY, /IF DEFINED, or a preprocessor directive, such as /EXEC SQL.
		+	The statement is a preprocessor continuation specification that began with /EXEC SQL on a previous line.

Table 2.16: Calculation Specification Summary, *continued*

Column	Title	Values	Description
7 - 8	Control level indicator or subroutine notation	Blank	The statement is a normal statement or normal subroutine statement. No special control is specified.
			Control-level indicators cannot be specified within a subprocedure.
		AN/OR	The indicator conditioning on the previous statement is continued onto this line. The indicator condition of the previous line and/or the indicator condition of this line must be met before the operation can be performed. When AN/OR is used, the operation must be specified on the last statement of the AN/OR group. There is no limit to the number of AN/OR continuations that can be specified for each operation.
		L0	Total-time calculation. Because level zero (L0) is always on, this controlling level indicator always tests true.
		L1 to L9	Total-time calculation. The control-level indicators are tested at total time (level break).
		LR	Total-time and last-record processing. The calculation statement is performed during total-time processing—after the last record indicator is set on.
		SR	Optional documentary notation to indicate a subroutine statement. Typically, SR is used only on the first and last statements of each subroutine to better identify the beginning and ending of the subroutine.
9 - 11	Conditioning indicators	Blank	No conditioning indicators are used to control whether or not this statement is performed. There should never be an entry in these columns if proper programming practices are followed.
		Any valid indicator(s)	The specified indicator(s) control the running of this calculation. If more than one indicator is required, the conditioning can be continued on subsequent calculation specifications by specifying an AN or an OR in the control level positions of the next calculation line. All valid indicators are allowed.
12 - 25	Factor 1	Blank	No factor 1 entry is specified. Several operations support an entry in factor 1, while others do not require factor 1.
		Any characters	The entry is used by the operation. The entry must match the requirements of the operation. All entries in factor 1 must be left-justified.

Table 2.16: Calculation Specification Summary, *continued*

Column	Title	Values	Description
26 - 35	Operation code and operation extender		The name of the RPG instruction (operation) that is to be performed. Most operations use factor 1, factor 2, or the result field.
		Operation [(ex)]	The operation extender is optional for operations that support an extender. The extender must be enclosed in parentheses. It can appear anywhere following the operation. Typical operation extenders include P (pad), N (no record lock), and H (half-adjust). *See* Table 5.8 for operation extender rules.

Extender	Description
D	Pass operation descriptors.
D	Test for valid date.
E	Activate %ERROR and %STATUS.
H	Half-adjust (round) result field.
M	Use max-digits precision rules.
N	Reset pointer to NULL.
N	Avoid locking the record.
P	Pad result field.
R	Use result-field length precision rules.
T	Test for valid time.
Z	Test for valid timestamp.

Column	Title	Values	Description
36 - 49	Factor 2	Blank	No factor 2 entry is specified. Several operations support an entry in factor 2, while others do not require factor 2.
		Any characters	The entry is used by the operation. The entry must match the requirements of the operation. All entries in factor 2 must be left justified.
36 - 80	Extended Factor 2	Any characters	Any natural expression is specified.
			It can span multiple lines by continuing the expression onto addition lines in the extended factor 2 area. Only certain operations support the extended factor 2, including the following:

Op Code	Description
CALLP	Call a prototyped procedure.
DOU	Do until.
DOW	Do while.
ELSEIF	Combined ELSE and IF operation
EVAL	Evaluate an expression.
EVALR	Evaluate, right adjust.
FOR	Iterative FOR loop
IF	Conditional IF.
RETURN	Return value to caller.
WHEN	Select/WHEN CASE.

Table 2.16: Calculation Specification Summary, *continued*

Column	Title	Values	Description
50 - 63	Result field	Blank	No result field entry is specified. Several operations support an entry in the result field, while others do not require the result field.
		Variable name	The entry is used as the target of the operation. The entry must match the requirements of the operation. All entries in the result field must be left justified. The result field is normally used as the target of the operation. For example, if it is the target of a MOVE operation, the content of factor 2 is copied to the result-field entry.
64 - 68	Result field length	Blank	The result field is defined elsewhere in the program or it is not a definable value (e.g., a label or subroutine name).
		1 to 30	For numeric fields, the length of the result field.
		1 to 65535	For character fields, the length of the result field.
		-65534 to +65534	Relative length of the result field based on the field specified for factor 2 for a *LIKE DEFINE operation. The result field's length is the length of the field specified in factor 2, plus or minus the value specified.
69 - 70	Decimal positions	Blank	If the result field is specified and a result field length is also specified, the new field's data-type is character. If the result field length is blank, then these columns must also be blank. For the *LIKE DEFINE operation, the result field decimal positions must be blank.
		0 to 30	Number of decimal positions for the result field. (Valid only for numeric result fields.)
71 - 76	Resulting indicators	Blank	No resulting indicators are set on as a result of the operation.
		Any valid indicator	The resulting indicators are set according to the results of the operation. All but the following can be specified as resulting indicators: 1P, MR.
77 - 80			Not used.

OUTPUT SPECIFICATION

Output specifications are used to define the output of the program. In the modern RPG language, output specifications are used for three purposes: defining program-defined printer files, releasing database record locks, and overriding the basic control for externally described output files. Figures 2.15 through 2.17 illustrate the output specifications.

```
.....OFormat++++DAddn01n02n03Except++++SpbSpaSkbSka
```

Figure 2.15: Output header specification.

```
.....O.........And..nØ1nØ2nØ3
```

Figure 2.16: Output header continuation specification.

```
.....O.............nØ1nØ2nØ3Field+++++++++YB?End++PConstant/Editword+++++++++++
```

Figure 2.17: Output field specification.

Program-Described Output File Control Entries

Table 2.17 summarizes output specification program-described file entries.

Column	Title	Values	Description
	Table 2.17: Output Specification Program-Described File Summary		
6	Form type	O	Identifies this statement as an output specification.
7 - 16	Output file name	Blank	The name used is the same as the more recently specified output file name.
		File name	Any file opened for output can be specified.
17	Output type	H	Heading records. For documentation purposes only. The H in this column is functionally equivalent to placing a D in this column. Heading records usually contain report column titles, page numbers, and date information.
		D	Detail records. Usually, detail records contain information that will be repeated on subsequent output records, such as a printed report. Additionally, detail records are used to write and update records in program-defined data files.
		T	Total-time records. Usually, total-time records are used to output the results of the program.
		E	Exception records. Exception records are written using the EXCEPT op code. Indicators or an exception name can condition exception output.
16 - 18	Conditioning continuation controls	AND/OR	The conditioning indicators are a continuation of the previous line. The indicator condition on the previous line and/or the indicator condition on this line must be satisfied for the output line to be written.
18 - 20	File addition and file deletion	ADD	For database (DISK) files only. Records are added to the file. File addition must be specified on the file specification for the file being written.
		DEL	For database (DISK) files only. The record is deleted from the file; it will no longer be accessible. The file must be declared as an UPDATE file on the file specification.

Table 2.17: Output Specification Program-Described File Summary, *continued*

Column	Title	Values	Description
18	Output control	Blank	No special controlling is specified for this output statement.
		F	Fetch overflow. When fetch is specified, RPG checks for overflow after each printed line. If the overflow indicator for this printer file is on and fetch has been specified, any detail and heading lines that are conditioned by that indicator are printed before this line.
		R	The WORKSTN file specified is released from the program. *See* REL operation.
21 - 29	Controlling indicators	Blank	No indicators condition this output line.
		1P	First page indicator (valid for heading and detail output only). Output lines conditioned with the 1P indicator are printed after the *INZSR subroutine is performed.
		Indicator	Any valid indicator (up to three) can be specified to control the output line. If more than three indicators are required, the continuation controls (AND/OR) can be specified.
30 - 39	Except name	Blank	No exception name controls the output line.
		Name	This line is exception output, and is controlled by the exception name. If conditioning indicators are specified, their condition must be satisfied for the line to be output. *See* EXCEPT operation.
40 - 42	Line spacing before printing	Blank	For PRINTER files only. The printer won't advance before printing the output line.
		0 to 255	The printer advances the number of lines specified before printing the output line.
43 - 45	Line spacing after printing	Blank	For PRINTER files only. The printer advances one line after printing the output line.
		0 to 255	The printer advances the number of lines indicated after printing the output line.
46 - 48	Line skipping before	Blank or 0	For PRINTER files only. The printer does not advance before printing the output line.
		1 to 255	The printer advances to the line on the current page before printing. If the current print line is beyond the line specified, the printer ejects the current page and advances to the line on the next page before printing.

Table 2.17: Output Specification Program-Described File Summary, *continued*

Column	Title	Values	Description
49 - 51	Line skipping after	Blank	For PRINTER files only. The printer won't advance after printing the output line.
		1 to 255	The printer advances to the line on the current page after printing. If the current print line is beyond the line specified, the printer ejects the current page and advances to the line on the next page after printing.
52 - 80			Not used.

Program-Described Output File Field Description

The advanced support for externally described files has led RPG programmers to rarely use program-described files. While the use of program-defined WORKSTN and DISK files is virtually nonexistent, it is quite common to find program-described PRINTER output files (see Table 2.18). This is probably due to the advanced support RPG has for printed output (a principle design element in the original RPG language).

Table 2.18: Output Specification Program-Described File Field Description Summary

Column	Title	Values	Description
6	Form type	O	Identifies this statement as an output specification.
7 - 20			Not used for program-defined output fields.
21 - 29	Controlling indicators	Blank	The output field is always written whenever the controlling output specification is written.
		1P	The output field is written only once—at first page output time (1P).
		Any valid indicator (up to three)	The output field is included in the output operation only when the test of the controlling indicators is true.
30 - 43	Output field name	Name	The name of the field to be output when the controlling output specification is written. The field name must have already been defined in the program or it must be a predefined name, such as *DATE, UDATE, PAGE, or *INxx.
		Name constant	The name of the named constant to be output when the controlling output specification is written.

Table 2.18: Output Specification Program-Described File Field Description Summary, *cont.*

Column	Title	Values	Description
30 - 43		PAGE, or PAGE1 to PAGE7	The current page number is output. The various PAGE fields include PAGE and PAGE*n*, where *n* is 1 to 7, giving a total of eight page-counter fields.
			Conditioning indicators condition the resetting, not the printing, of the page number fields. When the indicator condition is met, the PAGE*n* field is reset to zero. When the indicator condition is not met, the PAGE*n* field value is printed normally.
		*IN*xx*	The value of the indicator *xx* is output to the record; *xx* can be any valid RPG indicator.
		*IN,*xx*	The value of the indicator *xx* is output to the record; *xx* can be any general-purpose indicator (01 to 99).
		*PLACE	This reserved word causes the data that has been specified up to the first *PLACE to be repeated to the right of that same data. For example, if 4-up labels for the same name and address are required, the output specification contains the field for the name, followed by three *PLACE entries.
44	Edit code	Blank	No edit code is used for this output field.
		1 to 9 A, B, C, D, J, K, L, M, N, O, P, Q, X, Y, Z	The predefined edit code is used to mask the output field. The output field must be a numeric variable or a numeric named constant.
			For more information on edit codes and edit words, see Table 2.23.
45	Blank after	Blank	The field is output and no other action is taken.
		B	The field is output and then it is cleared. Numeric fields are set to zero and character fields are set to blanks.

Table 2.18: Output Specification Program-Described File Field Description Summary, *cont.*

Column	Title	Values	Description
40 - 43	Output positions	Blank	The output field is output to a relative position of +0. That is, it is output adjacent to the previous output field's right-most character.
	Ending position	1 to 65535	The ending (right-most) position of the output field.
	Relative position	- 65,534 to +65,534	The field is output relative to the previous field's ending position. The value of the relative position represents the number of spaces between the first character of this field and the last character of the previous field. For example, an ending position of +1 puts one space between this field and the previous field.
			The ± (plus or minus) sign must precede the relative number. The number itself, however, must be left justified.
		K1 to K10	For program-defined workstation device files, the K1 to K10 entry represents the length of the format name.
52	Data type	Blank	The output field is written as zoned decimal (if it is a numeric data-type) or character.
		A	(CHARACTER) character field. Default for fields with no decimal positions.
		B	(NUMERIC) binary field.
		C	(CHARACTER) UCS-2 field.
		D	(DATE) date field.
		F	(NUMERIC) floating-point numeric.
		G	(GRAPHIC) double-byte character set field.
		I	(NUMERIC) integer field.
		L	(NUMERIC) zoned decimal with a preceding sign.
		N	(CHARACTER) named indicator field.
		P	(NUMERIC) packed decimal field, the output field is written as packed decimal.
		R	(NUMERIC) zoned decimal with a trailing sign.
		S	(NUMERIC) zoned decimal.
		T	(TIME) time field.
		U	(NUMERIC) unsigned integer field.
		Z	(TIME) timestamp field.

Table 2.18: Output Specification Program-Described File Field Description Summary, *cont.*

Column	Title	Values	Description
53 - 80	Output constant or edit word	Blank	No constant or edit word is used with this output field. These columns must be blank when a non-numeric value is being output.
		Quoted literal	Any quoted character string can be specified. When the quoted character string contains embedded quotes, they must be doubled within the character string itself. So, O'Clock becomes 'O''Clock'.
		Edit word	Any valid edit word can be specified to format the output of a numeric field. See Table 2.23 for more information.
		Date or time format	Any valid date or time format can be specified to control the format of the date/time output field. These values are as follows:

Format	Description	Sep	Format
*MDY	Month Day Year	Yes	mm/dd/yy
*DMY	Day Month Year	Yes	dd/mm/yy
*YMD	Year Month Day	Yes	yy/mm/dd
*JUL	Juilian	Yes	yy/ddd
*ISO	ISO standard	No	ccyy-mm-dd
*USA	USA standard	No	mm/dd/ccyy
*EUR	European standard	No	dd.mm.ccyy
*JIS	Japan standard	No	ccyy-mm-dd

Format	Description	Sep	Format
*HMS	Standard	Yes	hh:mm:ss
*ISO	ISO standard	No	hh.mm.ss
*USA	USA standard	No	hh:mm AM
*EUR	European standard	No	hh.mm.ss
*JIS	Japan standard	No	hh:mm:ss

Column	Title	Values	Description
		Attribute	The data attribute for variable length fields can be specified. Use *VAR to indicate that the output field is a variable length field.
		Format name	The name of a format for a WORKSTN file. The name of the format must be left adjusted and enclosed in single quotation marks. Also, any length entry of K*n* (where *n* is the number of characters in the format name) must be specified.

Externally Described Output File Control Entries

Externally described output files can be controlled with RPG IV operations such as WRITE, UPDATE, DELETE, and EXCEPT, or by the RPG cycle. See Table 2.19.

Table 2.19: Output Specification Externally Described File Summary			
Column	Title	Values	Description
6	Form type	O	Identifies this statement as an output specification.
7 - 16	Record format name	Blank	The name used is the same as the more recently specified output format name.
		Format name	Any record format name opened for output can be specified.
17	Output type	H	Heading records. For documentation purposes only. The H in this column is functionally equivalent to placing a D in this column. Heading records usually contain report column titles, page numbers, and date information.
		D	Detail records. Usually, detail records contain information that is repeated on subsequent output records such as a printed report. Additionally, detail records are used to write and update records in program-defined data files.
		T	Total-time records. Usually, total-time records are used to output the results of the program.
		E	Exception records. Exception records are written using the EX-CEPT operation code. Indicators and/or an exception name can condition exception records.
16 - 18	Conditioning continuation controls	AND/OR	The conditioning indicators are a continuation of the previous line. The indicator condition on the previous line AND/OR the indicator condition on this line must be satisfied for the output line to be written.
18 - 20	File addition and file deletion	ADD	For database (DISK) files only. Records are added to the file. The file addition must be specified on the file description specification for the file being written.
		DEL	For database (DISK) files only. The record is deleted from the file; it is no longer accessible. The file must be declared as an UPDATE file on the file specification.

Table 2.19: Output Specification Externally Described File Summary, *continued*

Column	Title	Values	Description
18	Output control	Blank	No special controlling is specified for this output statement.
		F	Fetch overflow. When fetch is specified, RPG checks for overflow after each printed line. If the overflow indicator for this printer file is on and fetch has been specified, any detail and heading lines that are conditioned by that indicator are printed before this line.
		R	The WORKSTN file specified is released from the program. *See* REL operation.
21 - 29	Controlling indicators	Blank	No indicators condition this output line.
		1P	First page indicator (valid for heading and detail output only). Output lines conditioned with the 1P indicator are printed after the *INZSR subroutine is performed.
		Indicator	Any valid indicator (up to three) can be specified to control the output line. If more than three indicators are required, the continuation controls (AND/OR) can be specified.
30 - 39	Except name	Blank	No exception name controls the output line.
		Name	This line is exception output and it is controlled by the exception name. If conditioning indicators are specified, their condition must be satisfied for the line to be output. *See* EXCEPT operation.
40 - 80			Not used.

Externally Described Output File Field Description

Externally described file output fields are used to specify the fields to be output (Table 2.20).

Table 2.20: Output Specification Externally Described File Field Description Summary

Column	Title	Values	Description
6	Form type	O	Identifies this statement as an output specification.
7 - 20			Not used for program-defined output fields.
21 - 29	Controlling indicators	Blank	The output field is always written whenever the controlling output specification is written.
		1P	The output field is written only once—at first-page output time (1P).
		Any valid indicator (up to three)	The output field is included in the output operation only when the test of the controlling indicators is true.
30 - 43	Output field name	Name	The name of the field to be output when the controlling output specification is written. The field name must have already been defined in the program or it must be a predefined name, such as *DATE, UDATE, PAGE, or *INxx.
		Name constant	The name of the named constant to be output when the controlling output specification is written.
		*ALL	All fields in the externally described file are output.
30 - 43		PAGE, OR PAGE1 TO PAGE7	The current page number is output. The various PAGE fields include PAGE and PAGEn, where n is 1 to 7, giving a total of eight page-counter fields.
			Conditioning indicators condition the resetting, not the printing, of the page number fields. When the indicator condition is met, the PAGEn field is reset to zero. When the indicator condition is not met, the PAGEn field value is printed normally.
		*INxx	The value of the indicator xx is output to the record; xx can be any valid RPG indicator.
		*IN,xx	The value of the indicator xx is output to the record; xx can be any general-purpose indicator (01 to 99).
		*PLACE	This reserved word causes the data that has been specified up to the first *PLACE to be repeated to the right of that same data. For example, if 4-up labels for the same name and address are required, the output specification contains the field for the name, followed by three *PLACE entries.
45	Blank after	Blank	The field is output and no other action is taken.
		B	The field is output, then it is cleared. Numeric fields are set to zero and character fields are set to blanks.

PROCEDURE SPECIFICATION

The procedure specification is used to isolate the first and last statement of an RPG subprocedure. The procedure specification simply blocks the starting and ending source statements of the subprocedure and, optionally, identifies the procedure as being available to other procedures. The procedure specification ruler is shown in Figure 2.18.

```
.....PProcName+++++++..B.................Functions++++++++++++++++++++++++++++++
```

Figure 2.18: Procedure specification ruler.

Procedure Definition

A procedure definition is made up of three parts:

- Procedure prototype (specified with the definition specification).
- Procedure identification (specified with the procedure specification).
- Procedure interface (specified with the definition specification).

With only two exceptions, the procedure prototype and the procedure interface are similar interfaces. First, the type of definition specification is PR (for the procedure prototype) and PI (for the procedure interface). Second, the parameter names specified on the procedure interface are accessible by the procedure. The names specified on the procedure prototype, however, are optional and are used for documentation purposes only. They are not accessible by the calling procedure.

A procedure prototype is required within any program that calls the subprocedure and by the subprocedure itself. Procedure prototypes can be stored in a separate source file, and are included at compile time through the /COPY compiler directive. This allows the prototype to be inserted into any source file that requires it.

Procedure Specification Summary

Table 2.21 summarizes the procedure specification.

Column	Title	Values	Description
Table 2.21: Procedure Specification Summary			
6	Form type	P	Identifies this statement as a procedure specification.
7 - 21	Procedure name	Name	Name of the procedure being defined.
24		B	This procedure specification identifies the beginning of the subprocedure named in positions 7 to 21.
		E	This procedure specification identifies the ending of the subprocedure named in positions 7 to 21.
44 - 80	Functions	Keywords	Any valid procedure specification keyword can be specified. Currently, the EXPORT keyword is the only procedure keyword.

Procedure Specification Keyword Summary

Table 2.22 summarizes the keyword for the procedure specification.

Keyword	Parameters	Description
Table 2.22: Procedure Specification Keyword Summary		
EXPORT	['Exported procedure name']	The procedure is exported and made available to other "external" modules. The exported procedure name is optional and, if specified, indicates as the name of the procedure as it is exported. This exported name is the name used by other modules to import this procedure. Exported names specified on this keyword are enclosed in quotes and are exported case sensitive.

EDITING NUMERIC OUTPUT

The following sections describe various elements, options, and codes used to control editing patterns and special editing characters.

Edit Words

Edit words are patterns or *masks* that are specified in RPG output specifications. They are used to create ad hoc edits for numeric values, such as phone numbers, social security numbers, sales figures, and the time of day. Table 2.23 lists various edit-word masks.

Table 2.23: Examples of Edit Words

Description	Edit Word *...v....1....v...	Unedited Value	Edited Output
Large value	' , . '	00654321	6,543.21
Stop zero suppression	' , 0 . '	00000027	0.27
Time of day	'0 : : '	071223	07:12:23
Social Security number	'0 - - '	023456789	023-45-6789
Phone number	'0( )& - '	8005551212	(800) 555-1212
Floating currency symbol	' , , $0. '	000009402	$94.02

The number of blanks plus the zero suppression control code (i.e., the leading zero or asterisk) within an edit word must be greater than or equal to the number of digits for the field or named constant being edited.

Because editing a numeric value often changes the overall size of the value, RPG uses *ending positions* for the output location of fields in the output specification. This allows the right sides of numeric values to be aligned properly after editing.

> **TIP:** *To prevent zero suppression of output, specify a leading zero in the first (i.e., left-most) position of the edit word. This is typically used for editing values such as phone numbers where zero suppression is not desired.*

Edit Word Construction

The currency symbol and zero suppression character do not displace numbers within the edit word. The currency symbol, however, requires an additional position. This additional position is usually allocated as the left-most position of the edit word. Figure 2.19 illustrates the edit mask required to edit a numeric field with a floating currency symbol, commas, a decimal point, and zero suppression. The size of this numeric field is nine positions with two decimal positions.

		CS	1		2	3	4		5	6	7		8	9	
Output positions ➢		CS	1		2	3	4		5	6	7		8	9	
Edit word mask ➢	'	ƀ	ƀ	,	ƀ	ƀ	ƀ	,	ƀ	$	0	.	ƀ	ƀ	'
Unedited value ➢						7	6	5	4	3	2	1	2	1	
Output value ➢		$	7	,	6	5	4	,	3	2	1	.	2	1	

Figure 2.19: An edit-word example with the floating currency symbol.

Edit words consist of four optional elements:

- *Body*. The body is the area of the edit word where the numeric value is positioned.

- *Status*. The status is the area of the edit word consisting of the letters CR or a – (minus) sign. The status is used to indicate whether the value is negative or positive.

- *Expansion*. The expansion area follows the body and status (usually literal values).

- *Literal values*. Literal values can appear anywhere in the edit word. Literal values are included in the output only when significant digits appear to the left of the literal value. Note: While a named constant can be used as an edit word, named constants cannot be used within (i.e., as part of) the edit word itself.

Edit Word Control Codes

There are several control codes that can be inserted into an edit word to control zero suppression, leading asterisks, floating currency symbol, blanks, and decimal notation. The first occurrence of a *control code* is used as the control code. Except for the ampersand (&), which is always used as a control code, subsequent occurrences are treated as literal values. Table 2.24 contains a description of the edit word control codes that can be used in an edit word.

Table 2.24: Edit Word Control Codes

Control Code	Description
$	**Currency Symbol.** If the currency symbol is followed immediately by a zero, the currency symbol precedes the first significant digit. This is referred to as a *floating currency sign*. If the currency symbol is not followed by a zero, the currency symbol's position is fixed. When using the floating currency symbol, an available blank position is displaced. Typically, the displaced blank is shifted to the left of the currency symbol. The character used as the currency symbol is specified by the CURSYM keyword on the header specification.
*	**Asterisk.** Leading zeros are replaced with asterisks to the position of the asterisk. Zero suppression ends at the position of the asterisk.
&	**Ampersand.** Always replaced with a blank when output.
0	**Zero.** Ends zero suppression at the position of the zero. The zero is used as one of the output positions for digits to appear.
. (period) , (comma)	**Decimal Notation.** These characters are not actual control codes; they are treated as literal values. They are traditionally used for decimal notation and thousands notation.
ƀ	**Blanks.** Identifies available positions for the numeric value.
CR	**Status.** The literal value CR is output if the value is negative.
–	**Status.** The - (minus) sign is output if the value is negative.

TIP: *Be careful when using literal values in an edit word. Literal values can be any characters, including the letters CR. The first occurrence of the letters CR, however, is interpreted as the status code and will not appear when the number is greater than or equal to zero.*

Edit Words and Named Constants

To use an edit word, place the desired edit word—left justified—into output constant/edit word positions of the output specification for the field being edited. The RPG output specification accepts edit word literal values of up to 48 positions. For edit words that exceed 48 positions, the entry can be continued onto a second output line or a named constant can be used. Edit words can be up to 115 positions in length and can be specified—left justified—into output constant/edit word positions of the output specification. Figure 2.20 contains examples of edit-word usage.

```
.....FFileName++IFEASFRlen+LKeylnKFDevice+.Functions+++++++++++++++++++++++++++++++
     FQPRINT    O   F 132        PRINTER   OFLIND(*INOV)
.....DName++++++++++EUDS.......To/Len+TDc.Functions+++++++++++++++++++++++++++++++++
     D PhoneEdit       C                        Const('Ø(   )&  -    ')
.....CSRnØ1Factor1+++++++OpCode(ex)Factor2+++++++Result++++++++Len++DcHiLoEq
     C                   TIME                     Time             6 Ø
     C                   Z-ADD     *DATE          TodayIs          9 Ø
     C                   Z-ADD     8ØØ5551212     Phone           10 Ø
     C                   Z-ADD     654321         Sales           10 2
     C                   MOVE      Ø23456789      SSNBR            9 Ø
     C                   EXCEPT
     C                   SETON                                       LR
.....OFormat++++DAddnØ1nØ2nØ3Except++++SpbSpaSkbSka
     OQPRINT    E                         1
.....O..............nØ1nØ2nØ3Field+++++++++YB?End++PConstant/Editword++++++++++
     O                                        +Ø 'Soc Sec Nbr:'
     O                   SSNBR                +2 'Ø   -  - '
     OQPRINT    E                         1
     O                                        +Ø 'Phone:'
     O                   PhoneNum             +2 PhoneEdit
     OQPRINT    E                         1
     O                                        +Ø 'Date/Time:'
     O                   TodayIs        Y     +2
     O                   Time                 +2 'Ø & & '
     OQPRINT    E 1
     O                                        +Ø 'Salary:'
     O                   Sales                +2 '$   ,   , *. CR'
```

Figure 2.20: An example of edit-word usage.

Edit Codes

Edit codes are single-character codes that represent predefined editing patterns. These edit patterns are simply specific edit word masks that automatically adapt to the size of the numeric field or named constant being edited. This allows numeric fields of any size to be edited without concern for the particular semantics involved in using edit words.

To edit using an edit code, place the desired edit code into the edit-code position of the output specification for the field to be edited. Edit codes can be combined with special edit characters, such as the $ (floating currency) symbol and * (leading asterisk), to further edit numeric output. These special characters can be specified—left justified—into output constant/edit word positions of the output specification. The characters must be enclosed in single quotes (i.e., apostrophes), and only one of these characters can be specified for a field edited with an edit code.

To illustrate the output of numeric values edited with edit codes, three versions of edited output are listed in Table 2.25. The first version uses only the edit code, the second version uses the edit code and the floating currency symbol, and the third version uses the edit code with leading asterisks.

In each example, the data being output is a nine-digit numeric field with two decimal positions. For positive numbers, the value 0004567.89 is used; for negative output, the value -0004567.89 is used; and for zero output, the value 0000000.00 is used.

Edit Code	Thousands Notation	Output Zeros	Negative Sign	Positive Output	Negative Output	Zero Output
Table 2.25: Output Edit Codes						
1	Yes	Yes	No	4,567.89	4,567.89	.00
1 $				$4,567.89	$4,567.89	$.00
1 *				****4,567.89	****4,567.89	*********.00
2	Yes	No	No	4,567.89	4,567.89	
2 $				$4,567.89	$4,567.89	
2 *				****4,567.89	****4,567.89	************
3	No	Yes	No	4567.89	4567.89	.00
3 $				$4567.89	$4567.89	$.00
3 *				****4567.89	****4567.89	*********.00
4	No	No	No	4567.89	4567.89	
4 $				$4567.89	$4567.89	
4 *				****4567.89	****4567.89	**********
A	Yes	Yes	Yes CR	4,567.89	4,567.89CR	.00
A $				$4,567.89	$4,567.89CR	$.00
A *				****4,567.89	****4,567.89CR	*********.00
B	Yes	No	Yes CR	4,567.89	4,567.89CR	
B $				$4,567.89	$4,567.89CR	
B *				****4,567.89	****4,567.89CR	************
C	No	Yes	Yes CR	4567.89	4567.89CR	.00
C $				$4567.89	$4567.89CR	$.00
C *				****4567.89	****4567.89CR	*******.00
D	No	No	Yes CR	4567.89	4567.89CR	
D $				$4567.89	$4567.89CR	
D *				****4567.89	****4567.89CR	************

					Table 2.25: Output Edit Codes, *continued*		
Edit Code	Thousands Notation	Output Zeros	Negative Sign		Positive Output	Negative Output	Zero Output
J	Yes	Yes	Yes	–	4,567.89	4,567.89-	.00
J $					$4,567.89	$4,567.89-	$.00
J *					****4,567.89	****4,567.89-	*********.00
K	Yes	No	Yes	–	4,567.89	4,567.89-	
K $					$4,567.89	$4,567.89-	
K *					****4,567.89	****4,567.89-	************
L	No	Yes	Yes	–	4567.89	4567.89-	.00
L $					$4567.89	$4567.89-	$.00
L *					****4567.89	****4567.89-	*******.00
M	No	No	Yes	–	4567.89	4567.89-	
M $					$4567.89	$4567.89-	
M *					****4567.89	****4567.89-	************
N	Yes	Yes	Yes	–	4,567.89	-4,567.89	.00
N $					$4,567.89	-$4,567.89	$.00
N *					****4,567.89	****-4,567.89	*********.00
O	Yes	No	Yes	–	4,567.89	-4,567.89	
O $					$4,567.89	-$4,567.89	
O *					****4,567.89	****-4,567.89	************
P	No	Yes	Yes	–	4567.89	-4567.89	.00
P $					$4567.89	-$4567.89	$.00
P *					****4567.89	****-4567.89	*******.00
Q	No	No	Yes	–	4567.89	-4567.89	
Q $					$4567.89	-$4567.89	
Q *					****4567.89	****-4567.89	************
X	No	Yes	No		000456789	00045678R	000000000
Y	No	Yes	N/A		45/67/89	N/A	0/00/00
Z	No	No	No		456789	456789	

Custom Currency Symbol

The RPG header specification is used to control global editing values. The currency symbol, date format, date separator, and decimal notation are controlled by the header specification.

The character used as the currency symbol is controlled by the CURSYM keyword on the header specification. The character specified for the currency symbol can be used within edit words and with edit codes. For example, if the "at" sign (@) is specified, the @ symbol must be used wherever the currency symbol is normally used. Figure 2.21 illustrates the use of the @ symbol as the currency symbol.

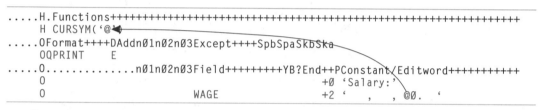

```
.....H.Functions+++++++++++++++++++++++++++++++++++++++++++++++++++++++++++++++++++
    H CURSYM('@
.....OFormat++++DAddn01n02n03Except++++SpbSpaSkbSka
    OQPRINT     E
.....O...............n01n02n03Field+++++++++YB?End++PConstant/Editword++++++++++
    O                                         +0 'Salary:'
    O                        WAGE             +2 '  ,  ,@0. '
```

Figure 2.21: An example using the custom currency symbol.

DATE EDIT CODE CONTROL SUMMARY

Table 2.26 lists various examples of how the header specification affects the date edit code (Y). The date edit code is, ironically, not used to edit fields that are type date, but rather to edit fields that are type numeric. The edited numeric output field is written in a date-formatted presentation.

The date 21 June, 1988 (or June 21, 1988, for those who live in the USA) is the basis for the examples used in Table 2.26.

Table 2.26: Controlling the Y (DATE) Edit Code					
Date Variable[1]	DATSEP Keyword	Date Edit Keyword (DATEDIT) Header Specification			
		Not Specified	*MDY	*DMY	*YMD
UDATE	Blank	6/21/88	6/21/88	21/06/88	88/06/21
UDATE	Blank	21/06/88	6/21/88	21/06/88	88/06/21
UDATE	Blank	21.06.88	6.21.88	21.06.88	88.06.21

Date Variable[1]	DATSEP Keyword	Date Edit Keyword (DATEDIT) Header Specification			
		Not Specified	*MDY	*DMY	*YMD
UDATE	–	6-21-88	6-21-88	21-06-88	88-06-21
UDATE	–	21-06-88	6-21-88	21-06-88	88-06-21
UDATE	–	21-06-88	6-21-88	21-06-88	88-06-21
*DATE	Blank	6/21/1988	6/21/1988	21/06/1988	1988/06/21
*DATE	/	21/06/1988	6/21/1988	21/06/1988	1988/06/21
*DATE	.	21.06.1988	6.21.1988	21.06.1988	1988.06.21
*DATE	–	6-21-1988	6-21-1988	21-06-1988	1988-06-21
*DATE	–	21-06-1988	6-21-1988	21-06-1988	1988-06-21
*DATE	–	21-06-1988	6-21-1988	21-06-1988	1988-06-21

Table 2.26: Controlling the Y (DATE) Edit Code, *continued*

[1] The UDATE field is a six-position numeric field with zero decimal positions. The *DATE field is an eight-position numeric field with zero decimal positions.

> **TIP:** To avoid zero suppression of the leading zero with the UDATE or *DATE values (e.g., to output the date as 06/21/88 instead of 6/21/88), use a 7- or 9-position numeric field for output instead of UDATE or *DATE. The Y edit code, by definition, "zero suppresses" only the first zero in the output field. Moving UDATE or *DATE to a larger field avoids zero suppression of the leading digit in the date.

TABLE AND ARRAY SPECIFICATION

Tables and arrays are declared with the definition specification. Specify the DIM keyword for a stand-alone field or data-structure subfield to declare the field as an array. If the table or array is loaded at compile time, the CTDATA keyword must be specified for the array declaration. In addition, the PERRCD keyword is used to indicate the number of array elements that are specified on each line of source code.

A compile-time table or array specification is identified by the **CTDATA keyword beginning in column 1 of the source line. The name of the compile-time table or array must appear beginning in position 10. Compile-time data must appear after all other source lines. The data to be loaded into the compile-time table or the array must begin on the line following the table or array specification. If multiple compile-time tables or arrays are used in a single program, each must begin with **CTDATA. For example, the program shown in Figure 2.22 contains two compile-time arrays.

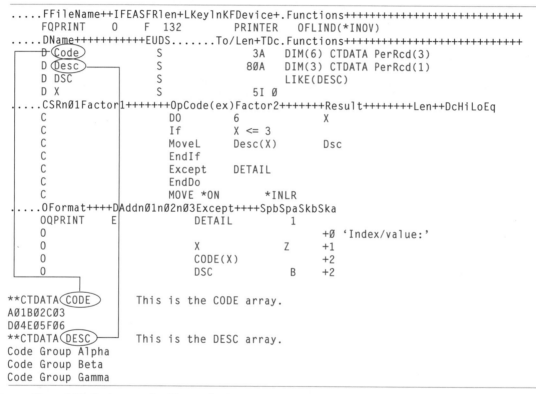

```
.....FFileName++IFEASFRlen+LKeylnKFDevice+.Functions++++++++++++++++++++++++++++
     FQPRINT    O  F  132          PRINTER    OFLIND(*INOV)
.....DName+++++++++++EUDS........To/Len+TDc.Functions++++++++++++++++++++++++++++
     D Code          S              3A   DIM(6) CTDATA PerRcd(3)
     D Desc          S             80A   DIM(3) CTDATA PerRcd(1)
     D DSC           S                   LIKE(DESC)
     D X             S              5I 0
.....CSRn01Factor1+++++++OpCode(ex)Factor2+++++++Result++++++++Len++DcHiLoEq
     C                    DO       6              X
     C                    If       X <= 3
     C                    MoveL    Desc(X)        Dsc
     C                    EndIf
     C                    Except   DETAIL
     C                    EndDo
     C                    MOVE *ON        *INLR
.....OFormat++++DAddn01n02n03Except++++SpbSpaSkbSka
     OQPRINT     E            DETAIL         1
     O                                                +0 'Index/value:'
     O                        X               Z       +1
     O                        CODE(X)                 +2
     O                        DSC             B       +2
**CTDATA CODE        This is the CODE array.
A01B02C03
D04E05F06
**CTDATA DESC        This is the DESC array.
Code Group Alpha
Code Group Beta
Code Group Gamma
```

Figure 2.22: Code example with compile-time arrays.

When the program shown in Figure 2.22 is run, the output shown in Figure 2.23 is generated.

```
*... ... 1 ... ... 2 ... ... 3 ... ... 4 ... ... 5 ... ... 6 ... ...
Index/value:  1  AØ1  Code Group Alpha
Index/value:  2  BØ2  Code Group Beta
Index/value:  3  CØ3  Code Group Gamma
Index/value:  4  DØ4
Index/value:  5  EØ5
Index/value:  6  FØ6
```

Figure 2.23: Sample output from program shown in Figure 2.22.

Chapter 3

EXPRESSIONS

Support for expressions in RPG IV extends normal conditional logic, keyword support, and calculations through the use of natural expressions. Natural expressions are used to simplify the programming of these components as well as the implementation of traditional business rules. Expressions can be used with conditional logic statements, assignment statements, or embedded as a parameter of a procedure. An expression matching the data type of a procedure's parameter can be specified as a parameter for the procedure, provided that the parameter is specified as being CONST or passed by VALUE. Unlike prior versions of RPG, the RETURN operation accepts expressions in the extended factor 2.

EXPRESSIONS in RPG

Expressions are used in the following areas of an RPG program:

- **Declaration.** Most definition specification keywords support expressions. This support provides referential referencing of related data items defined in the program and simplifies initialization of data items.

- **Assignment.** The calculation specification EVAL and EVALR operations fully support expressions of every type. Expressions can appear, in the assignment statements of the EVAL and EVALR operations, on either side of the = (equals) sign.

- **Comparison.** The conditional operations of the calculation specification include IF, WHEN, DOW, DOU, and FOR. These operations fully support conditional expressions. Note that assignment is never performed by conditional operations.

- **Procedures.** The CALLP and RETURN operations support expressions or parameters specified in factor 2.

NATURAL EXPRESSIONS

Expressions in RPG are specified in traditional mathematical infix notation. This kind of expression syntax is sometimes referred to as natural expression. Natural expressions allow basic mathematics to be written with RPG in a form similar to traditional mathematics. Bertrand Russell, the British philosopher and mathematician, once said, "Mathematics may be defined as the subject in which we never know what we are talking about, nor whether what we are saying is true." (Andrews, Robert. *The Columbia Dictionary of Quotations*. New York: Columbia University Press, 1993.)

In previous versions of RPG, the programmer always knew the outcome of an expression because only fixed-format, single-operator expressions were permitted. With natural expression support in RPG IV, programmers can write as complex or simple an algorithm as needed. As for complex algorithms, to paraphrase Bertrand, the programmer that follows the program author might never know what is expressed or if it is true. So write as basic an expression as possible.

Expressions are made up of *operands* and *operators*. Operands typically are data such as fields or numeric literals. Operators are mathematical symbols such as + (addition), - (subtraction), * (multiplication), or / (division); and conjuncts such as AND, OR, and NOT. The operators supported in RPG natural expressions are those listed in Table 3.1.

Table 3.1: Expression Operators		
Operator	Type	Description
+	Unary	Indicates positive numerical value
-	Unary	Indicates negative numerical value
NOT	Unary	Opposite of evaluated result
+	Binary (alpha)	Concatenation of two character strings
+	Binary (numeric)	Addition
-	Binary (numeric)	Subtraction
*	Binary	Multiplication
/	Binary	Division
**	Binary	Exponentiation (powers and roots)
=	Comparison	Equal
=	Assignment	Set values equal
>=	Comparison	Greater than or equal
>	Comparison	Greater than
<=	Comparison	Less than or equal
<	Comparison	Less than
<>	Comparison	Not equal
AND	Logical	AND conjunction comparison
OR	Logical	OR conjunction comparison

Priority of Operators

Expressions are parsed and then evaluated in a defined order. To ensure that the equation always results in the same value, a precedence of the operations is applied. Fortunately, this precedence is the same as that used by most other programming languages as well as mathematics. Table 3.2 lists the priority of the operators used in expressions in RPG.

The priority of parentheses and built-in functions is interpreted as meaning that the operations inside the parentheses are performed independently of the operations outside the parentheses. Use parentheses for clarity or when the priority of the equation is uncertain. Parentheses can be used to override the priority. Hence, parentheses can force an addition operation to be performed before a multiplication operation.

Table 3.2: Order of Evaluation of Operators		
Priority	Operator	Description
1	( )	Parentheses
2	Functions	Built-in functions or procedure functions
3	Unary operators	Unary +, -
3	Logical not	NOT
4	**	Powers and roots
5	* /	Multiplication and division
6	Binary operators	Binary +, -,
7	Comparison	Comparison operators, =, >=, >, <=, <,
8	Logical operators	Logical AND, logical OR
9	=	Assignment

The order of evaluation of an expression is important and is established with traditional mathematical precedence rules.

The power function ** is used for exponentiation. Mathematical rules state that, if a value is raised to the power of n, it is multiplied by itself n times. For example, 2**3 would result in 2*2*2, which evaluates to 8.

Mathematical rules also state that, if a value is raised to the power of $1/n$ (i.e., "one over n"), the result is the nth root of the value. For example, 16**(1/4) evaluates to the 4th root of 16, or 2. Table 3.3 lists a few examples of equations that use powers and roots.

Table 3.3: Powers and Roots Syntax	
Equation	Description
4**2	Result is 4 squared or 4x4 (16).
4**.5	Result is the square root of 4 (2).
27**(1/3)	Finds the cube root of 27 (3).
16**(1/2)	Finds the square root of 16 (4).

Expressions can be categorized into three types, *Boolean*, *numeric*, and *string*. An expression is any list of tokens that represents a value, either a character string or numeric value, or an operator (see Table 3.1). In other words, any character string or numeric value, be it a simple number or complex math formula, is an expression.

RPG support for natural expressions is similar to that of CL, BASIC, COBOL, C++, and PL/I. Expressions can be used in the extended factor 2 of the alternate calculation specification, and in the keyword section of the definition specification. Expressions can be used in assignment statements, compare statements, or in declarations.

Expressions, known as *tokens,* are made up of literal values, numbers, fields, and symbols. Symbols are used to perform operations on the various values. An expression can be as simple as the number 12 or as complex as the equation: (4*PI)*R**2.

Expression Continuation

To continue an expression, place the next token of the expression on the next line in the extended factor 2 or the function/keyword area of the definition specification.

To continue a quoted character string, use either a + (plus) or - (minus) sign to continue the string. This directs the compiler to concatenate the value together either on the first nonblank position when using the + sign or the first position of the extended factor 2 or function/keyword area when using the - sign.

Expressions in Assignment Statements

When one value is assigned to another, the EVAL and EVALR operation codes are used. These operations copy the value on the right side of the equal sign, known as the *r-value*, to the variable on the left of the equal sign, known as the *l-value*. The assignment must result in an r-value and an l-value that match. In other words, if the l-value is character, then the r-value must result in a character value.

The EVAL and EVALR operations work with all types of expressions. When used with character expressions, EVAL copies the value left justified. EVALR copies the value right justified.

The l-value can be an expression, but only when it is a character variable or an array name with an index value. The %SUBST() built-in function can be used as the l-value. In addition, numeric expressions can be used on the starting position and the length of the %SUBST() function. When an array index is specified, the index may be a literal, a field, or an expression. Figure 3.1 contains a sample of several expressions used in assignment statements.

```
.....CSRn01Factor1+++++++OpCode(ex)Factor2+++++++++++++++++++++++++++++++++++++++++
0001 C                    EVAL       A = B + C

0002 C                    EVAL       Amt_Due = Amt_Due - Amt_Paid

0003 C                    EVAL       PI = 3.1415926

0004 C                    EVAL       Area = 4 * PI * Radius ** 2

0005 C                    EVAL       Message = 'RPGIV is cool!'

0006 C                    EVAL       %subst(comp_name : start+3 : start+6) = 'Q38'

0007 C                    EVAL       ptrData = %ADDR(comp_name)

0008 C                    EVAL       Presidents(I + 1) = 'George '
0009 C                                  + 'Washington'

0010 C                    EVAL       *INLR = (%EOF(CUSTMAST) or %EOF(ITEMMAST))
0011 C                    EVAL       *IN32 = Amount > 100 and (Price - Cost) < 25.50
```

Figure 3.1: Examples of assignment expressions.

In Figure 3.1, line 1 computes the sum of B plus C and stores the result in A. In line 2, the AMT_DUE field is reduced by AMT_PAID. In line 3, the field named PI receives the value of 3.1415926. In line 4, the area of a sphere is computed as 4*PI*R2.

Line 5 copies a character string expression to the field named MESSAGE. Line 6 copies the character string expression 'Q38' to a substring location of the COMP_NAME field.

Line 7 retrieves the address of the field COMP_NAME and copies it into the pointer variable named PTRDATA. Line 8 concatenates the string 'George ' 'Washington' into 'George Washington' and copies it into an array element of the PRESIDENTS array. The element index is calculated from the expression I+1.

Line 10 is a Boolean expression. Indicator LR is set on if the end-of-file condition exists for either the CUSTMAST or ITEMMAST file. Line 11 sets on indicator 32 if the AMOUNT field is greater than 100 and the difference between PRICE and COST is less than 25.50.

Expressions in Compare Statements

The RPG operations DOW, DOU, IF, FOR, and WHEN allow the use of expressions as compare statements. Expressions used with these operations do not assign their result to a field. Rather, the values are used to compare one value to another.

The DOW, DOU, IF, FOR, and WHEN operations have identical support for expressions. Figure 3.2 illustrates various conditional expressions.

```
.....CSRnØ1Factor1+++++++OpCode(ex)Factor2+++++++Result++++++++Len++DcHiLoEq....
.....CSRnØ1..............OpCode(ex)Extended-factor2++++++++++++++++++++++++++++++
ØØØ1 C                   if          A = B

ØØØ2 C                   if          Amt_Due > 1ØØØØ and DaysOvrDue >= 3Ø
ØØØ3 C                   if          (Price - Cost) / Price < 1Ø or
ØØØ4 C                                Cost = Ø
ØØØ5 C                   select
ØØØ6 C                   when        *INØ1 = *ON

ØØØ7 C                   DOU         *INLR
ØØØ8 C                   read        Customer                             LR
ØØØ9 C                   endDo
ØØ1Ø C                   endSL
ØØ11 C                   Endif
ØØ12 C                   Endif
ØØ13 C                   Endif
```

Figure 3.2: Expressions on conditional statements.

In Figure 3.2, line 1 is a basic comparison expression. When the fields A and B are equal, the condition is considered TRUE. When they are not equal, the condition is FALSE.

Line 2 compares the AMT_DUE field to 10000. If AMT_DUE is greater than 10,000, it then evaluates the next condition. If DAYSOVRDUE is greater than or equal to 30, the entire conditional expression is considered true. If either the first condition or second condition is not true, the entire condition is considered false.

Lines 3 and 4 perform inline math. The equation of PRICE minus COST is performed first. The parentheses override the normal order of evaluation. The result of PRICE-COST is stored in a temporary result, and that result is divided by PRICE. The result of the division operation is stored in another temporary result. The next thing that happens is the comparison of the second temporary result to the number 10. If the result is less than 10, the condition is true. The OR operator is bypassed for now and the evaluation of COST = 0 is performed. If COST is equal to 0, that portion of the expression is true. The OR operator is used to test whether the left or right side operands evaluate to true. If either side is true, the condition is considered true.

Line 6 performs a WHEN (inline case), testing indicator 01 (*IN01) for an ON condition. If the indicator is on, the condition is considered true.

Line 7 performs a DOU (Do Until) operation. The expression used as the conditioning expression is simply *INLR. This is a valid condition, and evaluates to either a true or false condition. Because an indicator is either off or on, when its condition is tested, it returns true when the indicator is on and false when the indicator is off. To reverse this conditioning, specify the NOT operator in front of the indicator or simply evaluate the indicator to be equal to *OFF, as in DOU *INLR = *OFF.

Expressions in Declarative Statements

Built-in functions can be used in any expression. On the definition specification, basic expressions may be used as arguments for the various keywords. Expressions also are useful in establishing field referencing. When the properties of one item change, other items that depend on those properties also change. This is not the only use for expressions on the definition specification, but it is the most useful. Other uses include setting the initial value of a field, specifying the location of a data structure subfield, or calculating a mathematical formula.

Only expressions that can be analyzed at the time the source code is compiled may be specified. Hence, only literals, predefined values, and certain built-in functions are supported. Specifically, the value (content) of fields, arrays, and data structures cannot be used in an expression on the definition specification. Figure 3.3 illustrates several valid expressions as used on the definition specification function/keyword area.

```
.....DName++++++++++EUDS.......Length+TDc.Functions++++++++++++++++++++++++++++++
0001 D Amt_Len         S                5P 0 INZ(%size(AmountDue))
0002 D Dft_Comp        C                     Const('Skyline Pigeon Productions')
0003 D Company         S                     LIKE(CORP_NAME) INZ(DFT_COMP)
0004 D Radius          C                     Const(16)
0005 D PI              C                     Const(3.1415926)

0006 D CubeRoot        S                     LIKE(AMT_LEN)
0007 D NewName         S               +4A   LIKE(CORP_NAME)
```

Figure 3.3: Expressions on the definition specification.

Expressions in Parameters and Return Values

The CALLP and RETURN operations support expressions in the extended factor 2. The CALLP operation is used to evoke either a subprocedure or a separate program. The RETURN operation is used to specify the return value from a subprocedure to its caller. An expression can be specified for a parameter of a subprocedure call when that parameter is defined as CONST. In other words, the CONST keyword must be specified for the parameter in order for the RPG IV syntax checker to accept an expression for the parameter.

Expressions in Free Format Calculations

The free format version of RPG Calculation specifications is essentially expressions. While free format RPG syntax is not exactly the same as traditional RPG, expressions are used identically to traditional RPG. Free format expression may be specified in positions 8 to 80 of the source statement line.

To start using free format expressions, the /FREE-FORM directive must be specified on a line by itself in positions 7 through 16 of the RPG statement. Expressions may be specified on the line following the /FREE-FORM statement itself. The end free format expressions, a /END-FREE must be specified on a line by itself in positions 7 to 15.

Each free format expression must appear in positions 8 through 80 of the source statement and must be terminated with a semicolon (;).

Most traditional RPG operation codes may be used with free format expressions, however the syntax for operations is slightly modified. In free format, the operation code is specified first, followed by Factor 1, Factor 2, and the Result field. Resulting indicators are not supported in free format expressions. If an operation code does not require Factor 1, Factor 2 or the Result field, then those operands are not specified. Figure 3.4 illustrates the use of several free format expressions.

```
......_/Free-Form+++++++++++++++++++++++++++++++++++++++++++++++++++++++++++++++++++++++++++
      /FREE-FORM
0001      if      A = B;  // Check for Zero pricing
0002        if      Price > 0 and DaysOvrDue >= 30;
0003          if    (Price - Cost) / Price < 10 or Cost = 0;
0004          read    Customer;
0005          DOW    NOT %EOF(CustMast);
0006            TotalSales += CustSales;
0007            read    Customer;
0008          endDo;
0009        EndIf;
0010      EndIf;
0011      EndIf;
      /END-FREE
```

Figure 3.4: Expressions in free format RPG.

Note that the conditional statement on line 3 is followed by a comment. Two forward slash characters begin a comment in free format expressions. Comments may be the last item on a source line or the only item on a source line. Everything following the two forward slash characters on the source line is ignored by the compiler.

Expressions as Parameters

Normally expressions may not be used as the value of a parameter passed to a procedure or program. However, by specifying that a parameter is passed by value or is read-only, expressions are fully supported.

In order to allow an expression to be used as the value of a parameter, one of the following parameter keywords must be used.

VALUE – The parameter is passed by value instead of the default, by reference.

CONST – The parameter is read-only, the called procedure may not change the value.

When the VALUE keyword is used the system makes a copy of the value and passes the copy to the called procedure. Since the original parameter value's storage is not accessed by the called procedure, the compiler allows additional items to be passed on the parameter. Specifically, literals, named constants, and expressions are allowed.

 The following procedure does not use CONST or VALUE for its parameters, and therefore cannot accept expressions as parameter values.

```
.....PProcName+++++++..B.................Functions++++++++++++++++++++++++
0001 P Root              B                  Export

.....DName++++++++++++EUDS.......Length+TDc.Functions++++++++++++++++++++++
0002 D Root              PI              10I 0
0003 D nValue                             7P 0
0004 D nRoot                              5I 0

0005 D nRtnValue         S               10I 0

.....CSRn01.............OpCode(ex)Extended-factor2++++++++++++++++++++++++++
0006 C                   Eval      nRtnValue = %int(nValue ** (1/nRoot))
0007 C                   return    nRtnValue
0008 P Root              E
```

In order to permit expressions, either CONST or VALUE must be specified for the nValue and nRoot parameters. Neither parameter is modified by the procedure so both are candidates for these keywords.

Since the procedure does not modify the input parameters, the CONST keyword may be the better choice. The VALUE keyword would allow the parameter fields in the procedure to be modified within the procedure, but the modified values would not be passed back to the caller. The CONST keyword actually prohibits modification of the input parameters. Since the parameters are not modified, CONST is the correct choice. The following procedure has been modified to include the CONST keywords for its parameters.

```
.....PProcName+++++++..B.................Functions++++++++++++++++++++++++
0001 P Root              B                  Export

.....DName++++++++++++EUDS.......Length+TDc.Functions++++++++++++++++++++++
0002 D Root              PI              10I 0
0003 D nValue                             7P 0 CONST
0004 D nRoot                              5I 0 CONST

0005 D nRtnValue         S               10I 0

.....CSRn01.............OpCode(ex)Extended-factor2++++++++++++++++++++++++++
0006 C                   Eval      nRtnValue = %int(nValue ** (1/nRoot))
0007 C                   return    nRtnValue
0008 P Root              E
```

The ROOT procedure may now be called with any type of numeric data specified for its parameters, including expressions.

```
.....DName+++++++++++EUDS.......Length+TDc.Functions+++++++++++++++++++++++
0001 D Root               PR           10I 0
0002 D Value                            7P 0 Const
0003 D Root                             5I 0 Const

0004 D Var1               S             5I 0 Inz(3741)
0005 D nRoot              S             5I 0

.....CSRnO1.............OpCode(ex)Extended-factor2++++++++++++++
0006 C                   Eval         nRoot = Root(Var1 * 2 : 3)
```

An expression is specified on the first parameter of the ROOT procedure (line 6). The field VAR1 is multiplied by 2. The product of that expression is generated and is passed to the procedure. The literal 3 is specified on the second parameter. Then the procedure is called and the cubed root of 7482 is returned and assigned to NROOT variable.

Whether the CONST keyword is used or the VALUE keyword is used, the capability to specify expressions as parameters for procedures is allowed with either of these two keywords.

Chapter 4

BUILT-IN FUNCTIONS

BUILT-IN FUNCTIONS, *continued*

The RPG language contains a rich set of operations. In addition to these operations, RPG supports a set of functions. These functions, known as *built-in functions,* perform various tasks—much like that of an operation code. Unlike operations, however, built-in functions return a value and, therefore, can be used as the parameter of a keyword on the definition specification or within an expression in the extended factor 2.

Built-in functions can be used with the IF, DOW, DOU, EVAL, EVALR, FOR, WHEN, RETURN, and CALLP operations. These operations support the extended factor 2 calculation specification. In addition, built-in functions can be used in the function/keyword area of the definition specification. They cannot, however, be used in the function/keyword area of the header or file specifications, and they cannot be used with traditional RPG operations such as the DO, IFEQ, and COMP operations. The two types of built-in functions are those that return a value that can be interpreted at:

- Compile time.
- Runtime.

Currently, only %SIZE, %LEN, %DECPOS, %ADDR, %PADDR and %ELEM are capable of returning values at compile time. Therefore, these are the only built-in functions that can be used with definition specification keywords.

BUILT-IN FUNCTION SYNTAX

Built-in functions must begin with a % (percent) sign followed by the built-in function name. If the built-in function contains parameters, the function name is followed by the parameters enclosed in parentheses. Built-in function parameters are often referred to as *arguments*. These arguments can be any valid literal, field, expression, or another built-in function. When more than one argument is specified, they are separated by the : (colon) symbol. Spaces are not significant to built-in functions or expressions. All built-in functions have the following syntax:

```
%funct( arg1 : arg2 : ... argn )
```

For those built-in functions that do not support parameters, parentheses are not required. For example, %PARMS supports no parameters, so %PARMS or %PARMS() may be used. In earlier releases of RPG, (i.e., OS/400 Version 4 and earlier) empty parentheses were not allowed, so only %PARMS would be valid, and %PARMS() would be invalid. The syntax for built-in functions is the same as the syntax used when calling a subprocedure.

BUILT-IN FUNCTION SYNTAX SUMMARY

The original release of RPG IV included a set of built-in functions. Those built-in functions are: %ADDR, %PADDR, %SIZE, %ELEM, %SUBST, %TRIM, %TRIML, and %TRIMR.

In OS/400 V3R2 and V3R7, the %PARMS built-in function was introduced. Since then, several built-in functions have been added to RPG. Table 4.1 lists the syntax for each built-in function. In addition, the OS/400 version and release in which the specific built-in function was introduced or enhanced is specified.

All built-in functions may be used only in the calculation specifications. If noted with (D) in their description column, the build-in function may also be used on the Definition specifications. An (F) indicates that they may also be used on the file specification. And an (FD) indicates that they may be used on the file or definition specifications in addition to calculation specifications.

Table 4.1: Built-in Function Syntax Summary

Version Release	Built-in Function	Parameters	Return Value Description
V3R7	%ABS	numeric expression	(D) Absolute value of expression.
V3R1	%ADDR	variable name	(D) Address of variable.
V5R1	%ALLOC	bytes to allocate	Pointer to allocated memory.
V5R2	%BITAND	expression1 : expression2	(D) Returns a value whose bits are on (set to '1') when the bits in both expression1 and expression2 are on.
V5R2	%BITNOT	expression	(D) Retuns a value whose bits are the reverse of those in the expression.
V5R2	%BITOR	expression1 : expression2	(D) Returns a value whose bits are on (set to '1') when the bits in both expression1 and expression2 are on.
V5R2	%BITXOR	expression1 : expression2	(D) Returns a value where each bit of the return value is on if the corresponding two bits of expression1 and expression2 are opposite; that is one bit is on and the other bit is off.
V4R2 V4R4 V5R1	%CHAR	graphic, date, time, time stamp, or numeric expression { : date-format-code }	Value in character data type.
V5R1	%CHECK	compare-value : base-string {: starting-position }	The first position in the base-string that contains a character that does not appear in compare-value. If all of the characters in base-string also appear in compare-value, %CHECK returns 0.
V5R1	%CHECKR	compare-value : base-string {: starting-position }	The last position of the base-string that contains a character that does not appear in compare-value. If all of the characters in base-string also appear in compare-value, %CHECKR returns 0.
V5R1	%DATE	expression {: date-format }	A date value after converting the expression into the date format specified. The expression may be any valid RPG datatype, including character, numeric, date, time, or timestamp.
V5R1	%DAYS	number of days	A valid duration of the number of day specified. Use this to add the number-of-days to an existing date value.

	Table 4.1: Built-in Function Syntax Summary, *continued*		
Version Release	Built-in Function	Parameters	Return Value Description
V3R7 V5R2	%DEC	numeric expression {:digits : decpos}character-string : digits : decpos	Value in packed numeric format. If digits and DECPOS are specified, the result value is formatted to fit in a variable of the number of digits specified.If a character string is specified, the value is converted to packed decimal and returned based on the required digits and DECPOS parameters.
V3R7 V5R2	%DECH	numeric expression {:digits : decpos} character-string : digits : decpos	Half-adjusted value in packed numeric format. The length and decimal positions. If a character string is specified, the value is converted to packed decimal and returned based on the required digits and DECPOS parameters.
V3R7	%DECPOS	numeric expression	(D) Number of decimal digits.
V5R1	%DIFF	date1 : date2 : duration	The duration between two date, time or timestamp values. Valid duration codes include: *MSECONDS, *SECONDS, *MINUTES, *HOURS, *DAYS, *MONTHS, *YEARS. Alternatively the short-hand duration codes may be specified: *MS, *S, *MN, *H, *D, *M, *Y
V4R4	%DIV	Numerator : denominator	(D) Performs integer division and returns the quotient (result) of that division operation.
V3R7	%EDITC	non-float numeric expression : edit code {:*cursym | *astfill | currency symbol}	(D) String representing edited value.
V3R7	%EDITFLT	numeric expression	Character external display representation of float.
V3R7	%EDITW	non-float numeric expression : edit word	(D) String representing edited value.
V3R1	%ELEM	array, table, or multiple occurrence data structure name	(D) Number of elements or occurrences.
V4R2	%EOF	{file name}	'1' if the most recent file input operation or write to a subfile (for a particular file, if specified); | ended in an end-of-file or | beginning-of-file condition '0' otherwise.
V4R2	%EQUAL	{file name}	'1' if the most recent SETLL (for a particular file, if specified) or LOOKUP operation found an exact match; '0' otherwise.

Table 4.1: Built-in Function Syntax Summary, *continued*

Version Release	Built-in Function	Parameters	Return Value Description
V4R2	%ERROR		'1' if the most recent operation code with extender 'E' specified resulted in an error; '0' otherwise.
V5R2	%FIELDS	field1 {: field2 : ...}	Used with the UPDATE operation code to indicate the fields that should be updated by the operation. Only those fields enclosed within the %FIELDS built-in function are modified in the database record.
V3R7 V5R2	%FLOAT	numeric expression character-string	Value in float format. When a character value is specified, it is converted to floating point form. This is particularly useful when creating applications that accept only character data as input, such as EDI applications or CGI programs.
V4R2	%FOUND	{file name}	'1' if the most recent relevant operation (for a particular file, if specified) found a record (CHAIN, DELETE, SETGT, SETLL), an element (LOOKUP), or a match (CHECK, CHECKR, SCAN); '0' otherwise.
V4R4	%GRAPH	character value	(D) Converts character data to double-byte character set value.
V5R1	%HOURS	number of hours	A valid duration of the number of hours specified. Use this to add the number-of-hours to an existing date, time, or timestamp value.
V3R7 V5R2	%INT	numeric expression character-string	Value in integer format. When a character value is specified, it is converted to integer form. This is particularly useful when creating applications that accept only character data as input, such as EDI applications or CGI programs.
V3R7 V5R2	%INTH	numeric expression charater-string	Half-adjusted value in integer format. When a character value is specified, it is converted to integer form. This is particularly useful when creating applications that accept only character data as input, such as EDI applications or CGI programs.

Table 4.1: Built-in Function Syntax Summary, *continued*

Version Release	Built-in Function	Parameters	Return Value Description
V5R2	%KDS	data-structure { : field-cnt }	Used with the CHAIN, SETLL, SETGT, READE and READPE operation codes to allow a data structure to be used as a key list for file access. The first parameter is the name of a data structure whose subfields must match the key structure of the file being accessed. The second parameter is optional and, if specified, indicates the number of subfields used as the key list. If the second parameter is not specified, then all subfields in the data structure are used as the key list.
V3R7	%LEN	any expression	(D) Returns the length of a variable or literal value, or the current length of a varying length field. When used on the left side of the equal sign, sets the length of varying length fields.
V5R1	%LOOKUPXX	%LOOKUP(arg : array {: startindex {: numelems}}) %LOOKUPLT(arg : array {: startindex {: numelems}}) %LOOKUPGE(arg : array {: startindex {: numelems}}) %LOOKUPGT(arg : array {: startindex {: numelems}}) %LOOKUPLE(arg : array {: startindex {: numelems}})	Returns the array index of the LOOKUP built-in function.
V5R1	%MINUTES	number of minutes	A valid duration of the number of minutes specified. Use this to add the number-of-minutes to an existing date, time, or timestamp value.
V5R1	%MONTHS	number of months	A valid duration of the number of months specified. Use this to add the number-of-months to an existing date or timestamp value.
V5R1	%MSECONDS	number of microseconds	A valid duration of the number of microseconds specified. Use this to add the number-of-microseconds to an existing date, time, or timestamp value.
V3R7	%NULLIND	null-capable field name	Value in indicator format representing the null indicator setting for the null-capable field.

Table 4.1: Built-in Function Syntax Summary, *continued*

Version Release	Built-in Function	Parameters	Return Value Description
V5R1	%OCCURS	data structure name	If used on the left-side of the assignment operation, the data structure occurrence is set. If used on the right-side of the equals sign for assignment expressions or on either side of the comparator for a comparison operation, the current data structure occurrence is retrieved.
V4R2	%OPEN	file name	'1' if the specified file is open '0' if the specified file is closed.
V3R1	%PADDR	'procedure name' | prototype name	(D) Address of procedure.
V3R2 V3R6	%PARMS		Number of parameters passed to procedure.
V5R1	%REALLOC	ptr : number-of-bytes	Pointer to the newly allocated memory. The returned pointer may be the same as the original PTR parameter or it may be different. Up to 16776704 bytes of memory may be allocated.
V4R4	%REM	Numerator : Denominator	(D) Performs integer division and returns the remainder from the division operation.
V4R2	%REPLACE	replacement string: source string {:start position {:source length to replace}}	(D) String produced by inserting replacement string into source string, starting at start position and replacing the specified number of characters.
V3R7	%SCAN	search argument : string to be searched {:start position}	(D) First position of search argument in string or zero, if not found.
V5R1	%SECONDS	number of seconds	A valid duration of the number of seconds specified. Use this to add the number-of-seconds to an existing date, time or timestamp value.
V5R1	%SHTDN		*ON if job-end is requested, *OFF is job-end has not been requested.
V3R1	%SIZE	variable, data structure, array, or literal {: *ALL}	(D) Number of bytes used by variable or literal. *ALL returns the number of bytes used by all the elements of the array, or all the occurrences of the data structure.
V5R1	%SQRT	numeric expression	The square root of the numeric value.

Version Release	Built-in Function	Parameters	Return Value Description
		Table 4.1: Built-in Function Syntax Summary, *continued*	
V4R2	%STATUS	{file name}	Returns 0 if no program or file error occurred since the most recent operation code with extender 'E' specified as the most recent value set for any program or file status. If an error occurs as a file is specified, the value returned is the most recent status for that file.
V3R7	%STR	pointer{:maximum length}pointer : maximum length	Characters addressed by pointer argument up to but not including the first x'00' are retrieved or modified.
V5R1	%SUBDT	date1 : duration-component	The duration component of the date, time, or timestamp value. Valid duration components include: *MSECONDS, *SECONDS, *MINUTES, *HOURS, *DAYS, *MONTHS, *YEARS. Alternatively the short-hand duration components may be specified: *MS, *S, *MN, *H, *D, *M, *Y
V3R1	%SUBST	string:start{:length}	(D) Substring value. If length is not specified, the substring begins with start and continues through the end of the string.
V5R1	%THIS	reference to an object	Used only as a parameter to a procedure or method, this built-in function returns a reference pointer to the "this" object for those method calls.
V5R1	%TIME	expression {: time-format }	A time value after converting the expression from the time format specified. The expression may be any valid RPG datatype, including character, numeric, date, time, or timestamp.
V5R1	%TIMESTAMP	expression {: *ISO	*ISO0 }	A timestamp value after converting the expression from the timestamp format specified. The expression may be any valid RPG datatype, including character, numeric, date, time, or timestamp.

Table 4.1: Built-in Function Syntax Summary, *continued*

Version Release	Built-in Function	Parameters	Return Value Description
V5R1	%TLOOKUPXX	%TLOOKUP(arg : search-table {: alt-table}) %TLOOKUPLT(arg : search-table {: alt-table}) %TLOOKUPGE(arg : search-table {: alt-table}) %TLOOKUPGT(arg : search-table {: alt-table}) %TLOOKUPLE(arg : search-table {: alt-table})	*ON if a match is found; the table element is set to the found element. If a match is not found, *OFF is returned.
V3R1	%TRIM	string	(D) String with left and right blanks trimmed (removed).
V3R1	%TRIML	string	(D) String with left blanks trimmed.
V3R1	%TRIMR	string	(D) String with right blanks trimmed.
V4R4	%UCS2	Any character value	(D) Returns a varying-length value.
V4R2	%UNS	numeric expression character-expression	Value in unsigned format. When a character value is specified, it is converted to integer form. This is particularly useful when creating applications that accept only character data as input, such as EDI applications or CGI programs.
V4R2	%UNSH	numeric expression character-expression	Half-adjusted value in unsigned integer format. When a character value is specified, it is converted to integer form. This is particularly useful when creating applications that accept only character data as input, such as EDI applications or CGI programs.
V4R4	%XFOOT	Array name	Cross foots (totals) all the elements in an array.
V5R1	%XLATE	original-characters : translate-to-characters : data-to-translate {: start-pos}	Returns the data-to-translate after it is translated using the first and second parameters. The original data is not modified by the function.
V5R1	%YEARS	number of years	A valid duration of the number of years specified. Use this to add the number-of-years to an existing date or timestamp value.

The %FIELD and %KDS built-in functions are unique to specific operation codes. That is they cannot be used in any general RPG statement, but rather are allowed only with specification operation codes.

The syntax diagram for each built-in function appears on the pages that follow. An example use of a typical built-in function is illustrated in Figure 4.1. The built-in function is %SUBST. The first parameter is the variable CUSTNAME, the second parameter is the starting position (7), and the third parameter (5) is the number of bytes to extract.

```
.....CSRnØ1..............OpCode(ex)Extended-factor2+++++++++++++++++++++++++++++++
     C                   eval        lastname = %subst(custname : 7 : 5)
```

Figure 4.1: Example usage of a built-in function.

As shown in Figure 4.1, five characters of the CUSTNAME field, beginning at position 7, are assigned to the LASTNAME field. In all cases, built-in functions can appear on either side of the comparison operator for an IF, DOW, DOU, FOR, and WHEN operation. For assignments, however, only %SUBST and %STR have the ability to allow the target of the operation to be extracted. While most operations may appear within %SUBST, only %SUBST and %STR actually allows the value on the left side of the equals sign to be modified.

▶ %ABS (ABSOLUTE VALUE)

This function returns the absolute value of a given value.

%ABS Syntax Diagram

```
absolute value of variable = %ABS( variable or expression )
```

Specify any numeric expression or variable, data structure subfield, or array element on the %ABS function. The return value has the same properties as the variable specified for the %ABS function. In other words, a packed decimal value is returned when a packed decimal value is specified as the argument to the %ABS function.

Use this function to return the positive value of any number (negative or positive). The absolute value of a number is the non-negative value of the number. For example, the absolute value of -38 is 38 and the absolute value of 400 is 400. Figure 4.2 shows an example of the use of the %ABS built-in function. In Figure 4.2, the area of a sphere is calculated using the absolute value of its radius.

```
.....DName+++++++++++EUDS.......Length+TDc.Functions+++++++++++++++++++++++++++++
0010 D Radius          S              5I   INZ( -12 )
0020 D PI              C                    const( 3.1415926 )
0030 D Area            S              7P 3
.....CSRn01.............OpCode(ex)Extended-factor2+++++++++++++++++++++++++++++++
0040 C                 Eval       Area = 4 * PI * %Abs(Radius)**2
```

Figure 4.2: An example of the %ABS built-in function.

▶ %ADDR (GET ADDRESS)

The %ADDR function returns the memory location assigned to a variable. This memory location is known as the variable's *address*. It can be copied into a pointer variable, for further processing, or compared to another address.

%ADDR Syntax Diagram

```
pointer to variable = %ADDR( variable )
```

See also %PADDR and PROCPTR.

Specify any variable, data structure, subfield, array, or array element on the %ADDR function. The %ADDR function can be used to copy the address of the variable to a pointer variable or it can be used with a comparison operation, such as IF or WHEN.

Use this function to return the address of a variable when pointers are being used. For example, if a pointer variable named MYPOINTER is defined, store the address of another variable in MYPOINTER by using the %ADDR function as shown in Figure 4.3.

```
.....DName++++++++++EUDS.......Length+TDc.Functions++++++++++++++++++++++++++++++
0010 D Comp_Desc       S              35A
0020 D desc            S                  LIKE(Comp_Desc)

0030 D myPointer       S              *   INZ(%ADDR(Comp_Desc))
.....CSRn01.............OpCode(ex)Extended-factor2++++++++++++++++++++++++++++++++
0040 C                 Eval      myPointer = %ADDR( desc )
0050 C                 If        %addr( desc ) = MyPointer
```

Figure 4.3: An example of the %ADDR built-in function.

In Figure 4.3, the stand-alone field named COMP_DESC is defined as a 35-position character field (line 10). This variable's address in memory is allocated at runtime. Line 20 defines the DESC field with the same attributes as COMP_DESC.

The variable MYPOINTER is declared (line 30). Its data type is POINTER. Pointers contain the addresses of other variables. The address of COMP_DESC is stored in MYPOINTER by the INZ keyword.

Another method of assigning pointer values is the EVAL operation. Line 40 illustrates how the %ADDR built-in function can be used to assign the address of a variable to a pointer variable, while line 50 illustrates its use in a comparison operation.

%BITAND (BITWISE "ANDING" OF VALUES)

%BITAND returns the bit-wise ANDing of the bits of all the parameters. The result bit is on when all of the corresponding bits in the parameters are on; otherwise the resulting bit is off.

%BITAND Syntax Diagram

```
resulting-bit-pattern = %BITAND( expr1 : expr2 : expr3... )
```
See also: %BITXOR, %BITOR, %BITNOT

%BITAND can have two or more parameters. All parameters must be of the same datatype and must be either character or numeric.

The resulting value is the same datatype as the datatypes of the parameters, and its length is the same as the longest parameter value specified. If the parameter lengths are not the same, the longest length is used and the shorter parameters are padded on the left with X'00' if numeric, and on the right with X'FF' if character.

All bitwise built-in functions operate on fields of any length and may be specified in both the Calculation specifications and as a parameter of a keyword on the Definition and File specifications. When referring to the bits of a single byte, the 8 bits are enumerated as 0 through 7, starting with the high-order bit.

Bitwise operations are often used with single-byte character fields or values to test for or set a specific bit pattern. For example, to set the bits on in a result when all the bits of the comparison parameters are on, the %BITAND built-in function can be used as follows:

```
.....DName++++++++++EUDS.......Length+TDc.Functions++++++++++++++++++++
0001 D first           S              1A   Inz('1')
0002 D second          S              1A   Inz('2')
0003 D third           S              1A   Inz('3')
0004 D answer          S              1A   Inz(X'00')
.....CSRn01.............OpCode(ex)Extended-factor2++++++++++++++++++++
0005 C                 if           answer = %BitAND(first : second : third)
```

The ANSWER field is initialized to the bit pattern: 0000 0000 which is X'00' in hex. Line 5 performs a bitwise AND of the FIRST, SECOND and THIRD fields. The result is a bit pattern whose bits are set on if all the corresponding bits in the three parameters are also on; otherwise the resulting bit is off. The result of the %BITAND operation on line 5 is X'F0' or a bit pattern of 1111 0000.

	Bit Pattern	Hex Value
FIRST	1111 0001	X'F1'
SECOND	1111 0010	X'F2'
THIRD	1111 0011	X'F3'
%BITAND	AND	
Result	1111 0000	(X'F0')

%BITAND can also be used to set off specific bits within a field. To do this, create a secondary value that contains the bit pattern needed to set off the bits in the original value. For example, a value initialized to X'C4' represents a bit pattern of 1100 0100. To set off the low-order bits in this value, it can be ANDed with a value of 1111 0000 or X'F0'.

```
.....DName++++++++++++EUDS.......Length+TDc.Functions++++++++++++++++++++
0001 D myValue           S              1A    Inz(X'C4')
.....CSRn01.............OpCode(ex)Extended-factor2++++++++++++++++++++
0002 C                   if          myValue = %BitAND(myValue : X'F0')
```

Since bits 0 and 1 are the only two bits on in both values, the result of the %bitand built-in function is X'C0'.

	Bit Pattern	Hex Value
MYVALUE	1100 0400	X'F1'
%BITAND	AND	
Literal	1111 0000	X'F0'
Result	1100 0000	(X'C0')

▶ %BITNOT (BIT INVERSION)

%BITNOT returns the bit-wise inversion of the bits of the parameters. The resulting bit pattern is the opposite of the value specified on the parameter.

%BITNOT Syntax Diagram

```
resulting-bit-pattern = %BITNOT( expr1 )
```

See also: %BITXOR, %BITOR, %BITAND

%BITNOT accepts one parameter and returns a value with the same datatype as its parameter.

The resulting value is the same datatype as the datatypes of the parameter, and its length is the same as the parameter value specified. If the parameter is character, the result is character; if the parameter is numeric the result is either unsigned integer if the parameter is unsigned, otherwise the result is an 8-byte integer (20I 0) value.

All bitwise built-in functions operate on fields of any length and may be specified in both the Calculation specifications and as a parameter of a keyword on the Definition and File specifications. When referring to the bits of a single byte, the 8 bits are enumerated as 0 through 7, starting with the high-order bit.

Bitwise operations are often used with single-byte character fields or values to test for or set a specific bit pattern. For example, to reverse the bit pattern of a field the %BITNOT built-in function can be used as follows:

```
.....DName+++++++++++EUDS.......Length+TDc.Functions++++++++++++++++++
0001 D myValue          S             1A    Inz('1')
0002 D flip             S             1A    Inz(X'00')
.....CSRn01.............OpCode(ex)Extended-factor2++++++++++++++++++++
0003 C                  eval       flip = %BitNot(myValue)
```

The MYVALUE field is initialized to the bit pattern: 1111 0001 which is X'F1' in hex. Line 2 initializes the XVALUE field to hex zeros; if represents a bit pattern of 1111 1000. The %BITNOT operation (line 3) returns the bitwise NOTing of MYVALUE. The result is a bit pattern whose bits are the opposite of the original value in MYVALUE. The NOTing of MYVALUE produces the following result:

	Bit Pattern	Hex Value
MYVALUE	1111 0001	X'F1'
%BITNOT	NOT	
XVALUE	0000 0000	X'00'
Result	0000 1110	X'0E'

▶ %BITOR (BITWISE "ORING" OF VALUES)

%BITOR returns the bit-wise ORing of the bits of all the parameters. The result bits are on when any of the corresponding bits in the parameters are on. The resulting bits are off when all of the bits in the corresponding bit position of the parameters are off.

%BITOR Syntax Diagram

```
resulting-bit-pattern = %BITOR( expr1 : expr2 : expr3 ...)
```
See also: %BITXOR, %BITAND, %BITNOT

%BITOR can have two or more parameters. All parameters must be of the same datatype and must be either character or numeric.

The resulting value is the same datatype as the datatypes of the parameters, and its length is the same as the longest parameter value specified. If the parameter lengths are not the same, the longest length is used and the shorter parameters are padded on the left with X'00' if numeric, and on the right with X'FF' if character.

All bitwise built-in functions operate on fields of any length and may be specified in both the Calculation specifications and as a parameter of a keyword on the Definition and File specifications. When referring to the bits of a single byte, the 8 bits are enumerated as 0 through 7, starting with the high-order bit.

Bitwise operations are often used with single-byte character fields or values to test for or set a specific bit pattern. The %BITOR can be used to combined add bit values to existing values.

For example, to detect if some of the bits of one field are on in a second field, the %BITXOR built-in function can be used as follows:

```
.....DName++++++++++EUDS.......Length+TDc.Functions++++++++++++++++++
0001 D myValue         S              1A    Inz('1')
0002 D xValue          S              1A    Inz('8')

.....CSRn01..............OpCode(ex)Extended-factor2++++++++++++++++++++
0003 C                  if           myValue = %BitOR(myValue : xValue)
```

The MYVALUE field is initialized to the bit pattern: 1111 0001 which is X'F1' in hex. Line 2 initializes the XVALUE field to '8' which represents a bit pattern of 1111 1000 and a value of X'F8' in hex. The %BITOR operation (line 3) returns the bitwise ORing of MYVALUE with XVALUE. The result is a bit pattern whose bits are on if either of the two parameters' corresponding bits are on, otherwise the bit is off.

The ORing of MYVALUE with XVALUE produces the following results.

	Bit Pattern	Hex Value
MYVALUE	1111 0001	X'F1'
%BITOR	OR	
XVALUE	1111 1000	X'F8'
Result	1111 1001	X'F9'

▶ %BITXOR (BITWISE EXLUSIVE "ORING" OF VALUES)

%BITXOR returns the bit-wise XORing of the bits of all the parameters. The result bit is on when either of the corresponding bits in the parameters are on, but not both; otherwise the result bit is off.

%BITXOR Syntax Diagram

```
resulting-bit-pattern = %BITXOR( expr1 : expr2 )
```

See also: %BITAND, %BITOR, %BITNOT

%BITXOR must have two parameters. Both parameters must be of the same datatype, that is, character or numeric.

The resulting value is the same datatype as the datatype of the parameters, and its length is the same as the longest parameter value specified. If the parameter lengths are not the same, the longest length is used and the shorter parameters are padded on the left with X'00' if numeric, and on the right with X'FF' if character.

All bitwise built-in functions operate on fields of any length and may be specified in both the Calculation specifications and as a parameter of a keyword on the Definition and File specifications. When referring to the bits of a single byte, the 8 bits are enumerated as 0 through 7, starting with the high-order bit.

Bitwise operations are often used with single-byte character fields or values to test for or set a specific bit pattern. For example, to set off specific bits within a field, the %BIT the bit pattern of a field name MYVALUE and store that reversed pattern in a field named FLIP, following example may be used.

```
.....DName++++++++++EUDS.......Length+TDc.Functions++++++++++++++++++++
0001 D myValue          S             1A    Inz(X'FC')
0002 D flip             S             1A    Inz(X'00')

.....CSRn01.............OpCode(ex)Extended-factor2++++++++++++++++++++
0003 C                  Eval       flip = %BitXOR(myValue : X'FF')
```

The MYVALUE field is initialized to the bit pattern: 1111 1100 which is X'FC' in hex. The flip field is initialized to hex zeros, but that is irrelevant for this example.

On line 3, the MYVALUE field is exclusively ORed with the hex value X'FF'. Since X'FF' represents all the bits as being on, that is it is the same as a bit pattern of 1111 1111, the resulting bit pattern is the reverse of that in the MYVALUE field.

Exclusive ORing of MYVALUE with X'FF' produces the following results:

	Bit Pattern	Hex Value
MYVALUE	1111 1100	X'F0'
%BITXOR	XOR	
2nd Value	1111 1111	X'FF'
Result	0000 0011	X'03'

▶ %CHAR (CONVERT TO CHARACTER)

The %CHAR function returns the character form of a noncharacter value or expression.

%CHAR Syntax Diagram

```
character value = %CHAR( numeric-value or expression | date-value | :
                         date-format )
```

See also %EDITC and %EDITW.

The %CHAR function returns the numeric variable or expression or date value in character format. Any conventional noncharacter value—such as a date, time, timestamp, double-byte character, UCS-2, or numeric expression—may be specified.

For date, time, and timestamp values, the returned value includes the date, time, and timestamp value and the edit symbols. The edit symbols, or date separators, are based on the field's DATFMT (date format) keyword. The value is returned in the format of the date variable's DATFMT keyword unless the optional second parameter is specified.

The second parameter indicator, for date values, is the return-format of the date value. For example, if the date being converted is an *ISO date and the requirement is that the returned character value is to be formatted as *DMY, specifying *DMY on the second parameter will cause the returned value to be in *DMY format.

For numeric values and expressions, the returned value includes the decimal notation and, if applicable, the negative sign. Leading blanks and zeros are trimmed from the returned value. For example, a nine-digit number with two decimal positions, such as 000456789, would be returned as '4567.89' by %CHAR. If the numeric value is less than zero, a negative sign is inserted into the returned character string preceding the leading significant digit. Figure 4.4 shows an example of using %CHAR.

```
.....DName++++++++++EUDS.......Length+TDc.Functions++++++++++++++++++++++++++++
0010 D textDate        S            35A
0020 D textPrice       S            35A

0030 D ordDate         S            D    INZ(D'1999-02-14') DATFMT(*ISO)
0040 D ordTime         S            D    INZ(T'15:30:00') TIMFMT(*USA)
0050 D MarkUp          S          11P 2 INZ(11.25)
0060 D Cost            S          11P 2 INZ(37.50)
.....CSRn01.............OpCode(ex)Extended-factor2+++++++++++++++++++++++++++++
0070 C                 Eval      textDate = 'Order date and time is '
0080 C                                   + %Char(ordDate) + ' at '
0090 C                                   + %Char(ordTime)
```

```
       **   The value of textDate is 'Order date and time is 1999-02-14 at 03:30 PM'
0100 C                       Eval      textPrice = 'Your price is ' +
0110 C                                      + %Char( Cost + MarkUp )
       **   The value of textPrice is 'Your price is 48.75'
```

Figure 4.4: An example of the %CHAR built-in function.

▶ %CHECK (VERIFY FIELD CONTENT LEFT-TO-RIGHT)

The %CHECK function performs a character-by-character verification of a character value. Each character in the character field or value is tested to ensure that they are also in the verification list.

%CHECK Syntax Diagram

```
position = %CHECK( verification-list : searched-value {: start-position } )
```
See also: %CHECKR

The check function returns the first position of the searched-value that contains a character that does not appear in verification-list. If all of the characters in the searched-value also appear in verification-list, zero is returned.

The verification begins at the optional start-position and continues to the right until a character that is not contained in the comparator string is found or the end of the searched-value is detected.

The first parameter is the list of characters used as the verification-list and must be of a character field, expression, or named constant. In addition, it may be a graphic, UCS-2, fixed, or varying length field.

The second parameter must be of the same datatype (character, graphic, USC-2, etc.) as the first parameter. It is verified on a character-by-character basis against the verification-list.

The third parameter is optional and indicates the starting position as the verification. If unspecified, the verification begins with the first position of the searched-value.

▶ %CHECKR (VERIFY FIELD CONTENT RIGHT-TO-LEFT)

The %CHECKR function performs a character-by-character verification of a character value. Each character in the character field or value is tested, beginning with the right-most character, to ensure that each character is also in the verification list.

%CHECKR Syntax Diagram

```
position = %CHECKR( verification-list : searched-value
                  {: start-position } )
```

See also: %CHECK

The check-right function returns the right-most position of the searched-value that contains a character that does not appear in verification-list. If all of the characters in the searched-value also appear in verification-list, zero is returned.

The verification begins at the optional start-position and continues to the left until a character that is not contained in the comparator string is found or the end of the searched-value is detected.

The first parameter is the list of characters used as the verification-list and must be of a character field, expression, or named constant. In addition, it may be a graphic, UCS-2, fixed, or varying length field.

The second parameter must be of the same datatype (character, graphic, USC-2, etc.) as the first parameter. It is verified on a character-by-character basis against the verification-list.

The third parameter is optional and indicates the starting position to being the verification. If unspecified, the verification begins with the last (right-most) position of the searched-value.

▶ %DATE (CONVERT TO DATE VALUE)

The %DATE function converts a numeric, character or timestamp value to a valid date datatype value.

%DATE Syntax Diagram

```
date-value  = %DATE( { expression {: date-format-code }} )
```
                                                    See also: %TIME, %TIMESTAMP

The date function performs two functions: (1) It converts a non-date value into a date value using the optional date-format code, and (2) if no parameters are specified, it returns the current system date.

The date format codes that may be specified in parameter 2 of the %DATE function are as follows:

Format Code	Date Format
*YMD	YYMMDD
*DMY	DDMMYY
*MDY	MMDDYY
*CYMD	CYYMMDD
*CDMY	CDDMMYY
*CMDY	CMMDDYY
*ISO	YYYYDDYY
*USA	MMDDYYYY
*EUR	DDMMYYYY
*JIS	YYYYMMDD
*JUL	YYDDD
*LONGJUL	YYYYDDD

The date format code may be specified with a separator character when converting from a character value to a date value, to indicate that a separator other than the default separator is used in the character date value. The separator is not allowed when converting from a numeric value. In addition, a separator of 0 (zero) may be specified with the date-format code to indicate that the character date value contains no separators.

▶%DIFF (DIFFERENCE BETWEEN TWO DATE, TIME, OR TIMESTAMP VALUES)

The %DIFF function calculates the duration between two date, time, or timestamp values.

%DIFF Syntax Diagram

```
duration = %DIFF( date1 : date2 : duration-code )
```

See also: %SUBDT

The difference operation returns an integer (the duration value) that may be assigned to a numeric field, or added or subtracted from another date, time, or timestamp value. The first and second parameters must be the same or compatible date or time data types. That is, they must be both date values, or time values, or a date or time value and a timestamp value.

The duration code (parameter 3) is required and indicates the format for the returned value. The value duration codes are as follows:

*DAYS, *MONTHS, *YEARS or *D, *M, *Y

*MSECONDS, *SECONDS, *MINUTES, *HOURS, or *MS, *S, *MN, *H

▶%DEC and %DECH (CONVERT TO PACKED DECIMAL)

The %DEC and the %DECH functions convert a numeric value or expression to packed decimal notation.

%DEC Syntax Diagram

```
packed decimal value  = %DEC( numeric expression [: length : decimal positions ] )

packed decimal value  = %DEC( character-string : length : decimal positions )
```

or

```
packed decimal value  = %DECH( numeric expression : length : decimal positions  )

packed decimal value  = %DECH( character-string : length : decimal positions  )
```

%DEC converts the numeric value or expression to packed decimal. Alternatively, %DEC also converts a character string containing a number to a numeric value. The length and decimal positions are used to create the resulting value. If the length and decimal positions are not specified, the length and decimal positions of the expression arguments are used to determine a default length and decimal positions.

%DECH converts the numeric value or expression to packed decimal and performs the half adjust (rounding) of the result value. Alternatively, %DECH also converts a character string containing a number to a numeric value. Unlike %DEC, the %DECH built-in function requires the length and decimal positions in order to perform the half-adjust function.

▶%DECPOS (RETRIEVE DECIMAL POSITIONS)

The %DECPOS function retrieves the numeric decimal positions declared for any non-floating point numeric variable or expression.

%DECPOS Syntax Diagram

decimal positions = %DECPOS(numeric variable or expression)

See also %LEN

The %DECPOS function retrieves the number of decimal digits for a numeric variable. In addition, it can retrieve the decimal digits used to produce the temporary result of an expression. When multiple variables are specified for an expression, the result is the sum of the decimal positions.

```
.....DName++++++++++EUDS.......Length+TDc.Functions++++++++++++++++++++++++++++
0010 D Price           S              7P 2
0020 D Cost            S              5P 3
0030 D MarkUp          S              5P 2

0030 D PosA            S              5I 0
0030 D PosB            S              5I 0
0030 D PosC            S              5I 0
0030 D PosD            S              5I 0
.....CSRn01.............OpCode(ex)Extended-factor2++++++++++++++++++++++++++++++
0070 C                 Eval      PosA = %DECPOS( price )
     **   PosA = 2
0070 C                 Eval      PosB = %DECPOS( cost )
     **   PosB = 3
0070 C                 Eval      PosC = %DECPOS( MarkUp )
     **   PosC = 2
0070 C                 Eval      PosD = %DECPOS( Cost + MarkUp )
     **   PosD = 5
```

Figure 4.5: An example of the %DECPOS built-in function.

▶ %DIV (INTEGER DIVISION)

The %DIV function performs integer division on the two arguments. The first argument is the numerator and the second is the denominator.

%DIV Syntax Diagram

```
integer quotient  = %DIV( numerator  :  denominator )
```

See also %REM

The divide operation returns an integer (whole number) result value (quotient). The numerator and the denominator must be numeric values with no decimal digits. In other words, numeric variables cannot contain decimal positions.

The %DIV operation can be specified on the definition specification when the two arguments are constant values that fit within an 8-byte integer value (20 digits).

By definition, integer division doesn't perform rounding. Therefore, the half-adjust operation extender is not supported.

The %DIV operation is only for integer (whole number) division. For all other divide operations, the / operator or the DIV operation should be used. Figure 4.6 shows an example of use of %DIV.

```
.....DName++++++++++EUDS.......Length+TDc.Functions++++++++++++++++++++++++++++++
0010 D Cost            S             5P 3
0020 D MarkUp          S             5P 2
0030 D Count           S             7S 0 Inz(25)
0040 D Total           S             7P 0 Inz(220)

0050 D ValueA          S             5I 0
0060 D ValueB          S             5I 0
0070 D ValueC          S             5I 0
.....CSRn01.............OpCode(ex)Extended-factor2+++++++++++++++++++++++++++++++
0080 C                     Eval      valueA = %DIV( 15 : 5 )
     **   ValueA = 3
0090 C                     Eval      valueB = %DIV( MarkUp : Cost )
     **   ERROR ** MarkUp and Cost must have zero decimal positions.

0100 C                     Eval      valueC = %DIV( Total : Count )
     **   ValueC = 8
```

Figure 4.6: Example of %DIV built-in function.

▶ DURATION BUILT-IN FUNCTIONS

The duration built-in functions work with date arithmetic. That is, they convert a non-date value, such as a number, into a duration value, such as an hour, minute, day, or year.

Duration Built-in Functions' Syntax Diagrams

```
microseconds value  = %MSECONDS( numeric-value )
seconds value  = %SECONDS( numeric-value )
minutes value  = %MINUTES( numeric-value )
hours value  = %HOURS( numeric-value )
days value  = %DAYS( numeric-value )
months value  = %MONTHS( numeric-value )
years value  = %YEARS( numeric-value )
```

The first parameter can be any numeric value, expression, literal value, or named constant. That value is converted to the duration specified and the return value may be used with a corresponding date arithmetic or comparison operation.

▶ %EDITC (EDIT WITH EDIT CODE)

This function edits a numeric value and returns a character form of that value after applying the specified edit code.

%EDITC Syntax Diagram

```
character value = %EDITC( numeric exp : 'editcode' [:*ASTFILL | *CURSYM ] )
```
See also %EDITW, %EDITFLT, and %CHAR

The first parameter can be any numeric value, variable, literal, or expression.

The second parameter must be a valid edit code. The edit code must be a constant such as a quoted character or named constant. The valid edit codes are: 'A' through 'D', 'J' through 'Q', 'X', 'Y', 'Z' and '1' through '9'.

The third parameter can be one of the following values:

*ASTFILL — Leading asterisks are inserted in place of any leading zeros in the value.

*CURSYM — The currency symbol specified by the CURSYM keyword on the header specification is inserted into the edited value to the left of the first significant digit.

'quoted value' — This 1-byte quoted character value is used as the currency symbol for the edited value. The placement and function is the same as *CURSYM.

The length of the returned value is the length of the numeric value with the edit code applied. Leading blanks are included in the resulting edited value. When using %EDITC with the concatenation operator (+), use the %TRIML built-in function to trim off leading blanks.

Only one of the *CURSYM and *ASTFILL functions can be specified. It is often necessary to produce a result value that contains both leading asterisks and the currency symbol. This can be accomplished by using code similar to that shown in Figure 4.7.

```
.....DName++++++++++EUDS.......Length+TDc.Functions++++++++++++++++++++++++++++
0010 D MSG             S              40A
0010 D NetDue          S               7P 2 Inz(12.65)
0020 D Amount          S              11P 2 Inz(10500.00)
.....CSRn01.............OpCode(ex)Extended-factor2++++++++++++++++++++++++++++++
0020 C                 Eval      msg = 'Total due is '
0030 C                           + '$' + %EditC( netdue : 'J' : *ASTFILL)
     ** MSG = 'Total due is $***12.65'

0080 C                 Eval      MSG = %EditC( Amount : 'J' : *CURSYM)
     **  MSG = '    $10,500.00'
```

Figure 4.7: An example of the %EDITC built-in function.

▶ %EDITFLT (EDIT WITH FLOATING POINT)

The %EDITFLT function edits any numeric value and returns a character form of that value. The result is a 23-position character value, representing the numeric value in floating-point notation. If a 4-byte floating-point value is specified, the result value is 14 positions in length.

%EDITFLT Syntax Diagram

character value = %EDITFLT(*numeric expression*)

See also %EDITC

The first parameter can be any numeric value, variable, literal, or expression. It is converted into the external representation (character form) of a floating-point value.

▶ %EDITW (EDIT WITH EDIT WORD)

The %EDITW function edits a numeric value and returns a character form of that value after applying the specified edit word.

%EDITW Syntax Diagram

```
character value = %EDITC( numeric expression  :  'edit word' )
```
See also %EDITC, %EDITFLT, and %CHAR.

The first parameter can be any numeric value, variable, literal, or expression (except floating point). If a floating point value is required, the %DEC built-in function can be used to convert the floating point value to packed decimal.

The second parameter must contain a valid edit word mask. The edit word is applied to the numeric expression and the character form of the value is returned. The same editing rules that apply to output field edit words apply to the %EDITW built-in function. See the example shown in Figure 4.8.

```
.. ...CSRnØ1..............OpCode(ex)Extended-factor2++++++++++++++++++++++++++++++++
    C                     Eval      msg = 'Total due is '
    C                                    + %EditW( amount : '$ ,  Ø.  CR')
```

Figure 4.8: An example of the %EDITW built-in function.

%ELEM (GET NUMBER OF ELEMENTS)

The %ELEM function returns the number of elements declared for an array or table, or the number of occurrences of a multiple-occurrence data structure.

%ELEM Syntax Diagram

```
number of elements = %ELEM( array )

number of occurrences = %ELEM( data structure )
```
See also %SIZE and %LEN

Specify an array, table, or multiple-occurrence data structure name as the first argument of the %ELEM function.

Use %ELEM in place of "hard coding" a reference to the number of elements of an array or occurrences of a data structure. Figure 4.9 shows an example.

```
.....DName+++++++++++EUDSFrom+++To/Len+TDc.Functions++++++++++++++++++++++++++++
0010 D States          S             2A   DIM(50)
0020 D I               S             5I 0
.....CSRn01.............OpCode(ex)Extended-factor2++++++++++++++++++++++++++++++
0030 C                 For       I = 1 TO %ELEM(States)
0040 C                 MOVEL     States(I)     Where_Ever
0050 C* ....... other code can go here.......
0060 C                 endFOR
```
Figure 4.9: An example of the %ELEM built-in function.

In Figure 4.9, the number of elements in the STATES array sets the limit for the FOR/ENDFOR loop. Because there are 50 elements in the STATES array, the FOR loop is performed 50 times.

▶%EOF (END OF FILE STATUS)

The %EOF function checks the status of the last input operation for a file. If the beginning or end of the file has been reached as a result of that input operation, %EOF returns '1'; otherwise, %EOF returns '0'.

%EOF Syntax Diagram

```
boolean indicator = %EOF( [ file name ] )
```
See also %FOUND, %ERROR, and %OPEN.

The first parameter is optional and can specify the name of a file being checked for the beginning or end of file condition. If a file name is not specified, %EOF applies to the most recent file operation. Figure 4.10 shows an example.

Table 4.2: Use of %EOF in Place of Indicator		
Operation	Condition Tested	Description
READ	End of file.	Read next record.
READC	No more changed records.	Read next change subfile record.
READP	Beginning of file.	Read prior record.
READPE	Beginning of file.	Read prior record with equal key.
READE	End of file.	Read next record with equal key.
WRITE	Subfile full.	Write subfile detail record.

```
.....CSRnØ1Factor1++++++OpCode(ex)Factor2+++++++Result++++++++Len++DcHiLoEq
     C                     READ       ItemMast
     C                     READ       CustMast
     C                     IF         %EOF or %EOF(ItemMast)
     **...
     C                     endif
```

Figure 4.10: An example of the %EOF built-in function.

The %EOF built-in function can be used in place of resulting indicator 3 for any of the operation codes shown in Table 4.2.

▶%EQUAL (EQUAL CONDITION STATUS)

The %EQUAL function checks the status of the last SETLL or LOOKUP operation.

%EQUAL Syntax Diagram

```
boolean indicator = %EQUAL [ ( file name ) ]
```

See also %FOUND and %EOF

The first parameter is optional and can specify the name of a file of a previous SETLL operation. The %EQUAL checks for an equal key condition (SETLL) or an equal match on a array/table search (LOOKUP). If a file name is not specified, %EQUAL applies to the most recent SETLL or LOOKUP operation. Figure 4.11 shows an example.

Table 4.3: Use of %EQUAL in Place of Indicator		
Operation	Condition Tested	Operation Description
SETLL	Equal key condition	Set lower limits
LOOKUP	Equal element value	Look up with resulting indicator 3

```
.....CSRnØ1Factor1+++++++OpCode(ex)Factor2+++++++Result++++++++Len++DcHiLoEq
     C       ItemNo      SETLL       ItemMast
     C                   IF          %EQUAL( ItemMast )
     C       ItemNo      LOOKUP      SaveItems                          75
     C                   IF          %EQUAL
     C                   CallP       RestoreItem
     C                   endif
     C                   endif
```

Figure 4.11: An example of the %EQUAL built-in function.

The %EQUAL built-in function can be used in place of resulting indicator 3 for the SETLL operation (see Table 4.3). For the LOOKUP operation, resulting indicators are required because they control how the LOOKUP operation functions.

There is a subtle difference between the %EQUAL and the %FOUND built-in functions as they relate to the SETLL operation. The %FOUND condition means that a record with a key value equal to or less than that specified in Factor 1 has been detected. Whereas the %EQUAL condition is set only when a key with a value equal to that of Factor 1 of the SETLL operation has been detected.

▶ %ERROR (ERROR CONDITION STATUS)

The %ERROR function checks the status of the last operation that specified the E operation extender. If an error condition was set by that operation, %ERROR returns '1'. Otherwise, %ERROR returns '0'. Use %ERROR in place of resulting indicator 2.

%ERROR Syntax Diagram

boolean value = %ERROR

See also %FOUND, %EOF, and %STATUS

Any operation code that supports resulting indicator 2 supports the E operation extender. If the E operation extender is specified, %ERROR is set as a result of the operation. If the E operation extender and resulting indicator 2 are not specified, %ERROR is not set and the normal RPG error/exception handling routine is evoked. See Figure 4.12 for an example.

```
.....CSRnØ1Factor1+++++++OpCode(ex)Factor2+++++++Result++++++++Len++DcHiLoEq
     C     CustNo          CHAIN(E)  CustMast
     C                     SELECT
     C                     When      %ERROR
     C                     CallP     CheckForLock
     C                     When      %EOF
     C                     CallP     LastRecord
     C                     endSL
```

Figure 4.12: An example of the %ERROR built-in function.

Tip: *Remember, %ERROR and %STATUS are set only when the E operation extender is used for the operation. If the E operation extender is not used, the state of %ERROR and %STATUS does not change.*

▶%FIELDS (IDENTIFY FIELDS TO UPDATE)

%FIELDS isn't really a built-in function; it is a parameter keyword of the free-format version of the UPDATE and in the future, the WRITE operation codes.

%FIELDS identifies the field names of a database file that should be updated when an UPDATE operation code is performed.

%FIELDS Syntax Diagram

```
%FIELDS( field1 {: field2 {: field3...}} )
```

See also: %KDS

%FIELDS can accept any number of field names as parameters. Each field specified must be the name of a field within the database file being updated. When a field name has been renamed within the program, the new, internal name must be used. The following example illustrates the use of the %FIELDS built-in function.

```
.....C++++++++++++++++++++++++++++++++++++++++++++++++++++++++++++++++++++++
      /free
0001    chain %kds(Customer : 1) CustRec;
0002    ExFmt EditCust;
0003    if  %Found(CustMast);
0004       update CustRec  %fields(CustName : Addr1 : City : State: Zip);
0005    endif;
      /end-free
```

Line 4 contains the free-format UPDATE operation code. The %FIELDS built-in function acts as a parameter to that operation code, controlling which fields are to be updated in the database file.

▶ %FLOAT (CONVERT TO FLOATING POINT VALUE)

The %FLOAT function converts a numeric value, expression, or variable to floating point.

%FLOAT Syntax Diagram

```
floating point value = %FLOAT( numeric expression )
```

Any valid numeric expression or variable can be specified. The returned value is in floating-point notation and can be used in subsequent expressions. Use this built-in function when floating-point notation is required in mathematical expressions, as when a procedure requires a floating-point parameter value. Figure 4.13 shows an example.

```
.....DName+++++++++++EUDSFrom+++To/Len+TDc.Functions+++++++++++++++++++++++++++++
0010 D Amount          S             5P 2 INZ(27.50)
0020 D Term            S             3P 0 INZ(360)
0030 D Due             S             8F
.....CSRn01.............OpCode(ex)Extended-factor2+++++++++++++++++++++++++++++++
0040 C              Eval      Due =%Float(Amount) * %Float(Term)
```

Figure 4.13: An example of the %FLOAT built-in function.

▶ %FOUND (RECORD/STRING FOUND CONDITION)

The %FOUND function checks the status of the found condition for a file or string-operation code.

%FOUND Syntax Diagram

```
boolean indicator = %FOUND[ ( file name ) ]
```

See also %EQUAL and %EOF.

The first parameter is optional and can be the name of a file for a previous file operation. The %FOUND function checks for a record-found condition for the CHAIN, DELETE, SETGT, and SETLL operations. If a file name is not specified, %FOUND applies to the most recent file, string, or LOOKUP operation. See Figure 4.14 for an example.

Table 4.4: Use of %EQUAL in Place of Indicator		
Operation	Condition Tested	Description
SETLL	Equal key condition.	Set lower limits.
CHAIN	Record found.	Random access a file.
DELETE	Record found.	Delete database record.
SETGT	Record found.	Set greater than.
CHECK	Located alternate data.	Verify string.
CHECKR	Located alternate data.	Verify string reverse.
SCAN	Pattern found.	Scan string.
LOOKUP	Search specification.	Look up array element.

```
.....CSRnØ1Factor1+++++++OpCode(ex)Factor2+++++++Result++++++++Len++DcHiLoEq
      C      ItemNo        CHAIN      ItemMast
      C                    IF         %FOUND
      C                    CallP      ChangeItem
      C                    else
      C                    CallP      AddNewItem
      C                    endIf
      C      Category      LOOKUP     ItemCat                       71   75
      C                    IF         Not %FOUND
      C                    CallP      BadCategory
      C                    endif
```

Figure 4.14: An example of the %FOUND built-in function.

The %FOUND built-in function is used in place of resulting indicators for the file and string operation codes. For the LOOKUP operation, %FOUND is used in conjunction with the resulting indicators that control the LOOKUP operation itself.

▶%GRAPHIC (CONVERT TO DOUBLE-BYTE CHARACTER VALUE)

The %GRAPHIC function converts a character value or expression to graphic. %GRAPHIC is defined as DBCS (double-byte character set) data.

%GRAPHIC Syntax Diagram

graphic value = %GRAPHIC(character expression [: ccsid])

Any valid character expression or variable can be specified. The returned value is in graphic notation. The second parameter is the CCSID code that is used for the return value. Figure 4.15 shows an example.

```
.....DName++++++++++EUDSFrom+++To/Len+TDc.Functions++++++++++++++++++++++++++
ØØ1Ø D Name           S             12A    Inz('www.RPGIV.com')
ØØ2Ø D uName          S             2ØG
.....CSRnØ1.............OpCode(ex)Extended-factor2++++++++++++++++++++++++++++
ØØ4Ø C                 Eval       uName = %Graphic( name )
```

Figure 4.15: An example of the %GRAPHIC built-in function.

▶ %INT (CONVERT TO INTEGER VALUE)

The %INT function converts a numeric value, expression, or variable to integer format.

%INT Syntax Diagram

```
integer value  = %INT( numeric or character expression )
integer value  = %INTH( numeric or character expression )
```

See also %UNS.

Any valid numeric or character expression or variable can be specified. The returned value is in integer format and can be used in subsequent expressions. Use these built-in functions when integer notation is required in mathematical expressions, comparisons or assignments. For example, when specifying an array index, an integer is always required. See Figure 4.16.

```
.....DName+++++++++++EUDSFrom+++To/Len+TDc.Functions++++++++++++++++++++++++++++++
00001 D Amount          S              5P 2 INZ(27.50)
0002 D szOption         S             12A   Inz('12')
0003 D Index            S             10I 0
0004 D DiscRate         S              7P 2 Inz(0.15)
0005 D Discount         S              5I 0
.....CSRN01..............OpCode(ex)Extended-factor2++++++++++++++++++++++++++++++++
0006 C                  Eval       Index = %Inz(szOption)
0007 C                  Eval       Discount = %IntH( Amount * DiscRate)
```

Figure 4.16: Example of %INT built-in function.

▶ %KDS (USE A DATA STRUCTURE AS A KEY LIST)

%KDS isn't really a built-in function; it is a parameter keyword of the free-format version of the CHAIN, DELETE, READE, READPE, SETGT, and SETLL operations.

%KDS identifies a data structure whose subfields will be used as a key list to access the database file.

%KDS Syntax Diagram

```
%KDS( dsname { : subfield-count } )
```

See also: %FIELDS

%KDS accepts a data structure name. That data structure's subfields are used as a key list. Normally, key lists are defined using the KLIST and KFLD operation codes. Using %KDS a data structure can be used instead of a key list. %KDS converts the subfields of the data structure into an ad hoc key list.

The second parameter of %KDS is optional and, if specified, indicates the number of subfields to use as the key list. If unspecified, all subfields in the data structure are used for the ad hoc key list. %KDS can be used only with a data structure name.

```
.....DName+++++++++++EUDS.......Length+TDc.Functions++++++++++++++++++++
0001 D Customer       E DS                  ExtName(CustMast)
.....C++++++++++++++++++++++++++++++++++++++++++++++++++++++++++++++++++
0002  /free
0003     chain %kds(Customer : 2) CustRec;
0004     ExFmt EditCust;
0005     if  %Found(CustMast);
0006        update CustRec  %fields(CustName : Addr1 : City : State: Zip);
0007     endif;
0008  /end-free
```

Line 1 declares an externally described data structure based on the CUSTMAST database file. The first field in the CUSTMAST database file is the CUSTNO field, and the second is the REGION field. The key to the custmast file is a combination of the CUSTNO and REGION field.

Line 3 performs a CHAIN operation (database get-by-key) to the CUSTMAST file. The %KDS built-in function contains the CUSTOMER data structure as its first parameter. This would normally create an ad hoc database key made up of all the subfields of the CUSTOMER data structure. The second parameter, however, contains the number 2, which indicates the number of data structure subfields to use to create the ad hoc key list. Therefore the CUSTNO and REGION fields are used to access the file.

▶%LEN (SET/GET LENGTH)

The %LEN function retrieves the declared length of a variable or character expression, retrieves the current length of a variable length field, or sets the current length of a variable-length field.

%LEN Syntax Diagram

```
resulting-length = %LEN( numeric-expression )
field-length    = %LEN( character-field )
field-content-length  = %LEN( %Trim(character-field) )
current-length  = %LEN( varying-field )

%LEN( variable-field) = integer-expression
```

See also %SIZE, %DECPOS, and %ELEM

To retrieve the declared length of a variable, specify the variable within the %LEN built-in function. Any valid character expression or variable can be specified. The returned value is in integer format and can be used in subsequent expressions. Figure 4.17 shows an example.

For variable length fields, %LEN returns the current length of the field (not the declared maximum length). To set the length of a variable-length field, specify %LEN on the left side of the equal sign of the EVAL operations.

```
.....DName+++++++++++EUDSFrom+++To/Len+TDc.Functions++++++++++++++++++++++++++++
0010 D CustName       S              50A    Inz('The Lunar Spacecraft Co.')
0020 D CompName       S              50A    VARYING
0030 D myLength       S               5I 0
0040 D Amount         S               7P 2
.....CSRn01.............OpCode(ex)Extended-factor2+++++++++++++++++++++++++++++++
0050 C               Eval      myLength = %Len( Amount )
     **    The value of MYLENGTH = 7
0060 C               Eval      %Len( CompName ) = %Len( %TrimR( Custname ) )
     **    The new current length of COMPNAME is 24
```

Figure 4.17: Example of %LEN built-in function.

▶ %LOOKUPXX (ARRAY ELEMENT LOOKUP [SEARCH]))

The %LOOKUPXX function performs a case-sensitive search of an array for a search value. It returns the index of the array element that matches the search value and search condition.

%LOOKUPXX Syntax Diagram

```
index  = %LOOKUP(   search-value : array {: start-index {: num-elems }})
index  = %LOOKUPLT( search-value : array {: start-index {: num-elems }})
index  = %LOOKUPGT( search-value : array {: start-index {: num-elems }})
index  = %LOOKUPLE( search-value : array {: start-index {: num-elems }})
index  = %LOOKUPGE( search-value : array {: start-index {: num-elems }})
```

See also: %TLOOKUPXX

The lookup function returns the array index of the array element that matches the search condition. There are five forms of the %LOOKUP function.

- %LOOKUP – Search for an element that equals the search value.
- %LOOKUPLT – Search for an element that is less than the search value.
- %LOOKUPGT – Search for an element that is greater than the search value.
- %LOOKUPLE – Search for an element that is less than or equal to the search value.
- %LOOKUPGE – Search for an element that is greater than or equal to the search value.

The first parameter is the search value. The search is case-sensitive so the search value must be exactly the same as the pattern in the table. The variations of %LOOKUP that contain a Boolean search control will search for relative, or relative or equal matches.

The second parameter is the name of the array being searched (for table searches, use the %TLOOKUP function).

The third parameter is optional, and if specified, must be a numeric field or expression that indicates the first element in the array to begin the search.

The fourth parameter is optional, and if specified, must be a numeric field or expression that indicates the number of array elements to search.

If parameter 3 and parameter 4 are omitted, the entire array is searched beginning with the first element.

▶ %NULLIND (SET/GET NULL INDICATOR PROPERTY)

The %NULLIND function retrieves the null indicator property of a null-capable field. The %NULLIND built-in function can only be used when the program is compiled with the allow-null attribute set to ALWNUL (*USRCTL) *USRCTL.

%NULLIND Syntax Diagram

```
boolean value  = %NULLIND( null-capable field )

%NULLIND( null-capable field ) = boolean expression
```

To retrieve the null indicator, specify the variable within the %NULLIND built-in function (see Figure 4.18). The returned value is a Boolean value that is '1' or '0'.

To set the null indicator, specify the variable within the %NULLIND built-in function on the left side of the equal sign. Specify a Boolean expression on the right side of the equal sign. The Boolean value (*ON or *OFF can be used) is assigned to the null indicator for the field.

The null indicator is separate from the actual data stored in the field. The field's content is not changed by setting the null indicator.

```
.....DName+++++++++++EUDSFrom+++To/Len+TDc.Functions++++++++++++++++++++++++++++
0010 D ShipDate        S                D
0020 D DueDate         S                D
.....CSRn01..............OpCode(ex)Extended-factor2++++++++++++++++++++++++++++++
.....CSRn01Factor1+++++++OpCode(ex)Factor2+++++++Result++++++++Len++DcHiLoEq
0030 C                   IF            %NULLIND( ShipDate) = *OFF
0040 C       Shipdate    AddDur        15:*Days       DueDate
0050 C                   Else
0060 C                   Eval          %NULLIND( dueDate ) = *ON
0070 C                   Endif
```

Figure 4.18: An example of the %NULLIND built-in function.

▶ %OCCUR (SET/GET THE OCCURRENCE OF A DATA STRUCTURE)

The %OCCUR function changes the current occurrence of a data structure, or retrieves the current occurrence of a data structure.

%OCCUR Syntax Diagram

```
occurrence  = %OCCUR( data-structure )
%OCCUR( data-structure )
```

See also: %OCCUR operation

When used on the right-side of the equals sign on an assignment statement, or in a comparison operation, %OCCUR returns the current occurrence of the data structure specified in the first parameter.

When used on the left-side of the equals sign on an assignment statement %OCCUR will set the current occurrence to the value specified on the right-side of the equals sign.

Figure 4.19 illustrates the use of the %OCCUR built-in function.

```
.....DName+++++++++++EUDS.......Length+TDc.Functions++++++++++++++++++++++
0001 D MyDS            DS                  Occurs(20)
0002 D   CustNo                      7P 0
0003 D   Company                     30A
0004 D   Address                     25A
0005 D   City                        20A

0006 D nPos            S             5I 0

.....CSRn01.............OpCode(ex)Extended-factor2++++++++++++++++++++++++
0007 C                   Eval      nPos = %occur( myDS )
0008 C                   If        %occur( myDS ) = %size( myDS )
0009 C                   Eval      %occur( myDS ) = 1
0010 C                   Else
0011 C                   Eval      %occur( myDS ) = %occur( myDS ) + 1
0012 C                   endif
```

Figure 4.19: Multiple occurrence data structure use of %OCCUR function.

▶ %OPEN (CHECK FOR FILE OPEN CONDITION)

The %OPEN function returns the current open status of the specified file.

%OPEN Syntax Diagram

```
boolean value  = %OPEN( file name )
```

A file can be checked for an open or closed status using the %OPEN built-in function.
Simply prefix the %OPEN with the NOT operator to check for a closed condition (as shown
in Figure 4.20).

```
.....FFileName++IFEASFRlen+LKeylnKFDevice+.Functions++++++++++++++++++++++++++++
0010 FCustMast  UF A E              DISK     USROPN
.....CSRn01..............OpCode(ex)Extended-factor2+++++++++++++++++++++++++++++
0020 C                    IF        NOT %OPEN(CustMast)
0030 C                    Open      CustMast
0040 C                    EndIf
```

Figure 4.20: An example of the %OPEN built-in function.

The File specification keyword USROPN (line 10) causes the RPG cycle to avoid automatically opening the file when the program is first called. The IF condition (line 20) tests the
file to see if it has already been open. If is has not previously been open, the OPEN operation (line 30) opens the file.

▶ %PADDR (GET PROCEDURE ADDRESS)

The %PADDR function returns the address for a procedure. A procedure is similar to a
subroutine, except that other procedures and programs call procedures, procedures accept
parameters, and procedures support local variables.

%PADDR Syntax Diagram

```
pointer-to-procedure = %PADDR( 'quoted-literal' )
pointer-to-procedure = %PADDR( procedure-prototype )
```
See also %ADDR and PROCPTR

Specify a quoted character string, a hexadecimal value, or a named constant, or a prototype name for the %PADDR function. The compiler resolves a procedure pointer at compile time and stores it in the compiled object.

Procedure addresses are resolved when program modules are bound together. Therefore, the compiler must be able to resolve a procedure name during the bind phase. This is in contrast to the dynamic CALL operation that resolves program addresses at runtime. Consequently, a field name cannot be specified for the %PADDR function. See Figure 4.21 for an example of the use of the %PADDR built-in function.

When a prototype name is specified, the prototype must be a prototype for a procedure (not a program) written in a language other than Java.

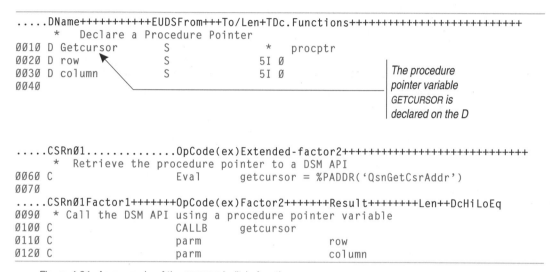

```
.....DName++++++++++++EUDSFrom+++To/Len+TDc.Functions++++++++++++++++++++++++++++
       *    Declare a Procedure Pointer
0010 D Getcursor        S                  *    procptr
0020 D row              S             5I 0
0030 D column           S             5I 0                    The procedure
0040                                                          pointer variable
                                                              GETCURSOR is
                                                              declared on the D


.....CSRn01..............OpCode(ex)Extended-factor2++++++++++++++++++++++++++++++
       *    Retrieve the procedure pointer to a DSM API
0060 C                     Eval       getcursor = %PADDR('QsnGetCsrAddr')
0070
.....CSRn01Factor1+++++++OpCode(ex)Factor2+++++++Result++++++++Len++DcHiLoEq
0090 * Call the DSM API using a procedure pointer variable
0100 C                     CALLB      getcursor
0110 C                     parm                    row
0120 C                     parm                    column
```

Figure 4.21: An example of the %PADDR built-in function.

▶ %PARMS (GET PARAMETER COUNT)

The %PARMS function returns the number of parameters passed to the procedure or program. When used in the mainline calcuations section of a program, the value returned for %PARMS is the same value that appears in the *PARMS locations of the program's Status Data Structure (SDS). For subprocedures, however, %PARMS returns the number of parameters passed to the subprocedure.

%PARMS Syntax Diagram

```
numeric return variable = %PARMS
```

The %PARMS function has no parameters of its own, and %PARMS cannot be used within a definition specification keyword. Specifically, it cannot be used to initialize a field. Figure 4.22 shows an example of its proper use.

```
.....DName+++++++++++EUDS.......Length+TDc.Functions++++++++++++++++++++++++++++
0010 D nParms         S              5I 0
0020 D i              S              3S 0
.....CSRn01..............OpCode(ex)Extended-factor2++++++++++++++++++++++++++++++
     * Get number of parameters passed to this procedure
0040 C                    If         %Parms > 0
0050 C                    Eval       nParms = %PARMS
     * Test %PARMS for specific value

0080 C                    Select
0090 C                    When       %Parms = 1
0100 C                    exsr       OneParm
0110 C                    When       %Parms = 2
0120 C                    exsr       TwoParms
0130 C                    When       %Parms = 3
0140 C                    exsr       ThreeParms
0150 C                    other
0160 C                    exsr       TooMany
0170 C                    endSL

0190 C                    endIf
```

> The WHEN statements on lines 90,110, and 130 use the %PARMS function to test for the number of parameters, then the appropriate subroutine is performed.
>
> The NPARMS field, initialized on line 50, could also have been used in this example.

Figure 4.22: An example of the %PARMS built-in function.

▶ %REM (Integer Division, Return Remainder)

The %REM function performs integer division on the two arguments. The first argument is the numerator and the second is the denominator. The remainder from this division operation is returned.

%REM Syntax Diagram

```
integer remainder  = %REM( numerator  :  denominator )
```

See also %DIV

The remainder operation returns an integer (whole number) result value. See Figure 4.23 for an example. The numerator and the denominator must be numeric values with no decimal digits. If numeric variables are used, they cannot contain decimal positions.

The %REM operation can be specified on the definition specification when the two arguments are constant values that fit within 8-byte integer values (20 digits).

By definition, integer division doesn't perform rounding. Therefore, the half-adjust operation extender is not supported.

```
.....DName++++++++++EUDS.......Length+TDc.Functions++++++++++++++++++++++++++++++
0010 D Count           S             7S 0 Inz(25)
0020 D Total           S             7P 0 Inz(220)

0030 D Quot            S             5I 0
0040 D Remain          S             5I 0
.....CSRn01.............OpCode(ex)Extended-factor2++++++++++++++++++++++++++++++++
0050 C                 Eval      quot = %DIV( Total : Count )
0060 C                 Eval      rem  = %REM( Total : Count )
0070 C                 Eval      msg  = 'Total divided by Count = ' +
0080 C                            %Char(quot) + ' remainder ' + %Char(rem)
     **   MSG = 'Total divided by Count = 8 remainder 20'
```

Figure 4.23: An example of the %REM built-in function.

▶ %REPLACE (REPLACE/INSERT CHARACTER STRING)

The %REPLACE function returns a character string that is created by replacing or inserting one character string in another.

%REPLACE Syntax Diagram

```
verifying-length value = %REPLACE( replacement string : source string
                         [: start position [: replacement length ]])
```
See also %SUBST and %SCAN

The first parameter, REPLACEMENT STRING, is the character string that will be inserted into the SOURCE STRING (the second parameter).

The second parameter, SOURCE STRING, is the string that contains the data that is the original or SOURCE STRING for the replacement. This string is modified using the first parameter.

The third parameter, START POSITION, identifies the starting position, within the SOURCE STRING (second parameter), where the insertion or replacement is to occur. If this parameter is not specified, the starting position defaults to position 1.

The fourth parameter, REPLACEMENT LENGTH, indicates the number of characters that are to be deleted from the source string before inserting the replacement string. This value can be 0 through the length of the source string. If not specified, the length of the replacement string is used as the replacement length.

When the replacement length is 0, the function inserts the replacement string into the source string at the start position.

When inserting, the replacement string is inserted into the source string prior to the starting position. When replacing, the replacement string is inserted into the source string, starting with the starting position, and continues for the number of characters specified for the replacement length.

▶ %SCAN (SCAN CHARACTER STRING)

The %SCAN function returns the location of the scan pattern, within the scanned data.

%SCAN Syntax Diagram

```
found position = %SIZE( scan pattern : scan data [ : start position ] )
```
                    See also %REPLACE, and SCAN, CHECK, CHECKR, and LOOKUP

The first parameter is the scan pattern that is searched for the value in the second parameter. The second parameter is the scan data that is searched for the scan pattern specified in the first parameter. The third parameter is optional and, if specified, indicates the starting position for the scan, within the scan data. Figure 4.24 shows a code example of %SCAN.

```
.....DName++++++++++EUDS.......Length+TDc.Functions+++++++++++++++++++++++++++++
0010 D CustName        S             35A  Inz('The Lunar Spacecraft Company')
0020 D POS             S              5P 0
.....CSRn01.............OpCode(ex)Extended-factor2+++++++++++++++++++++++++++++++
0050 C                     Eval      POS = %SCAN('craft' : CustName)
     **   POS = 16
0060 C                     Eval      POS  = %SCAN('Moon' : CustName)
     **   POS = 0   The search pattern data was not found in the CUSTNAME field.

0070 C                     IF        %SCAN('Company' : CustName) >0
     **   If CUSTNAME contains the string "Company" the IF condition is true.

     C                     EndIf
```
Figure 4.24: An example of the %SCAN built-in function.

▶ %SHTDN (CHECK FOR SYSTEM SHUT DOWN OR JOB END REQUEST)

The %SHDN function returns *ON if the job running the program has been issued an end request, otherwise the function returns *OFF.

%SHTDN Syntax Diagram

```
bool  = %shtdn( )
```

The shut down function returns true (i.e., *ON or '1') when the system operator has requested a shutdown of the job running the RPG program.

▶ %SIZE (GET SIZE IN BYTES USED)

This function returns the number of bytes of memory used by the value. For character and zoned numeric values, the value returned is also the length of the field. For packed numeric fields, the value returned is calculated using the packing algorithm.

%SIZE Syntax Diagram

```
numeric return value = %SIZE( variable [ : *ALL ] )
```

See also %LEN and %DECPOS

For tables and arrays, or multiple-occurrence data structures, the length of a single element or occurrence is returned unless *ALL is specified for the second argument. *ALL causes the size of the array element or data structure to be multiplied by the number of elements or occurrences. For all other data types, see Table 4.5.

Because %SIZE returns the number of bytes of memory allocated to a variable, the actual length of a field is not necessarily returned (as is the case with packed decimal fields). To determine the declared length of a variable, the %LEN built-in function can be used. Figure 4.25 illustrate the use of %SIZE.

Table 4.5: %SIZE Return Values		
Field Type	**Length**	**%SIZE Returns**
Char	1 to 65,535	Declared length.
Variable length	Variable	Declared length + 2.
Packed	1 to 30	((Declared length) / 2) + 1.
Zoned	1 to 30	Declared length.
Date	6, 8, or 10	Declared length.
Integer (U or I)	3	1
Integer (U or I)	5	2
Integer (U or I)	10	4
Integer (U or I)	20	8
Float	N/A	8
Binary	4	2
Binary	9	4
Pointer	N/A	16
Graphic	any	Declared length.
Array	any	Number of bytes used by a single array element.
Array : *ALL	any	Number of bytes used by the entire array.
Data structure	any	Number of bytes used by one occurrence of the data structure.
Data Struct:*ALL	any	Number of bytes used by all occurrences of the data structure.

```
.... DName++++++++++EUDS.......Length+TDc.Functions++++++++++++++++++++++++++++
0010 D Array            S            5A   DIM( %SIZE(CharField) )

0020 D DataF1           DS                Occurs(32)
0030 D  Field1                      10A
0040 D  Field2                       7P 2 INZ

0050 D CharField        S           35A
0060 D pkdDec           S            5P 0 INZ( %SIZE(CharField) )
0070 D zndNum           S            8S 0
0080 D bin2             S            4B 2
0090 D bin4             S            9B 2
0100 D int2             S            5I 0
0110 D int4             S           10I 0


0120 D Today            S             D   DATFMT(*ISO) INZ(*SYS)
0130 D ptr              S             *
0140 D VaryLen          S           50A   VARYING Inz('Chicago')
0150 D nSizeOf          S                 LIKE( int2 )
..  CSRn01..............OpCode(ex)Extended-factor2++++++++++++++++++++++.Size Is
0200 C                  Eval      nSizeOf = %size( Array )              5
0210 C                  Eval      nSizeOf = %size( Array : *ALL )     100
0220 C                  Eval      nSizeOf = %size( DataF1 )            14
0230 C                  Eval      nSizeOf = %size( DataF1 : *ALL )
0210 C                  Eval      nSizeOf = %size( CharField )         35
0210 C                  Eval      nSizeOf = %size( PkdDec )             3
0210 C                  Eval      nSizeOf = %size( ZndNum )             8
0210 C                  Eval      nSizeOf = %size( Bin2 )               2
0210 C                  Eval      nSizeOf = %size( Bin4 )               4
0210 C                  Eval      nSizeOf = %size( Int2 )               2
0210 C                  Eval      nSizeOf = %size( Int4 )               4
0210 C                  Eval      nSizeOf = %size( Today )             10
0210 C                  Eval      nSizeOf = %size( ptr )               16
0220 C                  Eval      nSizeOf = %size( VaryLen )           52

0220 C                  If        COUNT >= %size( COMPNAME)
0230 C*  TODO: Insert conditioned code here.
0240 C                  EndIf
```

%SIZE is being used to set the number of elements for an array.

%SIZE is being used to set the initial value of a packed decimal field.

Figure 4.25: An example of the %SIZE built-in function.

▶ %SQRT (COMPUTE SQUARE ROOT)

The %SQRT function calculates the square root of a number and returns that square root.

%SQRT Syntax Diagram

```
square-root  = %SQRT( expression )
```

See also: SQRT operation

The square root function returns the square root of the expression. The first parameter must be a numeric value, expression, field, or literal value whose square root is calculated by the function.

▶ %STATUS (FILE OR PROGRAM STATUS CODE)

The %STATUS function returns the status code for the most recent file operation or the status code for the program. This function is set only when the E operation extender is used.

%STATUS Syntax Diagram

```
boolean indicator = %STATUS[ ( file name ) ]
```

See also %ERROR.

The first parameter is optional and can be the name of a file for a previous file operation (see Figure 4.26). A separate area for each file declared in the program and an area for the program status code is created. Neither the INFDS nor PSDS is required to retrieve the file or program status. If the file name is not specified, the status code for the most recent file operation is returned. The status area for a file is reset to zero when an operation on that file is encountered that uses the E operation extender.

```
.....CSRnØ1Factor1+++++++OpCode(ex)Factor2+++++++Result++++++++Len++DcHiLoEq
ØØ1Ø C      ItemNo       CHAIN(E)  ItemMast
ØØ2Ø C                   IF        %ERROR
ØØ3Ø C                   Select
ØØ4Ø C                   When      %Status = 1211
ØØ5Ø C                   Exsr      FileNotOpen
ØØ6Ø C                   When      %Status = 1218
ØØ7Ø C                   Exsr      RecLocked
ØØ8Ø C                   endSL
ØØ9Ø C                   endIF
```

Figure 4.26: An example of the %STATUS built-in function.

File-related status codes are in the range 1000 to 9999. Program-related status codes are in the range 100 to 999.

Some of the file status codes are listed in the table that follows. For a complete list see Table X.Y.

Table 4.6: Common File Status Error Codes	
Status	**Description**
*FILE	Any file status code
01201	Record mismatch detected on input.
01211	I/O operation to a closed file.
01215	OPEN issued to a file already opened.
01216	Error on an implicit OPEN/CLOSE operation.
01217	Error on an explicit OPEN/CLOSE operation.
01218	Record already locked.
01221	Update operation attempted without a prior read.
01222	Record cannot be allocated due to referential constraint error
01231	Error on SPECIAL file.
01235	Error in PRTCTL space or skip entries.
01241	Record number not found. (Record number specified in record address file is not present in file being processed.)
01299	Other I/O error detected.

Several of the program status codes are listed in the table that follows. For a complete list see Table 4.7.

Table 4.7: Common Program Status Error Codes

Status	Description
00100	Value out of range for string operation.
00101	Negative square root.
00102	Divide by zero.
00103	An intermediate result is not large enough to contain the result.
00104	Float underflow. An intermediate value is too small to be contained in the intermediate result field.
00105	Invalid characters in character to numeric conversion functions.
00112	Invalid Date, Time or Timestamp value.
00113	Date overflow or underflow.
00114	Date mapping errors, where a Date is mapped from a 4-digit year to a 2-digit year, and the date range is not 1940-2039.
00115	Variable-length field has a current length that is not valid.
00120	Table or array out of sequence.
00121	Array index not valid.
00122	OCCUR outside of range.
00123	Reset attempted during initialization step of program.
00202	Called program or procedure failed; halt indicators (H1 to H9) are not on.
00211	Error calling program or procedure.
00222	Pointer or parameter error.
00231	Called program or procedure returned with halt indicator on.
00232	Halt indicator on in this program.
00233	Halt indicator on when RETURN operation run.
00299	RPG IV formatted dump failed.

%STR (GET/STORE NULL-TERMINATED C-STRING)

The %STR function does the following:

- Returns a normal character string value from a C-language–based, null-terminated string.
- Allows normal character data to be copied to a C-language, null-terminated string.

%STR Syntax Diagram

```
character value = %STR( base-pointer [ : length ] )

%STR( base-pointer : length  ) = character value
```

The first parameter is required and must contain a variable of type pointer. The pointer must contain the address of a memory location. Normally, the memory location is either the address of a variable in the program or the address of memory allocated with the ALLOC operation.

The second parameter indicates the number of bytes to extract or modify. Effectively, this is the maximum length of the data located at the address stored in the base-pointer (parameter 1). Figure 4.27 shows an example using the %STR built-in function.

```
.....DName++++++++++EUDS.......Length+TDc.Functions+++++++++++++++++++++++++++++
0010 D pCompany        S                  *
0020 D CustName         S               35A   Inz('The Lunar Spacecraft Company')
.....CSRn01Factor1+++++++OpCode(ex)Factor2+++++++Result++++++++Len++DcHiLoEq....
0030 C                     Alloc     100            pCompany
0040 C                     Eval      %STR( pCompany : 100 ) = %trimL(CustName)
```

Figure 4.27: An example of the %STR built-in function.

The result of the example shown in Figure 4.27 is that the value of CUSTNAME is copied to the 100 bytes of storage allocated by the ALLOC operation (line 30). The value is followed immediately by a X'00'. This X'00' is a null-terminator and is used by the C language. The X'00' value is moved to the position following the letter "y" in the word "Company" in the CUSTNAME field.

▶ %SUBDT (SUBSTRING DATE – EXTRACT A DATE OR TIME COMPONENT)

The %SUBDT function extracts a portion of a date, time, or timestamp value and returns that value as an unsigned numeric integer value.

%SUBDT Syntax Diagram

```
duration  = %SUBDT( dts : duration-code )
```

See also: %DIFF

The substring date operation returns an integer (the duration value) of a valid date, time, or timestamp value.

The first parameter must be a valid date, time, or timestamp datatype. The duration code (parameter 2) is required and indicates the format for the returned value. The value duration codes are as follows:

*DAYS, *MONTHS, *YEARS or *D, *M, *Y

*MSECONDS, *SECONDS, *MINUTES, *HOURS, or *MS, *S, *MN, *H

The *DAYS and *D duration codes always returns the day of the month, regardless of the date format of the *dts* (date, time or timestamp) value. The *YEARS and *Y duration codes always return a 4-digit year, regardless of the date format of the *dts* parameter.

▶ %SUBST (GET/SET A SUBSTRING OF A VALUE)

The %SUBST function:
- Returns a portion of a value or variable.
- Identifies a portion of a field as the target of an assignment operation.

%SUBST Syntax Diagram

```
return value = %SUBST( base-value : start [ : length ] )

%SUBST( base-value : start [ : length ] ) = value to assign
```

See also %REPLACE, %SCAN, and SUBS.

The %SUBST function accepts three parameters:
- The base value to be "substringed."
- The starting position within the base value.
- The number of bytes (including the starting position) to be included. This parameter is optional.

If the third parameter is omitted, the implied length is derived from the starting position to the end of the base value. For extraction (the first form of %SUBST), the base value can be any field or literal value. The start location and length can be a literal, a field, or a numeric expression. For assignment (the second form of %SUBST), the base value can be any character field, array, data structure, data structure subfield, or array element.

The %SUBST function is the only built-in function that can be specified on either side of the assignment symbol of the EVAL operation for assignment purposes. Figure 4.28 shows a code example of %SUBST.

```
.....DName++++++++++EUDS.......Length+TDc.Functions++++++++++++++++++++++++++++++
0000 D int2            S              5I 0
0010 D Company         S             35A   INZ('Skyline Pigeon Productions')
0020 D Address         S             35A   INZ('P.O. Box 964')
0030 D City            S             25A   INZ('St. Charles')
0040 D State           S              4A   INZ('IL')
0050 D PostalCode      S             10A   INZ('60174')
0060 D Country         S             25A

0110 D AddrLine1       S                   Like( Company )
0120 D AddrLine2       S                   Like( Company )
0130 D AddrLine3       S                   Like( Company )
0140 D AddrLine4       S                   Like( Company )

0210 D nStartPos       S                   LIKE( int2 )
0220 D nEndPos         S                   LIKE( int2 )
0230 D nLength         S                   LIKE( int2 )
.....CSRn01..............OpCode(ex)Extended-factor2+++++++++++++++++++++++++++++++
.....CSRn01Factor1++++++OpCode(ex)Factor2+++++++Result++++++++Len++DcHiLoEq
0310 C       '.,':' '   Xlate    Company      AddrLine1
0320 C       '.,':' '   Xlate    Address      AddrLine2
0330 C       '.,':' '   Xlate    City         AddrLine3

0350 C       ' '        Check    AddrLine1    nStartPos
0360 C                  Eval     AddrLine1 = %subst( AddrLine1 : nStartPos )
0370 C                  Eval     AddrLine1 = ToUpper(AddrLine1)

0390 C                  If       %subst( AddrLine1 : 1 : 4) = 'THE '
0400 C                  Eval     AddrLine1 = %subst(AddrLine1 : 5)
0410 C                  EndIf

0430 C       ' '        Check    AddrLine3    nStartPos
0440 C       ' '        CheckR   AddrLine3    nEndPos
```

This %SUBST function uses an expression for its length argument. It is itself part of a concatenation expression. It also is continued onto multiple source lines.

```
0460 C                    Eval      AddrLine3 = %Subst( AddrLine3 :
0470 C                                          nStartPos :
0480 C                                          nEndPos + 1 )
0490 C                                   + ', ' + State + PostalCode
```

Figure 4.28: Example of %SUBST built-in function.

%TIME (CONVERT TO TIME VALUE)

The %TIME function converts a numeric, character, or timestamp value to a valid time datatype value.

%TIME Syntax Diagram

```
time-value  = %TIME( { expression {: time-format-code }} )
```
See also: *%DATE, %TIMESTAMP*

The time function performs two functions: (1) It converts a non-time value into a time value using the optional time-format code, and (2) if no parameters are specified, it returns the current system time.

The time format codes that may be specified in parameter 2 of the %TIME function are as follows:

Format Code	Date Format
*HMS	HH:MM:SS
*ISO	HH.MM.SS
*USA	HH:MM AM
*EUR	HH.MM.SS
*JIS	HH:MM:SS

The time format code may be specified with a separator character when converting from a character value to a time value, to indicate that a separator other than the default separator is used in the character time value. The separator is not allowed when converting from a numeric value. In addition a separator of 0 (zero) may be specified with the time-format code to indicate that the character time value contains no separators.

%TIMESTAMP (CONVERT TO TIMESTAMP VALUE)

The %TIMESTAMP function converts a numeric, character, or timestamp value to a valid timestamp datatype value.

%TIMESTAMP Syntax Diagram

```
time-value  = %TIMESTAMP( { expression {: *ISO | *ISOØ }} )
```
See also: %DATE, %TIME

The %TIMESTAMP function performs two functions: (1) It converts a non-timestamp value into a timestamp value using the optional separator formatting code (parameter 2), and (2) if no parameters are specified, it returns the current system timestamp value.

The timestamp format codes that may be specified in parameter 2 of the %TIMESTAMP function are as follows:

Format Code	Date Format
*ISO	YYYY-MM-DD-HH.MM.SS.MMMMMM
*ISO0	YYYYMMDDHHMMSSMMMMMM

The timestamp format code of *ISO or *ISO0 may be specified when converting from a character value to a timestamp value, to indicate that no separator is used; a separator of 0 (zero) may be specified.

%TLOOKUPXX (TABLE ELEMENT LOOKUP [SEARCH]))

The %TLOOKUPXX function performs a case-sensitive search of a table for a search value. It returns *ON if the search is successful or *OFF is the search fails.

```
%TLookUpxx Syntax Diagram
bool  = %TLOOKUP(   search-value : table {: alt-table } )
bool  = %TLOOKUPLT( search-value : table {: alt-table } )
bool  = %TLOOKUPGT( search-value : table {{: alt-table } )
bool  = %TLOOKUPLE( search-value : table {{: alt-table } )
bool  = %TLOOKUPGE( search-value : table {: alt-table } )
```

See also: %LOOKUPXX

The table lookup function searches a table for the search-value. If the search is successful, the table's current element is set to the element matching the search condition. If an alt-table (parameter 3) is specified, then its current element is also set to the same element as the first table. There are five forms of the %TLOOKUP function.

- %TLOOKUP – Search for an element that equals the search value.
- %TLOOKUPLT – Search for an element that is less than the search value.
- %TLOOKUPGT – Search for an element that is greater than the search value.
- %TLOOKUPLE – Search for an element that is less than or equal to the search value.
- %TLOOKUPGE – Search for an element that is greater than or equal to the search value.

The first parameter is the search value. The search is case-sensitive so the search value must be exactly the same as the pattern in the table. The variations of %TLOOKUP that contain a Boolean search control, will search for relative, or relative or equal matches.

The second parameter is the name of the table being searched (for array searches, use the %LOOKUP function).

The third parameter is optional, and if specified, must be the name of another table whose element is set if the search is successful. In other words, the two tables are set to the same current element or index.

▶ %TRIM, %TRIML, %TRIMR
(TRIM LEADING AND/OR TRAILING BLANKS)

The %TRIM, %TRIML, and %TRIMR functions analyze a string value and return a string with its leading or trailing blank characters removed. Typically, these functions are used to concatenate a set of character string values or left justify a value:

- %TRIML   Removes leading blank characters.
- %TRIMR   Removes trailing blank characters.
- %TRIM   Removes both leading and trailing blank characters.

%TRIM Syntax Diagram

```
character return value = %TRIMx( base-value )
```

See also %CHAR and %EDITC

The value returned is a character string. It can be assigned to a variable or used in an expression. The base value must be a character value, expression, quoted character string, or variable. Figure 4.29 shows an example.

```
.....DName++++++++++EUDS.......Length+TDc.Functions++++++++++++++++++++++++++++
0010 D Lefty           S            25A
0020 D Name            S            25A    INZ
0030 D First           S            20A    INZ('    Bob      ')
0040 D Last            S            20A    INZ('    Cozzi')
.....CSRn01.............OpCode(ex)Extended-factor2++++++++++++++++++++++++++++++
0060 C                 EVAL        Name = %TRIMR(First) + ' ' + %TRIML(Last)
0070 C                 Eval        Lefty = %TrimL(Name)
```

Figure 4.29: An example of the %TRIM built-in function.

In the example shown in Figure 4.29, the interim value of the %TRIMR function is concatenated with the interim value of the %TRIML function (line 60). The blanks from the right side of the FIRST field are trimmed. The blanks from the left side of the LAST field are trimmed.

The trimmed value is copied to the NAME field. Then the blanks from the left side of the NAME field are trimmed, and the value is copied to the LEFTY field. This effectively left justifies the data that is copied to the LEFTY field (see Figure 4.30).

```
          1...v....1....v....2....v
NAME  = '      Bob Cozzi          '
LEFTY = 'Bob Cozzi                '
```

Figure 4.30: The result of the %TRIM function shown in Figure 4.29.

▶%UCS2 (CONVERT TO UCS-2)

The %UCS2 function converts a character string value to a UCS-2 varying length string.

%UCS2 Syntax Diagram

```
UCS-2 character value = %UCS2( character value [: ccsid ])
```
See also %CHAR and %EDITC

The first parameter is the character value that is to be converted to the UCS-2 value. The second parameter is optional, and indicates the CCSID code for the resulting converted value.

▶%UNS (CONVERT TO UNSIGNED INTEGER VALUE)

The %UNS function converts a numeric value, expression, or variable to integer format.

%UNS Syntax Diagram

```
unsigned integer value  = %UNS( numeric expression )

unsigned integer value with Half adjust  = %UNSH( numeric expression )
```
See also %INT.

Any valid numeric expression or variable can be specified. The returned value is an unsigned integer and can be used in subsequent expressions. Use this built-in function when integer notation is required in mathematical expressions or comparisons. Figure 4.31 shows a code example.

An unsigned integer has a numeric range roughly double that of signed integer values. For example, a 2-byte signed integer has a range of –32,768 to 32,767 whereas an unsigned integer has a range of 0 to 65,535.

```
.....DName++++++++++EUDSFrom+++To/Len+TDc.Functions++++++++++++++++++++++++++++
0010 D Amount           S             5P 2 INZ(27.50)
0020 D DiscRate         S             7P 2
0030 D Discount         S             7P 2 Dim(500)
.....CSRn01..............OpCode(ex)Extended-factor2++++++++++++++++++++++++++++
0040 C                  Eval          DiscRate = Discount( %UNS( Amount) )
```

Figure 4.31: An example of the %UNS built-in function.

▶%XFOOT (CROSS FOOT ARRAY ELEMENTS)

The %XFOOT function sums all the elements in the specified array and returns the product.

%XFOOT Syntax Diagram

```
sum of array elements  = %XFOOT( numeric array expression )
```

See also XFOOT

The first parameter is required and can be either of the following:

- An array name.
- An array-name expression.

An array-name expression is composed of multiple array names separated by standard arithmetic operations. Figure 4.32 shows a code example of using %XFOOT.

```
.....DName+++++++++++EUDSFrom+++To/Len+TDc.Functions++++++++++++++++++++++++++++
0010 D RemoteSales     S              7P 2 Dim(12)
0020 D LocalSales      S              5P 2 Dim( %elem( RegSales) )
0030 D TotSales        S              7P 2
0040 D RemoteTot       S                   Like(TotSales)
0050 D LocalTot        S                   Like(TotSales)
.....CSRn01.............OpCode(ex)Extended-factor2++++++++++++++++++++++++++++++++
0060 C                 Eval      LocalTot  = %XFoot( LocalSales )
0060 C                 Eval      RemoteTot = %XFoot( RemoteSales )
0060 C                 Eval      TotSales  = %XFoot( LocalSales + RemoteSales )
```

Figure 4.32: An example of the %XFOOT built-in function.

▶%XLATE (TRANSLATE CHARACTERS)

The %XLATE function translates a character value using a translation pattern.

%XLATE Syntax Diagram

```
translated-value = %XLATE(from-pattern : to-pattern : base-value
                        { : start-pos } )
```
See also: XLATE operation

The translate function translates the base-value using the translation patterns specified in the from-pattern and to-pattern parameters. Each character in the base-value is compared to the characters in the from-pattern. When a match is detected, the character is translated to the character in the corresponding position in the to-pattern value. If no match is detected, the original value is passed through unchanged.

The return value is the translated value; the original base-value is not changed.

The first parameter is a character value containing a list of characters, numbers, and symbols that will be matched against each character in the base-value.

The second parameter is a character value containing a list of characters, numbers and symbols that are inserted into the result value in place of the original characters.

The third parameter is the base character value that is translated using parameters 1 and 2.

The fourth parameter is optional, and if specified, indicates the starting position in the base-value for the translation to begin. Characters prior to start-pos are passed to the result unchanged.

```
.....DName+++++++++++EUDS.......Length+TDc.Functions+++++++++++++++++++++++++
0001 D UPPER           C                    'abcdefghijklmnopqrstuvwxyz'
0002 D lower           C                    'ABCDEFGHIJKLMNOPQRSTUVWXYZ'
0003 D Company         S             30A    Inz('The Lunar Spacecraft Company')
0004 D XComp           S                    Like(Company)

0005 C                     Eval      XComp = %xlate(lower:upper:Company)
        ** XCOMP = 'THE LUNAR SPACECRAFT COMPANY'
```

Chapter 5

OPERATION CODES

Operation Codes, *continued*

CLEAR	236	ON-ERROR	317
CLOSE	239	OPEN	319
COMMIT	240	ORxx	320
COMP	241	OTHER	321
DEALLOC	242	OUT	322
DEFINE	243	PARM	323
DELETE	246	PLIST	326
DIV	249	POST	329
DO	251	READ	331
DOUxx	253	READC	334
DOWxx	255	READE	335
DSPLY	258	READP	337
DUMP	260	READPE	340
ELSE	261	REALLOC	342
ELSEIF	262	REL	344
ENDxx	263	RESET	345
ENDSR	264	RETURN	348
EVAL	266	ROLBK	350
EVALR	268	SCAN	351
EXCEPT	269	SELECT	353
EXFMT	273	SETGT	354
EXSR	274	SETLL	356
EXTRCT	276	SETOFF	358
FEOD	277	SETON	359
FOR	278	SHTDN	360
FORCE	280	SORTA	361
GOTO	281	SQRT	362
IFxx	282	SUB	363
IN	285	SUBDUR	365
ITER	286	SUBST	367
KFLD	287	TAG	369
KLIST	288	TEST	370
LEAVE	289	TESTB	372
LEAVESR	290	TESTN	374
LOOKUP	291	TESTZ	375
MONITOR	293	TIME	376
MxxZO	295	UNLOCK	378
MOVE and MOVEL	296	UPDATE	380
MOVEA	300	WHENxx	382
MOVEL	304	WRITE	384
MULT	309	XFOOT	386
MVR	311	XLATE	387
NEXT	312	Z-ADD	390
OCCUR	314	Z-SUB	391

The RPG language contains a rich set of command functions. These functions are commonly referred to as *operation codes*, the abbreviated form *op codes*, or the simpler term *operations*. These operations provide a wide variety of processes within an application program. The programmer specifies these operations, left justified, in positions 26 to 35 of calculation specifications. The following list of terms is used when referring to the areas of the RPG calculation specification. When referring to columns:

- 7 to 8, the term *control-level indicator* is used.

- 9 to 11, the term *conditioning indicator* is used.

- 12 to 25, the term *factor 1* is used.

- 26 to 35, the term *operation* or *op code* is used.

- 36 to 49, the term *factor 2* is used.

- 36 to 80, the term *extended factor 2* is used.

- 50 to 63, the term *result field* is used.

- 64 to 68, the term *field length* is used.

- 69 to 70, the term *decimal positions* is used.

- 71 to 72, the term *resulting indicator 1* is used.

- 73 to 74, the term *resulting indicator 2* is used.

- 75 to 76, the term *resulting indicator 3* is used.

The preceding terms are used in place of column numbers to easily identify the areas of a calculation program statement.

ABBREVIATIONS USED THROUGHOUT THIS CHAPTER

Listed in Table 5.1 are the abbreviations and symbols (referred to here as tokens) that are used throughout this book.

Table 5.1: Standard Abbreviations and Symbols	
Token	**Description**
[0 or ƀ]	The result of the operation is zero or blank.
[+]	The result of the operation is positive.
[-]	The result of the operation is negative.
[0]	The result of the operation is zero.
[ ]	Brackets denote optional values.
bof	The result of the operation produces a beginning-of-file condition.
eof	The result of the operation produces an end-of-file condition.
[full]	The WRITE operation has filled up the subfile specified in factor 2.
[ind$n$]	Indicator n, where n is 1, 2, or 3.
[mix]	The result of a TESTB operation is some bits on and some off; the result of a TESTN operation is some characters are numeric and some are not.
[num]	The result of the TESTN operation is all numeric.
[other]	The result of the TESTZ operation indicates that the zone of the result field is neither positive nor negative; it is unknown.
1<2	Factor 1 is less than factor 2.
1=2	Factor 1 equals factor 2.
1>2	Factor 1 is greater than factor 2.
Char value	Character value, either literal or variable.
Char variable	Character variable—that is, a character field, array, array element, data structure, or data structure subfield.
Data struct	Data structure name.
Dec	Decimal digits (i.e., the number of digits to the right of the decimal point).
n / f	The result of the operation produces a not-found condition.
Num value	Numeric value (either literal or variable).
Num blanks	Number of blanks.
Num variable	Numeric variable—that is, a numeric field or array element.
Plist	Parameter list name.

OPERATION CODE SUMMARY

Table 5.2 lists RPG operations along with brief descriptions.

Op Code	Description
Table 5.2: Alphabetical List of Operation Codes	
ACQ	Acquire a program device.
ADD	Add two values together.
ADDDUR	Add duration to a DATE, TIME, or TIMESTAMP value.
ALLOC	Allocate memory and runtime.
AND*xx*	Extend IF*xx*, DOW*xx*, DOU*xx*, and WHEN*xx* conditioning.
BEGSR	Begin a subroutine.
BITOFF	Set off individual bits with a field.
BITON	Set on individual bits with a field.
CAB*xx*	Compare two values, then branch to a label.
CALL	Call another program.
CALLB	Call a bound-in procedure.
CALLP	Call with prototype.
CAS*xx*	Compare two values, then call a subroutine.
CAT	Concatenate factor 1 to factor 2.
CHAIN	Random file access by index.
CHECK	Verify the data in factor 2 against factor 1 (from left to right).
CHECKR	Verify the data in factor 2 against factor 1 (from right to left).
CLEAR	Clear data structure, variable, or record format.
CLOSE	Close a file.
COMMIT	Commitment control, commit group.
COMP	Compare two values and set on/off resulting indicators.
DEFINE	Define one field like another field.
DEALLOC	Release memory back to the system at runtime.
DELETE	Delete a database record.
DIV	Divide two values.
DO	Begin DO loop with an optional counter.
DOU	Begin DO UNTIL loop using expression conditioning.

Table 5.2: Alphabetical List of Operation Codes, *continued*

Op Code	Description
DOU*xx*	Begin DO UNTIL loop.
DOW	Begin DO WHILE loop using expression conditioning.
DOW*xx*	Begin DO WHILE loop.
DSPLY	Display a message at the workstation.
DUMP	Print a formatted dump.
ELSE	Else clause, used in conjunction with the IF*xx* operation.
ELSEIF	A combined ELSE and IF statement.
END	End a DO, DOW*xx*, DOU*xx*, CAS*xx*, IF*xx*, or SELECT group.
ENDCS	End a CAS*xx* group.
ENDDO	End a DO, DOW*xx*, or DOU*xx* loop.
ENDFOR	End a FOR loop.
ENDIF	End an IF*xx* group.
ENDMON	End a MONITOR/ON-ERROR group.
ENDSL	End a SELECT group.
ENDSR	End of a subroutine.
EVAL	Evaluate an expression. Left justifies result for character expressions.
EVALR	Evaluate an expression. Right justifies result for character expressions.
EXCEPT	Write a program-defined or externally described record format.
EXFMT	Write, and then read, a workstation device.
EXSR	Call an intra-program subroutine.
EXTRCT	Extract a component of a DATE, TIME, or TIMESTAMP value.
FEOD	Cause a file "cursor" reset; free locked records.
FOR	Begin a FOR loop using expression syntax.
FORCE	Force input priority alteration.
GOTO	Perform an unconditional branch to a label.
IF*xx*	Compare two values and perform a block of code.
IN	Retrieve an external data area's data.
ITER	Iterate a DO, DOW*xx*, or DOU*xx* loop.
KFLD	Define a key field of a key list.
KLIST	Define a key list used to access an indexed file.

Table 5.2: Alphabetical List of Operation Codes, *continued*

Op Code	Description
LEAVE	Leave a DO, DOW*xx*, or DOU*xx* loop.
LEAVESR	Leave the current subroutine and immediately return to its caller.
LOOKUP	Search an array or table for like or unlike elements.
MHHZO	Move high zone to high zone.
MHLZO	Move high zone to low zone.
MLHZO	Move low zone to high zone.
MLLZO	Move low zone to low zone.
MONITOR	Begin a block of code that is monitored for errors.
MOVE	Copy data, right-justified, from a field or constant to field.
MOVEA	Copy data, left-justified, to all successive array elements.
MOVEL	Copy data, left-justified, from a field or constant to a field.
MULT	Multiply two values.
MVR	Copy the remainder of a preceding division to a field.
NEXT	Force the next input cycle to read input from a specific device.
OCCUR	Set/get the occurrence of a multiple occurrence data structure.
ON-ERROR	Begin an error trap block of code.
OPEN	Open a file.
OR*xx*	Extend IF*xx*, DOW*xx*, DOU*xx*, and WHEN*xx* conditioning.
OTHER	Otherwise clause of a SELECT/WHEN group.
OUT	Update an external data area.
PARM	Define a parameter field within a parameter list.
PLIST	Define a parameter list.
POST	Retrieve and post device-specific information to a data structure.
READ	Read from a file.
READC	Read next changed subfile record.
READE	Read the next data file record with equal key index.
READP	Read previous data file record.
READPE	Read previous data file record with equal key index.
REALLOC	Reallocate memory of a new size at runtime.
REL	Release an acquired program device.

Table 5.2: Alphabetical List of Operation Codes, *continued*

Op Code	Description
RESET	Reset a variable to its initial value.
RETURN	Return to calling program.
ROLBK	Commitment control, roll back group.
SCAN	Scan argument for search pattern and return position.
SELECT	Begin an in-line SELECT/WHEN case group.
SETGT	Set the file cursor greater than the specified index.
SETLL	Set the file cursor less than the specified index.
SETOFF	Set an indicator off.
SETON	Set an indicator on.
SHTDN	Test for system shut down.
SORTA	Sort an array.
SQRT	Compute the square root of a number.
SUB	Subtract one value from another.
SUBDUR	1. Subtract a duration from a DATE, TIME, or TIMESTAMP value. 2. Calculate the duration between two DATE, TIME, or TIMESTAMP values.
SUBST	Copy substring value in factor 2 to the result field.
TAG	Define the location and name of a label.
TESTB	Test bit pattern.
TESTN	Test character field for numeric data.
TESTZ	Test the zone of the rightmost position of a field.
TEST	Test for a valid DATE, TIME, or TIMESTAMP value.
TIME	Retrieve the system time and date.
UNLOCK	1. Unlock an external data area object. 2. Unlock a database record.
UPDATE	Update a file.
WHEN*xx*	When select condition is true, then do.
WRITE	Write to a file.
XFOOT	Cross foot (sum up) an array.
XLATE	Translate factor 2 using translate data in factor 1.
Z-ADD	Zero and add numeric.
Z-SUB	Zero and subtract numeric.

UNCONDITIONABLE OPERATION CODES

Although conditioning indicators should not be used to control RPG operations, there are groups of operations that cannot be conditioned with indicators. Table 5.3 lists these operations. Most of these operations tolerate, but are not affected by, control-level indicators. The BEGSR and ENDSR operations do not support control-level indicators.

Table 5.3: Operation Codes That Do Not Support Conditioning Indicators	
Op Code	**Description**
AND*xx*	Continuation of the IF*xx*, DOW*xx*, DOU*xx*, and WHEN*xx* operations.
BEGSR	Begin subroutine.
DEFINE	Define variable; data area declaration.
ELSE	Else operation of the IF*xx* operation.
ENDIF	End IF*xx*.
ENDCS	End CAS*xx*.
ENDSL	End SELECT.
ENDSR	End subroutine.
KFLD	Index key field declaration.
KLIST	Index key list declaration.
OR*xx*	OR continuation of the IF*xx*, DOW*xx*, DOU*xx*, and WHEN*xx* operations.
OTHER	Otherwise clause of a SELECT/WHEN case group.
PARM	Parameter.
PLIST	Parameter list.
TAG	Target of a CAB*xx* or GOTO operation.
WHEN*xx*	When compare clause of a select CASE group.

DATE AND TIME FORMAT CODES

Date, time, and timestamp (DTS) values can be converted from character, numeric, or literal format to a valid date, time, or timestamp variable using the MOVE and MOVEL operations. In addition, character and numeric variables can be checked for valid date, time, or timestamp values using the TEST operation.

When moving a DTS variable's value to a non-DTS variable, factor 1 of the MOVE or MOVEL operations indicate the format of the result field's value. When moving a non-DTS value to a DTS variable, factor 1 of the MOVE and MOVEL operations indicates the format of the value in factor 2. Table 5.4 lists the supported date formats for these operations. For more information, see the definition of the MOVE operation in chapter 1.

Table 5.4: Date Format Codes					
Date Format	Description	Output Format	Separator	Length	Sample
*JOBRUN	Job runtime format	varies			
*JOB	Job start date	N/A			INZ(*JOB)
*SYS	Current system date	N/A			INZ(*SYS)
*MDY	Month, Day, Year	mm/dd/yy	/ - . , &	8	02/17/95
*DMY	Day, Month, Year	dd/mm/yy	/ - . , &	8	17/02/95
*YMD	Year, Month, Day	yy/mm/dd	/ - . , &	8	95/02/17
*CYMD	Century, Year, Month, Day	cyy/mm/dd	/ - . , &	9	095/02/17
*CMDY	Century, Month, Day, Year	cmm/dd/yy	/ - . , &	9	002/17/95
*CDMY	Century, Day, Month, Year	cdd/mm/yy	/ - . , &	9	017/02/95
*JUL	Julian (year, day of year 1 – 365)	yy/ddd	/ - . , &	6	95/048
*LONGJUL	Long Julian	yyyy/ddd		8	1999/048
*ISO	International Standards Organization	ccyy-mm-dd	- (fixed)	10	1995-02-17
*USA	IBM's USA Standard	mm/dd/ccyy	/ (fixed)	10	02/17/1995
*EUR	IBM's European Standard	dd.mm.ccyy	. (fixed)	10	17.02.1995
*JIS	Japanese Industrial Standard	ccyy-mm-dd	- (fixed)	10	1995-02-17

Although all date formats accept a separator character, only *MDY, *YMD, *DMY, *CMDY, *CYMD, and *CDMY date formats support various separators. In addition, a separator of 0 (zero) indicates that no separator is used and may be used with any date format.

Most time formats are similar. The only notable exception is the *USA format that is based on a 12-hour clock and includes AM/PM notation. Table 5.5 lists the time formats supported by the MOVE, MOVEL, and TEST operations.

Table 5.5: Time Format Codes					
Time Format	Description	Output Format	Separator	Length	Sample
*JOBRUN	Job runtime format	Varies			
*JOB	Job start time	N/A			INZ(*JOB)
*SYS	System time	N/A			INZ(*SYS)
*HMS	Hours, Minutes, Seconds	hh:mm:ss	: . , &	8	15:30:00
*ISO	International Standards Organization	hh.mm.ss	. (fixed)	8	15.30.00
*USA	IBM's USA Standard	Hh:mm am hh:mm pm	: (fixed)	8	03:30 pm
*EUR	IBM's European Standard	hh.mm.ss	. (fixed)	8	15.30.00
*JIS	Japanese Industrial Standard	hh:mm:ss	: (fixed)	8	15:30:00

Timestamp Format

The format of a timestamp field is fixed. It is a single-format data type that optionally includes microseconds. Timestamp variables occupy 26 bytes. The format of the timestamp data type follows:

```
CCYY-MM-DD-HH.MN.SS.MMMMMM
```

The format of the timestamp data type is the combination of the *ISO date format, the *ISO time format, and a 6-position microseconds entry. Note that only milliseconds are supported within the RPG IV language.

DATE AND TIME DURATION CODES

The date and time duration operations EXTRCT, ADDDUR, and SUBDUR and the built-in functions %DIFF and %SUBDT allow you to specify the duration code or extraction value. For example, you can subtract one date to control whether the return value is the number of days between the two

Table 5.6: Duration Codes		
Description of Duration	Duration Code	Short Form
Years	*YEARS	*Y
Months	*MONTHS	*M
Days	*DAYS	*D
Hours	*HOURS	*H
Minutes	*MINUTES	*MN
Seconds	*SECONDS	*S
Microseconds	*MSECONDS	*MS

dates, the number of months between the two dates, and so on. Table 5.6 lists the available duration codes.

Use one of these duration codes in factor 2 along with the corresponding duration value for the ADDDUR, SUBDUR, and EXTRCT operations. For additional information on the SUBDUR operation code, see the subheading SUBDUR (Subtract Duration).

Note that the MOVE and MOVEL operations don't use duration codes; they use date format codes. For more information, see Tables 5.4 and 5.5.

The duration code tells the compiler what type of code to generate for the ADDDUR, SUBDUR, and EXTRCT date operations. For example, when the number 30 is specified in factor 2 of the ADDDUR operation, the compiler needs to know whether that number represents 30 days, 30 minutes, 30 hours, or 30 years. If the date is July 23, 1996, adding one month to the date results in a date of August 23, 1996. If the date is July 31, 1996, adding one month to it results in a date of August 30, 1996.

There is no duration code for the century. This is an oversight. For date variables that include century, however, the *YEARS and *Y duration codes work with a four-digit year. This four-digit "year" includes the century in the first two positions.

OPERATION EXTENDER REFERENCE

Operation extenders provide a method to modify the behavior of the operation code. Note: All RPG IV operation codes that support resulting indicator 2—the error indicator—also support the E operation extender. Table 5.7 lists the operation extenders and their purposes.

Table 5.7: Operation Extenders

Operation Extender	Description
A	**Always Dump**. Cause the DUMP operation code to function even when the DUMP(*YES) keyword is not specified on the Header specification.
D	**Test Date**. Check the result field for a valid date (TEST opcode).
D	**Operand Descriptor**. Generates descriptive information about each parameter passed to the called procedure (CALLB opcode).
E	**Error Event**. This operation extender is used with operation codes that support error trapping. In traditional RPG III, resulting indicator 2 is used to signal that an error has occurred. In RPG IV, specifying the E operation extender allows the error event to be signaled via the %STATUS and %ERROR built-in functions. When the E operation extender is used, resulting indicator 2 is not required. If the E operation extender is not specified, the state of %ERROR and %STATUS does not change.
H	**Half-Adjust**. Used to round the result up to the nearest decimal value. This is accomplished by adding $5*10^{-(n+1)}$ to the absolute value of the result. Where n = number of decimal positions. For a DEC(5,2) field, the following applies: 1.006 half-adjust to 1.01; -1.006 half-adjust to -1.01
M	**Maximum Digits**. When computing numeric result values, the maximum number of allowable digits is used for intermediate result values. This is default behavior.
N	**Read without Locking**. Used when accessing database records from files that are opened for update. This operation extender allows records to be read, but does not place a lock on the record (database input opcodes only).
N	**Set pointer to *NULL**. Used with the DEALLOC operation code to cause *NULL (X'00') to move moved into the pointer specified on the Result field (DEALLOC opcode only).
P	**Pad Result**. Used to replace the data in the result field. The P operation extender allows a single operation to replace the contents of the result field. For character fields, blanks are used to pad the result. For numeric fields, zeros are used.
R	**Result Field Digits**. When computing numeric result values, the result field's decimal positions are used for the intermediate result values for the expression.
T	**Test Time**. Check the result field for a valid time.
Z	**Test Timestamp**. Check the result field for a valid timestamp.

RPG IV OPERATION CODE SUMMARY SYNTAX DIAGRAM LEGEND

Table 5.8 lists the operation code syntax diagram summary. Values in square brackets [ ] are optional. For example: [*NOKEY] means that the value *NOKEY is optional. The square brackets are not included when specifying these values in source code. In Table 5.8, as they are in the language, the operation code extenders are specified in parentheses. All operation extenders are optional, but for clarity they are illustrated here as they are specified in RPG IV (in parentheses) instead of brackets.

> **NOTE:** All operation codes that support resulting indicator 2 also support the E operation extender. For clarity purposes, the E operation extender has been omitted from the syntax diagram in this book.

Values in lowercase are variable values. For example, *compare value 2* means that a literal or variable (i.e., field) can be specified. Values in small capitals (for example, *LOCK) are constants. Values enclosed in single quotation marks represent a literal or named constant value.

The term *value*, as used in the syntax diagram (Table 5.8), generally means any field or literal value can be specified. If the value is enclosed in single quotation marks, only a literal or named constant is allowed.

The term *variable* generally means any field, data structure, array, or array element can be specified. For example: *char variable* refers to a field, data structure, or array element of type CHARACTER, whereas *num variable* refers to a field of type NUMERIC (such as packed, binary, integer, or signed numeric).

OPERATION CODE SYNTAX DIAGRAMS

Table 5.8: Operation Code Syntax Diagram Summary								
Factor 1	Op Code	Factor 2	Result	Length	Dec		Resulting Ind.	
workstn device ID	ACQ	workstn file name					[error]	
[numeric value]	ADD(H)	numeric value	sum	[size]	[dec]	[+]	[-]	[0]
[base date/time]	ADDDUR	duration:dur code	new date/time					
	ALLOC	num of bytes	pointer variable				[error]	
compare value 1	AND*xx*	compare value 2						
[subroutine name]	BEGSR							
	BITOFF	'bit nums to set off'	char variable	[size]				
	BITON	'bit nums to set on'	char variable	[size]				
compare value 1	CAB[1]	compare value 2	[label]			[1>2]	[1<2]	[1=2]
compare value 1	CAB*xx*	compare value 2	[label]			[1>2]	[1<2]	[1=2]
	CALL	program name	[plist]				[error]	[LR]
	CALLB(D)	'proc name' or ptr[2]	[plist]				[error]	
[compare value 1]	CAS*xx*	[compare value 2]	subroutine			[1>2]	[1<2]	[1=2]
	CALLP(E)	prototype-name[(*parm1 : parm2 : ...*])						
[operand 1]	CAT(P)	operand 2[:num blanks]	char variable	[size]			[error]	
key value or rec num	CHAIN(N)	record format			n/f		[error]	
key value or rec num	CHAIN(N)	file name	[data struct]		n/f		[error]	
check list	CHECK	base value[:start]	[position(s)]	[size]	[dec]		[error]	[found]
check list	CHECKR	base value[:start]	[position(s)]	[size]	[dec]		[error]	[found]
[*NOKEY]	CLEAR	[*ALL]	variable to clear	[size]	[dec]			
	CLOSE	file name					[error]	
	CLOSE	*ALL					[error]	
[boundary]	COMMIT						[error]	
compare value 1	COMP[3]	compare value 2				[1>2]	[1<2]	[1=2]
	DEALLOC(N)		pointer variable				[error]	
*LIKE	DEFINE	based-on variable	new variable	[±][size]	[dec]			
*DTAARA	DEFINE	[data area name][4]	assignment	[size]	[dec]			
[key value]	DELETE	file name			[n/f]		[error]	
[key value]	DELETE	record format			[n/f]		[error]	
[numerator]	DIV(H)	denominator	result	[size]	[dec]	[+]	[-]	[0]

Table 5.8: Operation Code Syntax Diagram Summary, *continued*						
Factor 1	Op Code	Factor 2	Result	Length	Dec	Resulting Ind.
[starting value]	DO	[iterations]	[counter]	[size]	[dec]	
	DOU	expression				
compare value 1	DOU*xx*	compare value 2				
	DOW	expression				
compare value 1	DOW*xx*	compare value 2				
[message ID]	DSPLY	[*EXT]	[response]	[size]		[error]
[message ID]	DSPLY	[message queue]	[response]	[size]		[error]
[descriptive text]	DUMP (A)					
	ELSE					
	ELSEIF	expression				
	END	[increment]				
	ENDCS					
	ENDDO	[increment][5]				
	ENDFOR					
	ENDIF					
	ENDMON					
	ENDSL					
[label]	ENDSR	[return point]				
	EVAL(HMR)	result-value = expression				
	EVALR(HMR)	result-value = expression				
	EXCEPT	[except output label]				
	EXFMT	record format				[error]
	EXSR	subroutine				
	EXTRCT	date var : dur code	extracted value	[size]	[dec]	[error]
	FEOD	file name				[error]
	FOR	Index = start TO | DOWNTO limit BY increment				
	FORCE	file name				
	GOTO	label				
	IF	expression				
Compare value 1	IF*xx*	compare value 2				
[*LOCK]	IN	data area				[error]
[*LOCK]	IN	*DTAARA				[error]
	ITER					

Table 5.8: Operation Code Syntax Diagram Summary, *continued*

Factor 1	Op Code	Factor 2	Result	Length	Dec		Resulting Ind.	
	KFLD		Key field					
Key list name	KLIST							
	LEAVE							
	LEAVESR							
Search pattern	LOOKUP	array(*starting elem*)				[high]	[low]	[equal]
Search pattern	LOOKUP	table 1	[Table 2]			[high]	[low]	[equal]
	MHHZO	source	Char variable	[size]				
	MHLZO	source	Char variable	[size]				
	MLHZO	source	Char variable	[size]				
	MLLZO	source	Char variable	[size]				
	MONITOR							
[Date format][sep][6]	MOVE(P)	source	target	[size]	[dec]	[+]	[-]	[0 or ƃ]
	MOVEA(P)	source	target	[size]	[dec]	[+]	[-]	[0 or ƃ]
[Date format][sep]	MOVEL(P)	source	target	[size]	[dec]	[+]	[-]	[0 or ƃ]
[Numeric value]	MULT(H)	numeric value	product	[size]	[dec]	[+]	[-]	[0]
	MVR		remainder	[size]	[dec]	[+]	[-]	[0]
workstn device ID	NEXT	workstn file name					[error]	
[occurrence to set to]	OCCUR	data structure	[occurrence]	[size]	[dec]		[error]	
	ON-ERROR	exception ID1 { : exception ID2...	*ALL	*PROGRAM	*FILE }					
	OPEN	file name					[error]	
compare value 1	OR*xx*	compare value 2						
	OTHER							
[*LOCK]	OUT	data area					[error]	
[*LOCK]	OUT	*DTAARA					[error]	
[Input value]	PARM	[output value]	parameter	[size]	[dec]			
Parameter list name	PLIST							
[Workstn device ID]	POST	workstn file name[7]	[infds]				[error]	
	READ(N)	record format					[error]	eof
	READ(N)	file name	[Data struct]				[error]	eof
	READC	subfile record format					[error]	eof
[Key value]	READE(N)	record format					[error]	eof
[Key value]	READE(N)	file name	[Data struct]				[error]	eof
	READP(N)	record format					[error]	bof

Factor 1	Op Code	Factor 2	Result	Length	Dec	Resulting Ind.		
	READP(N)	file name	[Data struct]				[error]	bof
[Key value]	READPE(N)	record format					[error]	bof
[Key value]	READPE(N)	file name	[Data struct]				[error]	bof
	REALLOC	num of bytes	Pointer variable				[error]	
Workstn device ID	REL	workstn file name					[error]	
[*NOKEY]	RESET	[*ALL]	Variable to reset	[size]	[dec]			
	RETURN							
	ROLBK						[error]	
Search pattern[:length]	SCAN	search var[:start]	[position(s)][8]	[size]	[dec]		[error]	[found]
	SELECT							
Key value	SETGT	file name				[n/f]	[error]	
Key value	SETGT	record format				[n/f]	[error]	
Key value	SETLL	file name				[n/f]	[error]	[found]
Key value	SETLL	record format				[n/f]	[error]	[found]
	SETOFF					[ind1]	[ind2]	[ind3]
	SETON					[ind1]	[ind2]	[ind3]
	SHTDN					yes		
	SORTA	array						
	SQRT(H)	numeric value	Square root	[size]	[dec]			
[Numeric value]	SUB(H)	numeric value	difference	[size]	[dec]	[+]	[-]	[0]
[Date / time]	SUBDUR	duration:dur code	Date / time				[error]	
Date / time	SUBDUR	date / time	Duration:dur code	[size]	[dec]		[error]	
[Length of source]	SUBST(P)	source var[:start]	Char variable	[size]			[error]	
label	TAG							
Format to test	TEST(D,T, Z)		Date / time variable				[error]	
	TESTB	'bit numbers to test'	Char variable	[size]		[xor]	[mix]	[equal]
	TESTN		Char variable	[size]		[num]	[mix]	[blank]
	TESTZ		Char variable	[size]		[+]	[-]	[other]
	TIME		Date/time/numeric val	[size]	[dec]			
	UNLOCK	data area | *DTAARA					[error]	
	UNLOCK	file name					[error]	

Table 5.8: Operation Code Syntax Diagram Summary, *continued*

Factor 1	Op Code	Factor 2	Result	Length	Dec		Resulting Ind.	
	UPDATE	record format					[error]	
	UPDATE	file name	[Data struct]				[error]	
	WHEN	expression						
Compare value 1	WHEN*xx*	compare value 2						
	WRITE	record format					[error]	[full][9]
	WRITE	file name	[Data struct]				[error]	
	XFOOT(H)	numeric array	Sum of array	[size]	[dec]	[+]	[-]	[0]
From value : to value	XLATE(P)	source[:start]	Char variable	[size]			[error]	
	Z-ADD(H)	numeric value	Num variable	[size]	[dec]	[+]	[-]	[0]
	Z-SUB(H)	numeric value	Num variable	[size[	[dec]	[+]	[-]	[0]

Table 5.8: Operation Code Syntax Diagram Summary, *continued*

[1] If the result field (label) is not specified, at least one resulting indicator is required.

[2] A procedure pointer can be a quoted procedure name, a named constant (representing a quoted procedure name), or a pointer variable that has been declared with the PROCPTR keyword specified.

[3] At least one resulting indicator is required.

[4] If factor 2 is not specified, the result field is used as the name of the data structure.

[5] The increment value is valid for END and ENDDO operations associated with a DO op code.

[6] The date format can be any format supported by RPG IV, such as *MDY, *YMD, or *ISO.

[7] Factor 2 is optional when a workstation device file's INFDS data structure name is specified for the result field.

[8] If the result field is omitted, resulting indicator 3 is required.

[9] Resulting indicator 2 [full] is valid only for WRITE operations to a WORKSTN subfile detail record format.

BOOLEAN OPERATION CODES

In the syntax diagrams throughout this chapter, several operation codes contain *xx* as part of the operation name. This indicates that a Boolean operator can be specified in place of the *xx*. Table 5.9 lists each of the Boolean operators. Listed in Table 5.10 are the operation codes that accept these Boolean operators.

FREE FORMAT OPERATION CODES

Most operations may be used in an alternate calculation specification syntax. This syntax is known as free-format. Free-format syntax does not use the traditional Factor 1, Factor 2, and the result field. Instead, positions 8 through 80 of the source line may be used specify the operation code and its parameters using free-format syntax.

Table 5.12 shows a list of the operation codes that may be used with the free format syntax. Values enclosed in {} are optional in the free-format syntax.

Table 5.9: Boolean Operations

Boolean	Description
EQ	Factor 1 is equal to factor 2.
GE	Factor 1 is greater than or equal to factor 2.
GT	Factor 1 is greater than factor 2.
LE	Factor 1 is less than or equal to factor 2.
LT	Factor 1 is less than factor 2.
NE	Factor 1 is not equal to factor 2.
blank	Unconditional comparison (for CAS*xx* and CAB*xx* only).

Table 5.10: Fixed-Format Conditional Operation Codes

Factor 1	Op Code	Factor 2
Compare value 1	AND*xx*	*Compare value 2*
Compare value 1	CAB*xx*	*Compare value 2*
Compare value 1	CAS*xx*	*Compare value 2*
Compare value 1	DOU*xx*	*Compare value 2*
Compare value 1	DOW*xx*	*Compare value 2*
Compare value 1	DOW*xx*	*Compare value 2*
Compare value 1	OR*xx*	*Compare value 2*
Compare value 1	WHEN*xx*	*Compare value 2*

Table 5.11: Operation Codes Supporting Natural Expressions

Op Code	Extended Factor 2
CALLP	Proc-name(parm1, parm2...)
DOU	Conditional expression
DOW	Conditional expression
EVALR	Result value = expression
EVAL	Result value = expression
FOR	Index [= start] [TO | DOWNTO limit] [BY increment]
IF	Conditional expression
ON-ERROR	error condition codes
WHEN	Conditional expression
RETURN	Return value expression

Table 5.12: Operation Codes Supporting Free Format Syntex

ACQ{(E)} *device-name workstn-file*	IN{(E)} {*LOCK} *data-area-name*
BEGSR *subroutine-name*	ITER
{CALLP{(EMR)}} *name({parm1{:parm2...}})*	LEAVE
CHAIN{(ENHMR)} *search-arg {data-structure}*	LEAVESR
CLEAR {*NOKEY} {*ALL} *name*	MONITOR
CLOSE{(E)} *file-name*	NEXT{(E)} *program-device file-name*
COMMIT{(E)} *{boundary}*	ON-ERROR *{exception-id1 {:exception-id2...}}*
DEALLOC{(EN)} *pointer-name*	OPEN{(E)} *file-name*
DELETE{(EHMR)} *{search-arg}*	OTHER
DOU{(MR)} *indicator-expression*	OUT{(E)} {*LOCK} *data-area-name*
DOW{(MR)} *indicator-expression*	POST{(E)} *{program-device} file-name*
DSPLY{(E)} *{message {output-queue {response}}}*	READ{(EN)} *name {data-structure}*
DUMP{(A)} *{identifier}*	READC{(E)} *record-name*
ELSE	READE{(ENHMR)} *search-arg|*KEY {data-structure}*
ELSEIF{(MR)} *indicator-expression*	READP{(EN)} *name {data-structure}*
ENDDO	READPE{(ENHMR)} *search-arg|*KEY {data-structure}*
ENDFOR	REL{(E)} *program-device file-name*
ENDIF	RESET{(E)} {*NOKEY} {*ALL} *name*
ENDMON	RETURN{(HMR)} *expression*
ENDSL	ROLBK{(E)}
ENDSR *{return-point}*	SELECT
{EVAL{(HMR)}} *result = expression*	SETGT{(EHMR)} *search-arg*
EVALR{(MR)} *result = expression*	SETLL{(EHMR)} *search-arg*
EXCEPT *{except-name}*	SORTA *array-name*
EXFMT{(E)} *format-name*	TEST{(EDTZ)} *{dtz-format} field-name*
EXSR *subroutine-name*	UNLOCK{(E)} *name*
FEOD{(EN)} *file-name*	UPDATE{(E)} *name {data-structure|%FIELDS(name{:name...})}*
FOR{(MR)} *index {= start} {BY increment} {TO|DOWNTO limit}*	WHEN{(MR)} *indicator-expression*
FORCE *file-name*	WRITE{(E)} *name {data-structure}*
IF{(MR)} *indicator-expression*	

NATURAL EXPRESSION OPERATION CODES

Several operations listed in Table 5.8 support the alternate calculation specification. This specification includes an extended factor 2 that begins where the normal factor 2 begins (column 36), but continues through column 80.

The extended factor 2 is used to specify a natural expression. Natural expressions can be specified anywhere within the extended factor 2, and can be continued onto subsequent alternate calculation source statements. Continuing a line is achieved by starting a new calculation specification, and by leaving all positions through the operation code (columns 7 through 35) blank. Table 5.11 lists the operations codes that support natural expressions.

PROGRAM STATUS CODES

Most operation codes support a *status error code*. When an operation code generates an exception/error, the program information data structure field *STATUS is updated. In addition, if the operation supports an error indicator (resulting indicator 2), that indicator is set on when an error is generated. Also, if the E operation extender is specified, the %STATUS built-in function is set to the status code listed in Table 5.13, and the %ERROR built-in function is set to *ON.

For operation codes that don't support the error indicator (e.g., SQRT, ADD, SUB, EVAL, MULT, DIV, MOVE, and MOVEA), the program exception/error subroutine (*PSSR) is automatically called (if it exists in the program). Example 5.1 illustrates how to code the *PSSR subroutine.

Example 5.1: Using the program status data structure to detect a divide-by-zero error.

```
.....DName++++++++++EUDSFrom+++To/Len+TDc.Functions++++++++++++++++++++++++++++
0010 D PSDS          SDS
0020 D  Status               *STATUS

0040 D Fact1        S              3P 0 Inz(5)
0050 D Fact2        S              3P 0 Inz(0)
0060 D Answer       S              3P 0 Inz(0)

.....CSRn01Factor1+++++++OpCode(ex)Factor2+++++++Result++++++++Len++DcHiLoEq
0070 C     Fact1        Div     Fact2        ANSWER
0080 C                  MOVE    *ON          *INLR
0090 CSR   *PSSR        BEGSR
0100 C                  If      Status = 102
```

```
0110 C                    Eval      Answer = 999
0120 C                    EndIf
0130 CSR    endPSSR       ENDSR
```

Table 5.13: Runtime Program Status Message Codes

Code	Description of Conditions
00000	No exception/error occurred.
00001	Called program ended with indicator LR on.
00100	String operation had range or subscript error.
00101	Square root of a negative number.
00102	Divide by zero.
00121	Invalid array index.
00122	OCCUR operation outside of data structure range.
00202	Called program failed with indicators H1 to H9 off.
00211	Program specified on CALL or FREE operation not found.
00221	Called program tried to access a parameter that was not passed to it.
00231	Called program failed with halt indicator (H1 to H9) on.
00232	Halt indicator (H1 to H9) on in current program.
00233	Halt indicator on when RETURN operation performed.
00299	RPG-formatted dump failed.
00333	Error occurred during DSPLY operation.
00401	Data area specified for IN/OUT operation not found.
00402	*PDA not valid for pre-start job.
00411	Attributes of data area specified for IN/OUT operation does not match actual data area.
00412	Data area specified for OUT operation was not locked.
00413	Error occurred during IN/OUT operation.
00414	Security authorization to access data area failed.
00415	Security authorization to change data area failed.
00421	Error occurred during UNLOCK operation.
00431	Data area is locked by another program and/or job.
00432	Data area is locked by another program in this job.
00907	Decimal data error.
00970	Compiler level does not match run-time subroutine level.
09998	Internal failure in RPG or generated run-time subroutines.
09999	Program exception in an operating system routine.

Note: These codes apply to RPG IV on IBM OS/400 and might differ with other compilers.

FILE-STATUS ERROR CODES

In addition to program status error codes, there are also file exception/error status codes. This type of code indicates when an error condition has been encountered after a file-specific operation is performed. An example is the CHAIN operation, where a record time-out error could occur.

Most operation codes set on resulting indicator 2 when an exception error is detected, however when the E operation extender is used, resulting indicator 2 is unnecessary. When the E operation extender is used, the %ERROR and %STATUS built-in functions may be used to detect the current status of the file (see Example 5.2). If the programmer has specified resulting indicator 2, the indicator is set on and control passes to the next RPG operation. If resulting indicator 2 is not specified and the E operation extender is not specified, but a file exception/error subroutine is specified, control automatically transfers to that subroutine. At that point, the value of *STATUS location may be interrogated. If resulting indicator 2 is not specified, the E operation extender is not specified, and a file exception/error subroutine is not specified, the RPG general exception/error handling subroutine receives control. The user or workstation operator is usually issued an error message at this point.

Example 5.2: Detecting a record lock/time-out condition.

```
.....FFileName++IFEASFRlen+LKeylnKFDevice+.Functions+++++++++++++++++++++++++++++
0010 FCUSTMAST  IF   E       K DISK


.....CSRn01Factor1+++++++OpCode(ex)Factor2+++++++Result++++++++Len++DcHiLoEq
0020 C     1234567       CHAIN(E)  CUSTMAST
0030 C                   If        %Status = 1218
0040 C                   Eval      Msg - 'DBF Timeout'
0050 C                   EndIf
0060 C                   MOVE      *ON            *INLR
```

Table 5.14 contains the definitions for the abbreviations used to describe the device types for the file status error codes that are listed in Table 5.14.

Table 5.14: Device Type Abbreviation Glossary

Abbreviation	Device Type	Description
WS	WORKSTN	Workstation device file. Used to access display files and ICF (communications) files.
DSK	DISK	Disk file. Used to access database physical, logical, or joined-logical files. Also, save files can be accessed through this device type.
PRT	PRINTER	Printer file. Used to output printed data to a print device. Typically, the data is spooled (stored on disk) for a time and then printed later.
SEQ	SEQ	Sequential file. Used to access diskette, tape, and save files. The files can be opened, read, written to, and closed, but not updated.
SPC	SPECIAL	Special file. Used to support user-written device file drivers. A device file driver is a user-written program that handles the file access requests, such as open, close, read, and write.

The built-in function, %STATUS and the INFDS subfield *STATUS may contain any of the status codes in the range 1000 to 9999. The specific status codes are listed in Table 5.15.

Table 5.15: File Status (Error) Code Descriptions

Code	Devices	Description of Conditions
00000		No exception/error occurred.
00002	WS	Function key used to input display.
00011	WS,DSK,SEQ	End of file detected on a READ (input) operation.
00012	WS,DSK,SEQ	No-record-found condition for a CHAIN, SETLL, or SETGT operation.
00013	WS	Subfile is full.
01011	WS,DSK,SEQ	Undefined record type (identifying indicators do not match record).
01021	WS,DSK,SEQ	Attempted to write to an existing record or duplicate index value.
01031	WS,DSK,SEQ	Matching record match field data out of sequence.
01041		Array/table load sequence error.

Table 5.15: File Status (Error) Code Descriptions, *continued*		
Code	**Devices**	**Description of Conditions**
01051		Too many array/table entries.
01052		Clearing of table prior to dump of data failed.
01071	WS,DSK,SEQ	Numeric sequence error.
01121	WS	Print key pressed with no resulting indicator.
01122	WS	Roll Up (Page Down) key pressed with no resulting indicator.
01123	WS	Roll Down (Page Up) key pressed with no resulting indicator.
01124	WS	Clear key pressed with no resulting indicator.
01125	WS	Help key pressed with no resulting indicator.
01126	WS	Home key pressed with no resulting indicator.
01201	WS	Workstation record mismatch detected on input.
01211	all	I/O operation to a closed file.
01215	all	OPEN operation issued to a file that was already opened.
01216	all	Error on an implicit OPEN/CLOSE operation (cycle oriented).
01217	all	Error on an explicit OPEN/CLOSE operation.
01218	DSK,SEQ	Unable to allocate record (record locked by another program).
01221	DSK,SEQ	Update operation without a prior successful read.
01231	SPC	Error on SPECIAL file.
01235	PRT	Error in PRTCTL data structure spacing or skipping entries.
01241	DSK,SEQ	ADDROUT record not found.
01251	WS	Permanent workstation I/O error detected.
01255	WS	Workstation session or device error occurred (recovery possible).
01261	WS	Attempted to exceed maximum number of acquired devices.
01281	WS	Operation to an acquired device.
01282	WS	Job ending (canceled) with controlled option.
01285	WS	Attempted to acquire an already acquired device.
01286	WS	Attempted to open shared file with SAVDS or IND file continuation.
01287	WS	Response indicators overlap IND continuation option indicators.
01299	WS,DSK,SEQ	Miscellaneous I/O error.
01331	WS	Wait-for-record time exceeded for READ or EXFMT operation.

NESTED CODE ILLUSTRATION

Nested DO, DOW*xx*, DOU*xx*, FOR, SELECT/WHEN*xx*, and IF/THEN/ELSE levels appear in several examples. Occasionally a graphic is used to illustrate nesting levels. The source code may be indented for clarity and does not represent exact coding statement, but rather the nesting level of the source code. Example 5.3 illustrates this indented nesting graphic. The operation code columns are extended in this nested view of RPG source code.

Example 5.3: Graphic illustration of RPG nesting.

```
.....CLØnØ1Factor1+++++++<26    to    35>Factor2+++++++Result+++++++++Len++DcHiLoEq
     C                    IF             %Status = Ø
     C                    | DOW          %eof(CUSTMAST) = *OFF AND Count <= 2Ø
     C                    | | WRITE      SFLØØ1
     C                    | | IF         NOT %EOF(SFLØØ1)
     C                    | | | ADD      1                COUNT
     C                    | | | READ     CUSTMAST
     C                    | | ENDIF
     C                    | ENDDO
     C                    ENDIF
```

FREE FORMAT NESTED CODE ILLUSTRATION

Typically free format code does not require a graphic illustrating the nesting levels since it can be written in an indented manner. However, Example 5.3b, below, illustrates this indented nesting graphic for free format RPG.

Example 5.3b: Graphic illustration of RPG nesting in free format.

```
....._++++++++++++++++++++++++++++++++++++++++++++++++++++++++++++++++++++++++++++
     /FREE-FORM
                   IF        %Status = Ø;
                   | DOW        %eof(CUSTMAST) = *OFF AND Count <= 2Ø;
                   | | WRITE     SFLØØ1;
                   | | IF     NOT %eof(SFLØØ1);
                   | | | Eval Count += 1;
                   | | | READ CUSTMAST;
                   | | ENDIF;
                   | ENDDO;
                   ENDIF;
     /END-FREE
```

▶ACQ (ACQUIRE)

The ACQ operation is used to grab or capture the program device (workstation/display station) specified in factor 1.

Factor 1	OpCode	Factor 2	Result Field	Resulting Indicators	
workstn device ID	ACQ(E)	workstn file name			[error]

See also REL

Factor 1 must contain a constant or a field that contains the name of the program device (workstation/display station) that is acquired by the program. Factor 2 must contain the name of the workstation file that is used to acquire the program device. When resulting indicator 2 is set on by the ACQ operation, one of the following conditions exists:

Resulting Indicator Legend			
Columns	Ind.	Usage	Set-On Condition
71 - 72	1	N/A	
73 - 74	2	[error]	An error occurred during the operation.
75 - 76	3	N/A	

- The device has already been acquired by another application (a user may have "signed on" to the system using that device).

- The device file specified in factor 2 already acquired the device.

- The device specified in factor 1 does not exist.

Once a device has been acquired, the program may read from the device or write to the device. To identify which device a program accesses, move the name of the device into the field specified for the program device ID. This field is specified on the DEVID keyword of the file specification. The maximum number of program devices a program can acquire is equal to the number of program devices specified for the MAXDEV keyword of the file specification.

In Example 5.4, line 10 contains the file specification for the workstation display file GLENTRY (G/L Entry). The MAXDEV keyword is used to indicate the maximum number of devices that may be acquired by the program for the GLENTRY workstation display file.

Example 5.4: Acquiring a workstation device.

```
.....FFileName++IFEASFRlen+LKeylnKFDevice+.Functions+++++++++++++++++++++++++++++
0010 FGLENTRY    CF    E                   WORKSTN MaxDev(*FILE) DEVID(wsid)


.....CSRn01Factor1+++++++OpCode(ex)Factor2+++++++Result++++++++Len++DcHiLoEq
0030 C      'DSP01'      ACQ(E)      GLENTRY
0040 C                   If          %ERROR
0050 C                   EXSR                         *PSSR
0060 C                   ENDIF
0070 C                   MOVEL       'DSP01'          WSID
0080 C                   EXFMT       PROMPT
```

In Example 5.4 , the file's description is used to set the number of devices. This value may be overridden to a different number outside of the program through a system function.

Line 10 also contains the DEVID keyword. This keyword is used to identify which device the program reads on the next I/O operation.

Line 30 uses the constant 'DSP01' as the name of the device that is acquired by the program. GLENTRY is the workstation file that acquires DSP01.

Line 70 moves the constant 'DSP01' into the field WSID to force the EXFMT (write/read format) operation on line 80 to write to and then read from the DSP01 device.

> **NOTE:** *Line 80 uses a record format name 'prompt' in place of the workstation file name.*

ADD (ADD NUMERIC)

The ADD operation is used to produce the sum of two numeric values. Add works with packed, signed, binary, or integer numeric data types. For DATE, TIME, and TIMESTAMP values, the ADDDUR operation must be used.

Factor 1	OpCode	Factor 2	Result Field	Resulting Indicators		
[numeric value 1]	ADD(H)	numeric value 2	sum	[+]	[-]	[0 or ꞗ]

See also EVAL, EVALR, SUB, MULT, DIV, SQRT, ADDDUR, and SUBDUR

If factor 1 is specified, factor 1 and factor 2 are added to produce a sum that is returned to the result field. If factor 1 is omitted, factor 2 and the result field are added and the sum is placed into the result field. The H operation extender can be specified to cause the result to be half-adusted (rounded up).

Resulting Indicator Legend			
Columns	Ind.	Usage	Set-On Condition
71 - 72	1	[+]	The result field is greater than zero.
73 - 74	2	[−]	The result field is less than zero.
75 - 76	3	[0]	The result field is equal to zero.

If you wrote the code shown in Example 5.5 in traditional mathematical expressions, it would appear as follows:

```
A + B = C

C + 1 = C
```

In this example, fields A and B are added, and the result is placed into field C. Then field C is incremented by 1. If C is greater than 0, resulting indicator 1 is set on. If C is less than 0, resulting indicator 2 is set on. If C is equal to 0, resulting indicator 3 is set on.

Example 5.5: Adding variables and constants.

```
.....CSRnØ1Factor1+++++++OpCode(ex)Factor2+++++++Result++++++++Len++DcHiLoEq
ØØ1Ø C     A              ADD       B             C
ØØ2Ø C                    ADD       1             C                   545658
```

▶ ADDDUR (ADD DURATION)

The ADDDUR operation adds the duration specified in factor 2 to the date, time, or timestamp variable specified in factor 1. The new value is returned in the result field. The value specified in factor 1 is referred to as the *base date* or *base time*. If factor 1 is not specified, the duration is added to the variable specified in the result field.

Factor 1	OpCode	Factor 2	Result Field	Resulting Indicators	
[date value]	ADDDUR(E)	duration : dur code	resulting date		[error]	

See also SUBDUR, EXTRCT, and TEST.

Factor 1 is optional and can contain a date, time, or timestamp value. If factor 1 is not specified, the date, time, or timestamp value specified in the result field is used.

Extender	Description
E	ERROR – Causes the %ERROR and %STATUS built-in functions to be set if an error occurs during the operation.

Factor 2 is required and must contain a variable or literal that represents a duration that is added to the value. Because factor 2 can be a positive or negative value, ADDDUR can be used to add or subtract a duration. The duration must be identified with a valid *duration code* (i.e., *YEARS, *MONTHS, *DAYS, *HOURS, *MINUTES, *SECONDS, *MSECONDS). See Table 5.6 for a description of these duration codes.

If the result field contains an array name (e.g., an array of dates), the duration is added to each element in the array. Example 5.6 illustrates the use of the ADDDUR operation code to add 30 days to the field named DUEDATE. In Example 5.6, the field DUEDATE is of type DATE. It is initialized to the 17th of February, 1996. After the ADDDUR operation on line 4 is performed, the DUEDATE variable is set to the 19th of March, 1996.

Example 5.6: Using ADDDUR to add 30 days to a date variable.

```
.....DName++++++++++EUDS.......Length+TDc.Functions+++++++++++++++++++++++++++++
0001 D DueDate          S            D   INZ (D'1996-02-17')
0002

.....CSRn01Factor1+++++++OpCode(ex)Factor2+++++++Result++++++++Len++DcHiLoEq
0003  *    Add 30 days to the due date
0004 C                     AddDur    30:*Days       DueDate
```

►ALLOC (ALLOCATE MEMORY)

The ALLOC operation is used to dynamically allocate storage (memory) at runtime. The number of bytes and a pointer variable to which the memory location is returned are passed to the ALLOC operation.

Factor 1	OpCode	Factor 2	Result Field	Resulting Indicators		
	ALLOC (E)	Length in bytes	Pointer variable		[error]	

See also REALLOC and DEALLOC.

Factor 1 is required and must contain a numeric field or literal value. Factor 1 indicates the number of bytes of memory to allocate. The number of bytes that can be allocated must be greater than 0 and less than 16 megabytes (16,776,704). If the number of bytes is outside this limit, status error code 0425 is returned to the %STATUS built-in function.

Resulting Indicator Legend			
Columns	Ind.	Usage	Set-On Condition
71 - 72	1	N/A	
73 - 74	2	[error]	An error occurred during the operation.
75 - 76	3	N/A	

The result field is required and must contain a field of type pointer. The address of the memory allocated is returned to this variable. There should be a variable with the BASED keyword referencing this pointer variable. The based variable can be used to access the newly allocated memory.

In Example 5.7, 500 bytes of memory are allocated on line 3. The pointer variable pSTRING is used to store the address of those 500 bytes of memory. Line 1 declares the based-on variable STRING. This variable declaration contains the BASED keyword. This indicates that the STRING variable is based on the pSTRING pointer. Note that RPG does not require pointer variables to be explicitly declared. Specifying the pointer variable in the BASED keyword causes the variable to be declared by the RPG language.

Example 5.7: Allocating 500 bytes of memory.

```
.....DName+++++++++++EUDS.......Length+TDc.Functions+++++++++++++++++++++++++++++
0001 D String          S            500A   Based( pString )

.....CSRn01Factor1+++++++OpCode(ex)Factor2+++++++Result++++++++Len++DcHiLoEq
0002 *    Allocate 500 bytes of memory
0003 C                  ALLOC(E)  500            pString
```

▶ ANDxx (AND CONDITION)

The ANDxx operation is used in conjunction with the IFxx, DOWxx, DOUxx, and WHENxx operations. ANDxx complements these other operations in that their conditioning is extended through the use of the ANDxx.

Conditioning indicators are not allowed for this operation. Resulting indicators are not valid for this operation.

Factor 1	OpCode	Factor 2	Result Field	Resulting Indicators		
Compare value 1	ANDxx	compare value 2				

See also ORxx, DOUxx, DOWxx, and IFxx

Factor 1 is required and must contain a field, literal value, array element, or figurative constant. Factor 2 is required and must contain a field, literal value, array element, or figurative constant.

Factor 1 is compared to factor 2 using the ANDxx Boolean operators EQ, GE, GT, LE, LT, and NE (see Table 5.9). Factor 1 and factor 2 must be similar data types. In other words, both must be character or numeric. Example 5.8 shows an example of using ANDLE to extend the DOWEQ operation.

Example 5.8: Using ANDLE to extend the DOWxx operation.

```
.....CSRnØ1Factor1+++++++OpCode(ex)Factor2+++++++Result++++++++Len++DcHiLoEq
ØØ10 C     *IN58      DOWEQ     *OFF
ØØ2Ø C        C       ANDLE     1Ø
ØØ3Ø C                ADD       1              C           3 Ø
ØØ4Ø C                READ      CUSTMAST                         58
ØØ5Ø C                ENDDO
```

In Example 5.8, indicator 58 is compared to the *OFF figurative constant. If indicator 58 is off, field C is compared to the constant 10. If it is less than or equal to 10, the ANDLE extension is satisfied, and the DO WHILE loop is performed.

▶BEGSR (BEGIN SUBROUTINE)

The BEGSR operation marks the beginning of a subroutine. Factor 1 must contain a unique name for the subroutine. That unique name is used as the target of the EXSR (perform subroutine) and CAS*xx* (compare factor 1 and factor 2, then perform subroutine) operations. Evoking a subroutine is faster than evoking a subprocedure or subprogram. Conditioning and control level-break indicators are not valid for this operation. Resulting indicators are not valid for this operation.

Factor 1	OpCode	Factor 2	Result Field	Resulting Indicators		
Subroutine name	BEGSR					

*See also ENDSR, EXSR, CASxx, *INZSR, and *PSSR*

Factor 1 is required and must contain a unique subroutine name. If factor 1 contains *PSSR, the subroutine is the program status subroutine and is called before the RPG exception/error handling routine to handle runtime exceptions. If factor 1 contains *INZR, the subroutine is the initialization subroutine and is called immediately after the RPG cycle completes the *INIT routine—before first page output (i.e., 1P output) is performed. If factor 1 contains *TERMSR, the subroutine is the termination subroutine and is automatically called when the program ends.

The control-level indicator can contain the subroutine identifying letters SR. This identifier is optional and is used only on the first and last lines of a subroutine for identification purposes.

Example 5.9: Performing a subroutine.

```
.....CSRn01Factor1+++++++OpCode(ex)Factor2+++++++Result++++++++Len++DcHiLoEq
0010 C                    EXSR      COUNT
0020 CSR    COUNT         BEGSR
0030 C                    READ      FILE                              75
0040 C                    IF        NOT %EOF
0050 C                    ADD       1              C
0060 C                    ENDIF
0070 CSR    ENDCNT        ENDSR
```

In Example 5.9, the subroutine COUNT is called from the "main line" calculations through the use of the EXSR operation. The subroutine COUNT is delimited with the BEGSR operation on line 20 and the ENDSR (End Subroutine) operation on line 70.

▶ BITOFF (SET BITS OFF)

The BITOFF operation causes the bits specified by factor 2 to be set to '0' in the result field. Bits that are not referenced in factor 2 are unchanged in the result field. This operation is normally used in conjunction with the BITON (Set Bits On) operation to build character values that are less than X'40'. Resulting indicators are not valid for this operation.

Factor 1	OpCode	Factor 2	Result Field	Resulting Indicators		
	BITOFF	'bits to set off'	char variable			

See also BITON and TESTB

Factor 2 can contain a *bit pattern*. The bit pattern can be a named constant or a literal value containing bit numbers, a one-position character field, or a hexadecimal literal value. If a field name or hexadecimal literal value is specified for factor 2, then the bits that are on in factor 2 are set on in the result field. For fields and hexadecimal literal values, bits that are off in factor 2 are not changed in the result field. The result field must contain a one-position character field or array element. For more information on bit patterns, see the subheading TESTB (Test Bit Pattern).

In Example 5.10, bit 1 in the first 35 elements of the array NAME is set off. If the array NAME contains some text, this routine would convert that text to lowercase.

Example 5.10: Converting the contents of an array to lowercase letters.

```
.....DName++++++++++EUDS.......Length+TDc.Functions++++++++++++++++++++++++++++
0010 D NAME            S             1    DIM( 35)


.....CSRn01Factor1+++++++OpCode(ex)Factor2+++++++Result++++++++Len++DcHiLoEq
0020 C                   DO        35         X
0030 C                   BITOFF    '1'        NAME(X)
0040 C                   ENDDO
```

▶ BITON (SET BITS ON)

The BITON operation causes the bits indicated in factor 2 to be set to '1' in the result field. Bits that are not referenced in factor 2 are unchanged in the result field.

This operation is normally used in conjunction with the BITOFF (Set Bits Off) operation to build character values that are less than X'40'. While it also can be used to convert lowercase letters to uppercase, the XLATE operation provides a more portable method of conversion. Resulting indicators are not valid for this operation.

Factor 1	OpCode	Factor 2	Result Field	Resulting Indicators		
	BITON	'bits to set on'	char variable			

See also %BITAND, %BITOR, %BITXOR, %BITNOT, BITOFF and TESTB

Factor 2 can contain a bit pattern. The bit pattern can be a named constant or a literal value containing bit numbers, a one-position character field, or a hexadecimal literal value. If a field name or hexadecimal literal value is specified for factor 2, then the bits that are on in factor 2 are set on in the result field. For fields and hexadecimal literal values, bits that are off in factor 2 are not changed in the result field.

The result field must contain a one-position character field or array element. For more information on bit patterns, see the subheading TESTB (Test Bit Pattern).

In Example 5.11, bit 1 in the first 35 elements of the array ITEM is set on. If the array ITEM contains some text, this routine converts that text to uppercase.

Example 5.11: Converting the contents of an array to uppercase letters.

```
.....DName++++++++++EUDS.......Length+TDc.Functions++++++++++++++++++++++++++++
0010 D ITEM            S             1    DIM(35)

.....CSRn01Factor1+++++++OpCode(ex)Factor2+++++++Result++++++++Len++DcHiLoEq
0020 C                   DO        35          X
0030 C                   BITON    '1'          ITEM(X)
0040 C                   ENDDO
```

If factor 2 contains a bit pattern literal value, it must conform to the following guidelines:

- It must be left-justified in factor 2.
- It must be enclosed in single quotation marks.
- It must contain one or more unique numerals ranging from 0 to 7.

Bits 0, 1, 2, and 3 are the top half of the byte. Bits 4, 5, 6, and 7 are the bottom half of the byte. Bits that are not referenced in factor 2 go unchanged. The bit pattern for factor 2 is described as follows:

Bit numbers that can be set ➔   Ø123 4567

Value of bits that are set ➔   8421 8421

In Example 5.12, Line 10 sets off all the bits in field FLDA. Line 20 sets on all the bits in the field FLDB. Line 30 sets off bits 0, 1, 3, 4, 5, and 7 in the field ATTR. Line 40 sets on bits 2 and 6 in field ATTR. Line 50 set on bits 0, 1, 2, and 3 (the mask for X'F0'). Bits 4, 5, 6, and 7 are not changed.

Example 5.12: More examples of bit manipulation.

```
.....CSRnØ1Factor1+++++++OpCode(ex)Factor2+++++++Result++++++++Len++DcHiLoEq
     *  Set off all the bits in FLDA.
ØØ1Ø C                    BITOFF    'Ø1234567'   FLDA               1
     *  Set on all the bits in FLDB.
ØØ2Ø C                    BITON     'Ø1234567'   FLDB               1
     *  Change field ATTR to x'22' (two operations required).
ØØ3Ø C                    BITOFF    'Ø13457'     ATTR               1
ØØ4Ø C                    BITON     '26'         ATTR               1
     *  Set on bits Ø to 3 in HEXVAL.
ØØ5Ø C                    BITON     X'FØ'        HEXVAL             1
```

In Example 5.12, Line 10 sets off all the bits in field FLDA. Line 20 sets on all the bits in the field FLDB. Line 30 sets off bits 0, 1, 3, 4, 5, and 7 in the field ATTR. Line 40 sets on bits 2 and 6 in field ATTR. Line 50 set on bits 0, 1, 2, and 3 (the mask for X'F0'). Bits 4, 5, 6, and 7 are not changed.

Use of the BITON and BITOFF operations has been substantially reduced since the introduction of hexadecimal literal values to the language. BITON and BITOFF traditionally have been used to create characters where the values are less than X'40' (a blank). With hexadecimal literal values, a simple MOVE or MOVEL accomplishes the same task and is much more readable.

▶ CABxx (COMPARE AND BRANCH)

The CABxx operation compares factor 1 to factor 2. If the relationship test is true, then a branch is performed to the label specified in the result field, and any resulting indicators are set on accordingly.

Factor 1	OpCode	Factor 2	Result Field	Resulting Indicators		
Compare value 1	CABxx	compare value 2	[label]	[1>2]	[1<2]	[1=2]

See also TAG, GOTO, ENDSR, and LEAVESR

The result field is optional and contains the label of a TAG or ENDSR statement that is the target of the branch. If the result field is omitted, at least one resulting indicator must be specified. Resulting indicators are optional unless no result field (label) is specified or when *xx* of the CAB*xx*

Resulting Indicator Legend			
Columns	Ind.	Usage	Set-On Condition
71 - 72	1	[1>2]	Factor 1 is greater than factor 2.
73 - 74	2	[1<2]	Factor 1 is less than factor 2.
75 - 76	3	[1=2]	Factor 1 is equal to factor 2.

operation is blank. Under these situations, at least one resulting indicator is required.

Example 5.13 shows several examples of the use of compare and branch operations.

Example 5.13: Branching to certain labels based on the contents of various fields.

```
.....CSRn01Factor1+++++++OpCode(ex)Factor2+++++++Result++++++++Len++DcHiLoEq
0010 C                    Z-ADD     100          A               3 0
0020 C                    Z-ADD     200          B               3 0
0030 C        A           CABEQ     B            LAB1
0040 C        A           CABLT     B            LAB2                 545658
0050 C        A           CAB       B            LAB3                 545658

0060 C  LAB1              TAG
0070 C  LAB2              TAG
0080 C  LAB3              TAG
```

▶ CALL (DYNAMIC CALL TO ANOTHER PROGRAM)

The CALL operation temporarily interrupts the program, and then dynamically loads and runs another program.

Factor 1	OpCode	Factor 2	Result Field	Resulting Indicators		
	CALL(E)	program name	[parameter list]		[error]	[LR}

See also CALLB, CALLP, PARM, and PLIST

Factor 2 must contain the name of the program to be run. Factor 2 can be either a quoted literal value, named constant, field, array element, data structure, or data-structure subfield name.

The result field is optional and may contain the name of a parameter list (PLIST) label. The parameter list is

Resulting Indicator Legend			
Columns	Ind.	Usage	Set-On Condition
71 - 72	1	N/A	
73 - 74	2	[error]	An error occurred during the operation.
75 - 76	3	[LR]	The called program ended with its LR indicator set on.

used to pass parameters between the programs. If the parameter list is omitted and parameters are required, the CALL operation may be immediately followed by the PARM operation to identify the parameters.

In Example 5.14, the program CUSTINQ is called and is passed two parameters: a customer number and some search data. The program CUSTINQ accepts parameters and those parameters are defined immediately following the CALL operation. Therefore, a parameter list (PLIST) is not needed in the result field of the CALL operation.

Example 5.14: Calling a program and passing two parameters.

```
.....CSRnØ1Factor1+++++++OpCode(ex)Factor2+++++++Result++++++++Len++DcHiLoEq
ØØ1Ø C                   CALL      'CUSTINQ'                        56
ØØ2Ø C                   PARM                    SEARCH
ØØ3Ø C                   PARM                    CSTNBR
```

In Example 5.15, the program name CUSTINQ is defined by the named constant PGMTOCALL (line 50) and is used by the CALL operation (line 60) to call the program CUSTINQ in the library ORDLIB. Because the data structure PARMDS is passed as the parameter (line 70), the data contained in all subfields within the data structure is accessible by the called program. The called program, CUSTINQ, should contain a parameter similar to PARMDS to receive the data.

Example 5.15: Calling a program and passing a data structure name as the parameter.

```
.....DName++++++++++EUDS.......Length+TDc.Functions++++++++++++++++++++++++++++++
0010 D ParmDS            DS
0020 D   CustNbr                      7p 0
0030 D   SearchData                   50A
0040 D   RtnCode                      1A

0050 D PgmToCall         C                        Const('ORDLIB/CUSTINQ')

.....CSRn01Factor1+++++++OpCode(ex)Factor2+++++++Result++++++++Len++DcHiLoEq
0060 C                   CALL      PgmToCall                              56
0070 C                   PARM                     PARMDS
```

In Example 5.15, the program name CUSTINQ is defined by the named constant PGMTOCALL (line 50) and is used by the CALL operation (line 60) to call the program CUSTINQ in the library ORDLIB. The data structure PARMDS is passed as the parameter (line 70), so the data contained in all subfields within the data structure is accessible by the called program. The *called* program, CUSTINQ, should contain a parameter similar to PARMDS to receive the data. (For more information on parameters and parameter lists, see the PARM and PLIST operation codes in Examples 5.104 and 5.105.)

Qualified Program Name

A called program can be qualified to a library by appending the library to the program name. If a library name is omitted, the library list or path is searched for the program name. Typically, a program is qualified to a library using one of the following methods:

- **library/program** Using the OS/400 convention, the forward slash qualifies the library to the program; the library name is followed by the program name.

- **d:\directory\program[.exe]** Using the SPEC 1170 convention, the back slash qualifies the program name to a directory or subdirectory. Also, a colon can be used to qualify the disk drive on which the program resides.

> **NOTE:** *The terms path and folder are sometimes used in place of directory. Also, the file suffix is optional.*

▶ CALLB (CALL A BOUND PROCEDURE/PROGRAM)

The CALLB operation evokes a subprogram or subprocedure that has been statically linked (bound) into the main program.

Factor 1	OpCode	Factor 2	Result Field	Resulting Indicators		
	CALLB(D E)	'procedure name'	[parameter list]		[error]	[LR}

See also CALL, CALLP, PARM, and PLIST

Factor 2 must contain the name of the procedure to be called. Factor 2 must contain a value that can be evaluated at compile time. This includes a quoted literal, a named constant, or a procedure pointer.

The name within the quotes (specified for factor 2) is case sensitive. It must be in the proper upper-/lowercase character mix to match the called procedure name. Factor 2 cannot contain a character field name.

The result field is optional and may contain the name of a parameter list (PLIST) label. The parameter list is used to pass parameters between the programs. If the parameter list is omitted and parameters are required, the CALLB operation may be immediately followed by one or more PARM operations to identify the parameters.

Resulting Indicator Legend			
Columns	Ind.	Usage	Set-On Condition
71 - 72	1	N/A	
73 - 74	2	[error]	An error occurred during the operation.
75 - 76	3	[LR]	The called program ended with its LR indicator set on.

Extender	Description
E	ERROR – Causes the %ERROR and %STATUS built-in functions to be set if an error occurs during the operation.
D	Operational Descriptor – Causes additional information about each parameter to be passed to the called procedure.

In Example 5.16, line 30 uses the named constant defined on line 10 to call the procedure. Note that, by using an RPG name in factor 2, uppercasing and lowercasing can be ignored. Line 40 uses the procedure pointer PGETCURSOR to call the procedure. Also, a parameter list is named in the result field. Line 50 uses the standard CALLB operation with a literal specified in factor 2. Note that the literal must be the correct uppercase/lowercase character pattern—matching the actual procedure name.

Example 5.16: Calling a bound procedure.

```
.....DName++++++++++EUDS.......Length+TDc.Functions++++++++++++++++++++++++++++++
0010 D  GetCsrLoc      C                      Const('QsnGetCsrLoc')
0020 D  pGetCursor     S                *     INZ('%paddr('QsnGetCsrLoc')) PROCPTR

.....CSRn01Factor1+++++++OpCode(ex)Factor2+++++++Result+++++++++Len++DcHiLoEq
0030 C                    CALLB      GETCSRLOC
0040 C                    CallB      pGetCursor      TheParms
0050 C                    CallB      'QsnGetCsrLoc'
```

In Example 5.16, lines 30, 40, and 50 all produce the same result. They illustrate the three basic methods of calling a bound procedure with the CALLB operation.

The names defined on lines 10 and 20 in Example 5.16 can be used in any combination of upper- and lowercase. However, the value they represent, 'QsnGetCsrLoc', must be in the correct uppercase/lowercase format or the compiler won't able to resolve the procedure's address correctly at compile time.

Any procedure can be called with the CALLB operation. The procedure must exist at compile time within a *MODULE object. That *MODULE object name is specified as an argument (parameter) of the compiler when the program/procedure containing the CALLB operation is compiled.

CALLP (CALL A PROTOTYPED PROCEDURE)

The CALLP operation evokes a statically bound procedure or dynamically calls a program. The procedure or program specified in factor 2 must be defined with a prototype on the definition specifications.

Factor 1	OpCode	Extended Factor 2
	CALLP(E M R)	procedure-name(parm1 : parm2 ...)

See also CALL and CALLB

Factor 2 must contain the name of a prototype. The prototype (which can also be a prototype for a procedure or program) must be prototyped on a definition specification. The actual name of the procedure or program to call is specified on the EXTPGM or EXTPROC keyword of the definition specification. If EXTPROC or EXTPGM is not specified,

Extender	Description
E	ERROR – Causes the %ERROR and %STATUS built-in functions to be set if an error occurs during the operation.
M	If expressions are specified for any of the parameters, the maximum-digits format for expressions is used.
R	If expressions are specified for any of the parameters, the result value's decimal positions are used for any intermediate result values. This is only useful, on this operation, when the %DEC built-in function is specified for one of the parameter values.

then EXTPROC is assumed and the name on the definition specification (positions 7 to 21) is used as the procedure name.

Use this operation in place of the CALL and CALLB operations. It combines the function of these other operations and provides a single, consistent method for calling other procedures and programs.

In Example 5.17, the AS/400 system API (QWCRSVAL) is used to retrieve the serial number of the system. Lines 120 to 170 are the prototype for QWCRSVAL. The EXTPGM keyword identifies the external name of the program that is being prototyped, and GETSYSVALUE is the name assigned to the prototype. The prototype name is the name that must be used within the RPG program.

Lines 20 and 21 use the CALLP operation to call QWCRSVAL. The prototype name GETSYSVALUE is used on line 20 to identify the program to call. The program parameters are specified as arguments of the GETSYSVAL program, and are separated by colons.

Example 5.17: Calling a procedure or program that has been prototyped.

```
.....DName+++++++++++EUDSFrom+++To+++++TDc.Functions+++++++++++++++++++++++++++++
0010 D APIerror   DS
0020 D* Number of bytes in error return code parameter
0030 D Length                     10i 0  INZ(%size(ApiError))
0040 D ByteAvail                  10i 0  INZ(0)
0050 D MsgID                       7A
0060 D MsgText                    80A
       *
0080 D nSysValLen     S           10I0   INZ(%Size(SRLNBR))
0090 D nCount         S           10I0   INZ(1)
0100 D SrlNbr         S            8A
       *
0120 D GetSysValue    PR                 ExtPgm('QWCRSVAL')
0130 D  gsvRtnVar                  8A
0140 D  gsvSVLen                  10I    Const
0150 D  gsvCount                  10I
0160 D  gsvSysVal                 10A    Const
0170 D  gsvApiErr                 96A

.....CSRn01..............OpCode(ex)Extended-factor2++++++++++++++++++++++++++++++++
0200 C                   CallP    GetSysvalue('QSRLNBR' : nSysValLen : nCount :
0210 C                                        SrlNbr : APIError )
```

▶ CAS*xx* (COMPARE AND PERFORM SUBROUTINE)

The CAS*xx* operation compares factor 1 to factor 2. If the result is true, one or both of the following occurs:

- The subroutine (internal call) named in the result field is performed.
- Any resulting indicators are set on.

Factor 1	OpCode	Factor 2	Result Field	Resulting Indicators		
[compare value 1]	CAS*xx*	[compare value2]	subroutine	[1>2]	[1<2]	[1=2]

See also EXSR, BEGSR, ENDSR, IF, SELECT, and WHEN

Factor 1 can contain any valid data type. Factor 2 must contain a value with attributes similar to factor 1. For example, if factor 1 contains a numeric field, factor 2 must contain a numeric value (such as another numeric field), a numeric literal, or a numeric-figurative constant.

Resulting Indicator Legend			
Columns	Ind.	Usage	Set-On Condition
71 - 72	1	[1>2]	Factor 1 is greater than factor 2.
73 - 74	2	[1<2]	Factor 1 is less than factor 2.
75 - 76	3	[1=2]	Factor 1 is equal to factor 2.

The *xx* is optional and can be any valid Boolean operator (EQ, GE, GT, LE, LT, NE, or blanks). See Table 5.9. The Boolean operator controls the comparison and whether the subroutine specified in the result field is called.

At least one resulting indicator must be specified when the *xx* operator is blank. The resulting indicator(s) is set on based on the result of the comparison. If factor 1 and factor 2 are not specified, then no resulting indicators can be specified.

If the comparison between factor 1 and factor 2 is met, the subroutine specified in the result field is called. Upon completion of the subroutine, control passes to the END or ENDCS statement associated with this CAS*xx* group. If the comparison is not met, control passes to the next sequential CAS*xx* operation. If no additional CAS*xx*

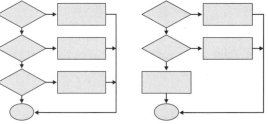

Figure 5.1: Logic flow of the two forms of CASxx.

operations are specified for this CASxx group, control passes to the END or ENDCS statement associated with this CASxx group.

If xx is blank, the subroutine named in the result field is performed unconditionally (after any comparison is made). This form of CASxx (the CAS operation) is often used as a catchall routine at the end of a CASxx group.

The IF and SELECT-WHEN-OTHER operations provide an in-line form of the CASE group. Whereas CASxx calls a subroutine, these other operations control operations that immediately follow them. When using the IFxx operation, try to avoid nesting the IF statements more than three levels deep. If further nesting is required, the CASxx and SELECT-WHEN-OTHER operations provide better readability. For more information on in-line CASE groups, see the subheadings IFxx (If Conditional Comparison) and SELECT (Start In-Line Case Group).

The CASE group of a CASxx operation is a list of one or more consecutive CASxx statements that conditionally perform (i.e., call) an internal subroutine. The CASE group is ended with a single ENDCS statement. An ENDCS statement must be used to close the CASE group, regardless of the number of CASxx statements. In Example 5.18, assume the fields are set to the following values:

```
QTYORD=100, QTYOH=200
ORDSTS='S', SHPSTS='S'
```

The result of the comparison (line 10) is true; therefore, subroutine SHIP is called.

Example 5.18: Testing for less than, equal, and a catch-all situation.

```
.....CSRn01Factor1+++++++OpCode(ex)Factor2+++++++Result++++++++Len++DcHiLoEq
0010 C       QTYORD       CASLT     QTYOH         SHIP
0020 C       ORDSTS       CASEQ     SHPSTS        BILL               545658
0030 C                    CAS                     POST
0040 C                    ENDCS
```

After subroutine SHIP has completed, control returns to the ENDCS statement associated with the CASE group (line 40); lines 20 and 30 are not performed. Figure 5.1 illustrates the logic of the two CASE constructs.

In Figure 5.1, the left-most flowchart illustrates the traditional CASE construct—a relationship test followed by a process; another relationship test is followed by a process, and is repeated as needed.

The right-most flowchart shown in Figure 5.1 illustrates an alternative form of the CASE construct—a relationship test followed by a process; another relationship test is followed by a process; and then a default process, which is performed when all of the CASE relationship tests are false.

Only one process of a CASE group is performed when the CASE group is entered. After a process is performed, control passes to the corresponding ENDCS statement for the CASE group.

▶ CAT (CONCATENATION)

The CAT operation concatenates factor 1 and factor 2, placing the concatenated string in the result field.

Factor 1	OpCode	Factor 2	Result Field	Resulting Indicators		
[string 1]	CAT (P)	string 2 [:blank-count]	concatenated result			

See also EVAL, +, MOVE, MOVEL, and %TRIM

Factor 1 is optional and can contain any character variable, constant, or named constant. If factor 1 is omitted, the result field is used in place of factor 1. Factor 2 is required and can contain any character variable, constant, or named constant.

Factor 2 accepts one optional parameter: BLANK-COUNT. This parameter is used to specify the number of blanks inserted between the last nonblank character of factor 1 and the first nonblank character of factor 2. If the BLANK-COUNT parameter is omitted, factor 2 is concatenated to the end of factor 1. BLANK-COUNT can be a literal value, named constant, numeric field, or numeric-data structure subfield.

The result field must be a character field, array element, data structure, or data-structure subfield. If the length of the result field is less than the sum of the result of the CAT operation, the concatenated value is stored left justified in the result field.

The P operation extender can be specified to cause the result to be padded; that is, the result field is replaced before the CAT operation is performed. In Example 5.19, the constant 'RPG   ' is concatenated with 'Lang':

- After line 10 is performed, NAME1 contains: 'RPG   Lang   '
- After line 20 is performed, NAME2 contains: 'RPGLang   '
- After line 30 is performed, NAME3 contains: 'RPGIV   '
- After line 40 is performed, NAME3 contains: 'RPGIV Language'

Example 5.19: Concatenating two values.

```
.....CSRn01Factor1+++++++OpCode(ex)Factor2+++++++Result++++++++Len++DcHiLoEq
0010 C      'RPG    '      CAT(p)    'Lang'       NAME1        15
0020 C      'RPG    '      CAT(p)    'Lang':0     NAME2        15
0030 C      'RPG    '      CAT(p)    'IV':0       NAME3        15
0040 C                     CAT       'Language':1 NAME3
```

The CAT operation is typically used to build proper salutations, such as: 'Dear President Kennedy,' or to format an address, such as: 'Washington, DC 20500'. In Example 5.20, the fields shown in Figure 5.2 are initialized as indicated.

```
Positions: *...v... 1 ...v... 2 ...v... 3 ...V
FNAME    = 'John                              '
MIDDLE   = 'F'
LNAME    = 'Kennedy                 '
ADDR     = '1600 Pennsylvania Ave         '
CITY     = 'Washington            '
STATE    = 'DC  '
ZIP      = '20500      '
```

Figure 5.2: Contents of fields used in Example 5.19.

The output from Example 5.20 is as follows:

President John F. Kennedy
1600 Pennsylvania Ave
Washington, DC 20500

Example 5.20: Using CAT to build an address line.

```
.....C*Rn01Factor1+++++++OpCode(ex)Factor2+++++++Result++++++++Len++DcHiLoEq
     C     'President'    CAT (p)  FNAME:1      ADDR1        35
     C                    If       MIDDLE  <> *Blanks
     C                    CAT      MIDDLE:1     ADDR1
     C                    CAT      '.':0        ADDR1
     C                    EndIf
     C                    CAT      LNAME:1      ADDR1
     *   Second, simply copy the street address.
     C                    MOVEL(p) ADDR         ADDR2        35
     *   Third, build the city, st zip line.
     C     CITY           CAT(p)   ',':0        ADDR3        35
     C                    CAT      STATE:1      ADDR3
     C                    CAT      ZIP:2        ADDR3
```

► CHAIN (RANDOM RECORD ACCESS/READ)

The CHAIN operation retrieves a single record using the key index or relative record number specified in factor 1 from the file represented in factor 2.

Factor 1	OpCode	Factor 2	Result Field	Resulting Indicators		
key value or record	CHAIN(N E)	format name		n/f	[error]	
key value or record	CHAIN(N E)	file name	[data structure]	n/f	[error]	

See also READ, READE, READPE, SETLL, SETGT, WRITE, UPDATE, DELETE, and UNLOCK

Factor 1 is required and must be a constant index, a constant relative record number, a field containing an index, a field containing a relative record number, or a key list. Factor 2 is required and must conform to the following rules:

- For an externally described file, a file or record format name may be specified.

- For a program-described file, only a file name may be specified.

- For a workstation file, only the name of a subfile record format may be specified.

Resulting Indicator Legend			
Columns	Ind.	Usage	Set-On Condition
71 - 72	1	n/f	The record identified by the key value or record number in factor 1 does not exist in the file specified in factor 2.
73 - 74	2	[error]	An error occurred during the operation.
75 - 76	3	N/A	Not used by this operation.

Extender	Description
E	ERROR – Causes the %ERROR and %STATUS built-in functions to be set if an error occurs during the operation.
N	NO LOCK – Causes the operation to avoid placing a record lock on records for files that have been open for update operations.

The result field can be specified for a program-described file only. The result field can contain the name of a data structure into which the retrieved record's data is placed. When a record is retrieved, the data is placed directly into the data structure.

The following characteristics apply when a database record is accessed with the CHAIN operation.

- For INPUT files, the record is retrieved, but no record locking occurs.
- For OUTPUT-only files, this operation is not valid.
- For UPDATE files, if the N operation extender is specified, no record locking is applied; if no operation extender is specified, the record is retrieved and locked until it is released by one of the following:
  - Another READ, READE, READP, READPE, or CHAIN operation.
  - The record is updated by an UPDATE or EXCEPT operation.
  - The record is deleted by the DELETE or the EXCEPT with DEL operations.
  - The record is implicitly released by one of the following operations:
    - Except operation to an empty output format (EXCEPT).
    - Unlock the record (UNLOCK).
    - Set lower limit (SETLL).
    - Set greater than (SETGT).
    - Force end of data (FEOD).
    - Close file (CLOSE).

In Example 5.21, the key list PART contains two key fields: the part number (PRTNBR) and the date sold (DTESLD). The key list PART is used to retrieve a record from the record format PARTFMT (line 40).

If a record does not exist with a matching index, resulting indicator 1 (indicator 54) is set on. That indicator is then placed into the field NF (line 50), which is subsequently used to control the flow of the program's logic.

Example 5.21: Accessing an externally described file using a key list.

```
.....CSRn01Factor1+++++++OpCode(ex)Factor2+++++++Result++++++++Len++DcHiLoEq
0010 C     PART           KLIST
0020 C                    KFLD                     PRTNBR
0030 C                    KFLD                     DTESLD

0040 C     PART           CHAIN     PARTFMT                              54

0050 C                    MOVE      *IN54          NF
0060 C     NF             CASEQ     *ON            ERROR
0070 C                    CAS                      UPDATE
0080 C                    END
```

In Example 5.22, a program-described file is accessed through the INDEX key field. The index value is assembled using the fields PRTNBR (part number) and DTESLD (date sold). Then the CHAIN operation is used to access the file PARTMST. If a record exists with an index value that matches factor 1, the data from that record is moved into the data structure PARTDS. Resulting indicator 1 (indicator 54) remains off.

Example 5.22: Reading a program-described file into a data structure.

```
.....CSRn01Factor1+++++++OpCode(ex)Factor2+++++++Result++++++++Len++DcHiLoEq
0010 C                    MOVEL     PRTNBR         INDEX
0020 C                    MOVE      DTESLD         INDEX

0030 C         INDEX      CHAIN     PARTMST        PARTDS              54

0040 C                    MOVE      *IN54          NF
0050 C         NF         CASEQ     *ON            ERROR
0060 C                    CAS                      UPDATE
0070 C                    END
```

▶ CHECK (VERIFY A CHARACTER STRING)

The CHECK operation verifies that each character of factor 2 is one of the list of characters in factor 1. This is accomplished by comparing the characters of factor 2, character by character, to the list of characters in factor 1 until a difference is detected or until the end of factor 2 is reached. If a difference is detected, its position is returned to the result field.

Factor 1	OpCode	Factor 2	Result Field	Resulting Indicators		
check list	CHECK (E)	base value [: start]	[position(s)]		[error]	[found]

See also CHECK, SCAN, and %FOUND

Factor 1 is required and must contain a character field, data structure, data structure subfield, array element, constant, or named constant. Factor 1 contains a list of one or more characters that is used to verify factor 2. Factor 2 is required and can contain a field, data structure, data-structure subfield, array element, constant, or named constant that is verified against factor 1.

Factor 2 accepts one optional parameter: START-POSITION. This parameter is used to specify the starting position of factor 2 where the verification begins. If the START-POSITION parame-

Resulting Indicator Legend

Columns	Ind.	Usage	Set-On Condition
71 - 72	1	N/A	Not used by this operation code.
73 - 74	2	[error]	The operation ended in error.
75 - 76	3	[found]	A character other than those specified in factor 1 is found in factor 2.

Extender	Description
E	ERROR – Causes the %ERROR and %STATUS built-in functions to be set if an error occurs during the operation.

ter is omitted, verification begins in position one of factor 2. START-POSITION can be a literal value, named constant, or numeric field.

The result field is optional and can contain a numeric field, array, or array element. The CHECK operation returns the position within factor 2 that is not contained in the list of characters located in factor 1. If all the characters of factor 2 match factor 1, zero is returned to the result field. If the result field contains an array, the positions of as many occurrences of invalid characters as there are array elements can be returned with one CHECK operation.

The CHECK operation is primarily used for two functions. One function is to find the first character position of factor 2 that is not in factor 1. An example would be to find the first nonblank character position of the field in factor 2. The second function is to verify that factor 2 contains valid characters—those specified in factor 1. An example would be to verify that factor 2 contains only numbers or only lowercase alphabetic characters.

In Example 5.23, the character field INPUT is verified against the named constant HEXCHARS.

Example 5.23: Verifying factor 2 against a list of characters.

```
.....DName++++++++++..C...................Functions++++++++++++++++++++++++++++++
0001 D HexChars        C              Const('1234567890ABCDEFabcdef')

.....CSRn01Factor1+++++++OpCode(ex)Factor2+++++++Result++++++++Len++DcHiLoEq
0002 C      HexChars    Check      Input        Pos             5 0
0003 C                  If         Pos > 0
0004 C                  EXSR                     Error
0005 C                  EndIF
```

If INPUT contains any characters other than those specified for HEXCHARS, the position within INPUT of the invalid character is returned in the POS field.

Before:
```
            *...v... 1 ...v... 2 ...v... 3
   INPUT =  'FDE6GE7B                    '
   POS   =  0
```
After:
```
            *...v... 1 ...v... 2 ...v... 3
   INPUT =  'FDE6GE7B                    '
   POS   =  5
```

In Example 5.24, the CHECK operation is used to locate the first nonblank position in the field LASTNAME.

Example 5.24: Using CHECK to find first nonblank character in a field.

```
.....CSRn01Factor1+++++++OpCode(ex)Factor2+++++++Result++++++++Len++DcHiLoEq
0001 C         ' '              CHECK     LASTNAME     NonBlank          5 0
       * Left justify the value within the field
0002 C                         If        NonBlank > 0
0003 C                         Eval      LastName = %subst(LastName : NonBlank)
0004 C                         EndIF
```

The %SUBST (substring) built-in function is used to left justify the value.

Before:

```
                    *...v... 1 ...v... 2 ...v... 3
    LASTNAME  =  '    Kennedy                    '
```

After:

```
                    *...v... 1 ...v... 2 ...v... 3
    LASTNAME  =  'Kennedy                        '
```

Example 5.25 begins by locating the first nonblank position of the LSTNAM field.

Example 5.25: Using CHECK to build a proper salutation.

```
.....C*Rn01Factor1+++++++OpCode(ex)Factor2+++++++Result++++++++Len++DcHiLoEq
0001 C         ' '              CHECK     LASTNAME     FirstBlank        5 0
0002 C                         Eval      LastName = %SUBST(lastname : FirstBlank)
0003 C         FIRSTNAME       CAT(p)    LASTNAME:1   NAME             30
```

Using the %SUBST built-in function, the value is left justified. Finally, the CAT operation is used to build the concatenated salutation.

Before:

```
                      *...v... 1 ...v... 2 ...v... 3
    FIRSTNAME  =  'Robert                         '
    LASTNAME   =  '    Kennedy                     '
    NAME       =  '                                '
```

After:

```
                      *...v... 1 ...v... 2 ...v... 3
    FIRSTNAME  =  'Robert                         '
    LISTNAME   =  'Kennedy                         '
    NAME       =  'Robert Kennedy                  '
```

▶CHECKR (VERIFY RIGHT TO LEFT)

The CHECKR operation verifies that each character of factor 2 is contained in the list of characters in factor 1. This is accomplished by comparing each character in factor 2, starting with the right-most position, to the list of characters in factor 1. The verification stops when a difference is detected or the first position of factor 2 is reached. If a difference is detected, its position is returned to the result field.

Factor 1	OpCode	Factor 2	Result Field	Resulting Indicators		
check list	CHECKR (E)	char value [: start]	[position(s)]		[error]	[found]

See also CHECK and SCAN

Factor 1 is required and must contain a character value. The character value identifies the valid characters that can appear in factor 2. Factor 2 is required and must contain a character value. This character value is verified against the list of characters specified in factor 1. Verifications begin with the right-most character in factor 2 or, if specified, with the *start position*.

Resulting Indicator Legend

Columns	Ind.	Usage	Set-On Condition
71 - 72	1	N/A	Not used by this op code.
73 - 74	2	[error]	The operation ended in error.
75 - 76	3	[found]	A character other than those specified in factor 1 is found in factor 2.

Extender	Description
E	ERROR – Causes the %ERROR and %STATUS built-in functions to be set if an error occurs during the operation.

Factor 2 accepts one optional parameter: START-POSITION. This parameter is used to specify the starting position where the verification begins in factor 2. If the START-POSITION is omitted, verification begins in the right-most position of the value specified for factor 2. The START-POSITION can be any numeric value.

The result field is optional and, if specified, must contain the name of a numeric field, array, or array element. The CHECKR operation returns the right-most position of factor 2 that is not listed in factor 1 to the result field. Multiple unmatched positions can be located with a single CHECKR operation by specifying a numeric array in the result field. If an array is specified for the result field, the operation is repeated until all available array elements have been filled or until the beginning of factor 2 is reached.

If no result field is specified, resulting indicator 3 is required and can be used to signal when a character other than those specified in factor 1 is found in factor 2. Alternatively, the %FOUND built-in function can be used to detect when the value in factor 1 is found in factor 2.

If the result field is not specified, resulting indicator 3 is required. Indicator 3 also is used to signal when a character is found in factor 2 that is other than those specified in factor 1. The CHECKR operation is the complement of the CHECK operation. The CHECK operation begins checking from the left and continues checking to the right. The CHECKR operation begins checking on the right and continues checking to the left.

The CHECKR operation is useful for determining the length of the data in a field. When variable-length data is used in an RPG program, the program must maintain the length of the data. The CHECKR operation can be used to retrieve the length of the data, and then store that length as a 2-byte integer field that precedes the variable-length field's data.

For example, by specifying a blank in factor 1, the CHECKR operation returns the position of the last nonblank in factor 2. This position is the length of the data in the field specified for factor 2 (see Example 5.26).

Example 5.26: Finding the length of data for a variable-length field.

```
.....DName+++++++++++EUDS.......To/Len+TDc.Functions+++++++++++++++++++++++++++++++
0001 D VarLenText      DS
0002 D   Length                        5I 0 INZ
0003 D   Title                       512A

.....C*Rn01Factor1+++++++OpCode(ex)Factor2+++++++Result++++++++Len++DcHiLoEq
0004 C        'President'   CAT (p)   'John':1       Title                 35
0005 C                      CAT       'F.':1         Title
0006 C                      CAT       'Kennedy':1    Title
0007 C               ' '    CHECKR    Title          LENGTH
```

After the CAT operations on lines 4 to 6 are performed, the length field is set to 25 and the title field contains the following:

```
 *...v....1....v....2....v....3....v
'President John F. Kennedy                 '
```

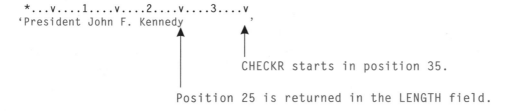

CHECKR starts in position 35.

Position 25 is returned in the LENGTH field.

▶ CLEAR (CLEAR DATA SET)

The CLEAR operation sets the result field to blanks, zeros, or the logical '0', depending on its attribute. The CLEAR operation is primarily used to clear all the subfields of a data structure or all the fields of a display-file record format.

Factor 1	OpCode	Factor 2	Result Field	Resulting Indicators		
[*NOKEY]	CLEAR	[*ALL]	variable to clear			

*See also RESET and *INZSR*

Factor 1 is optional and can contain the constant *NOKEY when the result field contains a record format of a keyed database (DISK) file. This indicates that the key fields of the record are to be preserved (i.e., not cleared) when the record format is cleared.

Factor 2 is optional and can contain the constant *ALL. When *ALL is specified and the result field contains an array, multiple-occurrence data structure, or a record format that is declared as input-only or output-only, all elements, occurrences, or fields are cleared in that object. The result field is required and can contain a field, data structure, data-structure subfield, record format, array, array element, table, or named indicator.

If the result field contains a record format, the corresponding file must be opened for update, output-only, or combined (input/output) processing, and must be used in the program with an output operation code or cycle output. The *ALL option in factor 2 is required in order to clear a record format for a file that is declared as input-only. If *ALL is not used, only fields defined as output or input/output are cleared. Fields declared as input-only are not cleared.

If the result field contains an array name, the entire array (every element) is cleared. When the result field contains an array element, such as ARR(3), only that element is cleared.

If the result field contains a multiple-occurrence data structure, the current occurrence of the data structure is cleared unless *ALL is specified in factor 2. When the result field contains a data structure, each subfield is cleared in order of its appearance in the data structure. The sequence in which the subfields are specified in the definition specifications controls the sequence of the clearing. The first field listed in the data structure definition specification is cleared first, followed by the second field, followed by the third field, etc.

CLEAR and Initial Values

The CLEAR operation ignores initial values because it moves either blanks or zeros into a variable based on the variable's attribute. If the application requires resetting a variable to its initial value, the RESET operation should be used. For more information, see the subheading RESET (Reset Variable to Its Initial Value).

Each data type supported by RPG is set to a specific low value when it is cleared. Table 5.16 lists the value to which each data type is set by the CLEAR operation.

Table 5.16: Cleared Values.	
Data Type	**Value Set by the CLEAR Operation**
Numeric	0
Character	Blanks
Indicator	'0'
Pointer	*NULL
Date	1st of January, 0001 (with century) 1st of January, 1940 (*MDY, *DMY, *YMD, and *CYMD formats)
Time	00:00:00 (*ISO format)12:00 AM (*USA format)
Timestamp	0001-01-01-00.00.00.000000

It should be pointed out that the default initial value for all data structure subfields is blanks. Unlike the RESET operation, which moves the initial value into a variable, the CLEAR operation moves the values listed in Table 5.16 to the various fields. When used in conjunction with a data structure, the CLEAR operation sets each subfield to an appropriate value versus the RPG initial value of blanks.

The initial value for data structure subfields also can be set to reflect the subfield's attribute by specifying the INZ keyword on the data structure header or on the individual subfields. Also, a distinct initial value can be specified as the parameter of the INZ keyword.

When the CLEAR operation is performed within the *INZSR subroutine, the cleared value becomes the initial value. Using CLEAR within the *INZSR subroutine overrides any initial value specified for the variable.

In Example 5.27, the subfields of the data structure named ITEM are cleared as follows:

1. Zeros are moved to the subfield PRICE.

2. Zeros are moved to the subfield COST.

3. Zeros are moved to the subfield ITEMNUM.

4. Blanks are moved to the subfield ITEMCHAR—replacing the zeros moved into the ITEMNUM subfield.

5. Blanks are moved to the subfield ITEMDESC.

Example 5.27: Clearing a data structure.

```
.....DName+++++++++++EUDS.......Length+TDc.Functions++++++++++++++++++++++++++++++
0001 D Item             DS
0002 D   Price                     7P 2
0003 D   Cost                      7P 2
0004 D   ItemNum                   4S 0
0005 D   ItemChar                  4A     Overlay(ItemNum)
0006 D   ItemDesc                 50A

.....CSRn01Factor1+++++++OpCode(ex)Factor2+++++++Result++++++++Len++DcHiLoEq
0007 C                   CLEAR                    Item
```

▶ CLOSE (CLOSE A FILE)

The CLOSE operation closes the file specified in factor 2 and optionally closes all opened files when *all is specified for factor 2.

Factor 1	OpCode	Factor 2	Result Field	Resulting Indicators	
	CLOSE(E)	file name		[error]	
	CLOSE(E)	*ALL		[error]	

See also OPEN and %OPEN.

Factor 2 must contain the name of the file being closed or *ALL. If factor 2 contains the value *ALL, all files currently opened in the program are closed. When a file is closed, it is disconnected from the program and can no longer be accessed by the program. If the file must be accessed again—in the same program—it must be opened with the OPEN operation.

A pre-runtime table or array file name (indicated by the FROMFILE keyword on the definition specifi-

Resulting Indicator Legend

Columns	Ind.	Usage	Set-On Condition
71 - 72	1	N/A	Not used by this operation.
73 - 74	2	[error]	An error occurred during the operation.
75 - 76	3	N/A	Not used by this operation.

Extender	Description
E	ERROR – Causes the %error and %status built-infunctions to be set if an error occurs during the operation.

cation) cannot be specified in factor 2. While an output table or array (indicated by the TOFILE keyword on the definition specification) can be specified in factor 2, its records aren't written out to disk until the program ends with the LR indicator on.

In Example 5.28, the file CUSTMAST is closed. If the CLOSE operation doesn't complete successfully, resulting indicator 2 (indicator 73 in this example) is set on, signaling that the close attempt failed.

Example 5.28: Closing a data file by naming the file.

```
.....CSRn01Factor1+++++++OpCode(ex)Factor2+++++++Result++++++++Len++DcHiLoEq
0010 C                    CLOSE           CUSTMAST                      73
```

▶COMMIT (COMMIT)

The COMMIT operation is a relational database management function. It performs the commitment function of the Relation Model by making all modifications that have been performed since the previous commit or ROLBK operation.

Factor 1	OpCode	Factor 2	Result Field	Resulting Indicators	
[boundary]	COMMIT(E)				[error]	

See also ROLBK

Factor 1 is optional and can contain a value that is used as a boundary identification. A recovery process can use this identification after an abnormal application termination occurs. The boundary identifier is logged to one of many optional locations, such as a data file, message queue, or data area. One optional location can be specified outside the RPG program to a system function.

Resulting Indicator Legend

Columns	Ind.	Usage	Set-On Condition
71 - 72	1	N/A	
73 - 74	2	[error]	An error occurred during the operation.
75 - 76	3	N/A	

Extender	Description
E	ERROR – Causes the %ERROR and %STATUS built-in functions to be set if an error occurs during the operation.

The COMMIT operation is performed on all files that currently are under commitment control for the session or activation group regardless of whether they are actually defined in the program performing the COMMIT operation.

When the COMMIT operation is performed, all records that have been locked during and by the commit process are released (including records that have been committed outside of the domain of the current program). The COMMIT and ROLBK operations are ignored at runtime when the value for the file continuation keyword for commitment control (COMMIT) has a value of '0' (such as *OFF) specified. Example 5.29 shows code to commit with a boundary identifier.

Example 5.29: Committing with a boundary identifier.

```
.....FFileName++IFEASFRlen+LKeylnKFDevice+.Functions++++++++++++++++++++++++++++++
0010 FCUSTMAST  IF   E           DISK    COMMIT

.....CSRn01Factor1+++++++OpCode(ex)Factor2+++++++Result++++++++Len++DcHiLoEq
0020 C                   MOVE      'POST03'        BNDRY           16
0030 C         BNDRY     COMMIT                                          56
```

▶ COMP (COMPARE)

The COMP operation compares factor 1 to factor 2. Resulting indicators 1, 2, and 3 are set on according to the outcome of the comparison. One or more resulting indicators are required for the COMP operation. If three resulting indicators are specified, no more than two may be the same indicator.

Factor 1	OpCode	Factor 2	Result Field	Resulting Indicators		
compare value 1	COMP	compare value 2		[1>2]	[1<2]	[1=2]

See also IFxx, CABxx, CASxx, and WHENxx.

Factor 1 can contain any RPG variable, including a literal value, field, data structure, data structure subfield, array, array element, or figurative constant such as *BLANKS.

Resulting Indicator Legend			
Columns	Ind.	Usage	Set-On Condition
71 - 72	1	[1>2]	Factor 1 is greater than factor 2.
73 - 74	2	[1<2]	Factor 1 is less than factor 2.
75 - 76	3	[1=2]	Factor 1 is equal to factor 2.

Factor 2 must contain a value with attributes similar to factor 1. For example, if factor 1 contains a numeric field, factor 2 must be a numeric field, a numeric constant, or a numeric-figurative constant (such as *ZEROS). If factor 1 is a character, factor 2 must also be a character.

In Example 5.30, the STATE field is compared to the constant 'IL' on line 10. If STATE is equal to 'IL', resulting indicator 3 (indicator 58 in this example) is set on. On line 20, the numeric field AMOUNT is compared to the constant 5000.00 and sets on the appropriate indicators.

Example 5.30: Comparing fields to constants.

```
.....CSRn01Factor1+++++++OpCode(ex)Factor2+++++++Result++++++++Len++DcHiLoEq
0010 C         STATE     COMP      'IL'                                 58
0020 C         AMOUNT    COMP      5000.00                          545658
```

▶ DEALLOC (RELEASE ALLOCATED MEMORY)

The DEALLOC operation is used to return storage (memory) allocated at runtime to the system. Only memory previously allocated with the ALLOC or REALLOC operations can be de-allocated.

Factor 1	OpCode	Factor 2	Result Field	Resulting Indicators		
	DEALLOC (E N)		Pointer variable		[error]	

See also ALLOC and REALLOC

The result field is required and must contain a field of type pointer. The address stored in the pointer must be that of memory allocated by an ALLOC or REALLOC operation. Any time storage is allocated, it should be deallocated (returned back to the system) before the program ends. The RPG language does not perform so-called garbage collections. In other words, RPG doesn't automatically return allocated storage to the system when the program ends.

Line 5 in Example 5.31 returns the memory allocated on line 3 to the

Resulting Indicator Legend			
Columns	Ind.	Usage	Set-On Condition
71 - 72	1	N/A	
73 - 74	2	[error]	An error occurred during the operation.
75 - 76	3	N/A	

Extender	Description
E	ERROR – Causes the %ERROR and %STATUS built-in functions to be set if an error occurs during the operation.
N	SET TO NULL – Causes the pointer variable specified in the result field to be set to null (X'00') after the storage is returned/released back to the system.

system. The pointer field pSTRING is set to null after the DEALLOC operation is performed.

Example 5.31: Using DEALLOC to return memory to the system.

```
.....DName++++++++++EUDS.......Length+TDc.Functions++++++++++++++++++++++++++++++
0001 D String           S            500A    Based( pString )

.....CSRn01Factor1+++++++OpCode(ex)Factor2+++++++Result++++++++Len++DcHiLoEq
0002  *    Allocate 500 bytes of memory
0003 C                      ALLOC(E)   500            pString
0004 C                      MoveL      'abcdefg'      STRING
0005 C                      DeAlloc(N)                pString
```

▶ DEFINE (DEFINE A FIELD OR DATA AREA)

The DEFINE operation can be used to declare new fields based on existing fields. DEFINE also is used to assign an external data area to a program variable. The data area is then accessible through the program variable. Conditioning indicators are not valid for this operation. Result indicators also are not valid for this operation.

Factor 1	OpCode	Factor 2	Result Field	Resulting Indicators		
*LIKE	DEFINE	based-on variable	variable			
*DTAARA	DEFINE	source	target			

*See also IN, OUT, *DTAARA, and the LIKE keyword*

The first form of DEFINE defines a derived field. It is a field based on the attributes of another field. The length and data-type are inherited. This form of the DEFINE operation is deprecated. See the LIKE keyword on the definition specification.

The second form of DEFINE assigns a field to an external data area. When the field is referenced by an IN, an OUT, or an UNLOCK operation, the data area assigned to the variable is read, written, or unlocked. Factor 1 is required and can contain one of the following:

Factor 1	Description
*LIKE	Defines a derived field. The field specified in the result field inherits the attributes of the field specified in factor 2. If factor 2 contains an array name, the result field is based on the attributes of an array element (not the array). If factor 2 contains a numeric field, the attribute of the new field is always (incorrectly) packed decimal. This is in contrast with the LIKE keyword, which correctly declares the new field with the same attributes as its "based on" field.
*DTAARA	Defines a field as a data area. The data in factor 2 is assigned to the field. When the variable specified in the result field is referenced by the IN, OUT, or UNLOCK operations, the data area specified in factor 2 is accessed.

The preferred method to declare a field reference or a data area is to use the LIKE and DTAARA keywords on the definition specification. While there is no performance or storage penalty for using the DEFINE operation, the definition specification is generally accepted as the preferred method of declaring derived fields. If *LIKE is specified for factor 1, the following conditions apply:

- Factor 2 must contain the name of a field, data structure, array, or array element that is used as a basis for a derived field.

- If factor 2 contains an array name, an element of the array is used as the basis for the derived field.

- The result field must contain the name of the field that is derived from (based on) factor 2.

- The derived field's length is equal to the length of the field specified in factor 2. The field's derived length can be overridden by specifying a relative or absolute field length in the result field length.

Relative size allows a shorter field length to be calculated by the compiler. To indicate a relative field length, prefix the derived field's length with a plus (+) or minus (-) sign. By specifying the plus or minus sign, the result field length is used as the relative size of the new field. Therefore, for example, a value of +5 in the result field length generates a derived field where the length is five positions longer than the based-on field's length.

On line 10 in Example 5.32, the field ACTNBR is defined and is three positions longer than the field CSTNBR. Line 20 defines the field OLDACT with a length of two positions less than CSTNBR, and line 30 defines the field SAVCST with the same attributes (i.e., length and type) as CSTNBR.

Example 5.32: Defining three derived fields.

```
.....CSRnØ1Factor1+++++++OpCode(ex)Factor2+++++++Result++++++++Len++DcHiLoEq
ØØ1Ø C     *LIKE        DEFINE    CSTNBR       ACTNBR          +3
ØØ2Ø C     *LIKE        DEFINE    CSTNBR       OLDACT          -2
ØØ3Ø C     *LIKE        DEFINE    CSTNBR       SAVCST
```

If *DTAARA is specified for factor 1, the following conditions apply:

- Factor 2 may optionally contain the name of an external data area. If the system supports a Local Data Area, *LDA may be specified in factor 2. If the system supports the program information Parameters Data Area, *PDA may be specified for factor 2. If factor 2 is omitted, then the value specified in the result field is used as the name of the external data area.

- The result field is required and must contain the name of a field, data structure, data structure subfield, or data area data structure. The entry in the result field is used to access the external data area's data. The result field is "assigned" to the data area and is used by the IN and OUT operations.

- The length of the field being assigned to the data area may be specified in the result field length

An external data area can be retrieved (read) and rewritten (updated) with the IN and OUT operations. See the subheadings IN (Read in a Data Area) and OUT (Output an External Data Area).

In Example 5.33, Line 10 defines the external data area CONTROL and assigns it to the CTRL field. In this example, the attributes (i.e., length and type) of CTRL are defined as a seven-digit packed numeric. However, the result field can be a field, data structure, or data structure subfield.

Line 20 retrieves (i.e., reads) the external data area CONTROL into the CTRL field. The data in the CTRL field can be used (moved, copied, changed, or deleted) without affecting the data contained in the external data area. The data in the external data area is not affected until an OUT operation to CTRL is performed.

Example 5.33: Defining an external data area and assigning the data area to the field named.

```
.....CSRnØ1Factor1+++++++OpCode(ex)Factor2+++++++Result++++++++Len++DcHiLoEq
ØØ1Ø C     *DTAARA      DEFINE    CONTROL      CTRL             7 Ø
ØØ2Ø C                  IN        CTRL                             56
```

If the data area doesn't exist or if it has been locked by another process, resulting indicator 2 (indicator 56 in this example) is set on by the IN operation on line 20.

▶ DELETE (DELETE DATA FILE RECORD)

The DELETE operation deletes a single record from the file specified in factor 2. Factor 2 can be a file name or a record-format name.

Factor 1	OpCode	Factor 2	Result Field	Resulting Indicators	
[key value]	DELETE (E)	file name		[n/f]	[error]
[key value]	DELETE (E)	format name		[n/f]	[error]

See also WRITE, UPDATE, READ, READPE, and CHAIN.

Indexed files may contain the following in factor 1:

- A field or data structure name containing the key value.

- A key-list name whose key fields contain the key or partial key value.

- A constant representing the key value.

- Blanks, which cause the DE-LETE operation to delete the record currently locked by the program.

Resulting Indicator Legend

Columns	Ind.	Usage	Set-On Condition
71 - 72	1	[n/f]	Record not found.
73 - 74	2	[error]	Error occurred during the operation.
75 - 76	3	N/A	Not used by this operation code.

Extender	Description
E	ERROR – Causes the %ERROR and %STATUS built-in functions to be set if an error occurs during the operation.

Relative record number accessed files may contain the following in factor 1:

- A numeric field with zero decimal positions that contains a positive nonzero number.

- An integer constant such as 27 for record number 27.

- Blanks, which cause the DELETE operation to delete the record currently locked by the program.

For externally described files, factor 2 can be either the name of the file containing the record that is deleted or the name of a file's record format whose record is deleted.

The file represented in factor 2 must be declared as an update file (i.e., the letter U must appear in position 17 of the file's file specification) to allow the DELETE operation to function. When factor 1 is used to access the record, resulting indicator 1 must be specified to signal a record-not-found condition.

In Example 5.34, the examples use the file ORDERS. The file ORDERS contains a record format name of HEADER. The file's index is made up of the key fields CSTNBR and ORDNBR. Access by CSTNBR is all that is needed in these examples.

Example 5.34: Deleting a record by specifying a key list in factor 1.

```
.....FFileName++IFEASFRlen+LKeylnKFDevice+.Functions++++++++++++++++++++++++++++++
0010 FORDERS    UF   E          K DISK


.....CSRn01Factor1+++++++OpCode(ex)Factor2+++++++Result++++++++Len++DcHiLoEq
0030 C*  Key list by customer number only.
0040 C       CSTKEY       KLIST
0050 C                    KFLD                   CSTNBR
0060 C*  Delete first order for customer = 200
0070 C                    Z-ADD    200           CSTNBR
0080 C       CSTKEY       DELETE   HEADER                       5456
```

In Example 5.34, the key list CSTKEY is used by the DELETE operation to access the file ORDERS by key. If a matching key is found, its corresponding record is deleted. If no matching key is found, resulting indicator 1 is set on. If the record exists but could not be allocated, resulting indicator 2 is set on. Factor 2 of the DELETE operation contains the record format name HEADER. This is the name of the record format for the file named ORDERS.

Optionally, resulting indicator 2 may be used to signal errors that might occur during the attempt to delete the record. Possible errors that would set on resulting indicator 2 are: record allocation time-out or lack of proper authority to delete records from the file. The *STATUS variable should be checked to identify the error that caused resulting indicator 2 to be set on. See Table 5.15 for specific error codes.

In Example 5.35, the key list CSTKEY is used to access the file ORDERS through the CHAIN operation on line 80. If a record is found, the DELETE operation on line 130 deletes the record from the file.

> **NOTE:** The file ORDERS is accessed through the record format HEADER on line
> 80 and deleted through its file name on line 150. The DELETE deletes
> the last record read by the program. Also, line 150 avoids using result-
> ing indicator 2 or checking for an error condition because the CHAIN
> operation on line 80 retrieves and locks the record for update.

Unlike the CHAIN, READ, and READP operations, the DELETE operation does not copy the
contents of a file's fields to the input buffer. Therefore, when the program knows the index of a record, using only the DELETE operation with factor 1 specified yields better
performance.

When the DELETE operation deletes a record, that record is permanently erased from storage. Also, a subsequent READ operation reads the record following the deleted record,
and a READP operation reads the record prior to the deleted record.

Example 5.35: Deleting a record using CHAIN/DELETE combination.

```
.....FFileName++IFEASFRlen+LKeylnKFDevice+.Functions++++++++++++++++++++++++++++++
0010 FORDERS    UF   E         K DISK


.....CSRn01Factor1+++++++OpCode(ex)Factor2+++++++Result++++++++Len++DcHiLoEq
0030 C*  Key list by customer number.
0040 C     CSTKEY       KLIST
0050 C                  KFLD                      CSTNBR
0060 C*  Delete first order for customer = 200
0070 C                  Z-ADD      200            CSTNBR
0080 C     CSTKEY       CHAIN(E)   HEADER
0090 C                  If         %ERROR
0100 C                  If         %STATUS = 1218
0110 C                  EXSR       TIMOUT
0120 C                  ENDIF
0130 C                  ENDIF
0140 C                  If         %FOUND
0150 C                  DELETE     ORDERS
0160 C                  ENDIF
```

▶ DIV (DIVIDE)

The DIV operation is used to produce the quotient (result) of a divide operation in the form factor 1 divided by factor 2 (F1/F2)—long form—or result field divided by factor 2 (RF/F2)—short form.

Factor 1	OpCode	Factor 2	Result Field	Resulting Indicators		
dividend	DIV(H)	divisor	quotient	[+]	[-]	[0]
	DIV(H)	divisor	quotient and dividend	[+]	[-]	[0]

See also ADD, SUB, MULT, EVAL, MVR, %DIV, and %REM.

If factor 1 contains a value, factor 1 is the dividend, factor 2 is the divisor, and the result field is the quotient. If factor 1 is blank, the result field is used as the dividend, factor 2 is the divisor, and the result field is the quotient.

The H operation extender can be specified to cause the result to be half-adjusted—that is, rounded up. If the DIV operation is immediately followed by the MVR operation, the operator extender cannot be specified for the DIV operation.

Resulting Indicator Legend			
Columns	Ind.	Usage	Set-On Condition
71 - 72	1	[+]	The result field is greater than zero.
73 - 74	2	[–]	The result field is less than zero.
75 - 76	3	[0]	The result field is equal to zero.

If the dividend (factor 1, long form; result field, short form) is 0, the result is 0. If the divisor (factor 2) is 0, a "divide by zero error" occurs. In this case, the default exception/error handling subroutine receives control. Therefore, the exception/error handling subroutine must be coded in the program or factor 2 must be tested before performing the divide operation. Normally, the program would compare the divisor (factor 2) to zero before the DIV operation is performed, thus avoiding a divide-by-zero error.

To capture the remainder of a DIV operation, the MVR (Move Remainder) operation must immediately follow the DIV operation. If MVR is specified, the remainder from the DIV operation is placed into the result field of a MVR operation; the H operation extender (half-adjust) cannot be specified for the DIV operation. For more information, see the sub-heading MVR (Move Remainder of Division).

In Example 5.36, the first DIV operation divides field A by field B, and the quotient is placed in field C.

Example 5.36: Long and short forms of division.

```
.....CSRnØ1Factor1+++++++OpCode(ex)Factor2+++++++Result++++++++Len++DcHiLoEq
ØØ10 C                    If         B  Ø
ØØ20 C      A             DIV        B          C
ØØ30 C                    DIV        B          C                      545658
ØØ40 C                    ENDIF
```

In the second DIV operation, field C is divided by field B, and the quotient replaces the value in field C. Also, if the quotient is greater than zero (i.e., a positive number), resulting indicator 1 is set on. If the quotient is less than zero (i.e., a negative number), resulting indicator 2 is set on. If the quotient is equal to zero, resulting indicator 3 is set on.

In Example 5.37, the remainder of A/B is stored into the field REMAINDER. If A = 5 and B = 3, then as a result of the calculations in Example 5.37, C = 1 and REMAINDER = 2.

Example 5.37: Long form division with remainder.

```
.....CSRnØ1Factor1+++++++OpCode(ex)Factor2+++++++Result++++++++Len++DcHiLoEq
ØØ10 C      A             DIV        B          C
ØØ20 C                    MVR                   Remainder        3 Ø
```

In Example 5.38, the H operation extender causes the quotient (result field) to be rounded. For example, if A = 7 and B = 4, then A/B = 1.75; with half-adjust in effect; the quotient is C = 2. The quotient varies based on the number of decimal positions of the result field. For example, if the quotient is defined with one decimal position, the result of the calculation would be C = 1.8 (rounding to the tenths position).

Example 5.38: Division with rounding (half-adjust).

```
.....CSRnØ1Factor1+++++++OpCode(ex)Factor2+++++++Result++++++++Len++DcHiLoEq
ØØ20 C      A             DIV(H)     B             C
```

DO (BEGIN DO LOOP)

The DO operation begins a DO/ENDDO loop. The code between the DO and the ENDDO statement is called the DO group and is performed a number of times. The END or ENDDO statements close a DO/ENDDO loop. The DO operation is a structured programming construct. It contributes to, but does not cause, structured programming.

Factor 1	OpCode	Factor 2	Result Field	Resulting Indicators		
[starting value]	DO	[limit]	[counter variable]			

See also FOR, DOW, DOU, and ENDDO

The structure of the DO/ENDDO loop is shown in Example 5.39.

Example 5.39: Structure of a DO/ENDDO loop.

```
.....CSRnØ1Factor1+++++++OpCode(ex)Factor2+++++++Result++++++++Len++DcHiLoEq
     C   in1Start            DO         Limit          Count
     C                                  .
      *          Do group code goes here.
     C                                  .
     C   in2                 ENDDO      Increment
```

START is an optional starting value of COUNT. When the DO loop is entered, the value of START is placed into COUNT. If START is omitted, 1 is used as the starting value.

LIMIT is the optional upper limit of the number of times the DO loop is performed. LIMIT is compared to COUNT at the "top" of the DO loop. If COUNT is greater than LIMIT, the DO group is not performed. If LIMIT is omitted, 1 is used as the upper-limit value.

COUNT is the index or counter of the DO loop. COUNT is increased by INCREMENT at the end of each pass through the DO loop. At the top of each pass of the DO loop, COUNT is compared to LIMIT. If COUNT is greater than LIMIT, the DO loop is ended. If COUNT is omitted, an internal variable is used for the counter.

INCREMENT is factor 2 of the ENDDO statement, which contains the value that is added to COUNT when the ENDDO statement is encountered. If INCREMENT is not specified, a value of 1 is used as the INCREMENT.

IN1 is an optional indicator or set of indicators that controls the entry into the DO loop. If the conditioning indicator test is met when the DO loop is encountered, the DO loop is entered. If the conditioning indicator test is not met, the program branches to the statement following the ENDDO statement.

IN2 is an optional indicator that controls the unnatural exit from the DO loop. When the ENDDO statement is encountered and one or more conditioning indicators are present, the indicator conditions are tested. If the condition is met, the ENDDO statement is performed and control passes back up to the DO statement. If the condition is not met, control passes to the statement following the ENDDO statement, and the DO loop is exited.

The ENDDO statement is the DO loop's *end marker*. The end marker defines the end of the block of code controlled by the DO operation. When used in conjunction with the DO statement, ENDDO adds INCREMENT to COUNT, and then branches to the top of the DO loop.

In Example 5.40, line 40 begins the DO loop. Factor 2 of line 40 indicates that the DO loop is performed 12 times. The result field on line 40 is the field X. Defined on line 20, the X field is the counter for the DO loop. Each iteration through this DO loop increments X by 1. Lines 50 and 60 use X as an index of the ARRAY array.

Each time the DO loop is encountered (i.e., each time the program flow causes the DO loop to be processed), the count field (the result field of the DO operation) is automatically initialized to the value specified in factor 1 of the DO operation.

Example 5.40: Performing a DO group multiple times.

```
.....DName+++++++++++EUDS.......Length+TDc.Functions++++++++++++++++++++++++++++++
0010 D Array           S              10A   Dim(12)
0020 D X               S              10I 0
0030 D ArrayCount      C                    Const(%elem(Array)

.....CSRn01Factor1+++++++<—OpCode(ex)—>Factor2+++++++Result++++++++Len++DcHiLoEq
0040 C                  DO              ArrayCount    X
0050 C                  | If            Array(x) = 'Q38'
0060 C                  | | MOVEL       'Midrange'    ARRAY(X)
0070 C                  | ENDIF
0080 C                  ENDDO
```

In Example 5.41, lines 10 and 20 set the outer DO...END loop START and INCREMENT fields to 5. When the DO group is started, Y is set to 5, and then it is increased by 5 during each pass through the DO loop. The limit for the outer loop is 15 and the DO group is performed three times. Because the inner loop (lines 40 to 80) is performed 12 times the number of times the outer DO loop is performed, the inner DO loop is performed 36 times.

Example 5.41: Nested DO...END groups.

```
.....CSRn01Factor1+++++++<—OpCode(ex)—>Factor2+++++++Result++++++++Len++DcHiLoEq
0010 C                    Z-ADD         5              Start          5 0
0020 C                    Z-ADD         5              Increment      5 0
0030 C       Start        DO            15             Y              5 0
0040 C                    | DO          12             X              5 0
0050 C                    | | IF        OLD(Y) = 'Q38'
0060 C                    | | | MoveL   'Midrange'     NEW(X)
0070 C                    | | EndIf
0080 C                    | EndDo
0090 C                    EndDo         Increment
```

DOU*xx* (BEGIN DO UNTIL LOOP)

The DOU*xx* operation begins a DO UNTIL loop. The code between the DOU*xx* and the ENDDO statement is called the DO group and is performed at least once. Conditioning indicators, if specified, are tested once before entry into the DO UNTIL group. The DOU*xx* operation is a structured operation. It contributes to, but does not cause, structured programming. The fixed-format versions of DOU*xx* (DOWEQ, DOUNE, DOULT, DOULE, DOUGT, and DOUGE) have been deprecated by the DOU operation.

Factor 1	OpCode	Factor 2	Result Field	Resulting Indicators		
compare value 1	DOU*xx*	compare value 2				
	DOU	conditional expression				

See also IF, DOW, DO, FOR, WHEN, and ENDDO

The DOU*xx* operation performs a relationship test *xx*, where *xx* may be any one of the Boolean operators (EQ, GE, GT, LE, LT, and NE). See Table 5.8 for details. Factor 1 is compared to factor 2 based on the *xx* operator. Factor 1 and factor 2 must be similar data types. For the secondary form of DOU, the extended factor 2 must contain a conditional expression.

The DO UNTIL construct logically tests its condition at the bottom of the DO loop (i.e., when the ENDDO statement is encountered) and, therefore, always performs its DO group at least once. Indicators can condition the ENDDO statement. If the indicator condition is true, the ENDDO is performed normally. If the indicator condition is false, the ENDDO is not performed, and control passes to the statement following the ENDDO.

The DOU*xx* Boolean test can be extended with the AND*xx* or OR*xx* operations. AND*xx* allows compound conditions to be tested and OR*xx* allows distinct conditions to be tested.

The ANDxx and ORxx operations cannot be used in conjunction with the DOU form of this operation.

In Example 5.42, the DO group is performed until A is equal to B and D is greater than C, but it is always performed at least once.

Example 5.42: DOUxx with ANDxx extension.

```
.....CSRnØ1Factor1+++++++OpCode(ex)Factor2+++++++Result++++++++Len++DcHiLoEq
ØØ1Ø C     A          DOUEQ      B
ØØ2Ø C     D          ANDGT      C
ØØ3Ø C                ADD        1           B
ØØ4Ø C                ADD        2           D
ØØ5Ø C                ENDDO
```

In Example 5.43, the database file named DATAFILE is accessed on line 10 with the CHAIN operation. If an index exists for the key value contained in CSTNBR, the record is retrieved. The DOU operation on line 40 begins the DO loop and controls the iterations through the DO loop. The ENDDO operation on line 100 is where the logical occurrence of the relationship test is performed.

Example 5.43: DOU with OR extension to fill a subfile with 20 records.

```
.....CSRnØ1Factor1+++++++<—OpCode(ex)—>Factor2+++++++Result++++++++Len++DcHiLoEq
ØØ1Ø C     CSTNBR       CHAIN          DATAFILE
ØØ2Ø C                  IF             %FOUND
ØØ3Ø C                  | Z-ADD        Ø             RELNO        3 Ø
ØØ4Ø C                  | DOU          %EOF or RELNO >= 2Ø
ØØ5Ø C                  | | ADD        1             RELNO
ØØ6Ø C                  | | WRITE      SUBFILE
ØØ7Ø C                  | | If         NOT %EOF(subfile)
ØØ8Ø C                  | | | READ     DATAFILE
ØØ9Ø C                  | | endif
Ø1ØØ C                  | ENDDO
Ø11Ø C                  ENDIF
```

In Example 5.44, the DOU operation checks the variable named KEYPRESSED (line 10). If it is equal to the named constant F3, the DOU loop is ended. On line 70, the variable I is set to ZERO, and then the DOU loop is entered. This DOU loop is performed until the variable I is greater than or equal to the number of elements in the ARR array.

Example 5.44: DOU with extended factor 2 to condition a DO UNTIL loop.

```
.....CSRnØ1Factor1+++++++OpCode(ex)Factor2+++++++Result++++++++Len++DcHiLoEq
ØØ1Ø C                    dou        KeyPressed = F3
ØØ2Ø C                    EXFMT      OrdEntry
ØØ3Ø C                    If         NOT (KeyPressed = F3 )
ØØ4Ø C                    Exsr       Process
ØØ5Ø C                    endif
ØØ6Ø C                    enddo

ØØ7Ø C                    eval       i = Ø
ØØ8Ø C                    dou        i >= %elem(arr) or *IN56
ØØ9Ø C                    Eval       ARR (i + 1) = 'TK421'
Ø1ØØ C                    Add        1              i                      56
Ø11Ø C                    enddo
```

▶ DOW*xx* (Begin Do While Loop)

The DOW*xx* operation begins a DO WHILE loop. The code between the DOW*xx* and the ENDDO statement is called the DO group. Conditioning indicators, if specified, are tested once before entry into the DO group. The DOW*xx* operation is a structured operation. It contributes to, but doesn't cause, structured programming. The fixed-format versions of DOW*xx* (DOWEQ, DOWNE, DOWLT, DOWLE, DOWGT ,and DOWGE) have been deprecated by the DOW operation.

Factor 1	OpCode	Factor 2	Result Field	Resulting Indicators		
compare value 1	DOW*xx*	compare value 2				
	DOW	conditional expression				

See also IFxx, DOUxx, DO, WHENxx, and ENDDO

The DOW*xx* operation performs a relationship test *xx*, where *xx* may be any one of the Boolean operators (EQ, GE, GT, LE, LT, and NE). See Table 5.8 for details. Factor 1 is compared to factor 2 based on the *xx* operator. Factor 1 and factor 2 must be similar data types. For the secondary form of DOW, the extended factor 2 must contain a conditional expression.

The DO WHILE construct logically tests its condition at the top of the DO loop and, therefore, only performs its DO group when the condition is true. The ENDDO statement can be conditioned by indicators. If the indicator condition is true, the ENDDO is performed normally. If the indicator condition is false, the ENDDO is not performed, and control passes to the statement following the ENDDO.

The DOW*xx* test can be extended with the AND*xx* or OR*xx* operations. AND*xx* allows compound conditions to be tested; OR*xx* allows additional, but separate, conditions to be tested. The AND*xx* and OR*xx* operations cannot be used in conjunction with the DOW form of this operation.

In Example 5.45, the DO loop is performed while A is equal to B or C is not equal to D.

Example 5.45: DOWxx with ORxx extension.

```
.....CSRn01Factor1+++++++OpCode(ex)Factor2+++++++Result++++++++Len++DcHiLoEq
0010 C     A           DOWEQ      B
0020 C     C           ORNE       D
0030 C                 ADD        1           B
0040 C                 ADD        2           D
0050 C                 ENDDO
```

In Example 5.46, the database file named CUSTMAST is accessed on line 10 with the CHAIN operation. If an index exists for the key value contained in CSTNBR, the record is retrieved and the field EOF is set off.

Example 5.46: DOWxx with ANDxx extension to fill a subfile with 20 records.

```
.....CSRn01Factor1+++++++<–OpCode(ex)–>Factor2+++++++Result++++++++Len++DcHiLoEq
0010 C     CSTNBR       CHAIN        CUSTMAST                          54
0020 C                  Eval         EOF = *IN54
0030 C                  Z-ADD        0             RELNO             3 0
0040 C     EOF          DOWEQ        *OFF
0050 C     RELNO        ANDLT        20
0060 C                  | ADD        1             RELNO
0070 C                  | WRITE      SUBFILE
0080 C                  | READ       CUSTMAST                          58
0090 C                  | Eval       EOF = *IN58
0100 C                  ENDDO
```

The DOWEQ ANDLT operations control entry into the DO group. First, the field RELNO (subfile relative record number) is increased on line 60, and then a SUBFILE (or tabular list panel) detail record named subfile is written. Finally, the database file CUSTMAST is read, and the DO loop is performed again. If end-of-file is reached or RELNO is equal to 20, the DO loop ends.

Normally, when processing a database file with this operation, the file is positioned to the first record to be processed before entering into the DO WHILE group.

In Example 5.47, the DOW operation checks the variable named INDEX to see if it is less than the number of elements in the STATES array (line 10). If it is less than the number of elements of STATES, the DO WHILE loop is entered. Note that the LEAVE operation (line 50) is used to exit the DO WHILE loop when the end-of-file condition is detected.

On line 10, the file CUSTMAST's record (CUSTREC) is read. Then the DOW operation (line 11) is performed. The DO WHILE loop is performed while there are records read from the CUSTMAST file and while the subfile is not full.

Example 5.47: DOW with extended factor 2 to condition a DO WHILE loop.

```
.....CSRn01Factor1+++++++OpCode(ex)Factor2+++++++Result++++++++Len++DcHiLoEq
0010 C                   Eval      Index = 1
0020 C                   dow       Index < %elem(States)
0030 C                   READ      CustRec                              58
0040 C                   If        *IN58
0050 C                   Leave
0060 C                   EndIf
0070 C                   Eval      States(Index) = CM_State
0080 C                   Eval      Index = Index + 1
0090 C                   enddo

0100 C                   read      CustRec                              58
0110 C                   dow       NOT %EOF(CUSTMAST) and NOT %EOF(subfile)
0120 C                   write     subfile                              58
0140 C                   read      CustRec                              58
0150 C                   enddo
```

▶ DSPLY (DISPLAY WORKSTATION MESSAGE)

The DSPLY operation provides a primitive form of message-level communication between the workstation operator or the system operator and the RPG program. A message can be sent (up to 52 characters) so that it returns an operator response. A message not requiring a response is also supported.

Factor 1	OpCode	Factor 2	Result Field	Resulting Indicators	
[message text]	DSPLY(E)	[message queue]	[reply variable]		[error]	

See also DEBUG

Factor 1 is optional and can contain a message ID, a literal value, or a field with information to be displayed. If a message ID is specified, it must conform to one of the following formats:

Resulting Indicator Legend			
Columns	Ind.	Usage	Set-On Condition
71 - 72	1	N/A	
73 - 74	2	[error]	An error occurred during the operation.
75 - 76	3	[0]	

- *Myyyy—Where *M is constant and *yyyy* is a user-defined message ID. For example, *M10 generates user message USR0010.

The yyyy message ID must be one to four characters in length, left-justified against the *M constant.

- *Mxxxyyyy—Where *xxx* is a message prefix such as USR, RPG, or MCH, and *yyyy* is a user-defined message ID. For example, *MRPG400 would generate user message RPG0400. The *xxx* must be three characters in length, left justified against the *M constant. The yyyy message ID must be one to four digits in length, left justified against the *Mxxx constant.

Factor 2 is optional and can contain the name of the message queue that receives the message. For example, 'QSYSOPR' causes the message to be sent to the system operator, and '*EXT' causes the message to be sent to the workstation operator. For interactive jobs, factor 2 defaults to '*EXT'. For batch jobs, factor 2 defaults to 'QSYSOPR'.

The result field can contain the name of a field that receives the workstation or system operator's reply. If the result field is omitted, the operator is not allowed to type in a reply.

If factor 1 contains a message ID, RPG retrieves the message text of the message ID from the message file named QUSERMSG. This message file name can be overridden to some other name by running the OS/400 command OVRMSGF. This command can be run outside of the RPG program or by calling a system-command processing program (e.g., QCMDEXC on AS/400) from within RPG, and passing it a string containing the OVRMSGF command.

The message ID text, constant, or field specified in factor 1 is displayed at the workstation or system operator message queue, along with any data that is contained in the result field when the DSPLY operation is performed.

If factor 1 is blank and the result field is specified, only the data contained in the result field is displayed. If the result field is blank and factor 1 is omitted, nothing is displayed.

In Example 5.48, the user-defined message USR0010, indicated by *MUSR010 in factor 1, is sent to the workstation operator. The value *EXT in factor 2 of line 10 controls where the message is sent.

Any response the workstation operator types in is returned to the program in the field RE-PLY, which is specified in the result field.

Example 5.48: Display a message at the workstation.

```
.....CSRn01Factor1+++++++OpCode(ex)Factor2+++++++Result++++++++Len++DcHiLoEq
0010 C     *MUSR010     DSPLY              '*EXT' REPLY              1
0020 C                  IF        Reply ='C'
0030 C                  Eval      *inlr = *ON
0040 C                  Return
0050 C                  EndIf
```

▶ DUMP (PRINT FORMATTED DUMP)

The DUMP operation generates a list of all fields, data structures, indicators, internal fields, pointers, storage areas, tables, and arrays. The DUMP operation is valid only when the DEBUG keyword is specified on the header specification. Resulting indicators are not valid for this operation.

Factor 1	OpCode	Factor 2	Result Field	Resulting Indicators		
[descriptive text]	DUMP					

See also DEBUG keyword

Factor 1 is optional and may contain a dump identifier that is printed on the generated dump listing. The dump listing is quite similar to the formatted dump generated by the operating system.

Example 5.49 produces a formatted dump listing with 'DivBYZER' as its identifier. The fields TOTAL, ORDQTY, UNIT, and STATUS, and the indicator LR are included in the formatted dump listing along with several compiler-generated fields.

Example 5.49: Producing a dump when divide by zero occurs.

```
      H.Functions++++++++++++++++++++++++++++++++++++++++++++++++++++++++++++++++++
0010 H DEBUG(*YES)

.....DName+++++++++++EUDS.......Length+TDc.Functions+++++++++++++++++++++++++++++++
0020 D              SDS
0030 D   Status         *STATUS

.....CSRn01Factor1+++++++OpCode(ex)Factor2+++++++Result++++++++Len++DcHiLoEq
0040 C                Z-ADD     123        TOTAL          7 0
0050 C                Z-ADD     0          ORDQTY         7 0
0060 C     TOTAL      DIV(H)    ORDQTY     UNIT           5 2
0070 C                MOVE      *ON        *INLR

.....CSRn01Factor1+++++++OpCode(ex)Factor2+++++++Result++++++++Len++DcHiLoEq
0080 CSR   *PSSR      BEGSR
0090 C                IF         Status = 0102
0100 C     'DivByZer' DUMP
0110 C                EndIf
0120 CSR   ENDPSR     EndSR
```

▶ELSE (ELSE CLAUSE)

The ELSE operation is used with the IF*xx* operation. The ELSE operation follows the IF*xx* group and precedes the corresponding ENDIF statement. The group of statements between the ELSE operation and the corresponding ENDIF statement is performed when the condition specified for the IF*xx* is false. Conditioning indicators are not valid for this operation.

Factor 1	OpCode	Factor 2	Result Field	Resulting Indicators		
	ELSE					

See also IF and ENDIF

In Example 5.50, the field DAYS is compared to 30 and 60 days. When the IFLE operation is true, the MOVEL operation that immediately follows the IFLE operation is performed. Control then passes to the ENDIF statement associated with the IFLE operation. When the IFLE operation tests false, control passes to the ELSE statement within the IFLE group. In the example, this performs a subsequent IFLE operation.

Example 5.50: Using ELSE for conditioning.

```
.....CSRn01Factor1+++++++<-OpCode(ex)->Factor2+++++++Result++++++++Len++DcHiLoEq
0010 C                    IF           Days <= 30
0020 C                    | MOVEL      '0-30'        AGING
0030 C                    +ELSE
0040 C                    | IF         Days <= 60
0050 C                    | | MOVEL    '31-60'       AGING
0060 C                    | +ELSE
0070 C                    | | MOVEL    'Over-Due'    AGING
0080 C                    | ENDIF
0090 C                    ENDIF
```

▶ ELSEIF (ELSE IF CONDITIONAL COMPARISON)

The ELSEIF operation evaluates the conditional expression in the extended factor 2. If the comparison is true, the group of calculations between the ELSEIF and its associated ENDIF operation (or another ELSEIF operation) are performed. Conditioning indicators are not valid for the ELSEIF operation.

Factor 1	Op Code	Factor 2	Result Field	Resulting Indicators
	elseif (m r)	conditional expression		

See also IF, SELECT, WHEN, ELSE, DOWxx, DOUxx, CASxx, and FOR

The ELSEIF operation requires a relationship test in the extended factor 2. If the condition is true the set of operations following the ELSEIF and the corresponding ENDIF or secondary ELSEIF statement are performed. The IF operation supports the M and R operation extenders:

Extender	Description
M	If expressions are specified for any of the arguments of the operation, the maximum-digits format for intermediate results is used.
R	If expressions are specified for any of the arguments of the operation, the result value's decimal positions are used for intermediate result values. This extender is useful only when the %DEC built-in function is specified for the argument.

The ELSEIF operation is used within an if statement to allow alternative operations to be perform, should the IF statement condition fail. When an ELSEIF is used instead of separate ELSE and IF statements, only a single ENDIF statement is required. The result is that the IF/ELSEIF/ENDIF clause is an in-line case similar in functionality to the SELECT/WHEN/ENDSL CLAUSE.

In Example 5.51 that follows the ELSEIF operation is used on line 30 to test for an alternate condition. Note the use of a single ENDIF statement (line 70) for the IF/ELSEIF/ELSE/ENDIF clause.

Example 5.51: Using elseif for conditioning.

```
.....CSRnØ1Factor1+++++++<-OpCode(ex)->Factor2+++++++Result++++++++Len++DcHiLoEq
ØØ1Ø C                   IF            Days <= 3Ø
ØØ2Ø C                   | MOVEL       '0-3Ø'          AGING
ØØ3Ø C                   +ELSEIF       Days <= 6Ø
ØØ4Ø C                   | | MOVEL     '31-6Ø'         AGING
ØØ5Ø C                   +ELSE
ØØ6Ø C                   | | MOVEL     'Over-Due'      AGING
ØØ7Ø C                   ENDIF
```

▶ ENDxx (END DO GROUP, MONITOR GROUP, SELECT GROUP, CAS, and IF)

The ENDxx operation closes a DO, DOUxx, DOWxx, CASxx, IFxx, or SELECT group.

Factor 1	OpCode	Factor 2	Result Field	Resulting Indicators		
	ENDxx	[increment]				

See also SELECT, WHENxx, IFxx, DO, DOWxx, DOUxx, ENDSR, and CASx

The *xx* of the ENDxx operation is optional and can be specified to document the type of END operation.

Op Code	Description
END	End an IFxx, DOxxx, SELECT, or CAS operation.
ENDCS	End a CASxx operation.
ENDDO	End a DO, DOWxx, or DOUxx operation.
ENDIF	End an IFxx operation.
ENDFOR	End a FOR operation.
ENDMON	End a MONITOR/ON-ERROR group.
ENDSL	End a SELECT operation.

Factor 2 (allowed only when closing a DO...ENDDO group) is optional and may contain the increment value for a DO loop counter.

Conditioning indicators are optional when closing a DO, DOWxx, or DOUxx group. If the conditioning indicator test is true, the ENDDO statement is performed and control passes back to the top of the loop. If the conditioning indicator test is false, control passes to the operation following the ENDDO statement. See Example 5.52.

Example 5.52: Ending a DOU loop and an IF.

```
.....CSRnØ1Factor1+++++++<—OpCode(ex)—>Factor2+++++++Result++++++++Len++DcHiLoEq
ØØ1Ø C     CSTNBR        CHAIN        CUSTMAST
ØØ3Ø C                   IF           %EOF = *OFF
ØØ4Ø C                   | DOU        %EOF = *ON
ØØ5Ø C                   |               or RelNo >= 2Ø
ØØ6Ø C                   | | ADD      1             RELNO
ØØ7Ø C                   | | WRITE    SUBFILE
ØØ8Ø C                   | | READ     CUSTMAST
Ø1ØØ C                   | ENDDO
Ø11Ø C                   ENDIF
```

▶ENDSR (END SUBROUTINE)

The ENDSR operation marks the end of a subroutine. It must be the last statement of a subroutine. Factor 1 is optional and may contain a label that is used as the target of a GOTO or CAB*xx* operation.

Factor 1	OpCode	Factor 2	Result Field	Resulting Indicators		
[label]	ENDSR	[return point]				

See also BEGSR, EXSR, LEAVESR, CABxx, and CASxx

Controlling level indicators, conditioning indicators, and resulting indicators are not valid for this operation. Columns 7 and 8 must contain either the constant SR or blanks. The letters SR can be used in columns 7 and 8 of this operation to provide a visual indication of the end of a subroutine. Example 5.53 shows an example using a label. Example 5.54 shows how to cancel the program using *CANCL.

Table 5.17: Exception/Error Return Points for ENDSR

Routine	Description
*DETC	Beginning of detail-time calculations.
*DETL	Beginning of detail-time output.
*GETIN	Get input routine (read next record).
*TOTC	Beginning of total-time calculations.
*TOTL	Beginning of total-time output.
*OFL	Beginning of overflow lines.
*CANCL	Abnormal end of program.
blanks	Return to statement following interruption.

Example 5.53: Ending subroutine with a label.

```
.....CSRnØ1Factor1+++++++OpCode(ex)Factor2+++++++Result++++++++Len++DcHiLoEq
ØØ1Ø C                   EXSR      COUNT
ØØ2Ø C     ENDPGM        TAG
ØØ3Ø C                   MOVE      *ON            *INLR

ØØ4Ø CSR   COUNT         BEGSR
ØØ5Ø C                   ADD       1              Cnt
ØØ6Ø C                   MOVE      'MIDRANGE'     NEW(Cnt)
ØØ7Ø CSR   EndCount      ENDSR
```

Example 5.54: Exception/error subroutine with program cancel.

```
.....CSRn01Factor1+++++++OpCode(ex)Factor2+++++++Result++++++++Len++DcHiLoEq
0010 C                     READ      CUSTMAST                               5658
0020 C       *IN56         CASEQ     *ON             *PSSR
0030 C                     END

0040 CSR     *PSSR         BEGSR
0050 C                     IF        Status = TIMOUT
0060 C                     MOVE      *ON             *INLR
0070 C                     ENDIF
0080 CSR     EndPSSR       EndSR     '*CANCL'
```

Factor 2 may contain a six-position field, constant, or named constant when the subroutine is an exception/error handling subroutine. Factor 2 can contain a field name or a constant that identifies the returning point after the subroutine is performed. If the exception/error handling routine is called with either the EXSR or CAS*xx* operations and factor 2 is blank, control returns to the statement following the EXSR or CAS*xx* operation.

The valid exception/error return points that can be specified in factor 2 for the ENDSR operation are listed in Table 5.17.

▶EVAL (EVALUATE AN EXPRESSION)

The EVAL operation evaluates a mathematical equation or string expression and assigns the result to the variable specified on the left side of the equals (=) sign. For a description of RPG IV expressions and expression syntax, see chapter 4.

Factor 1	OpCode	Extended Factor 2
	EVAL(H)	Variable or expression = variable or expression

See also: EVALR, ADD, SUB, MULT, DIV, MVR, and MOVEL

Factor 2 is required and must contain either a string expression or a numeric equation. The expression consists of three components: the l-value, the assignment symbol, and the r-value. The l-value is the term used to describe the value to the left of the assignment symbol. The r-value is the term used to describe the value to the right of the assignment symbol. The *assignment symbol* is the special symbol use to separate the l-value and r-value. The equals sign (=) is used as the assignment symbol for the EVAL operation in RPG.

The result (i.e., the l-value) can be any type of variable. Also, the %SUBST built-in function can be used on either side of the assignment. When an array name is specified or an array name with an index value of * is specified for the l-value, the value specified for the r-value is copied to each element of the array. Remember the following when using the EVAL operation:

- Numeric expressions that require the half-adjust operation extender can be specified.

- The MVR (Move Remainder) operation is not supported following an EVAL operation. Use the %REM built-in function if a remainder is required.

- Data is stored right adjusted in the resulting field.

- Expressions can be used within array indexes and in %SUBST subscripts when used on the left side or right side of the expression.

- Date and time data types can be used in an expression, but format conversion of date and time values to character values requires the use of the %CHAR built-in function.

- The result of a conditional expression can be assigned to an indicator or named indicator variable.

The EVAL operation is the general-purpose assignment operation. It can be used to copy data from one variable to another or to perform complex mathematical and string expressions.

Example 5.55 illustrates various uses of expressions with the EVAL operation. For a description of RPG IV expressions and expression syntax, see chapter 3.

Example 5.55: Using an expression on the EVAL operation.

```
.....CSRnØ1.............OpCode(ex)Extended-factor2+++++++++++++++++++++++++++++++
        * Character string assignments
ØØØ1 C                  Eval      Message = YourName + ' Ph.D'
ØØØ2 C                  Eval      %SUBST( name : 7 : 5 ) = 'Cozzi'
ØØØ3 C                  Eval      name ='Bob' + ' ' + 'Cozzi'
ØØØ4 C                  Eval      msg = ItemDesc + %CHAR(ItemNo) + ' is out +
ØØØ5 C                             of stock.'
        * Numeric assignments
ØØØ6 C                  Eval      Result = (1 - (Term * Principal) * Interest)/2
ØØØ7 C                  Eval(h)   Profit = SalesQTY * (Price - Cost)

ØØØ8 C                  Eval      area = 4*PI*Radius**2

ØØØ9 C                  Eval      *IN58 = (Amt_Due > 1000 AND Price > 500)
ØØ1Ø C                  Eval      *INLR = count <= 30 or count > 10000
        * Date/Time assignments
ØØ11 C                  Eval      dateSold = D'1996-06-01'
```

The following is a description of what occurs in Example 5.55.

Line	Description
1	The YOURNAME field is concatenated together with the literal ' PH.D' and stored in MESSAGE.
2	The %SUBST built-in function is used to copy 'COZZI' to positions 7 through 11 of the NAME field.
3	Two literals and a blank are concatenated together.
4 and 5	The ITEMNO field is converted to character and then concatenated with the ITEMDESC field. Then a literal is concatenated to it and copied to the result.
6	A typical mathematical equation is performed.
7	The PROFIT field is assigned the value of PRICE minus cost, multiplied by SALESQTY.
8	The area of a sphere is calculated as $4\pi R2$.
9 and 10	The indicator *IN58 is set on when the conditional expression is TRUE.
11	The DATESOLD field (which is of type DATE) is assigned a date literal.

▶ EVALR (EVALUATE AN EXPRESSION, RIGHT-ADJUST)

The EVALR operation evaluates a mathematical equation or string expression and assigns the result to the variable specified on the left side of the equals (=) sign. The resulting value is stored right justified in the variable specified to the left of the equals sign. For a description of RPG IV expressions and expression syntax, see chapter 4.

Factor 1	OpCode	Extended Factor 2
	EVAL(E H M R)	Variable or expression = variable or expression

See also EVALR, ADD, SUB, MULT, DIV, MVR, and MOVEL

Factor 2 is required and must contain either a string expression or a numeric equation. The expression consists of three components: the l-value, the assignment symbol, and the r-value. The l-value is the term used to describe the value to the left of the assignment symbol. The r-value is the term used to describe the value to the right of the assignment symbol. The assignment symbol is the special symbol use to separate the l-value and r-value. The equals sign (=) is used as the assignment symbol in RPG.

The result (i.e., the l-value) can be any type of variable. The resulting value is stored in the l-value right justified. The %SUBST built-in function can be used on either side of the assignment. When an array name is specified or an array name with an index value of * is specified for the l-value, the value specified for the r-value is copied to each element of the array. Remember the following when using the EVALR operation:

- Numeric expressions that require the half-adjust operation extender can be specified.
- The MVR (move remainder) operation is not supported following an EVALR operation. Use the %REM built-in function if a remainder is required.
- Data is stored right adjusted in the resulting field.
- Expressions can be used within array indexes and in %SUBST subscripts when used on the left side or right side of the expression.
- Date and time data types can be used in an expression, but format conversion for date and time values to character values requires the use of the %CHAR built-in function.
- The result of a conditional expression can be assigned to an indicator or named indicator variable.

The EVALR operation is the general-purpose assignment operation. It can be used to copy data from one variable to another or to perform complex mathematical and string expressions. The EVAL operation is the primary assignment operation code. EVALR is used when the need to store a result value right adjusted is required.

Example 5.56 illustrates the use of the EVALR operation. For a description of RPG IV expressions and expression syntax, see chapter 4.

Example 5.56: Using an expression on the EVAL operation.

```
.....DName++++++++++EUDS.......Length+TDc.Functions++++++++++++++++++++++++++++
     D Website          S            35A

.....CSRn01..............OpCode(ex)Extended-factor2++++++++++++++++++++++++++++
     * Character string assignments
0002 C                   EvalR     website = 'www.RPGIV.com'

       *...v....1....v....2....v....3....v....
website = '             www.RPGIV.com'
```

▶ EXCEPT (EXCEPTION OUTPUT)

The EXCEPT operation performs an immediate write to either a program-defined output file or an externally described file's record format.

Factor 1	OpCode	Factor 2	Result Field	Resulting Indicators		
	EXCEPT	[except label]				

See also WRITE and UNLOCK

Factor 2 can contain the name of an EXCEPT label. EXCEPT labels are used to control the output to the output record. When an EXCEPT label is present, only those output specifications that contain the EXCEPT label are written. More than one output specification can contain the same EXCEPT label.

When an EXCEPT label is not used, only those exception output records without an EXCEPT label are written, provided that the output format conditioning indicators are true. The EXCEPT operation can be used to release records of a database file that have been locked by another operation.

When an EXCEPT operation is performed on an externally described file and database fields are specified on the output specification, only those fields specified are written to the database record. Other fields within the record go unchanged. To write out all fields in the record format, the figurative constant *ALL must be the first and only field specified for the exception output.

When updating a record, fields not specified for output go unchanged. When writing a new record, fields that are not specified for output are set to their default value, typically zero or blanks—depending on their attribute. For date and time variables, they are set to their default value. If no default value has been specified in the file description (DDS) for a date or time field, the current date or time is inserted.

Examples 5.57 through 5.60 illustrate four uses of the EXCEPT operation:

- EXCEPT output to a program-defined printer file.
- EXCEPT output with an EXCEPT label to a program-defined print file.
- EXCEPT output to an externally described database file format.
- EXCEPT output to release a locked record.

In Example 5.57, the first record matching the key value in the field INDEX is retrieved from the customer master file CUSTMAST. Next, an exception output line is printed (printing the customer number and customer name). Because the EXCEPT operation on line 40 contains no except name, the output specifications on lines 80 to 100 are output and lines 110 to 120 are not.

Example 5.57: Exception output to a program-defined printer file.

```
.....CSRnØ1Factor1+++++++OpCode(ex)Factor2+++++++Result++++++++Len++DcHiLoEq
ØØ1Ø C     INDEX         CHAIN    CUSTMAST
ØØ3Ø C                   DOW      %Found

ØØ4Ø C                   EXCEPT

ØØ5Ø C     INDEX         READE CUSTMAST                                  58
ØØ7Ø C                   ENDDO

.....OFormat++++DAddnØ1nØ2nØ3Except++++SpbSpaSkbSka
ØØ8Ø OQPRINT     E                            1

.....O.............nØ1nØ2nØ3Field+++++++++YB?End++PConstant/Editword+++++++++++
ØØ9Ø O                        CUST#       Z   1Ø
Ø1ØØ O                        CSTNAM          +2
Ø11Ø OQPRINT     E            DETAIL      1
Ø12Ø O                        BALDUE      3   1Ø
```

In Example 5.58, the exception label DETAIL is used to control the output of the printer file. The output specifications on lines 110 and 120 print the balance due. The output specifications on lines 80 to 100 are not output because they are not conditioned by the DETAIL exception name.

Example 5.58: Exception output with an EXCEPT label to a program-described file.

```
.....CSRnØ1Factor1+++++++OpCode(ex)Factor2+++++++Result++++++++Len++DcHiLoEq
ØØ1Ø C         INDEX          CHAIN     CUSTMAST
ØØ3Ø C                        DOW       %Found

ØØ4Ø C                        EXCEPT    DETAIL

ØØ5Ø C         INDEX          READE     CUSTMAST
ØØ7Ø C                        ENDDO

.....OFormat++++DAddnØ1nØ2nØ3Except++++SpbSpaSkbSka
ØØ8Ø OQPRINT     E            DETAIL         1

.....O..............nØ1nØ2nØ3Field+++++++++YB?End++PConstant/Editword+++++++++++
ØØ9Ø O                        CUST#           Z    1Ø
Ø1ØØ O                        CSTNAM               +2
Ø11Ø OQPRINT     E            DETAIL         1
Ø12Ø O                        BALDUE         3    1Ø
```

In Example 5.59, the first record matching the key value in the field INDEX is retrieved from the customer orders file CUSTINV. Then, the balance-due field BALDUE is zeroed, giving the customer a zero-balance-due account. To update only that field, an exception label is used on line 70 to update the customer record with a zero balance.

Example 5.59: Exception output to an externally described database file format.

```
.....FFileName++IFEASFRlen+LKeylnKFDevice+.Functions+++++++++++++++++++++++++++++
ØØ1Ø FCustInv   IF   E          K DISK

.....CSRnØ1Factor1+++++++OpCode(ex)Factor2+++++++Result++++++++Len++DcHiLoEq
ØØ2Ø C         INDEX          CHAIN     CUSTINV
ØØ4Ø C                        DOW       %Found
ØØ5Ø *    Zero out the existing balance due field.
ØØ6Ø C                        Eval      BalDue = Ø

ØØ7Ø C                        EXCEPT    NewBalDue

ØØ8Ø C         INDEX          READE     CustRec
Ø1ØØ C                        EndDo

.....OFormat++++DAddnØ1nØ2nØ3Except++++SpbSpaSkbSka
Ø11Ø OCustRec    E            NewBalDue
Ø12Ø O                        BALDUE
```

In Example 5.60, the record matching the key value in the field INDEX is retrieved from the customer master file CUSTMAST. Because CUSTMAST is opened for update, data management locks the record. To release this record lock, the EXCEPT operation can be used, although the UNLOCK operation is more intuitive.

Example 5.60: Exception output to release a locked record.

```
.....FFileName++IFEASFRlen+LKeylnKFDevice+.Functions++++++++++++++++++++++++++++
0010 FCustMast  UF   E          K DISK

.....CSRn01Factor1+++++++OpCode(ex)Factor2+++++++Result++++++++Len++DcHiLoEq
0020 C        INDEX        CHAIN     CUSTMAST

0040 C                     IF        %Found
0050 C                     EXCEPT    Release
0060 C                     ENDIF

0070 C                     EXFMT     DISPLAY

.....OFormat++++DAddn01n02n03Except++++SpbSpaSkbSka
0080 OCustRect   E            RELEASE
```

To release the record lock, an EXCEPT operation is performed on line 50. The EXCEPT label RELEASE is specified. RELEASE is an empty output format (that is, it contains no output fields). This is the key to this technique. By specifying no output fields, the system performs an "empty" output operation and releases the record lock. Note that the exception label name "RELEASE" is used for easy identification of the release function.

This technique works with program-defined and externally described database files that are open for UPDATE. It's functionally equivalent to the UNLOCK operation. The UNLOCK operation is better suited for releasing records because it was designed for this purpose.

> **WARNING:** When an EXCEPT name is used on a file that has been opened for OUTPUT only and no output fields have been specified for the exception output—as described in Example 5.57—a record containing blank and zero fields (depending on the field attribute) is written to the database file.

▶ EXFMT (WRITE/READ A WORKSTATION FILE FORMAT)

The EXFMT operation performs a WRITE followed by a READ to the same WORKSTN file record format. The EXFMT operation is a combined and optimized form of WRITE followed by READ.

Factor 1	OpCode	Factor 2	Result Field	Resulting Indicators	
	EXFMT (E)	workstn format			[error]	

See also READ and WRITE

Factor 2 must contain the name of a WORKSTN file record format. Resulting indicator 2 is optional and, if specified, it signals when a workstation error has occurred. EXFMT, however, cannot be used for workstation timeout. See the subheading READ (Read from a File) for information on workstation timeout.

Resulting Indicator Legend			
Columns	Ind.	Usage	Set-On Condition
71 - 72	1	N/A	
73 - 74	2	[error]	An error occurred during the operation.
75 - 76	3	N/A	

In Example 5.61, the database fields in the file CUSTMAST are the same as those used in the workstation file format CUSTFMT. Consequently, no MOVE operations need to be performed to get the database information into the workstation record format.

Example 5.61: Retrieving and displaying a data file record.

```
.....FFileName++IFEASFRlen+LKeylnKFDevice+.Functions+++++++++++++++++++++++++++++
0010 FCustMast  IF   E           K DISK
0020 FCUSTINQ   CF   E                     WORKSTN

.....CSRn01Factor1+++++++OpCode(ex)Factor2+++++++Result++++++++Len++DcHiLoEq
0030 C     INDEX        CHAIN    CustRec
     *  If the customer is not found, add a new customer
0040 C                  IF       NOT %Found
0050 C                  EXFMT    NEWCUST
0060 C                  ELSE
     *  If the customer is found, display the existing record
0070 C                  EXFMT    UPDCUST
0080 C                  ENDIF
```

▶EXSR (PERFORM SUBROUTINE)

The EXSR operation calls an internal subroutine (known as a procedure in some languages). After the subroutine has completed, or the LEAVESR operation is performed, control returns to the statement following the EXSR operation.

If a GOTO operation within the subroutine caused branching outside of the domain of the subroutine, or an exception/error handling subroutine caused branching to a different part of the program cycle, control doesn't return to the statement following the EXSR operation.

Factor 1	OpCode	Factor 2	Result Field	Resulting Indicators		
	EXSR		Subroutine			

See also BEGSR, ENDSR, CASxx, and LEAVESR

Factor 2 can contain a user-written subroutine name, the name of the exception/error subroutine (*PSSR), or the initialization subroutine (*INZSR). It also can contain a file exception/error subroutine (INFSR) name. The subroutine name can be up to 14 characters in length for fixed format operations, and any length for free-format operations.

In Example 5.62, the database file ITEMMAST (item master) is accessed on line 10. The subroutine PROFIT is then performed on line 50 to compute the gross profit of the item retrieved by the CHAIN operation on line 10. The subroutine PROFIT begins on line 80 with the BEGSR operation. The gross profit is calculated. The subroutine ends with the ENDSR operation (line 120). Control returns to line 60.

Example 5.62: Performing a subroutine to compute profit.

```
.....CSRn01Factor1+++++++OpCode(ex)Factor2+++++++Result++++++++Len++DcHiLoEq
0010 C     INDEX          CHAIN     ITEMMAST                             54
0030 C                    IF        %FOUND
0040 C                    MOVEL     'FOUND'        MSG

0050 C                    EXSR      PROFIT

0060 C                    ENDIF
0070 C                    MOVE      *ON            *INLR

0080 CSR   PROFIT         BEGSR
0090 C     PRICE          MULT      QTYORD         EXTEND
0100 C     ITMCST         MULT      QTYORD         EXTCST
0110 C     EXTPRC         SUB       EXTCST         GRSPFT
0120 CSR                  ENDSR
```

Subroutine Considerations

Each subroutine must be outside the domain of other subroutines. In other words, a subroutine cannot contain another subroutine—although a subroutine can call another subroutine.

Any RPG operation may be specified with a subroutine, including the EXSR and CAS*xx* operations. Therefore, a subroutine can call another subroutine. However, recursive calls to a subroutine can cause the program to loop.

Control level-break indicators are not allowed. The constant SR can be specified in the control level-break indicator columns 7 and 8 to indicate that this is a subroutine. Most programs contain the SR only on the BEGSR and ENDSR statements. This visually identifies the beginning and end of the subroutine.

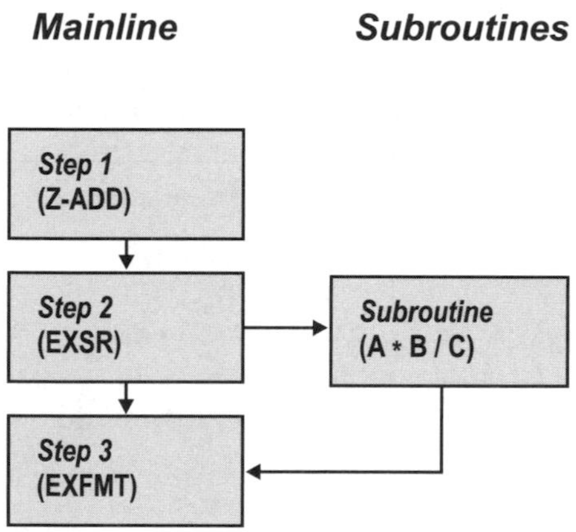

The GOTO operation can be used to branch within the subroutine (such as to a LABEL on a TAG or ENDSR statement). It also can branch to a location outside of the subroutine's domain, within the *mainline calculations*. The GOTO operation cannot, however, branch to a label contained within another subroutine. Figure 5.3 shows a diagram of the mainline and subroutines.

Mainline **Subroutines**

Step 1 (Z-ADD)

Step 2 (EXSR) → Subroutine (A * B / C)

Step 3 (EXFMT)

Figure 5.3: Diagram of mainline flow with EXSR.

▶ EXTRCT (EXTRACT A PORTION OF A DATE, TIME, OR TIMESTAMP)

The EXTRCT operation code can be used to extract a part of a date, time, or timestamp value. The extracted *date component* is copied into the result field.

Factor 1	OpCode	Factor 2	Result Field	Resulting Indicators		
	EXTRCT(E)	Date : duration	numeric variable		[error]	

See also %SUBDT, ADDDUR, SUBDUR, and TEST

The date, time, or timestamp value is specified in factor 2 and is followed immediately by a duration code. The duration code identifies which part is to be extracted. Valid duration codes are *YEARS, *MONTHS, *DAYS, *HOURS, *MINUTES, *SECONDS, *MSECONDS, and the shorthand forms *Y, *M, *D, *H, *MN, S, *MS. For a description of each duration code, see Table 5.6.

The result field can be either a character or a numeric variable. If the result field is a character, the extracted value is copied left justified and zero suppressed; unneeded positions in the character field are filled with blanks. If the result field is numeric, the extracted value replaces the value of the result field.

In Example 5.63, the EXTRCT operation on line 4 extracts the day of the month from the DUEDATE field. Because DUEDATE has been initialized to February 17, 1996, the day of the month is 17. On line 6, a similar EXTRCT operation also retrieves 17. Note that, regardless of the date format of factor 2, the day of the month is retrieved.

Example 5.63: Using EXTRCT to retrieve the day of the month.

```
.....DName++++++++++EUDSFrom+++To/Len+TDc.Functions++++++++++++++++++++++++++++++
0001 D DueDate         S              D    INZ(D'1996-02-17')
0002 D JuliDate        S              D    DatFmt(*JUL) INZ(D'1996-02-17')

.....CSRn01Factor1+++++++OpCode(ex)Factor2+++++++Result++++++++Len++DcHiLoEq
0003  *   Extract the day from the date. The field THEDAY receives the value 17.
0004 C                    Extrct    DueDate:*Days theDay            2 0
0005  *   Extract the day from the date. Field JULIDAY also receives the value 17.
0006 C                    Extrct    JuliDate:*DaysJuliDay           2 0
```

FEOD (FORCE END OF DATA)

The FEOD operation positions a file's "cursor" to the end-of-file, releases any record locks that exist, and force any buffered data to be written to the device. For example, the last few lines of a printed report are normally not sent to the printer until after the print file is closed. The FEOD operation forces those last few printed lines to the printer device (output queue) without requiring the file to be closed.

Factor 1	OpCode	Factor 2	Result Field	Resulting Indicators	
	FEOD(E)	File name		[error]	

See also CLOSE, SETLL, and OPEN

Factor 2 must contain the name of the file for the FEOD operation. If the FEOD fails, resulting indicator 2 is set on.

The FEOD operation differs from the CLOSE operation in that acquired device files (see the subheading ACQ [Acquire]) are not released (i.e., disconnected) from the program. The file must be repositioned before any subsequent read operation can access the file's data.

Resulting Indicator Legend			
Columns	Ind.	Usage	Set-On Condition
71 - 72	1	N/A	
73 - 74	2	[error]	An error occurred during the operation.
75 - 76	3	N/A	

In Example 5.64, the file CUSTMAST is forced to the end of data. Any CUSTMAST records locked by the program are released. Resulting indicator 2 (indicator 56 in this example) is set on if the FEOD fails.

Example 5.64: Forcing the end of data of a data file.

```
.....CSRn01Factor1+++++++OpCode(ex)Factor2+++++++Result++++++++Len++DcHiLoEq
0010 C                   FEOD      CUSTMAST                            56
```

▶FOR (FOR LOOP)

The FOR operation begins an iterative group of operations. An index, increment, and limit are specified to control the iterative process.

Factor 1	OpCode	Extended Factor 2
	FOR	Index [= start] [TO | DOWNTO limit] [BY increment]

See also LEAVE, ITER, DO, and ENDFOR

The FOR operation begins a FOR/ENDFOR loop. The operations enclosed within the FOR and ENDFOR operations are performed a number of times. The number of times the operations are performed is controlled by the *limit*. Each iteration through the FOR/ENDFOR loop increments or decrements the *index* by *increment value* until the limit is breached.

When the FOR operation is encountered, the *start value* is assigned to the index variable. The index value is compared with the limit. When the TO keyword is specified, and if the index is greater than the limit, control is passed to the statement following the ENDFOR operation. When the DOWNTO keyword is specified, and if the index is less than the limit, control is passed to the statement following the ENDFOR operation. Otherwise, the operations enclosed within the FOR/ENDFOR operations are performed.

The FOR operation supports three parameters. Index is a type of loop counter variable. It can be assigned an initial *start* value when the FOR/ENDFOR loop is started. Limit is the threshold for the loop. It represents the minimum or maximum value allowed for the index variable. Increment is the value that is added to or subtracted from the index variable after each pass through the FOR/ENDFOR loop.

The TO keyword indicates that the index is incremented on each pass; whereas, the DOWNTO keyword indicates that the index is decremented on each pass. The BY keyword identifies the amount added to or subtracted from the index on each pass through the FOR/ENDFOR loop. Normally, the BY value is a positive value.

Figure 5.4 shows the full syntax of the FOR/ENDFOR operations. Conditioning indicators on the FOR operation are tested when the FOR operation is initially performed. They are not tested as the FOR/ENDFOR loop is iterating. Conditioning indicators control whether or not the FOR/ENDFOR is performed at all, but not whether the iterations themselves are performed. Conditioning indicators are tested each time the ENDFOR operation is encountered.

```
.....CSRnØ1..............OpCode(ex)Extended-factor2++++++++++++++++++++++++++++++
C                      FOR        index [= start value ]
C                                 TO [DOWNTO] limit ]
C                                 [ BY increment ]
C
C                      endfor
```

Figure 5.4: Syntax of the FOR/ENDFOR operation.

Example 5.65 shows an example of the operation codes. Upon normal completion of the FOR/ENDFOR loop, the value of the index is one more than the limit for the TO keyword or one less than the limit for the DOWNTO keyword. This is always true unless the LEAVE operation is used to prematurely exit the FOR/ENDFOR loop.

Example 5.65: An example of the FOR/ENDFOR operation.

```
.....CSRnØ1..............OpCode(ex)Extended-factor2++++++++++++++++++++++++++++++
.....CSRNØ1Factor1+++++++OpCode(ex)Factor2+++++++Result++++++++Len++DcHILOEQ....
     **  Do the routine 5Ø times, adding 1 to I each time.
C                      FOR        i=1 to 5Ø
C                      add        i              Counter
C                      endfor
     ** NOTE: X = 51 after this statement.

     **  Start at 1Ø, do until X is 1.

.....CSRnØ1..............OpCode(ex)Extended-factor2++++++++++++++++++++++++++++++
C                      for        X = 1Ø DownTo 1
C                      if         %Subst(Name : X : 1) = *BLANK
C                      eval       %subst(Name : X : 1) = '_'
C                      else
C                      Leave
C                      endIF
C                      endFOR
     **  NOTE:  X=Ø after this statement.
```

▶ FORCE (FORCE INPUT PRIORITY)

The FORCE operation controls the sequence in which records are read by the RPG cycle. Only primary and secondary files are read by the RPG cycle. The FORCE operation is valid within detail-time calculations only.

Factor 1	OpCode	Factor 2	Result Field	Resulting Indicators		
	FORCE	File name				

See also NEXT.

Factor 2 must contain the name of the primary or secondary file that is read on the next RPG cycle. If the file specified in factor 2 is at end of file, the FORCE operation is ignored and the RPG cycle selects the next file to be read.

When more than one FORCE operation occurs during the same RPG cycle, the final FORCE operation has priority over all other FORCE operations. In Example 5.66, the file ORDERS is read on the next input cycle, bypassing the normal primary/secondary selection priority.

Extender	Description
M	If expressions are specified for any of the arguments of the operation, the maximum-digits format for intermediate results is used.
R	If expressions are specified for any of the arguments of the operation, the result value's decimal positions are used for intermediate result values. This extender is useful only when the %DEC built-in function is specified for the argument.

Example 5.66: Forcing input from a secondary file.

```
.....FFileName++IFEASFRlen+LKeylnKFDevice+.Functions+++++++++++++++++++++++++++++++
0010 FCustMast  IPE  E            DISK
0020 FITEMMAST  ISE  E            DISK
0030 FORDERS    ISE  E            DISK


.....CSRn01Factor1+++++++OpCode(ex)Factor2+++++++Result++++++++Len++DcHiLoEq
0040 C                   IF        Count = 0
0050 C                   ADD       1             COUNT           3 0
0060 C                   FORCE     ORDERS
0070 C                   ENDIF
        *   Additional code would go here...
```

▶GOTO (GO TO)

The GOTO operation allows branching to different areas of the program. A label, called a *tag* in RPG, is the target of the GOTO operation. Labels are declared with the TAG and ENDSR operation.

Factor 1	OpCode	Factor 2	Result Field	Resulting Indicators		
	GOTO	label				

See also TAG, CABxx, IF, SELECT, WHEN, DO, DOW, DOU, LEAVESR, and ENDSR

The GOTO operation performs a permanent branch to the label specified in factor 2. Control never returns to the GOTO statement. For the most part, the GOTO can branch anywhere in the program from anywhere in the program. However, a subroutine cannot be branched into from outside of that subroutine. Also, detail-time calculations cannot be the target of a branch operation from within total-time calculations. In Example 5.67, the GOTO operation on line 500 performs an unconditional branch to the label READ on line 10.

Example 5.67: GOTO controlled looping.

```
.....CSRn01Factor1+++++++OpCode(ex)Factor2+++++++Result++++++++Len++DcHiLoEq
0010 C        READ         TAG
0020 C                     READ      CUSTMAST                            LR
0030 C        *INLR        CABEQ     *ON         ENDPGM

     C*... user code ........
0500 C                     GOTO      READ

     C*... more user code.....
0900 C        ENDPGM       TAG
```

▶ IF*xx* (IF CONDITIONAL COMPARISON)

The IF*xx* operation compares the value in factor 1 to the value in factor 2. If the comparison is true, the group of calculations between the IF*xx* and its associated ENDIF operation (or ELSE operation) are performed. Conditioning indicators are valid for the IF*xx* operation. However, conditioning indicators cannot be used on AND*xx* and OR*xx* operations.

Factor 1	OpCode	Factor 2	Result Field	Resulting Indicators		
Compare value 1	IF*xx*	compare value 2				
	IF (M R)	conditional expression				

See also ELSEIF, SELECT, WHEN, ELSE, DOWxx, DOUxx, CASxx, and FOR

The IF*xx* operation requires a relationship test *xx*, where *xx* may be any one of the Boolean operators (EQ, GE, GT, LE, LT, and NE). See Table 5.9 for details. Factor 1 is compared to factor 2 based on the *xx* operator. Factor 1 and factor 2 must be similar data types. For the secondary form of IF, the extended factor 2 must contain a conditional expression. The IF operation supports the M and R operation extenders.

If a conditioning indicator is used, it is tested before the IF*xx* operation. When the indicator condition is false, the IF*xx* operation is not performed. Control passes to the associated ENDIF operation for this IF*xx* operation even if an ELSE operation is specified. When the indicator condition is true, the IF*xx* operation, along with any AND*xx* and OR*xx* conditioning, is performed.

The IF*xx* operation can be used to conditionally perform a group of operations by testing a range, a list of values, a single value, or a compound set of values. See Examples 5.68 through 5.72 for details.

The IF*xx* test can be extended with the AND*xx* or OR*xx* operations. The AND*xx* operation allows compound conditions to be tested; OR*xx* allows additional, but separate, conditions to be tested. The AND*xx* and OR*xx* operations cannot be used in conjunction with the IF form of this operation.

In Example 5.68, the CHAIN operation on line 10 accesses the database file CUSTMAST. If a record is found, resulting indicator 1 (if specified) is set off. The IF operation on line 20 tests the %FOUND status and performs an EXFMT operation if the condition is true.

Example 5.68: Conditioning a group of operations on a single comparison.

```
.....CSRnØ1Factor1+++++++OpCode(ex)Factor2+++++++Result++++++++Len++DcHiLoEq
ØØ1Ø C     INDEX        CHAIN     CUSTMAST
ØØ2Ø C                  IF        %FOUND
ØØ3Ø C                  EXFMT     DISPLAY
ØØ4Ø C                  ENDIF
```

In Example 5.69, the EXFMT operation prompts the user. The format DISPLAY is written to and read from the display device. After the format is read, the compound IF*xx* operation on lines 20 to 40 compares the field OPTION to 'A1', 'B1', or 'C1'. If the field OPTION is equal to any of these values, the MOVE operation on line 50 is performed.

Example 5.69: Using the IFxx and the ORxx to test for a list of values.

```
.....CSRnØ1Factor1+++++++OpCode(ex)Factor2+++++++Result++++++++Len++DcHiLoEq
ØØ1Ø C                  EXFMT     DISPLAY
ØØ2Ø C     OPTION       IFEQ      'A1'
ØØ3Ø C     OPTION       OREQ      'B1'
ØØ4Ø C     OPTION       OREQ      'C1'
ØØ5Ø C                  MOVE      'OK'            STATUS
ØØ6Ø C                  ENDIF
```

In Example 5.70, the workstation format DISPLAY is sent to and read from the display through the EXFMT operation. When the workstation file is read, the IF operation on line 20 compares the field OPTION to be between 1 and 9. If the field OPTION satisfies this condition, the EVAL operation on line 30 is performed.

Example 5.70: Using the IF and the AND to test for a range.

```
.....CSRnØ1..............OpCode(ex)Extended-factor2++++++++++++++++++++++++++++++
ØØ1Ø C                  EXFMT     DISPLAY
ØØ2Ø C                  IF        Option > = 1 and Option <= 9
ØØ3Ø C                  EVAL      Status = 'OK'
ØØ4Ø C                  ENDIF
```

To rewrite Example 5.71 with the alternate form of IF, the code in Example 5.72 can be specified.

Example 5.71: Using the compound form of IFxx to control entry into a subroutine.

```
.....CSRnØ1Factor1+++++++<—OpCode(ex)—>Factor2+++++++Result++++++++Len++DcHiLoEq
ØØ1Ø C                  EXFMT     DISPLAY
ØØ2Ø C     OPTION       IFEQ      '9'
ØØ3Ø C     FILE         ANDNE     *BLANKS
ØØ4Ø C     LIBR         ANDNE     *BLANKS
ØØ5Ø C     FILE         ANDNE     '*DELETED'
ØØ6Ø C     USERID     | IFEQ      'SECURITY'
```

```
0070 C     USERID      | OREQ        'MANAGER'
0080 C     AUT         | ANDEQ       'DELRGHT'
0090 C                 | | EXSR      DeleteUser
0100 C                 | ENDIF
0110 C                 ENDIF
```

In Example 5.72, the workstation format DISPLAY is written to and read from the workstation using the EXFMT operation. When the workstation file is read, the IF operation on lines 20 and 30 is tested. When the condition is met, the nested IF operation that begins on line 50 is tested. If that condition is met, the user's record is retrieved. If the retrieval is successful, the EXSR operation (line 90) is performed.

Example 5.72: Using alternate IF to control entry into a subroutine.

```
.....CSRn01..............OpCode(ex)Extended-factor2+++++++++++++++++++++++++++++
0010 C                 EXFMT       DISPLAY
0020 C                 If          Option = 9 and (FileName   *Blanks
0030 C                              and LibName   *Blanks and FileName   '*DELETED')

0050 C                 If          (userID = 'SECURITY' or userID='MANAGER')
0060 C                              and authority = 'DELRIGHTS'
0070 C     USERID      CHAIN       UserFile
0080 C                 If          %FOUND
0090 C                 EXSR        DeleteUser
0100 C                 EndIf
0110 C                 EndIf
0120 C                 EndIf
```

Figure 5.5 shows diagrams of the two forms of IF-THEN-ELSE. The left-most flowchart in Figure 5.5 illustrates a traditional IF-THEN operation. If the test is true, the process is performed; if the test is false, the process is bypassed. The right-most flowchart illustrates the IF-THEN-ELSE operation. If the test is true, the process is performed; if the test is false, an alternate process is performed.

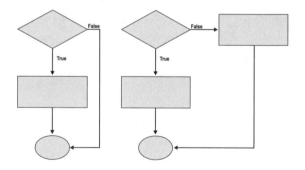

Figure 5.5: The two forms of IF-THEN-ELSE.

IN (READ IN A DATA AREA)

The IN operation retrieves one or all of the data areas defined in the program. Optionally, it also allows the data area to be locked. When a data area is locked, no other program can access that data area until an UNLOCK (unlock data area) operation is performed.

Factor 1	OpCode	Factor 2	Result Field	Resulting Indicators	
[*LOCK]	IN (E)	data area variable		[error]	
[*LOCK]	IN (E)	*DTAARA		[error]	

See also OUT, *DTAARA DEFINE, and DTAARA keywords

Factor 1 can contain the constant *LOCK, which causes the data area specified in factor 2 to be locked. Factor 1 can be blank, causing the data area specified in factor 2 to be retrieved without being locked. If factor 1 is blank for an IN operation, the previous IN operation dictates the lock/no-lock status. The first IN operation of a succession of IN operations for a specific data area controls the object lock placed on the data area.

Resulting Indicator Legend			
Columns	Ind.	Usage	Set-On Condition
71 - 72	1	N/A	
73 - 74	2	[error]	An error occurred during the operation.
75 - 76	3	N/A	

Factor 2 can contain a data area name or the constant *DTAARA. When a data area name is specified, the data area is retrieved and optionally locked by the program. When *DTAARA is specified, all data areas declared to the program are retrieved.

Example 5.73: Defining then retrieving a data area.

```
.....CSRn01Factor1+++++++OpCode(ex)Factor2+++++++Result++++++++Len++DcHiLoEq
0010 C     *DTAARA     DEFINE    ACCTCTL      CTLNBR
0020 C     *LOCK       IN        CTLNBR
```

In Example 5.73, the data area ACCTCTL is defined to the program on line 10. The field CTLNBR is the field that is assigned to the data area. Line 20 retrieves the data area ACCTCTL into the field CTLNBR. The data area is locked.

▶ITER (ITERATE A LOOP)

The ITER operation can be used within a DO, DOWxx, and DOUxx to cause the iteration of the loop being processed. Iteration is accomplished by transferring control to the logical "top" of the DO loop.

Factor 1	OpCode	Factor 2	Result Field	Resulting Indicators		
	ITER					

See also DO, DOW, DOU, and LEAVE

The ITER operation is used within a DO or FOR loop, typically in conjunction with the LEAVE operation, to enhance control of the loop. To control the ITER operation, conditioning indicators or more properly, an IF operation can be used.

In Example 5.74, the I (index) field is initialized to the length of the ITEMDS variable (a data structure name, not shown). Then, each character of ITEMDS is compared to a blank. Any position of ITEMDS that is blank is bypassed. The ITER operation on lines 3, 4, 5 is used to bypass the blanks in the field. All other characters are processed by the remaining operations of the FOR group.

Example 5.74: Using ITER to bypass unnecessary code.

```
.....CSRn01Factor1+++++++<-OpCode(ex)->Factor2+++++++Result++++++++Len++DcHiLoEq
0002 C                    FOR           Count = 1 TO %len(ITEMDS) BY 1
0003 C                    | If          %SUBST(ITEMDS : Count:1) = *Blank
0004 C                    | | ITER
0005 C                    | EndIf
     C                    | .
     C*   additional code can go here.
     C                    | .
     C                    ENDFOR
```

▶KFLD (KEY FIELD)

The KFLD operation is a declarative operation that defines an element of a key list. Multiple successive KFLD operations are used to define a key list, which is used in accessing keyed database files. The KFLD operation may appear anywhere in the calculation specifications, but it must follow a KLIST operation (see the subheading KLIST [Key List]) or another KFLD operation code. Conditioning indicators are not valid for this operation.

Factor 1	OpCode	Factor 2	Result Field	Resulting Indicators		
	KFLD		key field			

See also %KDS, KLIST, CHAIN, SETLL, and DELETE

The result field must contain the name of the field that defines the key field. This field is used with other key fields (if specified) to form a key list (KLIST). The key list is used to access a database file.

One or more KFLD operation codes are needed to define a key list. The attributes of each key field must match those of the database file that is accessed by the key list. The number of KFLD operations that is permitted per key list depends on the index (i.e., access path) of the database file that is being accessed. The key list may contain as many KFLD operation codes as there are key fields defined for the database file's index. If fewer KFLD operation codes appear on the key list than are actually contained in the database file's index, then that subset is used to access the file. See Example 5.75.

Example 5.75: Using a key field for access by warehouse and part number.

```
.....CSRn01Factor1+++++++OpCode(ex)Factor2+++++++Result++++++++Len++DcHiLoEq
0010 C     PART          KLIST
0020 C                   KFLD                      WHSNBR
0030 C                   KFLD                      PRTNBR
0040 C     PART          CHAIN     PARTMAST                           54
```

▶ KLIST (KEY LIST)

The KLIST operation defines a composite key or key list made up of one or more KFLD operation codes. The key list is used to access a database file by an index. Conditioning indicators are not valid for this operation.

Factor 1	OpCode	Factor 2	Result Field	Resulting Indicators		
key list name	KLIST					

See also KFLD, %KDS, CHAIN, SETLL, and DELETE

Factor 1 must contain the name of the key list that is being defined. The KLIST operation must be followed by one or more KFLD operation (see the preceding subheading). The KLIST operation defines the key list name; the KFLD operations define the key fields. For externally described files only, the key list name can appear in factor 1 of the CHAIN, DELETE, READE, READPE, SETGT, and SETLL operation codes.

In Example 5.76, line 10 defines the key list WHSE consisting of the field WHSNBR. Line 30 defines the key list PART consisting of the fields WHSNBR and PRTNBR.

Example 5.76: Accessing a part master file via a key list.

```
.....CSRn01Factor1+++++++OpCode(ex)Factor2+++++++Result++++++++Len++DcHiLoEq
0010 C     WHSE          KLIST
0020 C                   KFLD                      WHSNBR

0030 C     PART          KLIST
0040 C                   KFLD                      WHSNBR
0050 C                   KFLD                      PRTNBR

0060 C     PART          CHAIN     PARTMAST                      54
0070 C     WHSE          CHAIN     PARTMAST                      54
```

▶LEAVE (LEAVE A DO GROUP)

The LEAVE operation can be used to exit a DO, DOW*xx*, and DOU*xx* group. The LEAVE operation transfers control to the statement following the DO group's ENDDO operation.

Factor 1	OpCode	Factor 2	Result Field	Resulting Indicators		
	LEAVE					

See also ITER, DO, DOW, DOU, and FOR

The LEAVE operation is used within a DO loop, to enhance control of the DO loop. To control performing the LEAVE operation, conditioning indicators or the IF operation can be used.

In Example 5.77, the FOR group fills a subfile with up to 20 orders for a given customer. If the end of orders indicator is detected (line 4), the LEAVE operation (line 5) is performed and control is transferred to the statement following the ENDDO operation. In other words, control is transferred to line 9.

Example 5.77: Using LEAVE to exit a DOUEQ loop.

```
.....CSRnØ1Factor1+++++++<—OpCode(ex)—>Factor2+++++++Result++++++++Len++DcHiLoEq
ØØØ1 C                    Eval          CustNo = 911
ØØØ2 C                    FOR           SFLRecNo = 1 to 2Ø
ØØØ3 C       CustNo       | ReadE       ORDERS
ØØØ4 C                    | IF          NOT %FOUND
ØØØ5 C                    | | LEAVE
ØØØ6 C                    | ENDIF
ØØØ7 C                    | WRITE       SubFile
ØØØ8 C                    ENDFOR
ØØØ9 C                    EXFMT         OrdPanel
```

▶ LEAVESR (EXIT SUBROUTINE)

The LEAVESR operation can be used to immediately exit a subroutine. The LEAVESR operation transfers control to the ENDSR operation for the subroutine in which the LEAVESR operation is performed. This causes control to return to the caller of the subroutine.

Factor 1	OpCode	Factor 2	Result Field	Resulting Indicators		
	LEAVESR					

See also ITER, DO, DOW, DOU, and FOR

The LEAVESR operation can be used only within the BEGSR and ENDSR operations (shown in Example 5.78). Use the LEAVESR operation within a conditional expression to cause a branch to the end of the subroutine. Unlike the GOTO operation, the ENDSR operation doesn't need to contain a label in factor 1 in order for the LEAVESR operation to function properly.

Example 5.78: Using LEAVESR to exit a subroutine.

```
.....CSRnØ1Factor1+++++++OpCode(ex)Factor2+++++++Result++++++++Len++DcHiLoEq
ØØ1Ø CSR    AddMarkUp    BegSR
ØØ2Ø C                   If        Cost <= Ø
ØØ3Ø C                   LeaveSR
ØØ4Ø C                   endIf
ØØ5Ø C      Cost         Div       1Ø            MarkUp
ØØ6Ø C                   If        MarkUp < 1.ØØ
ØØ7Ø C                   LeaveSR
ØØ8Ø C                   endIf
ØØ9Ø C                   Eval      Price = cost + Markup
Ø1ØØ CSR    endMarkUp    endSR
```

▶ LOOKUP (LOOKUP ARRAY OR TABLE)

The LOOKUP operation searches an array or table for a search argument. At least one resulting indictor is required with this operation.

Factor 1	OpCode	Factor 2	Result Field	Resulting Indicators		
search argument	LOOKUP	array[(search index)]		[HI]	[LO]	[EQ]
search argument	LOOKUP	table to search	[alternate table]	[HI]	[LO]	[EQ]

See also %LOOKUPXX, %TLOOKUPXX, SORTA, SCAN, and CHAIN.

Factor 1 must contain a search argument. The search argument must be the same attribute as the elements of the array or table. When a lookup is performed on an array, factor 2 can contain an optional starting index. If a starting index is specified, the lookup begins with that array element. If the starting index is specified as a numeric field, when the search is successful, the index field is set to the element where the search was satisfied.

Resulting Indicator Legend			
Columns	Ind.	Usage	Set-On Condition
71 - 72	1	[HI]	Causes LOOKUP to search for the first element greater than factor 1.
73 - 74	2	[LO]	Causes LOOKUP to search for the first element less than factor 1.
75 - 76	3	[EQ]	Causes LOOKUP to search for the first element equal to factor 1. Sets the %EQUAL built-in function to *ON or *OFF.

When a lookup is performed on a table, the result field can contain an alternate table name. If the lookup operation is successful, the table in the result field is set to the corresponding element where the search argument is located.

Resulting indicators control the type of search that is performed by LOOKUP. At least one, and no more than two, resulting indicators can be specified for the LOOKUP operation.

Resulting indicators 1 and 3 can both be specified to cause the LOOKUP to search for the first element that is greater than or equal to factor 1. Resulting indicators 2 and 3 can both be specified to cause the LOOKUP to search for the first element that is less than or equal to factor 1. When resulting indicator 3 is specified, the %EQUAL built-in function is set using the same conditions as resulting indicator 3.

The LOOKUP operation is widely used in RPG. Although more flexible string-handling operation codes have been added to the language in recent years, LOOKUP still proves valuable. Example 5.79 shows a typical use of the LOOKUP operation.

Example 5.79: Searching an array for a valid code.

```
.....DName++++++++++++EUDS.......Length+TDc.Functions++++++++++++++++++++++++++++++
0010 D ValidCode       S              1    DIM(4) PerRcd(4) CTDATA
0020 D CodeText        S             20    DIM(4) PerRcd(1) CTDATA

.....CSRn01Factor1+++++++OpCode(ex)Factor2+++++++Result++++++++Len++DcHiLoEq
0030 C                   Eval      Inx = 1
0040 C         Code      LOOKUP    ValidCode(Inx)                            58
0050 C                   If        *IN58
0060 C                   MOVEL     CodeText(Inx) MsgLine
0070 C                   ENDIF

**CTDATA VALIDCODE
ABCD
**CTDATA CODETEXT
Advanced lesson
Beginner lesson
Change answers
Delete test results
```

In Example 5.79, line 10 defines the four-element array named VALIDCODE. Line 20 defines the four-element array named CODETEXT. The array VALIDCODE is a valid code array, and CODETEXT is the code's text description. A description of each code stored in the VALIDCODE array is located in the corresponding element of the CODETEXT array.

When the LOOKUP operation on line 40 is successful, the variable IDX is set to the index of the located value. By using that variable as the array element of the CODETEXT array, the code's description is copied to the MSGLINE field.

► MONITOR (BEGIN A MONITOR GROUP)

The MONITOR operation is used perform error handling for a group of operation codes. The operation codes between the MONITOR and the first ON-ERROR operation are monitored for error conditions.

Factor 1	Op Code	Factor 2	Result Field	Resulting Indicators
	MONITOR			

See also ON-ERROR, ENDMON, %ERROR, %STATUS

The MONITOR operation creates a boundary around one or more regular operation codes. When an error condition is signaled by any of those operations, the ON-ERROR operations that are also part of the MONITOR group are tested. If the error is trapped by an ON-ERROR operation, then the corresponding operations below the ON-ERROR operation are performed until another ON-ERROR operation or an ENDMON operation is detected.

If the operations within the ON-ERROR statements run without error, then control continue by branching to the ENDMON statement for the MONITOR group.

Example 5.80: Monitor Group.

```
.....CSRnØ1..............OpCode(ex)Extended-factor2++++++++++++++++++++++++
ØØØ1 C                   Monitor
ØØØ2 C                   Eval      X = A + B / C
ØØØ3 C        CustNo     Chain     CustMast
ØØØ4 C                   If        %Found
ØØØ5 C                   Eval      BalDue = X
ØØØ6 C                   Endif

ØØØ7 C                   On-Error  Ø1Ø2
ØØØ8 C        'Divisor err' Dsply
ØØØ9 C                   On-Error  1218 : 1222
ØØ1Ø C        'Locked Rec' Dsply
ØØ11 C                   EndMon
```

In Example 5.80, the MONITOR statement (line 1) and the ENDMON statement (line 11) create a monitor group. This monitor group consists of the regular operation codes on lines 2 through 6, and the ON-ERROR error-trapping statements on lines 7 through 10.

The operation codes on lines 2 through 6 are performed. If any error occurs during those operations, the list of ON-ERROR operation codes enclosed in the monitor group is tested. If an error matching factor 2 of one of the ON-ERROR statements is detected, the statements following that On-Error statement are performed up to the next On-Error statement or the ENDMON statement.

Monitor groups may monitor for any valid program status error or file status error. In addition, generic "catch-all" figurative constants may be used to trap messages of any given type. These figurative constants that may be tested on the On-Error operation are as follows:

Figureative Constant	Description
*PROGRAM	All program status error codes. The range tested is 100 to 999.
*FILE	All file status error codes. The range is tested is 1000 to 9999.
*ALL	Both program status and file status errors. The range tested is 100 to 9999.

▶ MxxZO (Move Zone to Zone)

The four MxxZO operations copy the specified zone of either the left-most or right-most character of factor 2 to the left-most or right-most character of the result field. Except when the program is processing data from a system other than the host computer, this operation is rarely used.

Factor 1	OpCode	Factor 2	Result Field	Resulting Indicators		
	MxxZO	source	target			

See also BITON and BITOFF

The four Move Zone to Zone operations are as follows:

- The MHHZO (Move High to High Zone) operation copies the zone portion (i.e., bits 0, 1, 2, and 3) of the left-most character in factor 2 to the zone portion of the left-most character of the result field. Factor 2 must contain a character field. The result field must contain a character field.

- The MHLZO (Move High to Low Zone) operation copies the zone portion (i.e., bits 0, 1, 2, and 3) of the left-most character in factor 2 to the zone portion of the right-most character of the result field. Factor 2 must contain a character field. The result field can contain either a character or numeric field.

- The MLHZO (Move Low to High Zone) operation copies the zone portion (i.e., bits 0, 1, 2, and 3) of the right-most character in factor 2 to the zone portion of the left-most character of the result field. Factor 2 can contain either a character or numeric field. The result field must contain a numeric field.

- The MLLZO (Move Low to Low Zone) operation copies the zone portion (i.e., bits 0, 1, 2, and 3) of the right-most character in factor 2 to the zone portion of the right-most character of the result field. Factor 2 can contain either a character or numeric field. The result field also can contain a character or numeric field.

▶ MOVE AND MOVEL (COPY DATA)

The MOVE operation copies the data from factor 2 right-justified to the result field. The MOVEL operation copies the data from factor 2 left justified to the result field. For the remainder of this operation description, the MOVE operation is used. However, unless otherwise noted, everything listed here applies to both the MOVE and MOVEL operations. The only difference is that MOVEL moves data left justified whereas MOVE moves data right justified.

The MOVE operation copies data and automatically performs data-type conversion when necessary. Specific operations performed are character to numeric, numeric to character, and date and time to non-date and time.

Resulting indicators are valid only when moving data to a numeric or character field and indicate whether the result field is positive, negative, zero, or blank.

Factor 1	OpCode	Factor 2	Result Field	Resulting Indicators		
[date format][sep]	MOVE(P)	source	target	[+]	[-]	[0 or ƀ]
[date format][sep]	MOVEL(P)	source	target	[+]	[-]	[0 or ƀ]

See also EVAL, EVALR, SUBST, MOVEL, CLEAR, and CAT

Factor 1 is optional and is supported only when factor 2 or the result field (but not both) contains a date or time value. The format of the non-date or time value is specified in factor 1. If factor 1 is omitted for MOVE operations involving date and timedata types, the date or time format specified for the DATFMT keyword on header specification is used. Factor 2 can be any data type—literal value or variable. The result field variable can be any data type. When the result field is an array, factor 2 is

Resulting Indicator Legend

Columns	Ind.	Usage	Set-On Condition
71 - 72	1	[+]	The numeric result field is greater than zero.
73 - 74	2	[–]	The numeric result field is less than zero.
75 - 76	3	[0 or]	The numeric result field is equal to zero or the character result field is blank.

Extender	Description
P	PAD – Causes the result field's value to be cleared before the MOVE or MOVEL operation is performed. This has the same effect as performing the CLEAR operation immediately before performing the MOVE or MOVEL operation.

moved into each element of the array. Factor 2 and the result field cannot be overlapping data-structure subfields.

When the length of factor 2 is less than the length of the result field, the number of characters replaced in the result field is equal to the length of factor 2. Unless the P (pad) operation extender is specified, other positions within the result field are not affected.

When the length of factor 2 is greater than or equal to the length of the result field, a complete replacement of the result field with factor 2 is performed. Any additional data in factor 2 is not moved.

The MOVE operation traditionally has been used to clear the contents of the character-result field by moving *BLANKS to the result field. The CLEAR operation, however, accomplishes the same task and is data-type independent. Therefore, character, numeric, date, and time fields as well as data structures, record formats, arrays, and array elements can be cleared with a single CLEAR operation.

In addition to the standard date and time formats (see Tables 5.4 and 5.5), several date format codes that are unique to MOVE and MOVEL are supported. This allows simple conversion between date and non-date fields. Table 5.18 lists the set of date format codes that are supported by the MOVE and MOVEL operations.

The *CYMD, *CMDY, and *CDMY date format codes support a one-position century digit in the first position in the date. This digit can be 0 through 9. The value 0 equates to 1900, the value 1 equates to 2000, the value 2 equates to 2100, and so on. By adding the year to these values, the true four-digit year is calculated.

Date/Time Format Code	Description	Format
Table 5.18: Date Format Codes Supported by MOVE and MOVEL		
*CDMY	CL Date Century-digit, Day, Month, Year	CDDMMYY
*CMDY	CL Date Century-digit, Month, Day, Year	CMMDDYY
*CYMD	CL Date Century-digit, Year, Month, Day	CYYMMDD
*JOBRUN	Runtime job DATFMT attribute	Runtime job DATFMT
*JUL	Julian (2-digit year)	YY/DDD
*LONGJUL	Long Julian (4-digit year).	YYYY/DDD
*MDY	Month, Day, Year (2-digit year)	MM/DD/YY
*DMY	Day, Month, Year (2-digit year)	DD/MM/YY
*YMD	Year, Month, Day (2-digit year)	YY/MM/DD
*ISO	International Standards Organization Standard	YYYY-MM-DD
*USA	United States Standard	MM/DD/YYYY
*EUR	European Standard	DD.MM.YYYY
*JIS	Japanese International Standard	YYYY-MM-DD

Examples of MOVE and MOVEL

Examples 5.81 through 5.83 illustrate the MOVE and MOVEL operations. Figure 5.6 shows the type and lengths that are assumed for each field name.

```
.....DName+++++++++++EUDS.......Length+TDc.Functions+++++++++++++++++++++++++++
      D ARR             S              7P 0 DIM(5)
      D ErrMsg          S             30A    INZ('The customer number is 1234567')
      D MsgLine         S             10A
      D MsgCon          S              4A
      D CstNbr          S              7P 0
```

Figure 5.6: Definitions of fields used in MOVE and MOVEL examples.

Example 5.81: Various MOVE operations.

```
.....CSRn01Factor1+++++++OpCode(ex)Factor2+++++++Result++++++++Len++DcHiLoEq
0010 C                   MOVE      ERRMSG       MsgLine
0020 C                   MOVE      ERRMSG       CSTNBR
0030 C                   MOVE      CSTNBR       ARR
```

After line 10 in Example 5.81 is performed, the field MSGLIN contains the following:

```
MSGLINE = ' is 1234567'
```

After line 20, the field CSTNBR contains the following:

```
CSTNBR = 1234567
```

After line 30, each element in the ARR array contains the value 1234567. The value of CSTNBR is moved to each array element as though independent MOVE operations to each ARR(x) were performed (with x being the array index).

```
ARR     = 1234567,1234567,1234567,1234567,1234567
```

Example 5.82: Moving with length of factor 2 greater than the result field.

```
.....CSRnØ1Factor1+++++++OpCode(ex)Factor2+++++++Result++++++++Len++DcHiLoEq
ØØ10 C                    MOVE      MsgLine      MsgCon
```

In Example 5.82, after the MOVE operation is performed, the result field contains the following:

```
MSGCON = '4567'
```

Example 5.83: Moving with length of factor 2 shorter than the result field.

```
.....CSRnØ1Factor1+++++++OpCode(ex)Factor2+++++++Result++++++++Len++DcHiLoEq
ØØ10 C                    MOVE      'XXXX'       MSGCON
ØØ20 C                    MOVE      MSGCON       ERRMSG
```

In Example 5.83, after the MOVE operation on line 20 is performed, the ERRMSG result field contains the following:

```
            *... ... 1 ... ... 2 ... ... 3

ERRMSG = 'The customer number is 123XXXX'
```

▶ MOVEA (MOVE WITH ARRAY)

The MOVEA operation is a string manipulation operation code. It copies the contents of factor 2 and is left justified to the result field. Factor 2 or the result field or both must be an array.

Factor 1	OpCode	Factor 2	Result Field	Resulting Indicators		
	MOVEA(P)	source	target	[+]	[-]	[0 or ƀ]

See also MOVEL, MOVE, SUBST, LOOKUP, and SORTA

Factor 2 can contain a field, data structure, data structure subfield, array, array element, constant, or named constant. The result field can contain a field, data structure, data structure subfield, array, or array subscript. However, it cannot contain the same array name as factor 2.

An array or array subscript must be specified in factor 2 or the result field. If an array subscript is specified, the move operation begins with the specified array element. For example, if the array subscript ARR(3) is used with the MOVEA operation, the move begins with the third element of the ARR array.

Resulting Indicator Legend			
Columns	Ind.	Usage	Set-On Condition
71 - 72	1	[+]	The result field is greater than zero.
73 - 74	2	[–]	The result field is less than zero.
75 - 76	3	[0 or ƀ]	The result field is equal to zero or if the result field is character-based, the result field contains blanks.

Extender	Description
P	PAD – The result field is cleared before the MOVEA operation is performed. Numeric fields are set to zero and character fields are set to blanks.

The MOVEA operation operates with either character or zoned numeric arrays. It does not operate on arrays where elements are defined as binary or packed numeric. The MOVEA operation operates on a byte-by-byte basis. It aligns factor 2 and the result field based on any array index, and then performs the equivalent of the MOVEL (move left) operation code. Except when an array index is used as a starting point for the MOVEA operation code, the length of array elements is meaningless.

The shorter length of factor 2 and the result field determines the length of the string that is moved. The length of the string can be calculated with the following formula:

```
E = The number of elements in the array.
L = Length of a single array element.
I = The index of the array.

Length = E * L - ((I - 1) * L)
```

For example, if an array consists of 10 elements of 5 characters each and the array index is 4, then the length of the string moved is 35.

```
10 * 5 - ((4 - 1) * 5) = 35
```

There is no way to control the ending element for the move. If the field in factor 2 is longer than the total length of the array specified in the result field, the move continues through the last element in the array. In Example 5.84, the MSG field is moved into the STRING array.

Example 5.84: Moving a field to an array—no indexing.

```
.....DName++++++++++EUDS.......Length+TDc.Functions++++++++++++++++++++++++++++++
0010 D String          S              1A   DIM(256)
0020 D Msg             S            512A   INZ(*ALL'Q')

.....CSRn01Factor1+++++++OpCode(ex)Factor2+++++++Result++++++++Len++DcHiLoEq
0030 C                   MOVEA     MSG           String
```

While the STRING array contains 256 single-character elements, each position of the MSG field occupies a single-array element. If the defined length of the MSG field is less than 256, the balance of the array remains as it was before the MOVEA operation was performed. If the defined length of the MSG field is greater than 256 (the number of elements in STRING times their length), every array element is replaced. The data in positions beyond 256 in the MSG field is not moved, and the storage beyond the last element in STRING is not touched by the operation. In Example 5.83, the MSG field is moved into the STRING array starting with array element *x* as the index. Because *x* is set to 45 on line 20, the move replaces data in the STRING array beginning with the 45th element.

Example 5.85: Moving a field to an array with indexing in the result field.

```
.....DName++++++++++EUDS.......Length+TDc.Functions++++++++++++++++++++++++++++
0010 D String           S            1A   DIM(256)

.....CSRn01Factor1+++++++OpCode(ex)Factor2+++++++Result++++++++Len++DcHiLoEq
0020 C                   Eval      X = 45
0030 C                   MOVEA     MSG             String(X)
```

In Example 5.86, the array STRING is moved, beginning with its 128th element, to the MSG field. Because you are starting with the 128th array element, 127 array elements are not eligible to be moved. Therefore, the length of the move does not exceed 129 characters.

Example 5.86: Moving an array to a field with indexing in factor 2.

```
.....DName++++++++++EUDS.......Length+TDc.Functions++++++++++++++++++++++++++++
0010 D String           S            1A   DIM(256)

.....CSRn01Factor1+++++++OpCode(ex)Factor2+++++++Result++++++++Len++DcHiLoEq
0020 C                   Eval      X = 128
0030 C                   MOVEA     String(X)       MSG
```

In Example 5.87, the EXTRACT array is moved to the STRING array. The move begins with the 128th element of the EXTRACT array, which is moved into the 211th element of the STRING array.

Example 5.87: Moving an array to an array with indexing in factor 2 and the result field.

```
.....DName++++++++++EUDS........Length+TDc.Functions++++++++++++++++++++++++++++
0010 D String           S            1A   DIM(256)
0020 D Extract          S            1A   DIM(256)

.....CSRn01Factor1+++++++OpCode(ex)Factor2+++++++Result++++++++Len++DcHiLoEq
0030 C                   Eval      X = 128
0040 C                   Eval      Y = 211
0050 C                   MOVEA     Extract(Y)      String(X)
```

MOVEA with Figurative Constants

It is often useful to move a repeating string to an array. This enables all zeros, blanks, or other characters to be moved to each element of an array. The MOVEA operation used in conjunction with figurative constants provides this function.

In Example 5.88, the figurative constant *ZEROS is used on line 30 to move zeros into all locations of each element of the array ARR1. After the MOVEA operation on line 30 is performed, each array element of the array ARR1 contains '000'.

Example 5.88: Moving a value repeatedly to an array.

```
.....DName+++++++++++EUDS.......Length+TDc.Functions+++++++++++++++++++++++++++++
0010 D Arr1            S               3A   DIM(50)
0020 D Arr2            S               5A   DIM(8)

.....CSRn01Factor1+++++++OpCode(ex)Factor2+++++++Result++++++++Len++DcHiLoEq
0030 C                   MOVEA     *ZEROS        Arr1
0040 C                   MOVEA     *ALL'XYZ'     Arr1
0050 C                   MOVEA     *ALL'XYZ'     Arr2
```

The figurative constant *ALL is used with XYZ on line 40 to move a literal value of 'XYZ'
to each element of the array ARR1. After this MOVEA operation is performed, each array
element of the array ARR1 contains 'XYZ'. The figurative constant *ALL is used with XYZ
on line 50 to move a repeating literal value to the array ARR2. After the MOVEA operation
is performed, each element of the array ARR2 contains the following pattern:

ARR2 Element Values after MOVEA							
1	2	3	4	5	6	7	8
XYZXY	ZXYZX	YZXYZ	XYZXY	ZXYZX	YZXYZ	XYZXY	ZXYZX

▶ MOVEL (COPY DATA LEFT JUSTIFIED)

The MOVEL operation copies the data from factor 2, left justified, to the result field. When the result field is an array, resulting indicators are not valid for this operation.

Factor 1	OpCode	Factor 2	Result Field	Resulting Indicators		
[date format][sep]	MOVEL(P)	source	target	[+]	[-]	[0 or ƀ]

See also MOVE, MOVEA, SUBST, CAT, CLEAR, and EVAL

Factor 1 is optional, and is supported only when factor 2 or the result field (but not both) contain a date or time value. The format of the non-date or time value must be specified in factor 1. The MOVE and MOVEL operations support additional format codes. See Tables 5.4 and 5.18.

When the length of factor 2 is greater than or equal to the length of the result field, a complete replacement of the result field with factor 2 is performed, regardless of the presence of the operation extender. The data in factor 2 extending beyond the length of the result field is not copied. This is known as low-order truncation.

Resulting Indicator Legend			
Columns	Ind.	Usage	Set-On Condition
71 - 72	1	[+]	The numeric result field is greater than zero.
73 - 74	2	[–]	The numeric result field is less than zero.
75 - 76	3	[0 or ƀ]	The numeric result field is equal to zero or the character result field is blank.

Extender	Description
P	PAD – Causes the result field's value to be cleared before the MOVE or MOVEL operation is performed. This has the same effect as performing the CLEAR operation immediately before performing the MOVE or MOVEL operation.

When the length of factor 2 is less than the length of the result field and the operation extender is not specified, the number of characters replaced in the result field is equal to the length of factor 2 unless the P operation extender is specified.

Factor 2 can be a data structure, data structure subfield, literal value, named constant, figurative literal value, array, or array element. Factor 2 and the result field cannot be overlapping data structure subfields.

The result field can be any variable data type. When the result field is an array, factor 2 is moved into each element of the array.

The MOVEL operation differs from the MOVE operation in that the MOVEL operation copies data from factor 2, placing it left justified in the result field. In contrast, the MOVE operation copies data from factor 2, placing it right-justified in the result field. For more information on MOVE, see the subheading MOVE (Copy Data).

When data is moved to a numeric field, if the length of factor 2 is greater than or equal to the result field, the sign of factor 2 is used as the sign for the result field. If the length of factor 2 is less than the result field, the sign of the result field is retained.

In Example 5.89, after the MOVEL operation is performed, the AREACODE field contains the following:

```
*... ... 1 ... ... 2 ... ... 3
   AREACODE = 630
```

Example 5.89: Moving a 10-digit phone number to an area-code field.

```
.....DName+++++++++++EUDS.......Length+TDc.Functions++++++++++++++++++++++++++++++
0010 D Phone           S              10A   INZ('6305551212')
0020 D AreaCode         S              3S 0

.....CSRn01Factor1+++++++OpCode(ex)Factor2+++++++Result++++++++Len++DcHiLoEq
0030 C                  MOVEL     PHONE         AreaCode
```

In Example 5.908, after the MOVEL operation is performed, the result field contains the following:

```
Partial = 'The customer'
```

Example 5.90: Moving left with factor 2 longer than the result field.

```
.....DName+++++++++++EUDS.......Length+TDc.Functions++++++++++++++++++++++++++++++
0010 D Text           S              30A   INZ('The customer number is 1234567')
0020 D Partial        S              12A

.....CSRn01Factor1+++++++OpCode(ex)Factor2+++++++Result++++++++Len++DcHiLoEq
0030 C                  MOVEL     TEXT          Partial
```

In Example 5.91, after the MOVEL operation is performed, the result field contains the following:

```
        *... ... 1 ... ... 2 ... ... 3
   TEXT = 'XXXXcustomer number is 1234567'
```

Example 5.91: Moving left with factor 2 shorter than the result field.

```
.....DName+++++++++++EUDS.......Length+TDc.Functions++++++++++++++++++++++++++++++
0010 D Text            S            30A   INZ('The customer number is 1234567')

.....CSRn01Factor1+++++++OpCode(ex)Factor2+++++++Result++++++++Len++DcHiLoEq
0020 C                   MOVEL       'XXXX'        TEXT
```

In Example 5.92, after the MOVEL operation with the operation extender is performed, the result field contains the following:

```
        *... ... 1 ... ... 2 ... ... 3
   TEXT = 'ZZZZZ                        '
```

Example 5.92: Moving left with factor 2 shorter than the result field with pad.

```
.....DName+++++++++++EUDS.......Length+TDc.Functions++++++++++++++++++++++++++++++
0010 D Text            S            30A   INZ('The customer number is 1234567')

.....CSRn01Factor1+++++++OpCode(ex)Factor2+++++++Result++++++++Len++DcHiLoEq
0020 C                   MoveL(P)    'ZZZZZ'       TEXT
```

MOVEL with DATE and TIME Variables

In addition to the standard date and time formats (see Table 5.4), several date and time format codes that are unique to the MOVE and MOVEL operations are supported. This allows simple conversion between date and non-date fields. Table 5.19 lists the set of date format codes that are supported by the MOVE and MOVEL operations. The most notable additions are the AS/400 CL date formats.

	Table 5.19: Format Codes for Date and Time Conversion		
Format Code	Description	Year Length	Format[1]
*CDMY	CL Date Century-digit, Day, Month, Year	3	CDD/MM/YY
*CMDY	CL Date Century-digit, Month, Day, Year	3	CMM/DD/YY
*CYMD	CL Date Century-digit, Year, Month, Day	3	CYY/MM/DD
*JOBRUN	Job runtime DATFMT attribute	2	Job Runtime DATFMT
*JUL	Julian (2-digit year)	2	YY/DDD
*LONGJUL	Long Julian (4-digit year)	4	YYYY/DDD
*MDY	Month, Day, Year (2-digit year)	2	MM/DD/YY
*DMY	Day, Month, Year (2-digit year)	2	DD/MM/YY
*YMD	Year, Month, Day (2-digit year)	2	YY/MM/DD
*ISO	International Standards Organization Standard	4	YYYY-MM-DD
*USA	United States Standard	4	MM/DD/YYYY
*EUR	European Standard	4	DD.MM.YYYY
*JIS	Japanese International Standard	4	YYYY-MM-DD

[1]The example with the separators is valid for moves from/to character fields. Moves between date/time fields and numeric fields are the same format as depicted. However, separators are not part of the move.

The TIME format codes that can be used with MOVE and MOVEL include *HMS, *USA, and *JIS that use the colon as a separator, and *ISO and *EUR that use a period as a separator. In addition, all time formats except *USA are in a 24-hour clock format of HHMMSS. In contrast, *USA uses AM/PM notation to indicate time.

The *CYMD, *CMDY, and *CDMY date format codes support a one-position century digit in the first position in the date. This digit can be 0 through 9. The value 0 equates to 1900, the value 1 equates to 2000, the value 2 equates to 2100, and so on. By adding the year to these values, the true four-digit year is calculated.

When moving data from a numeric or character field to a date or time field, the format code (see Table 5.19) in factor 1 identifies the format of the non-date value of factor 2. When moving data from a date or time field to a numeric or character field, the format code in factor 1 identifies the format of the resulting non-date value stored in the result field.

Example 5.93 illustrates the use of the MOVE and MOVEL operations with date fields.

Example 5.93: Using MOVE and MOVEL with date fields.

```
.....DName++++++++++EUDS.......Length+TDc.Functions++++++++++++++++++++++++++++++
0010 D InvDate         S                 D    DATFMT(*ISO)
0020 D OrdDate         S                 D    DATFMT(*MDY)
0030 D DueDate         S                 D    DATFMT(*USA)
0040 D Message         S               30A    Inz('The date value is...xx yy zzzz')
0060 D dbDate          S                8S 0

.....CSRn01Factor1+++++++OpCode(ex)Factor2+++++++Result++++++++Len++DcHiLoEq
0070 C     *MDY         MoveL     '12/31/98'    InvDate
     **  The result is, INVDATE = D'1998-12-31'
0080 C     *USA         Move      '12/31/98'    Message
     **  The result is, Message = 'The date value is...12/31/1998')
     C                  Reset                   Message
0090 C     *USA         MoveL     '12/31/98'    Message
     **  The result is, Message = '12/31/1998alue is...xx yy zzzz')
0100 C     *ISO         MoveL     INVDATE       dbDate
     **  The result is, dbDATE = 19981231
```

▶MULT (MULTIPLY)

The MULT operation is used to calculate the product (result) of the multiplication of two operands.

Factor 1	OpCode	Factor 2	Result Field	Resulting Indicators		
multiplier	MULT(H)	multiplicand	product	[+]	[-]	[0]
	MULT(H)	multiplicand	multiplier and product	[+]	[-]	[0]

See also ADD, SUB, DIV, SQRT, and EVAL.

Factor 1 is optional and, if specified, is multiplied by the value specified for factor 2. The product is stored in the result field. If factor 1 is not specified, the result field is used in place of factor 1 and is multiplied by factor 2. The product is returned to the result field.

Resulting Indicator Legend

Columns	Ind.	Usage	Set-On Condition
71 - 72	1	[+]	The result field is greater than zero.
73 - 74	2	[-]	The result field is less than zero.
75 - 76	3	[0]	The result field is equal to zero.

Extender	Description
H	HALF ADJUST – The result field value is rounded after the mathematical operation is performed.

Example 5.94, if written in traditional mathematical expressions and using the asterisk as the multiplication symbol, would read as follows:

```
A * B = C

C * B = C
```

In Example 5.94, the MULT operation on line 10 multiplies field A by field B, and the product is placed in field C.

On line 20, field C is multiplied by field B and the product replaces the value in field C. If the product is greater than zero, resulting indicator 1 is set on. If the product is less than zero, resulting indicator 2 is set on. If the product is equal to zero, resulting indicator 3 is set on.

Example 5.94: Long and short forms of multiply.

```
.....CSRn01Factor1+++++++OpCode(ex)Factor2+++++++Result++++++++Len++DcHiLoEq
0010 C     A              MULT      B              C                  3 0
0020 C                    MULT      B              C
```

In Example 5.95, the H operation extender (half-adjust) causes the product (result field) to be rounded. The product varies based on the decimal positions of the result field. For example:

```
If A = 3 and B = 4.25, then A * B = 12.75
```

With half-adjust in effect, the product would be:

```
C = 13
```

If the product were defined as a three-digit variable with one decimal position, the result would be:

```
C = 12.8 (rounding to the tenths position)
```

Example 5.95: Multiplication with rounding.

```
.....CSRn01Factor1+++++++OpCode(ex)Factor2+++++++Result++++++++Len++DcHiLoEq
0010 C     A              Mult(H)   B              C                  3 0
```

▶ MVR (MOVE REMAINDER OF DIVISION)

The MVR operation moves the remainder of a division operation to the result field. The MVR operation must immediately follow a DIV operation code (see the DIV [Divide] subheading). If it does not, the RPG runtime exception/error handling routine is called. The half-adjust operation extender cannot be specified for this operation. Nor can it be specified for the DIV operation that immediately precedes the MVR operation.

Factor 1	OpCode	Factor 2	Result Field	Resulting Indicators		
	MVR		remainder	[+]	[-]	[0]

See also DIV and %REM.

Factor 1 and factor 2 must not contain an entry. The remainder of the previous DIV operation is stored in the result field.

In Example 5.96, suppose A = 10 and B = 4. If A, B, and C are defined as three-digit numeric fields with no decimal positions, the result of the MVR operation stores a value of 2 in the REMAINDER field.

Resulting Indicator Legend			
Columns	Ind.	Usage	Set-On Condition
71 - 72	1	[+]	The result field is greater than zero.
73 - 74	2	[–]	The result field is less than zero.
75 - 76	3	[0]	The result field is equal to zero.

Example 5.96: Integer division with remainder.

```
.....CSRnØ1Factor1+++++++OpCode(ex)Factor2+++++++Result++++++++Len++DcHiLoEq
ØØ1Ø C     A          DIV       B              C              3 Ø
ØØ2Ø C                MVR                      Remainder      3 Ø
```

▶ NEXT (FORCE NEXT INPUT FROM A SPECIFIC DEVICE FILE)

The NEXT operation forces input from a specific device file. For example, if a single program is communicating with multiple workstations, the NEXT operation can be used to force a READ operation to read from a specific workstation.

Factor 1	OpCode	Factor 2	Result Field	Resulting Indicators	
workstn device ID	NEXT (E)	workstn file			[error]	

See also ACQ and FORCE

Factor 1 must contain the name of the device that is read from by the next explicit READ operation or cycle read. Factor 1 must be either a quoted constant or a 10-position character-field name containing the name of the device. Factor 2 must contain the name of the device file from which the READ operation is requested.

Resulting Indicator Legend			
Columns	Ind.	Usage	Set-On Condition
71 - 72	1	N/A	
73 - 74	2	[error]	An error occurred during the operation.
75 - 76	3	N/A	

Extender	Description
E	ERROR – Causes the %ERROR and %STATUS built-in functions to be set if an error occurs during the operation.

After the NEXT operation is issued, a read is issued to the program device specified in factor 1. The read function must be either an RPG cycle read or the READ operation. The NEXT operation is often used in conjunction with the ACQ operation. The ACQ operation acquires the devices for the program; the NEXT operation is used to control the input sequence.

A file specification keyword—MAXDEV, DEVID, or SAVEDS—is required to define a workstation file as a multiple device file. In Example 5.97, lines 30 and 40 acquire the workstation devices named DSP01 and DSP02. Lines 50 and 60 send the workstation file record format named PROMPT to the device named DSP01. Lines 70 and 80 do the same for the device named DSP02.

Example 5.97: Controlling input sequence with the NEXT operation.

```
.....FFileName++IFEASFRlen+LKeylnKFDevice+.Functions+++++++++++++++++++++++++++++
0010 FGLENTRY   CF    E              WORKSTN MaxDev(*FILE) DevID(WSID)

.....CSRnØ1Factor1+++++++OpCode(ex)Factor2+++++++Result++++++++Len++DcHiLoEq
0030 C      'DSPØ1'     ACQ         GLENTRY                           56
0040 C      'DSPØ2'     ACQ         GLENTRY                           56

0050 C                  MOVEL       'DSPØ1'         WSID
0060 C                  WRITE       PROMPT
0070 C                  MOVEL       'DSPØ2'         WSID
0080 C                  WRITE       PROMPT

0090 C      'DSPØ1'     NEXT        GLENTRY                           56
0100 C                  READ        PROMPT
0110 C                  EXSR        DoTheWork

0120 C      'DSPØ2'     NEXT        GLENTRY                           56
0130 C                  READ        PROMPT
0140 C                  EXSR        DoTheWork
```

Line 90 in Example 5.97 issues the NEXT operation code. Factor 1 contains the constant 'DSP01', which conditions the program to access the DSP01 device. When line 100 is performed, the READ operation issues its read to the device named DSP01. Line 110 processes the data received on that read operation. Lines 120 to 140 do the same for the device named DSP02.

 OCCUR (SET/RETRIEVE DATA STRUCTURE OCCURRENCE)

The OCCUR operation code performs one of two functions:

- It sets the *occurrence index* of the multiple-occurrence data structure specified in factor 2. Once the occurrence index is set, all subsequent RPG operations performed against the data structure affect that occurrence until another OCCUR operation changes the occurrence index.

- It retrieves the current occurrence index for a multiple-occurrence data structure specified in factor 2.

The OCCUR operation can be used within the *INZSR subroutine to assign unique initial values to each data-structure occurrence. The OCCUR operation can only be used on data structures that are declared as multiple occurrence (using the OCCURS keyword) and not when they are declared as arrays (using the DIM keyword).

Factor 1	OpCode	Factor 2	Result Field	Resulting Indicators	
[occurrence to set]	OCCUR (E)	data structure	[occurrence]		[error]	

See also OCCUR and DIM keywords and %ELEM.

Factor 1 is optional; if specified, it causes the OCCUR operation to set the occurrence of the data structure specified in factor 2 to the occurrence specified by factor 1. Factor 1 can be a numeric field (with zero decimal positions), a numeric constant (e.g., 15), or another multiple-occurrence data structure.

If factor 1 contains a constant or a numeric field, the value of factor 1 is used to set the occurrence of the data structure specified in factor 2.

Resulting Indicator Legend			
Columns	Ind.	Usage	Set-On Condition
71 - 72	1	N/A	
73 - 74	2	[error]	An error occurred during the operation.
75 - 76	3	N/A	

Extender	Description
E	ERROR – Causes the %ERROR and %STATUS built-in functions to be set if an error occurs during the operation.

For example, if factor 1 contains the number 12, the occurrence of the data structure specified in factor 2 is set to its 12th occurrence.

If factor 1 contains another data structure name, that data structure's occurrence is used to set the occurrence of the data structure specified in factor 2. For example, if the data structure in factor 1 is set to its 14th occurrence, the occurrence of the data structure in factor 2 is set to 14. Factor 2 must contain the name of a multiple occurrence data structure, the occurrence of which is set or retrieved by the OCCUR operation.

The result field is optional unless factor 1 is omitted. It can contain a numeric field name (with zero decimal positions) that receives the number of the current occurrence of the data structure specified in factor 2.

Resulting indicator 2 can be specified to signal when the value specified in factor 1 is less than or equal to zero, or greater than the maximum number of occurrences for the data structure.

The OCCUR operation provides a high level of function. For example, because arrays can be specified as a data-structure subfield, two-dimensional arrays can be created. See Example 5.98.

Example 5.96: Illustrating the use of the OCCUR operation.

```
.....DName++++++++++EUDS.......Length+TDc.Functions++++++++++++++++++++++++++++
0020 D TwoDims         DS                    Occurs(10)
0030 D  Arr                         10       DIM(10)

0040 D DataF2          DS                    Occurs(10)
0050 D  FieldD                      6A
0050 D  FieldE                      6A

.....CSRn01Factor1+++++++OpCode(ex)Factor2+++++++Result++++++++Len++DcHiLoEq
0070 C      3          OCCUR     TWODIMS

0080 C                 Z-ADD     4              INDEX          3 0
0090 C      INDEX      OCCUR     DATAF2

0100 C                 Occur     TwoDims        CurOccur       3 0

0110 C                 Eval      NumOccurs = %Elem(DataF2)

0120 C      DATAF2     OCCUR     TWODIMS        NEWOCR         3 0    56
0130 C      *IN56      CASEQ     *ON            OnDSError
0140 C                 END
```

In Example 5.98, line 70 sets the occurrence of the data structure TWODIMS to its third occurrence. Line 80 initializes the field INDEX to 4 and line 90 sets the occurrence of the data structure DATAF2 to the value contained in the field INDEX. Line 100 contains no value for factor 1; therefore, the occurrence of the data structure TWODIMS is unchanged and its occurrence is placed into the CUROCCUR result field.

Line 110 retrieves the number of occurrences declared for the DATAF2 data structure. The %ELEM built-in function is used to extract the occurrences and store them in the numeric field named NUMOCCURS.

Line 120 sets the occurrence of the data structure TWODIMS to the same occurrence as the data structure DATAF2, specified in factor 1. Line 120 also stores the occurrence set by the operation in the result field NEWOCR. If the occurrence set on line 120 is outside the range of the TWODIMS data structure, resulting indicator 2 (indicator 56 in our example) is set on, and subroutine ONDSERROR is called (line 130).

Single-occurrence data structures don't need to be named. If a data structure is a multiple-occurrence data structure, it must be named. For example, a multiple-occurrence data structure consisting of four occurrences, each containing two fields, is described in Example 5.99.

Example 5.99: A multiple occurrence data structure.

```
.....DName+++++++++++EUDS.......Length+TDc.Functions++++++++++++++++++++++++++++++
0010 D Company          DS                      Occurs(4)
0020 D   ActNbr                      7P 0
0030 D   CstNam                     20A
```

Line 10 of Example 5.99 defines the data structure name as COMPANY. The OCCURS keyword indicates that there are four occurrences. Lines 20 and 30 define the two fields that make up the data-structure format. If this data structure is filled with data, it might look like the data listed in Table 5.20.

Table 5.20: Example of Data in Data Structure		
Occurrence	ACTNBR	CSTNAM
1	05320	PeaTree.com Corp.
2	05340	Skyline Pigeon Productions
3	01207	Maui Pineapple
4	09404	Cozzi Research

▶ON-ERROR (TEST ERROR STATUS CONDITION)

The ON-ERROR operation is used perform error tests within an error monitor group. When an operation within a monitor group generates an error, is transferred to the first ON-ERROR operation for the monitor group.

Factor 1	Op Code	Factor 2	Result Field	Resulting Indicators
	On-Error	{ error status code1 {: error status code2 : ... })		

See also MONITOR, ENDMON, %ERROR, %STATUS

The ON-ERROR operation specifies the exception/error status codes that are being monitored by the monitor group. If the error status code is not included in one of the ON-ERROR statements within this monitor group, then the normal RPG exception/error handling routines are called.

Multiple status codes may be specified on each ON-ERROR statement, or one of the figurative constants listed below may be specified to monitor for a range of error status conditions. If more than one error status code is specified, separate each status code with a colon. The figurative constants that may be monitored on the ON-ERROR operation are as follows:

Error Status Code	Description
*PROGRAM	All program status error codes. The range tested is 100 to 999.
*FILE	All file status error codes. The range is tested is 1000 to 9999.
*ALL	Both program status and file status errors. The range tested is 100 to 9999.

Multiple ON-ERROR statements are allowed within an monitor group. Error status codes are tested on a first come, first served basis. That is the first ON-ERROR statement is tested first. If it handles the particular status code, then its group of error handling operations is performed. Then control is passed to the ENDMON statement. Consequently, no other ON-ERROR statements are called. If, however, the error status code is not being monitored by the ON-ERROR statement, control passes to the next ON-ERROR statement (if any). If all ON-ERROR statements have been tested and the error status code is not trapped by one of the statements, control passes to the normal RPG exception/error handling routines.

Example 5.100: Monitor Group.

```
.....CSRn01..............OpCode(ex)Extended-factor2+++++++++++++++++++++++
0001 C                    Monitor
0002 C                    Eval       X = A + B / C
0003 C       CustNo       Chain      CustMast
0004 C                    If         %Found
0005 C                    Eval       BalDue = X
0006 C                    Endif

0007 C                    On-Error   0102
0008 C       'Divisor err' Dsply
0009 C                    On-Error   1218 : 1222
0010 C       'Locked Rec'  Dsply
0011 C                    EndMon
```

In Example 5.100, the MONITOR statement (line 1) and the ENDMON statement (line 11) create a monitor group. This monitor group consists of the regular operation codes on lines 2 through 6, and the On-Error error-trapping statements on lines 7 through 10. The operation codes on lines 2 through 6 are performed.

The ON-ERROR operation codes that appear on lines 7 and 9 check for a divide-by-zero error (line 7) and a record locking or other locking condition (line 9).

OPEN (OPEN A FILE)

The OPEN operation opens the *full procedural file* specified in factor 2. The file must be closed in order to avoid an error. The User Controlled Open (USROPN) keyword can be specified for the file on its file specification. When the USROPN keyword is specified, the OPEN operation is normally required to open the file.

Factor 1	OpCode	Factor 2	Result Field	Resulting Indicators	
	OPEN (E)	file name			[error]	

See also CLOSE, FEOD, ACQ, and %OPEN.

Factor 2 must contain the name of the file being opened. The file must be closed; otherwise an exception/error is generated. When RPG programs start, unless the USROPN keyword is specified, the RPG cycle automatically opens files for processing. In this situation, the file must be closed with the CLOSE operation before an OPEN operation will succeed.

Resulting Indicator Legend

Columns	Ind.	Usage	Set-On Condition
71 - 72	1	N/A	
73 - 74	2	[error]	An error occurred during the operation.
75 - 76	3	N/A	

Extender	Description
E	ERROR – Causes the %ERROR and %STATUS built-in functions to be set if an error occurs during the operation.

When a WORKSTN device file is opened and the DEVID keyword is specified, the associated workstation ID field is set to blanks. For more information, see the ACQ (Acquire) subheading.

In Example 5.101, the file CUSTMAST is opened. If the OPEN operation (line 50) doesn't complete successfully, resulting indicator 2 (indicator 56 in the example) is set on, signaling that the open attempt failed. The remainder of the program reads and prints each record in the file CUSTMAST. The file is then closed and a line of totals is printed.

Example 5.101 uses the DOW loop and READ operation to set on and test the condition of indicator LR, which controls the ending of the DO loop—and the program.

Example 5.101: Opening a file, printing it, then closing the file.

```
.....FFileName++IFEASFRlen+LKeylnKFDevice+.Functions++++++++++++++++++++++++++++++
0010 FCUSTMAST   IF    E                DISK      USROPN
0020 FPRINTER    O     E                PRINTER

.....CSRn01Factor1+++++++OpCode(ex)Factor2+++++++Result++++++++Len++DcHiLoEq
0030 C                   If            NOT %OPEN(CUSTMAST)
0040 C                   OPEN          CUSTMAST                          56
0050 C                   ENDIF
0060 C                   If            *IN56
0070 C                   READ          CUSTMAST                                LR
0080 C                   Dow           *INLR = *OFF
0090 C                   ADD           AMOUNT          TOTAL
0100 C                   WRITE         DETAIL
0110 C                   READ          CUSTMAST                                LR
0120 C                   ENDDO
0130 C                   CLOSE         CUSTMAST
0140 C                   WRITE         TOTALS
0150 C                   ENDIF
```

▶ OR*xx* (OR CONDITION)

The OR*xx* operation is used in conjunction with the IF*xx*, DOU*xx*, DOW*xx*, and WHEN*xx* operations. The OR*xx* operation complements these other operation codes in that their conditioning is extended through the use of the OR*xx* operation. Conditioning indicators aren't allowed for this operation.

Factor 1	OpCode	Factor 2	Result Field	Resulting Indicators		
compare value 1	OR*xx*	compare value 2				

See also ANDxx, IFxx, DOWxx, DOUxx, and WHENxx

Factor 1 and factor 2 are required and must contain a variable, literal value, array element, or figurative constant. Factor 1 is compared to factor 2 using the OR*xx* operation Boolean operator. See Table 5.9 for information on the Boolean operators (GE, GT, LE, LT, EQ, and NE). Factor 1 and factor 2 must be the same type.

Example 5.102: Using OREQ to extend the DOUxx operation.

```
.....CSRn01Factor1+++++++OpCode(ex)Factor2+++++++Result++++++++Len++DcHiLoEq
0010 C       *IN58       DOUEQ         *ON
0020 C                   OREQ          10
0030 C                   ADD           1             C            3 0
0040 C                   READ          CUSTMAST                               58
0050 C                   ENDDO
```

In Example 5.102, the DO UNTIL loop is performed until indicator 58 is set on or field C equals 10. Note that this form of OR cannot be used with the IF, DOW, DOU, and WHEN natural expression operations.

OTHER (OTHERWISE)

The OTHER operation is used to perform a default or "catch all" routine within an in-line case group delimited with the SELECT/ENDSL operations. Conditioning indicators are not valid for this operation.

Factor 1	OpCode	Factor 2	Result Field	Resulting Indicators		
	OTHER					

See also SELECT, WHEN, and ENDSL.

The OTHER operation identifies one or more operations that are run when no WHEN*xx* (When) condition within the case group has been satisfied. Only one OTHER operation can be specified per in-line case group. An in-line case group is defined by the SE-LECT-WHEN-OTHER-ENDSL operations.

Most operation codes can appear within an in-line case group, including another in-line case group. The BEGSR and ENDSR operations cannot appear within an in-line case group.

Example 5.103 shows how to code the OTHER operation.

Example 5.103: Testing input and performing a routine.

```
.....CSRnØ1Factor1+++++++<—OpCode(ex)—>Factor2+++++++Result++++++++Len++DcHiLoEq
      *  Stay in loop until exit is requested
     C                    DOU           Funct = Exit
     C                    | EXFMT        INQUIRY                            58
     C                    | EXSR         RTVMAC
     C                    | SELECT
      *  If the exit key was pressed, then leave the Do loop
     C                    | When         Funct = EXIT
     C                    | | Eval       *INLR = *ON
     C                    | | LEAVE
      *  If the OPTION is B to Z, then send an error
     C                    | When         Option >= 'B' and Option <= 'Z'
     C                    | | Eval       Msg = 'ERROR'
      *  Otherwise, ask the user to confirm their choice
     C                    | OTHER
     C                    | | EXFMT      CONFIRM
     C                    | ENDSL
     C                    ENDDO
```

▶OUT (OUTPUT AN EXTERNAL DATA AREA)

The OUT operation code sends data to the data area named in factor 2. Before an OUT operation can be used on a data area, the data sent to the data area replaces all data in the data area.

Factor 1	OpCode	Factor 2	Result Field	Resulting Indicators	
[*LOCK]	OUT (E)	data area field			[error]
[*LOCK]	OUT (E)	*DTAARA			[error]

See also IN and UNLOCK

Factor 1 can contain the reserved word *LOCK to retain the lock on the data area.

Factor 2 is required and must contain the name of the field assigned to the data area being written. Optionally, all data areas can be output with a single OUT operation by specifying *DTAARA in factor 2.

In Example 5.104, lines 10 and 20 define the data structure CONTROL. The DTAARA keyword is used to assign the CTRLDATA data area to the CONTROL data structure. The data area is input to the program on line 40. The contents of the data area is altered (line 50) and output with the OUT operation (line 70).

Resulting Indicator Legend			
Columns	Ind.	Usage	Set-On Condition
71 - 72	1	N/A	
73 - 74	2	[error]	An error occurred during the operation.
75 - 76	3	N/A	

Extender	Description
E	ERROR – Causes the %ERROR and %STATUS built-in functions to be set if an error occurs during the operation.

Example 5.104: Using a data area to store a control number.

```
.....DName++++++++++EUDS.......Length+TDc.Functions++++++++++++++++++++++++++++
0010 D Control         DS                     Dtaara(CtrlData)
0020 D  NextNbr                        5S 0 INZ

.....CSRn01Factor1+++++++OpCode(ex)Factor2+++++++Result++++++++Len++DcHiLoEq
0040 C      *LOCK       IN        Control
0050 C                  ADD       1             NextNbr
0060 C                  Eval      ActNbr = NextNbr
0070 C                  OUT       Control
```

▶PARM (PARAMETER DECLARATION)

The PARM operation is used to define a parameter. A parameter is a method used to pass data between programs. Parameters are passed between programs using the CALL or CALLB operation. A parameter can be defined on a parameter list with the PLIST operation or directly following a CALL or CALLB operation. If the PARM operation follows a CALL or CALLB operation, that PARM operation is associated with the CALL or CALLB operation. If the PARM operation follows a PLIST operation, the parameter is associated with the PLIST. To use the parameter list, the name of the PLIST must appear in the result field of the CALL or CALLB operation.

Parameters are used extensively in the modern RPG language. Modular program design, structured programming, and flexible systems design all contribute to the need for the program-to-program CALL operation. The parameter is a useful part of this operation.

Factor 1	OpCode	Factor 2	Result Field	Resulting Indicators		
input from parm	PARM	output to parm	parameter | *OMIT			

See also PLIST, CALL, CALLB, and CALLP

Factor 1 and factor 2 are optional and, if present, must be the same type of field as the result field. Factor 1, if present, must be a field, (i.e., it cannot be a constant). Factor 2 can be a field or a constant.

Factor 1 can be used to receive the value of the parameter. If factor 1 is specified, data passed to the program by a CALL or CALLB operation from another program is moved to the field in factor 1 from the result field. This technique is often used to move data into a data structure subfield, indicator variable, or array element.

Factor 2 can be used to place data into the parameter when a program ends or calls another program. The data in factor 2 is moved into the result field when the program ends or calls another program. This technique is often used to move a data structure subfield, indicator variable, constants, or array elements into the result field before calling another program and upon program completion.

The parameters of a CALLB operation can be omitted by specifying the *OMIT value. This value indicates that no value is being passed to the called program/procedure. When *OMIT is specified, a *NULL value is passed to the called program. Checking for a *NULL in the called procedure will indicate whether *OMIT was specified.

The effect on the result field when using factor 2 with the PARM operation is equivalent to using a MOVEL or Z-ADD operation. Character fields are moved to the result field, left justified, and padded with blanks. Numeric data is moved to the result field, right justified, and padded with zeros.

The result field is required and must conform to the following criteria: If factor 1 is specified, the result field must match its type and length. It must match the type and length of factor 2 when factor 2 contains a field name, and it must match the type of factor 2 when factor 2 is a literal value, figurative constant, or reserved word.

When used as an *ENTRY PLIST parameter, the result field can be a field name, array name, or data structure name, but cannot be a data structure subfield name or an array element.

When used as a parameter of the CALL or CALLB operation, the result field can be a field name, data structure name, data structure subfield name, array name, or an array element.

Parameters are passed by reference, not value. The address or *pointer* of the parameter is passed to the program being called. The called program references the parameter by defining a parameter of its own. Both parameters address the same memory location. Therefore, if the value of a parameter in one program is changed, the value in the second program also is changed.

The program status data structure can be used to determine the number of parameters passed to a program. A predefined subfield location, referred to as *PARMS, provides a value for the number of parameters passed to the RPG program. If no parameters are passed, *PARMS equals zero. In addition, the %PARMS built-in function can be used to retrieve the number of parameters passed to a procedure.

> **NOTE:** *Numeric fields that are defined within the scope of a calculation specification default to packed numeric in RPG III and RPG IV, and to zoned numeric in RPG II. This can cause problems when passing parameters between programs. To avoid these problems, ensure that numeric parameters are of the same type (e.g., zoned, packed, binary) and length.*

In Example 5.105, lines 60 to 100 move the parameters into fields that are used in the program. If the number of parameters passed to a program is different from the number of parameters defined on the *ENTRY PLIST parameter list, %PARMS can be used to avoid referencing parameters that are not passed. For example, if only one parameter (the field PACCT) is received by the program, and the field PMODE (the second parameter) is addressed in any way by the RPG code, a runtime error is generated.

In Example 5.105, note that the comparison for the number of parameters (line 60) uses the operation IF GREATER THAN OR EQUAL TO. This operation is used instead of the EQUAL operation to ensure that the program continues to function without changing line 60 should additional parameters be added in the future.

Example 5.105: Passing parameters to a called program.

```
.....CSRn01Factor1+++++++OpCode(ex)Factor2+++++++Result++++++++Len++DcHiLoEq
0010 C        *ENTRY       PLIST
0020 C                     PARM      PACCT
0030 C                     PARM      PMODE
     *    If two parms are passed in, then use parm 2,
     *    else, use a default value for MODE.
0060 C                     If        %Parms >= 2
0070 C                     MOVE      PMODE           MODE
0080 C                     ELSE
0090 C                     MOVE      'INQUIRY'       MODE
0100 C                     ENDIF
0110 C                     DOU       Funct = 'EXIT'
     C                     Select
0120 C                     When      Mode = 'INQUIRY'
0130 C                     CALL      'CUSTINQ'
0140 C                     PARM      ACTNBR
0150 C                     PARM      SEARCH
0160 C                     ELSE
0170 C                     When      Mode = 'UPDATE'
0180 C                     CALL      'CSTUPD'        PLIST1
0190 C                     ELSE
0200 C                     When      Mode = 'DELETE'
0210 C                     CALL      'CSTDEL'        PLIST1
0220 C                     endsl
0240 C                     ENDDO
0250 C        PLIST1       PLIST
0260 C                     PARM                      ACTNBR
0270 C                     PARM      MODE            FUNCT
0280 C        RETURN       PARM                      RTNCOD
```

Parameters are a part of a parameter list. See the following subheading, PLIST (Parameter List Declaration) for more information. A named parameter list is produced with the PLIST operation. An unnamed parameter list is a parameter list built by placing PARM operations immediately following a CALL or CALLB operation. Examples of each of these methods are shown in Examples 5.106 and 5.107.

Example 5.106: Defining a parameter list.

```
.....CSRn01Factor1+++++++OpCode(ex)Factor2+++++++Result++++++++Len++DcHiLoEq
0010 C     GETPRT       PLIST
0020 C                  PARM                      PRTNBR
0030 C                  PARM                      CMPNTS
     ... program code can go here.
xxxx C                  CALL      'PARTINQ'       GETPRT                  56
```

Example 5.107: Specifying parameters without a parameter list.

```
.....CSRn01Factor1+++++++OpCode(ex)Factor2+++++++Result++++++++Len++DcHiLoEq
0010 C                  CALL      'PARTINQ'                               56
0020 C                  PARM                      PRTNBR
0030 C                  PARM                      CMPNTS
```

▶ PLIST (PARAMETER LIST DECLARATION)

The PLIST operation defines a list of parameters (PARM) that is used when the program is called, when a program calls another program, and when an I/O operation to a SPECIAL device is performed. At least one PARM operation must appear immediately following the PLIST operation.

A parameter list can be specified as the result field of a program-to-program CALL or CALLB operation. It also can be specified as a value for the PLIST keyword of the file specification for SPECIAL device files.

Factor 1	OpCode	Factor 2	Result Field	Resulting Indicators		
parameter list name	PLIST					

See also PARM, CALL, CALLB, and CALLP

Factor 1 must contain a unique name of the parameter list being defined. Optionally, the reserved word *ENTRY can be specified in factor 1. *ENTRY is a special parameter list. It defines the parameters that are received by the program when it is called.

There are two kinds of parameter lists: named and unnamed. *Named parameter* lists are defined with the PLIST operation. The name of the parameter list is specified in factor 1 of the calculation specification. A named parameter list can be used by one or more CALL or CALLB operations, or as the parameter list of a SPECIAL device file.

Placing the PARM operation immediately following the CALL or CALLB operations specifies an *unnamed parameter list*. Unnamed parameter lists do not use the PLIST operation.

Examples 5.108 through 5.110 illustrate the three areas where a PLIST is used. Example 5.108 contains an entry parameter list. When this program is called, a single parameter, ACCT#, is received by the program.

Example 5.108: Defining a program-entry parameter list.

```
.....CSRn01Factor1+++++++OpCode(ex)Factor2+++++++Result++++++++Len++DcHiLoEq
0010 C     *ENTRY         PLIST
0020 C                    PARM                     ACCT#
```

Example 5.109 contains a named parameter list termed GETPRT. Any number of CALL or CALLB operations can use the parameter list. Line 256 uses the parameter list as the result field. All parameters of the parameter list GETPRT are passed to the called program RTVPART.

Example 5.109: Defining a parameter list for a program call.

```
.....CSRn01Factor1+++++++OpCode(ex)Factor2+++++++Result++++++++Len++DcHiLoEq
0010 C     GETPRT         PLIST
0020 C                    PARM                     PRTNBR
0030 C                    PARM                     CMPNTS
xxxx  *    ... additional program code goes here.
0256 C                    CALL      'RTVPART'      GETPRT              56
```

Example 5.110 illustrates the SPECIAL device file use of the PLIST. When a SPECIAL device is used, RPG automatically constructs a parameter list. When additional parameters are required for the SPECIAL device routine, a user-written PLIST has to be created.

Example 5.110: Additional parameters of a SPECIAL device file.

```
.....FFileName++IFEASFRlen+LKeylnKFDevice+.Functions++++++++++++++++++++++++++
0010 FTAPEDRV   IF   E                 SPECIAL PGMNAME(TAPEIO) Plist(TapeDrive)

.....CSRn01Factor1+++++++OpCode(ex)Factor2+++++++Result++++++++Len++DcHiLoEq
0020 C     TapeDrive      PLIST
0030 C                    PARM                     TIMDTE
0040 C                    PARM                     USERID
0050 C                    READ      TAPEDRV                            58
```

The additional parameters are appended to the parameter list that RPG automatically generates. Example 5.108 illustrates the appending of a date/timestamp and user ID to the SPECIAL device-parameter list.

RPG automatically creates a parameter list consisting of the following parameters for SPECIAL device files:

- *Operation Code*. A single character that identifies the operation that is being requested. Table 5.21 contains a list of possible operations.

Table 5.21: Operation Codes for Special Device Files	
Operation Code	Description
O	Open the file.
C	Close the file.
R	Read the file and move the contents of the next record read into the DATA AREA parameter (parameter 4).
W	Write to the file, using the DATA AREA parameter (parameter 4) as the output data.
D	Delete the current record from the file.
U	Replace (update) the current record's data with the data from the DATA AREA parameter (parameter 4).

- *Return Code*. A single-character parameter that contains the status of the operation request. Table 5.22 contains a list of return codes.

Table 5.22: Return Codes for Special Device Files	
Return Code	Description
0	Normal completion of requested operation.
1	End of file detected.
2	The operation did not run—an error has occurred.

- *Error Code*. A five-digit zoned numeric field that contains an error code. When parameter 2, the return code, equals '2', the error code (parameter 3) is moved into the field specified for *RECORD in the file information data structure.

- *Data Area*. A character field that contains the data that is transferred between the program and the SPECIAL device routine. The length of this parameter is equal to the record length of the SPECIAL file.

▶ POST (POST DEVICE INFORMATION)

The POST operation places status or input/output information into the file information data structure.

Factor 1	OpCode	Factor 2	Result Field	Resulting Indicators		
workstn device ID	POST (E)	workstn file name	[file info data struc]		[error]	

See also ACQ and REL.

Factor 1 is optional and can contain a field name or quoted constant containing a program device name. Specifying factor 1 causes the POST operation to place status information into the information data structure. If factor 1 is omitted, the POST operation places input/output information into the information data structure.

Resulting Indicator Legend			
Columns	Ind.	Usage	Set-On Condition
71 - 72	1	N/A	
73 - 74	2	[error]	An error occurred during the operation.
75 - 76	3	N/A	

Extender	Description
E	ERROR – Causes the %ERROR and %STATUS built-in functions to be set if an error occurs during the operation.

Factor 2 and the result field are mutually optional; one or the other or both must be specified. Factor 2 can contain the name of the workstation file about which the POST operation places information into the information data structure. If the result field is blank, the information data structure associated with the file specified in factor 2 is used as the target of the POST operation.

The result field can contain the name of an information data structure into which the POST operation places the status or input/output information. If both factor 2 and the result field are specified, the result field must contain the name of the information data structure associated with the file specified in factor 2. If factor 2 is blank, the result field is required and the information data structure's associated file name is used as the file for the POST operation.

In Example 5.111, the workstation file GLENTRY is the target of the POST operation.

Example 5.111: POST status information to an information data structure.

```
.....FFileName++IFEASFRlen+LKeylnKFDevice+.Functions++++++++++++++++++++++++++++++
0010 Fglentry   CF   E             WORKSTN  Infds(GL_Infds)

.....DName+++++++++++EUDsFrom+++To/L+++TDc.Functions++++++++++++++++++++++++++++++
0020 D PSDS            SDS
0030 D  WSID                 244      253A

0040 D GL_Infds        DS
0050 D  Status          *Status
0060 D  Device               272      275A
0070 D  Model                276      277A
0075 D  Fkey                 369      396A

.....CSRn01Factor1+++++++OpCode(ex)Factor2+++++++Result++++++++Len++DcHiLoEq
0080 C      WSID          POST      glentry                          56

0090 C                    If        Device =  '3180' or Device = '3477'
0100 C                    Move      *ON         DS4               1
0110 C                    else
0120 C                    Move      *ON         DS3               1
0130 C                    Endif

0150 C                    If        DS4 = *ON
0160 C                    EXFMT     Panel4
0170 C                    else
0180 C                    EXFMT     Panel3
0190 C                    EndIf
```

NOTE: *The information data structure for* WORKSTN *device files differs from system to system. The file information data structure positions in this example are for RPG IV on the IBM AS/400 and may differ on other systems.*

▶ READ (READ FROM A FILE)

The READ operation reads a record from a full-procedural file (i.e., the letter F appears in column 18 of the file specification for the file). For data files, the record that is read is the next record in the file. For workstation file formats, the record format specified in factor 2 is the record that is read. And for workstation files, the record format that was sent to the workstation last is read.

Factor 1	OpCode	Factor 2	Result Field		Resulting Indicators	
	READ (N E)	format name			[error]	[EOF]
	READ (N E)	file name	[data structure]		[error]	[EOF]

See also READP, READPE, READE, CHAIN, WRITE, UPDATE, DELETE, and UNLOCK

Factor 2 is required and can contain the name of the file or file record format that is read. If a record format name is specified, the file must be an externally described file.

The result field can contain the name of a data structure when factor 2 contains a program-described file name. When the READ operation completes successfully, the content of the record is copied to the data structure specified in the result field. This technique provides support of external file definitions for program-described files through the use of an externally described data structure.

Resulting Indicator Legend

Columns	Ind.	Usage	Set-On Condition
71 - 72	1	N/A	
73 - 74	2	[error]	An error occurred during the operation.
75 - 76	3	[EOF]	Set on when the end of file is reached.

Extender	Description
E	ERROR – Causes the %ERROR and %STATUS built-in functions to be set if an error occurs during the operation.
N	NO LOCK – Causes the database record to be read without placing a record lock on the record. This is useful for files that have been open for update operations.

When a READ operation fails to read a record, as is the case when the end of file is reached, resulting indicator 3 (if specified) and the %EOF built-in function are set on. The following characteristics apply when a record is accessed with the read operation:

- For INPUT files, the record is retrieved, but no record locking occurs.
- For OUTPUT-only files, this operation is not valid.

- For UPDATE files, if no operation extender is specified, the record is retrieved and locked until it is released through one of the following:
  - Another READ, READE, READP, READPE, or CHAIN operation.
  - The record is updated by an UPDATE or EXCEPT operation.
  - The record is deleted by a DELETE or EXCEPT with DEL operation.
  - The record is implicitly released by one of the following operations:
    - Except to an empty output format (EXCEPT).
    - Unlock the record (UNLOCK).
    - Set lower limit (SETLL).
    - Set greater than (SETGT).
    - Force end of data (FEOD).
    - Close file (CLOSE).

In Example 5.112, the READ operation on line 10 reads the first record in the file CUSTMAST. The DOW operation (line 20) begins the DO WHILE group that processes each record in the file. Resulting indicator 3 (LR in the example) is set on if the file is at end of file when the READ operation is performed (line 40). The %EOF built-in function is set to *ON when end of file is reached.

Example 5.112: Reading a file until end of file is detected.

```
.....CSRnØ1Factor1+++++++OpCode(ex)Factor2+++++++Result++++++++Len++DcHiLoEq
       *   Read the first record in the file.
ØØ1Ø C                  READ      CUSTMAST                              LR
       *   If records exist, then enter the read/print loop
       *   and print the first record.
ØØ2Ø C                  dow       NOT %EOF
       *   Print the record's data.
ØØ3Ø C                  Except    REPORT
       *   Read the next record in the file.
ØØ4Ø C                  READ      CUSTMAST                              LR
ØØ5Ø C                  EndDo
```

When a workstation device file format is specified in factor 2 and the format has not been written to the workstation, the following occurs: If the Write-Before-Read keyword exists in the file definition, the record format is written to the workstation, and then the READ option is performed. If the Write-Before-Read keyword is not specified, resulting indicator 2, if specified, is set on. If resulting indicator 2 is not specified, control is passed to the RPG exception/error routine.

If factor 2 contains a workstation file name, the last workstation file record format written to the device is read. When factor 2 contains a workstation file name, workstation *timeout* can be detected.

A workstation timeout occurs after a period of inactivity at the workstation. For example, if the workstation operator hasn't pressed <Enter> for a period of time (say 5 minutes), the workstation times out and resulting indicator 2 is set on. After a workstation record format is written, a workstation timeout can be detected by issuing a READ to the workstation file. See Example 5.113.

To support the workstation timeout feature, the INVITE (Invite from Device) keyword must exist in the device file. Also, a MAXDEV(*ONLY) keyword must be specified.

Example 5.113: Reading a workstation file with timeout support.

```
.....FFileName++IFEASFRlen+LKeylnKFDevice+.Functions++++++++++++++++++++++++++++
0010 FCUSTINQ   CF  E              WORKSTN MaxDev(*Only)
0020 FCUSTMAST  IF  E           K DISK    INFDS(CM_INFDS)

.....DName++++++++++EUDS.......Length+TDc.Functions++++++++++++++++++++++++++++
0030 D CM_INFDS         DS
0040 D   Status           *STATUS

.....CSRnØ1Factor1+++++++OpCode(ex)Factor2+++++++Result++++++++Len++DcHiLoEq
0050 C      ACTNBR        CHAIN     CUSTMAST                       54
0060 C                    IF        %FOUND
0070 C                    WRITE     Inquiry
0080 C                    READ      CUSTINQ                              5658
0090 C                    If        %ERROR = *ON and %STATUS = 1331
0100 C                    Exsr      TimeOut
0110 C                    Endif
0120 C                    EndIf
        *... the program continues.
```

► READC (READ NEXT CHANGED WORKSTATION RECORD)

The READC operation reads the changed records from a subfile. A record is read only if its data has been changed.

Factor 1	OpCode	Factor 2	Result Field	Resulting Indicators		
	READC	subfile format name			[error]	[EOF]

See also EXFMT and SFILE keywords

Factor 2 is required and must contain the name of a WORKSTN device file record format that is defined as a subfile. A WORKSTN record format is declared a subfile by specifying the SFILE keyword on the file specification.

In Example 5.114, line 10 defines the record format CUSTLIST as a subfile. Line 20 issues an EXFMT operation that displays the subfile. The READC operation on line 30 reads the first changed record in the subfile. The DO WHILE loop on

Resulting Indicator Legend			
Columns	Ind.	Usage	Set-On Condition
71 - 72	1	N/A	
73 - 74	2	[error]	An error occurred during the operation.
75 - 76	3	[EOF]	The end of subfile has been reached.

Extender	Description
E	ERROR – Causes the %ERROR and %STATUS built-in functions to be set if an error occurs during the operation.

lines 40 to 70 processes each changed subfile record.

Example 5.114: Displaying a subfile then reading all changed records.

```
.....FFileName++IFEASFRlen+LKeylnKFDevice+.Functions++++++++++++++++++++++++++++
0010 FCUSTINQ   CF   E             WORKSTN Sfile(Custlist : rrn )

.....CSRn01Factor1+++++++OpCode(ex)Factor2+++++++Result++++++++Len++DcHiLoEq
0020 C                  EXFMT      LISTCTL
0030 C                  ReadC      CUSTLIST                          58
0040 C                  dow        NOT %EOF(CustList)
0050 C**   Code to process the changed record goes here.
0060 C                  ReadC      CUSTLIST                          58
0070 C                  EndDo
```

READE (READ NEXT RECORD WITH AN EQUAL KEY)

The READE operation uses the full-key value or partial-key value specified in factor 1 to sequentially retrieve a record from the keyed file specified in factor 2.

Factor 1	OpCode	Factor 2	Result Field	Resulting Indicators		
[key value]	READE (N E)	format name			[error]	[EOF]
[key value]	READE (N E)	file name	[data structure]		[error]	[EOF]

See also READPE, READP, READ, CHAIN, WRITE, UPDATE, DELETE, and UNLOCK

Factor 1 is optional and can contain the key value for the READE operation. If factor 1 is blank, the next record with a key equal to the current record is retrieved. If a record with an equal key does not exist, resulting indicator 3 is set on. Factor 2 is required and must contain a database file or format name to be read.

The result field can contain the name of a data structure into which the data from the file is copied. This option is valid only for program-defined database files.

Resulting Indicator Legend			
Columns	Ind.	Usage	Set-On Condition
71 - 72	1	N/A	
73 - 74	2	[error]	An error occurred during the operation.
75 - 76	3	[EOF]	Set on when the end of file is reached.

Extender	Description
E	ERROR – Causes the %ERROR and %STATUS built-in functions to be set if an error occurs during the operation.
N	NO LOCK – Causes the database record to be read without placing a record lock on the record. This is useful for files that have been open for update operations.

When a READE operation fails to read a record, as is the case when the end of file is reached, resulting indicator 3 (if specified) and the %EOF built-in function are set on.

The following characteristics apply when a record is accessed by the READE operation:

- For INPUT files, the record is retrieved, but no record locking occurs.
- For OUTPUT-only files, this operation is not valid.
- For UPDATE files, if no operation extender is specified, the record is retrieved and locked until it is released through one of the following:

- ◆ Another READ, READE, READP, READPE, or CHAIN operation.
- ◆ The record is updated by an UPDATE or EXCEPT operation.
- ◆ The record is deleted by a DELETE or EXCEPT with DEL operation.
- ◆ The record is implicitly released by one of the following operations:
  - ➧ Except to an empty output format (EXCEPT).
  - ➧ Unlock the record (UNLOCK).
  - ➧ Set lower limit (SETLL).
  - ➧ Set greater than (SETGT).
  - ➧ Force end of data (FEOD).
  - ➧ Close file (CLOSE).

The READE operation is used when a data file contains non-unique full keys or partial keys. The READE operation provides sequential access to those non-unique keys. When the READE operation is the first input/output operation after an OPEN operation, the first record that matches the key value specified in factor 1 is retrieved. Example 5.115 shows an example of using the READE operation.

Example 5.115: Adding up the quantity on hand for a specific part number.

```
.....FFileName++IFEASFRlen+LKeylnKFDevice+.Functions+++++++++++++++++++++++++++++
0010 FPARTMAST  IF   E        K DISK

.....CSRn01Factor1+++++++OpCode(ex)Factor2+++++++Result++++++++Len++DcHiLoEq
0020 C     PART#        KLIST
0030 C                  KFLD                     PART           10
     * Establish the part number to total.
0040 C                  MOVEL(p)  'CEC01'        PART
     * Position the file to the first record for this PART number.
0050 C     PART#        SetLL    PARTMAST                          58
0060 C                  Eval     QtyOh = 0
0070 C                  dow      NOT %EOF
0080 C                  ADD      QTYOH           PARTOH         7 0
     * Retrieve the next record contain the same part number.
0090 C     PART#        READE    PARTMAST                          58
0110 C                  ENDDO
```

▶ READP (READ PRIOR RECORD FROM A DATA FILE)

The READP reads the previous record from the database file specified in factor 2.

Factor 1	OpCode	Factor 2	Result Field		Resulting Indicators	
	READP (N E)	format name			[error]	[BOF]
	READP (N E)	file name	[data structure]		[error]	[BOF]

See also READ, READE, READPE, CHAIN, WRITE, UPDATE, DELETE, and UNLOCK

Factor 2 is required and must contain the name of a database file or an externally described, database file-format name.

The result field can be specified for a program-described file only. The result field can contain the name of a data structure into which the retrieved record's data is placed. When the record is retrieved, the data is copied into the data structure.

When a READP operation fails to read a record, as is the case when the beginning of file is reached, resulting indicator 3 (if specified) and the %EOF built-in function are set on.

Resulting Indicator Legend

Columns	Ind.	Usage	Set-On Condition
71 - 72	1	N/A	
73 - 74	2	[error]	An error occurred during the operation.
75 - 76	3	[BOF]	Set on when the beginning of the file is reached.

Extender	Description
E	ERROR – Causes the %ERROR and %STATUS built-in functions to be set if an error occurs during the operation.
N	NO LOCK – Causes the database record to be read without placing a record lock on the record. This is useful for files that have been open for update operations.

After an unsuccessful READP operation, resulting indicator 3 is set on. A CHAIN, SETLL, or SETGT operation must be used to reposition the file before any other input operation can be performed on the file. The following characteristics apply when a record is accessed with the READP operation:

- For INPUT files, the record is retrieved, but no record locking occurs.
- For OUTPUT-only files, this operation is not valid.
- For UPDATE files, if no operation extender is specified, the record is retrieved and locked until it is released using one of the following:

- Another READ, READE, READP, READPE, or CHAIN operation.
- The record is updated by an UPDATE or EXCEPT operation.
- The record is deleted by a DELETE or EXCEPT with DEL operation.
- The record is implicitly released by one of the following operations:
    - Except to an empty output format (EXCEPT).
    - Unlock the record (UNLOCK).
    - Set lower limit (SETLL).
    - Set greater than (SETGT).
    - Force end of data (FEOD).
    - Close file (CLOSE).

In Example 5.116, the workstation file defined on line 20 is used to display a customer master file. Line 40 positions the file to end of file (with the *HIVAL figurative constant). Line 50, therefore, reads the last record in the file CUSTMAST.

Example 5.116: Reading a data file backwards and filling a subfile with the data.

```
.....FFileName++IFEASFRlen+LKeylnK.Device+.Functions++++++++++++++++++++++++++++
0010 FCUSTINQ   CF   E             WORKSTN Sfile(Custlist : rrn )
0010 FCUSTMAST  IF   E          K DISK

.....CSRn01Factor1++++++++<-OpCode(ex)->Factor2+++++++Result++++++++Len++DcHiLoEq
0040 C      *HIVAL         SetGT       CUSTMAST
0050 C                     ReadP       CUSTMAST                               58
0060 **  In this case, %EOF indicates beginning-of-file
0070 C                     dow         NOT %EOF
0080 C                     | Add       1              RRN           5 0
0090 C                     | Write     CUSTLIST
0100 C                     | ReadP     CUSTMAST                               58
0120 C                     EndDo
0130 C                     EXFMT       CustPanel
0140 C                     EXSR        RtvMacro
```

The DO WHILE loop (lines 70 to 120) writes to the subfile CUSTLIST, and then reads the next previous record in the file CUSTMAST (line 10).

The subfile CUSTLIST uses the relative record number field RRN to control the records that are written. Line 80 increments the subfile relative record. Line 90 writes the data retrieved by the previous READP operation to the subfile. This technique assumes that the subfile record contains the same field names as the data file CUSTMAST and that the subfile should be filled completely before presenting the information to the user.

To improve performance, the subfile could be filled with a few records—a page at a time—and then displayed to the user. The code shown in Example 5.117 would replace the DO WHILE loop in the previous example.

Example 5.117: Reading a data file backwards and filling a subfile one page at a time.

```
.....CSRnØ1Factor1+++++++<–OpCode(ex)–>Factor2+++++++Result++++++++Len++DcHiLoEq
ØØ2Ø C                   dow           Funct = 'ROLLDOWN'
ØØ3Ø C                   | Eval        rrn = Ø
ØØ4Ø C                   | dow         NOT %EOF and RRN <= 2Ø
ØØ5Ø C                   | | add       1                   RRN
ØØ6Ø C                   | | Write     CustList
ØØ7Ø C                   | | ReadP     CustMast                          58
ØØ9Ø C                   | enddo
Ø1ØØ C                   | Exfmt       CustPanel
Ø11Ø C                   | exsr        RtvMacro
Ø12Ø C                   enddo
```

In Example 5.117, the DO WHILE loop (line 20) causes the looping processes to occur each time the user presses the ROLLDOWN function key. In addition, only 20 subfile records are written each time this process is performed. (The subroutine RTVMACRO, on line 120, sets the value of the FUNCT field.)

READPE (READ PRIOR RECORD WITH AN EQUAL KEY)

The READPE operation uses the key value specified in factor 1 to sequentially retrieve the prior record from the keyed file specified in factor 2. The READPE operation provides sequential access to records with non-unique keys in descending order ("up" through the file). The full or partial index of the record is equal to the key value specified in factor 1.

Factor 1	OpCode	Factor 2	Result Field	Resulting Indicators		
[key value]	READPE (N E)	format name			[error]	[BOF]
[key value]	READPE (N E)	file name	[data structure]		[error]	[BOF]

See also READ, READE, READP, CHAIN, WRITE, UPDATE, DELETE, and UNLOCK

Factor 1 is optional and can contain the key value for the READPE operation. If factor 1 is blank, the previous record with a key equal to the current record is retrieved. Resulting indicator 3 is set on when a record with an equal key does not exist in the file.

Factor 2 is required and must contain the name of a file or a format of an externally described file. If factor 2 contains a file name, the result field can contain the name of a data structure into which the input data from the file is copied. This option is valid only for program-defined database files.

Resulting Indicator Legend			
Columns	Ind.	Usage	Set-On Condition
71 - 72	1	N/A	
73 - 74	2	[error]	An error occurred during the operation.
75 - 76	3	[BOF]	Set on when the beginning of the file is reached.

Extender	Description
E	ERROR – Causes the %ERROR and %STATUS built-in functions to be set if an error occurs during the operation.
N	NO LOCK – Causes the database record to be read without placing a record lock on the record. This is useful for files that have been open for update operations.

When a READPE operation fails to read a record, as is the case when the beginning of file is reached, resulting indicator 3 (if specified) and the %EOF built-in function are set on.

The following characteristics apply when a record is accessed with the READPE operation:

- For INPUT files, the record is retrieved, but no record locking occurs.
- For OUTPUT-only files, this operation is not valid.

- For UPDATE files, if no operation extender is specified, the record is retrieved and locked until it is released through one of the following:
  - ◆ Another READ, READE, READP, READPE, or CHAIN operation.
  - ◆ The record is updated by an UPDATE or EXCEPT operation.
  - ◆ The record is deleted by a DELETE or EXCEPT with DEL operation.
  - ◆ The record is implicitly released by one of the following operations:
    - → Except to an empty output format (EXCEPT).
    - → Unlock the record (UNLOCK).
    - → Set lower limit (SETLL).
    - → Set greater than (SETGT).
    - → Force end of data (FEOD).
    - → Close file (CLOSE).

Example 5.118 shows an example of coding the READPE operation.

Example 5.118: Adding the quantity on hand for a specific item number.

```
.....FFileName++IFEASFRlen+LKeylnKFDevice+.Functions+++++++++++++++++++++++++++++
0010 FITEMMAST  IF   E         K DISK


.....CSRn01Factor1+++++++OpCode(ex)Factor2+++++++Result++++++++Len++DcHiLoEq
0020 C     ITEM#         KList
0030 C                   KFld                    ITEM
     * Establish the item number to total.
0040 C                   MoveL(p) 'CEC01'        ITEM
     * Retrieve the last record for the item number
0050 C     ITEM#         ReadPE   ITEMMAST                          58
0060 C                   move     *IN58          NotFound
0070 C                   dow      NotFound = *OFF
0080 C                   add      QTYOH          ITEMOH
     * Retrieve previous record containing same item number
0090 C     ITEM#         ReadPE   ITEMMAST                          58
0100 C                   move     *IN58          NotFound
0110 C                   enddo
```

► REALLOC (REALLOCATE MEMORY)

The REALLOC operation is used to dynamically allocate storage (memory) at runtime. The number of bytes and a pointer variable to which the memory location is returned are passed to the REALLOC operation. Data currently stored at the existing pointer variable address is copied to the newly allocated storage location.

Factor 1	OpCode	Factor 2	Result Field	Resulting Indicators		
	REALLOC (E)	Length in bytes	Pointer variable		[error]	

See also ALLOC and DEALLOC

Factor 1 is required and must contain a numeric field or literal value. Factor 1 indicates the number of bytes of memory to allocate. The number of bytes that can be allocated must be greater than 0 and less than 16 megabytes (16,776,704). If the number of bytes is outside this limit, status error code 0425 is returned to the %STATUS built-in function.

The result field is required and must contain a field of type pointer. This pointer must contain a storage address returned by a

Resulting Indicator Legend			
Columns	Ind.	Usage	Set-On Condition
71 - 72	1	N/A	
73 - 74	2	[error]	An error occurred during the operation.
75 - 76	3	N/A	

Extender	Description
E	ERROR – Causes the %ERROR and %STATUS built-in functions to be set if an error occurs during the operation. Status code 0425 is returned if a memory allocation error occurs. Status code 0426 is returned if the existing pointer value is not valid.

previous ALLOC or REALLOC operation. A new memory address is returned to this variable. The storage at the original address is copied to the storage in the new location. Use this operation code to change the size of allocated storage.

In example 5.119, the number of bytes required to allocate 100 array elements is calculated on line 4. Because the %SIZE built-in function returns the number of bytes required for a single array element, it is used in this calculation.

Line 5 allocates 300 bytes of memory (100 elements times 3 bytes per element). Line 6 recalculates the number of bytes needed to allocate an additional 250 elements. Line 7 allocates the new memory size. The original pARR value is passed to the REALLOC operation. The storage at the address stored in pARR prior to the first REALLOC operation is copied to the storage at the new location.

If the size of the new storage location is less than the original location, only enough bytes to fill the new storage size are copied. Line 8 returns the storage to the operating system and sets the pARR pointer to null.

Example 5.119: Reallocating memory based on a calculated value.

```
.....DName+++++++++++EUDS.......Length+TDc.Functions++++++++++++++++++++++++++++++
0001 D pARR            S               *
0002 D ARRAY           S               5P 0 Dim(5000) Based( pArr )
0003 D nSize           S              10i 0

.....CSRn01Factor1+++++++OpCode(ex)Factor2+++++++Result++++++++Len++DcHiLoEq
       *    Allocate 100 elements for the array.
0004 C                 Eval      nSize = %Size(Array) * 100
0005 C                 ALLOC(E)  nSize          pArr
       **   Do something with the array data.
       **   But be sure not to touch outside the 100 allocated elements.
0006 C                 Eval      nSize = nSize + (%size(Array) * 250)
0007 C                 ReAlloc   nSize          pArr
       **   Do something with the 350 elements now allocated to the array
0008 C                 DeAlloc(N)               pArr
0009 C                 SetOn                                             LR
```

REL (RELEASE AN ACQUIRED DEVICE FILE)

The REL operation releases the WORKSTN device ID specified in factor 1. The device ID can be one acquired by the ACQ operation (see the subheading ACQ [Acquire]) or it can be the WORKSTN device running the program.

Factor 1	OpCode	Factor 2	Result Field	Resulting Indicators		
workstn device ID	REL	workstn file name			[error]	

See also ACQ

Factor 1 is required and must contain the name—for example, 'DSP12'—of the program device that is released. Factor 1 can be a 10-character field or constant enclosed in apostrophes. Factor 2 is required and must contain the name of the WORKSTN device file that previously has acquired the WORKSTN device ID.

Resulting Indicator Legend			
Columns	Ind.	Usage	Set-On Condition
71 - 72	1	N/A	
73 - 74	2	[error]	An error occurred during the operation.
75 - 76	3	N/A	

Extender	Description
E	ERROR – Causes the %ERROR and %STATUS built-in functions to be set if an error occurs during the operation.

In Example 5.120, the acquired program device DSP01 is released from the program on line 80. The field WSID contains the name of the previously acquired device. The MAXDEV keyword for the GLENTRY file (line 10) controls the number of devices that can be acquired for the program.

Example 5.120: Releasing an acquired workstation device.

```
.....FFileName++IFEASFRlen+LKeylnKFDevice+.Functions++++++++++++++++++++++++++++
0010 Fglentry   CF   E            WORKSTN MaxDev(*File)

.....CSRn01Factor1+++++++OpCode(ex)Factor2+++++++Result++++++++Len++DcHiLoEq
0030 C     'DSP01'      ACQ       glentry                             56
0040 C     *IN56        caseq     *ON          *PSSR
0050 C                  endcas
0060 C                  moveL(p)  'DSP12'      WSID           10
0070 C                  EXFMT     PROMPT
0080 C     WSID         REL       GLENTRY                             56
```

▶RESET (RESET VARIABLE TO ITS INITIAL VALUE)

The RESET operation changes the value of the variable specified in the result field to its initial value. The RESET operation can be run anywhere in the RPG program except within the *INZSR subroutine or any subroutine that is called by *INZSR.

Factor 1	OpCode	Factor 2	Result Field	Resulting Indicators	
	RESET	[*ALL]	variable to reset		[error]	
[*NOKEY]	RESET	[*ALL]	record format		[error]	

*See also: CLEAR and *INZSR*

Factor 1 is optional and can be specified only when the result field is a record format for a keyed database file. When a keyed database file is specified, factor 1 can contain the constant *NOKEY. This indicates that the key field values for the record are to be preserved (i.e., not reset) when the record format is reset.

Resulting Indicator Legend

Columns	Ind.	Usage	Set-On Condition
71 - 72	1	N/A	
73 - 74	2	[error]	An error occurred during the operation.
75 - 76	3	N/A	

Extender	Description
E	ERROR – Causes the %ERROR and %STATUS built-in functions to be set if an error occurs during the operation.

Factor 2 can contain the optional *ALL value. When factor 2 contains *ALL, the result field must contain a data structure, array or table, or workstation device file record format. When a multiple occurrence data structure is specified, all occurrences are reset. When an array or table is specified, all elements are reset. And when a workstation device file record format is specified, all fields (regardless of input/output status) are reset to their initial value.

The result field is required and can contain any variable, including a field name, data structure, data structure subfield, record format, array, array element, table, or named indicator.

If the result field contains a record format, the corresponding file must be opened for update, output-only, or combined (input/output) processing. The RESET operation cannot be used on a record format for a file that is opened for input only. Only fields defined as output or input/output are reset. Input-only fields are not reset in the record format.

If the result field contains a multiple occurrence data structure, only the current occurrence of the data structure is reset. If an array is specified, the entire array (every element) is reset. If an array element is specified, such as ARR(3), only that element is reset. When the RESET operation is performed on a data structure, each subfield is reset in order of its appearance in the data structure.

The RESET operation is intended to be used with initial values because it moves the initial value of a variable into the variable. In general, the variable must have been declared within the scope of the routine that contains the RESET operation. For example, when a variable is declared within a subprocedure, the RESET must also appear in that same subprocedure.

Because the RESET operation uses "hidden" storage to reset a field to its initial value, RESET cannot be used on any variable that has been declared with the IMPORT keyword.

When the RESET operation is specified, the compiler allocates storage containing a copy of the variable's initial value. Whenever the RESET operation is performed, the initial value is copied to the variable.

You should note, however, that the default initial value for a data structure subfield (regardless of type) is blank. Therefore, unlike the CLEAR operation, the RESET operation typically moves blanks into data structure subfields unless those subfields have been explicitly initialized.

A specific initial value can be specified by the INZ keyword or within the *INZSR subroutine. Additional storage is allocated containing a copy of the initialized data structure, its subfields, and their initial values. This causes program sizes to be larger than when RESET is not used.

In Example 5.121, the compiler initializes each data structure subfield in the ITEMS data structure (line 10) based on their data type. An exception is the ITEMCHAR subfield. The ITEMCHAR subfield contains its own INZ keyword and is initialized to '0100' (line 50).

Example 5.121: Resetting a data structure.

```
.....DName++++++++++++EUDS.......Length+....Functions++++++++++++++++++++++++++++++
0010 D ITEMS           DS                    INZ


.....DName++++++++++++EUDsFrom+++To/L+++TDc.Functions++++++++++++++++++++++++++++++
0020 D Price                      1      4P 2
0030 D Cost                       5      8P 2
0040 D ItemNum                    9     12S 0
0050 D ItemChar                   9     12A    INZ('0100')
0060 D ItemDesc                  13     62A
```

> The INZ keywords on lines 10 and 50 cause initialization code for the data structure to be generated.

```
.....CSRn01Factor1+++++++OpCode(ex)Factor2+++++++Result++++++++Len++DcHiLoEq
0080 C                   Eval      ItemNum = 9402
0090 C                   RESET                    Items
0100 C        *INZSR     BEGSR
0110 C                   Eval      *in88 = *ON
0120 C        endINZ     EndSr
```

The *INZSR subroutine (line 100) is called when the program is started. Indicator 88 is set to *ON, making its status *ON, when the main line calculations are entered.

The EVAL operation (line 80) places 9402 into the ITEMNUM subfield.

The RESET operation (line 90) resets the ITEMS data structure and, therefore, all of its subfields based on their data type. When the RESET operation is performed, the subfield ITEMCHAR (which occupies the same positions within the data structure as ITEMNUM) is set to '0100'.

Under this scenario, even if ITEMNUM had some other explicit initial value, the initial value for ITEMCHAR would supersede it because it appears later in the source code than the ITEMNUM field. The initial value for any field, data structure, data structure subfield, array, array element, or indicator is established (logically speaking) after the *INZSR subroutine is performed for the first time. Because data-structure subfield initialization occurs before the *INZSR subroutine is performed, the initial value of a data structure subfield can be overridden by altering the data-structure subfield's value during the *INZSR subroutine.

▶RETURN (RETURN TO CALLING PROGRAM)

The RETURN operation returns control to the caller of the program or procedure in which it is used. For programs, if the halt and LR indicators are off when the RETURN is performed, the program is suspended, but remains resident. For subprocedures, the RETURN operation returns control to the caller and optionally returns a value to the caller. Resulting indicators are not valid for this operation.

Factor 1	OpCode	Extended Factor 2
	RETURN (H M R)	return value or expression

*See also *INLR*

For RETURN operations to programs, the operation works as follows:

Extender	Description
H	HALF ADJUST – Any mathematical result from the expression in the result field is calculated using half-adjust (rounding) routines.
M	Maximum Digits
R	Result Value Digits

- If any halt indicator (H1 to H9) is on, the program ends abnormally.

- If indicator LR is on and the halt indicators are off, the program ends normally and returns to the calling program.

- If indicator LR is off and the halt indicators are off, the program remains active in memory, but control returns to the calling program. When this condition occurs, open files remain open; fields, data structures, arrays, and indicators retain their value, and the program remains active, but suspended. The next time the program is called, control is transferred to the program much faster than to an inactive program.

When a subprocedure performs a RETURN operation, the value specified in the extended factor 2 is returned to the caller. The value specified on the subprocedure's prototype and procedure interface control the format of the returned value.

In Example 5.122, the RETURN operation (line 100) is used to return to the caller of the program. Also, note the GETINTEREST function on line 80. Example 5.123 illustrates using the RETURN operation to return a value to the caller.

Example 5.122: Returning to caller from a dynamically called program.

```
.....H.Functions+++++++++++++++++++++++++++++++++++++++++++++++++++++++++++++++++
0010 H DatFmt(*ISO)

.....DName++++++++++EUDS.......To/Len+TDc.Functions++++++++++++++++++++++++++++
          * prototype for GetInterest procedure
0030 D GetInterest     PR            32A    ExtProc
0040 D   NumInput                    30P 4 Value

.....DName++++++++++EUDS.......Length+TDc.Functions++++++++++++++++++++++++++++
0060 D InvAmt          S              7P 0
0070 D Message         S            255A

.....CSRn01.............OpCode(ex)Extended-factor2+++++++++++++++++++++++++++++
0080 C                 Eval      Message = 'Amount Due: ' + GetInterest(InvAmt)
     C* the program continues...
0090 C                 Eval      *INLR = *ON
0100 C                 RETURN
```

In Example 5.123, the procedure GETINTEREST is defined. The procedure interface (line 20) indicates that a 32-byte character value must be returned to the caller of this procedure. Lines 100 and 110 build a value that is returned to the caller by the RETURN operation on line 120. This is the GETINTEREST procedure that is called by the EVAL operation on line 80 in Example 5.122.

Example 5.123: Returning a value to the caller with a procedure interface.

```
.....PProcname+++++++..B...................Functions++++++++++++++++++++++++++++
0010 P GetInterest     B             Export

.....DName++++++++++EUDS.......To/Len+TDc.Functions++++++++++++++++++++++++++++
0020 D GetInterest     PI            32A
0030 D   NumInput                    30P 4 Value

0040 D Interest        S            30P 4
0050 D RATE            C                   Const(.12)
0060 D CharVal         S            32A

.....CSRn01Factor1+++++++OpCode(ex)Factor2+++++++Result++++++++Len++DcHiLoEq
0070 C                 If        NumInput = 0
0080 C                 RETURN    '0'
0090 C                 EndIf

0100 C                 eval      Interest = NumInput * Rate
0110 C                 evalR     CharVal = %Char(Interest + NumInput)
0120 C                 RETURN    CharVal

.....PProcname+++++++..B...................Functions++++++++++++++++++++++++++++
0130 P GetInterest     E
```

▶ROLBK (ROLLBACK)

The ROLBK operation is a relational database management function. It performs the roll-back function of the relation model by abandoning all changes made to files since the prior COMMIT or ROLLBACK operation.

Factor 1	OpCode	Factor 2	Result Field	Resulting Indicators	
	ROLBK (E)				[error]

See also COMMIT.

The ROLLBACK and COMMIT operations are performed on all files that are under commitment control for a process (i.e., job), regardless of whether they are actually defined in the program performing the ROLBK or COMMIT operation.

In Example 5.124, the COMMIT keyword (line 10) specifies that the CUSTMAST file is under commitment control. Line 20 issues the ROLBK operation, causing all changes made to the CUSTMAST file—since the previous commit or rollback operation—to be abandoned.

Resulting Indicator Legend

Columns	Ind.	Usage	Set-On Condition
71 - 72	1	N/A	
73 - 74	2	[error]	An error occurred during the operation.
75 - 76	3	N/A	

Extender	Description
E	ERROR – Causes the %ERROR and %STATUS built-in functions to be set if an error occurs during the operation.

Example 5.124: Rolling back a file under commitment control.

```
.....FFileName++IFEASFRlen+LKeylnKFDevice+.Functions++++++++++++++++++++++++++++
0010 FCUSTMAST  UF   E           DISK      COMMIT('1')

.....CSRn01Factor1+++++++OpCode(ex)Factor2+++++++Result++++++++Len++DcHiLoEq
0020 C      'REGION6'      DELETE(E) CUSTMAST
0030 C                     If        NOT %ERROR
0040 C                     ROLBK(E)
0050 C                     endif
```

SCAN (SCAN STRING OR ARRAY)

The SCAN operation scans the character variable or array specified in factor 2 for the argument specified in factor 1. If the argument is found, the position of the first character of the argument is returned to the result field. If a numeric array is specified as the result field, each occurrence of the argument found in factor 2 is returned in a corresponding array element. A successful result of a SCAN operation can be checked using any of the following three techniques:

- The result field (if specified) will contain a value greater than zero.

- Resulting indicator 3 (if specified) will be equal to *ON.

- The %FOUND built-in function will be equal to *ON.

Factor 1	OpCode	Factor 2	Result Field	Resulting Indicators		
argument[:length]	SCAN(E)	search var[:start]	[position(s)]		[error]	[found]

See also LOOKUP, %FOUND, and %SCAN

Factor 1 is required and must contain a field, data structure, data structure subfield, array element, constant, or named constant that contains the search argument.

Factor 1 has one optional parameter: ARGUMENT-LENGTH. This parameter is separated from the argument in factor 1 by a colon (:). This parameter indicates how many characters of the search argument can be used for the scan. The ARGUMENT-LENGTH parameter can be any valid numeric value. The ARGUMENT-LENGTH must be

Resulting Indicator Legend

Columns	Ind.	Usage	Set-On Condition
71 - 72	1	N/A	
73 - 74	2	[error]	An error occurred during the operation.
75 - 76	3	[FOUND]	The SCAN operation located the data specified in factor 1 in the variable specified in factor 2.

Extender	Description
E	ERROR – Causes the %ERROR and %STATUS built-in functions to be set if an error occurs during the operation.

greater than 0 and less than or equal to the length of the search argument. If the ARGUMENT-LENGTH parameter is omitted, the entire search argument is used.

Factor 2 is required and must contain the value to be scanned. Factor 2 can be any valid data type except a figurative constant. Factor 2 has one optional parameter: START-POSITION. Separated from the entry in factor 2 by a colon (:), this parameter indicates the starting position of the scan within the scan data. If the START-POSITION parameter is omitted, the starting position for the scan is 1.

The result field is optional and can contain a numeric variable that receives the position of the left-most character of the search argument within the scan data. If a numeric array is specified, each occurrence of the search argument within the scan data is stored in a corresponding array element.

If the search argument is not found, the result field is set to zero. If the result field contains an array, each array element is set to zero. If the result field is not specified, resulting indicator 3 is required unless the %FOUND built-in function is used. See Example 5.125.

Example 5.125: Finding a search argument in a character variable.

```
.....FFileName++IFEASFRlen+LKeylnKFDevice+.Functions++++++++++++++++++++++++++++++
     FQRPGSRC   IF   F   112          DISK

.....DName++++++++++++EUDS.......To/Len+TDc.Functions++++++++++++++++++++++++++++++
     D Len          S              10I 0
     D StrPos       S              10I 0 Inz(1)
     D POS          S              10I 0
     D Counter      S               5I 0

.....IName++++++NS10INPos1+NCVPos2+NCVPos3+NCV
     IQRPGSRC    NS

.....I.....................Fmt+/TFrom+To+++D+Field+++++++++L1M1FRPLMNZB
     I                        13   112   SRCDTA

.....CSRn01Factor1+++++++OpCode(ex)Factor2+++++++Result++++++++Len++DcHiLoEq
     **   Scan argument.
     C                    MOVEL    'DISK'       Pattern          45
     **   Argument length.
     C                    Eval     Len = %TRIMR(Pattern)

     **   Search each record in an RPG source member for the word 'DISK'.
     C                    READ     QRPGSRC
     C                    DOW      NOT %EOF

     *   Scan the source record for the argument 'DISK'.
     C      Pattern:Len   SCAN     SRCDTA:StrPos Pos

      *   Count how many times the work DISK is used in the program.
     C                    IF       Pos > 0
     C                    Eval     StrPos = Pos
     C                    ADD      1            Counter
     C                    EndIf
     C                    READ     QRPGSRC
     C                    ENDDO
```

▶SELECT (START IN-LINE CASE GROUP)

The SELECT operation is used to begin an in-line case group. In-line case groups contain one or more WHENxx operations and an optional OTHER operation. The SELECT and ENDSL operations define the scope of the in-line case group.

Factor 1	OpCode	Factor 2	Result Field	Resulting Indicators		
	SELECT					

See also WHEN, OTHER, and ENDSL.

The SELECT operation must be followed immediately by one or more WHEN operations. Both forms of WHEN are supported by the SELECT operation. An in-line case group is defined by either the SELECT/WHEN/OTHER/ ENDSL case group or the IF/ELSE/ENDIF operations.

Differences between SELECT/WHENxx and IFxx/ELSE

The SELECT/WHEN/OTHER/ENDSL operations require only one ENDSL operation for the entire case group. The IFxx operation requires one ENDIF operation for each IFxx operation. The WHEN operation incorporates an implicit ELSE-like operation. A sequential ELSE and IFxx sequence provides function similar to the WHENxx operation.

The OTHER operation is the functional equivalent of the "catch all" or "final" ELSE operation of an IFxx/ELSE/ENDIF group. If the previous WHEN statement condition is not satisfied, the statements following the OTHER (Otherwise) operation are performed. Any RPG operation, except BEGSR and ENDSR, can be specified within an in-line case group, including another in-line case group.

Example 5.126: Using a SELECT statement to delimit an in-line case group.

```
.....CSRnØ1Factor1+++++++OpCode(ex)Factor2+++++++Result++++++++Len++DcHiLoEq
ØØØ1 C                   Read      ORDERS
ØØØ2 C                   SELECT
ØØØ3 C                   When      %EOF
ØØØ4 C                   exsr      AllDone
ØØØ5 C                   When      Region = MIDWEST
ØØØ6 C                   add       Amount        MWSALE
ØØØ7 C                   When      Region = CENTRAL
ØØØ8 C                   add       Amount        CTSALE
ØØØ9 C                   When      Region = WESTERN
ØØ1Ø C                   add       Amount        WCSALE
ØØ11 C                   Other
ØØ12 C                   add       Amount        HQSALE
ØØ13 C                   EndSl
```

In Example 5.126, the READ operation on line 1 reads a record from the orders file. Then, the SELECT group is entered. The WHEN operation (line 3) checks for end of file. If the end-of-file indicator is on, subroutine ALLDONE is performed, and then control transfers to the ENDSL operation (line 13).

If the test performed by the WHEN operation on line 3 is false, control passes to the next WHEN operation to perform its test. This continues until a WHEN test is true. Then the statements associated with the WHEN operation are performed. If none of the tests of the WHEN operations are true, control passes to the default routine associated with the OTHER operation.

▶ SETGT (SET GREATER THAN)

The SETGT operation positions the file specified in factor 2 to the record that is greater than the index or relative record number specified in factor 1. The file's data is not returned to the program by this operation.

Factor 1	OpCode	Factor 2	Result Field	Resulting Indicators		
key value	SETGT (E)	file name		[n/f]	[error]	
key value	SETGT (E)	format name		[n/f]	[error]	

See also SETLL, READ, READE, READP, READPE, CHAIN, and %FOUND

Factor 1 is required and must contain a record index or a record number. The key value or record number is used to position the file so that a subsequent READ operation retrieves records with a key value or relative record number greater than factor 1. A subsequent READP operation retrieves the previous record in the file. Factor 2 is required and must contain a full procedural file name or an externally described file's format name.

Resulting Indicator Legend			
Columns	Ind.	Usage	Set-On Condition
71 - 72	1	[n/f]	No records were found matching the index value in factor 1.
73 - 74	2	[error]	An error occurred during the operation.
75 - 76	3	N/A	

Extender	Description
E	ERROR – Causes the %ERROR and %STATUS built-in functions to be set if an error occurs during the operation.

The %FOUND built-in function is set to *ON when the SETGT operation successfully locates a record in the file with an index greater than the value specified in factor 1.

In Example 5.127, the file CUSTMAST is positioned to the index value that is greater than 'C999999'. If the end-of-file indicator is set on, the file is repositioned by the SETLL operation to beginning of file.

Example 5.127: Positioning a file with SETGT.

```
.....FFileName++IFEASFRlen+LKeylnKFDevice+.Functions++++++++++++++++++++++++++++
0010 FCUSTMAST  IF   E              DISK

.....CSRn01Factor1+++++++OpCode(ex)Factor2+++++++Result++++++++Len++DcHiLoEq
0020 C          'C999999'   SETGT    CUSTMAST
0030 C                      If       NOT %FOUND
0040 C          *LOVAL      Setll    CUSTMAST
0050 C                      EndIf
```

▶SETLL (SET LOWER LIMIT)

The SETLL operation positions the full procedural file specified in factor 2 to the record that is greater than or equal to the index or relative record number specified in factor 1. A subsequent READ operation retrieves the next record in the file; a subsequent READP operation retrieves the previous record in the file. The file's data is not returned to the program with this operation.

Factor 1	OpCode	Factor 2	Result Field	Resulting Indicators		
key value	SETLL (E)	file name		[n/f]	[error]	[equal]
key value	SETLL (E)	format name		[n/f]	[error]	[equal]

See also SETGT, READ, READE, READP, READPE, CHAIN, %FOUND, and %EQUAL

Factor 1 is required and must contain an index value (field, literal value, figurative constant, or key list) or a relative record number. The value of the index or relative record number is used to position the file so that a subsequent READ operation retrieves the record with an index value or relative record number greater than or equal to factor 1. Factor 2 is required and must contain the name of a full procedural file or externally described, file-record format.

Resulting Indicator Legend			
Columns	Ind.	Usage	Set-On Condition
71 - 72	1	[n/f]	The key value in factor 1 is greater than the highest corresponding key value in the file. The file cursor is positioned to end of file.
73 - 74	2	[error]	An error occurred during the operation.
75 - 76	3	[equal]	A key exists in the file that equals the key value specified in factor 1.

The %FOUND built-in function is set to *ON when the SETLL operation successfully locates a record in the file with an index less than or equal to the value specified in factor 1. The %EQUAL built-in function is set to *ON when the SETLL operation successfully locates a record in the file with an index exactly equal to the value specified in factor 1.

In Example 5.128, the file CUSTMAST is positioned to the 22nd relative record number (line 20). If relative record number 22 exists in the file CUSTMAST, resulting indicator 3 (indicator 58) is set on and subroutine GETREC (Get Record) is performed (line 30).

Example 5.128: Positioning a file with SETLL.

```
.....FFileName++IFEASFRlen+LKeylnKFDevice+.Functions++++++++++++++++++++++++++++++
0010 FCUSTMAST  IF  E              DISK

.....CSRn01Factor1+++++++OpCode(ex)Factor2+++++++Result++++++++Len++DcHiLoEq
0020 C     22            SETLL     CUSTMAST                                58
0030 C     *IN58         CASEQ     *ON          GetRecord
0040 C                   EndCS
0050 C*... the program continues...
```

If relative record number 22 doesn't exist, but relative record number 23 does, the file is positioned to relative record 23 and resulting indicator 3 (indicator 58) is not set on. Graphically, if the file is positioned to relative record number 22 using SETLL, the file cursor is positioned between records 21 and 22. See Figure 5.7.

As shown in Figure 5.7, the SETLL operation from Example 5.128 positions the file cursor after record 21 and before record 22. A subsequent READ operation retrieves record 22; a subsequent READP operation retrieves record 21.

SETOFF (SET OFF AN INDICATOR)

The SETOFF operation sets off (i.e., sets to '0') the indicator(s) specified in the resulting indicators. At least one resulting indicator must be specified.

Factor 1	OpCode	Factor 2	Result Field	Resulting Indicators		
	SETOFF			[ind1]	[ind2]	[ind3]

See also SETON, MOVE, MOVEL, and EVAL

Resulting indicators 1, 2, and 3 are optional, but at least one must be specified. The resulting indicator(s) specified is set off. The SETOFF operation performs the equivalent of a MOVE '0' or MOVE *OFF operation to a named indicator variable or an EVAL operation that has an indicator variable as its l-value. When indicators are set to one ('1'), they are considered on. When they are set to zero ('0'), they are off. The figurative constant *ON is the same as '1' and the figurative constant *OFF is the same as '0'.

Cursor Location	Record Number
	19
	20
	21
→	22
	23
	24

Figure 5.7:The SETLL operation by relative record number.

In Example 5.129, line 10 sets off indicators 54, 56, and 58. Line 20 sets off indicators 01 and 02. Because the SETOFF operation is functionally equivalent to a MOVE operation to a named indicator variable, lines 30, 40, and 50 perform the same function as line 10. Line 60 uses the MOVEA operation with the indicator array to set off indicators 01 and 02; this is the equivalent of line 20. Line 70 uses the EVAL operation to set off indicator 33 and line 80 sets indicator LR to the opposite setting of indicator 15.

Example 5.129: Setting off various indicators.

```
.....CSRn01Factor1+++++++OpCode(ex)Factor2+++++++Result++++++++Len++DcHiLoEq
0010 C                   SETOFF                                       545658
0020 C                   SETOFF                                       01  02
0030 C                   MOVE       '0'            *IN54
0040 C                   MOVE       *OFF           *IN56
0050 C                   MOVE       '0'            *IN,58
0060 C                   MOVEA      '00'           *IN,01
0070 C                   Eval       *IN33 = *OFF
0080 C                   Eval       *inlr = NOT *IN15
```

▶ SETON (Set On an Indicator)

The SETON operation sets on (i.e., sets to '1') the indicator(s) specified in the resulting indicators. At least one resulting indicator must be specified.

Factor 1	OpCode	Factor 2	Result Field	Resulting Indicators		
	SETON			[ind1]	[ind2]	[ind3]

See also SETON, MOVE, MOVEL, and EVAL.

Resulting indicators 1, 2, and 3 are optional, but at least one must be specified. The resulting indicator(s) specified is set on. The SETON operation performs the equivalent of a MOVE '1' or MOVE *ON operation to a named indicator variable or an EVAL operation that has an indicator variable as its l-value. When indicators are set to one ('1'), they are considered on. When they are set to zero ('0'), they are off. The figurative constant *ON is the same as '1' and the figurative constant *OFF is the same as '0'.

Example 5.130: Setting on various indicators.

```
.....CSRnØ1Factor1+++++++OpCode(ex)Factor2+++++++Result++++++++Len++DcHiLoEq
ØØ1Ø C                   SETON                                      545658
ØØ2Ø C                   SETON                                      Ø1  Ø2
ØØ3Ø C                   MOVE      '1'          *IN54
ØØ4Ø C                   MOVE      *ON          *IN56
ØØ5Ø C                   MOVE      '1'          *IN,58
ØØ6Ø C                   MOVEA     '11'         *IN,Ø1
ØØ7Ø C                   Eval      *IN33 = *ON
```

In Example 5.130, line 10 sets on indicators 54, 56, and 58. Line 20 sets on indicators 01 and 02. Because the SETON operation is functionally equivalent to a MOVE operation to a named indicator, lines 30, 40, and 50 perform the same function as line 10. Line 60 uses the MOVEA operation to the indicator array to set on indicators 01 and 02; this is the equivalent of line 20. Line 70 uses the EVAL operation to set on indicator 33.

▶ SHTDN (TEST FOR SHUTDOWN REQUEST)

The SHTDN operation tests for a system shutdown request. This can be any function that requests the program to end, including, but not limited to, system power down and an end-session request. Note: The SHTDN operation is obsolete and should be phased out of existing applications.

Factor 1	OpCode	Factor 2	Result Field	Resulting Indicators		
	SNTDN	label		true		

See also %SHTDN, RETURN and *INLR

Resulting indicator 1 is required and is set on if the shutdown test is successful. Specifically, it is set on when session shutdown has been requested.

Resulting Indicator Legend			
Columns	Ind.	Usage	Set-On Condition
71 - 72	1	True	A shut down request has been detected by the operation.
73 - 74	2	N/A	
75 - 76	3	N/A	

The SHTDN operation will set on resulting indicator 1 when one of the following AS/400 commands have been issued: PWRDWNSYS, ENDJOB, SIGNOFF, or ENDSBS.

In Example 5.131, the program normally ends with the LR indicator off. This would leave the program suspended, but resident. However, when session shutdown has been requested, indicator LR is set on (line 50), causing the program to be removed from memory when it returns to its caller (line 60).

Example 5.128: Testing for a session shutdown request.

```
.....CSRn01Factor1+++++++OpCode(ex)Factor2+++++++Result++++++++Len++DcHiLoEq
0010 C     *ENTRY        PLIST
0020 C                   PARM                     TIME           6 0
0030 C                   TIME                     TIME
0040 C     ENDPGM        TAG
0050 C                   SHTDN                                        LR
0060 C                   RETURN
```

▶SORTA (SORT ARRAY)

The SORTA operation arranges an array in the order specified by the ASCEND or DESCEND keywords on the array's definition specification.

Factor 1	OpCode	Factor 2	Result Field	Resulting Indicators		
	SORTA	Array name				

See also LOOKUP

Factor 2 is required and must contain the name of the array that is sorted. The indicator array *IN cannot be sorted. If the array being sorted has an associated *alternate array*, the alternate array is not sorted.

The SORTA operation supports both ascending and descending sorting. Specify the AS-CEND keyword for the array (on the definition specification) to sort in ascending order. Specify the DESCEND keyword to sort the array in descending order. If neither ASCEND nor DESCEND is specified, the array is sorted in ascending order.

In Example 5.132, the four-element, compile-time array LETTER (line 10) is initialized to DCAB when the program is started. The SORTA operation (line 20) sorts the array LETTER in ascending order.

Example 5.132: Sorting the array ALPHA in ascending order.

```
.....DName++++++++++EUDS.......Length+TDc.Functions+++++++++++++++++++++++++++++
0010 D Letter          S              1A    Dim(4) CTDATA PerRcd(4)

.....CSRn01Factor1+++++++OpCode(ex)Factor2+++++++Result++++++++Len++DcHiLoEq
0020 C                   SORTA      LETTER
0030 C                   MOVE       *ON           *INLR
**CTDATA LETTER
DCAB
```

Before SORTA

D,C,A,B

After SORTA

A,B,C,D

▶ SQRT (SQUARE ROOT)

The SQRT operation calculates the square root of the value specified in factor 2 and places the result into the result field. The EVAL operation supports the square root function in a much easier format. See the subheading EVAL (Evaluate an Expression) for more information.

Factor 1	OpCode	Factor 2	Result Field	Resulting Indicators		
	SQRT(H)	numeric value	square root			

See also ADD, SUB, MULT, DIV, and EVAL.

Factor 2 is required and must contain a numeric field, literal value, array, or array element. The square root of the value in factor 2 is placed in the result field. The value specified in factor 2 must be greater than or equal to zero. If factor 2 is less than zero, the exception/error routine is called. If factor 2 is an array, the result field must also be an array because the square root of each element is placed into the corresponding element in the array specified in the result field.

Extender	Description
H	HALF ADJUST – Causes the result value to be rounded.

The result field is required and must contain the name of a numeric field, array, or array element that receives the square root of the value specified in factor 2.

In Example 5.133, the field VALUE is initialized to 16 (line 10). On line 20, the square root of the field VALUE is calculated (4) and placed into the result field ANSWER. As an alternative, the square root of a number can be calculated using natural expression support (line 30).

Example 5.133: Calculating the square root of a value.

```
.....CSRn01Factor1+++++++OpCode(ex)Factor2+++++++Result++++++++Len++DcHiLoEq
0010 C                   Z-add     16            Value          3 0
0020 C                   SQRT      Value         Answer         7 5
0030 C                   Eval      Answer = Value ** (1/2)
```

►SUB (SUBTRACT)

The SUB operation is used to produce the difference of two values. Factor 2 is subtracted from factor 1 (long form); the difference is placed into the result field.

Factor 1	OpCode	Factor 2	Result Field	Resulting Indicators		
[minuend]	SUB(H)	subtrahend	difference	[+]	[-]	[0]

See also ADD, MULT, DIV, SQRT, and EVAL

Factor 1 is optional and, if specified, it is used as the basis for the subtraction. In other words, factor 2 is subtracted from factor 1. This is known as a *long-form subtract.* If factor 1 is omitted, factor 2 is subtracted from the current value of the result field. The difference replaces the value of the result field. This is known as a *short-form subtract.*

Resulting Indicator Legend			
Columns	Ind.	Usage	Set-On Condition
71 - 72	1	[+]	The result field is greater than zero.
73 - 74	2	[–]	The result field is less than zero.
75 - 76	3	[0]	The result field is equal to zero.

Extender	Description
H	HALF ADJUST – Causes the result value to be rounded up to the nearest decimal position.

Factor 2 is required and is subtracted from factor 1, if specified, or from the current value of the result field if factor 1 is omitted. The result field is required. The result of the SUB operation (the *difference*) is stored in the result field.

Example 5.134, if written in traditional mathematical expressions, would read as follows:

```
A - B = C

C - 1 = C
```

In Example 5.134, field B is subtracted from field A (line 10) and the difference is stored in field C. Then field C is decremented by 1 (line 20).

After the second SUB operation (line 20) is performed, if field C is greater than zero (i.e., a positive number), resulting indicator 1 (indicator 54) is set on. If field C is less than zero (i.e., negative), resulting indicator 2 (indicator 56) is set on. If field C equals zero, resulting indicator 3 (indicator 58) is set on.

Example 5.134: Subtracting factor 2 from factor 1 and then decrementing the result.

```
.....CSRn01Factor1+++++++OpCode(ex)Factor2+++++++Result++++++++Len++DcHiLoEq
0010 C     A            SUB     B            C               5 0
0020 C                  SUB     1            C                 545658
```

In Example 5.135, each element of the ARR1 array has 3 subtracted from it (line 40), and it is placed into the corresponding element in the DIFF array. On line 50, each element of ARR2 array is subtracted from the corresponding element of ARR1 array, and the difference is placed into the corresponding elements of DIFF array. On line 60, the constant 5 is subtracted from each element of the DIFF array. On line 70, the 5th element of the ARR2 array is subtracted from the 4th element of the ARR1 array. The difference is placed into the ANSWER field.

Example 5.135: Illustrating array handling with the SUB operation.

```
.....DName++++++++++EUDS.......Length+TDc.Functions+++++++++++++++++++++++++++++++
0010 D Arr1                    3S 0 Dim(5)
0020 D Arr2                    3S 0 Dim(5)
0030 D Diff                    3S 0 Dim(5)

.....CSRn01Factor1+++++++OpCode(ex)Factor2+++++++Result++++++++Len++DcHiLoEq
0040 C     Arr1         SUB     3            Diff
0050 C     Arr1         SUB     Arr2         Diff
0060 C                  SUB     5            Diff
0070 C     Arr1(4)      SUB     Arr2(5)      Answer          3 0
```

SUBDUR (SUBTRACT DURATION)

The SUBDUR operation code can be used to calculate a new date or calculate the period between two dates. SUBDUR has all the function of ADDDUR, plus the capability to calculate a period between two date values.

Factor 1	OpCode	Factor 2	Result Field	Resulting Indicators		
date value	SUBDUR (E)	date value	duration : dur code		[error]	[0]
[date value]	SUBDUR (E)	duration: :dur code	resulting date		[error]	

See also ADDDUR, EXTRCT, TEST, and MOVE

To calculate the period between two date or time values, specify the starting date or time value in factor 1 and the ending date or time value in factor 2. The result field receives the duration between the two values. Use the duration code parameter in the result field to indicate the type of duration you want. For a list of valid duration codes, see Table 5.4.

Resulting Indicator Legend			
Columns	Ind.	Usage	Set-On Condition
71 - 72	1	N/A	
73 - 74	2	[error]	An error occurred during the operation.
75 - 76	3	N/A	

Extender	Description
E	ERROR – Causes the %ERROR and %STATUS built-in functions to be set if an error occurs during the operation.

To calculate a new date, specify the starting date in factor 1, and the period to be subtracted from this date (i.e., the *duration*) in factor 2. Specify the duration code parameter in factor 2 to indicate the type of duration you want to subtract.

> **NOTE:** The duration can be a negative value, effectively performing the same function as the ADDDUR operation code.

If factor 1 is not specified, the date value in the result field is used as the starting date. In the result field, specify a date or time variable that receives the result of the operation.

In Example 5.136, today's date is moved into the TODAY field (line 50). The special date format *JOBRUN is used in factor 1 to indicate the format for the *DATE field. Line 70 uses the SUBDUR operation to subtract the DUEDATE value from today's date. The number of days since the due date is stored in PASTDUE. Note the use of the *DAYS duration code.

Example 5.136: Using SUBDUR to calculate past-due invoices.

```
.....DName++++++++++++EUDSFrom+++To/Len+TDc.Functions+++++++++++++++++++++++++++++
0010 D DueDate         S               D   INZ(D'1996-02-17')
0020 D Today           S               D

.....CSRn01Factor1+++++++OpCode(ex)Factor2+++++++Result++++++++Len++DcHiLoEq
0040  *   Convert today's date to a date data-type field.
0050 C     *JOBRUN       MOVE      *DATE           ToDay
0060  *   Calculate the number of days past-due.
0070 C     ToDay         SubDur    DueDate         PastDue:*DAYS     3 0
0080 C                   if        PastDue > 30
0090  *   TODO: insert code for past due invoices here.
0100 C                   endif
```

Example 5.137 shows how to use SUBDUR to calculate durations and dates.

Example 5.137: Using SUBDUR to calculate various durations and new dates.

```
.....DName++++++++++++EUDSFrom+++To/Len+TDc.Functions+++++++++++++++++++++++++++++
0010 D DayOne          S               D   INZ(D'1900-01-01')
0020 D NextCent        S               D   INZ(D'2000-01-01')
0030 D ToDay           S               D
0040 D ClockIn         S               T   INZ(T'07:00:00')
0050 D ClockOut        S               T   INZ(T'16:30:00')
0060 D LoanDue         S               D   INZ(D'2020-07-04')

.....CSRn01Factor1+++++++OpCode(ex)Factor2+++++++Result++++++++Len++DcHiLoEq
      * Number of days months, weeks, and years since first day of 19th century.
0100 C     NextCent      SubDur    DayOne          Days:*Days        5 0
0110 C     Days          Div       7               Weeks             5 0
0120 C     NextCent      SubDur    DayOne          Months:*Months    5 0
0130 C     NextCent      SubDur    DayOne          Years:*Years      3 0
      * Number hours and minutes worked this week
0150 C     ClockIn       SubDur    ClockOut        Hours:*H          3 0
0160 C     ClockIn       SubDur    ClockOut        Mins:*MN          5 0
      * Set a loan's due date back by 15 years.
0180 C                   SubDur    15:*Years       LoanDue
```

▶ SUBST (SUBSTRING THEN MOVE LEFT)

The SUBST operation copies a portion of the value in factor 2 to the result field.

Factor 1	OpCode	Factor 2	Result Field		Resulting Indicators	
[length]	SUBST (P E)	source [:start]	target		[error]	

See also MOVE, MOVEL, CAT, EVAL, and %SUBST

Factor 1 is optional and can contain the length for the substring. Factor 1 can be a numeric field, data structure subfield, array element, or constant. If factor 1 is omitted, the length is automatically calculated by the operation; the length is calculated through the end of the variable specified in factor 2.

Factor 2 is required and must contain a character field, data structure, data-structure subfield, array, array element, or constant that is copied.

Resulting Indicator Legend

Columns	Indy	Usage	Set-On Condition
71 - 72	1	N/A	
73 - 74	2	[error]	An error occurred during the operation.
75 - 76	3	N/A	

Extender	Description
P	PAD – Causes the result field to be cleared before the subst operation is performed.
E	ERROR – Causes the %ERROR and %STATUS built-in functions to be set if an error occurs during the operation.

Factor 2 has one optional parameter: START-POSITION. This parameter is separated from the entry in factor 2 by a colon (:). START-POSITION indicates the starting position for the substring. If the START-POSITION parameter is omitted, the starting position for the substring is 1. START-POSITION can be a literal value, named constant, numeric field, or numeric data-structure subfield.

The result field is required and must contain a character field, data structure, data structure subfield, array element, or table name. If no operation extender is specified and the substring length is less than that of the result field, the field is moved, left justified, into the result. Any data in the result field that is not overlaid by the substring is unchanged.

The %SUBST built-in function performs the same function as the SUBST operation. However, %SUBST also can be used by the EVAL statement and with conditional expressions.

The SUBST operation is useful when a value needs to be separated from within a field. Traditional RPG programming would dictate moving a value into an array, and then using that array to select the substring value for the field. The SUBST operation eliminates the need for most array-handling techniques for non-array fields, array elements, data structures, and data-structure subfields.

In Example 5.138, the SCAN operation locates the first blank after the first name (line 10). That value is used to calculate the length of the first name (line 30). The SUBST operation is used to extract the first name from NAME (line 40). In addition, the first character of the last name is located (lines 50 to 110) and the last name is extracted. The result of this process is the following:

```
           *...v ...1... v ...2... v
 FIRST  =  'Robert                '
 LAST   =  'Kennedy               '
```

Example 5.138: Using SUBST with SCAN to split a name into first and last names.

```
.....DName++++++++++EUDS.......To/Len+TDc.Functions++++++++++++++++++++++++++++++
     D Name            S             30     INZ('Robert Kennedy')
     D Len             S             5P 0
     D Pos             S             5P 0


.....CSRnØ1Factor1+++++++OpCode(ex)Factor2+++++++Result++++++++Len++DcHiLoEq
         *    Find the first blank following the first name
ØØ1Ø C        *BLANK:1    SCAN      NAME          POS
ØØ2Ø C                    If        POS > 1
         *    Subtract 1 from the position to compute its length
ØØ3Ø C                    Eval      Len = Pos - 1
         *    Pull out the first name
ØØ4Ø C        LEN         SUBST(p)  NAME:1        FIRST            25
ØØ5Ø C                    CLEAR                   POS
         *    Locate the first non-blank character of the last name
ØØ6Ø C        *BLANK      CHECK     NAME          POS
ØØ7Ø C                    If        POS > Ø
         *    Compute the remaining length as the (field length of Name) - POS
ØØ8Ø C                    eval      Len = %Size(Name) - POS
         *    Pull out the last name
ØØ9Ø C        LEN         SUBST(p)  NAME:Pos      Last             25
Ø1ØØ C                    EndIf
Ø11Ø C                    EndIf
```

▶ TAG (LABEL)

The TAG operation defines a label. A label can be used as the target of a GOTO or CAB*xx* operation. A TAG can be specified anywhere in the program. Conditioning indicators are not valid for this operation. Resulting indicators are not valid for this operation.

Factor 1	OpCode	Factor 2	Result Field	Resulting Indicators		
label	TAG					

See also LABEL, ENDSR, GOTO, and CABxx

Factor 1 is required and must contain a label name of up to six characters. The label must be unique—that is, no other field, array, data structure, data structure subfield, or subroutine can have the same name as a TAG label.

The label is specified in factor 2 of the GOTO operation and in the result field of the CAB*xx* operation. More than one GOTO and CAB*xx* operation can branch to the same label. Factor 1 of an ENDSR operation also can function as a target of a GOTO or CAB*xx* operation, and has restrictions similar to the TAG operation.

In Example 5.139, the CABEQ (Compare and Branch Equal) operation (line 20) branches to the label ENDPGM (line 501) when the end of file is detected (i.e., the READ operation on line 10 sets on the LR indicator).

Example 5.139: Branching to a label when end of file is detected.

```
.....CSRnØ1Factor1+++++++OpCode(ex)Factor2+++++++Result++++++++Len++DcHiLoEq
ØØ1Ø C                     READ      CUSTMAST                              LR
ØØ2Ø C        *INLR        CABEQ     *ON          ENDPGM
xxxx C*.... additonal user-code goes here.
Ø5Ø1 C        ENDPGM       TAG
Ø5Ø2 C                     RETURN
```

▶ TEST (TEST DATE/TIME/TIMESTAMP)

TEST verifies the contents of the result field. Verification is performed based on the operation extender. A valid date, time, or timestamp value can be tested with the TEST operation.

Factor 1	OpCode	Factor 2	Result Field	Resulting Indicators	
l[date format[sep]]	TEST (D E)		date variable		[error]
[time format[sep]]	TEST (T E)		time variable		[error]
[*ISO	*ISO0]	TEST (Z E)		timestamp variable		[error]
	TEST (E)		date/time/timestamp		[error]

See also EXTRCT, SUBDUR, and ADDDUR

Factor 1 is optional and identifies the date or time format of the value in the result field. Factor 1 can be used when the field being tested (the result field) is either a character or numeric field. Factor 1 cannot be specified when the result field contains an actual date, time, or timestamp variable.

Resulting Indicator Legend			
Columns	Ind.	Usage	Set-On Condition
71 - 72	1	N/A	
73 - 74	2	[error]	An error occurred during the TEST operation. The result field's value did not pass the format test for the type of data indicated by the operation extender.
75 - 76	3	N/A	

The result field can contain a date, time, timestamp, character, or numeric field. When a character or numeric field is specified for the result field, an operation extender must be used to indicate the kind of testing being formed. In addition, an optional format code can be specified in factor 1.

Resulting indicator 2 is set on when the TEST operation fails (when the result field contains an invalid date, time, or timestamp value).

There are three operation extenders that control the TEST operation. An operation extender must be specified when the result field contains either a character or numeric variable. The valid operation extenders are described as follows:

Extender	Description
E	ERROR – Causes the %ERROR built-in function to be set on if the result field fails the TEST operation. This operation extender can be used in place of resulting indicator 2, and can be specified along with any one of the other operation extenders.
D	DATE TEST – Checks the value in the result field for a valid date format. The date format code can be specified in factor 1. If factor 1 is blank, the date format specified for the DATFMT keyword on the header specification is used. If no DATFMT keyword is specified, then *ISO is the default date format code.
T	TIME TEST – Checks the value in the result field for a valid time format. The time format code can be specified in factor 1. If factor 1 is blank, the time format specified for the TIMFMT keyword on the header specification is used. If no TIMFMT keyword is specified, then *ISO is the default time format code.
Z	TIMESTAMP TEST – Checks the value in the result field for a valid timestamp format. The timestamp format code can be specified in factor 1 as *ISO or *ISO0. If no timestamp format code is specified, then *ISO is the default timestamp format.

In Example 5.140, line 10 tests the INVDATE field (which is a DATE variable) for a valid date. If the date is valid, the date is moved into a six-digit numeric field named ORDDTE. ORDDTE is a field used in the database record ORDREC (line 60). To be certain ORDDTE contains a valid date in Month-Day-Year format, a second TEST operation is performed on that field (line 40). If the field is invalid, an error routine is called and the database record is not written out.

Example 5.140: Testing for various date values.

```
.....CSRnØ1Factor1+++++++OpCode(ex)Factor2+++++++Result++++++++Len++DcHiLoEq
ØØ1Ø C                   Test                     InvDate
ØØ2Ø C                   If         NOT %ERROR
ØØ3Ø C      *MDY         Move       InvDate       ORDDTE          6 Ø
ØØ4Ø C      *MDY         Test(DE)                 ORDDTE                   56
ØØ5Ø C                   If         NOT %ERROR
ØØ6Ø C                   Write      OrdRec
ØØ7Ø C                   else
ØØ8Ø C                   CallB      'DateError'
ØØ9Ø C                   EndIf
Ø1ØØ C                   EndIf
```

TESTB (TEST BIT PATTERN)

The TESTB operation compares the bits specified in factor 2 to the result field. Bits that are not referenced in factor 2 go untested in the result field.

Factor 1	OpCode	Factor 2	Result Field	Resulting Indicators		
	TESTB	'bits to test'	1-byte char variable	[xor]	[mix]	[equal]

See also TEST, BITON, BITOFF, TESTN, and TESTZ

Factor 2 is required and must contain one of the following: a bit number or numbers, a 1-byte character field, or a 1-byte hexadecimal literal. The bit configuration in factor 2 is compared to the bit configuration of the result field.

The result field is required and must contain a 1-byte character variable. At least one resulting indicator must be specified for this operation. If factor 2 contains only one bit, then resulting indicator 2 cannot be specified.

Resulting Indicator Legend			
Columns	Ind.	Usage	Set-On Condition
71 - 72	1	[xor]	All the bits specified in factor 2 are off in the result field.
73 - 74	2	[mixed]	Mixed bit matching between factor 2 and the result field.
75 - 76	3	[equal]	All the bits specified in factor 2 are on in the result field.

There are eight bits in an EBCDIC byte. When addressing a bit with a TESTB operation, the bits are numbered from the top down as 0 through 7. Unofficially referred to as *nibbles*, the bits are grouped into two logical units—the top half and bottom half. Their numeric value is reversed (the value of bit 0 is 8, the value of bit 7 is 1, as follows):

Bit	Value
0	8
1	7
2	6
3	5
4	4
5	3
6	2
7	1

Because RPG is written horizontally, addressing bits vertically would be awkward. Therefore, RPG uses a horizontal method of addressing bits, as follows:

```
Bit Number ➜     0123 4567
Bit Value  ➜     8421 8421
```

Remember that bits can be either on or off (they are equal to X'1' or X'0' respectively). When a bit is on, it is equal to X'1' and represents the value for its bit number. When a bit is off, it is equal to X'0' and represents a value of zero. For example, if bits 5 and 7 are on and all the other bits are off, the byte is represented as a hex value of X'05', a binary value of B'00000101', and a numeric value of 5.

In Example 5.141, the bit pattern in factor 2 is different than the result field (line 10). Only resulting indicator 2 (indicator 56) is set on. On line 20, bits 1, 2, and 7 are tested, and the bits that are on in FIELDA are on in FIELDB. Therefore, only resulting indicator 3 (indicator 58) is set on. On line 30, all of the bits specified in factor 2 are off in the result field. Therefore, resulting indicator 1 (indicator 54) is set on.

Bit Number ➜	0123 4567
Bit pattern for FIELDA	0100 0001
Bit pattern for FIELDB	0101 1101

Example 5.141: Testing various field bit values.

```
.....CSRn01Factor1+++++++OpCode(ex)Factor2+++++++Result++++++++Len++DcHiLoEq
0010 C                   TESTB     '127'         FIELDA           545658
0020 C                   TESTB     FIELDA        FIELDB           545658
0030 C                   TESTB     '026'         FIELDA           54  58
```

TESTN (TEST CHARACTER FIELD FOR NUMERIC DATA)

The TESTN operation tests the value of the result field for valid zoned numeric data. At least one resulting indicator must be specified for this operation.

Factor 1	OpCode	Factor 2	Result Field	Resulting Indicators		
	TESTN		char variable	[num]	[mix]	[blank]

See also TEST, TESTZ, and TESTB

The result field is required and must be a character variable. The content of the result field is tested for numeric data and resulting indicators are set on accordingly. Except when the result field is blank, no resulting indicators are set on when the result field contains invalid numeric data.

Resulting Indicator Legend			
Columns	Ind.	Usage	Set-On Condition
71 - 72	1	[num]	All the characters in the result field are numeric.
73 - 74	2	[mixed]	The result field is numeric with one or more leading blanks.
75 - 76	3	[blank]	The result field contains blanks.

Numeric data in the result field can be positive or negative. If the data is negative, the right-most character of the result field contains the letters J to R.

In Example 5.142, the TESTN operation on line 50 sets on resulting indicator 1. The TESTN operation on line 60 sets on resulting indicator 2. The TESTN operation on line 70 sets on resulting indicator 3. The TESTN operation on line 80 sets on no resulting indicators because FLDD doesn't contain valid numeric data.

Example 5.142: Illustrating the TESTN operation.

```
.....DName++++++++++++EUDS.......Length+TDc.Functions+++++++++++++++++++++++++++++
0010 D FieldA          S             5A    INZ('12345')
0020 D FieldB          S             5A    INZ('  345')
0030 D FieldC          S             5A    INZ(*BLANKS)
0040 D FieldD          S             7A    INZ('400 Q38')

.....CSRn01Factor1+++++++OpCode(ex)Factor2+++++++Result++++++++Len++DcHiLoEq
0050 C                   TESTN                    FieldA                545658
0060 C                   TESTN                    FieldB                545658
0070 C                   TESTN                    FieldC                545658
0080 C                   TESTN                    FieldD                545658
```

TESTZ (TEST THE ZONE OF A FIELD)

The TESTZ operation tests the zone of the left-most character of the result field. At least one resulting indicator must be specified with this operation.

Factor 1	OpCode	Factor 2	Result Field	Resulting Indicators		
	TESTZ		char variable	[+]	[-]	[other]

See also TEST, TESTN, and TESTB.

The result field is required and must contain a character variable. The zone of the left-most character of the result field is tested.

In Example 5.143, the TESTZ operation on line 10 sets on resulting indicator 1 (indicator 54). The TESTZ operation on line 20 sets on resulting indicator 2 (indicator 56). The TESTZ operation on line 30 sets on resulting indicator 3 (indicator 58).

Resulting Indicator Legend			
Columns	Ind.	Usage	Set-On Condition
71 - 72	1	[+]	The right-most character of the result field contains an ampersand (&), the letter A to I, or any character with the same zone as the letter A.
73 - 74	2	[–]	The right-most character of the result field contains a minus sign (–), the letters J to R, or any character with the same zone as the letter J.
75 - 76	3	[other]	The right-most character contains a value that is not represented by either resulting indicator 1 or 2.

Example 5.143: Illustrating the TESTZ operation.

```
.....DName+++++++++++EUDS........Length+TDc.Functions++++++++++++++++++++++++++++++
0010 D FieldA          S              5A    INZ('ABCDE')
0020 D FieldB          S              5A    INZ('0200J')
0030 D FieldC          S              5A    INZ(*BLANKS)

.....CSRn01Factor1+++++++OpCode(ex)Factor2+++++++Result++++++++Len++DcHiLoEq
0010 C                   TESTZ                    FIELDA                  545658
0020 C                   TESTZ                    FIELDB                  545658
0030 C                   TESTZ                    FIELDC                  545658
```

▶TIME (RETRIEVE SYSTEM TIME AND DATE)

The TIME operation retrieves the system time and, optionally, the system date. The retrieved time is stored in the result field. The length of the result field determines whether TIME returns only the system time or the system time and system date.

Factor 1	OpCode	Factor 2	Result Field	Resulting Indicators		
	TIME		numeric variable			
	TIME		date variable			
	TIME		time variable			
	TIME		timestamp variable			

See also *DATE, *TIME, and TIMESTAMP

The result field is required and must contain either a 6-, 12-, or 14-position numeric field, or a date, time, or timestamp variable. If a 6-position field is specified, the current system time is retrieved. If a 12-position numeric field is specified, the current system time and current system date are retrieved. If a 14-position numeric field is specified, the current system time and current system date (including the century) are retrieved.

When both time and date are retrieved, the time is returned in positions 1 through 6, and the date is returned in positions 7 to 12 or 7 to 14. The time is returned in the format HHMMSS and is based on a 24-hour clock.

If the date is also retrieved, it is returned in the format specified for the job running on the system. If the job's date format is *MDY, the date is returned as MMDDYY for a 12-position result field and MMDDCCYY for a 14-position result field. For Julian dates, the format is YY0DD and CCYY0DDD. The embedded zero is a placeholder because Julian days range from 1 to 366.

The format of the date/time value returned by the TIME operation is based on the length and type of the result field. The format is always HHMMSSddddddd, where HHMMSS is the time, and ddddddd is the date. The value is truncated as necessary by the TIME operation before it is stored in the result field. Table 5.23 lists the return value for the TIME operation. The date used in this illustration is the 31st of December 1998 at 13:45:00 (1:45 P.M.).

	Table 5.23: Various Result Field Types for TIME Operation		
Result Field Type	**Time Returns**	**Format**	**Example Value Datfmt**
Dec(6,0)	System Time	HHMMSS	124500
Dec(12,0)	System Time, System Date	HHMMSSMMDDYY	124500123198
Dec(14,0)	System Time, System Date	HHMMSSMMDDYYYY	12450012311998
DATE	System Date	Result field's format	1998-12-31
TIME	System Time	Result field's format	13:45:00
TIMESTAMP	System Date, System Time	*ISO	1998-12-31-13.45.00.000000

When the date format is *YMD and the time and date are returned together in a 12-position field, the format is HHMMSSYYMMDD. For a 14-position field, the format is HHMMSSYYYYMMDD. Example 5.141 illustrates the TIME operation. The date used in these examples is the 31st of December 1998 at 13:45:00 (1:45 P.M.). The date format for the session (job) running the program is *MDY. Example 5.144 shows various ways to code the TIME operation.

Example 5.144: Retrieving the system time and the system time and date.

```
.....DName++++++++++EUDS.......Length+TDc.Functions+++++++++++++++++++++++++++
0010 D myTime          S              6S 0
0020 D myDate          S             12S 0
0030 D myDateTime      S             14S 0
0040 D theTime         S               T   TIMFMT(*USA)
0050 D theDate         S               D   DATFMT(*ISO)
0060 D theTimeStamp    S               Z

.....CSRn01Factor1+++++++OpCode(ex)Factor2+++++++Result++++++++Len++DcHiLoEq
0070 C                   TIME                     myTime
     **   MYTIME = 134500
0080 C                   TIME                     myDate
     **   MYDATE = 123198
0090 C                   TIME                     myDateTime
     **   MYDATETIME = 134500123198
0010 C                   TIME                     theTime
     **   THETIME = T'01:45 PM'
0011 C                   TIME                     theDate
     **   THEDATE = D'1998-12-31'
0012 C                   TIME                     theTimeStamp
     **   THETIMESTAMP = Z'1998-12-31-13.45.00.000000'
```

UNLOCK (UNLOCK DATA AREA/RELEASE RECORD LOCK)

The UNLOCK operation releases a lock applied to one or all data areas that are locked by the program. In addition, the UNLOCK operation unlocks a database file record. For the UNLOCK operation to be used on a data area, the *DTAARA DEFINE operation must have been used to assign the data area to a variable within the program. For the UNLOCK operation to be used on a file, the file must have been opened for update processing and a record must be locked.

Factor 1	OpCode	Factor 2	Result Field	Resulting Indicators	
	UNLOCK	data area name		[error]	
	UNLOCK	*DTAARA		[error]	
	UNLOCK	database file name		[error]	

*See also *DTAARA, IN, OUT, *LOCK, READ, and CHAIN*

For data areas, factor 2 is required and must contain the name of the data area that is released. The reserved word *DTAARA can be specified to indicate that all data areas locked by the program are to be released. The local data area (*LDA) cannot be unlocked by this operation.

Resulting Indicator Legend			
Columns	Ind.	Usage	Set-On Condition
71 - 72	1	N/A	
73 - 74	2	[error]	An error occurred during the operation.
75 - 76	3	N/A	

Extender	Description
E	ERROR – Causes the %ERROR and %STATUS built-in functions to be set if an error occurs during the operation.

For database files, factor 2 is required and must contain the name of the file with an unlocked record. The file must have been opened for update processing and a record must be locked.

In Example 5.145, two data areas (CTRLDTA and NEXTCUST) are defined to the program (lines 10 and 20), and then retrieved and locked (line 30). After some data manipulation, the data areas are rewritten (lines 50 and 70). In addition, the data areas are unlocked with the UNLOCK operation (line 80).

Example 5.145: Releasing all data area locks for a program.

```
.....CSRnØ1Factor1+++++++OpCode(ex)Factor2+++++++Result++++++++Len++DcHiLoEq
ØØ1Ø C      *DTAARA    DEFINE   CTRLDATA     CONTROL       9 Ø
ØØ2Ø C      *DTAARA    DEFINE                NextCust      9 Ø
ØØ3Ø C      *LOCK      IN       *DTAARA
ØØ4Ø C                 ADD      1            NextCust
ØØ5Ø C                 OUT      NextCust
ØØ6Ø C                 Eval     Control = NextCust
ØØ7Ø C                 OUT      Control
ØØ8Ø C                 UNLOCK   *DTAARA
```

Example 5.146 shows how to unlock records that have been previously locked.

Example 5.146: Unlocking a record previously locked.

```
.....FFileName++IFEASFRlen+LKeylnKFDevice+.Functions+++++++++++++++++++++++++++
     FCUSTMAST  UF   E        K DISK     INFDS(INFDS)


.....CSRnØ1Factor1+++++++OpCode(ex)Factor2+++++++Result++++++++Len++DcHiLoEq
     C                 dou      %EOF
     C                 READ     CUSTOMER                           58
      *   If at EOF, then leave the DO loop
     C                 if       %EOF
     C                 LEAVE
     C                 ENDIF
      *   Print an invoice based on the region
     C                 SELECT
     C                 WHEQ     Region = MIDWST or Region = PACIFIC
     C                 EXSR     INVBLU
     C                 When     REGION = CENTRAL
     C                 EXSR     INVRED
     C                 OTHER
      *   If we're not printing invoices for this customer's region
      *   then unlock the customer record.
     C                 Unlock   CUSTMAST
     C                 EndSl
     **   Additional code should go here.
     C                 EndDO
```

UPDATE (UPDATE A FILE)

The UPDATE operation rewrites the data-file record currently retrieved and locked by the program. The file specified in factor 2 must be opened for update (i.e., the letter U must be specified in position 15 of the file's file specification). In addition, the record must have been previously read and locked by a CHAIN, READ, READE, READP, or READPE operation.

Factor 1	OpCode	Factor 2	Result Field	Resulting Indicators	
	UPDATE (E)	format name		[error]	
	UPDATE (E)	file name	[data structure]	[error]	

See also UNLOCK, EXCEPT, WRITE, READ, and DELETE

Factor 2 is required and must conform to the following rules:

Resulting Indicator Legend			
Columns	Ind.	Usage	Set-On Condition
71 - 72	1	N/A	
73 - 74	2	[error]	An error occurred during the operation.
75 - 76	3	N/A	

- For an externally described file, a record format name must be specified.

- For program-described files, a file name is required. The result field is also required for program-described files.

- For workstation files, only a subfile record format name can be specified.

The result field is optional for externally described files and is required for program-described files. When the result field is specified, it must contain the name of a data structure from which the file is updated. Resulting indicator 2 is optional and can be used to signal when the UPDATE operation doesn't complete successfully (for example, when the record being rewritten is not the last record retrieved from the file).

Before an UPDATE operation can be issued, a record must have been retrieved for update by the program. The READ, READC, READE, READP, and CHAIN operations can be used to retrieve the record for update. The UPDATE operation can be used on any file opened for update. However, unpredictable results can occur if the operation is issued at *total-time calculations*.

In Example 5.147, line 20 defines the data file CUSTMAST as an UPDATE file and line 30 defines the workstation file DISPLAY as a COMBINED file. This allows the subfile records in the subfile PANEL02 (line 30) to be written to and updated.

Example 5.147: Updating a master data file and a subfile.

```
.....FFileName++IFEASFRlen+LKeylnKFDevice+.Functions++++++++++++++++++++++++++++++
0010 FCODETBL    IF   E          K DISK
0020 FCUSTMAST   UF   E          K DISK
0030 FDISPLAY    CF   E            WORKSTN Sfile(Panel02 : rrn)


.....CSRnØ1Factor1+++++++OpCode(ex)Factor2+++++++Result++++++++Len++DcHiLoEq
0050 C       CustID       CHAIN     CustRec                          54
0070 C                    IF        %Found
0080 C                    EXSR      FillSFL
0090 C                    EXFMT     PANELØ1
0100 C                    EXSR      RTVFunct
0110 C                    If        FUNCT = 'UPDATE'

0120 C                    UPDATE    CustRec

0130 C                    EXSR      UpdSFL
0140 C                    endIf
0150 C                    endIf
```

Line 50 retrieves the record with the index value stored in CUSTID. If the record is found, the FILL-SUBFILE routine is called. Then the subfile control record (PANEL02 on line 80) is displayed.

The record's data and the subfile are displayed at the workstation by the EXFMT operation on line 90. If the user modifies the data, the file CUSTMAST is rewritten (line 120) and the subfile is updated through a subroutine (line 130).

▶ WHEN*xx* (INLINE CASE SELECTION/WHEN TRUE THEN SELECT)

The WHEN*xx* operation is used to perform the selection within an in-line case group of the SELECT-WHEN-OTHER-ENDSL operations. The WHEN*xx* operation compares the value in factor 1 to the value in factor 2. If the comparison is true, the group of calculations between the WHEN*xx* and the next WHEN*xx*, OTHER, or ENDSL operation is performed. The WHEN operation performs a test in the extended factor 2.

Factor 1	OpCode	Factor 2	Result Field	Resulting Indicators		
compare value 1	WHEN*xx*	compare value 2				
	WHEN (M R)	conditional expression				

See also SELECT, OTHER, ENDSL, DOWxx, DOUxx, and CASxx

The WHEN*xx* operation requires a relationship test *xx*, where *xx* may be any one of the Boolean operators (EQ, GE, GT, LE, LT, and NE). See Table 5.9 for details. Factor 1 is compared to factor 2 based on the *xx* operator. Factor 1 and factor 2 must be similar data types. The natural expression form of WHEN uses the conditional expression specified in the extended factor 2.

The WHEN*xx* test can be extended with the AND*xx* or OR*xx* operations. AND*xx* allows compound conditions to be tested; OR*xx* allows additional, but separate, conditions to be tested. The AND*xx* and OR*xx* operations cannot be used in conjunction with the WHEN form of this operation.

The WHEN*xx*, OTHER, and SELECT operations define an in-line case group. The SELECT operation is used to identify the case group. The WHEN*xx* operation is used to conditionally perform specific blocks of code. An OTHER operation identifies the block of code to be performed when all of the conditions for the WHEN*xx* operations are false. The OTHER operation can be thought of as a "catch all" routine.

In Example 5.148, the WHEN*xx* operation is used to condition various program statements. Also, several levels of nested IF, SELECT/WHEN*xx*, and DO*xx* loops are featured.

Example 5.148: In-line case group with SELECT/WHENxx/OTHER statements.

```
.....CSRn01Factor1+++++++<—OpCode(ex)—>Factor2+++++++Result++++++++Len++DcHiLoEq
0001 C                    dou          Funct = EXIT
0002 C                    | EXFMT      PANEL01                               56
0003 C                    | EXSR       RTVMacro
0004 C                    | SELECT
0005 C          FUNCT     | WHENEQ     EXIT
0006 C                    | | MOVE     *ON                     *INLR
0007 C                    | | LEAVE
0008 C          CODE      | WHENEQ     '2'
0009 C                    | | MOVEL    'ADD'                   OPTION
0010 C                    | | ADD      5000                    AMOUNT
0011 C          CODE      | WHENEQ     '9'
0012 C          OBMNAM    | ANDNE      '*DELETED'
0013 C                    | | MOVEL    'DELETE'                OPTION
0014 C                    | | SELECT
0015 C                    | | WHEN     Type = '*PGM'
0016 C                    | | | EXFMT  CFMPGM
0017 C                    | | WHEN     Type = '*LIB'
0018 C                    | | | EXFMT  CFMLIB
0019 C                    | | ENDSL
0020 C          CONFRM    | | IFEQ     'Y'
0021 C                    | | | CALL(E) 'DLTOBJ'
0022 C                    | | | PARM                          OBJNAM
0023 C                    | | +ELSE
0024 C                    | | | CLEAR                         OPTION
0025 C                    | | ENDIF
0026 C                    | OTHER
0027 C                    | | MOVEL    'UNKNOWN'               FUNCT
0028 C                    | ENDSL
0029 C                    ENDDO
```

> The two forms of WHEN*xx* can be intermixed within a SELECT group.
>
> Lines 5, 10, and 11-12 use the fixed-form, while lines 17 and 17 use the contemporary form of WHEN.

WRITE (WRITE TO A FILE)

The WRITE operation outputs a record to a file. If the file is a data file, then a new record is created in the file. If the file is a device file, the record is sent to the device.

Factor 1	OpCode	Factor 2	Result Field	Resulting Indicators		
	WRITE (E)	format name			[error]	[full][1]
	WRITE (E)	file name	[data structure]		[error]	
[1]Valid when Factor 2 contains the name of a subfile detail record format.						

See also READ, READE, READP, READPE, CHAIN, UPDATE, DELETE, UNLOCK, and EXCEPT

Factor 2 is required and must conform to the following rules:

- For an externally described file, a record format name must be specified.
- For program described files, a file name is required. The result field is also required and must contain the name of a data structure, from which the file's data is retrieved and written to the file.

Resulting indicator 3 is optional and can be specified when factor 2 contains a subfile record format name. The indicator signals when the subfile is full. In addition, the %EOF built-in function is set on when the subfile is full.

Resulting Indicator Legend			
Columns	Ind.	Usage	Set-On Condition
71 - 72	1	N/A	
73 - 74	2	[error]	An error occurred during the operation.
75 - 76	3	[full]	The WRITE operation to a subfile detail record did not complete because the subfile is full. The %EOF built-in function is set on when this condition occurs.

Extender	Description
E	ERROR – Causes the %ERROR and %STATUS built-in functions to be set if an error occurs during the operation.

If resulting indicator 3 is omitted for subfile record formats, the following applies:

- For extendible subfiles—those where the subfile page size is less than the total subfile size—the subfile is automatically extended.
- For fixed-size subfiles—those where the subfile page equals the subfile size—the program's exception/error routine is called (unless the E operation extender is also

specified). If the E operation extender is specified, the %ERROR and %STATUS built-in functions are initialized.

The WRITE operation adds records to database files and outputs formats to WORKSTN device files. Depending on the external attributes of the WORKSTN file, device file formats are sent to the device.

In Example 5.149, a new record is added to the file CUSTMAST (line 120). A record is added to the subfile PANEL02 (line 180) using the WRITE operation. The subfile relative record number is incremented (line 170). It contains the number of the record to be added to the subfile (line 180).

Example 5.149: Writing to a master data file and a subfile.

```
.....FFileName++IFEASFRlen+LKeylnKFDevice+.Functions+++++++++++++++++++++++++++++
0010 FCODETBL    IF   E          K DISK
0020 FCUSTMAST   UF A E          K DISK
0030 FDISPLAY    CF   E            WORKSTN  SFILE(Panel02 : rrn)

.....CSRn01Factor1+++++++OpCode(ex)Factor2+++++++Result++++++++Len++DcHiLoEq
0050 C       CustID         CHAIN      CustRec
0070 C                      If         %FOUND
0080 C                      exsr       FillSFL
0090 C                      ExFmt      PANEL01
0100 C                      exsr       RTVFunct
0110 C                      If         Funct = 'WRITE'

0120 C                      WRITE      CustRec

0130 C                      endIf
0140 C                      endIf

0150 CSR    FillSFL         BEGSR
0160 C                      dou        %EOF = *ON
0170 C                      ADD        1                  RRN
     ** Add to the subfile, and ignore the subfile-full message.
0180 C                      WRITE      PANEL02

0190 C                      Read       CODETBL
0210 C                      endDo
0220 CSR    endFillSFL      endsr
```

▶ XFOOT (CROSS FOOT AN ARRAY)

The XFOOT operation adds all the elements of the numeric array specified in factor 2 and places the sum into the result field.

Factor 1	OpCode	Factor 2	Result Field	Resulting Indicators		
	XFOOT(H)	numeric array	sum of array	[+]	[-]	[0]

See also SORTA, SORTD, and %XFOOT

Factor 2 is required and must contain a numeric array name where the elements are added together. The result field is required and must contain a numeric field or array element. An element of the array specified in factor 2 can be used as the result field. The sum of all the elements of the array specified in factor 2 is placed into the result field.

Resulting Indicator Legend

Columns	Ind.	Usage	Set-On Condition
71 - 72	1	[+]	The result field is greater than zero.
73 - 74	2	[−]	The result field is less than zero.
75 - 76	3	[0]	The result field is equal to zero.

Extender	Description
H	HALF ADJUST – Causes the result value to be half-adjusted (rounded) off to the nearest decimal point.

In Example 5.150, the array MONTHSALES (line 10) contains the monthly sales figures. The XFOOT operation (line 30) sums the monthly sales figures and stores the total in the YEARSALES field. Then, on line 40, the %XFOOT built-in function is used to perform the equivalent task.

Example 5.150: Illustrating XFOOT with a numeric array.

```
.....DName+++++++++++EUDS.......Length+TDc.Functions++++++++++++++++++++++++++++++++
0010 D Months          S              7P 2 Dim(12)
0020 D YearSales       S              +2   Like(MonthSales)

.....CSRn01Factor1+++++++OpCode(ex)Factor2+++++++Result++++++++Len++DcHiLoEq
0030 C                   XFOOT     MONTHSALES    YearSales
0040 C                   Eval      YearSales = %XFoot(MonthSales)
```

▶ XLATE (TRANSLATE A CHARACTER STRING)

The XLATE operation translates each character of factor 2 based on the 'from' and 'to' translation values specified in factor 1. The translated value is placed in the result field.

Factor 1	OpCode	Factor 2	Result Field	Resulting Indicators		
from value : to value	XLATE (P E)	source [:start pos]	target		[error]	

See also SCAN and IFxx

Factor 1 is required and must contain the 'from' and 'to' values that are used to translate the value specified in factor 2. The from and to values can be a literal value, named constant, field, array element, data structure, or data-structure subfield. For long translation values, it is beneficial to use a named constant or field in factor 1.

Resulting Indicator Legend			
Columns	Ind.	Usage	Set-On Condition
71 - 72	1	N/A	
73 - 74	2	[error]	An error occurred during the operation.
75 - 76	3	N/A	

Extender	Description
P	PAD – Causes the result field to be cleared before the translate operation is performed.
E	ERROR – Causes the %ERROR and %STATUS built-in functions to be set if an error occurs during the operation.

Factor 2 is required and must contain a literal value, named constant, field, array element, data structure, or data-structure subfield that is used as the source of the translation. The translated value is placed in the result field.

Factor 2 accepts one optional parameter: START-POSITION. This parameter is used to specify the starting-position in factor 2 where translation begins. If the START-POSITION parameter is omitted, translation begins in position one of factor 2. START-POSITION can be a literal value, named constant, numeric field, or numeric data-structure subfield.

Translation occurs by substituting each character of factor 2 (beginning with the START-POSITION) that matches a character of the 'from' value with the corresponding character of the 'to' value. The result of the translation, including any positions of factor 2 that are bypassed (i.e., through the START-POSITION), are moved and left adjusted to the result field.

In Example 5.151, the named constants LOWER and UPPER are used to translate lowercase letters in the field NAME to uppercase. Note that any characters of factor 2 that are not represented in the *from* value go unchanged when moved to the result field. An example of the results from this routine follows:

```
Before    *...v... 1 ...v... 2 ...v... 3
NAME  =  'Robert F. Kennedy             '

After     *...v... 1 ...v... 2 ...v... 3
NAME  =  'ROBERT F. KENNEDY             '
```

Example 5.151: Translating lowercase characters to uppercase characters.

```
.....DName++++++++++++EUDS.......Length+TDc.Functions+++++++++++++++++++++++++++++++
0010 D Lower           C                    Const('abcdefghijklmnopqrstuvwxyz')
0020 D Upper           C                    Const('ABCDEFGHIJKLMNOPQRSTUVWXYZ')

.....CSRn01Factor1+++++++OpCode(ex)Factor2+++++++Result++++++++Len++DcHiLoEq
0030 C     lower:UPPER  XLATE     NAME        NAME
```

In the previous example, lowercase characters are translated to uppercase. By reversing the order of these named constants, translation from uppercase to lowercase would be performed. In the following example, all occurrences of blanks are translated to periods. In Example 5.152, blank characters in the field PROMPT are translated to periods.

Example 5.152: Translating blanks to periods.

```
.....CSRn01Factor1+++++++OpCode(ex)Factor2+++++++Result++++++++Len++DcHiLoEq
     C     ' ':'.'     XLATE     PROMPT      PROMPT
```

A before-and-after example of the data used by this example follows:

Before:
```
              *...v... 1 ...v... 2 ...v... 3
  PROMPT  =  'Customer name                '
```
After:
```
              *...v... 1 ...v... 2 ...v... 3
  PROMPT  =  'Customer.name................'
```

In the preceding example, a period appears between the words 'Customer' and 'name'. If the desired result is to begin substitution after the two words, 'Customer name', the START-POSITION parameter can be used. See Example 5.153.

Example 5.153: Translating with starting position.

```
.....CSRnØ1Factor1+++++++OpCode(ex)Factor2+++++++Result++++++++Len++DcHiLoEq
     C       ' '        CHECKR    PROMPT         S                  5 Ø
     C                  ADD       1              S
     C       ' ':'.'    XLATE     PROMPT:S       PROMPT
```

The results of the routine in Example 5.150 are as follows:

Before:

```
                 *...v... 1 ...v... 2 ...v... 3
     PROMPT  =  'Customer name                ',
```
After:

```
                 *...v... 1 ...v... 2 ...v... 3
     PROMPT  =  'Customer name................'
```

▶ Z-ADD (ZERO AND ADD)

The Z-ADD operation moves the value specified in factor 2 to the result field. Any data in the result field, including the sign, is replaced with the new value.

Factor 1	OpCode	Factor 2	Result Field	Resulting Indicators		
	Z-ADD(H)	numeric value	numeric variable	[+]	[-]	[0]

See also Z-SUB, CLEAR, EVAL, RESET, and MOVE

Factor 2 is required and must contain the name of a numeric field, array element, or the constant with the data that replaces the data in the result field. The result field is required and must contain the name of a numeric field or numeric array element that receives the value specified in factor 2.

The Z-ADD operation has traditionally been used to clear the contents of a numeric field. The CLEAR operation accomplishes the same task and is data-type independent.

Resulting Indicator Legend			
Columns	Ind.	Usage	Set-On Condition
71 - 72	1	[+]	The result field is greater than zero.
73 - 74	2	[–]	The result field is less than zero.
75 - 76	3	[0]	The result field is equal to zero.

Extender	Description
H	HALF ADJUST – Causes the result value to be rounded to the nearest decimal position.

In Example 5.154, the value 3 replaces the contents of the field FIELDA (line 10). The value of field FIELDA replaces the value of the result field FIELDB (line 20). The value 0 replaces the value of the result field TOTAL (line 30).

Example 5.154: Illustrating the Z-ADD operation.

```
.....CSRnØ1Factor1+++++++OpCode(ex)Factor2+++++++Result++++++++Len++DcHiLoEq
ØØ1Ø C                   Z-ADD    3             FIELDA
ØØ2Ø C                   Z-ADD    FIELDA        FIELDB
ØØ3Ø C                   Z-ADD    Ø             TOTAL
```

▶ Z-SUB (ZERO AND SUBTRACT)

The Z-SUB operation subtracts the value of factor 2 from zero, and then moves the result into the result field. Any data in the result field, including the sign, is replaced with the new value.

Factor 1	OpCode	Factor 2	Result Field	Resulting Indicators		
	Z-SUB(H)	numeric value	numeric variable	[+]	[-]	[0]

See also Z-ADD, CLEAR, EVAL, RESET, and MOVE

Factor 2 is required and must contain the name of a numeric field, the array element, or the constant where the data is subtracted from zero and is then placed into the result field. The result field is required and must contain the name of a numeric field or numeric array element that receives the result of the subtraction operation.

Resulting Indicator Legend

Columns	Ind.	Usage	Set-On Condition
71 - 72	1	[+]	The result field is greater than zero.
73 - 74	2	[–]	The result field is less than zero.
75 - 76	3	[0]	The result field is equal to zero.

Extender	Description
H	HALF ADJUST – Causes the result value to be rounded to the nearest decimal position.

In Example 5.155, after the Z-SUB operation on line 10 is performed, FIELDA equals -3. After the Z-SUB operation on line 20 is performed, FIELDB equals 2. After the Z-ADD operation on line 30 is performed, TOTAL equals 0. Line 40 illustrates a primary use of the Z-SUB operation. The sign of FIELDC is reversed.

Example 5.155: Illustrating the Z-SUB operation.

```
.....CSRn01Factor1+++++++OpCode(ex)Factor2+++++++Result++++++++Len++DcHiLoEq
0010 C                   Z-SUB     3              FIELDA
0020 C                   Z-SUB     -2             FIELDB
0030 C                   Z-SUB     0              TOTAL
0040 C                   Z-SUB     FIELDC         FIELDC
```

Chapter 6

Program Organization

The procedure specification is used to name and delineate RPG subprocedures. See chapter 2 for more information on all RPG IV specifications. Zero or more subprocedures can be included in a source file. The term *source file*, as used in this text, refers to a single container of RPG source. It relates directly to an AS/400 source file member or to a plain ASCII text file on another computer operating system. When a source file is compiled, an object of type *MODULE is created. A machine-readable RPG program is created by linking (referred to as *program binding*) one or more modules.

Machine-readable RPG IV programs consist of one or more *mainline procedures* and zero or more subprocedures. The mainline procedure is the entry point of an RPG program. It is the area traditionally referred to as the mainline calculations, but also includes the file, input, definition, and output specifications. The mainline procedure is the same as the program name. Hence, when an RPG program is called, the mainline procedure is being evoked.

Subprocedures are isolated by beginning and ending procedure specifications. These subprocedures can be called through the CALLP or CALLB operations. In addition, when a procedure is prototyped, it is also considered a function, and can be evoked similarly to RPG built-in functions.

SOURCE FILE LOCATION

Contemporary RPG IV compilers accept source code from the highly structure database native to IBM's OS/400 operating systems (on which RPG IV originated) or from the flat-file systems such as those available under Linux, UNIX and Microsoft Windows operating systems. A version of the flat-file systems, referred to as the Integrated File System or "IFS", is also built into OS/400.

The OS/400 RPG IV compiler accepts and compiles source code from either file system.

Under the native OS/400 database, source code is stored in source file members. Under this database structure, database files contain members, members are the final element in the structure and members contain the actual data. Whereas under a flat-file system, the source file contains the actual source code.

To resolve this difference when using the flat-file system to store and compile source, most application development environments encourage the programmer to create a directory structure that simulates the native OS/400 database file structure. For example:

Under OS/400, the database file named QRPGLESRC has been created in the library named ORDENTRY. Within QRPGLESRC there are five source members that contain RPG IV source code. Those member names are as follows:

1. ORDERS
2. CUSTMAINT
3. CUSTSCH
4. PRTORD
5. SHIPORD

To identify one of these source members to the compiler, the following command parameter syntax would be specified:

```
CRTBNDRPG  PGM(CUSTMAINT)   SRCFILE(ORDENTRY/CUSTMAINT) SRCMBR(CUSTMAINT)
```

Using the IFS to store source code is relatively uncommon in the OS/400 world, although flat-file systems are the standard practice for storing source code on all other operation systems. The CRTBNDRPG and CRTRPGMOD commands accept source from the IFS through the use of the SRCSTMF parameter.

The SRCSTMF parameter identifies the source file and the location of the source file in the IFS. When the SRCSTMF parameter is used the SRCFILE and SRCMBR parameters are not allowed. An error will occur if SRCFIEL and SRCMBR are specified with the SRCSTMF parameter. By default, the SRCSTMF parameter defaults to SRCSTMF(*NONE).

If an IFS directory structure named */mysrc/qrpglesrc* has been created to store source code, and the source files named ORDERS, CUSTMAINT, CUSTSCH, PRTORD, SHIPORD are stored in the directory, the file names should be suffixed with the traditional SEU source type. In the case of RPG IV, this would be RPGLE. So these files would be referred to as follows:

```
/mysrc/qrpglesrc/orders.rpgle
/mysrc/qrpglesrc/custmaint.rpgle
/mysrc/qrpglesrc/custsch.rpgle
/mysrc/qrpglesrc/prtord.rpgle
/mysrc/qrpglesrc/shipord.rpgle
```

To compile any of these source members using the CRTRPGMOD command, the following command could be used:

```
CRTRPGMOD MODULE(SHIPORD) SRCSTMF('/mysrc/qrpglesrc/shipord.rpgle')
```

SOURCE FILE MEMBER CONTENTS

A source file can contain just the mainline procedure, the mainline procedure and one or more subprocedures, or only subprocedures. When only subprocedures exist within a source file, a header specification within that source file must include the NOMAIN keyword. Figure 6.1 illustrates the structure of a source file that contains a mainline procedure and two subprocedures.

MODULE DEFINITION

RPG IV programs consist of one mainline procedure and zero or more subprocedures. A source file can contain just the mainline procedure, the mainline procedure and one or more subprocedures, or only subprocedures. When only subprocedures exist within a source file, the header specification within that source file should include the NOMAIN keyword. This keyword instructs the compiler to avoid automatically inserting the RPG runtime support for the *program logic cycle*. The program logic cycle typically is not required and it adds unnecessary overhead to the compiled object.

Source files that contain only subprocedures are permitted to contain data definitions outside the scope of any of the subprocedures.

Variables declared within the mainline procedure are called *global variables*. Variables declared outside of any subprocedure (where the mainline procedure would normally be placed) also are called global variables. Variables declared within subprocedures are called *local variables*. See the subheading Scope for more information on global and local variables.

Figure 6.2 contains the annotated source for an RPG program that contains a mainline procedure and one subprocedure.

Header specification
Global variables
Mainline calculations
Begin Procedure specification
Local variables
Procedure calculations
End Procedure specification
Begin Procedure specification
Local variables
Procedure calculations
End Procedure specification

Figure 6.1: Source file structure with mainline procedure.

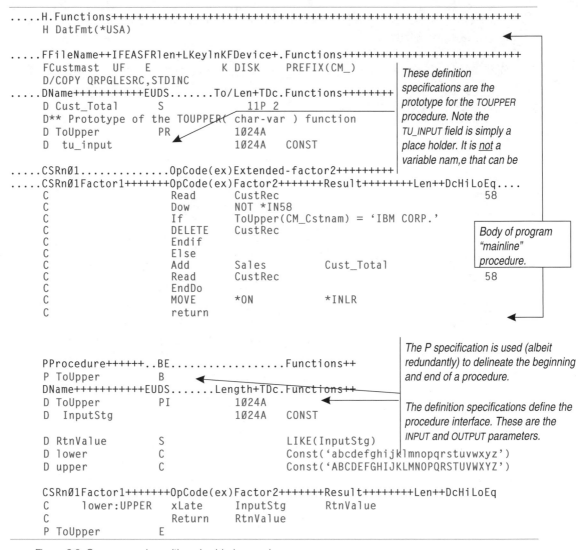

```
.....H.Functions+++++++++++++++++++++++++++++++++++++++++++++++++++++++++++++++++++
     H DatFmt(*USA)

.....FFileName++IFEASFRlen+LKeylnKFDevice+.Functions++++++++++++++++++++++++++++++
     FCustmast  UF   E           K DISK      PREFIX(CM_)
     D/COPY QRPGLESRC,STDINC
.....DName++++++++++EUDS.......To/Len+TDc.Functions++++++++++
     D Cust_Total      S             11P 2
     D** Prototype of the TOUPPER( char-var ) function
     D ToUpper         PR            1024A
     D   tu_input                    1024A    CONST

.....CSRnØ1..............OpCode(ex)Extended-factor2+++++++++
.....CSRnØ1Factor1+++++++OpCode(ex)Factor2+++++++Result++++++++Len++DcHiLoEq....
     C                   Read      CustRec                              58
     C                   Dow       NOT *IN58
     C                   If        ToUpper(CM_Cstnam) = 'IBM CORP.'
     C                   DELETE    CustRec
     C                   Endif
     C                   Else
     C                   Add       Sales         Cust_Total
     C                   Read      CustRec                              58
     C                   EndDo
     C                   MOVE      *ON           *INLR
     C                   return



     PProcedure++++++..BE.................Functions++
     P ToUpper         B
     DName++++++++++EUDS.......Length+TDc.Functions++
     D ToUpper         PI            1024A
     D   InputStg                    1024A    CONST

     D RtnValue        S                       LIKE(InputStg)
     D lower           C                       Const('abcdefghijklmnopqrstuvwxyz')
     D upper           C                       Const('ABCDEFGHIJKLMNOPQRSTUVWXYZ')

     CSRnØ1Factor1+++++++OpCode(ex)Factor2+++++++Result++++++++Len++DcHiLoEq
     C       lower:UPPER  xLate     InputStg      RtnValue
     C                    Return    RtnValue
     P ToUpper         E
```

These definition specifications are the prototype for the TOUPPER procedure. Note the TU_INPUT field is simply a place holder. It is not a variable nam,e that can be

Body of program "mainline" procedure.

The P specification is used (albeit redundantly) to delineate the beginning and end of a procedure.

The definition specifications define the procedure interface. These are the INPUT and OUTPUT parameters.

Figure 6.2: Source member with embedded procedures.

Modules are defined at the source file level. RPG programs can call other programs dynamically or statically. They also can call subprocedures; however, all subprocedures require the static call interface.

As shown in Figure 6.2, variables can be defined within the mainline RPG code or in a subprocedure. In this example, the subprocedure TOUPPER is embedded within the same source file as the mainline program. The TOUPPER procedure is called to convert a character string to capital letters.

When source files are compiled, the output from the compiler is a module. If a program is made up of only one source file, then only one module is generated. If a program is made up of multiple source files, multiple modules are generated. Those modules must be bound together to create a single program object that can be called and run. This program object is referred to as a *machine readable object* or as *executable*. Figure 6.3 illustrates this source-to-module-to-program transition.

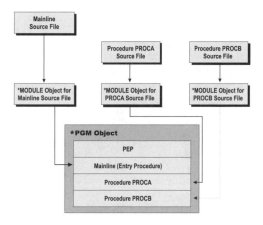

*Figure 6.3: Source file transition to *PGM object.*

RPG allows separately compiled and independent programs to be bound together to form a single program object. The source file for each program is compiled to generate a module. Each module can be bound to create independent program objects. The individual modules, however, also can be bound together to create one larger program object.

There are two distinctions between separately compiled, independent programs and single programs that are composed of several bound modules:

- The single bound program is larger and is, by definition, a single-program object. In contrast, the separately compiled and separately bound programs are independent objects.

- The method of evoking one program from the other for a single-bound program is through the CALLB operation. For independent programs, the CALL operation is used.

There are four types of RPG IV source program organizations that can generate an object module. These types of source programs, and the commands used to compile them, are listed in Table 6.1 and explained in the text that follows.

Table 6.1: Source Program Structures			
Description	Compiler Command	Service Program[1]	Activation Group
Traditional, single-source file (all in one) RPG program.	CRTBNDRPG	No	*DFTACTGRP
Single-source file that utilizes one or more embedded subprocedures.	CRTBNDRPG	Yes	QILE (i.e., named activation group)
Source file that uses zero or more embedded subprocedures, and one or more external subprocedures.	CRTRPGMOD	Yes	*NEW
Source files containing only subprocedures.	CRTRPGMOD	N/A	N/A

[1]Indicates whether the generated *MODULE can be bound into a service program. Also requires the NOMAIN keyword on the Header specification.

Traditional, Single-Source File RPG Program

The traditional, single-source file RPG type of program organization is typically used in legacy applications or in new applications that have a limited scope. These kinds of programs can be statically bound together by using the CRTRPGMOD and the CRTPGM commands instead of the single-source-to-program CRTBNDRPG command. If one large bound program is created, the CALL operations must be changed to the CALLB operation.

Single-Source File Using Embedded Subprocedures

The single-source file with embedded subprocedures is another kind of all-in-one program. The program is contained within a single source file and contains one or more subprocedures to perform various tasks. This type of program can be compiled using the single-source-to-program CRTBNDRPG command. However, the defaults for the command need to be changed. Specifically, on the AS/400, programs that contain subprocedures cannot be run in the default activation group. They must be run in another activation group. When compiling this type of source file, typically, the QILE activation group is specified.

Multiple Source Files with Embedded or External Subprocedures

For new applications, the most common type of program has multiple source files with embedded or external subprocedures. Typically, there is a main *application source file*. It contains call interfaces (i.e., CALL, CALLB, CALLP, or prototypes) to the other programs and subprocedures. The CRTRPGMOD compiler command is used to generate modules for each separate source file. Procedures used by the application should probably be exported with the EXPORT keyword. This allows them to be evoked from other modules within the application.

A typical scenario for this type of application is one where the application source file contains the mainline procedure and controls the program's flow (logic). The other source files contain supporting subprocedures. Normally, the header specification is embedded in the secondary source files with the NOMAIN keyword specified. This allows the compiler to avoid generating redundant RPG program cycle code directly into each module. Only the mainline procedure requires the RPG program cycle code.

SCOPE

As illustrated in Figure 6.1, a source file containing the mainline RPG program code (mainline procedure) includes all global data. This includes fields, arrays, data structures, constants, files, input fields, and output fields.

The term *scope* is used to define the limit of visibility of a program item such as a field. For example, all fields have a scope based on the program structure. A field has a scope, which is global or local, that limits visibility of the field as follows:

Scope	Visibility
Local	Subprocedure
Global	Source file/module

If a subprocedure is specified, it has access to all global variables within the same source file. In addition, it has its own local variables. Local variables are available only to the subprocedure in which they are declared. Figure 6.4 illustrates the scope of variable definitions within RPG IV modules and subprocedures. Remember, for purposes of this text, the term source file means AS/400 source file member.

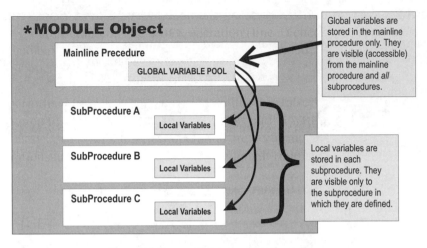

Figure 6.4: Scope of global and local variables.

Local variables of the same name as a global variable are supported in RPG. In this situation, within the subprocedure, the local variable has precedence over the global variable. The properties of the local and global variables of the same name need not be similar. For example, a global field named ITEM could be defined as a 10-position character field within the mainline procedure. Within a subprocedure, the ITEM field (such as a five-digit packed decimal field) can be defined differently. Typically, this kind of situation is avoided through program design.

All global variables within a source file are visible only to the mainline procedure and the subprocedures that are embedded in that source file. For example, an application is made up of two source files named MYAPP and TOOLS. The source file named MYAPP contains a global variable named CUSTNAME. Subprocedures included in the MYAPP source file have access to CUSTNAME.

The mainline procedure (if one exists) and all subprocedures specified in the TOOLS source file do not have access to the CUSTNAME field.

STATIC AND AUTOMATIC STORAGE

Static storage is part of the program's memory that is retained for the duration of the program's or procedure's runtime. *Automatic storage* is part of the program's memory that is automatically allocated and released each time the procedure in which it is declared is called and ended respectively. Within a subprocedure, local variables are, by default, declared in automatic storage.

The STATIC keyword can be used on the definition specification within a subprocedure to force a local variable to have the STATIC storage attribute. When a local variable is set to STATIC, its content remains unchanged each time the subprocedure is evoked. There is only one copy of the variable for the duration of the entire runtime of the program. This includes recursively called subprocedures.

For example, if subprocedure P1 calls subprocedure P2, and P2 calls P1 (which is perfectly valid in RPG IV), variables declared as automatic storage (which is the default property) have new instances created (i.e., a second copy of the variable is automatically generated). Variables declared as static storage are assigned a storage location only the first time the subprocedure is evoked. Subsequent invocations use the original storage locations. This process doesn't affect the data within that location. Hence, the data stored within a static storage variable is available to each invocation.

IMPORT AND EXPORT

Any global variable (declared with the definition specification) can be exported for use by other modules with the same application program. The EXPORT keyword is used to export a global variable. This property makes the variable available to separately compiled source modules. Figure 6.5 illustrates how to code EXPORT and IMPORT keywords in separate source files.

Figure 6.5 illustrates two independent RPG source files. The first source file, STATUSONE (on the left of Figure 6.5), contains a variable named STATUSCODE. This variable has the EXPORT keyword specified. This field property means that the field is defined in STATUSCODE and resides within it, but is available for importing by any other module.

The other source file, STATUSCHK (shown on the right in Figure 6.5), is called by STATUSONE. The CALLP operation on line 5 performs the CALL operation to the STATUSCHECK file. Within the STATUSCHK module, the field STATUSCODE is also defined (line 2). In STATUSCHK, however, the STATUSCODE field contains the keyword IMPORT. This field property indicates that storage for the field is not allocated within the STATUSCHK module, but rather is located (i.e., *resolved*) when the related modules are bound together.

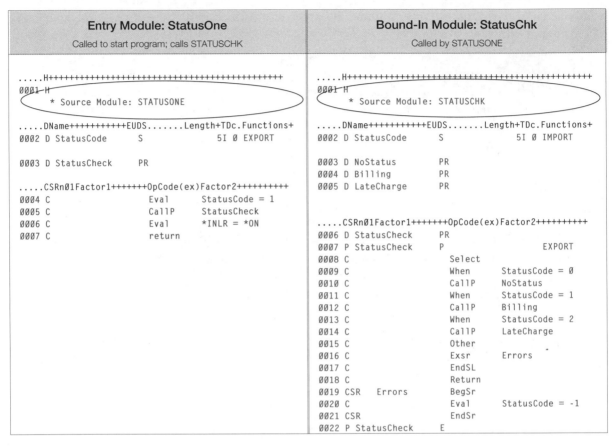

Figure 6.5: Independent source files.

Only one copy of STATUSCODE exists, and its storage is allocated within STATUSONE. Any changes to this field in any module are immediately, and instantly, reflected in the other modules. They all reference the same storage location.

Figure 6.6 shows how modules within a single program share exported variables. The module in which the variable is defined is the module where the variable resides. Other modules that want to access the exported variable declare a variable with the same properties and specify the IMPORT keyword. When the modules are combined by the program binder, references to the exported variable (that is, all imported variables) are resolved. The imported variables are, essentially, pointers to the exported variable. Keep in mind the following points when using IMPORT and EXPORT:

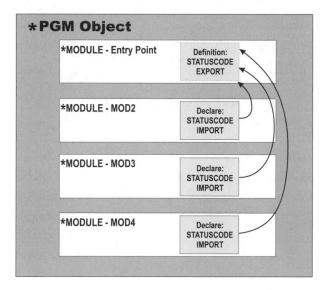

Figure 6.6: Modules sharing IMPORT/EXPORT data.

- Only global variables can be imported or exported. Local variables (fields declared within a subprocedure) cannot be exported.

- The module that contains the variable definition and storage is the one that contains the EXPORT keyword.

- To access an exported variable from within a subprocedure in a separate module, declare a global variable in the second module, specify the IMPORT keyword, and refer to that global variable within the subprocedure.

- Subprocedure names must be exported (using the EXPORT keyword) in order to access them from other modules.

Chapter 7

MODERN OPERATION CODE USAGE

Structured programming is a way of life for many programmers. New structure-based and object-oriented languages such as ADA, C++, and Modula-2 are becoming increasingly popular. PL/I, which is one of the most structured programming languages, was developed by IBM during the early '60s and introduced to the data-processing community in 1966. PL/I supports more structured-programming constructs than any other popular language. However, PL/I never made a strong stand in the data-processing community. The exact reasons for this are a matter of controversy, but the most common speculation is that it was just too big. PL/I tried to do too much and be all things to all people. At the time, magnetic media was new and not very dense. Therefore, a "big" language was not practical.

RPG was also developed in the early '60s. It, too, contains most—but certainly not all—structured-programming constructs. There are, however, major differences between PL/I and RPG. One primary difference is size: RPG is a small language. Its code can be considered "tight." It was designed for small diskless machines like the 1400 and 360 model 20.

This chapter describes the use of RPG operation codes in the modern RPG language. The structured constructs such as IF-THEN-ELSE, WHEN DO, DO WHILE, and DO UNTIL are covered in addition to the other operations. Structured operations support the top-down approach to structured program design and development. Additionally, a comparison of the modern RPG language to traditional RPG coding is provided for experienced RPG programmers who are learning the modern RPG language.

Each example in this chapter can be considered a task within a larger program or system. Some are fully functional, and others illustrate a more specific operation.

OPTIMIZING

Optimizing application code is a popular topic. Ironically, most of the optimizing has focused more on the performance of the compiler and not on application programs. Application programmers should, of course, be concerned with the application's performance more than the compiler's thoroughness.

With RPG, using indicators can lead to poor application performance. A conditioning indicator entry on the calculation specification generates one "compare" instruction for each indicator used. Therefore, each indicator used to condition an operation generates an independent compare instruction.

You could surmise that the use of RPG indicators is not good for performance. That's actually true. The modern RPG programmer avoids the use of indicators and, in their place, uses the IF, DOW, DO, DOU, FOR, CASxx, and SELECT/WHEN operations to control program flow.

Most operation codes generate a corresponding machine instruction. A MOVE generates a COPY instruction, an ADD generates an add-numeric instruction, a COMP generates a compare instruction, an IF generates a compare instruction, and so on.

Subscript fields (i.e., arrays and multiple occurring data structures) generate additional overhead. Therefore, when the same array element is used throughout a routine—moving the array element to a field—then performing the operations on the field can improve runtime performance.

Some operations, such as the SQRT, LOOKUP, and dynamic CALL operations, generate entire subroutines containing dozens of machine instructions. For example, if a program uses the dynamic CALL operation to evoke an external program at eight different locations, the CALL operation is inserted into the program at each of those eight locations. The compiler generates the same CALL-related instructions—eight times. This can lead to larger program sizes.

The dynamic CALL can be placed into a subroutine and performed through the EXSR (Perform Subroutine) or CASxx (Compare and Perform Subroutine) operations. The subroutine would then be called each time the subprogram is needed. The code needed to call the subprogram is not used in multiple locations. Therefore, the program is smaller and provides fewer chances for programming errors.

The overhead for a call to an RPG subroutine is minimal. The overhead for a call to an external program is huge. Program modularity, however, must be taken into consideration. Both in size and performance, using a subprocedure can be a good compromise, and so can a bound call (through the CALLB operation) to another program.

Other considerations for program speed are the use of MULT (multiply) and DIV (divide) operations. On most computers, these instructions are transients that can cause the machine to "burp" slightly whenever they are performed. For example, the MOVE, ADD, and SUB operations run several times faster than the MULT, DIV, and SQRT operations. The number of times an operation code is performed per transaction also must be taken into consideration. If the code is only performed once or twice per transaction, there is no need to worry about how fast a specific operation code runs.

As new compiler architectures are introduced into the RPG language, the issue of optimization in specific areas is being reduced. Compilers, or rather optimizers, are getting more and more intelligent. As they become smarter, the optimizer is performing more of the optimization traditionally performed by hand by a programmer.

INDICATOR-CONTROLLED LOGIC

RPG II programmers have traditionally used indicators to control program logic:

- Read a record, turn on an indicator.
- Compare two values, turn on an indicator.
- Search an array, turn on an indicator.
- Terminate the program, turn on an indicator.

Indicators were the most consistent way to control program logic. An indicator takes up only two positions on a coding specification and, because the fixed-format column design of RPG severely limited the amount of space per line of code, indicators were a logical solution.

Today, however, RPG has been enhanced to support structure operations similar to those found in PL/I. New operations, such as IF-THEN-ELSE-END, DO, DOW, DOU, and SELECT-WHEN-OTHERWISE, provide RPG with full structured-programming support.

When an indicator is used, RPG generates a compare-and-branch instruction. If multiple indicators control an operation code, multiple compare-and-branch instructions are generated. This effect was minimized in RPG II by reversing the indicators and using them to control a GOTO operation that jumps around the program code. Figures 7.1 and 7.2 illustrate this "RPG II-style" of coding in the RPG IV language.

```
.....CSRn01Factor1+++++++OpCode(ex)Factor2+++++++Result++++++++Len++DcHiLoEq
     C     FIELDA      COMP      '01'                              22
     C N22             GOTO      NOTOT1
     C                 ADD       QTY         TQTY
     C                 ADD       QTY         GQTY
     C                 MOVE      '**'        FLAG2
     C                 MOVE      '***'       FLAG3
     C     NOTOT1      TAG
```

Figure 7.1: Indicator-controlled branching.

```
.....CSRn01Factor1+++++++OpCode(ex)Factor2+++++++Result++++++++Len++DcHiLoEq
     C     FIELDA        COMP      '01'                             22
     C     22            ADD       QTY          TQTY
     C     22            ADD       QTY          GQTY
     C     22            MOVE      '**'         FLAG2
     C     22            MOVE      '***'        FLAG3
```

Figure 7.2: Traditional RPG II-style indicator usage.

Figure 7.1 shows the preferred method of controlling the program logic before modern operation codes became available. Figure 7.2 illustrates the original method of controlling program logic. Neither technique, however, represents a viable coding practice in today's world of advanced application programming.

When multiple indicators are needed to condition the same section of a program, the OR condition (columns 7 and 8) can be used. See Figures 7.3 and 7.4.

```
.....CSRn01Factor1+++++++OpCode(ex)Factor2+++++++Result++++++++Len++DcHiLoEq
     C     FLDA          COMP      'A'                              21
     C     FLDB          COMP      'B'                              22
     C  N21
     CORN22              GOTO      NOTOT2
     C                   ADD       QTY          TQTY
     C                   ADD       QTY          GQTY
     C                   MOVE      '**'         FLAG2
     C                   MOVE      '***'        FLAG3
     C     NOTOT2        TAG
```

Figure 7.3: Multi-indicator controlled branching.

```
.....CSRn01Factor1+++++++OpCode(ex)Factor2+++++++Result++++++++Len++DcHiLoEq
     C     FLDA          COMP      'A'                              21
     C     FLDB          COMP      'B'                              22
     C  21
     CAN 22              ADD       QTY          TQTY
     C  21
     CAN 22              ADD       QTY          GQTY
     C  21
     CAN 22              MOVE      '**'         FLAG2
     C  21
     CAN 22              MOVE      '***'        FLAG3
```

Figure 7.4: Traditional multi-indicator control logic

Figure 7.3 illustrates the preferred method of controlling program logic with multiple indicators before modern operation codes became available. The technique shown in Figure 7.4, unfortunately, is used more often. This code is actually converted from a previous version of RPG. Once again, neither of these techniques is useful for today's advanced application-programming needs.

INDICATORLESS CONTROLLED LOGIC

There are two inherent problems with using the traditional indicator methods for controlling operations and branching:

1. It can lead to *spaghetti code*—unreadable programs that are harder to debug, modify, or enhance. For example, is indicator 38 used for the same thing in every program?

2. It isn't long before meaningful names for labels give way to less useful names. For example, what function is performed at the SKIP2 or SKIP3 tags?

To follow a more structured approach, the IF, DO, and SELECT-WHEN-OTHERWISE operation codes are used to produce more readable programs. Structured conditional logic using IF and SELECT-WHEN removes the need for any indicator-controlled logic, and most GOTO — TAG operations.

For example, the RPG code shown in Figures 7.3 and 7.4 should be written using modern operation codes. See Figures 7.5 and 7.6.

```
.....CSRn01Factor1+++++++OpCode(ex)Factor2+++++++Result++++++++Len++DcHiLoEq
.....CSRn01..............OpCode(ex)Extended-factor2++++++++++++++++++++++++++
     C                   IF        FieldA = 'A' and FieldB = 'B'

     C                   ADD       QTY          TQTY
     C                   ADD       QTY          GQTY
     C                   MOVE      '**'         FLAG2
     C                   MOVE      '***'        FLAG3

     C                   endIf
```

Figure 7.5: An example of "IF" controlled program logic.

```
.....CSRn01Factor1+++++++OpCode(ex)Factor2+++++++Result++++++++Len++DcHiLoEq
     C     FieldA        COMP      'A'                              21
     C     FieldB        COMP      'B'                              22
     C  21
     CAN 22              DO

     C                   ADD       QTY          TQTY
     C                   ADD       QTY          GQTY
     C                   MOVE      '**'         FLAG2
     C                   MOVE      '***'        FLAG3

     C                   endDo
```

Figure 7.6: Combined indicator/DO controlled logic.

Figure 7.5 shows the preferred method of controlling program logic. Although the style in Figure 7.6 is more popular with some traditional RPG programmers, the method shown in Figure 7.5 is preferable because it:

- Provides immediate identification of conditions that control the code.

- Takes indicators out of the conditioning.

If performance is a concern, Figure 7.5 contains the most optimized code. In contrast, Figure 7.6 performs redundant comparisons:

- The COMP operations that will set on the indicators.

- Testing the indicator condition before entering the DO loop.

DO LOOPS

DO loops make it much easier to write routines that are performed more than once. For example, to count the occurrences of a character in a character string, the DO and IF operations can be used to process an array. See Figure 7.7.

```
.....DName+++++++++++EUDS.......Length+TDc.Functions++++++++++++++++++++++++++++++++
0001 D Text            S            1A    DIM(80) CTDATA PerRcd(80)

.....CSRn01Factor1+++++++OpCode(ex)Factor2+++++++Result++++++++Len++DcHiLoEq
0002 C                  Do          80            X                  3 0
0003 C                  If          text(x) = 'Q'
0004 C                  ADD         1             Count              3 0
0005 C                  EndIf
0006 C                  endDo
**CTDATA TEXT
Quality Programmers write Quality code, not Quantity code.
```
Figure 7.7: Combining DO and IF operations.

Figure 7.7 illustrates a typical programming task: counting the occurrences of a letter contained in an array. The array TEXT defined on line 1 is an 80-element array. Each element is one character in length.

The DO loop started on line 2 is performed 80 times. The field X is used as the counter index of the DO loop and is used for the index of the array TEXT (line 3).

The array element *x* is compared to the letter Q on line 3. If the array element equals the letter Q, the value 1 is added to the field COUNT (line 4). When the DO loop completes its 80th pass, the field COUNT is set to the number of occurrences of the letter Q that are found in the array TEXT.

Do Loops with Level-Break Processing

DO loops can be used in several areas. For example, if an older program that uses level-break processing is in need of maintenance, the DO operation can be used to improve performance.

As mentioned earlier, one compare instruction is generated for each conditioning and level-break indicator. Therefore, programs using level-break processing—which uses the same level-break indicator on several consecutive program lines—will perform poorly.

The DO operation can be used to condition level-break processing. By conditioning only the DO operation on the level-break indicator and the subsequent operations on indicator L0, the program's performance improves. See Figures 7.8 and 7.9.

```
.....CSRnØ1Factor1+++++++OpCode(ex)Factor2+++++++Result++++++++Len++DcHiLoEq
      CL1              DO
      CLØ              MOVE        FLDA         FLDB
      CLØ              ADD         AMT          TOTAL
      CLØ              MOVE        '**'         FLAG2
      CLØ              MOVE        '***'        FLAG3
      CLØ              EXCEPT      SubTotal
      CLØ              Eval        Tqty = Ø
      CLØ              Eval        Gqty = Ø
      CLØ              ENDDO
```

Figure 7.8: DO-loop controlled level-break processing.

```
.....CSRnØ1Factor1+++++++OpCode(ex)Factor2+++++++Result++++++++Len++DcHiLoEq
      CL1              MOVE        FLDA         FLDB
      CL1              ADD         AMT          TOTAL
      CL1              MOVE        '**'         FLAG2
      CL1              MOVE        '***'        FLAG3
      CL1              EXCEPT      SubTotal
      CL1              Eval        Tqty = Ø
      CL1              Eval        Gqty = Ø
```

Figure 7.9: Traditional level-break processing.

Figure 7.8 is the preferred technique because only one indicator test is performed. L0 (an indicator that is, by definition, always on) is used in place of redundant L1 indicators. Therefore, the compiler avoids generating code that tests the status of the indicator on each line of code.

In Figure 7.9, one compare instruction is generated for each occurrence of indicator L1. Thus, seven indicators are present and so seven compare operations are generated.

Do WHILE and Do UNTIL Operations

The DO WHILE and DO UNTIL operations provide a high-level of flexibility for application development. DOW (DO WHILE) is used, while a condition is true, to perform a routine repetitively. DOU (DO UNTIL) is used, until a condition is true, to perform a routine repetitively. For example, the DOU operation can be used with the READ operation to read a file until a field contains a specific value. See Figure 7.10.

```
.....CSRnØ1Factor1+++++++OpCode(ex)Factor2+++++++Result++++++++Len++DcHiLoEq
     C                    Dou         Dept = 'Q38' or %EOF = *ON
     C                    Read        EMPLOYEE
     C                    endDo
```

Figure 7.10: DO UNTIL controlled logic

In Figure 7.10, the DOU operation is used to find the first occurrence of the department 'Q38' in the file EMPLOYEE. The OR operation extends the DO UNTIL to include a test for an end-of-file condition.

The same function can be performed using the DOW operation. The condition test must be reversed, however, because the loop is performed while the condition is true. See Figure 7.11.

```
.....CSRnØ1Factor1+++++++OpCode(ex)Factor2+++++++Result++++++++Len++DcHiLoEq
     C                    DoW         Dept  'Q38' AND NOT %EOF
     C                    Read        EMPLOYEE
     C                    endDo
```

Figure 7.11: DO WHILE controlled logic.

When using these techniques, be certain to specify each condition that controls the looping process. Poorly coded DO WHILE and DO UNTIL loops are major causes of never-ending loops. For example, if the EOF condition is not tested and department 'Q38' doesn't exist, the DO WHILE loop will loop endlessly. See Figure 7.11.

COMPARE AND BRANCH

The compare operation evaluates the relationship between two items. The branch operation performs a transfer to another part of the program. The COMP and GOTO operations in conjunction with conditioning indicators have a significant number of alternatives in the modern RPG language. Table 7.1 lists these alternatives with a brief description.

Table 7.1: Conditioning and Branching Operations.	
Op Code	Description
ANDxx	Extend IFxx, DOWxx, and DOUxx conditioning.
CABxx	Compare two values then branch to a label.
CASxx	Compare two values then call a subroutine.
COMP	Compare two values and set resulting indicators on/off.
DO	Begin DO loop with an optional counter.
DOUxx	Begin DO UNTIL loop.
DOWxx	Begin DO WHILE loop.
ELSE	Else clause, used in conjunction with the IFxx operation.
ELSEIF	Combines the functionality of the ELSE and IF opcodes
ENDxx	Ends a DO, DO WHILE, DO UNTIL, CASE, SELECT, and IF/THEN/ELSE group.
GOTO	Performs an unconditional branch to a label.
IFxx	Compares values and performs a block of code.
ITER	Branch to the top of the DO loop.
LEAVE	Exit a DO loop.
ORxx	Extend IFxx, DOWxx, and DOUxx conditioning.
OTHER	Otherwise clause of the SELECT/WHEN group.
WHENxx	Within a SELECT group, compares two values and performs a block of code.

Figures 7.12, 7.13, and 7.14 are examples of the various compare and branch operations.

```
.....CSRnØ1Factor1+++++++OpCode(ex)Factor2+++++++Result++++++++Len++DcHiLoEq
     C     FLDA          CABEQ     'A'            LABEL              21
```

Figure 7.12: Compare and branch operations.

```
.....CSRnØ1Factor1+++++++OpCode(ex)Factor2+++++++Result++++++++Len++DcHiLoEq
     C     FieldA         COMP       'A'                                  21
     C   21              GOTO       label
```

Figure 7.13: Compare and GOTO operations.

```
.....CSRnØ1Factor1+++++++OpCode(ex)Factor2+++++++Result++++++++Len++DcHiLoEq
     C                    IF         Field = 'A'
     C                    SETON                                           21
     C                    GOTO       Label
     C                    EndIf
```

Figure 7.14: IF and GOTO operations.

All three of these examples perform the same task. Figure 7.12 is the preferred technique for several reasons:

- It is a single RPG operation code.
- It generates the least number of instructions.
- The CABxx operation (illustrated in Figure 7.12) replaces the technique featured in Figure 7.13.

When the technique featured in Figure 7.12 is used, resulting indicators are not normally used unless the program is communicating with an externally described file. For example, the indicator may control the attributes of a field in a workstation device file.

COMPARE OPERATION

As previously mentioned, the COMP operation is normally not often used in the modern RPG language. It is, however, often overlooked when communicating with an externally described workstation or printer file. When an indicator is needed to communicate with an external file, the COMP operation is used to test the condition and set on a resulting indicator. The resulting indicator can be used by the externally described file to issue an error message, change the color of a field, or cause additional fields to be written to the display or printer. See Figure 7.15 and 7.16.

```
.....CSRnØ1Factor1+++++++OpCode(ex)Factor2+++++++Result++++++++Len++DcHiLoEq
     C     FieldA         COMP       'A'                                  21
     C                    EXFMT      DspError
```

Figure 7.15: COMP operation used to communicate with a DEVICE file.

```
.....CSRnØ1Factor1+++++++OpCode(ex)Factor2+++++++Result++++++++Len++DcHiLoEq
     C                   IF          FieldA = 'A'
     C                   SETON                                           21
     C                   EndIf
     C                   EXFMT       DspError
```

Figure 7.16: IF and SETON used to communicate with a DEVICE file.

Figure 7.15 shows the simpler technique. The COMP operation compares factor 1 to factor 2 and sets on the appropriate resulting indicators. Figure 7.16 illustrates an alternate and less-used technique.

RANGES, LISTS, AND SELECT/OMIT

Testing for a range, a list, or specific select/omit values is a tradition in programming. The modern RPG language provides limited support for these operations with the IF operation.

For a simple range, traditional RPG programs have used various techniques (as shown in Figure 7.17 and 7.18). Whenever possible, the modern RPG language programmer avoids using indicators and uses the technique illustrated in Figure 7.17. The COMP operation, as shown in Figure 7.18, is less desirable.

```
.....CSRnØ1Factor1+++++++OpCode(ex)Factor2+++++++Result++++++++Len++DcHiLoEq
     C                   Do          35          X                      3 Ø
     C                   Move        Name(x)     CHAR                    1
     C                   If          Char >= 'a' and Char <= 'z'
     C                   BitOn       '1'         NAME(x)
     C                   Endif
     C                   EndDo
```

Figure 7.17: Using IF to test a range of values.

The code in Figure 7.17 states that:

```
If CHAR is Greater than or Equal to 'a'
    AND it is Less than or Equal to 'z', then...
```

```
.....CSRnØ1Factor1+++++++OpCode(ex)Factor2+++++++Result++++++++Len++DcHiLoEq...
     C     LOOP          tag
     C                   Add         1           X                      3 Ø
     C                   Move        NAME(X)     char                   1
     C     char          comp        'a'                               21 21
     C   21char          comp        'z'                                  2323
     C   21
   CAN 23                BitOn           '1'     Name(x)
     C    X              comp        35                                    56
     C n56               GOTO        LOOP
```

Figure 7.18: Traditional RPG code used to test a range of values.

Figure 7.17 is the preferred technique because it says exactly what it does. The technique shown in Figure 7.18 performs exactly the same function, but it is convoluted and inflexible. At best, maintenance is complicated. Testing a list of values requires the use of the IF operation along with the OR operator. For example, to test for the occurrence of the letters R, P, G, or the number 4 in the NAME array, the IF operation is used in conjunction with the OR operation. See Figure 7.19 and 7.20.

```
.....CSRnØ1Factor1+++++++OpCode(ex)Factor2+++++++Result++++++++Len++DcHiLoEq...
 C                      DO          35             X                3 Ø
 C                      Move        NAME(x)        char              1
 C                      If          Char='R' OR char='P' OR char='G' or Char='4'
 C                      EXSR        RPG4
 C                      EndIf
 C                      EndDo
```

Figure 7.19: IF with OR to test for a list of values.

```
.....CSRnØ1Factor1+++++++OpCode(ex)Factor2+++++++Result++++++++Len++DcHiLoEq
 C        LOOP          tag
 C                      ADD         1              X                3 Ø
 C                      Move        NAME(x)        char              1
 C        CHAR          COMP        'R'                                   75
 C      N75CHAR         COMP        'P'                                   75
 C      N75CHAR         COMP        'G'                                   75
 C      N75CHAR         COMP        '4'                                   75
 C       75            EXSR        RPG4
 C        X             COMP        35                                 75
 C       75            GOTO        LOOP
```

Figure 7.20: Traditional RPG COMP operation to test a list of values.

Figure 7.19 shows the preferred technique. Its straightforward approach is concise and can be modified easily. On the other hand, the technique shown in Figure 7.20 is complex and cumbersome. Care should be taken when modifications are made.

RPG IV STYLE

The overall programming style used in any programming is a matter of personal taste. Normally, a programming environment has established procedures and standards to be followed. The use of the RPG IV language should influence the standards and programming practices of the RPG programmer. The following recommendations are conventions that can be considered and implemented with good RPG IV-style programming practices.

- Use structured operation codes whenever possible.

- Avoid the use of indicators, except when communicating with external files that require indicator conditioning.

- Use top-down logic. Implement a mainline section in the RPG calculations and call important tasks.

- Write tasks as subroutines or subprocedures and take advantage of independent source files.

- Where appropriate, use traditional RPG math operation codes (for example, when adding a single value to an accumulator).

- Use subprocedures in place of complex subroutines.

- Where appropriate, convert existing RPG code to modern RPG programming practices.

- Keep routines (i.e., subroutines, subprocedures, subprograms) to a single task.

- Build hierarchical subprocedures to perform complex tasks.

Each of the preceding recommendations is described in more detail as follows:

Use Structured Operation Codes. Whenever possible, take advantage of the natural expression support provided by the IF, DOW, DOU, and WHEN operations. Most expressions and conditional logic can be expressed much more simply using these operation codes.

Avoid the Use of Indicators. Except when communicating with an external device file that requires indicator conditioning, avoid using indicators. It is difficult to avoid using indicators when communicating with an interactive workstation (WORKSTN) device file. This is due to the nature of that device's definition language (which is indicator-controlled). It also is difficult to avoid the use of indicators when processing any type of external file (such as a database file). Today, signaling—when the end-of-file is reached or when an error occurs—is done through the use of built-in functions such as %EOF and %FOUND.

Use Top-Down Logic. Implement a mainline section in the RPG calculations and call most important tasks. Design and write RPG applications that have the mainline calculations of the main program control the logic of the application. Rather than inserting them within the mainline code itself, write all tasks that are called as subprocedures or subroutines.

Write Tasks as Subroutines or Subprocedures. Take advantage of independent source files. Writing most tasks as subprocedures or subroutines allows the program logic to be specified in the mainline calculations. All work is performed inside the subprocedures or subroutines. This can lead to easier maintenance, and the reuse of program code is greatly simplified.

Use Traditional RPG Math Operation Codes. Where appropriate, such as when adding a single value to an accumulator, use the ADD operation and other traditional RPG math operation codes. The traditional RPG operations for math includes ADD, SUB, MULT, and DIV. These operation codes are still important in light of the EVAL operation. For example, it is often easier, and frequently more accurate, to write a simple expression using the ADD operation. The two lines of code shown in Figure 7.21 perform the same task.

```
.....CSRnØ1.............OpCode(ex)Extended-factor2++++++++++++++++++++++++++++++
.....CSRnØ1Factor1+++++++OpCode(ex)Factor2+++++++Result++++++++Len++DcHiLoEq
     C                   Add        1             Count
     C                   Eval       Count = Count +1
```

Figure 7.21: Equivalent mathematical operations.

When considering the use of the MULT or DIV operations, accuracy can become an issue. The EVAL operation tends to use a intermediate result field for mathematical operations. This result field is normally a floating-point numeric field. This can lead to results that are different from traditional MULT and DIV operations, particularly where the half-adjust operation extender is used. Figure 7.22 illustrates the MULT, DIV, and EVAL operations with the rounding (i.e., "half adjust") operation extender in use.

```
.....DName+++++++++++EUDS.......Length+TDc.Functions++++++++++++++++++++++++++++
     D Count         S              5p Ø  INZ(15)
     D Sum           S              7p 2  INZ(32.78)
     D Average       S              7P 2

.....CSRnØ1.............OpCode(ex)Extended-factor2++++++++++++++++++++++++++++++
.....CSRnØ1Factor1+++++++OpCode(ex)Factor2+++++++Result++++++++Len++DcHiLoEq...
     C     Sum       Div(H)     Count         Average
     C               Mult       1ØØ           Average
     **   AVERAGE = 219.ØØ
     C               Eval(H)    Average = Sum / Count * 1ØØ
     **   AVERAGE = 218.53
```

Figure 7.22: Mathematical operations with rounding.

Use Subprocedures in Place of Complex Subroutines. The use of subprocedures opens up an entirely new dimension to RPG programming. Local variables (i.e., fields that are "visible" only to the subprocedure), functions, and parameters are just a few advantages to using subprocedures. Create subprocedures where subroutines of any significant length or reusability would normally be used. This allows parameters to be passed to the subprocedure while allowing the subprocedure to retain access to the fields and files declared in the so-called mainline calculations.

Where Appropriate, Convert Existing RPG Code to Modern RPG Programming Practices. The use of indicators, COMP operations, and even nested IF*xx* operations can be difficult to read and maintain. As programs are modified, attempt to correctly modify this existing code to conform to modern RPG constructs. Convert nested IF*xx*-AND*xx*-OR*xx*-ENDIF statements to SELECT-WHEN-OTHERWISE constructs. Convert COMP statements and indicator conditioning to IF statements with natural expressions.

Keep Routines (e.g., Subroutines, Subprocedures) to a Single Task. Avoid lengthy subroutines or subprocedures. Attempt to design and write subroutines and subprocedures that perform one and only one main task, and then return. Lengthy subroutines can be burdensome, inflexible, and difficult to enhance. When a task comprises several smaller tasks, create a subprocedure for each smaller task. Then create a functional subprocedure that calls each smaller task in the proper controlling sequence. See the following programming convention for more information.

Build Hierarchical Subprocedures to Perform Complex Tasks. A high level of modularization can be more beneficial than creating larger, more monolithic subprocedures. Each part of a program, (i.e., a *task*) can be placed into its own stand-alone subprocedure or subroutine. Subprocedures should be used for algorithms and routines that stand on their own. Subroutines, which can be called from mainline calculations or subprocedures, should be used to reduce redundant coding within a procedure.

The boundaries of definition between a subprocedure and subroutine are not thick. Subroutines have been with the RPG language since its inception. Subprocedures are new to the RPG language. Subprocedures allow additional support for parameters, local variables (scope), importing and exporting data, and full modularity. Subroutines, on the other hand, are evoked (i.e., loaded) faster than subprocedures, but are limited in scope to global variables. Subroutines cannot be exported; they can be called only by the procedure (either mainline procedure or subprocedure) in which they are included.

Chapter 8

STRUCTURED PROGRAMMING

This chapter describes how to write structured programs. In dealing with this subject, the application of structured programming to the modern RPG language is presented. The traditional approach to RPG programming has been to take advantage of the RPG cycle, indicators, and branching (i.e., GOTO). This approach has led to a stockpile of RPG programs that, to the new RPG programmer, are difficult to understand, hard to explain, and contain more comments than code. This has resulted in the inability of programmers to differentiate the logic portion of the program from the program process itself.

THE STRUCTURED APPROACH

Structured programming is not new. The concept has been around since the early 1970s. RPG, born in the early 1960s, is even older than structured programming. The Modern RPG Language, released in 1978, is a relatively new language that includes many features necessary to write structured programs. The current version of RPG—RPG IV—contains a full set of structured programming constructs.

As more object-based programming practices are performed, RPG should be able to keep up with the latest in object-based programming. After all, the primary platform on which RPG is used (the IBM AS/400) has the original object-based operating system architecture that has been in use for over 20 years.

Programming itself is both an art (creativity) and a science. Structured programming is a method of programming. Programming methods are bred from learning experiences and practice—not from trends.

Programming style is a highly personal matter. Programmers solve programming problems much like mathematicians solve equations. Unlike mathematicians, however, few programmers agree on the best method for solving a problem. This is a primary cause for programming errors—programmers interjecting their own personality into the programs they're writing.

Like a general practitioner who must first go through internship and residency prior to becoming a family doctor, a programmer must first learn structured technologies and the vocabulary. Then the programmer must practice the art of structured programming before writing a major application using the structured approach.

The structured approach to program design consists of a set of related technologies for designing and writing application programs. Through a series of formulas and guidelines, these related technologies help reduce program errors while still providing for programmer creativity.

Some of the technology relating and contributing to structured programming include the following:

Structured Analysis. Structured analysis includes the techniques used to separate a system into base components. This allows the most complex problem to be broken down into simple items. Each item by itself becomes a simple programming task. When these tasks are properly combined, the complex problem is solved.

Structured Design. Structured design includes the methods used to take the results of the structured analysis (i.e., its components) and build program specifications. For example, a customer master inquiry application consists of a user interface, a full-record display panel, a multi-record list panel, and a method of querying the data.

Program Design. Program design includes the methods used to translate a piece of structured design into a series of program or module definitions. One example is the logic behind a customer master inquiry. Most programming errors are actually created in this phase. Poorly thought-out logic tasks that are too large and inflexible to communicate with other program modules are major causes of programming errors.

Top-Down Program Development. Top-down program development includes the technique used for developing programs in an incremental manner. The modules of a program design are broken down into individual functions or tasks. The program developer simply presumes each task will function properly, leaving lower-level analysis for later.

Top-Down Programming

Top-down program design, by definition, is performed before any programs are written. Currently, several billion lines of RPG code exist. Most of this code was written before the introduction of structured constructs into RPG. With so many lines of code already written, there must be several billion lines of unstructured code already in existence.

As existing programs are maintained, structured programming constructs should be used to maintain the program code. These changes should be more readable and should greatly reduce the possibility of introducing errors into the program.

Naming conventions also are important. Clear and consistent names for fields, files, and routines should be used at all times. For example, you could name a procedure "Update an Order's Line Item" and name a field "Customer Number."

As a by-product, all names depict their unique function. A routine named "Update an Order's Line Item" performs the stated function.

To begin top-down development, first define the major requirements of the module being created. The customer master inquiry example could be broken down into six primary elements. See Figure 8.1.

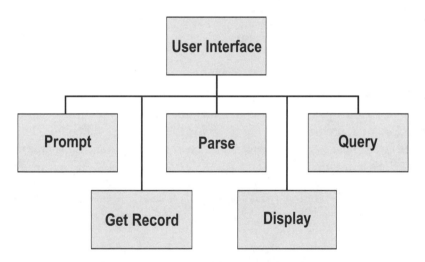

Figure 8.1: Hierarchy chart of a top-down design.

The primary functions of the user interface of the customer master inquiry have been outlined without concern for the detail behind the functions. Once the functions have been specified, each can be treated as an individual, less-complex task. See Figure 8.2.

```
Step 1:
        Open the workstation device file.

Step 1A:
        Send the prompt panel to the workstation.
        Read the user's request from the workstation.
        If 'EXIT' requested, end the program.

Step 2:
        Parse the data the user has entered.
        Return the result to the main line.

Step 3:
        If the parser returns a customer number:
                Retrieve the customer record.
                Display the customer data.

Step 4:
        Else, if the parser returns search data:
                Query the customer file with the
        user's search criteria.
        GO TO Step 1A.
```

Figure 8.2: An outline for a top-down development approach.

As shown in Figure 8.2, the outlining process can be used for top-down program development. The benefit of using an outline is that the programmer is led from the major functions of the structured programming design to the low-level program code. For example, to further define the basic steps in this design, the controlling logic's program code would be written as shown in Figure 8.3.

```
.....CSRn01Factor1+++++++OpCode(ex)Factor2+++++++Result++++++++Len++DcHiLoEq
0001 C                   Open       CustInq
0002 C                   Dou        Function = 'EXIT'
0003 C                   ExFmt      Panel1
0004 C                   exsr       RtvMacro
     *     Step 2
0005 C                   exsr       Parse
0006 C                   TestN      RqsData                              5456
0007 C                   Move       *IN54          CustRqs
0008 C                   Move       *IN56          QryRqs
     *     Step 3
0009 C     CustRqs       casEQ      *ON            DSPCST
     *     Step 4
0010 C     QryRqs        casEQ      *ON            QUERY
0011 C                   EndCS
0012 C                   EndDo
```

Figure 8.3: Program code for customer inquiry.

As mentioned earlier, structured programming is a method of programming. The mere use of structured operations such as IF-THEN-ELSE, DO, SELECT-WHEN-OTHERWISE doesn't, in and of itself, constitute structured programming. Structured programming is the linking of a set of single-function routines that perform to the design specification. These routines are the result of structured analysis, structured design, and a top-down development specification.

Characteristics of a Well-Formed Routine

A properly structured routine exhibits these characteristics:

- One, and only one, entry and exit point is used. An escape clause is permitted, provided the escape clause branches to the one and only exit point.

- All program code in the routine is necessary. No unusable code exists.

- Infinite loops are absent from the routine.

- Redundant code doesn't exist in the routine.

- Only structured constructs are used for logic control.

Remember, however, that these are the outward characteristics of a properly structured procedure. The use of these characteristics as a guideline for programming routines doesn't warrant that properly structured routines are being written. In other words, don't confuse the results of hard work with the work itself.

The following rules should be known and respected when taking the structured approach to program development stage.

1. All procedures must be broken down into single-function routines. These routines consist of the lowest-level program code or program statements.

2. The function control routines (logic modules) contain conditional logical, testing, repetition, and *flag setting*.

3. The low-level functions (subprocedures) are controlled (i.e., called upon) by higher-level logic modules.

4. Low-level functions (subprocedures) are defined in one and only one location and are called upon whenever and wherever needed.

To achieve cohesion between the low-level modules, each routine performs one, and only one, task. The binding of the routines is controlled by high-level logic.

Remember, though, the mere use of structured operation codes doesn't mean well-formed structured programs are being written. They are only the tools used to write programs. The structure of those programs depends on the programmer.

According to a structured programming theorem, only sequence, choice, and repetition are needed to solve any logic problem. Sometimes, however, the efficiency of a procedure is achieved at the expense of structure. When a procedure or program has to conform to rigid size restrictions and still perform efficiently, techniques other than structured techniques may be required (i.e., the branch operation).

Control Flow Constructs

Structured programming consists of three components or *constructs*:

- **Sequence**—The processes or operations of an application.

- **Choice**—The decision or conditional logic of an application. This control structure is sometimes referred to as *selection*.

- **Repetition**—The looping or consecutive rerunning of a sequence of operations. This construct is sometimes referred to as *iteration*.

The following sections offer descriptions and examples of each of these control-flow constructs.

Sequence

Sequence is defined as one or more processes of an application. Flow passes from one process to another without concern. In the RPG language, a process can be a series of one or more successive operations: a subroutine, a subprocedure, or an entire program. For example, the "Update an Order's Line Item" routine shown in Figure 8.4 contains only sequence operations. Most RPG operation codes are considered sequence operations.

```
.....CSRnØ1Factor1+++++++OpCode(ex)Factor2+++++++Result++++++++Len++DcHiLoEq
     C     PriceItem      BEGSR
      *   Price an Order's Line Item
     C     ORDQTY         MULT      Price          Extension
     C     Extension      MULT      DiscPrice      Discount
     C                    SUB       Discount       Extension
     C     ENDPrice       ENDSR
```

Figure 8.4: Program code to update an order's line item.

Choice

Choice is defined as control structures or decisions that control sequence operations. If the decision is true, one path is taken. If the decision is false, a different path is taken. These control structures are known as IF-THEN-ELSE and CASE structures. The CASE structure is a special form of IF-THEN-ELSE. It provides a more readable method of composing thick nests of choice constructs. The SELECT-WHEN-OTHERWISE operations are used for this type of CASE.

The RPG language supports a third type of choice constructs with the CAS*xx* (CASE) operation code. For example, the IF-THEN-ELSE control structure could be used to condition a pricing routine based on the item ordered being available and the quantity ordered being greater than zero (see Figure 8.5).

```
.....CSRnØ1Factor1+++++++OpCode(ex)Factor2+++++++Result++++++++Len++DcHiLoEq
     C     ITEM         CHAIN      ITEMMAST                           54
     C                  EVAL       NotFound = *in54
     C                  If         (NotFound = *OFF) and (QtyOrd > Ø)
     C                  Exsr       PriceItem
     C                  endif
```

Figure 8.5: The IF operation used in choice selection.

Table 8.1 lists the RPG operation codes that support the choice construct.

The COMP operation is typically avoided in modern RPG. The IF and SELECT-WHEN constructs are heavily used throughout most applications. The CAS*xx* operation is used in applications where more traditional subroutines are included instead of the more modern subprocedures.

Table 8.1: RPG Operation Codes That Perform Choice Functions	
Operation	Description
IF	IF then ELSE... ENDIF.
CAS*xx*	Compare, then perform subroutine.
COMP	Compare factor 1 to factor 2.
CAB*xx*	Compare factor 1 to factor 2, then branch.
SELECT	Select — Begin an in-line case group.
WHEN	Compare factor 1 to factor 2 in a case group.

Repetition

Repetition is defined as looping control of a sequence. A routine is performed a specified number of times, as long as a condition is true, or until a condition is true. The RPG language supports repetition with the DOW*xx* (DO WHILE), DOU*xx* (Do Until), DO (Do repeated), and FOR (Do repeated) operations. For example, the "Price an Ordered Item" routine shown in Figure 8.6 could price all items of an order by using the DOW*xx* construct for repetition.

```
.....CSRnØ1Factor1+++++++OpCode(ex)Factor2+++++++Result++++++++Len++DcHiLoEq
ØØØ1 C        ORDNBR      Chain     OrdFile                                54
ØØØ2 C                    Eval      eof = *IN54
ØØØ3 C                    Dow       NOT (eof)
ØØØ4 C        ORDQTY      casGT     Ø              PRICEORDER
ØØØ5 C                    endcs
ØØØ6 C        ORDNBR      ReadE     OrdFile                                58
ØØØ7 C                    Move      *IN58          eof              1
ØØØ8 C                    endDo
```

Figure 8.6: The DOW operation used as repetition.

RPG includes several operations to perform repetition. These are traditional format operations and repetition operations that work with expressions. See Table 8.2.

Operation	Description
Table 8.2: Repetition Operation Codes	
DO	DO... ENDDO (repeat process *n* times).
DOU	DO UNTIL... ENDDO expression version (repeat process until condition is true).
DOU*xx*	DO UNTIL... ENDDO fixed-format version (repeat process until condition is true).
DOW	DO WHILE... ENDDO expression version (repeat process while condition is true).
DOW*xx*	DO WHILE... ENDDO fixed-format version (repeat process while condition is true).
FOR	FOR / ENDFOR expression version (repeat process *n* times).
ITER	Iteration loop (stop processing DO loop at current step and branch up to the top of the DO loop to perform the next iteration).
LEAVE	Leave loop (leave the DO loop by branching to the statement following the corresponding ENDDO operation).

The FOR operation is used to repeat a series of program statements. There is a counter, limit, and increment value associated with each FOR operation. The counter can be incremented or decremented. In addition to standard expression syntax, the FOR operation supports the following infix operators:

- BY – Identifies the increment or decrement value.

- TO – Identifies the limit. The maximum value the index can be before the FOR loop ends.

- DOWNTO – Identifies the limit. The minimum value the index can be before the FOR loop ends.

These three operators control the FOR loop. They identify two of the three components of a FOR loop. The entire FOR loop syntax is as follows:

```
0010 C        FOR         counter = start TO limit  BY increment-value
```
or
```
0020 C        FOR         counter = start DOWNTO limit  BY increment-value
```

The first line illustrates the traditional FOR loop structure: a start, an upper limit, and an increment value. This is effectively the traditional "FOR i = 1 to 10 by 1" syntax. The second line illustrates the decrement FOR loop. The decrement FOR loop starts at a higher value and decrements the counter on each pass through the FOR loop, as in "FOR i = 10 DOWNTO 1 by 1" syntax. Figure 8.7 illustrates the RPG IV code syntax of the FOR/ENDFOR loop.

```
.....DName++++++++++EUDS.......Length+TDc.Functions++++++++++++++++++++++++++++++
0010 D Index          S            5P 0
0020 D CustName       S           35A    Inz('The Lunar Spacecraft Company')

.....CSRn01..............OpCode(ex)Extended-factor2++++++++++++++++++++++++++++++
0030 C                    FOR       Index = 1 TO %Len(CustName)  by 1

0040 C                    If        %Subst(CustName : Index : 1) = ' '
0050 C                    Eval      %Subst(CustName : Index : 1) = '_'
0060 C                    Endif
0070 C                    endfor
```

Figure 8.7: The FOR loop used for repetition.

Structured Operation Codes

A program of structure results when coherent logic and organizational skills are used in the analysis and design phases of program development. Program language operation codes are used to build the low level of a program. For more information on all RPG operations, see chapter 5. These operations are essential in structured programming. While featured in chapter 5, they are reviewed here under the context of top-down structured programming.

Boolean Operators

The operation codes IF*xx*, CAS*xx*, DOU*xx*, DOW*xx*, and WHEN*xx* support Boolean operators. Boolean operators are used to control the type of relationship test that is performed between factor 1 and factor 2. The Boolean operators are listed in Table 8.3. The traditional RPG operations use the operator letters. In contrast, the modern operations (those supporting natural expressions) use the symbol form of the operator. The Boolean operator is appended to the operation code itself.

Table 8.3: Boolean Operations		
Operator	Symbol	Relationship Test
EQ	=	Factor 1 is equal to factor 2.
NE	<>	Factor 1 is not equal to factor 2.
GE	>=	Factor 1 is greater than or equal to factor 2.
GT	>	Factor 1 is greater than factor 2.
LE	<=	Factor 1 is less than or equal to factor 2.
LT	<	Factor 1 is less than factor 2.
Blank	N/A	Relationship test result is used to set on resulting indicators.

THE IF-THEN-ELSE STRUCTURE

The IF-THEN-ELSE structure is used to control the process section of a program. The Boolean comparison operator is used to control the relationship test between two operands. The available IF-THEN-ELSE Boolean operators are listed in Table 8.3.

The IF operation can test a relationship and evaluate an expression. For example, to test the relationship between two fields, the following logic applies:

```
IF  A = B  THEN...
```

To evaluate an expression within a conditional statement, the following logic applies:

```
IF A = (B + C) THEN...
```

To evaluate an expression, an RPG compiler generates code that calculates the result of the expression, and then uses that result to perform the comparison. For example:

```
temp = B + C

IF A = temp THEN...
```

The temporary result, commonly referred to as the *intermediate result*, is normally a floating-point numeric field. If the expression is character-string based, the intermediate result is, of course, a character field. The RPG code shown in Figure 8.8 illustrates this technique.

```
.....CSRnØ1Factor1+++++++OpCode(ex)Factor2+++++++Result++++++++Len++DcHiLoEq
      *****************************
      *  If A = (B + C) then... *
      *****************************
ØØØ1 C         B            ADD       C             TEMP              7 2
ØØØ2 C         A            IFEQ     •TEMP
ØØØ3 C                       .
ØØØ4 C                       .
ØØØ5 C                       .
ØØØ6 C                      ENDIF
```

Figure 8.8: Coding an intermediate result for comparison.

The IF*xx* operation works as follows: When the relationship test between factor 1 and factor 2 is true, the statements following the IF*xx* operation are performed until an associated ELSE or ENDIF operation is encountered. At this point, control passes to the statement following the associated ENDIF operation. If the relationship test is false, the program branches to the associated:

1. ELSE operation if one exists.
2. ENDIF statement, if an ELSE operation doesn't exist.

Using the modern IF operation instead of the traditional IF*xx* operation, the same type of program code can be written as shown in Figure 8.9.

```
.....CSRnØ1Factor1+++++++OpCode(ex)Factor2+++++++++++++++++++++++++++++++++++
      *****************************
      *  If A = (B + C) then... *
      *****************************
ØØØ1 C                      If        A = B + C
ØØØ2 C                       .
ØØØ3 C                       .
ØØØ4 C                       .
ØØØ5 C                      ENDIF
```

Figure 8.9: Using IF to eliminate the need for an intermediate result field.

The modern IF operation used in Figure 8.10 illustrates the preferred coding style. In Examples 8.1 through 8.9, you should presume fields A, B, C, and D are set as shown in Figure 8.10.

```
.....DName+++++++++++EUDS.......Length+TDc.Functions++++++++++++++++++++++++++++++
     D A              S              5p Ø Inz(1ØØ)
     D B              S              5p Ø Inz(2Ø)
     D C              S              5p Ø Inz(3Ø)
     D D              S              5p Ø Inz(4Ø)
     D Message        S             35A
```

Figure 8.10: An example of preferred coding.

In Example 8.1, the relationship test between field A and the numeric constant 5 is true. Therefore, lines 2 and 3 are performed. If the relationship is false, control would pass to the associated ENDIF operation on line 4, and lines 2 and 3 would not be performed.

Example 8.1: A simple relationship test.

```
.....CSRnØ1..............OpCode(ex)Extended-factor2+++++++++++++++++++++++++++++++
.....CSRnØ1Factor1+++++++OpCode(ex)Factor2+++++++Result++++++++Len++DcHiLoEq....
ØØØ1 C                   If        A > 5
ØØØ2 C                   Add       2Ø                  C
ØØØ3 C                   Eval      message = 'Current'
ØØØ4 C                   endIf
```

In Example 8.2, the relationship test between field B and field C is false. An ELSE operation exists for this IF operation. Therefore, control passes to the ELSE operation on line 4, and lines 5 and 6 are performed. If the relationship test between fields B and C were true, however, lines 2 and 3 would be performed. Then control would pass to the ENDIF operation on line 7.

Example 8.2: A relationship test, with branching to an ELSE operation.

```
.....CSRnØ1..............OpCode(ex)Extended-factor2+++++++++++++++++++++++++++++++
.....CSRnØ1Factor1+++++++OpCode(ex)Factor2+++++++Result++++++++Len++DcHiLoEq....
ØØØ1 C                   If        B > C
ØØØ2 C                   ADD       1Ø                  C
ØØØ3 C                   Eval      message = 'OVERDUE'
ØØØ4 C                   ELSE
ØØØ5 C                   ADD       1Ø                  B
ØØØ6 C                   Eval      message = 'Current'
ØØØ7 C                   endIf
```

IF*xx* operations can be extended to form more complex conditioning. AND*xx* and OR*xx* operations can be used with the IF*xx* operation to extend the relationship test.

In Example 8.3, the IF and AND operation on line 1 states: If A is greater than B and D and C, then perform statements 2 and 3.

Example 8.3: Testing for a list of values.

```
.....CSRn01..............OpCode(ex)Extended-factor2+++++++++++++++++++++++++++++++
.....CSRn01Factor1+++++++OpCode(ex)Factor2+++++++Result++++++++Len++DcHiLoEq....
0001 C                   If        A > b AND A > D AND A > C
0002 C                   Eval      message = 'A High'
0003 C                   Eval      A = 20
0004 C                   endIf
```

Relationship tests can be nested by using multiple IF operations. The outer-level IF-THEN-ELSE structure is tested first and, if it proves true, the next level IF-THEN-ELSE structure is tested. See Example 8.4.

Example 8.4: Compound relationship test with nesting.

```
.....CSRn01..............OpCode(ex)Extended-factor2+++++++++++++++++++++++++++++++
.....CSRn01Factor1+++++++OpCode(ex)Factor2+++++++Result++++++++Len++DcHiLoEq....
0001 C                   If        A > b AND A > D AND A > C
0002 C                   Eval      message = 'A High'
0003 C                   If        C < D
0004 C                   Eval      message = 'C Low'
0005 C                   Add       50              AcctBal
0006 C                   endIf
0007 C                   endIf
```

In Example 8.4, the same conditioning used in Example 8.3 is used to control the IF-THEN-ELSE structure. However, when line 3 is reached, if its relationship test is true, lines 4 and 5 are performed. If its relationship test is false, control passes to the ENDIF statement on line 6, ending the inner IF-THEN-ELSE structure. Additional operations can be specified between the ENDIF statements. See Example 8.5.

Example 8.5: Perform operations between ENDIF statements.

```
.....CSRn01..............OpCode(ex)Extended-factor2+++++++++++++++++++++++++++++++
.....CSRn01Factor1+++++++OpCode(ex)Factor2+++++++Result++++++++Len++DcHiLoEq....
0001 C                   If        A > b AND A > D AND A > C
0002 C                   Sub       10              C
0003 C                   If        D < C
0004 C                   Add       50              C
0005 C                   Eval      message = 'D Low'
0006 C                   endIf
0007 C                   ADD       20        B
0008 C                   ADD       30        C
0009 C                   ADD       40        D
0010 C                   endIf
```

Example 8.5 contains three ADD operations on line 7 to line 9. They are performed when the outer IF-THEN-ELSE structure is entered and after the inner IF-THEN-ELSE structure has been performed or bypassed. IF-THEN-ELSE structures can be nested to a high level (at least 100 levels with most RPG compilers). While there is no hard and fast rule, readability tends to deteriorate when more than three levels of IF-THEN-ELSE structures are nested. If more than three levels of nesting is required, the CASE structure can be used to improve readability.

THE CASE STRUCTURE

The CASE structure is used to control sections of the program. CASE offers greater readability than IF-THEN-ELSE when a high level of nesting is required or when the control structure is controlling several dozen lines of code. This is, in part, due to the inherent nature of CASE to separate the logic from the processes.

RPG supports both in-line and subroutine forms of CASE. The CAS*xx* operation performs subroutines while the SELECT-WHEN-OTHER operations perform in-line code. The Boolean operators for CAS*xx* and WHEN operations are the same as those listed in Table 8.3. The CASE operations are considered choice constructs. Figure 8.11 shows the logic flow for the CASE structure.

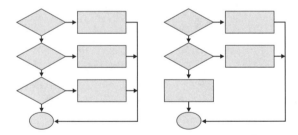

Figure 8.11: The two forms of CASE.

The primary difference between the two forms of CASE (shown in Figure 8.11) is that the logic flow illustrated to the right includes a default process and the logic flow to the left has no default process.

In Example 8.6, the WHEN operations, like the IF-ELSE-ENDIF operations, can be difficult to distinguish from the other operations. This can force the programmer to interpret each line of code (i.e., the process) even if all that is needed is to check the logic (i.e., choice) of the program.

Example 8.6: In-line CASE using SELECT/WHENxx/OTHER.

```
.....CSRnØ1..............OpCode(ex)Extended-factor2+++++++++++++++++++++++++++++++
.....CSRnØ1Factor1+++++++OpCode(ex)Factor2+++++++Result++++++++Len++DcHiLoEq....
     C                   Select
     C                   When      FieldA = FieldB
     C                   Eval      Answer = 'A = B'
     C                   Add       A         B
     C                   Div       Cost            MARKUP
     C                   When      FieldA > FieldB
     C                   Eval      Answer = 'A > B'
     C                   Sub       A         B
     C                   Div       Cost            PRICE
     C                   When      FieldA < FieldB
     C                   Eval      Answer = 'A < B'
     C                   Eval      MarkUp = Price - Cost
     C                   If        MarkUp  Ø
     C                   Div       MarkUp          PRICE
     C                   endIf
     C                   When      FieldA  FieldB
      *                            *** This WHEN block would never run
     C                   Eval      Answer = 'A  B'
     C                   Add       MarkUp          YTDProfit
     C                   endSl
```

Complex or multiple conditions, such as those illustrated in Example 8.6, are necessary from time to time. In-line CASE statements can add power to the application. When the in-line CASE gets too complex, however, its power tends to be offset by complexity. At this point, it is important to consider using the CAS*xx* operation or a WHEN-EXSR operation set.

The form of CASE shown in Example 8.7 can provide an alternative to the standard in-line form of CASE (i.e., SELECT-WHEN-OTHER-ENDSL) logic. This form takes advantage of the SELECT-WHEN constructs while placing the process within subroutines or subprocedures.

Example 8.7: The SELECT-WHEN-EXSR-CALLP form of case.

```
.....CSRnØ1Factor1+++++++OpCode(ex)Factor2+++++++Result++++++++Len++DcHiLoEq....
     C                   Select
     C                   When      FieldA = FieldB
     C                   Exsr      Equal
     C                   When      FieldA > FieldB
     C                   Exsr      Greater
     C                   When      FieldA < FieldB
     C                   CallP     LessThan
     C                   When      FieldA  FieldB
     C                   CallP     NotEqual
     C                   EndSl
```

The WHEN-EXSR and WHEN-CALLP operation codes provide the RPG programmer with a powerful programming tools.

The traditional form of CASE, using the CASxx operation, was often used in place of the technique illustrated in Example 8.7. Example 8.7 contains the much simpler CASxx structure. The logic flow of the program is the same as in Example 8.6. Example 8.8, however, allows the programmer to concentrate on the logic (i.e., choice) of the program.

Example 8.8: The subroutine CASxx operation.

```
.....CSRn01Factor1+++++++OpCode(ex)Factor2+++++++Result+++++++++Len++DcHiLoEq
     C      FieldA       casEQ      FieldB         Equal
     C      FieldA       casGT      FieldB         Greater
     C      FieldA       casLT      FieldB         LessThan
     C      FieldA       casNE      FieldB         NotEqual
     C                   endCS
```

In Example 8.9, the field named FUNCT (Function) is compared to the literal 'DELETE' on line 1. The CASEQ operation is used to test for the equal condition. If the test is true (i.e., FUNCT equals 'DELETE'), the subroutine DELETERCD (Delete a Record) is performed.

Example 8.9: A basic CASE structure.

```
     .....CSRn01Factor1+++++++OpCode(ex)Factor2+++++++Result+++++++++Len++DcHiLoEq
0001 C      Funct        casEQ      'DELETE'       DeleteRcd
0002 C                   endCS

     C*.....the program continues...

0003 Csr    DeleteRcd    BEGSR
0004 C      Index        Delete     CUSTMAST                                      56
0005 Csr                 endSR
```

Upon completion of the subroutine DLTRCD, control returns to the END statement associated with the CASE structure (line 2 in Example 8.9). The next successive operation is performed as the program continues.

Successive CASE Operations

As mentioned earlier, CASE is the preferred control structure for choice constructs. Successive CASE structures are easy to read and understand. They support top-down program design by allowing the programmer to concentrate on the logic of the program (i.e., the *logic modules*) until the detail (i.e., the *function modules*) must be written. See Figure 8.13, for example, if the design of a routine calls for the type of code shown in Figure 8.12.

```
PROMPT the workstation operator for the FUNCTION request.
READ the Operator's RESPONSE.
PARSE the Operator's RESPONSE.
BUILD the requested FUNCTION.
IF FUNCTION equals 'DELETE' then
    Perform the DELETE-RECORD routine.
ELSE, IF FUNCTION equals 'UPDATE' then
    Perform the UPDATE-RECORD routine.
ELSE, IF FUNCTION equals 'ADDNEW' then
    Perform the ADD-RECORD routine.
ELSE, IF FUNCTION equals 'SEARCH' then
    Perform the SEARCH routine.
ELSE, IF FUNCTION equals 'EXIT' then
    Perform the END-PROGRAM routine.
ELSE, perform the DEFAULT handler.
```

Figure 8.12: Successive CASE operations sample code.

The RPG code that supports the design shown in Figure 8.12 is featured in Figure 8.13.

```
.....CSRnØ1..............OpCode(ex)Extended-factor2++++++++++++++++++++++++++++++
.....CSRnØ1Factor1+++++++OpCode(ex)Factor2+++++++Result++++++++Len++DcHiLoEq....
ØØØ1 C                   Dou        Funct = 'EXIT'
     * Prompt the workstation operator for a response.
ØØØ2 C                   Exsr       Prompt
     * Parse (interpret) the Operator's response.
ØØØ3 C                   EXSR       Parse
     * Finish up the PARSE by converting the request to FUNCT.
ØØØ4 C                   EXSR       BuildFunct
     ** Select the subroutine when the relationship is met.
ØØØ5 C                   SELECT
ØØØ6 C                   When       Funct = 'DELETE'
ØØØ7 C                   CallP      DeleteRcd
ØØØ8 C                   When       Funct = 'UPDATE'
ØØØ9 C                   CallP      UpdateRcd
ØØ1Ø C                   When       Funct = 'ADDNEW'
ØØ11 C                   CallP      AddRcd
ØØ12 C                   When       Funct = 'SEARCH'
ØØ13 C                   CallP      SearchFile
ØØ14 C                   When       Funct = 'EXIT'
ØØ15 C                   CallP      EndProc
ØØ16 C                   Other
ØØ17 C                   Exsr       DefaultRtn
ØØ18 C                   endSL
ØØ19 C                   endDo
```

Figure 8.13: CASE-controlled logic module.

As shown in Figure 8.13, the CASE structure makes this logic control module easy to read and comprehend. On the other hand, if an IF-THEN-ELSE structure is used, it could lead to a much more complex module.

Upon entry into the CASE structure, the relationship between the field FUNCT and the constant 'DELETE' is performed. If the relationship is true, the subroutine DLTRCD is performed. Upon completion of the subroutine DLTRCD, control passes to the END statement associated with the CASE structure.

If the relationship test on line 6 is false, control passes to the WHEN operation on line 6. If that relationship test is true, the subroutine UPDRCD is performed. Upon completion of the subroutine, control passes to the CASE structure ENDSL statement on line 18.

This process is repeated for each CASE structure in this CASE group. If none of the CASE comparisons are true, the "catch all" OTHER (otherwise) operation on line 16 performs the subroutine DFTRTN.

Compare and Branch Operations

The CABxx (Compare and Branch) operation is unique to the RPG language. It differs from the CASxx operation in that the CASxx operation performs a subroutine and returns to the same point in the program. The CABxx operation branches to a label and does not return.

The CABxx operation supports the complete set of Boolean operators listed in Table 8.3. When the relationship test is true, a branch to the label specified in the result field is performed. When the relationship test is false, the program continues with the next successive instruction following the CABxx operation. If resulting indicators are specified, they are set on accordingly—regardless of the Boolean operator used with the operation.

Other RPG operations are required to provide a target for the CABxx operation. The TAG and ENDSR operation provide this function. Table 8.4 lists the RPG operations that support branching.

	Table 8.4: RPG Branching Operations
Operation	**Description**
CAB*xx*	Compare and branch.
GOTO	Go to (i.e., branch to) a label identified by a TAG or ENDSR operation.
ENDSR	End subroutine. Factor 1 can contain a label that can be used as the target of a CAB*xx* or GOTO operation.
TAG	Label. Factor 1 contains a label that can be used as the target of a CAB*xx* or GOTO operation.
ITER	Iterate a DO loop. Branch to the top of the DO loop for the next iteration.
LEAVE	Exit a DO loop. Branch to the corresponding ENDDO statement of a DO loop.
LEAVESR	Exit subroutine. Branch to the ENDSR statement of the current subroutine.

The CAB*xx* operation should be used primarily as an escape clause in order to branch to an exit routine or to the end of a subroutine or program. Never use CAB*xx* or GOTO to exit a subroutine. Branching to a label on the ENDSR operation is acceptable, however.

The GOTO operation should be avoided as much as possible. Actually, many programming shops have standards and conventions that prohibit the use of GOTO. The GOTO operation is an unconditional branch to another location of the RPG program.

The ENDSR and TAG operations are declarative operations that identify a label to the RPG program. A label is the target of a CAB*xx* or GOTO operation. The content of factor 1 is used as the label of the TAG operation.

The ITER (iterate) operation causes control of a DO loop (DO, DOW, or DOU) to be transferred to the top of the DO loop. The next iteration of the DO loop is evoked. Condition the ITER operation, when necessary, with an IF statement.

The LEAVE operation causes control of a DO loop (DO, DOW, or DOU) to be terminated. In other words, the program branches to the corresponding ENDDO statement. This operation can be considered an "Exit DO Loop" operation. Condition the LEAVE operation, when necessary, with an IF statement.

The LEAVESR operation causes a branch to the ENDSR operation for the current subroutine. This, in turn, causes the subroutine to return.

Chapter 9

INTER-MODULE COMMUNICATION

A primary characteristic of structured programming is that it comprises modular programs. Modular programs consist of a series of mainline routines, subroutines, subprograms, and subprocedures—all referred to as modules. The term *module*, used throughout this chapter, refers to an independent section of program code (i.e., a task). There is not necessarily a one-to-one correspondence between the AS/400 *MODULE object and the term module used in this chapter. However, isolating application modules at the *MODULE level can be beneficial.

With traditional programming, an application and all of its components are placed into a few large multifunction programs. With modular programming, an application is broken into multiple, single-function modules. Whether a module is a subroutine or a subprogram depends on its complexity and the requirements of the application.

BENEFITS OF MODULAR PROGRAMMING

Modular programming provides several benefits that contribute to reduced cost and simplification of the programming task. For example:

- Applications are broken into multiple modules and the programming tasks required for different modules can be spread among several programmers. Therefore, an application program often can be completed more quickly.

- Modules that consist of a few functions often can be developed more reliably. This is primarily due to reduced opportunity for errors that normally occur during module development. Once the module performs correctly, it can be "put away" without impact to the other modules in the application.

- Individual modules can be maintained with little or no impact to the other modules. For example, if the aging routine in an invoicing application needs maintenance, it can be revised without impact to the rest of the application. In addition, if the module is used by more than one application, program maintenance need be performed only once.

- Occasionally, modules can be reused by other applications. For example, a set of program utility functions that simplifies data translation, program-to-program communication, or Internet access would be of use in several applications.

Modular programs consist of two types of modules:

- Logic control modules.

- Function modules.

Logic control modules contain mostly *choice constructs* and *repetition constructs* (see chapter 8 for more information on constructs). The logic of a routine is driven by logic control modules. There is little or no work, in the traditional sense, performed in a logic control module. Only relationship testing (choice), looping (repetition), and conditional branching through structured operations are performed.

Function modules consist primarily of *sequence constructs*. The processes of the application are performed by function modules. A function module also contains choice and repetition constructs that control branching and looping within the function module. Function modules exist at the lowest level of the program design. They perform one and only one task, and then return to the logic control module.

To guarantee the top-down (i.e., vertical) relationship between logic control modules and function modules, a hierarchy chart should be created that illustrates the module relationship. A proper program and, consequently, a proper module exhibits the following characteristics:

- One entry and one exit point.

- No unusable program code.

- No infinite loops.

In addition, to ensure correctness in the application module hierarchy, the following guidelines should be kept in mind when designing an application:

- Logic control modules control access to all lower-level modules.

- Module access is always vertical (never horizontal). A module can call only lower-level modules (not modules at the same or higher level). An exception is that any module may call itself when recursive programming is required.

- Modules are reusable. In other words, modules may be called by multiple modules.

Figure 9.1 shows a hierarchy chart. Each module is depicted by a rectangle. When a module is reused, additional vertical lines on the left and right edge of the rectangle identify the module as reusable (see module B).

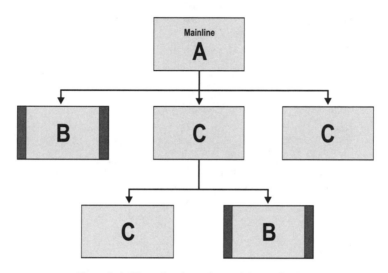

Figure 9.1: Hierarchy chart of a modular application.

Each module can be a subroutine, a subprocedure, or a subprogram. When a module is a subprogram, it can be further defined by a *program hierarchy chart*. The top-most box of the program's hierarchy is the core of the program. It exhibits the functionality of the module. A program hierarchy chart is essentially the same as an *application hierarchy chart*. A program hierarchy chart, however, supports an additional symbol that identifies a module as being further defined by a flowchart. See Figure 9.2. The additional horizontal line at the top of the rectangle identifies the module as one that is further defined by a flowchart.

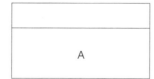

Figure 9.2: Flowchart definition symbol.

COMMON TECHNIQUES FOR INTER-MODULE COMMUNICATION

With so many modules making up an application, inter-module communication becomes an important issue. The most common AS/400 techniques for passing information between modules include:

- Parameter passing.

- Reading and writing to an external data area.

- Exporting and importing variables.

- Stacks and data queues.

- Message sending.

Data queues are considered to be the fastest way to send large volumes of information between applications. This chapter, however, discusses parameter passing, data area handling, and exporting and importing variables.

Parameter Passing

Parameter passing is perhaps the most effective method for communicating between program modules. Most operating systems, such as the AS/400 Operating System/400 (OS/400), support parameters in a consistent manner throughout all high-level languages. This makes it easy to send data from RPG programs to other programs and procedures regardless of the language in which they are written.

When a program transfers control to another program, it is referred to as *calling a procedure* or *calling a program*. The program doing the calling is referred to as the *calling program* or by the simpler term *caller*. The program that receives control is referred to as the *called program* or by the simpler term *callee*.

For example, if a program named PGMA (pronounced "program A") calls a program named PGMB (pronounced "program B"), PGMA is the calling program, and PGMB is the called program. See Figure 9.3.

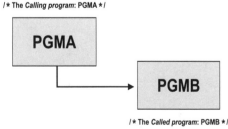

Figure 9.3: Program-to-program call.

Parameter Passing with PLIST

Parameters are passed between program modules and procedures. RPG cannot pass parameters to subroutines. For program-to-program calls, the PLIST (parameter list) operation normally defines the parameter interface for the call. Factor 1 of the PLIST operation, in the calculation specifications, identifies the name of the parameter list that is being defined. Figure 9.4 shows the syntax for a named parameter list.

```
.....CSRnØ1Factor1+++++++OpCode(ex)Factor2+++++++Result++++++++Len++DcHiLoEq...
     C     MATH          PLIST
     C                   PARM                     Result          7 2
     C                   PARM                     Value1          5 2
     C                   PARM                     Value2          5 2
     C                   PARM                     Operation       1
```

Figure 9.4: Parameter list definition using a named parameter list.

In Figure 9.4, the parameter list named MATH is defined. The individual fields that are passed between modules are called parameters and are defined by the PARM (Parameter Declaration) operation. In this example, four fields (RESULT, VALUE1, VALUE2, and OPERATION) are declared as parameters on the parameter list MATH. The number of parameters passed between programs is implied by the number of PARM operations.

A special-purpose parameter list, known as the *entry parameter list*, is used to receive parameters into a called program and return them to the calling program. An entry parameter list (often referred to as the *entry PLIST*) is identified with *ENTRY in factor 1 of the PLIST operation. For example, if the parameter list MATH is used to call a program named PGMB, the entry parameter list for PGMB is written as shown in Figure 9.5.

```
.....CSRnØ1Factor1+++++++OpCode(ex)Factor2+++++++Result++++++++Len++DcHiLoEq...
     C     *ENTRY        PLIST
     C                   PARM                     p1_Result       7 2
     C                   PARM                     p2_Value1       5 2
     C                   PARM                     p3_Value2       5 2
     C                   PARM                     p4_Oper         1
```

Figure 9.5: Entry parameter list.

Figure 9.5 shows a typical entry PLIST. The name implies that the entry PLIST is the entry point into the program; it is not. While the entry PLIST can appear anywhere in the program, RPG always starts processing at the beginning of the RPG cycle.

Each parameter of the parameter list MATH, shown in Figure 9.4, has a corresponding parameter in the called program shown in Figure 9.5. Typically, identical parameter lists are defined in the calling and called programs. Field names used on the entry parameter list normally match those of the calling program's parameter list. In the example shown in Figure 9.5, however, this is not illustrated.

On the System/38 and AS/400, parameters are traditionally passed by reference, not value. The parameter's address in memory (a pointer) is transferred between programs. The data itself is accessed through a field, array, or data structure. Internally, RPG accesses the data through the address; however, this is entirely transparent to the application program.

Parameters also can be passed by value. This causes the system to make a copy of the parameter's data and store that data in a temporary location. A pointer to that temporary location is then passed to the called procedure. Parameters that are passed by value are referred to as *read-only parameters*. Parameters passed by value can be transferred only between procedures, not programs.

When a program is called, the fields specified on the entry PLIST are assigned the address of the parameters being passed to the program. This means that fields on the entry PLIST in the called program actually point to the original data in the calling program. Any changes to the data, made by the called program, automatically affect the field values in the calling program.

For example, assume a field named RESULT in PGMA has a memory address of X'00287DC0' and is a parameter used on a call operation to the PGMB program. In PGMB, the ANSWER field is specified in the same relative position on the *ENTRY parameter list as the RESULT field.

When PGMA calls PGMB, the address of the field RESULT from PGMA is assigned to the ANSWER field in PGMB. As shown in Figure 9.6, the ANSWER field is assigned an address of X'00287DC0'. This is referred to as *parameter passing by reference*.

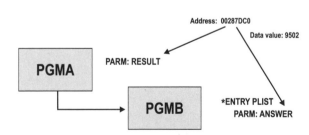

Figure 9.6: Parameter passing by reference.

The called program should define a parameter list that can accommodate (i.e., receive) all of the incoming parameters. The names and attributes (e.g., length, type) of the fields being used as parameters in the calling program do not have to match those defined in the called program. However, if the attribute of the parameters in the calling and called programs do not match, data integrity can be compromised. For example, a character field containing blanks could be passed to a numeric field, which would cause an error.

This style of call interface (parameter lists) is referred to as the *weak parameter module*. There is no compile-time parameter checking, validation, or integrity. For this reason, the *prototyped call interface* exists as an alternative call interface. For more information, see the subheading Prototyped Call.

Assume the parameters of the MATH parameter list are assigned the values shown in Figure 9.7.

```
RESULT    = 0.0        /* This value is returned from the called program. */
VALUE1    = 3.5
VALUE2    = 6.0
OPERATION = *
```

Figure 9.7: MATH parameter values.

Both the calling program and the called program reference these values. If the value of one of the fields is changed by the called program, the field in the calling program is also changed because both fields reference the same memory location.

When a program is called and the MATH parameter list is passed to it, a series of four parameter addresses is transferred to the called program. Those addresses represent the location in memory of the values assigned to the parameter fields.

Table 9.1 lists an example memory address for each field used on the MATH parameter list (see also Figure 9.4) and the data represented by those fields.

As mentioned earlier, the name of the fields used for the called program's parameter list don't have to match those used in the calling program's parameter list. The sequence of the parameters is important, however. Corresponding parameters in different programs must be in the same relative location on the parameter list.

Table 9.1: Memory Location for Fields Used on the MATH Parameter List		
Field Name on PLIST	Memory Address	Data
RESULT	X'00003618'	X'0000000F'
VALUE1	X'000046C5'	X'00350F'
VALUE2	X'000046C8'	X'00600F'
OPER	X'000052D6'	*

For example, if a program named PGMA uses the MATH parameter list (see Figure 9.4) to call the program named PGMB, the fields used on the entry parameter list in PGMB are assigned the same address as the corresponding parameter in PGMA. Therefore, the fields of the entry parameter list in PGMB have access to the same physical data as the corresponding fields in PGMA. See Table 9.2.

Table 9.2: Parameter Field Address in Called Program		
Field Name on Plist	Memory Address	Data
ANSWER	X'003618'	X'0002100F'
FACT1	X'0046C5'	X'00350F'
FACT2	X'0046C8'	X'00600F'
OPER	X'0052D6'	*

In Table 9.2, note that the value for the ANSWER field is specified. This assumes that PGMB has finished processing and is about to return to its caller. The memory location of each parameter is not affected, but the data itself can be modified.

Figure 9.8 contains the program listing for the example PGMA. It contains the parameter list definition for the MATH parameter list. Because parameter lists are declarations, they can be specified anywhere in the program. The technique shown in Figure 9.8 uses a named parameter list. The MATH parameter list is defined independently from the CALL operation and, therefore, can be used by more than one CALL operation.

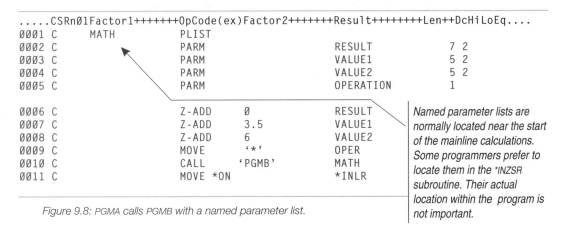

```
.....CSRnØ1Factor1+++++++OpCode(ex)Factor2+++++++Result++++++++Len++DcHiLoEq....
ØØØ1 C     MATH          PLIST
ØØØ2 C                   PARM                     RESULT        7 2
ØØØ3 C                   PARM                     VALUE1        5 2
ØØØ4 C                   PARM                     VALUE2        5 2
ØØØ5 C                   PARM                     OPERATION     1

ØØØ6 C             Z-ADD    Ø      RESULT
ØØØ7 C             Z-ADD    3.5    VALUE1
ØØØ8 C             Z-ADD    6      VALUE2
ØØØ9 C             MOVE     '*'    OPER
ØØ1Ø C             CALL     'PGMB' MATH
ØØ11 C             MOVE *ON        *INLR
```

Named parameter lists are normally located near the start of the mainline calculations. Some programmers prefer to locate them in the *INZSR subroutine. Their actual location within the program is not important.

Figure 9.8: PGMA calls PGMB with a named parameter list.

Figure 9.9 illustrates a called program. The entry parameter list (lines 1 to 5) contains four parameters. While this program uses all of the parameters passed to it, only the first parameter—the ANSWER field—is modified by the program.

```
.....CSRnØ1Factor1+++++++OpCode(ex)Factor2+++++++Result++++++++Len++DcHiLoEq
ØØØ1 C     *ENTRY       PLIST
ØØØ2 C                  PARM                        Answer            7 2
ØØØ3 C                  PARM                        Fact1             5 2
ØØØ4 C                  PARM                        Fact2             5 2
ØØØ5 C                  PARM                        OpCode            1

ØØØ6 C                  SELECT
ØØØ7 C                  When        OpCode = '+'
ØØØ8 C                  Eval        Answer = Fact1 + Fact2
ØØØ9 C                  When        OpCode = '-'
ØØ1Ø C                  Eval        Answer = Fact1 - Fact2
ØØ11 C                  When        OpCode = '*'
ØØ12 C                  Eval        Answer = Fact1 * Fact2
ØØ13 C                  When        OpCode = '/'
ØØ14 C                  Eval        Answer = Fact1 / Fact2
ØØ15 C                  EndSL

ØØ16 C                  MOVE        *ON             *INLR
```

*Figure 9.9: P*GMB *source—the called program.*

A parameter list can be specified immediately following a CALL operation. In this situation, the parameter list is assigned exclusively to the CALL operation that precedes it. See Figure 9.10.

```
.....CSRnØ1.............OpCode(ex)Extended-factor2+++++++++++++++++++++++++++++
ØØØ1 C                  EVAL        Result = Ø
ØØØ2 C                  EVAL        Value1 = 3.5
ØØØ3 C                  EVAL        Value2 = 6
ØØØ4 C                  EVAL        Operation = '*'

.....CSRnØ1Factor1+++++++OpCode(ex)Factor2+++++++Result++++++++Len++DcHiLoEq....
ØØØ5 C                  CALL        'PGMB'
ØØØ6 C                  PARM                        RESULT            7 2
ØØØ7 C                  PARM                        VALUE1            5 2
ØØØ8 C                  PARM                        VALUE2            5 2
ØØØ9 C                  PARM                        OPERATION         1
ØØ1Ø C                  MOVE        *ON             *INLR
```

*Figure 9.10: P*GMA *source—unnamed parameter list.*

Factor 2 can be specified for a PARM operation. When a program calls another program, the content of factor 2 of the PARM operation (if present) is copied into the result field. This allows the program to avoid explicitly moving the parameter data into the parameter fields. See Figure 9.11.

```
.....CSRnØ1Factor1+++++++OpCode(ex)Factor2+++++++Result++++++++Len++DcHiLoEq....
ØØØ1 C                    CALL       'PGMB'
ØØØ2 C       ANSWER       PARM                     RESULT          7 2
ØØØ3 C                    PARM       3.5           VALUE1          5 2
ØØØ4 C                    PARM       6             VALUE2          5 2
ØØØ5 C                    PARM       '*'           OPERATION       1
```

Figure 9.11: Parameter movement upon calling a program.

Factor 1 can be specified for a PARM operation. When a program is called, the contents of the result fields of the entry parameter list are copied into factor 1. See Figure 9.12.

```
.....CSRnØ1Factor1+++++++OpCode(ex)Factor2+++++++Result++++++++Len++DcHiLoEq....
ØØØ1 C       *ENTRY       PLIST
ØØØ2 C       Answer       PARM       Answer        Result          7 2
ØØØ3 C                    PARM                     Fact1           5 2
ØØØ4 C                    PARM                     Fact2           5 2
ØØØ5 C                    PARM                     Operation       1
```

Figure 9.12: Parameter movement upon entering a called program.

A program ends when it returns to its caller. The content of factor 2 of its entry parameter list is copied into the result field. See Figure 9.13.

```
.....CSRnØ1Factor1+++++++OpCode(ex)Factor2+++++++Result++++++++Len++DcHiLoEq....
ØØØ1 C       *ENTRY       PLIST
ØØØ2 C       Answer       PARM       Answer        Result          7 2
ØØØ3 C                    PARM                     Fact1           5 2
ØØØ4 C                    PARM                     Fact2           5 2
ØØØ5 C                    PARM                     Operation       1
```

Figure 9.13: Parameter movement upon exiting a called program.

Upon leaving a program, factor 2 is copied to the result field. This effect, shown in Figure 9.13, is similar to the one shown in Figure 9.11.

When a called program returns control to its caller, the result fields of the parameter list in the calling program are copied into factor 1. See Figure 9.14.

```
.....CSRnØ1Factor1+++++++OpCode(ex)Factor2+++++++Result++++++++Len++DcHiLoEq....
ØØØ1 C                   CALL      'PGMB'
ØØØ2 C        ANSWER      PARM                      RESULT          7 2
ØØØ3 C                    PARM      3.5             VALUE1          5 2
ØØØ4 C                    PARM      6               VALUE2          5 2
ØØØ5 C                    PARM      '*'             OPERATION       1
```

Figure 9.14: Parameter movement upon returning to the calling program.

Table 9.3 lists a cross reference of the figures that illustrate program-to-program call operations with parameters being passed between the programs.

Table 9.3: Cross Reference of CALL/PARM Movement

Call/Return Action	Figure Illustrating Action in PGMA	Figure Illustrating Action in PGMB
PGMA calls PGMB	Figure 9.11	Figure 9.12
PGMB ends; control returns to PGMA	Figure 9.14	Figure 9.13

Passing Data Structures as Parameters

Parameters can be virtually any RPG field, data structure, or array name. A technique often used to pass multiple fields involves using a data structure. The fields are defined as data-structure subfields. This avoids having to code a PARM operation for each parameter that is passed. Data-structure subfields cannot be passed as parameters themselves; passing a data structure avoids this restriction. For example, if the fields RESULT, VALUE1, VALUE2, and OPERATION need to be passed, a single parameter can be defined that passes a data structure. The data structure would be made up of the four subfields. See Figure 9.15.

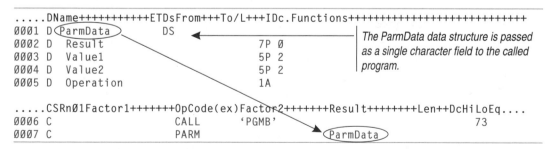

```
.....DName+++++++++++ETDsFrom+++To/L+++IDc.Functions++++++++++++++++++++++++++++
ØØØ1 D ParmData        DS
ØØØ2 D   Result                        7P Ø                The ParmData data structure is passed
ØØØ3 D   Value1                        5P 2                as a single character field to the called
ØØØ4 D   Value2                        5P 2                program.
ØØØ5 D   Operation                     1A

.....CSRnØ1Factor1+++++++OpCode(ex)Factor2+++++++Result++++++++Len++DcHiLoEq....
ØØØ6 C                   CALL      'PGMB'                                73
ØØØ7 C                   PARM                      ParmData
```

Figure 9.15: Data structure used as a parameter.

The data structure PARMDATA (line 1) is made up of four data structure subfields: RESULT, VALUE1, VALUE2, and OPERATION (lines 2 to 5, respectively). When PGMB is called (line 6) and is passed its single parameter, all the data stored in each of the four subfields becomes available to the called program PGMB. To address the four subfields of the data structure, a parameter should be declared by the called program as a data structure. See Figure 9.16.

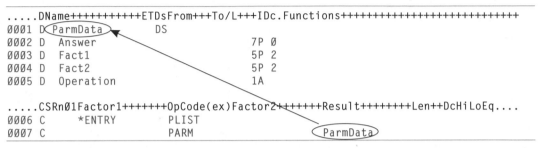

```
.....DName++++++++++++ETDsFrom+++To/L+++IDc.Functions++++++++++++++++++++++++++++++++++
0001 D ParmData          DS
0002 D   Answer                          7P 0
0003 D   Fact1                           5P 2
0004 D   Fact2                           5P 2
0005 D   Operation                       1A

.....CSRn01Factor1+++++++OpCode(ex)Factor2+++++++Result++++++++Len++DcHiLoEq....
0006 C       *ENTRY        PLIST
0007 C                     PARM                       ParmData
```

Figure 9.16: Program receiving a data structure as a parameter.

When the program listed in Figure 9.16 receives control, the PARMDATA parameter is assigned the address of the corresponding parameter in the caller program. The PARMDATA data structure is then used to access the data at that address in memory. Note that, because this is an *ENTRY PLIST parameter, the PARMDATA data structure cannot be initialized with the INZ keyword.

PROTOTYPED CALL

The prototyped call interface provides a way to declare the number and type of parameters that are required by a program or procedure. Prototypes are declared with the definition specification. This permits a wide variety of data types to be specified as parameters.

All data types, with the exception of data structures, can be declared as a parameter of a procedure prototype. Data structures can be passed as character strings and then referenced using a based variable in the subprocedure. See the following subheading, Data Structures and Prototyped Procedures, for information on passing data structures to subprocedures. Figure 9.17 shows the call interface to a prototyped procedure.

```
.....H.Functions++++++++++++++++++++++++++++++++++++++++++++++++++++++++++++++++
0001 H DATFMT(*MDY)

.....DName++++++++++EUDS.......Length+TDc.Functions+++++++++++++++++++++++++++++++
0002 D NAME            S            35A    INZ('Skyline PigeON ComPANY')
0003 D CompName        S            32A    INZ('skyline pigeon company')

       ** Include prototypes for letter conversion
0004  /COPY cvtcase

.....CSRn01.............OpCode(ex)Extended-factor2+++++++++++++++++++++++++++++++++
0005 C                 CallP      MakeUpper( Name )
0006 C                 IF         ToUpper(CompName) = Name
0007 C       'They match!' Dsply
0008 C                 EndIf
0009 C                 Eval       *INLR = *ON
```

Prototype Call through the CALLP operation.

Prototype call as a function.

Figure 9.17: Passing data to subprocedures.

Figure 9.17, line 4, includes the CVTCASE source file. (Note: The source code for CVTCASE is listed in Figure 9.19.) These prototypes are necessary to allow the compiler to do parameter-type checking at compile time. On line 5, the procedure MAKEUPPER is called. This procedure converts the data in the parameter passed to it to uppercase. The NAME field is passed and converted to uppercase.

Line 2 indicates the NAME field's initial value for this field. After the CALLP operation is performed on line 5, the data in NAME is converted to uppercase. Figure 9.18 illustrates the conversion.

```
Position        *....v....1....v....2....v....3....v

Before          'Skyline PigeON ComPANY'

After           'SKYLINE PIGEON COMPANY'
```

Figure 9.18: Before-images and after-images of the name field.

In Figure 9.17, on line 6, the IF operation is used to compare two values for equality. The TOUPPER procedure is called, with the COMPNAME field being passed to it. The TOUPPER function reads the input parameter (i.e., COMPNAME) and returns the uppercase equivalent. The returned value is actually inserted into the expression at the location of the subprocedure call. In this example, the returned value is then compared to the value on the right side of the equals sign. The content of the COMPNAME field is unchanged by the TOUPPER procedure. Figure 9.19 shows the source code for CVTCASE.

```
.....DName++++++++++EUDS.......Length+TDc.Functions++++      The CONST keyword indicates that
     *** -Prototype of TOUPPER( const char-var )           this parameter is read-only.
0001 D ToUpper          PR         1024A
0002 D  tu_input                   1024A    CONST ◄

     *** -Prototype of ToLower( const char-var )            The first line of a prototype is referred to as
0003 D ToLower          PR         1024A ◄                  the Prototype Name Definition Statement. It
0004 D  tl_input                   1024A    CONST           is where the procedure is named, and the
                                                            return value's properties are specified.
     *** -Prototype of MAKEUPPER( char-var )
0005 D MakeUpper        PR                   OPDESC
0006 D  mu_input                   1024A     OPTIONS(*VARSIZE)
```

Figure 9.19: Prototypes for three conversion procedures.

Figure 9.19 contains the source code of the prototypes for the TOUPPER, TOLOWER, and MAKEUPPER procedures. The properties of the parameters passed to these procedures are declared within the prototype. Any names assigned to the parameters, on the prototype statements, are discarded by the compiler. The remaining parameter information must match the properties specified for the *procedure interface*. The procedure interface for these procedures is listed in Figure 9.20.

```
.....H.Functions+++++++++++++++++++++++++        The NOMAIN keyword indicates that the RPG program
0001 H NOMAIN ◄                                  cycle code is not inserted into the complied module.

0002  /COPY sysInline
0003  /COPY cvtcase ◄                            The prototype for the procedure is
                                                 included by the /COPY directive.

.....PProcName+++++++..B.................Functions+++++++++++++++++++++++++++++
0004 P ToUpper          B                EXPORT

.....DName++++++++++EUDS.......Length+TDc.Functions+++++++++++++++++++++++++++++
0005 D ToUpper          PI         1024A
0006 D  InputStg                   1024A    CONST

0007 D RtnValue         S                   LIKE(InputStg)

0008 D lower            C                   Const('abcdefghijklmnopqrstuvwxyz')
0009 D UPPER            C                   Const('ABCDEFGHIJKLMNOPQRSTUVWXYZ')

.....CSRn01Factor1+++++++OpCode(ex)Factor2+++++++Result++++++++Len++DcHiLoEq....
0010 C        lower:UPPER   xLate      InputStg      RtnValue
0011 C                      Return     RtvValue

.....PProcName+++++++..B.................Functions+++++++++++++++++++++++++++++
0012 P ToUpper          E
```

Figure 9.20: Procedure interface for TOUPPER.

The procedure prototype is similar to a named parameter list. It defines the parameter interface of a called procedure. The procedure interface is functionally similar to the *ENTRY PLIST used by the traditional RPG call interface. One additional function of a prototyped procedure is that the called procedure can return a value. When the prototyped procedure is used in an expression (see line 5 in Figure 9.17), the called procedure is expected to return a value. In the example TOUPPER procedure, the returned value is the uppercase equivalent of the input parameter.

The returned value can be used in an expression. The EVAL, IF, DOW, DOU, and WHEN operations support conditional expressions. The EVAL operation supports assignment expressions. In addition, if a procedure returning a value is evoked through the CALLP operation, the return value is ignored.

The return value is declared on the procedure *prototype name definition statement*. This source statement contains the letters PR in positions 24 and 25. The name of the procedure is identified on this line along with the properties of the return value.

Figure 9.20 contains the start of the CVTTOOLS source file. For purposes of explanation, this source file is divided into two sections.

In Figure 9.19, lines 4 to 12 define the TOUPPER procedure. The procedure interface is declared on lines 5 and 6. The letters PI, in positions 24 and 25 of line 5, indicate that line 5 is the *procedure interface definition statement*. The name of the procedure and the properties of the return value (if any) are specified on this statement.

On line 6, the first (and only) parameter is defined. This parameter's properties must exactly match those of the procedure prototype. The names of the parameters are used by the procedure to access the parameter data. This is in contrast to the parameter names on prototype statements, which are discarded by the compiler.

Figure 9.21 lists the MAKEUPPER source code. This is a continuation of the CVTTOOLS source file that begins in Figure 9.20.

```
.....PProcName+++++++..B...................Functions+++++++++++++++++++++
0013 P MakeUpper        B

.....DName++++++++++++EUDS.......Length+TDc.Functions++++++++++++++++++++
0014 D MakeUpper        PI                   OPDESC         ◄
0015 D   InputStg                    1024A   OPTIONS(*VARSIZE)

0016 D   WorkVar        S                    LIKE(InputStg)
```

> *The procedure interface for MAKEUPPER includes the OPDESC keyword. This causes operational descriptions for each parameter to be available to the procedure.*

```
0017 D lower            C                    Const('abcdefghijklmnopqrstuvwxyz')
0018 D UPPER            C                    Const('ABCDEFGHIJKLMNOPQRSTUVWXYZ')

0019 D descType         S         10I 0
0020 D dataType         S         10I 0
0021 D descInf1         S         10I 0   ◄
0022 D descInf2         S         10I 0
0023 D strlen           S         10I 0
```

> *These fields are used by the CEEDOD (operational description) procedure. All but the STRLEN field are ignored by the MAKEUPPER procedure.*

```
.....CSRn01Factor1+++++++OpCode(ex)Factor2+++++++Result++++++++Len++DcHiLoEq....
0024 C                    CALLP      CEEDOD(1 : descType : datatype :
0025 C                                   descInf1 : descInf2 : strlen)
0026 C                    Eval       workvar = %subst(InputStg : 1 : strlen)
0027 C       lower:UPPER  xLate      workvar      workvar
0028 C                    Eval       %subst(InputStg : 1 : strlen) = workvar
0029 C                    return

.....PProcName+++++++..B...................Functions+++++++++++++++++++++++++
0030 P MakeUpper        E
```

Figure 9.21: Procedure interface for MAKEUPPER.

The MAKEUPPER procedure accepts one character field as a parameter (line 15), processes the data (lines 26 and 27), and then returns the modified value to the caller (lines 28 and 29).

In order to correctly access this data, the length of the value passed to the procedure must be determined. This is accomplished with a system function named CEEDOD. In order to call this procedure with the CALLP operation (line 24), a prototype for CEEDOD must be included in the source file. The prototypes for this and several other system functions are included in a source file named SYSINLINE. This source file is included using the /COPY compiler directive on line 2 of Figure 9.20. It is also listed in its entirety in Appendix D.

DATA STRUCTURES AND PROTOTYPED PROCEDURES

Prototyped procedures do not allow data structures to be declared as parameters. This is due to the syntax of the definition specification. Data structures, however, are allowed as parameter arguments (values) when the parameter is declared as a character field. Additional work must be performed within the procedure to map the incoming parameter to a data structure.

Specifically, within the subprocedure, the input parameter's address can be assigned to a pointer field. That pointer must be specified as the value of the BASED keyword for a data structure. Once the pointer is assigned the address of the input parameter, the based-on data structure overlays the input parameter in memory. At this point, the procedure's data structure can be used to access the parameter. Figure 9.22 and its related comments provide more details on this technique.

In Figure 9.22, the data structure named MYSTRUCT is passed to the PRINTADDR subprocedure. When PRINTADDR is evoked, it copies the address of the first (and only) parameter to the PSTRUCT field. This is a pointer field that is implicitly declared by the RPG compiler. It is used on line 12 to base the THESTRUCT data structure.

The THESTRUCT data structure is based on the PSTRUCT pointer. While no explicit definition of the PSTRUCT pointer is specified, the compiler generates a declaration for it. RPG implicitly declares pointer variables when used in this manner. Once the address of INADDRESS (the input parameter) is copied into the PSTRUCT pointer (line 17), the memory of the variable passed to the procedure is accessible through the THESTRUCT data structure (lines 12 to 15).

```
.....DName+++++++++++EUDS.......Length+TDc.Functions++++++++++++++
0001 D MyStuct          DS  ◄
0002 D   CustNo                       7P 0
0003 D   CustName                          LIKE(CORP_NAME)
0004 D   Address                      35

0005 D bOkay            S            10I 0

0006 D PrintAddr        PR            1N
0007 D   p1_Address                       Like(myStruct)
.....CSRn01..............OpCode(ex)Extended-factor2++++++++++++++++++++++++++
0008 C                   Eval       bOkay = PrintAddr(MyStruct)


0009 P PrintAddr        B

.....DName+++++++++++EUDS.......Length+TDc.Functions+++++++++++
0010 D PrintAddr        PI            1N
0011 D   InAddress                        Like(myStruct)  ◄

0012 D LCLStruct        DS                Based(pStruct)
0013 D   CustNo                       7P 0
0014 D   CustName                          LIKE(CORP_NAME)
0015 D   Address                      35

0016 D bFailed          S             1N

0017 C                   Eval       pStruct = %Addr(InAddress)
     C** TODO: Insert code to print the address here.
0018 C                   Return     bFailed
0019 P PrintAddr        E
```

The MYSTRUCT data structure needs to be passed to the subprocedure.

The data structure is passed to the procedure. The compiler treats data structures as character fields.

The input parameter is a character field. Its length is inherited from the global MYSTRUCT data structure.

The LCLSTRUCT data structure is based on the PSTRUCT pointer. When an address is moved into PSTRUCT, the data at that address is available through LCLSTRUCT.

Figure 9.22: Passing a data structure to a subprocedure.

In order to get the data from the INADDRESS input parameter (line 11) into the THESTRUCT data structure (lines 12 to 15), the address of INADDRESS is moved to the PSTRUCT field (line 17). PSTRUCT is the pointer on which THESTRUCT is based. Therefore, the data located at the memory address stored in PSTRUCT is accessible through this based-on data structure.

Prototyped Procedure Keywords

Several standard definition specification keywords can be used to enhance the properties of parameters passed to prototyped procedures. Table 10.1 lists the keywords that have a distinct effect on prototyped procedure parameters.

DATA AREAS

A data area is a persistent (permanent) location on the computer that is used to store information. A data area is separate from a program and can be used for communication between program modules.

Data areas are communicated between modules through system functions and RPG operations. Unlike parameters, the data contained in the data area is never passed between modules. Instead, a data area is retrieved from the system and a copy of its data is placed into a field or data structure within the procedure. Any manipulation of the data is performed on the program's copy of the data. The data area is updated with new information when data is written to the data area.

Data areas can be implicitly or explicitly read and written. A data area is implicitly read and written at the start and end of a program by defining a data structure as a *data area data structure*. The DTAARA keyword is used to associate a field, data structure, or data structure subfield with a data area. The name of the data area is specified as the parameter of the DTAARA keyword. See Figure 9.23.

```
.....DName+++++++++++EUDS........Length+TDc.Functions++++++++++++++++++++++++++++++
0001 D MyDataArea      UDS                    DTAARA(LastUsed)
0002 D  1_CustNo                      7S 0
0003 D  1_InvNo                       7S 0
0004 D  1_AcctNo                      7S 0

0005 D Company         S             50A      DTAARA(compname)

0006 D PurchOrder      DS                     DTAARA(Purchasing)
0007 D  NextPO#                       7S 0
0008 D  PODueDate                     10D      DATFMT(*USA)
```

External data area.

Figure 9.23: Data area declarations.

Once a data area is associated with a program variable, the data area can be read and written. The RPG data area operation codes IN, OUT, and UNLOCK are used to access data areas. Factor 2 of these operations must contain the name of the program variable that is associated with the data area (not the data area name itself).

Data Area Data Structures

To define an implicit data area read/write, the data structure must be defined as a cycle-controlled data structure (see Figure 9.24). The letter U in position 23 of the data structure name definition specification identifies the data structure as a cycle-controlled data area data structure. When the letter U is specified, the RPG compiler generates code that automatically reads the data area's content into the data structure when the program is first called, and automatically writes the content of the data structure to the data area when the program ends. This code (the letter U) is a carry-over from the RPG II language.

```
.....DName+++++++++++EUDS.......Length+TDc.Functions++++++++++++++++++++++++++++
0001 D MyDataArea     UDS                   DTAARA(LastUsed)
0002 D   1_CustNo                     7S 0
0003 D   1_InvNo                      7S 0
0004 D   1_AcctNo                     7S 0
```

Figure 9.24: Data area data structure specification.

When a data area data structure is defined, RPG implicitly retrieves the data area into the data structure when the program is started and writes the data structure to the data area when the program ends. If the data area doesn't exist when the program is run, it is created. On the AS/400, the data area is created in the QTEMP library with the same properties (e.g., name, length, type) as the corresponding data structure. If the DTAARA keyword is not specified, the name of the data structure is used as the name for the data area.

A data area data structure, like all data structures, can be externally described. Specify the letter E in position 22 of the data structure name definition specification. Optionally, the EXTNAME keyword can be used to name an externally described database file on which the format of the data structure is based. If the EXTNAME keyword is not specified, the name of the data structure is used as the name of the externally described database file. See Figure 9.25.

```
.....DName+++++++++++EUDS.......Length+TDc.Functions++++++++++++++++++++++++++++
0001 D MyDataArea     EUDS                  DTAARA(LastUsed)
0002 D                                      EXTNAME(LUFmt)   PREFIX(LU_ : 2)
```

Figure 9.25: Externally described data area.

Figure 9.25 defines a data area data structure named MYDATAAREA. The data area is externally described. Its format is based on the record format of the LUFMT database file. The name of the data area is LASTUSED.

Note the use of the PREFIX keyword (line 2). This keyword causes the renaming of every field of the LUFMT. In this example, the first two characters of the external field name are removed, and then the leading characters 'LU_' are appended to the field name. Hence, a field named LUCUSTNO is renamed to LU_CUSTNO.

IN and OUT Operation

Data areas can be explicitly read and written with the IN and OUT operations. Four RPG operations provide complete access to data areas:

- DEFINE — Assigns a host variable that is used to transfer data between the data area and the program. This is functionally equivalent to the DTAARA keyword.

- IN — Reads the data area's data and stores it in the associated host variable. The host variable is specified in factor 2 of this operation.

- OUT — Writes the contents of the host variable to the data area. The host variable is specified in factor 2 of this operation.

- UNLOCK — Releases the data area from a locked state.

The DEFINE operation names a data area and associates a field, data structure, or data structure subfield to the data area. That field is referred to as a *host variable.* It is where the data area's data is stored when an IN operation is used to read the data area. It is also the source of the data written to the data area by an OUT operation.

The IN operation reads one or all data areas defined in the program into their associated host variables. Factor 2 identifies the data area(s) to be read. If factor 2 contains the name of a host variable, its associated data area is copied into the host variable. If factor 2 contains *DTAARA, all data areas defined in the program are read into their associated host variables.

Factor 1 can be used to control object locking on the data area. By specifying *LOCK in factor 1, the data area associated with the host variable specified in factor 2 is locked by the program. The data area remains locked until an OUT operation is performed. Optionally, the UNLOCK operation can be used to release the lock.

The OUT operation writes the data contained in the data area's host variable to the data area. The name of the data area's host variable is specified in factor 2. If factor 2 contains the *DTAARA option, all data areas defined in the program are written. If factor 1 is blank, any lock placed on the data area is released when the data area is written. If factor 1 contains the *LOCK option, the data area lock is not released.

Figure 9.26 shows a data area data structure. The data structure name definition (line 1) contains the DTAARA keyword and the U in position 23. The program automatically reads the COMPINFO data area when the program starts. The data area's data is copied to the HOSTDS data structure.

```
.....DName+++++++++++EUDS.......Length+TDc.Functions++++++++++++++++++++++++++++++
0001 D HostDS           UDS                   DTAARA(CompInfo)
0002 D   CompName                  35A
0003 D   Rpt_Title                 50A
```

Figure 9.26: Data area data structure.

Figure 9.27 illustrates an assignment of a data area to a host data structure. Position 23 of line 1 is blank. Therefore, the data area is not automatically read and written when the program starts and ends. The IN operation (line 4) reads the COMPINFO data area into the HOSTSTUC data structure.

```
.....DName+++++++++++EUDS.......Length+TDc.Functions++++++++++++++++++++++++++++++
0001 D HostStruc        DS                    DTAARA(CompInfo)
0002 D   CompName                  35A
0003 D   Rpt_Title                 50A

.....CSRn01Factor1+++++++OpCode(ex)Factor2+++++++Result++++++++Len++DcHiLoEq....
0004                     IN          HostStruc
```

Figure 9.27: Data structure as data area host variable.

Figure 9.28 illustrates an assignment of a data area to a host field. Line 1 contains the definition for the NEXTCUST field. It is a stand-alone field, with the DTAARA keyword identifying the data area to be assigned. The CUSTNUMBER data area is assigned (line 1) to the NEXTCUST field. The IN operation (line 2) is used to read the data area's data into the NEXTCUST field. Note that, once a data area is assigned to a host variable, only the host variable is referenced in the data area operations.

```
.....DName+++++++++++EUDS.......Length+TDc.Functions++++++++++++++++++++++++++++++
0001 D NextCust         S                7S 0 Dtaara(CustNumber)

.....CSRn01Factor1+++++++OpCode(ex)Factor2+++++++Result++++++++Len++DcHiLoEq....
0002 C     *LOCK         IN          NextCust
0003 C                   Eval        NextCust = NextCust +1
0004 C     *LOCK         OUT         NextCust
```

Figure 9.28: Stand-alone field as data area host variable.

On line 3, the host variable is modified. Then, on line 4, the host variable is written out to the data area. Note that the *LOCK option is specified on line 4. This maintains the lock on the data area, preventing others from modifying it while this program is running.

Figure 9.29 shows an assignment of a data area to a host data structure subfield. Line 2 contains the subfield declaration. It is a subfield of the TEXT data structure (line 1). The IN operation (line 3) is used to read the data area's data into the NEXTACCT subfield.

```
.....DName++++++++++EUDS.......Length+TDc.Functions+++++++++++++++++++++++++++++
0001 D Text            DS
0002 D   NextAcct                      7S 0 Dtaara(CustNumber)

.....CSRn01Factor1+++++++OpCode(ex)Factor2+++++++Result++++++++Len++DcHiLoEq....
0003                     IN        NextAcct
```

Figure 9.29: Data structure subfield as data area host variable.

Figure 9.30 illustrates an assignment of a data area to a host field. This technique uses the DEFINE operation for this association. In Figure 9.30, line 2 is similar to line 1 in Figure 9.28. A stand-alone field is associated with the data area. However, the DEFINE operation instead of the DTAARA keyword is use to perform the association. The DEFINE operation is included in RPG IV for compatibility with prior versions of RPG. The DTAARA technique shown in Figure 9.28 is the preferred RPG IV technique.

```
.....DName++++++++++EUDS.......Length+TDc.Functions+++++++++++++++++++++++++++++
0001 D NextNum         S             7S 0

.....CSRn01Factor1+++++++OpCode(ex)Factor2+++++++Result++++++++Len++DcHiLoEq....
0002 C     *DTAARA      Define    CustNumber     NextNum
0003 C     *LOCK        IN        NextNum
0004 C                  Eval      NextNum = NextNum +1
0005 C     *LOCK        OUT       NextNum
```

Figure 9.30: The DEFINE operation used in defining data area.

Chapter 10

PROCEDURES

The RPG IV language provides a rich set of features that allow the programmer to modularize any application. Part of that feature set is the user-written function or, more properly, the procedure. Procedures are independent processes that typically are called to perform a specific task. The terms *procedure* and *subprocedure* are used interchangeably in RPG.

USER-WRITTEN PROCEDURES

When a procedure is written, it is referred to simply as a procedure. When a higher-level process calls the procedure, it becomes a subprocedure of that higher-level process. The main entry point into a program is referred to as the mainline procedure. All other procedures within the RPG program are referred to as subprocedures.

Header, definition, and procedure specifications are used to create procedures for RPG programs. The actual work of a procedure is performed by calculation specifications.

The procedure specification is used to name and delineate procedures within the RPG source code. A source file can contain only a mainline procedure, a mainline procedure and one or more subprocedures, or subprocedures only. When a source file is made up of only subprocedures, a header specification should be specified with the NOMAIN keyword. This ensures that the RPG program cycle code is not inserted into the compiled *MODULE. If NOMAIN is not specified, the procedures work the same as if NOMAIN were specified, but the overall module size is increased unnecessarily.

Procedures can exist in any number of program modules. A program is made up of one or more modules. Each module can export any of its subprocedures. Exported subprocedures can be called by procedures in other modules within the same program. This process is shown in Figure 10.1.

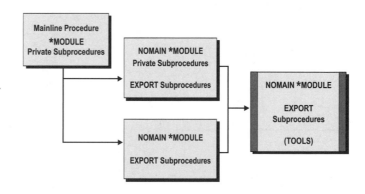

Figure 10.1: Procedures stored in separately compiled modules.

The logical path followed when a subprocedure is evoked is shown in Figure 10.1. In reality, the independent modules are statically bound into a single program object.

When a source file is compiled, the compiler generates a module object. On the AS/400, the CRTRPGMOD is used to generate a module. To create a program, one or more modules are bound together by the program binder. On the AS/400, the CRTPGM command evokes the program binder.

Figure 10.2 illustrates the structure of a source file that contains a mainline procedure and two subprocedures.

RPG program source code is organized in modules. A module can be a stand-alone program, a mainline procedure, or a procedure module. A stand-alone program is all-inclusive. It contains all the program statements required to perform its task.

A mainline procedure contains the process logic, support code, and RPG program cycle. This includes database file declarations and, perhaps, the user-interface components. A mainline procedure typically calls subprocedures, either statically or dynamically, to perform the detail work of the various processes.

A procedure module contains subprocedures that are called by higher-level programs or procedures. Typically, these subprocedure modules are one of two types, as follows:

- **Application-Specific Subprocedures**. Application-specific subprocedures are unique to the application in which they are bound.

- **General-Purpose Subprocedures**. General-purpose subprocedures perform more programmatic tasks such as converting a character string to all uppercase letters or formatting a date into a textual representation.

| Header specification |
| Global variables |
| Mainline calculations (mainline procedure) |
| |
| Begin Procedure specification |
| Local variables |
| Procedure calculations |
| End Procedure specification |
| |
| Begin Procedure specification |
| Local variables |
| Procedure calculations |
| End Procedure specification |

Figure 10.2: Source file structure with mainline procedure.

CALLING A PROCEDURE

The syntax for evoking a procedure or subprocedure is the same as that of a built-in function. Procedures are sometimes referred to as *user-written functions*. In this case, the user is the RPG programmer.

There are two basic techniques used to evoke (i.e., CALL) subprocedures. The first type is as the value of the extended factor 2 entry of the CALLP operation. This operation accepts subprocedure names that have been prototyped. The parameters of the subprocedure are specified similarly to that of a built-in function. See Figure 10.3.

```
.....CSRnØ1..............OpCode(ex)Extended-factor2++++++++++++++++++++++++++++++
     C                   CallP      myFunct( p1 : p2 : p3 : p4)
```

Figure 10.3: Calling a subprocedure with CALLP.

As shown in Figure 10.3, the CALLP operation accepts the name of a prototype that identifies a subprocedure to call in factor 2. If parameters can be required, they are specified on the same line as the CALLP operation and enclosed in parentheses.

The second type of subprocedure call is within an expression. This can be a conditional expression (such as the IF, DOW, DOU, and WHEN operations), in an assignment expression on the EVAL operation, or as the return value for the RETURN operation. Figure 10.4 shows three examples of how to evoke a subprocedure from within an expression.

```
.....CSRnØ1..............OpCode(ex)Extended-factor2++++++++++++++++++++++++++++++
ØØØ1 C                   IF         myFunct( p1 ) = myFunct2( p2 )

ØØØ2 C                   DOW        myFunct3( p3 * 5Ø ) < 1ØØØØ

ØØØ3 C                   EVAL       var = myFunct4( p4 )

ØØØ4 C                   RETURN     myFunct5( p5) + 7
```

Figure 10.4: Calling a subprocedure within an expression.

In Figure 10.4, the subprocedures MYFUNCT and MYFUNCT2 (line 1) are used in a conditional expression. On line 2, MYFUNCT3 is used to condition a DOW loop by comparing its return value to the literal 10000. The parameter of the MYFUNCT3 subprocedure also is an expression. On line 3, the subprocedure MYFUNCT4 is used to assign its return value to the VAR field on line 4; MYFUNCT5 is used to calculate the value returned to the calling procedure.

When a subprocedure is evoked through a conditional or assignment operation, a return value is expected. When a subprocedure is evoked using the CALLP operation, a return value is optional and is ignored by the operation. Normally, the CALLP operation is used to call a subprocedure that has no return value or to evoke a stand-alone program that has been prototyped.

In addition to subprocedures, stand-alone programs can be prototyped. This allows a program to be called through the CALLP operation, and to have strong parameter-type checking performed by the compiler.

In Figure 10.5, two prototypes are specified. The first (lines 1 and 2) is for a subprocedure named TOUPPER. The second (lines 3 to 6) is for a stand-alone program named QCMDEXC. The name used to call QCMDEXC in this program is RUN. The EXTPGM keyword (line 3) names the external program to be evoked and the prototype name (positions 7 to 21 of line 3) is used in the program.

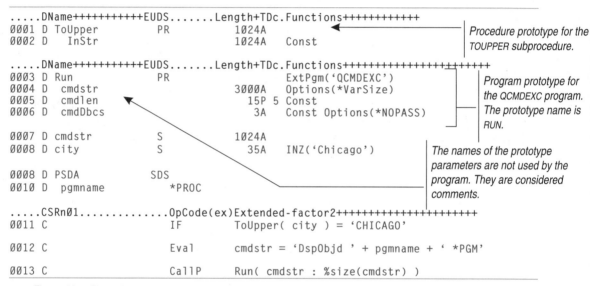

```
.....DName++++++++++EUDS.......Length+TDc.Functions+++++++++++++
0001 D ToUpper       PR          1024A
0002 D   InStr                   1024A    Const
```
Procedure prototype for the TOUPPER subprocedure.

```
.....DName++++++++++EUDS.......Length+TDc.Functions++++++++++++++++++++++
0003 D Run           PR                   ExtPgm('QCMDEXC')
0004 D   cmdstr                  3000A    Options(*VarSize)
0005 D   cmdlen                  15P 5    Const
0006 D   cmdDbcs                    3A    Const Options(*NOPASS)

0007 D cmdstr        S           1024A
0008 D city          S             35A    INZ('Chicago')

0008 D PSDA          SDS
0010 D   pgmname        *PROC
```
Program prototype for the QCMDEXC program. The prototype name is RUN.

The names of the prototype parameters are not used by the program. They are considered comments.

```
.....CSRn01.............OpCode(ex)Extended-factor2++++++++++++++++++++++++
0011 C                   IF         ToUpper( city ) = 'CHICAGO'

0012 C                   Eval       cmdstr = 'DspObjd ' + pgmname + ' *PGM'

0013 C                   CallP      Run( cmdstr : %size(cmdstr) )
```

Figure 10.5: Procedure and program prototypes.

The compiler ignores the names specified for the parameters of a prototype (lines 4 to 6). In Figure 10.5, line 4 specifies the name CMDSTR as the first parameter of the RUN prototype. The stand-alone field (line 7) is also named CMDSTR. The compiler throws out the name on line 4; therefore, it can be reused on line 7.

PROCEDURE DEFINITION

A procedure definition is made up of three parts:
- Procedure prototype — Specified with the definition specification.
- Procedure identification — Specified with the procedure specification.
- Procedure interface — Specified with the definition specification.

With only two exceptions, the procedure prototype and the procedure interface are similar interfaces. First, the type of definition specification is PR (for the procedure prototype) and PI (for the procedure interface). Second, the parameter names specified on the procedure interface are accessible by the procedure. The names specified on the procedure prototype, however, are optional and are used for documentation purposes only. They are not accessible by the calling procedure.

A procedure prototype is required within any program that calls the subprocedure and by the subprocedure itself. Procedure prototypes can be stored in a separate source file and are included at compile time through the /COPY compiler directive. This allows the prototype to be inserted into any source file that requires it.

Figure 10.6 shows a simple procedure prototype. The definition type is PR (positions 24 and 25). The procedure name is TOUPPER and it accepts one parameter named INSTR that is a read-only character string of up to 1.024 bytes in length. The INSTR field is only for documentation and is not inserted into the program. The procedure has a return value that is a character string of up to 1,024 bytes in length.

```
.....DName++++++++++EUDS.......Length+TDc.Functions++++++++++++++++++++++++++++
     D ToUpper          PR           1024A
     D    InStr                      1024A    Const
```

Figure 10.6: Simple procedure prototype.

To evoke a prototyped procedure, the CALLP operation is used. If the procedure returns a value, the procedure can be used in an expression just like a built-in function. In Figure 10.7, the three basic forms of evoking a procedure are illustrated on lines 5, 6, and 7.

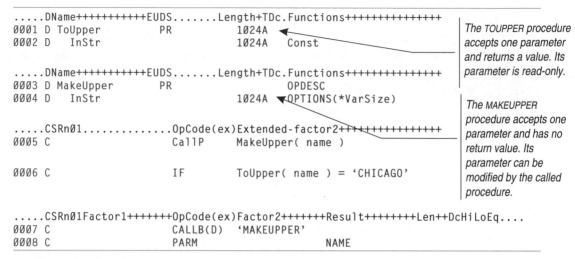

```
.....DName+++++++++++EUDS.......Length+TDc.Functions++++++++++++++++
0001 D ToUpper         PR             1024A  ◄
0002 D   InStr                        1024A    Const

.....DName+++++++++++EUDS.......Length+TDc.Functions++++++++++++++++
0003 D MakeUpper       PR                     OPDESC
0004 D   InStr                        1024A  ◄OPTIONS(*VarSize)

.....CSRn01.............OpCode(ex)Extended-factor2++++++++++++++++++
0005 C                     CallP     MakeUpper( name )

0006 C                     IF        ToUpper( name ) = 'CHICAGO'


.....CSRn01Factor1+++++++OpCode(ex)Factor2+++++++Result+++++++++Len++DcHiLoEq....
0007 C                     CALLB(D)  'MAKEUPPER'
0008 C                     PARM                     NAME
```

The TOUPPER procedure accepts one parameter and returns a value. Its parameter is read-only.

The MAKEUPPER procedure accepts one parameter and has no return value. Its parameter can be modified by the called procedure.

Figure 10.7: Example use of prototyped procedure.

In Figure 10.7, lines 1 and 2 are the prototype for the TOUPPER procedure. The length and data type attributes on line 1 indicate that this procedure returns a value. Lines 3 and 4 are the prototype for the MAKEUPPER procedure. Because there is no length or data-type attribute for this procedure, it doesn't return a value. This type of procedure can be called through the CALLP or CALLB operations. It cannot, however, be used within an expression of a conditional or assignment statement.

The first (and only) parameter of the MAKEUPPER procedure contains the OPTIONS (*VARSIZE) keyword. This indicates that the length of the parameter represents the longest argument length accepted by the procedure. Arguments of shorter length are accepted, but longer-length arguments are not. This option allows variable-length parameters to be passed to subprocedures.

There is no RPG interface to access the attributes of variable-length parameters. However, there are several system interface APIs that provide this support.

If the *VARSIZE option is not specified, and the CONST keyword also is not specified, the length of the argument being passed must exactly match that of the parameter definition.

PROTOTYPED PROCEDURE KEYWORDS

Several standard definition specification keywords can be used to enhance the properties of parameters passed to prototyped procedures. Table 10.1 lists the keywords that have a distinct effect on prototyped procedure parameters.

Table 10.1: Definition Specification Keywords for Prototyped Parameters			
Keyword	**Parameters**	**Used By**	**Description**
CONST		PARM	For procedure parameters, the value being passed is constant. It is considered read-only and is not changed by the called procedure.
			When a parameter is CONST, the compiler performs a small level of "type casting." If the value specified is similar to the data type and length required by the parameter, the system does some conversion to convert the value to the format required by the parameter.
			This is especially apparent for numeric parameters where a length is specified for the parameter, but a numeric value of any length can be specified.
			For date parameters, CONST allows the system to convert date values (of any format) to the format required by the prototype parameter.
DATFMT	Format [separator]	PARM RETURN	The date format expected for the parameter. The date format of the value passed must match this format unless the parameter is read-only (i.e., it is not changed by the called procedure), and the CONST keyword is specified for the parameter.
			For return values, this is the format of the date value being returned by the called procedure.
EXTPGM	*external program name*	Prototype	The name of the program being prototyped. Either a quoted character literal or a named constant can be specified. This keyword is typically used for calling operating system APIs, but it can also be used to provide a prototyped interface to custom application programs.
			The prototype name (specified in positions 7 to 21) does not have to match the value specified for this keyword. The prototype name is the name used within the program to evoke the subprogram.
EXTPROC	*external procedure name*	Prototype	The name of the procedure being prototyped. Either a quoted character literal, a named constant, or a procedure pointer can be specified.
			The name of the prototype (positions 7 to 21) is used as the procedure name if neither EXTPROC nor EXTPGM is specified.

Table 10.1: Definition Specification Keywords for Prototyped Parameters, *continued*			
Keyword	**Parameters**	**Used By**	**Description**
EXTPROC *continued*	*external procedure name*	Prototype	The prototype name does not have to match the value specified for this keyword. The prototype name is the name used within the program to evoke this subprocedure. This can be useful for renaming unusually named subprocedures. For example, CEEDOD can be renamed as GETOPDESC. Then GETOPDESC is used to evoke the CEEDOD procedure.
LIKEREC	*based-on variable*	PARM	Use this keyword to assign the attribute of the referenced variable to the new variable. Only the size, decimal positions (if any), and data type are inherited. The initial value is not inherited. If the referenced variable is the name of a procedure prototype, the new field inherits the properties of the prototype's return value. If the referenced variable is an array, the properties of an array element are inherited. Specify DIM(%elem(based-on VAR)) to also inherit the number of elements. If the referenced variable is a data structure, a character field is created with a length equal to that of the data structure.
NOOP		PARM	Used when calling OPM (i.e., RPG III) programs. Most OPM programs may be called using the EXTPGM keyword without the NOOPT keyword specified. However, if problems with passing values occur, add the NOOPT key to each parameter.
OPDESC		Prototype Proc-Interface	Operational descriptors are passed to the called procedure or program. All system APIs expect operation descriptors. An operational descriptor can be useful in other procedures as well. The length and type of character fields are passed to the called procedure.This is useful for string manipulation and variable length parameters. When this keyword is used, it must be specified on both the procedure prototype and the procedure interface definition. *See also* OPTIONS(*VARSIZE).
OPTIONS	[opt1 : opt2 : opt3]	PARM	Parameter passing options. On a prototype, use the OPTIONS keyword on any of the parameters that require special consideration.
	*NOPASS		The parameter is optional. It does not have to be specified wn the procedure is called. All subsequent parameters must also include the option OPTIONS(*NOPASS).he
	*OMIT		The *OMIT option is allowed for the parameter. Use *OMIT in place of a parameter value when the procedure is called. In other languages, the NULL value is normally passed in this situation. *OMIT is similar to passing a null value as a place holder for a parameter.

Keyword	Parameters	Used By	Description
OPTIONS *continued*	*OMIT *continued*		To determine whether or not a parameter is specified as *OMIT, compare the parameter's address to the *NULL built-in constant. For example:
			`CSRn01..............OpCode(ex)Extended-factor2++++++`
			`C                        If        %addr(p1) = *NULL`
			Where P1 is the parameter being passed into the procedure or program.
	*VARSIZE		The character, array, or graphic parameter value can be shorter than the length defined in the prototype for the parameter. If *VARSIZE is not specified, the value passed must match the length of the parameter declaration.
			The *VARSIZE option allows a parameter to be passed that is of varying size. Contrast this with the CONST keyword, which allows the length to differ, but does not allow the called procedure to modify the parameter's data.
			The actual length of the parameter can be determined by calling a system interface API. On the AS/400, this information is retrieved from the sixth parameter of the CEEDOD API.
			See also CONST.
	*STRING		Pass the value as a null terminated string. The parameter value is converted to a null terminated string automatically by the compiler.
	*RIGHTADJ		The data in the character parameter is right justified
VALUE		PARM	Pass parameter argument by value. The value passed on the parameter is copied to a temporary location, and a reference to the copy is passed to the called procedure. The called program can make changes to the value, but those changes are not reflected in the calling program.
VARYING		PARM	Pass the parameter as variable length field. When used in conjunction with the CONST or the VALUE keywords, any character string expression (variable length or fixed length) may be passed as the parameter value.

Table 10.1: Definition Specification Keywords for Prototyped Parameters, *continued*

PROGRAM ENTRY POINT

For stand-alone programs, the area of the RPG program commonly referred to as the mainline calculations is known as the *mainline procedure.* This is also referred to as the *program entry point.* The program entry point is different from the generic *program entry procedure* (PEP) that is inserted into every program by the OS/400 binder.

The PEP receives control from a static or dynamic call to a program. It, in turn, transfers control to the *user entry procedure* (UEP). The UEP is the program's starting point. In stand-alone RPG programs, the UEP is the start of the RPG program cycle, which eventually leads to the first detail-time calculation, also known as the the *mainline* calculations.

In Table 10.2, three RPG program source code structure types are listed. These structures illustrate how procedures can be specified in RPG source files.

Type 1 is either a stand-alone source program or the program entry-point module for a larger application. For stand-alone programs, it can be called directly and run from a command line. The module object from this type of program can be bound to run on its own or it can be statically bound to another module. The call interface to this type of program is through the dynamic CALL operation or the static CALLB and CALLP operations.

Type 2 is a procedure-only source program. It is used to store procedures that are called by other programs. The module object created from this type of source program must be statically bound to another module. Other programs or procedures may call this module's exported procedures. A major shortcoming with this type of source file is that the RPG program cycle is embedded into its *MODULE by the compiler. This additional overhead is unnecessary considering the Type 3 source file.

Type 3 is a procedure-only source file, similar to Type 2. It is used to store procedures that are called by other programs. The module object created from this type of source program must be statically bound to another module. Other programs or procedures may call this module's exported procedures. The main difference is the NOMAIN keyword. This keyword directs the compiler to avoid embedding the RPG program cycle overhead into the *MODULE. Type 3 is preferred over Type 2.

Table 10.2: Three Types of Source File Structures

Type	Source Code Structure	Description	Caveats

1	`H`
	`F (global files)`
	`D (global data)`
	`C (mainline calcs)`
	`O (global output)`
	
	`P (begin proc1)`
	`D`
	`C`
	`P (end proc1)`
	
	`P (begin proc2)`
	`D`
	`C`
	`P (end proc2)`
		Stand-alone program.
		
		Evoked via call to the program name. Call must be dynamic, unless module is bound with other modules, in which case the static call is required.
			Procedures are essentially replacements for subroutines, or no procedures are specified.
			
			Entry point is the mainline procedure via a static or dynamic call to the program name.
			
			Subprocedures can be called if they are exported, but typically they are not exported.

2	`F (global files)`
	`D (global data)`
	
	`P (begin proc1) EXPORT`
	`D`
	`C`
	`P (end proc1)`
	
	`P (begin proc2)`
	`D`
	`C`
	`P (end proc2)`
		Procedure module.
		
		Evoked via call to any exported procedure.
		
		Global data is available to each procedure.
		
		No mainline calculations are specified.
		
		Most procedures are exported.
		
		RPG program cycle overhead is inserted into the module.
			The NOMAIN keyword is omitted but only procedures are included (no mainline calculcations).
			
			Use as a subprocedure library.
			
			The overhead of the RPG program cycle is not necessary; files are automatically opened and closed anyway.
			
			Larger-than-necessary module size.
			
			Can be used to create a service program.

3	`H NOMAIN`
	`F (global files)`
	`D (global data)`
	
	`P (begin proc1) EXPORT`
	`D`
	`C`
	`P (end proc1)`
	
	`P (begin proc2) EXPORT`
	`D`
	`C`
	`P (end proc2)`
		Procedure module.
		
		Evoked via call to any exported procedure.
		
		Global data is available to each procedure.
		
		No mainline calculations are specified.
		
		The NOMAIN keyword on the header specification directs the compiler not to insert the RPG program cycle overhead.
			NOMAIN keyword is included (no mainline calculations).
			
			Use as a subprocedure library.
			
			Smaller module size.
			
			Can be used to create a service program.
			
			Procedures intended for public use must include the EXPORT keyword on their procedure specification.
			
			Global data usually is not required.

There is another type of module that can be generated. However, it is similar in structure to the Type 1 source file. When the CALLB operation is used, the module name can be used as the name of the program to call. This allows independent programs to be statically bound into one physical program object. With the exception of the CALLB operation, however, the interface between the two programs is the same as for the CALL operation:

- Full RPG cycle code is embedded into the generated module.

- The subprogram can be called via the mainline program.

- The program entry point in the subprogram is the first line of its mainline calculation specifications.

To further illustrate the Type 1 and Type 3 source file structures, an example Type 1 source file is shown in Figure 10.8 and an example Type 3 source file is shown in Figure 10.9.

```
.....H.Functions+++++++++++++++++++++++++++++++++++++++++++++++++++++++++++++++++++
0001 H DatFmt(*USA)


.....FFileName++IFEASFRlen+LKeylnKFDevice+.Functions++++++++++++++++++++++++++++++
0002 FCustMast  IF   E           K DISK     PREFIX(CM_)                    ◄─────────┐


.....DName+++++++++++EUDS.......Length+TDc.Functions++++++++++++++++++++++++++++++  │
     *** -Prototype of the TOUPPER( char-var ) function                            │
0003 D ToUpper         PR            1024A                                          │
0004 D  tu_input                     1024A     CONST                               │


.....CSRnØ1..............OpCode(ex)Extended-factor2++++++++++++++++++++++++++++++++ │
.....CSRnØ1Factor1+++++++OpCode(ex)Factor2+++++++Result++++++++Len++DcHiLoEq....    │
0005 C                   READ       CustRecd                              LR        │
0006 C                   Dow        NOT *INLR                     ┌──────────────────────────┐
                                                                  │ Mainline procedure.       │
0007 C                   IF         ToUpper(CM_City) = 'ROCHESTER'└──────────────────────────┘
0008 C                   DELETE     CustRecd           ┌── Call to subprocedure                │
0009 C                   endif                         │   named TOUPPER.          LR          │
0010 C                   READ       CustRecd       ◄───┘                                       │
0011 C                   EndDo                                                                 │
0012 C                   return                                            ◄──────────────────┘


.....PProcName+++++++..B.................Functions++++++++++++++++++++++++++++++  ◄──────┐
0013 P ToUpper         B                                                                 │


.....DName+++++++++++EUDS.......Length+TDc.Functions++++++++++++++++++++++++++++++        │
0014 D ToUpper         PI            1024A                                                │
0015 D  InputStg                     1024A     CONST                  ┌──────────────────────────┐
                                                                      │ TOUPPER subprocedure.     │
0016 D RtnValue        S                       LIKE(InputStg)         └──────────────────────────┘

0017 D lower           C                       Const('abcdefghijklmnopqrstuvwxyz')          │
0018 D upper           C                       Const('ABCDEFGHIJKLMNOPQRSTUVWXYZ')          │


.....CSRnØ1Factor1+++++++OpCode(ex)Factor2+++++++Result++++++++Len++DcHiLoEq....            │
0019 C     lower:UPPER  xLate      InputStg        RtnValue                                 │
0020 C                  Return     RtvValue                                                 │


.....PProcName+++++++..B.................Functions++++++++++++++++++++++++++++++            │
0021 P ToUpper          E                                                        ◄──────────┘
```

Figure 10.8: Type 1 source file.

```
.....H.Functions++++++++++++++++++++++++++++++++++++++++++++++++++++++++++++++++
      H DATFMT(*ISO) NOMAIN

        /COPY ZINCLUDE    ◄────────────────────  Note: Protoypes can be stored in separate source files.

.....PProcName+++++++..B.................Functions++++++++++++++++++++++++++++++
      P DayOfWeek      B                  EXPORT                               ◄──────┐
      **                                                                              │
      ** Procedure interface for the get DayOfWeek function                           │
      **                                                                              │
                                                                                      │
.....DName++++++++++EUDS.......Length+TDc.Functions++++++++++++++++++++++++++++++     │
      D DayOfWeek      PI            10I 0                                            │
      D  InDate                      D    CONST DATFMT(*ISO)                          │
                                                            ┌─────────────────────┐  │
      D BaseDate       S             D    INZ(D'1582-10-14')│ DAYOFWEEK Subprocedure│  │
      D                                    STATIC           └─────────────────────┘  │
      D nDayOfWeek     S             10I 0                                           │
      D nDays          S             10I 0                                          │
                                                                                    │
.....CSRn01Factor1+++++++OpCode(ex)Factor2+++++++Result++++++++Len++DcHiLoEq....    │
      C               TEST                    InputDate              73             │
                                                                                    │
      C               If        *IN73                                              │
      C               Return    -1                                                 │
      C               Endif                                                        │
      C     InDate    SubDur    BaseDate      nDays:*Days                          │
      C               CALLB     'CEEDYWK'                            73             │
      C               Parm                    nDays                                │
      C               Parm                    nDayofWeek                           │
      C               return    nDayOfWeek                                         │
      P DayOfWeek      E                                              ◄─────────────┘
```

Figure 10.9: Type 3 source file with NOMAIN (part 1 of 2).

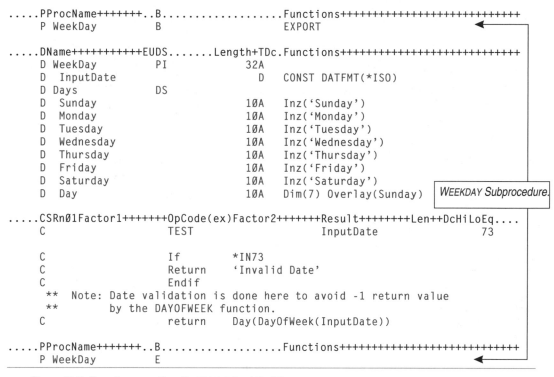

```
.....PProcName+++++++..B..................Functions+++++++++++++++++++++++++++++
     P WeekDay          B                  EXPORT

.....DName+++++++++++EUDS.......Length+TDc.Functions+++++++++++++++++++++++++++++
     D WeekDay          PI            32A
     D  InputDate                      D   CONST DATFMT(*ISO)
     D Days              DS
     D  Sunday                        10A   Inz('Sunday')
     D  Monday                        10A   Inz('Monday')
     D  Tuesday                       10A   Inz('Tuesday')
     D  Wednesday                     10A   Inz('Wednesday')
     D  Thursday                      10A   Inz('Thursday')
     D  Friday                        10A   Inz('Friday')
     D  Saturday                      10A   Inz('Saturday')
     D  Day                           10A   Dim(7) Overlay(Sunday)

.....CSRn01Factor1+++++++OpCode(ex)Factor2+++++++Result+++++++++Len++DcHiLoEq....
     C                  TEST                      InputDate                  73

     C                  If         *IN73
     C                  Return     'Invalid Date'
     C                  Endif
      **  Note: Date validation is done here to avoid -1 return value
      **        by the DAYOFWEEK function.
     C                  return     Day(DayOfWeek(InputDate))

.....PProcName+++++++..B..................Functions+++++++++++++++++++++++++++++
     P WeekDay          E
```

Figure 10.9: Type 3 source file with NOMAIN (part 2 of 2).

A SYSTEM INTERFACE FOR PROCEDURES

There are several useful system interfaces (APIs) provided on the IBM AS/400 system. These interfaces provide access to the properties of parameters passed to subprocedures. All of these interfaces begin with the letters CEE. When an API begins with these letters, it is bound into the program as an in-line function. This means that the actual code for the API is embedded into the program module; a call to the API is not generated.

When a subprocedure requirement calls for an optional parameter, or a variable-length parameter, the OPDESC keyword should be specified on the procedure name definition statement. This keyword is required on both the prototype and the procedure interface.

The OPDESC keyword causes additional information about each parameter to be passed to the called procedure. RPG IV does not provide conventional methods for accessing this information. Therefore, system interfaces must be called to retrieve the operational descriptions.

The basic operational description API is CEEDOD (Retrieve Operational Descriptor). This API has seven parameters (six of which are required). The sixth parameter is the one that is frequently used within RPG programs.

The naming for this API is generic to the AS/400 ILE runtime environment. It is possible to use an alternative name, however, to evoke this API. Rather than call CEEDOD directly using the CALLB(D) operation, a prototype for the API can be created and used to evoke the interface. That prototype can be named more clearly than the API name. A simple prototype for CEEDOD is shown in Figure 10.10.

```
.....DName+++++++++++EUDS.......Length+TDc.Functions++++++++++++++++++++++++++++++++
0001 D GetOpDesc       PR                    ExtProc('CEEDOD')
0002 D  ParmPos                      10I 0 Const
0003 D  o_desctype                   10I 0
0004 D  o_datatype                   10I 0
0005 D  o_descinf1                   10I 0
0006 D  o_descinf2                   10I 0
0007 D  o_fieldlen                   10I 0
0008 D  o_errors                     12A   OPTIONS(*OMIT)
```

Figure 10.10: Prototype for the operational description API.

To call CEEDOD using the prototype shown in Figure 10.10, specify the CALLP operation with GETOPDESC specified for the procedure name. Figure 10.11 shows this technique using the MAKEUPPER user-written subprocedure.

See Appendix D for a complete listing of the examples used in this chapter.

```
.....DName++++++++++++EUDS.......Length+TDc.Functions++++++++++++++++++++++++++
0001 D MakeUpper       PR           1024A  OPDESC
0002 D  InputStg                    1024A  OPTIONS(*VARSIZE)

0003 D GetOpDesc       PR                  ExtProc('CEEDOD')
0004 D  ParmPos                    10I 0   Const
0005 D  o_desctype                 10I 0
0006 D  o_datatype                 10I 0
0007 D  o_descinf1                 10I 0
0008 D  o_descinf2                 10I 0
0009 D  o_fieldlen                 10I 0
0010 D  o_errors                    12A    OPTIONS(*OMIT)
```

The MAKEUPPER prototype requires the OPDESC keyword. Its sole parameter is a *VARSIZE PARM.

The CEEDOD API is accessed via the GETOPDESC name. Note the parameters specified for the prototype are for documentation purposes only.

```
.....PProcName+++++++..B...................Functions++++++++++++++++
0011 P MakeUpper        B
```

```
.....DName++++++++++++EUDS.......Length+TDc.Functions++++++++++++++++++++++++++
0012 D MakeUpper       PI           1024A  OPDESC
0013 D  InputStg                    1024A  OPTIONS(*VARSIZE)

0014 D RtnValue        S                   LIKE(InputStg)

0015 D lower           C                   Const('abcdefghijklmnopqrstuvwxyz')
0016 D UPPER           C                   Const('ABCDEFGHIJKLMNOPQRSTUVWXYZ')

0017 D  nDescType                  10I 0
0018 D  nDataType                  10I 0
0019 D  nDescInf1                  10I 0
0020 D  nDescInf2                  10I 0
0021 D  nLength                    10I 0
```

To call CEEDOD, the CALLP operation is used with GETOPDESC specified in factor 2. The length of the input parameter is returned as the 6th parameter (to the nlength field).

```
.....CSRn01Factor1+++++++OpCode(ex)Factor2+++++++++Result++++++++++Len++DcHiLoEq....
.....CSRn01..............OpCode(ex)Extended-factor2++++++++++++++++++++++++++++++++
0022 C                   CallP    GetOpDesc( 1 : nDescType : nDataType :
0023 C                                       nDescInf1 : nDescInf2 :
0024 C                                       nLength   : *OMIT )

0025 C                   Eval     RtnValue = %Subst(InputStg : 1 : nLength)

0026 C      lower:UPPER  xLate    RtnValue        RtnValue
0027 C                   Return   RtvValue

.....PProcName+++++++..B...................Functions++++++++++++++++++++++++++++
0028 P MakeUpper
```

Figure 10.11: Using operational descriptor.

Chapter 11

FILE PROCESSING

This chapter focuses on full-procedural file processing. Full-procedural files are files in which input and output operations to the file are controlled completely by RPG op codes. Contrast that with cycle-bound files where the RPG cycle controls most of the input and output processing. Also remember that the modern RPG language supports several types of file access:

- Primary/secondary processing through the RPG cycle.
- Demand file processing.
- Record address file (ADDROUT) processing.
- Special file processing.
- Pre-runtime table and array processing.
- Embedded SQL file processing.
- Full-procedural processing.

FULL-PROCEDURAL FILE PROCESSING

Full-procedural files are defined by placing the letter F into column 16 of the file specification. A typical declaration for a full procedural file is shown in Figure 11.1.

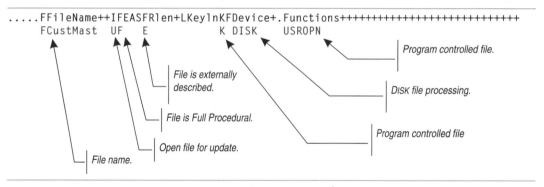

Figure 11.1: File description for a full-procedural DISK file.

Both program-described and externally described database files can be declared as full procedural. Full-procedural file processing is performed by several RPG op codes. For example, to read a record from a file, the READ operation is used. To write a new record to a file, the WRITE operation is used. Table 11.1 lists RPG op codes that can be used with full-procedural files.

Table 11.1: File-Based Op Codes	
Op Code	Description
ACQ	Acquire program device.
CHAIN	Random file access by index.
COMMIT	Commitment control, commit group.
DELETE	Delete database file record.
EXCEPT	Write program-defined or externally described record format.
EXFMT	Write, then read, a workstation device-file record format.
FEOD	Reset the file "cursor." Unlock any locked records.
KFLD	Define a key field of a key list.
KLIST	Define key list.
OPEN	Open file.
POST	Retrieve and post device-specific information to a data structure.
READ	Read record.
READC	Read next changed subfile record.
READE	Read next database file record with matching index.
READP	Read previous database file record.
READPE	Read previous database file record with matching index.
REL	Release acquired program device.
ROLBK	Commitment control, roll back group.
SETGT	Set file cursor greater than the specified index.
SETLL	Set file cursor less than the specified index.
UNLOCK	Release record lock.
UPDATE	Update record.
WRITE	Write record.

In discussing file processing, several database terms are used. These terms are general to the topic of databases and specific to the AS/400 system. Here's a look at a brief glossary of file terminology:

access path: An object used to access data in a file in a specific sequence.

cross reference: A set of files containing fields for where and how information is used.

library: A directory of a group of related and unrelated objects that have been placed into a specific context.

field: In a record, one or more bytes of information that make up a single fact.

File: A directory of members and formats. Typically referred to as *physical files, logical files*, or *join logical files*, file is a generic term for *database file.*

member: The entity within a database file that contains the actual data. A set of fields and records.

index: *See* access path.

join logical file: A subset of fields and records from two or more files.

Key: *See* access path.

key field: A field in a physical or logical file used to determine the order of entries in an access path.

logical file: A subset of fields and records from a file.

physical file: A database file containing records of real data.

record: A horizontal line of data in a physical or logical file.

random access: A method of processing a file randomly by its access path through its key fields.

view: A subset of fields and records from a file.

PHYSICAL FILES

Full-procedural file processing provides access to disk files and workstation files. *Disk files* contain data and are referred to as *database files*. Database files are files that have been defined to the operating systems by the data definition services. This allows RPG programs to access the file with operating-system services. Database files consist of a group of related data records. Data records consist of one or more fields. Database files are defined with a data definition language such as SQL—which is available on most computer systems—and DDS, which is available on the AS/400 for data definition.

To define a file using DDS, source code describing the file must be created. File definition source is created in much the same way as an RPG source program; a source-code editor is used to create data definition source code. For example, a file named CUSTMAST, consisting of five fields and a key field, can be created with the DDS source code shown in Figure 11.2.

```
.....AanØ1nØ2nØ3R.Format++++.Len++TDPURowColKeywords+++++++++++++++++++
ØØØ1 A          R CUSTREC                    TEXT('Customer file')
ØØØ2 A            ACTNBR        5P Ø          TEXT('Account Number')
ØØØ3 A            CSTNAM        3Ø            TEXT('Customer Name')
ØØØ4 A            CSTADR        3Ø            TEXT('Street Address')
ØØØ5 A            CSTCTY        2Ø            TEXT('City')
ØØØ6 A            CSTSTE         2            TEXT('State')
ØØØ7 A          K ACTNBR
```

Figure 11.2: DDS source to define a database file.

In Figure 11.2, line 1 specifies the name CUSTREC for the record format of the file. Lines 2 to 6 define each field of the file. Line 7 specifies that the field ACTNBR (account number) is used as a key field.

Similar to program source code, data-definition source code must be compiled before it can be used by RPG. On the IBM AS/400, DDS is compiled to create a *file object*. This file object is referred to as a database file.

When the DDS shown in Figure 11.2 is compiled, a file consisting of five fields is created. When the file object is created, only its description is actually created. There is no data in a newly created file object; data must be added to the file through some other method.

Assume that four records have been added to the CUSTMAST database file. These records are accessible by RPG and other high-level languages. Table 11.2 lists the file CUSTMAST after four records have been added.

Table 11.2: Illustration of CUSTMAST Database File

ACTNBR	CSTNBR	CSTADDR	CSTCTY	CSTSTE
01207	Skyline Pigeon Co.	Kauai Blvd.	Maui	HI
05320	Perlman-Rocque	103rd Street	Lemont	IL
05340	Champion Parts	22nd Street	Oak Brook	IL
05381	Luna Spacecraft	12 Artemis Drive	Geneva	IL

The field ACTNBR (account number) is the key field for the file. Therefore, when the file is accessed through its key, it is arranged in order of the data stored in the ACTNBR field. Additionally, a record can be accessed randomly by its key-field value. For example, to retrieve the record for "Luna Spacecraft," the key field ACTNBR is set equal to 5381. See Figure 11.3.

```
.....FFileName++IFEASFRlen+LKeylnKFDevice+.Functions++++++++++++++++++++++++++++
0001 FCUSTMAST  IF   E        K DISK

.....CSRn01Factor1+++++++OpCode(ex)Factor2+++++++Result++++++++Len++DcHiLoEq....
0002 C     *LIKE      DEFINE   ACTNBR       ACTKEY
0003 C     ACCT       KLIST
0004 C                KFLD                  ACTKEY

0005 C                Z-ADD    5381         ACTKEY
0006 C     Acct       CHAIN    CustRec                              54
0007 C                MOVE     *IN54        NOTFOUND        1
0008 C                .
0009 C                . (the program continues)
0010 C                .
```

Figure 11.3: Random access of a database file using the CHAIN operation.

In Figure 11.3, line 1 defines CUSTMAST as an externally described, full-procedural, keyed file. Line 2 defines the ACTKEY field as having the same attributes as the ACTNBR field. ACTNBR is defined in the CUSTMAST file. Line 3 defines the ACCT key list (which is used to access the file randomly by key). Line 4 defines the sole key field ACTKEY.

Line 5 initializes the ACTKEY field with the value of the key to be retrieved. Line 6 randomly accesses the CUSTMAST file using the key list ACCT. If a record exists with a key that matches the key list specified in factor 1, processing continues. If a record with a matching key doesn't exist, indicator 54 is set on.

Figure 11.3 illustrates random file access using a key list. Because the file CUSTMAST has only one key field, a key list is optional. The field ACTKEY could have been used in factor 1 of line 6, producing the same results. When a file's index is made up of multiple key fields, however, a key list is the easiest method to access its records.

Multiple Key Fields

Sometimes more than one key field is necessary for file access. For example, if the customer master file listed in Table 11.2 requires an access path by CSTSTE (state) and ACTNBR, two key fields are necessary.

Figure 11.4 illustrates the DDS for a multi-key database file. Line 7 contains the primary key field and line 8 contains the secondary key field. When records from this file are retrieved, they are ordered by state, and then by account number within the state.

```
.....AanØ1nØ2nØ3R.Format++++.Len++TDPURowColKeywords+++++++++++++++++++
ØØØ1 A         R CUSTREC                    TEXT('Customer file')
ØØØ2 A           ACTNBR        5P Ø         TEXT('Account Number')
ØØØ3 A           CSTNAM        30           TEXT('Customer Name')
ØØØ4 A           CSTADR        30           TEXT('Street Address')
ØØØ5 A           CSTCTY        20           TEXT('City')
ØØØ6 A           CSTSTE         2           TEXT('State')
ØØØ7 A         K CSTSTE
ØØØ8 A         K ACTNBR
```

Figure 11.4: Database file with multiple key fields.

Table 11.3 lists how the database records in the database file are ordered when the file is indexed by the CSTSTE and ACTNBR fields.

Table 11.3: Multi-Keyed Database File				
ACTNBR	CSTNBR	CSTADDR	CSTCTY	CSTSTE
01207	Skyline Pigeon Co.	Kauai Blvd.	Maui	HI
05320	Perlman-Rocque	103rd Street	Lemont	IL
05340	Champion Parts	22nd Street	Oak Brook	IL
05381	Luna Spacecraft	12 Artemis Drive	Geneva	IL

When the file CUSTMAST is processed, both key fields can be used to access the file or only the primary key can be used. For example, to retrieve the record for

"Perlman-Rocque," the primary key field must be set to IL, and the secondary key field must be set to 05320. See the example source code shown in Figure 11.5.

```
.....FFilename++IFEASFRlen+LKeylnKFDevice+.Functions++++++++++++++++++++++++++++++
0001 FCustMast  IF   E           K Disk      Rename(CustMast : Customer)

.....DName++++++++++EUDS.......Length+TDc.Functions++++++++++++++++++++++++++++++
0002 D State            S                     Like(CstSte)
0003 D AcctKey          S                     Like(ActNbr)
0004 D NotFound         S              1A     INZ(*OFF)

.....CSRnØ1Factor1+++++++OpCode(ex)Factor2+++++++Result++++++++Len++DcHiLoEq....
0005 C     ACCT          KLIST
0006 C                   KFLD                         STATE
0007 C                   KFLD                         ACCTKEY

0008 C                   EVAL       AcctKey = 5360
0009 C                   EVAL       State = 'IL'
0010 C     ACCT          CHAIN      CUSTMAST                        71
0011 C                   EVAL       NotFound = *IN71
0012 C                    .
0013 C                    . (the program continues)
0014 C                    .
```

Figure 11.5: Random access of a database file with multiple key fields.

Figure 11.5 illustrates random file access using two key fields. A key list is the preferred method for accessing files by key when multiple key fields exist for a file.

When multiple key fields exist, the number of key fields on a key list can be less than or equal to the number of key fields that make up the access path. When the number of key fields of a key list is less than the number of key fields for the file, that key list is called a *partial key list*.

Partial key lists are useful when non-unique primary keys exist in the file. For example, in the file CUSTMAST, three records exist for the state of Illinois. If the RPG program must process all records for the state of Illinois, a partial key can be used to position the file to the first record with CSTSTE equal to IL, and then read all records where CSTSTE equals IL. See Figure 11.6.

```
.....FFileName++IFEASFRlen+LKeylnKFDevice+.Functions++++++++++++++++++++++++++++++
0001 FCustMast  IF   E           K Disk      Rename(CustMast : Customer)

.....DName++++++++++EUDS.......Length+TDc.Functions++++++++++++++++++++++++++++++
0002 D State            S                     Like(CstSte)
0003 D AcctKey          S                     Like(ActNbr)
0004 D NotFound         S              1A     INZ(*OFF)
```

Figure 11.6: Random access of a database file by partial key (part 1 of 2).

```
.....CSRn01Factor1+++++++OpCode(ex)Factor2+++++++Result++++++++Len++DcHiLoEq....
0005 C       ByState       KLIST
0006 C                     KFLD                      State

0007 C                     Eval       State = 'IL'

0008 C       ByState       Chain      Customer                          71
0009 C                     EVAL       NotFound = *IN71

0010 C                     Dow        NotFound = *OFF
0011 C                     EXSR       PRINT
0012 C       ByState       ReadE      Customer                          75
0013 C                     EVAL       NotFound = *IN75
0014 C                     endDo
0015 C                        .
0016 C                        . (the program continues)
0017 C                        .
```

Figure 11.6: Random access of a database file by partial key (part 2 of 2).

In Figure 11.6, the partial key list BYSTATE (line 5) is used to access records in the CUSTMAST file. The access path for CUSTMAST consists of two key fields: CSTSTE and ACTNBR. The key list BYSTATE is made up of the single key field STATE. This provides file access by only the CSTSTE key field.

Line 2 defines the STATE field with the same attributes as the field CSTSTE (the primary key field for the file CUSTMAST). Line 5 defines the BYSTATE key list with one key field STATE (line 6). No other key fields are specified. Therefore, the key list becomes a partial key list.

Line 7 sets the STATE field equal to IL. This sets the value of the key list, which is used later to access the file. Line 8 chains to the file using the BYSTATE key list. A partial key list is used. Therefore, if records with duplicate keys exist, the first record in the file whose key matches the key list is retrieved.

Lines 10 to 14 read all records in the file where the key equals that of the key list. Line 12 retrieves the next record where the key equals the value of the partial BYSTATE key list. When no more records exist that match the key list, resulting indicator 3 (indicator 75) is set on.

Partial key file processing is common in the modern RPG language. For example, in a manufacturing application a *product structure file* typically contains two key fields—the item number and the subitem number.

When an item is manufactured, it is assembled into a "finished good" using subitems. A product-structure file contains the finished-goods assembly. Table 11.4 lists a typical product-structure file.

The ITMNBR field is the primary key and the SUBITM field is the secondary key. In order to process an item, a partial key list is used. See Figure 11.7.

Table 11.4: A Product-Structure File	
ITMNBR	SUBITM
101	127
101	501
101	602
201	127
201	333
201	402
201	602
450	101
450	333

```
.....FFileName++IFEASFRlen+LKeylnKFDevice+.Functions++++++++++++++++++++++++++++
0001 FProdStructIF   E           K DISK    Rename(ProdStruct : Products )

.....DName++++++++++EUDS.......Length+TDc.Functions++++++++++++++++++++++++++++++
0002 D NotFound        S              1A   INZ(*OFF)

.....CSRn01Factor1+++++++OpCode(ex)Factor2+++++++Result++++++++Len++DcHiLoEq....
0003 C        Primary      KList
0004 C                     KFld                   Item
0005 C                     Eval       Item = 201
0006 C        Primary      Chain      Products                        71
0007 C                     Eval       NotFound = *IN54

0008 C                     Dow        NotFound = *OFF
0009 C                     ExSr       Print
0010 C        Primary      ReadE      Products                        75
0011 C                     Eval       NotFound = *IN75
0012 C                     endDo
0013 C                     .
0014 C                     . (the program continues)
0015 C                     .
```

Figure 11.7: Sequential access by key of the product structure file.

Figure 11.7 processes the PRODSTRUCT file. Item number 201 is moved into the key list PRIMARY (line 5). That key list is used to retrieve the first record (subitem 127) in the product-structure file for item 201 (line 6). The DO WHILE loop (lines 8 to 12) processes the remainder of the product structure with the READE operation.

LOGICAL FILES

Sometimes it is necessary to process a portion or *subset* of a database file. A logical file can be used to create a subset of the file. A logical file is a view of a physical file. It can contain some or all of the fields and records of the physical file. Additionally, an access path (i.e., key fields) can be specified for the logical file.

Logical files don't contain data; they are vehicles through which data from physical files is supplied to an application program. Application programs treat both physical and logical files exactly the same. It is the operating system's responsibility to maintain the proper link between the logical file and the physical file's data.

As mentioned, logical files represent a subset of a physical file. For example, if an application requires only two fields of a five-field physical file, a logical file can be created to present only those two fields to the program. This technique is referred to as *mapping*. Table 11.5 shows the relationship between the physical file data and a logical file based on the physical file.

Table 11.5: Physical File Mapped to a Logical File

Physical File

ACTNBR	CSTNBR	CSTADDR	CSTCTY	CSTSTE
01207	Skyline Pigeon Co.	Kauai Blvd.	Maui	HI
05320	Perlman-Rocque	103rd Street	Lemont	IL
05340	Champion Parts	22nd Street	Oak Brook	IL
05381	Luna Spacecraft	12 Artemis Drive	Geneva	IL

Logical file

ACTNBR	CSTCTY
05381	Geneva
01207	Maui
05320	Lemont
05340	Oak Brook

Logical files are created with DDS source in the same manner as physical files. Logical file DDS, however, contains only the field names needed for the subset. For example, the DDS necessary to create the logical file listed in Table 11.5 is featured in Figure 11.8.

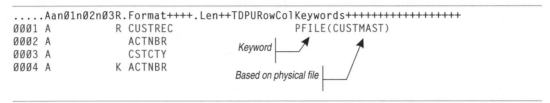

```
.....AanØ1nØ2nØ3R.Format++++.Len++TDPURowColKeywords++++++++++++++++++++
ØØØ1 A              R CUSTREC                  PFILE(CUSTMAST)
ØØØ2 A                ACTNBR
ØØØ3 A                CSTCTY
ØØØ4 A              K ACTNBR
```

Keyword

Based on physical file

Figure 11.8: Logical file DDS.

In Figure 11.8, line 1 defines the record format name for the logical file and the physical file on which the logical is based. The PFILE keyword identifies the based-on physical file.

Lines 2 and 3 identify the fields that are included in the logical file. The field properties (e.g., type, length) don't need to be specified. The properties of the fields in the physical file are inherited by the field names in the logical file. The field properties can, however, be overridden in the logical file.

Line 4 defines the key field that is used as the access path for the logical file. If the key field of the logical file is the same as that of the physical file or some other logical file, the access path is shared. When an access path is shared, only one copy of the access path exists. This saves time when the access path is built and improves performance when records are added to the file.

As stated, the DDS shown in Figure 11.9 is for a logical file that contains a subset of fields of the physical file. If a subset of records is required, select/omit specifications can be added to the DDS for the logical file. Table 11.6 lists DDS for a typical logical file with select/omit statements. Although both SELECT and OMIT operations are supported, traditionally only SELECT statements are used.

```
.....AanØ1nØ2nØ3R.Format++++.Len++TDPURowColKeywords++++++++++++++++++++
ØØØ1 A                                         DYNSLT
ØØØ2 A              R CUSTREC                  PFILE(CUSTMAST)
ØØØ3 A                ACTNBR
ØØØ4 A                CSTCTY
ØØØ5 A              K ACTNBR
ØØØ6 A              S ACTNBR                   COMP(GT 5ØØØ)
```

Figure 11.9: Logical file DDS with dynamic SELECT/OMIT.

Line 1 specifies that the select/omit specifications are dynamic. In other words, the select/omit is not combined with the access path but is performed by the operating system as the records are read by a high-level language.

Table 11.6: Subset of Fields and Records of a Logical File	
ACTNBR	CSTCTY
05381	Geneva
05320	Lemont
05340	Oak Brook

Line 6 contains the select/omit specification. The field ACTNBR must be greater than 5,000 for the record to be included in this logical file. The resulting view of the physical file's data is listed in Table 11.6. Note that account number 1207 is not included because its ACTNBR doesn't match the select/omit criteria.

Join Logical Files

The topic of relational database and join logical files has filled several volumes. AS/400 join logical files are similar to logical files in that they provide a subset of a physical file. However, join logical files can represent a subset of multiple physical files.

An *equi-join file* is a join logical file that joins two or more files by a common value. For example, an inventory file (consisting of part number, quantity on-hand, and part description) and a customer-order history file (consisting of customer number, part number, and quantity ordered) can be joined by part number, forming a join-logical view of the two files.

When files are joined, a single join record is created. The join record can contain any or all of the fields from the files being joined. Figures 11.10 through 11.12 illustrate the DDS necessary to create a join logical file. Table 11.9 provides an example of data mapped through the join logical file that is created.

```
.....AAnØ1nØ2nØ3T.Name++++++RLen++TDcBRowColKeywords++++++++++++++++++
      *** Physical file: INVMAST
     A           R INVENTRY
     A             PARTNO        5P Ø        COLHDG('Part' 'Number')
     A             QTYOH         7P Ø        COLHDG('Qty' 'On' 'Hand')
     A             DESC         5ØA          COLHDG('Part' 'Desc.')
```

Figure 11.10: DDS of a primary physical file.

Figure 11.10 illustrates the DDS for a physical file containing the part number, quantity on hand, and part description.

```
.....AAnØ1nØ2nØ3T.Name++++++RLen++TDcBRowColKeywords++++++++++++++++++++
    *** Physical file: ORDHIST
  A           R HISTREC
  A             CUSTNO         5P Ø        COLHDG('Part' 'Number')
  A             PARTNO    R                REFFLD(PARTNO INVMAST)
  A             QTYORD    R                REFFLD(QTYOH  INVMAST)
  A                                        COLHDG('Qty' 'Ordered')
```

Figure 11.11: DDS of a secondary physical file.

Figure 11.11 illustrates the DDS for a physical file containing the customer number, part number, and quantity ordered.

```
.....AAnØ1nØ2nØ3T.Name++++++RLen++TDcBRowColKeywords++++++++++++++++++++
    *** Join-Logical file: INVORDHST
ØØØ1 A                                     JDFTVAL
ØØØ2 A           R INORHIST                JFILE(INVMAST ORDHIST)
ØØØ3 A           J                         JOIN(1 2)
ØØØ4 A                                     JFLD(PART PART)
ØØØ5 A             PARTNO                   JREF(1)
ØØØ6 A             CUSTNO                   JREF(2)
ØØØ7 A             QTYORD                   JREF(2)
ØØØ8 A             DESC                     JREF(1)
ØØØ9 A           K PARTNO
```

Figure 11.12: DDS of a join logical file.

Figure 11.12 illustrates the DDS for the join logical file. This file, or *view*, contains fields from the files of both Figures 11.10 and 11.11. The JFILE keyword (line 2) identifies the physical files on which the logical file is based.

The JOIN keyword (line 3) indicates the primary-to-secondary file sequence. In other words, the join is from file number 1 to file number 2. This means that a record from the INVMAST file (file 1) is retrieved, and then an equal record from the ORDHIST file (file 2) is retrieved.

On line 4, the JFLD keyword is used to identify the fields names from the INVMAST and ORDHIST files that are used to connect (i.e., join) the two files.

The fields used for the join logical file are listed on lines 5 to 8. The JREF keyword identifies the file from which the field's content is retrieved. This is important when a file name exists in more than one of the based-on physical files.

Finally, line 9 identifies the file name used for the key to the join logical file. The field name doesn't require the JREF keyword because it must (currently) be a name that exists in the primary physical file. An example of two physical database files and a join logical file is listed in Tables 11.7, 11.8, and 11.9, respectively. When the data from the INVMAST file (file 1, as listed in Table 11.7) is joined with the ORDHIST file (file 2, listed in Table 11.8), the resulting join-logical view, as listed in Table 11.9 is created.

Inventory File (INVMAST)

Customer Order History (ORDHIST)

Table 11.7: Example Physical File Data for File 1		
PART	QTYOH	DESC
100	5000	VGA Display
200	6	Hi-gain Antennas
300	1	OS/2 Applications

Table 11.8: Example Physical File Data for File 2		
CUST	PART	QTYORD
1207	100	50
5340	100	1000
5381	200	1
5382	200	1

Resulting Join Logical File: INVORDHST
(File INVMAST Joined to ORDHIST)

Table 11.9: Join Logical File View of Data			
PART	CUST	QTYORD	DESC
100	1207	50	VGA Display
100	5340	1000	VGA Display
200	5381	1	Hi-gain Antennas

FILE ACCESS

File access within RPG programs is consistent with each type of file. All RPG database file-operation codes function identically on physical, logical, and join-logical files. The only exception to this is when a file has been defined to the operating system as read-only. In this situation, output operations aren't allowed.

When a file is defined to a program as a keyed file (i.e., the letter K is specified in column 31 of the file specification), RPG processes the file by the file's access path. When a file is defined as a sequential file (i.e., column 31 contains a blank), RPG processes the file's records in the order in which they appear in the file.

When a file is defined as a keyed file to the RPG program, the operations that retrieve records from a file can access those records randomly through the access path. With some operations, the record's data is copied to the input (buffer) area for the file, while others simply reposition the file cursor. Table 11.10 lists the effect of the file operations on a database file when the operation is successful.

Table 11.10: Cursor Positioning after Successful Operation			
Op Code	Data Returned	Record Status	Cursor Positioning
CHAIN	Yes	Locked	To record
DELETE	No	Deleted	To no record
EXCEPT	No	Released	To same record
FEOD	No	Released	To no record
OPEN	No	None	Beginning of file
READ	Yes	Locked	To record
READE	Yes	Locked	To record
READP	Yes	Locked	To record
READPE	Yes	Locked	To record
SETGT	No	Released	After record
SETLL	No	Released	Before record
UNLOCK	No	Released	To same record
UPDATE	No	Released	To same record
WRITE	No	Released	To same record

When any operation causes the file cursor to be positioned to the record or before the record, a subsequent READ or READE operation retrieves the next record in the file. A subsequent READP or READPE retrieves the prior record in the file. Additionally, if the N (no lock) operation extender is used with any of the input operations, no record lock is applied to the retrieved record.

Read Equal Key Anomaly

The READE (Read Next Record with Equal Key) and READPE (Read Prior Record with Equal Key) operations can cause record-lock contention under the following conditions:

- When the operation reads a record, the record is reviewed for the equal-key condition. If the key value for the record doesn't match the value in factor 1, the record is released, and data is never copied to the input (buffer) area.

- During the review of the key value for the record, the record is locked based on the conditions specified for the file on the file specification.

- If the record is already locked by another application, the READE or READPE operation waits for the record to be released for a time specified by the file's description. This wait period is specified external to the RPG program.

- When the wait-time expires, the RPG exception/error handling routine receives control unless resulting indicator 2 is specified. If resulting indicator 2 is specified, it is set on. To avoid the record lock, the N operation extender (NO LOCK) can be used. Specify READE(N) or READPE(N) to avoid placing the lock on the database record.

Tables 11.11 through 11.26 list the position of the file cursor after the specified operation code has been performed successfully.

The file PARTMAST is used in these examples. It contains the key field PART (part number). Only the key field is depicted in the figures. Prior to each operation, the record containing the part number 5738SS1 has been successfully retrieved with the CHAIN operation. Tables 11.11 through 11.26 diagram what happens to the file cursor and the part number record after the specified operation has been performed.

Table 11.11: CHAIN Operation	
File Cursor Position	**Part (Index) Number**
	*START
	LBY17YR
	Q385381
→	5738SS1
	84VETTE
	*END
	*NORECORD

Table 11.12: DELETE Operation	
File Cursor Position	**Part (Index) Number**
	*START
	LBY17YR
	Q385381
→	. . .
	84VETTE
	*END
	*NORECORD

Table 11.13: EXCEPT (to Add) Operation	
File Cursor Position	**Part (Index) Number**
	*START
	LBY17YR
	Q385381
	5738SS1
→	
	84VETTE
	*END
	*NORECORD

Table 11.14: EXCEPT (to Delete) Operation	
File Cursor Position	**Part (Index) Number**
	*START
	LBY17YR
	Q385381
→	. . .
	84VETTE
	*END
	*NORECORD

Table 11.15: EXCEPT (to Release) Operation	
File Cursor Position	**Part (Index) Number**
	*START
	LBY17YR
	Q385381
	5738SS1
→	
	84VETTE
	*END
	*NORECORD

Table 11.16: EXCEPT (to Update) Operation	
File Cursor Position	**Part (Index) Number**
	*START
	LBY17YR
	Q385381
	5738SS1
→	
	84VETTE
	*END
	*NORECORD

Table 11.17: FEOD Operation	
File Cursor Position	**Part (Index) Number**
	*START
	LBY17YR
	Q385381
	5738SS1
	84VETTE
→	*END
	*NORECORD

Table 11.18: OPEN Operation	
File Cursor Position	**Part (Index) Number**
→	*START
	LBY17YR
	Q385381
	. . .
	84VETTE
	*END
	*NORECORD

Table 11.19: READ Operation	
File Cursor Position	Part (Index) Number
	*START
	LBY17YR
	Q385381
	5738SS1
➔	84VETTE
	*END
	*NORECORD

Table 11.20: READE Operation	
File Cursor Position	Part (Index) Number
	*START
	LBY17YR
	Q385381
	5738SS1
	84VETTE
	*END
➔	*NORECORD

Table 11.21: READP Operation	
File Cursor Position	Part (Index) Number
	*START
	LBY17YR
➔	Q385381
	5738SS1
	84VETTE
	*END
	*NORECORD

Table 11.22: READPE Operation	
File Cursor Position	Part (Index) Number
	*START
	LBY17YR
	Q385381
	5738SS1
	84VETTE
	*END
➔	*NORECORD

Table 11.23: SETGT Operation	
File Cursor Position	**Part (Index) Number**
	*START
	LBY17YR
	Q385381
	5738SS1
→	84VETTE
	*END
	*NORECORD

Table 11.24: SETLL Operation	
File Cursor Position	**Part (Index) Number**
	*START
	LBY17YR
	Q385381
→	5738SS1
	84VETTE
	*END
	*NORECORD

Table 11.25: UPDATE Operation	
File Cursor Position	**Part (Index) Number**
	*START
	LBY17YR
	Q385381
	5738SS1
→	84VETTE
	*END
	*NORECORD

Table 11.26: WRITE Operation	
File Cursor Position	**Part (Index) Number**
	*START
	LBY17YR
	Q385381
	5738SS1
→	84VETTE
	*END
	*NORECORD

ACCESS PATH PROCESSING

Database file record access can be performed by record number, sequentially, or by access path. An index is used to process a file by its access path. The index used in an RPG program to access a database file can be a field, constant, or key list.

When a field or constant is used as an index in factor 1 of an input file, the entire composite key of the file is referenced. In other words, all key fields for the file are treated as one large key field by RPG. When a key list is used as the index by RPG, each key field must correspond to a key field in the database file. For example, the order history file consists of three fields: PART, CUST, and QTYORD. The access path for the file consists of two key fields: PART and CUST. The DDS to create this file is listed in Figure 11.13.

```
.....AanØ1nØ2nØ3R.Format++++.Len++TDPURowColKeywords+++++++++++++++++++
ØØØ1 A          R ORDREC              TEXT('Order History')
ØØØ2 A            PART        3P Ø    TEXT('Part Number')
ØØØ3 A            CUST        5P Ø    TEXT('Customer Number')
ØØØ4 A            QTYORD      7P Ø    TEXT('Quantity Ordered')
ØØØ5 A          K PART
ØØØ6 A          K CUST
```

Figure 11.13: DDS for the order history file.

Assuming four records are written to the file—two for part number 100 and two for part number 200—the data in the file appears as listed in Table 11.27. RPG can process this file by its access path (in order according to the file's key fields) or sequentially (by the way the records are physically arranged).

Figure 11.14 shows how the file ORDHIST is declared in a program. The file is declared as an input, full-procedural, externally described, keyed file.

Table 11.27: Order History File with Four Records		
PART	CUST	QTYORD
100	1207	50
100	5340	1000
200	5381	65
200	5382	30

```
.....FFileName++IFEASFRlen+LKeylnKFDevice+.Functions++++++++++++++++++++++++++++
0001 FORDHIST    IF   E          K DISK
0002 FREPORT     O    E            PRINTER OFLIND(*INOV)

.....DName++++++++++++EUDS.......Length+TDc.Functions++++++++++++++++++++++++++++
0003 D EoKey            S            1A   INZ(*OFF)
0004 D EoFile           S            1A   INZ(*OFF)

     ***********************************
     *  Print each part number and the  *
     *  customers that have ordered it. *
     ***********************************

.....CSRn01Factor1+++++++OpCode(ex)Factor2+++++++Result++++++++Len++DcHiLoEq....
0005 C      PART#        KLIST
0006 C                   KFLD                     PART
0007 C                   DOU       EoFile = *ON
0008 C                   READ      ORDHIST                            58
0009 C                   EVAL      EoKey = *IN58
0010 C                   DOW       EoKey = *OFF
0011 C                   EXCEPT    DETAIL
0012 C      PART#        READE     ORDHIST                            58
0013 C                   EVAL      EoKey = *IN58
0014 C                   ENDDO
0015 C      PART#        SETGT     ORDHIST                       54
0016 C                   EVAL      EoFile = *IN54
0017 C                   ENDDO

.....OFormat++++DAddn01n02n03Except++++SpbSpaSkbSka..........................
0018 OREPORT    E            DETAIL         1

.....O.............n01n02n03Field+++++++++YB?End++PConstant/Editword+++++++++++
0019 O                       PART            +   1
0020 O                       CUST            +   1
0021 O                       QTYORD     Z    +   1
```

Figure 11.14: Processing by access path with a key list.

In Figure 11.14, the key list PART# is used to access the file ORDHIST. The key list consists of a single key field (PART). Because only one key field is specified for the key list PART#, only the first key field of the access path is referenced.

The READE operation (line 12) is used to access the file with the key list. Each time the READE operation is performed, the next record in the file where the key matches the value of the key list PART# is read. When no more keys match the key list value, resulting indicator 3 (indicator 58) is set on.

When a CHAIN operation is used with a partial key list, the first record in the file that matches the key list is returned to the program. For example, if the key list field PART equals 200, record 3 of the order history file (from Table 11.27) is retrieved.

Fields of a key list correspond to the key fields of an access path. For example, the order history file consists of two key fields: PART and CUST. A key list consisting of two key fields would correspond to those two access path key fields specified in the DDS for the file. Figure 11.15 contains the related DDS, RPG key list, and RPG file specifications.

Key field specification excerpt from the DDS of the ORDHIST file:
```
.....AanØ1nØ2nØ3R.Format++++.Len++TDPURowColKeywords++++++++++++++++++++
     A           K PART
     A           K CUST
```

Declaration of the ORDHIST file as a keyed file in the file specification:
```
.....FFileName++IFEASFRlen+LKeylnKFDevice+.Functions+++++++++++++++++++++++++++++
     FOrdHist   IF   E         K DISK
```

Key list definition used to access records in ORDHIST by key:
```
.....CSRnØ1Factor1+++++++OpCode(ex)Factor2+++++++Result++++++++Len++DcHiLoEq....
     C      PRTCST       KLIST
     C                   KFLD                     PART
     C                   KFLD                     CUST
```

Use of the PRTCST key list to access the ORDHIST file in RPG:
```
.....CSRnØ1Factor1+++++++OpCode(ex)Factor2+++++++Result++++++++Len++DcHiLoEq....
     C      PRTCST       Chain     OrdRec                                71
```

Figure 11.15: Associated file access source code.

A key list can contain as many key fields as the access path. It also can contain fewer key fields than the access path. It cannot, however, contain more key fields than the access path. Key lists and key fields can be used for all indexed file processing. They are flexible, clear, and provide a consistent method for specifying access path (index) structures.

WORKSTATION DEVICE FILE PROCESSING

Workstations are display terminals, CRTs, video display stations, or personal computers. The keyboard is the means through which we typically interact with a computer. Workstations come in two varieties: intelligent and dumb. Dumb workstations are the original workstations for RPG programs.

The IBM 5250 family of workstations is considered to have *dumb terminals*. The contemporary name is *nonprogrammable terminals* or NPT. Intelligent workstations are *personal computers* or PCs. When RPG programs are run from intelligent workstations, those workstations are normally PCs emulating a dumb terminal. Hence, the intelligence isn't being utilized.

RPG supports workstation display devices through the WORKSTN device file. Workstation device files can be defined to the RPG program as an input, output, or combined file on the file specification. Table 11.28 lists the RPG operation codes that can be used with workstation files.

Table 11.28: Workstation Device File Operations	
Op Code	Description
ACQ	Acquire a device.
CHAIN	Random access of subfile records.
CLOSE	Close file.
EXFMT	Write and then read a workstation device.
OPEN	Open file.
POST	Retrieve workstation device information into a data structure.
READC	Read next changed subfile record.
REL	Release an acquired device.
UPDATE	Update subfile record.
WRITE	Write workstation file format (including a subfile record format).

In Examples 11.1 through 11.8, each workstation operation code is shown as it relates to workstation device files. The RPG source code listed in the figures contains only that which is necessary to illustrate the operation code. Complete and fully functional programs are not featured.

> **NOTE:**   *ACQ and REL operations seldom are used in modern RPG programs and aren't covered in this section.*

CHAIN (RANDOM FILE ACCESS)

In Example 11.1, the file CUSTINQ is defined on line 1 as a combined, full-procedural, workstation file. The SFILE keyword defines the DISPLIST subfile and assigns the RRN field as the relative record number field used when processing this subfile. Lines 2 to 9 fill the subfile with information from a database file. Line 10 uses the CHAIN operation to randomly access the fifth subfile record. If the record exists, data is returned to the program. If the record does not exist, resulting indicator 1 (indicator 71) is set on.

Example 11.1: Random access of a subfile record.

```
.....FFileName++IFEASFRlen+LKeylnKFDevice+.Functions++++++++++++++++++++++++++++++
0001 FCUSTINQ   CF   E              WORKSTN SFILE(DISPLIST : RRN)

     C*                   .
     C*                   .
     C*                   .

.....CSRn01Factor1+++++++OpCode(ex)Factor2+++++++Result++++++++Len++DcHiLoEq....
0002 C                    READ      CUSTMAST                          58
0003 C                    EVAL      EoFile = *IN58

0004 C                    DOW       EoFile = *OFF and Count < 6
0005 C                    ADD       1            RRN              3 0
0006 C                    WRITE     DISPLIST
0007 C                    READ      CUSTMAST                          58
0008 C                    EVAL      EoFile = *IN58
0009 C                    ENDDO
     C*                   .
     C*                   .
     C*                   .
0010 C        5           CHAIN     DISPLIST                          71
```

OPEN AND CLOSE (OPEN AND CLOSE A FILE)

In Example 11.2, the HELPTEXT file is defined on line 1 as a combined, full-procedural, workstation file. Also, the file HELPTEXT is a user-controlled file open. The USROPN keyword indicates that the file is opened by the program code (not by the RPG cycle). The USROPN isn't required for the OPEN or CLOSE operations to be used on a file after the file is opened by RPG. Therefore, when a file is opened by RPG (i.e., the USROPN keyword is not specified) and then closed with the CLOSE operation, the OPEN operation should successfully open the file.

Line 2 opens the file HELPTEXT. Line 6 closes the file HELPTEXT.

Example 11.2: Open and close a workstation file.

```
.....FFileName++IFEASFRlen+LKeyInKFDevice+.Functions+++++++++++++++++++++++++++++
0001 FHELPTEXT  CF    E              WORKSTN USROPN

.....CSRn01Factor1+++++++OpCode(ex)Factor2+++++++Result++++++++Len++DcHiLoEq....
0002 C                   OPEN        HELPTEXT                        73
0003 C                   EVAL        IOError = *IN73
0004 C                   IF          NOT (IOError)
0005 C                   EXFMT       HELPRECD
     C                     .
     C                     .
     C                     .
0006 C                   CLOSE       HELPTEXT
0007 C                   ENDIF
```

Remember, if the OPEN operation attempts to open a file that has already been opened, an error occurs. Resulting indicator 2, if it is specified, is set on. If the CLOSE operation attempts to close a file that is already closed, an error occurs. Resulting indicator 2, if it is specified, is set on. *ALL can be specified for factor 2. When *ALL is specified, all open files are closed by the operation.

EXFMT (WRITE THEN READ WORKSTATION DEVICE)

The EXFMT operation performs the functional equivalent of a WRITE operation followed immediately by a READ operation. This operation can be used with a device (i.e., nondatabase) file only. Example 11.3 illustrates the use of the EXFMT operation.

Example 11.3: Retrieve and display a database record.

```
.....FFileName++IFEASFRlen+LKeyInKFDevice+.Functions+++++++++++++++++++++++++++++
0001 FCUSTINQ   CF    E              WORKSTN
0002 FCUSTMAST  IF    E            K DISK

.....CSRn01Factor1+++++++OpCode(ex)Factor2+++++++Result++++++++Len++DcHiLoEq....
0003 C     INDEX         CHAIN       CustRec                         71
0004 C                   EVAL        NotFound = *IN71
0005 C                   IF          NotFound = *OFF

0006 C                   EXFMT       DSPCUST                         73

0007 C                   ENDIF
```

In Example 11.3, a record from the CUSTMAST database file (line 2) is retrieved (line 3). The workstation file CUSTINQ (line 1) is written to and read from with the EXFMT (line 6). The DSPCUST workstation file format is used in factor 2 of the EXFMT operation.

When several workstation file formats are needed on the display, the additional formats must be written with the WRITE operation. The final format (the one after which an input operation is required) can be written to the workstation file with the EXFMT operation. This effectively performs a WRITE followed by a READ.

POST (POST DEVICE SPECIFIC INFORMATION)

In Example 11.4, the Program Status Data Structure (PSDS), defined on lines 2 and 3, is used by the POST operation (line 7) to write device-dependent feedback information to the information data structure (WSDS on lines 4 to 6) for the CUSTINQ workstation file. The WSID subfield (lines 3 and 7) contains the name of the device that is being used to run the RPG program.

The DISPMODE field contains a special code that indicates whether the display is capable of displaying 132 characters. When DISPMODE equals hexadecimal '17' the display device supports 132 characters.

Example 11.4: POST status information to the INFDS.

```
.....FFileName++IFEASFRlen+LKeylnKFDevice+.Functions++++++++++++++++++++++++++++++
0001 FCUSTINQ   CF   E              WORKSTN Infds(wsds)

.....DName++++++++++EUDSFrom+++To+++++TDc.Functions++++++++++++++++++++++++++++++
0002 D PSDS          SDS
0003 D   wsid                  244    253A

0004 D Wsds          DS
0005 D   Status           *STATUS
0006 D   DispMode             252    252A

.....CSRn01Factor1+++++++OpCode(ex)Factor2+++++++Result++++++++Len++DcHiLoEq....
       *  POST the workstation device information to the DS
0007 C      WSID          POST      CUSTINQ                              73

       *  Test for a device that supports 132-columns
0008 C                    If        DispMode = X'17' and (*IN73 = *OFF)
0009 C                    z-add     132         SIZE              3 0
0010 C                    else
0011 C                    z-add     80          SIZE
0012 C                    EndIf

0013 C                    select
0014 C                    When      Size = 132
0015 C                    ExFmt     PANEL4
0016 C                    When      Size = 80
0017 C                    ExFmt     PANEL3
0018 C                    endSL
```

READ (READ A RECORD FROM A FILE)

In Example 11.5, the workstation file format or panel, PANEL1, is written to the workstation file (line 2). The READ operation on line 3 reads the format PANEL1. The READ operation waits for the user to respond to the panel by pressing the Enter key or a function key.

Two workstation file formats are written to the workstation file on lines 4 and 5. Line 6 uses the EXFMT operation to write and then read a third panel, PANEL3. These read operations wait for a user response (pressing of the Enter key or a function key). In other words, the EXFMT operation waits for the user to respond. When a response is detected, the PANLE3 input is returned to the program. Subsequent READ operations, however, are required to return the input data from the other panels.

After the user responds, other panels currently active in the workstation file are read (lines 7 and 8). These READ operations don't wait for a user response because the READ operation (the EXFMT operation on line 6) releases all workstation formats.

Line 9 writes the format PANEL3. The CUSTINQ file itself is read by the READ operation on line 10. This technique causes the workstation file to timeout after an inactivity threshold has been reached. The MAXDEV keyword (line 1) indicates that the device can be "invited," thus allowing this timeout technique to be used.

Example 11.5: READ a workstation device file.

```
.....FFileName++IFEASFRlen+LKeylnKFDevice+.Functions++++++++++++++++++++++++++++
0001 FCUSTINQ   CF   E            WORKSTN MAXDEV(*ONLY)

.....CSRn01Factor1+++++++OpCode(ex)Factor2+++++++Result++++++++Len++DcHiLoEq....
0002 C                   WRITE     PANEL1
0003 C                   READ      PANEL1                              75
     *    This routine writes, then reads three
     *    workstation file formats.
0004 C                   WRITE     PANEL1
0005 C                   WRITE     PANEL2
0006 C                   EXFMT     PANEL3
0007 C                   READ      PANEL1                              75
0008 C                   READ      PANEL2                              75
     *    This routine writes the PANEL3 format,
     *    then reads the workstation file. If the
     *    workstation time-out threshold is reached,
     *    resulting indicator 2 is set on.
0009 C                   WRITE     PANEL3
0010 C                   READ      CUSTINQ                           7375
```

READC (READ NEXT CHANGED SUBFILE RECORD)

In Example 11.6, line 2 uses the EXFMT operation to write and then read the subfile control record SFLCTL. When the subfile control record is written to the workstation file, the subfile detail records also are written.

The READC operation (line 4) reads each record of the subfile that has been modified. Technically, each record that has the *modify data tag* set on is returned with the READC operation. The modify data tag is a 5250 data-stream flag that is switched on when the workstation user types data into a field that is displayed on the workstation.

The subfile relative record number field RRN is updated with the relative record number of the subfile record just processed by the READC operation.

Example 11.6: Read next changed subfile record.

```
.....FFileName++IFEASFRlen+LKeylnKFDevice+.Functions++++++++++++++++++++++++++++++
0001 FCustInq    CF   E               WORKSTN SFile(DispList : RRN)

.....CSRn01Factor1+++++++OpCode(ex)Factor2+++++++Result++++++++Len++DcHiLoEq....
0002 C                       EXFMT     SFLCTL

0003 C                       Dou       EndOfSFL = *ON
0004 C                       ReadC     DispList                              75
0005 C                       Eval      EndOfSFL = *IN75
0006 C         OPTION        casEQ     '1'           Select
0007 C         OPTION        casEQ     '9'           Delete
0008 C                       endcs
0009 C                       endDo
```

UPDATE (UPDATE A RECORD)

In Example 11.7, the subfile DISPLIST is read with the READC operation (lines 4 and 11). The subfile records are processed (lines 6 to 8), and then the subfile record is updated with the UPDATE operation (line 9). The logic of this example is as follows:

1. Display the subfile control record and the subfile.

2. Read the first changed subfile record.

3. If there are changed records, process the first record.

4. Update the record (line 9).

5. Read the next changed subfile record (line 10).

6. Branch to the top of the DO loop (line 12 branch to line 5).

Example 11.7: Update subfile record.

```
.....FFileName++IFEASFRlen+LKeylnKFDevice+.Functions+++++++++++++++++++++++++++++
0001 FCUSTINQ   CF    E              WORKSTN SFile(DispList : rrn)

.....CSRn01Factor1+++++++OpCode(ex)Factor2+++++++Result++++++++Len++DcHiLoEq....
0002 C                    EXFMT      SFLCTL

0003 C                    ReadC      DispList                               75
0004 C                    Eval       EndOfSFL = *IN75

0005 C                    Dow        EndOfSFL = *OFF
0006 C      Option        casEQ      '1'          Select
0007 C      Option        casEQ      '9'          Delete
0008 C                    ENDcs

0009 C                    Update     DispList

0010 C                    ReadC      DispList                               75
0011 C                    Eval       EndOfSFL = *IN75
0012 C                    endDo
```

WRITE (WRITE A RECORD)

In Example 11.8, the subfile DISPLIST is activated and initialized when the SFLCTL subfile control-record format is written (line 5). The database file CUSTMAST is initially read (line 6). The data from the file CUSTMAST is written to the DISPLIST subfile (line 10) after the subfile record number (RRN) is incremented (line 9). The next CUSTMAST database record is read (line 11) and the DO loop branches to the top of the loop, increments the RRN field, and writes the next subfile record (line 10).

The workstation format HEADING is written (line 16), and then the subfile control record and subfile are sent to, and read from, the workstation (line 17).

Example 11.8: Write a workstation subfile record.

```
.....FFileName++IFEASFRlen+LKeylnKFDevice+.Functions++++++++++++++++++++++++++++
0001 FCUSTINQ   CF   E              WORKSTN SFile(DispList : rrn)
0002 FCUSTMAST  IF   E            K DISK

.....CSRn01Factor1+++++++OpCode(ex)Factor2+++++++Result++++++++Len++DcHiLoEq....
0003 C     ACCT          KLIST
0004 C                   KFLD                     CSTNBR

0005 C                   write     SFLCTL
0006 C     ACCT          Chain     CustRec                          71
0007 C                   Eval      EOF = *IN71

0008 C                   dow       EOF = *OFF
0009 C                   add       1              RRN          5 0

0010 C                   write     DISPLIST
0011 C     ACCT          ReadE     CustRec                          75
0012 C                   eval      EOF = *IN75
0013 C                   endDo

0014 C                   If        RRN > 0
0015 C                   eval      *IN21 = *ON
0016 C                   write     Heading
0017 C                   exfmt     SFLCTL
0018 C                   endIf
```

Chapter 12

ALTERNATE SYNTAX OPTIONS

The RPG IV language accepts operation codes on its calculation specifications, but there are actually three distinct syntax structures for calculation specifications. The first structure is the traditional fixed-format syntax that has been a part of RPG since it was first introduced. Fixed format syntax is still supported in RPG IV. The second format is the enhanced or alternate calculation specification that supports what is called the Extended factor 2. The extended factor 2 allows natural expressions to be performed. The first structure is free-format syntax. In Free-format syntax only natural expressions are supported and the entry of the natural expressions is permitted from position 8 through 80 of the source line.

FIXED-FORMAT CALCULATION SPECIFICATIONS

Traditional fixed-format calculations are the most widely used form of statement. This is due primarily to the legacy of RPG and its original fixed-format only coding. Today, RPG IV programmers primarily use a combination of the traditional fixed-format specifications along with the enhanced specifications.

Figure 12.1 contains an example of using the traditional fixed-format calculation specifications.

```
.....CSRn01Factor1+++++++OpCode(ex)Factor2+++++++Result++++++++Len++DcHiLoEq
0001 C     CustNo        Chain     CustRec                              71
0002 C     *IN71         ifeq      *OFF
0003 C                   Add       1              Visits
0004 C                   Update    CustRec
0005 C                   endif
```

Figure 12.1: Traditional fixed-format calculations.

In Figure 12.1, line 1 illustrates the CHAIN operation code, which is the common file access method used in RPG programs. Line 2 uses the deprecated IFEQ operation code to check for a record found condition. If the CHAIN operation is successful, *IN71 will be equal to *OFF, otherwise if the record is not found *IN71 will be equal to *ON. Line 3 increments the field named VISITS which is a field in the customer master file. And finally, on Line 4, the customer master file record CUSTREC is updated; all the fields of the file are rewritten to the database.

ENHANCED-FORMAT CALCULATION SPECIFICATIONS

Enhanced-format calculation specifications have been available since RPG IV was introduced. This style specification is the most popular for new applications and for maintenance (i.e., program changes) to existing applications. This style can be easier to use and may provide a level of productivity far beyond that of the traditional fixed-format specification. Figure 12.2 contains an example use of the enhanced-format specifications.

```
.....CSRn01Factor1+++++++OpCode(ex)Factor2+++++++Result++++++++
0001 C        CustNo       Chain      CustRec
0002 C                     if         %Found
0003 C                     Eval       Visits = Visits + 1
0004 C                     Update     CustRec
0005 C                     endif
```

Figure 12.2: Enhanced/alternative format calculations

In Figure 12.2, line one accesses the Customer master file using the traditional CHAIN operation; however no resulting indicators are used. Instead, line 2 uses the %FOUND built-in function to test the result of the CHAIN operation. This built-in function equates to *ON if the CHAIN operation is successful, otherwise it is set to *OFF. Line 3 performs the arithmetic add operation, replacing the ADD operation code. Then, on line 4 the update operation is performed; all the fields of the customer master file are rewritten to the database.

FREE-FORMAT CALCULATION SPECIFICATIONS

The free-format specifications are a contemporary feature to the RPG language. They provide a syntax that is relaxed compared to traditional RPG.

Free-format specifications allow RPG operations to be specified in positions 8 through 80 of the source line. Free format statements may extend across multiple lines, if necessary. All RPG statements must be terminated with a semicolon (;). The letter "C", normally specified in position 6 of RPG calculation statements, is not specified on free format statements. Positions 6 and 7 must be blank in free format syntax. Traditional comments (an asterisk in column 7) are not allowed in free format syntax.

Free-format operations must be specified between a /FREE and /END-FREE compiler directive. These directives must appear on a line by themselves. This allows the compiler to process all traditional RPG specifications normally, while also supporting free-format statements as needed.

Figure 12.3 illustrates an example of the free-format specifications. Note that the code is the same as in the example listed in Figure 12.2, but has been reformatted to the free-format syntax.

```
.....C/FREE++++++++++++++++++++++++++++++++++++++++++++++++++++++++++
      C/Free
0001      Chain  CustNo CustRec;
0002      If     %Found();
0003      Visits += 1;
0004      Update CustRec  %Fields(Visits);
0005      endif;
      C/End-Free
```

Figure 12.3: Free-format calculations

Line 1, in Figure 12.3 performs a CHAIN operation to the customer master file. Note the arrangements of the file name and key field. This illustrates how all operation codes are altered for free-format, that is the opcodes name appears first, followed by factor 1 (if necessary), followed by factor 2 (if necessary), and the result field (if necessary). Should any factor or the result field be unnecessary, it is omitted. In addition, the semi-colon must be specified at the end of all free-format RPG statements. This includes all operation codes as well as the ELSE, OTHER and ENDxx operations.

Free-Format Operation Code Syntax

Operation code syntax on free-format specification is substantially different from traditional fixed-format syntax. The following diagram illustrates the difference in syntax between these two specifications.

Traditional Syntax	Factor 1	OpCode	Factor 2	Result
Free format Syntax	OpCode	Factor 1	Factor 2	Result ;

Free format syntax requires a terminating semicolon at the end of all free format RPG IV statements. If a semicolon is not specified, a compile error will occur. The semicolon is required at the end of all operation code statements.

```
.....CSRn01Factor1+++++++OpCode(ex)Factor2+++++++Result++++++++
    C     CustNo      Chain     CustRec

....../FREE++++++++++++++++++++++++++++++++++++++++++++++++++++++
      Chain  CustNo CustRec;
```

Not all operation codes may be used in free-format. Most notably are the MOVEL and MOVE, and there is no direct replacement for them in free-format. Although the EVAL and EVALR operations do most of the function of MOVEL and MOVE respectively, they are not equivalent functions. Therefore a direct translation is not always available. If factor 2 and the result field of the MOVEL operation are the same datatype and length, then EVAL and MOVEL are equivalent. Likewise, if factor 2 and the result of the MOVE operation are the same length, then EVALR and MOVE are equivalent.

The primary difference between MOVEL and EVAL is that MOVEL is effectively a substring-like function. That is, if factor 2 is shorter than the result filed, the number of bytes replaced in the result field is equal to the length of factor 2. Whereas EVAL is an assignment operation, consequently EVAL replaces the contents of the target field. The MOVEL(P) operation using the pad operation extender is equivalent to the EVAL operation.

Myriad Math Syntax Options

Contemporary RPG IV contains a number of syntaxes to perform simple math. Originally, the ADD, SUB, MULT, DIV, and SQRT operation codes were used to do arithmetic. Today, the EVAL operation can be used along with expressions to perform any mathematical formula. In addition, free-format syntax allows assignment statements (i.e., the EVAL operation) to be used with or without the EVAL operation code named. That is, the EVAL operation code name is optional on the free format specification. The following two statements are equivalent free-format syntax mathematical operations:

```
.....C/FREE++++++++++++++++++++++++++++++++++++++++++++++++++++++++
      /Free
0001            Eval  C = A + B;
0002            C = A + B;
      /End-free
```

There are several syntaxes that may be used to perform math. In fact, there are no less than eight methods that may be used to add one value to another giving a result. The eight RPG IV statements in figure 12.4 perform identical functions; they add X to Y giving X.

```
.....CSRn01Factor1+++++++OpCode(ex)Factor2+++++++Result++++++++
0001 C        X         Add        Y             X
0002 C                  Add        Y             X
0003 C                  Eval       X = X + Y
0004 C                  Eval       X + = Y
```

```
.....C/FREE+++++++++++++++++++++++++++++++++++++++++++++++++++++++++
      /Free
0005           Eval  X = X + Y;
0006           Eval  X += Y;

0007           X = X + Y;
0008           X += Y;
      /End-free
```

Figure 12.4: Adding X to Y

The /FREE and /END-FREE statements are required to start and end free-format syntax and are not strictly counted as program statements. Lines 5 and 6 are the same as lines 7 and 8 respectively; note that the EVAL operation code has been omitted from lines 7 and 8.

Commenting RPG IV Source Code

Traditional comments in RPG appeared on lines that contain an asterisk in position 7 of the source line. Figure 12.5 illustrates traditional comments.

```
.....CSRn01Factor1+++++++OpCode(ex)Factor2+++++++Result++++++++
        *   Retrieve the customer record. If found, increment
        *   the customer's visit counter and update the record.
0001 C       CustNo        Chain     CustRec
0002 C                     if        %Found
0003 C                     Eval      Visits = Visits + 1
0004 C                     Update    CustRec
0005 C                     endif
```

Figure 12.5: Traditional commants

The first two lines of the source in Figure 12.5 are comments. The asterisk in position 7 causes the compiler to ignore the entire line.

With free-format RPG, an alternate comment syntax is provided that allows comments to be intermixed with the actual statements themselves.

```
.....C/FREE+++++++++++++++++++++++++++++++++++++++++++++++++++++++++
      C/Free
               // Retrieve the customer record.
0001      Chain  CustNo CustRec;
0002      If     %Found();
0003      Visits  += 1;  // Increment visits
               // Update the customer file
0004      Update  CustRec  %Fields(Visits);
0005      endif;
      C/End-Free
```

Figure 12.6: Free-format comments

In Figure 12.6 three comment statements are embedded within the source code. Note the double forward slash (//), that indicates the beginning of a comment. When // is detected, the compiler ignores the rest of the physical line on which the // appears. An example of combination statement and comment line appears on line 3 of Figure 12.6.

The alternate syntax for comments may be used within /FREE and /END-FREE statements and in place of traditional comments. Figure 12.7 illustrates using the alternate style comments with traditional RPG statements.

```
.....CSRnØ1Factor1+++++++OpCode(ex)Factor2+++++++Result++++++++
                 // Retrieve the customer recordd.
ØØØ1 C       CustNo       Chain      CustRec
ØØØ2 C                    if         %Found
               // If it is an existing customer
               // increment the Visits field
ØØØ3 C                    Eval       Visits = Visits + 1
               // then update the file
ØØØ4 C                    Update     CustRec
ØØØ5 C                    endif
```

Figure 12.7: Traditional syntax RPG with alternate comment syntax

Note that the appearance of the // symbols may occur at any point on the line. Unlike free format syntax, however, when // comments are intermixed with traditional RPG calculation specifications, they must appear on a line by themselves.

Addressing Data Structures and Arrays

Data structures and arrays have different syntax grammars when they are addressed by traditional RPG calculation specifications. The enhanced and free-format RPG syntax however supports a unified data structure and array syntax. This syntax is referred to as "data structures as arrays" or the simpler "array data structures." Figure 12.8 illustrates using data structures as arrays with the enhanced syntax.

```
.....DName+++++++++++EUDSFrom+++To+++++TDc.Functions++++++++++++++++++++
ØØØ1 D myStruct      DS                      Dim(3Ø) QUALIFIED
ØØØ2 D   ItemNo                       5I Ø
ØØØ3 D   ItemPrice                    7P 2
ØØØ4 D   Desc                        2ØA

ØØØ5 D Prices        S                       Dim(3Ø) Like(myStruct.Price)
ØØØ6 D i             S               1ØI Ø

ØØØ7 C                    for        i = 1 to %elem(myStruct)
ØØØ8 C                    eval       Prices(i) += myStruct(i).ItemPrice
ØØØ9 C                    endfor
```

Figure 12.8: Array and data structure syntax in enhanced calculation syntax

Figure 12.9 illustrates the same source code rewritten using free-format syntax.

```
.....DName++++++++++++EUDSFrom+++To+++++TDc.Functions++++++++++++++
0001 D myStruct        DS                      Dim(30) QUALIFIED
0002 D  ItemNo                         5I 0
0003 D  ItemPrice                      7P 2
0004 D  Desc                          20A

0005 D Prices          S                       Dim(30) Like(myStruct.Price)
0006 D i               S               10I 0
     /FREE
0007      For i = 1 to %elem(myStruct);
0008          Prices(i) += myStruct(i).ItemPrice;
0009      endfor;
     /END-FREE
```

Figure 12.9: Array and Data Structure Syntax in Free Format Syntax

In the examples in Figures 12.8 and 12.9 the data structure myStruct is a multiple occurrence data structure. In this syntax, however, these types of data structures are referred to as data structure arrays and may contain an array index in places the complex OCCURS operation. The DIM keyword (line 1) declares the number of elements for the data structure array named myStruct. When the DIM keyword is used, the data structure may be used within the RPG source member like an array. The SORTA and MOVEA operations may not be used with data structure arrays. In addition, only qualified data structures may be declared as an array. To declare a qualified data structure the QUALIFIED keyword is use. In addition, the LIKEDS or LIKEREC keywords may be used; with these keywords, the QUALIFIED keyword is implied.

To access individual elements of a data structure array or regular array, parentheses are used (see line 8 in Figure 12.8 or 12.9). Within the parentheses a literal, named constant, field name, or procedure that returns a numeric value or a mathematical expression may be specified.

Date and Time Data Type Usage

Manipulating date, time, or timestamp variables, referred to collectively as "date" value in free-format syntax is somewhat different from traditional fixed-format calculations. The arithmetic date operators are replaced by the + and – symbols. In addition, the duration codes have been replaced in free-format with built-in functions of a similar name.

Table 12.1 summarizes the differences between traditional fixed-format calculation specification date manipulation and free-format syntax.

Table 12.1: Date, Time, and Timestamp Differences in Free-form vs. Fixed format	
Fixed-format Operation	Free-format Syntax
ADDDUR and SUBDUR – Add or subtract a duration. (Add a period of time to a date.)	+ or – symbols along with the %YEARS, %MONTHS, %DAYS, %HOURS, %MINUTES, %SECONDS, and %MSECONDS built-in functions. e.g., StartTime = StartTime + %Hours(HRSWRK)
SUBDUR – Subtract two date values. (Find the difference between two dates.)	%DIFF built-in function. e.g., nHoursWorked = %DIFF(nClockIn : nClockOut : *HOURS)
EXTRCT – Extract a component of a date.	%SUBDT built-in function. e.g., nDayofMonth = %SUBDT(InvDate : *DAYS)
TEST – Checking a variable for a valid date value.	TEST opcode e.g., TEST(DE) *YMD ORDDTE // check non-date for date TEST(E) INVDATE // check date variable for valid date
Duration codes	Whenever a duration is needed, one of the duration code built-in functions may be used, including: %YEARS, %MONTHS, %DAYS, %HOURS, %MINUTES, %SECONDS, and %MSECONDS built-in functions.
MOVE – Move a date value to a non-date value, or move a non-date value to a date value.	The built-in functions %DATE, %TIME, and %TIMESTAMP may be used to copy a non-date value to a date field. The %CHAR built-in function may be used to copy a date, time or timestamp value to a non-date field.

The bottom line is that date, time, and timestamp variables are manipulated with built-in functions when used in free-format syntax, and with operation codes when used with traditional syntax. Figure 12.10 illustrates the use of many of the date built-in functions.

```
.....DName++++++++++EUDS.......Length+TDc.Functions++++++++++++++++++
     D DueDate         S               D
     D DueDte          S               6S 0
     D InvDate         S               D    INZ(D'2003-03-15')
     D Today           S               D    Inz(*SYS)
     D nDayOfMonth     S               5I 0
     D nDays           S               5I 0
      /FREE
0001    Test(DE) *YMD DueDte;
0002    if NOT %Error;
0003      DueDate = %Date(DueDte : *YMD);
0004      nDayofMonth  = %SUBDT(DueDate : *DAYS);
```

```
0005    endif;

0006    nDays = %DIFF(Today : DueDate : *DAYS);
0007    if (nDays > 30);
0008      DueDate = InvDate + %Month(1);
0009      DueDte  = %Char(DueDate : *YMD);
0010    endif;
      /END-FREE
```

Figure 12.10: Date Manipulation using free-format syntax.

In Figure 12.10, free-format line 1 uses the TEST operation to check the non-date field named DUEDTE field for a valid date value. If the date is valid, the %DATE built-in function is used to convert the non-date value to the real date field named DUEDATE. Then the day of the month is extracted from the DUEDATE field (line 4) and assigned to the nDayofMonth field.

On line 6 the number of days between the TODAY and DUEDATE fields is calculated using the %DIFF built-in function. On line 7 the number of days is compared to 30, and if greater than 30, one month is added to the value in the INVDATE field and the result is assigned to the DUEDATE field..

On line 9, the 6-digit zoned numeric field named DUEDTE is assigned the date value currently stored in the DUEDATE field. The format of the date value in copied to DUEDTE is set to YMD (year, month, day) by the %CHAR built-in function.

Retrieving Date Values at Runtime

The TIME operation code is traditionally used to retrieve the current system date, time, or timestamp value at runtime. TIME is not supported in free-format syntax. In place of the time operation, the %DATE, %TIME, and %TIMESTAMP built-in functions may be used.

Normally these built-in functions are used to convert a non-date, time or timestamp values into real date, time, or timestamp values. When used without a parameter, they return the current system date, time, or timestamp value.

```
.....DName++++++++++EUDS.......Length+TDc.Functions+++++++++
      D Yesterday       S              D
      D Today           S              D
      D Tomorrow        S              D
      D RightNow        S              T
      D DTS             S              Z
       /FREE
0001      dts = %Timestamp();
0002      rightNow = %Time();
0003      yesterday = %Date() - %days(1);
0004      today = %Date();
0005      Tomorrow = %Date() + %days(1);
       /End-Free
```

Figure 12.11: Using %DATE, %TIME, and %TIMESTAMP

On line 1 in Figure 12.11, the current system date and timestamp is assigned to the DTS field. On line 2 the current system time is assigned to the RIGHTNOW field. Then on lines 3, 4, and 5, the fields YESTERDAY, TODAY, and TOMORROW are assigned corresponding date values.

```
.....FFileName++IFEASFRlen+LKeylnKFDevice+.Functions++++++++++++++
      FDSPCUST    CF   E              WORKSTN SFILE(CUSTLIST : RRN)
      FCUSTMAST   IF   E          K DISK

       /COPY FKEYS

.....C*Rn01..............OpCode(ex)Extended-factor2++++++++++
      C                    EVAL      *INLR = *ON
      C                    EXFMT     PROMPT
      C                    if        FKEY = F3
      C                    RETURN
      C                    endif
      C         CUSTNO     SetLL     CustMast
      C                    if        %FOUND
      C                    Read      CustRec
      C                    DOW       NOT %EOF
      C                    Add       1                   RRN
      C                    Write     CUSTLIST
      C         CUSTNO     ReadE     CustRec
      C                    enddo
      C                    endif
```

Figure 12.12: Traditional RPG IV code to fill a subfile.

Figure 12.12 illustrates a traditional RPG IV routine to fill up a subfile with records from a database file.

Listed in Figure 12.13 is the identical routine rewritten in RPG IV free-format syntax.

```
.....FFileName++IFEASFRlen+LKeylnKFDevice+.Functions++++++++++++++
    FDSPCUST   CF    E                WORKSTN SFILE(CUSTLIST : RRN)
    FCUSTMAST  IF    E            K DISK

     /COPY FKEYS

     /FREE
         *INLR = *ON;
         Exfmt  Prompt;
         If       FKey = F3;
           return;
         endif;
         Setll  CustNo  CustMast;
         if      %Found();
           Read    CustRec
           dow     NOT %eof();
             rrn   += 1;
             Write CustList;
             ReadE  CustNo CustRec;
           enddo;
         endif;
     /End-Free
```

Figure 12.13: Fixed-format RPG IV code to fill a subfile.

Alternative Syntax Summary

The free-format syntax of RPG IV provides more room on each line for expressions. Programmer habits may or may not lead to more readable code when using either syntax. One disadvantage of the free-format syntax is that none of the RPG editors on the market today support prompting of free-format syntax statements. Most editors do, however, allow traditional syntax RPG to be translated to free-format syntax through a keyboard macro. None of these editors, however, provides the ability to convert free-format RPG syntax statements back into traditional syntax.

There are several basic issues that may arise as a result of using free-format syntax for the first time. The following list may be helpful to those who have never used a noncolumnar language.

- Always include a semicolon at the end of every RPG IV free-format statements. This includes conditional statements as well as all other statements, such as assignments and looping. Never include a semicolon at the end of traditional syntax RPG IV statements.

- Start all RPG IV free-format statement groups with the /FREE compiler directive and end them with an /END-FREE compiler directive.

- Embedded SQL statements may not be embedded between /FREE and /END-FREE statements.

- The CALLP and EVAL operation codes are optional when used with free-format syntax. If unspecified, they are implied.

- Parentheses are optional when used on parameterless built-in functions and procedure calls. However, it is highly recommended to use empty parentheses in order to visually distinguish between variables and procedures.

Appendix A

COMPILER OPTIONS

There are two options for compiling RPG programs on the IBM AS/400 system. The first option involves a direct source-to-program process. The second option is a two-phase process that involves creating an intermediate *MODULE object, and then binding that object into a program. The normal approach for compilation of RPG IV programs is a two-phased process. This uses the CRTRPGMOD (Create RPG Module) and the CRTPGM (Create Bound Program) commands.

COMPILER CHOICES FOR RPG IV PROGRAMS

The CRTRPGMOD command syntax checks and compiles a single source file. The output is a *MODULE object. The CRTPGM command accepts one or more *MODULE objects and binds them into a single executable program.

The other approach to compiling RPG program is to use the CRTBNDRPG (Create Bound RPG Program) command. This command performs a source-to-program compilation of a single source file. The normal two-phase compile process is automated. The intermediate *MODULE object is deleted upon successful binding of the program. This appendix describes the CRTBNDRPG command parameters in detail.

The CRTBNDRPG Command

The CRTBNDRPG command performs a single source-file-to-program compilation. It checks the syntax source file for errors and, upon successful syntax checking, it generates a *MODULE object. The command automatically evokes the CRTPGM command upon successful *MODULE generation. After a successful bind, a *PGM is generated. This *PGM object can be called through the conventional program interfaces, such as the CL CALL command of the OS/400 operating system.

Note that the actual native AS/400 interface displays full-text descriptions for command parameters. These keywords are the CL command interface to the various parameters. For example, the CL command prompter displays "Program . . . . . ." for the program name parameter, but the keyword for this parameter is PGM. The keyword form of the parameter name is used in this appendix.

PGM (Program Name)

The name of the program and library of the program (*PGM) being created. The program name and library name must conform to AS/400 naming conventions. If no library is specified, the created program is stored in the current library.

*CTLSPEC The name of the program object is retrieved from the DFTNAME keyword of the header specification of the source file member.

program-name The name of the program object to create. The special value *CTLSPEC can be specified. When *CTLSPEC is specified, the program name is retrieved from the DFTNAME keyword of the header specification of the source file.

library-name The name of the library where the created program is stored. The special value *CURLIB can be specified. When *CURLIB is specified, the program is stored in the library assigned to the current library position in the job's library list. This library can be established with the CHGCURLIB or CHGLIBL commands.

SRCFILE (Source File Name)

Specify the name of the source file that contains the RPG IV source member being compiled. A fully qualified source file name can be specified. The default source file name is QRPGLESRC. Other names, such as QRPGSRC, also are used.

If a program-development environment is being used, such as Program Development Manager (PDM), the source file name is generally established based on the source file being worked with.

SRCMBR (Source File Member)

Specify the name of the member of the file specified on the SRCFILE parameter. The member name is where the RPG IV source code resides.

*PGM The special value *PGM can be specified. This indicates that the name of the source member is derived from the PGM parameter. If *PGM is specified and PGM(*CTLSPEC) is also specified, the generated program name is RPGPGM.

source-file-member-name Specify the name of the source file member containing the RPG IV source code to be compiled.

GENLVL (Generation Severity)

Specify the maximum error severity that is acceptable while still generating the program object. The program is created only when any errors generated are less than or equal to the generation severity.

10 Severity 10 creates programs when the error severity level is 10 or less. Severity 11 or higher messages cause the compile to fail.

severity-level-value Specify a severity between 0 and 20. In most cases the default of 10 is sufficient. In some situations, however, a severity of 20 is necessary. Severity higher than 20 with program creation is not supported under this version of the RPG IV compiler.

TEXT

Specify some descriptive text for the program being compiled. This text is embedded into the program object, and is visible through several system interfaces, such as DSPOBJD, WRKOBJ, DSPPGM, and PDM.

*SRCMBRTXT The special value *SRCMBRTXT can be specified to cause the text description for the program to be retrieved from the text description of the source-file member being compiled.

*BLANK Specify *BLANK when no text description should be embedded into the compiled program.

'description' Specify the text description that is embedded within the compiled program object. Up to 50 characters can be specified. The description is normally enclosed in single quotes (i.e., apostrophes). However, the apostrophes are not part of the text description.

DFTACTGRP (Default Activation Group)

Specify *YES for this option when the program must be run in the default activation group. The default activation group name is *DFTACTGRP. DFTACTGRP(*NO) is recommended for RPG IV programs that take advantage of procedures. Activation groups are an *integrated language environment* (ILE) construct and are beyond the scope of this appendix.

*YES Specify DFTACTGRP(*YES) to force the program to run in the default activation group. When DFTACTGRP(*YES) is specified, the ACTGRP parameter is ignored.

Specifying DFTACTGRP(*YES) causes the RPG IV program to behave like traditional RPG III program objects. The override scoping, open scoping, and resource use are the same as that of RPG III programs. This option allows programmers to plug-in replacements for legacy RPG III and RPG II applications with RPG IV without concern for the common runtime environment built around the newer AS/400 compilers.

Stand-alone RPG IV programs without procedure calls can typically use this option without impacting performance or runtime. There are several limitations in this configuration, however. These limitations may cause the experienced RPG IV programmer to choose DFTACTGRP(*NO). The following restrictions are placed on an RPG IV program when DFTACTGRP(*YES) is specified:

◆ ILE static binding is not available when a program is created with DFTACTGRP(*YES). This means the CALLB and CALLP operations are not supported.

◆ The BNDDIR parameter cannot be specified. Hence, binding directories are not supported.

◆ User-written functions, commonly known as procedures, cannot be used. Procedures are statically bound and, because static binding is not supported, procedures cannot be called.

DFTACTGRP(*YES) is useful when moving an application to the RPG IV environment. By using the CVTRPGSRC command to convert RPG III source code to its equivalent RPG IV source code, the CRTBNDRPG with DFTACTGRP(*YES) specified is one method to do a plug-in replacement of the original program.

*NO Specify DFTACTGRP(*NO) for most RPG IV compiles. When *NO is specified, the program runs in the activation group specified on the ACTGRP parameter.

DFTACTGRP(*NO) is useful when you intend to take advantage of advanced RPG IV features, such as procedure calls or ILE features such as named activation groups, calling service programs, or binding directories.

BNDDIR (Binding Directory)

Specify the name of one or more binding directories. These directories are used to locate *MODULE and *SRVPGM objects for binding with the compiled program. Several binding directory names can be specified.

*NONE Specify *NONE when no binding directories are needed.

binding-directory-name Specify the fully qualified name of one or more binding directories required by the program. Binding directories contain references to external symbols, service programs, and procedures.

ACTGRP (Activation Group)

Specify the ACTGRP parameter to indicate the activation group in which this program runs.

QILE Specify QILE (the default) as the name of the activation group. QILE is a normal activation group and it is typically used when DFTACTGRP(*NO) is required. The QILE name provides a suggestion for a default *named activation group*. The default name could be any name, but QILE is the name shipped with the RPG IV compiler.

*NEW Specify *NEW to cause OS/400 to generate a temporary activation group name. Use this option when the program should run in its own activation group.

*CALLER Specify *CALLER to cause the program to run in the same activation group as the program that evoked it. *CALLER should not be used when the caller's activation group is the default activation group.

activation-group-name Specify a unique name for the activation group to be created when this program is called. Suggested names for activation groups centers around the application. For example, all the programs for the accounts receivable application might be associated with the ACCTREC activation group. Payroll and human resources might be associated with a PAYROLL activation group. The name of the activation group is only important to the programmer.

OPTION

Specify the compile listing and object generation options to use when the source is compiled. Specify one or more of the following options in any order. Separate the individual options with one or more blanks or use the command prompter. When multiple or contra-dictory options are specified, the last option specified is used for the compile.

*XREF Produce a name (fields, files, data structure, tokens, etc.) to the line number, cross-reference listing.

*NOXREF No cross-reference listing is produced.

*GEN Create the program object if the program compiles successfully. A program compiles successfully when the highest message severity level does not exceed the GENLVL option.

*NOGEN Perform preprocessing and syntax checking only. Essentially, this option does everything except generate the compiled program. When only checking for syntax errors or producing a cross-reference listing, OPTION(*NOGEN) substantially improves the amount of time required to generate the desired output. No program object is created.

*SECLVL The second-level message text is generated along with the message text description. The second-level message text is normally much more descriptive than the standard first-level message text that normally appears on the compiler listing.

*NOSECLVL Second-level message text is not generated.

*SHOWCPY The source code of all /COPY source-file members, included in place, on the compiler listing.

*NOSHOWCPY /COPY compiler directives are printed as is, and are not included on the compiler listing.

*EXPDDS The input and output specifications of externally described files is generated and included on the compiler listing.

*NOEXPDDS The input and output specifications of externally described files are not included on the compiler listing.

*EXT Generate a list of external references (procedures and field names) on the compile listing.

*NOEXT Don't generate a list of external references (procedures and field names) on the compile listing.

*NOEVENTF The events file is not generated.

*EVENTF The events files is generated. The events file contains information, useful to client-server development environments, such as IBM CODE/400 (OS/2) and COZZI CodeStudio (Windows). The events file name is EVFEVENT. The member name is the same as the name specified on the PGM parameter. It is stored in the same library as the program object.

*EXT External fields and procedures are included on the compiler listing.

*NOEXT External fields and procedures are not included on the compiler listing.

DBGVIEW (Debug View Level)

Specify the level of debugging that will be available to debug the compiled program.

*STMT Specify *STMT to allow debugging at the source-statement, line-number level. This view does not support the full-screen, source-level debugger of the AS/400.

*SOURCE Specify *SOURCE to generate a source view for debugging the compiled program. When debugging the program, the source-level debugger uses the actual source file member specified on the SRCFILE and SRCMBR parameters.

*COPY Specify *COPY to generate a source view for debugging that includes in-line /COPY directive source. The source code of each /COPY source member is inserted into the debug view. Specifying *COPY also implies the *SOURCE view.

*LIST Specify *LIST to generate a listing of the compiled source-file member that is used by the debugger. The listing is embedded into the compiled program object and used by the source-level debugger when the program is debugged. This is the most common and useful debugging option. When used in conjunction with the OPTION(*NODEBUGIO) option on the program's source header specification, DBGVIEW(*LIST) provides the highest level of debugging capability.

*ALL Specify *ALL to generate all available debug views.

*NONE Specify *NONE to avoid generating any debug views. This option is normally used for a production release of the program. Debug views add unnecessary program-size overhead, and can cause security problems where source code should not be available.

OUTPUT (Compiler Output Listing)

Specify the output listing option to generate a listing or avoid generating a listing.

*PRINT Specify *PRINT to have the compiler print the compiler listing.

*NONE Specify *NONE to avoid having the compiler listing generated.

OPTIMIZE (Optimization Level)

Specify the level of optimization to be performed on the program. Optimization on the AS/400 is generally technologically superior to other compilers. The overall throughput of the program, however, is not always dependent on the level of optimization. Actually, for general-purpose business applications, optimizing RPG IV programs is only marginally affective.

*NONE Specify *NONE to avoid any level of optimization. Avoiding optimization allows for a faster compile than optimizing. Also, OPTIMIZE(*NONE) should be specified when a debug view has been specified during development.

*BASIC Specify *BASIC to perform some basic level of optimization on the generated program. This level of optimization is performed much more quickly than OPTIMIZE(*FULL). In addition, debugging can be performed on the program, as with OPTIMIZE(*NONE). A program variable, however, cannot be modified during debug when *BASIC is specified.

*FULL Specify *FULL when a program is ready to be placed into the production environment. Fully optimized code takes the longest time to generate. Programs can still be debugged if necessary. However, the content of variables is not reliable under full optimization.

INDENT (Indented Compiler Listing)

Specify the INDENT option to control whether structured operations are printed in an indented source-listing format. The character used to highlight the indent levels also is specified on this parameter.

> **NOTE:** *Any indentation you request here will not be reflected in the listing debug view, which is created when you specify DBGVIEW(*LIST).*

*NONE Specify *NONE to have the normal (nonindented) compiler listing generated.

'character-value' Specify a character string (up to two characters) that is used to generate the indented compiler listing. By specifying these characters, an indented compiler listing is generated. The characters connect the beginning and ending lines of the structured operations, such as IF, DO, and SELECT-WHEN.

CVTOPT (Data Type Conversion Options)

Specify the CVTOPT option to control how certain data types of externally described files are handled by the compiled program. Each option converts its corresponding data type to a fixed-length character field.

*NONE Specify *NONE for normal processing. No data type conversion is generated.

*DATETIME Specify *DATETIME to convert externally described date, time, and timestamp database fields to fixed-length character fields.

*GRAPHIC Specify *GRAPHIC to convert double-byte character set (DBCS) graphic data types to fixed-length character fields.

*VARCHAR Specify *VARCHAR to convert variable-length character data types to fixed-length character fields.

*VARGRAPHIC Specify *VARGRAPHIC to convert variable-length double-byte character set (DBCS) graphic data types to fixed-length character fields.

SRTSEQ (Sort Sequence Table)

Specify the SRTSEQ option to control the sort sequence table that is used in the RPG IV source program.

*HEX No sort sequence table is used.

*JOB Specify *JOB to retrieve the SRTSEQ setting from the job running when the program is compiled.

*JOBRUN Specify *JOBRUN to retrieve the SRTSEQ setting from the job runtime environment when the program is run.

*LANGIDUNQ Specify *LANGIDUNQ to use a unique weighted table, based on the language ID specified for the LANGID parameter.

*LANGIDSHR Specify *LANGIDSHR to use a shared weighted table, based on the language ID specified for the LANGID parameter.

sort-table-name Specify the fully qualified sort sequence table name.

LANGID (Language Identifier)

Use the LANGID parameter to specify the language identifier used when the sort sequence (SRTSEQ) parameter is *LANGIDUNQ or *LANGIDSHR. The LANGID parameter is used with the SRTSEQ parameter to specify the sort sequence table.

*JOBRUN Specify *JOBRUN to retrieve the language identifier setting from the job runtime environment when the program is run.

*JOB Specify *JOB to retrieve the language identifier setting from the job running when the program is compiled.

language-identifier Specify the language identifier for the program.

REPLACE (Replace Existing Program upon Successful Compile)

Specify the REPLACE option to have the compiler replace an existing compiled program after this program compiles successfully.

*YES Specify *YES to have an existing program (of the same name as the program being compiled) replaced with the newly compiled program. The existing program is moved to the QRPLOBJ (Replace Object) library and renamed. The renamed program's text description identifies the original program name.

*NO Specify *NO to terminate the compilation if a program already exists with the same name and library as the program being compiled.

USRPRF (User Profile Authority Adoption)

Specify the USRPRF parameter to control how the program runs. The authority of the program's owner can be used when the program runs or the authority of the user running the program can be used.

*USER Specify *USER to have the program run with the authority of the user running the program.

*OWNER Specify *OWNER to have the program run with the authority of the program object's owner. Each object on the AS/400 has an associated owner. This owner is a user profile on the system. When *OWNER is specified, the program runs under the combined authority of both the user running the program and the program's owner. The combined authority of both user profiles is used to access objects while the program is running. Objects created during the program runtime are owned by the program's user.

AUT (User Authority)

Specify the AUT parameter to control the authority given to user profiles that don't have explicit authority to the program.

*LIBCRTAUT Specify *LIBCRTAUT to grant user profiles authority to the program based on the CRTAUT (Object Creation Authority) from the library in which this program is being stored.

*ALL Specify *ALL to grant user profile authority for all operations on the program except ownership authority, which is reserved to the owner of the program.

*CHANGE Specify *CHANGE to grant user profiles all data access authorities and limited operations authority. This is the traditional authority granted to user profiles, and is typically that specified on the CRTAUT parameter for the library. Hence, AUT(*LIBCRTAUT) typically means AUT(*CHANGE).

*USE Specify *USE to grant user profiles object-operational authority and read authority.

*EXCLUDE Specify *EXCLUDE to avoid granting user profiles any access to the compiled program.

authorization-list name Specify the name of the authorization list to which the program is added. The program is secured to this authorization list. The authorization list must exist when this program is created.

TRUNCNBR (Truncate Numbers on Overflow)

Specify the TRUNCNBR parameter to issue a message when a number is truncated during a move to the result field. This parameter applies only to traditional fixed-format operations and is for backward compatibility. Previous versions of RPG ignored truncation. The default for this parameter also causes truncation to be ignored. However, specifying TRUNCNBR(*NO) causes a message to be issued when truncation occurs.

*YES Specify *YES to ignore numeric overflow (sometimes referred to as *high-order truncation*). Values are moved to the result field without notification. This is compatible with previous versions of RPG.

*NO Specify *NO to cause a message to be generated when numeric overflow is detected. An RPG runtime error message is generated. This error can be trapped within the *PSSR subroutine of the RPG program. If it is noted, the operator (i.e., the end user of the program) is notified in a terse manner.

FIXNBR (Fix Decimal Data Errors for Zoned Numeric Fields)

Specify the FIXNBR parameter to cause the compiler to generate code that allows zoned numeric fields containing blanks or other non-numeric data to be converted to valid data.

*NONE Specify *NONE to avoid fixing zoned decimal fields that contain decimal data errors. If decimal data errors are detected, an error is issued during program runtime.

*ZONED Specify *ZONED to generate code that fixes decimal data errors detected in zoned decimal fields. This fix is performed when the zoned decimal data is being moved to a packed decimal field.

*INPUTPACKED Specify *INPUTPACKED to generate code that fixes decimal data errors detected in packed decimal input fields. This fix is performed when the data is read into the program. Decimal data errors aren't allowed in on-input packed decimal fields, regardless of the option specified for the FIXNBR parameter.

TGTRLS (Target Operating System Release)

Specify the TGTRLS parameter to target prior versions and releases of the operating system. This option directs the compiler to generate code that is backward compatible with the targeted release. The IBM OS/400 operating system doesn't allow programs to run on back-releases. Only current and future versions and releases are reasonably guaranteed.

*CURRENT Specify *CURRENT to indicate the current version and release is the target of the compiled program.

*PRV Specify *PRV to indicate that the previous release of the operating system is the target of the compiled program.

release-level Specify the version and release-level in the format VxRxMx, where Vx is the version, Rx is the release, and Mx is the modification level. For example, V3R7M0 is Version 3, Release 7, Modification level 0. The program can be used on an AS/400 running OS/400 with the specified release or with any subsequent release, unless program observability has been removed.

ALWNULL (Allow Null-Capable Fields in Database Records)

Specify the ALWNULL parameter to control whether the program allows records with null-capable fields to be read. Files declared as input-only support nulls in this manner. No other file processing supports nulls.

*NO Specify *NO to restrict processing of null-capable fields. If the program reads a record containing a null value, a data-mapping error is issued and the record in not retrieved.

*YES Specify *YES to allow processing of null-capable fields. To support null-capable fields, when a null value is detected, the default value for the field replaces the null value. For example, if a field containing a date is null-capable, and is null, when that field is retrieved, the default date value (either the current system date, or D'0001-01-01') replaces the null value for the field.

Appendix B

DECIMAL DATA ERRORS

Decimal data is at the heart of most business applications. Floating point and binary numbers are not as incorporated into business applications as decimal data. With the possible exception of the banking industry, floating point and binary fields are not widely used to calculate amounts, quantities, dollars, etc. in the vast majority of business applications. This appendix describes decimal data errors and shows how the system handles decimal data errors when the FIXNBR(*ZONED) and the FIXNBR (*INPUTPACKED) option is specified when an RPG source file member is compiled.

DECIMAL DATA OVERVIEW

There are two forms of decimal data:

- *Zoned decimal data* — Occupying 1 byte for every digit declared.

- *Packed decimal data* — Occupying approximately 1 byte for every two digits declared.

The AS/400 is strict when it comes to valid decimal data. The predecessor of the AS/400, the System/38, had no mechanism to handle invalid decimal data. RPG programs written for System/38 had to completely control the handling of invalid decimal data messages or they stopped running.

Because much of the data contained on the AS/400 has been "migrated" from other systems such as the System/36, the capability to easily handle invalid decimal data has become a requirement. The capability to handle decimal data errors is easier with RPG IV than with previous versions of RPG.

Decimal data errors occur during program runtime when a packed or zoned decimal field contains data that is invalid. An example of invalid data can be a zoned decimal field containing blanks or the letters 'ABCD'. This is clearly not valid numeric data and causes a decimal data error to be generated.

Fix Decimal Data Errors

The AS/400 RPG IV compiler provides an option to ignore decimal data errors. The CRTBNDRPG and CRTRPGMOD commands support the FIXNBR parameter as follows:

```
FIXNBR(*NONE | *ZONED | *INPUTPACKED)
```

The default option, FIXNBR(*NONE), causes decimal data errors to generate an exception/error. In this situation, the default RPG exception/error handling routine is called when an error occurs. If the *PSSR subroutine is specified in the RPG program, that subroutine is called when the exception/error occurs. The default of FIXNBR(*NONE) is appropriate when processing AS/400 database files containing valid numeric data.

The FIXNBR(*ZONED) option causes decimal data errors within zoned decimal numeric fields to be corrected. This is performed by the underlying AS/400 system licensed internal code (SLIC). When an RPG program is run, the AS/400 system prefers to use packed decimal fields. This means that *binary fields* and *zoned fields*, declared within an RPG IV program, are internally mapped to packed decimal fields. Except when decimal data errors are detected, this mapping is transparent to the RPG program.

Using FIXNBR(*ZONED) causes the SLIC to test the zoned decimal fields during this translation. If the zoned decimal field contains all blanks, for example, the blanks are converted to zeros. This special case is the most common type of decimal data error. The process of fixing zoned decimal fields containing blanks is known as *blank transparency*.

In another situation, when a zoned decimal field contains non-numeric data, the SLIC ignores the top half of each byte (the *zone*), except for the right-most byte. The right-most byte contains the sign of the number. If the sign is invalid, it is set to positive.

The bottom half of each byte (the *digit*) is tested for a value of 0 through 9. If the digit portion of the byte is not 0 through 9, the byte is set to zero (i.e., X'F0'). Note that the original zoned decimal field, however, is not converted. Only the targeted (and often temporary) packed decimal field receives the translated value.

Typically, FIXNBR(*ZONED) is used in programs with zoned decimal input fields or data structures that contain numeric subfields.

Because data structures, by default, are initialized to blanks, decimal data errors can occur. To correct the decimal data error that occurs frequently in data structures, the INZ keyword can be specified. This initializes each data structure subfield to the default initial value based on the field's data-type. The FIXNBR(*ZONED) keyword can virtually eliminate the most common form of decimal data errors.

The FIXNBR(*INPUTPACKED) option causes decimal data errors within packed decimal input fields, read from the database, to be corrected. This is performed by the underlying

AS/400 system licensed internal code (SLIC). When an RPG program is run and a record is read, the system checks packed input fields for invalid packed decimal data. If there is a decimal data error, the system sets the field's value to zero.

DATABASE FILE MODELS

The IBM System/34 and System/36 use a *flat file system*. All files are linear, or nonrelational. This is in sharp contrast to the System/38 and AS/400 *relational database management system*, where fields are used to define the representation of the file.

When a file is created with the flat file model, its records are created as one large "field." There are no database field definitions. This is similar to the default method RPG uses to initialize data structures.

When a file is created with the relational model, its records are created as a collection of *columns*. These columns are known as *fields* to RPG programmers. The file's record length is calculated by the sum of the lengths of the fields. In essence, the record length becomes unimportant to the application developer.

When moving from a flat file system, such as the System/36, to a relational database system, such as the AS/400, several data integrity problems can arise.

- When an RPG program writes a record using the System/36 flat file model, only the fields specified in RPG output specifications are written to the file. The remainder of the record is padded with blanks.

- When a file from the System/36 flat file model is moved to the AS/400, the file is generally created with one large field. The length of this field equals that of the file's record length.

Decimal data errors can occur when a record is read from a file (i.e., during a CHAIN, READ, or RPG cycle input operation). When an error occurs and FIXNBR(*ZONED) is specified, the record is returned and any zoned decimal fields are fixed as previously described. Packed decimal fields are not fixed, however. Hence, decimal data errors can still occur in a program that has been created with the FIXNBR(*ZONED) option.

Zoned Decimal Data

Zoned decimal is a carry-over from the old 80-column, punch-card era. Essentially, each digit of a decimal number occupies 1 byte of a zoned decimal field. The top four bits (the zone) are set on in a normal zoned decimal number. The default hexadecimal value for the zone is X'F'. The bottom four bits (the digit) of the byte represent the numeric value. For example, a value of 3 would be X'F3', a value of 4 would be X'F4', and so on.

The *sign* (sometimes referred to as the *status*) of a zoned decimal field is stored in the top four bits of the right-most byte of a zoned decimal field. The sign can be X'C' or X'D' for negative values (X'D' is the default), and X'A', X'B', X'E', or X'F' for positive values (X'F' is the default). The dual negative signs are a result of the way the COBOL language sets the bits for negative values. COBOL uses X'C' for its negative sign; RPG and other AS/400 languages use X'D'. Both are supported by all AS/400 languages and system functions. The multiple positive signs result from treating any non-negative number as positive.

Figure B.1 shows the storage for a typical five-position zoned decimal field. The value of the field below is set to 3741.

The digit portion of a zoned decimal field identifies the numeric value. The zone portion of each byte (except the sign byte) can contain any value. During an RPG operation, the zone of each byte (except the sign byte) is set on (i.e., set to B'1111' or X'F'). This includes mathematical, move, copy, and output operations.

Byte Position	1	2	3	4	5
Zone	F	F	F	F	F
Digit	0	3	7	4	1

Figure B.1: Storage for a five-position zoned decimal field (value 3741).

The zone of a zoned decimal field is ignored (except for the sign). Consequently, operations on zoned decimal fields are forgiving when some invalid data appears. For example, a five-position zoned decimal field with a value of 3741 could appear as shown in Figure B.2 without any errors occurring.

This value is tolerated because the zone portion of a zoned decimal field is ignored. The sign is also tolerated because it is between X'A' and X'F' (i.e., X'E'). When

Byte Position	1	2	3	4	5
Zone	A	8	8	D	E
Digit	0	3	7	4	1

Figure B.2: Another representation of a zoned decimal field with a value of 3741.

this zoned decimal field is used, the operating system translates the zone of each byte (except for the sign) to X'F'. Consequently, the value is treated as though it were coded as X'F0F3F7F4F1'.

The sign of a zoned decimal field is handled a little more strictly. The zone portion of the right-most byte (i.e., the sign of the zoned value) must be one of the entries in Table B.1.

Table B.1: Valid Sign Values of a Zoned Decimal Field			
Zone Value (in Hex)	Zone Value (in Binary)	Sign (Status)	Description
X'F'	B'1111'	+	All bits are on, the sign is positive (DEFAULT).
X'D'	B'1101'	–	Bit 2 is off, the sign is negative (DEFAULT).
X'A'	B'1010'	+	Bits 1 and 3 are off, the sign is considered positive.
X'B'	B'1011'	+	Bit 1 is off, the sign is considered positive.
X'C'	B'1100'	–	Bits 2 and 3 are off, the sign is negative.
X'E'	B'1110'	+	Bit 3 is off, the sign is considered positive

If the right-most byte's zone is not one of the values listed in Table B.1, and FIXNBR(*ZONED) is specified, the sign is translated to a positive sign (i.e., X'F').

Zoned Decimal Data Errors

There are two situations that cause decimal data errors for a zoned decimal field. Decimal data errors occur when FIXNBR(*NONE) is specified when the source file is compiled.

- When a sign value other than X'A' to X'F' is used. Any other value, that is X'0' to X'9', in the sign location generates a decimal data error.

- When any digit in the zoned decimal field contains a value other than X'0' to X'9', a decimal data error is issued. Any other value, that is X'A' to X'F', in the digit location generates a decimal data error.

This creates a problem with the use of zoned decimal fields in data structures. A data structure subfield of type zone decimal is, by default, initialized to blanks—which is X'40'. This is, by its very nature, invalid decimal data. There are several methods to prevent this type of decimal data error, including:

- Specify the INZ keyword on the numeric data structure subfield. This initializes the subfield based on its data type. Hence, numeric fields are initialized to zero instead of blanks.

- Move zeros or some other valid numeric value into the subfield prior to using the subfield in another operation.

- Clear the subfield with the CLEAR operation. The CLEAR operation is a "smart" op code (in that it is context sensitive). When it is used on a decimal field, it is smart enough to move zeros into the field.

- Clear the data structure containing the subfield with CLEAR operation code. The CLEAR operation moves either blanks or zeros to each data structure subfield based on the data type of the subfield. However, because data-structure subfields can, and often do, overlap one another, the CLEAR operation can cause a decimal data error to occur in a later operation. The CLEAR operation clears subfields in the order they appear in the RPG program (not by their physical location within the data structure). Therefore, should both a zoned decimal subfield and a character subfield occupy the same physical location, the subfield that appears last in the definition specifications dictates the value moved into the positions within the data structure.

- Specify that the data structure containing the subfield is initialized at program start time. This can be accomplished by specifying the INZ keyword on the data structure name definition specification. Again, subfields are initialized based on their occurrence in the RPG definition specifications. Therefore, the same criteria as the CLEAR operation applies to the INZ keyword.

PACKED DECIMAL DATA

A packed decimal field occupies 1 byte for every 2 digits, except for the right-most digit, which shares its byte with the sign. The formula used to calculate the number of bytes occupied by a packed decimal field is a follows:

```
bytes = (declared length / 2) + 1
```

Consider a 5-position packed decimal field with four decimal positions. Using the above formula to calculate the number of bytes occupied, gives:

```
bytes = (5 / 2) + 1
```

The number of bytes occupied by this packed decimal field is three. Note that the number of decimal positions (four in this example) has no impact on the bytes occupied.

Figure B.3 shows the storage allocation of a seven-position packed decimal field, with two decimal positions. The value is set to zero.

Byte Position	1	2	3	4
Bits 0-3 (in hex)	0	0	0	0
Bits 4-7 (in hex)	0	0	0	F

Figure B.3: Storage for a seven-position packed decimal field (value 0).

Each number of a decimal value is coded into its binary form when copied to a packed decimal field. The values are copied starting with the sign. Then the numeric digits are copied, starting with the right-most number and continuing to the left.

Figure B.4 shows a seven-position packed decimal field with two decimal positions. The field is set to 1207.38 with a positive sign.

Byte Position	1	2	3	4
Bits 0-3 (in hex)	0	2	7	8
Bits 4-7 (in hex)	1	0	3	F

Figure B.4: Storage for a seven-position packed decimal positive field (value 1207.38).

This spelunking storage technique is the most common format for decimal data on the IBM AS/400. The AS/400 SLIC has been optimized to handle packed decimal data.

Although the sign is stored in bits 4 to 7 of the right-most byte for packed decimal fields, and in bits 0 to 3 of the right-most byte for zoned decimal fields, it is handled basically the same for both.

The sign for a packed decimal field (i.e., bits 4 to 7 of the rightmost byte) must be X'A' to X'F', with X'F' being the default value for a positive sign, and X'D' being the default value for a negative sign. Table B.2 describes the valid signs for a packed decimal field.

Note that the declared length of a packed decimal field is the value that is returned by the %SIZE built-in function. If the field's length is five-positions with two decimal positions, the %SIZE built-in function returns 5 as the field's size.

		Table B.2: Valid Sign Values for Packed Decimal Fields	
Sign (in Hex)	Sign (in Binary)	Sign (Symbol)	Description
X'F'	B'1111'	+	All bits are on, the sign is positive (DEFAULT).
X'D'	B'1101'	−	Bit 2 is off, the sign is negative (DEFAULT).
X'A'	B'1010'	+	Bits 1 and 3 are off, the sign is considered positive.
X'B'	B'1011'	+	Bit 1 is off, the sign is considered positive.
X'C'	B'1100'	−	Bits 2 and 3 are off, the sign is negative.
X'E'	B'1110'	+	Bit 3 is off, the sign is considered positive.

CONDITIONS FOR DECIMAL DATA ERRORS

Depending on the conditions where a decimal data error occurs, results vary. In most situations, however, the result can be predicted. There are two primary conditions under which decimal data errors occur. They are:

- On a read to a database file (externally described or program described).

- On an operation code that attempts to copy invalid decimal data to a numeric field.

Decimal Data Error upon an Input Operation to a Database File

When a record is read from a database file, its data is copied to an "input buffer." This buffer is separate from the file's input specifications. After the data from the file is copied to the input buffer, it is copied, on a field-by-field basis, to the input area of the program. The input area is the file's input specifications.

At the point at which data is copied from the input buffer to the input area, decimal data errors do not occur. If the database record contains invalid data, it is copied to the input buffer as is. Decimal data errors can occur when one of the numeric input fields (for example, a packed decimal field) is copied to another packed decimal field. Another time a decimal data error occurs is when a field containing invalid decimal data is written to the database.

Unlike previous versions of RPG, RPG IV always returns the data from an input operation even when a decimal data error could be detected. This means the data in the input area of the program always represents the actual data in the database file.

Data is returned regardless of the FIXNBR option. In previous versions of RPG, when a decimal data error occurred during an input operation, the data from the previous input operation was retained—causing some interesting side effects. The RPG IV method of handling decimal data, while not as complete as it could be, is certainly a major step in correcting data problems.

Appendix C

DDS DATE AND TIME FORMAT CONSIDERATIONS

T he OS/400 database, known as *DB2 for OS/400* or the *universal database*, supports many types of field attributes, including integrated DATE, TIME and TIMESTAMP data types. To declare a field as being of type DATE, the L data type is specified. To declare a field as being of type TIME, the T data type is specified. To declare a field as being of type TIMESTAMP, the Z data type is specified. The data type for a field is specified in column 35 of the OS/400 data description specification. The DDS ruler used to identify the layout of a database field specification follows:

```
1...v....1....v....2....v....3....v....4....v....5....v....6....v....7....v....8
.....A..........R.Fieldname+RLen++TDc.......Functions++++++++++++++++++++++++++++
```

DATABASE DATE AND TIME OVERVIEW

Date and time data types support several formats. These formats control how the date or time value is presented at a high-level. Internally, all DATE fields are stored as a 4-byte value. All TIME fields are stored as a 3-byte value. The TIMESTAMP data type supports one format and is stored internally as a 10-byte value. For example, the date July 23, 1958, is stored as 714982 in the internal 4-byte format. See Figure C.1. This format is often referred to as *Super Julian*. Super Julian is the number of days since January 1, 0001. The date 0001-01-01 (in ISO format) is the base date used by RPG IV.

0	7	4	8
0	1	9	2

Figure C.1: Internal storage format for date values.

The internal date, time, and timestamp formats cannot be accessed through conventional programming. It is documented here for completeness.

Because the external date and time formats don't affect the internal date format, the external format is not a consideration when designing access paths or selecting key fields for a file. Also, because it is the default value used throughout the RPG IV and DDS languages, the *ISO date format offers the fewest compatibility problems.

The standard for specifying the length of a date, time, or timestamp field in RPG is to not specify the length. The format of the field determines its length. The compiler generates a length entry, automatically, as follows:

- DATE fields allocate 6, 8, or 10 bytes in a database file.
- TIME fields allocate 8 bytes in a database file.
- TIMESTAMP fields allocate 26 bytes in a database file.

For more information on the attributes of DATE, TIME, and TIMESTAMP fields, see Tables C.1 and C.2

DATABASE DATE FORMAT AND SEPARATOR (Edit Character)

To specify the format for a date field, use the DDS keyword DATFMT, as follows:

```
DATFMT( *JOB | *MDY | *YMD | *DMY | *ISO | *USA | *EUR | *JIS | *JUL )
```

The DDS DATFMT keyword accepts the date format codes listed in Table C.1.

Table C.1: Date Formatting Codes					
Date Format	Description	Output Format	Separator	Length	Sample
*JOB	job attribute	compile-time			
*MDY	Month, Day, Year	mm/dd/yy	/ - . , &	8	02/17/95
*DMY	Day, Month, Year	dd/mm/yy	/ - . , &	8	17/02/95
*YMD	Year, Month, Day	yy/mm/dd	/ - . , &	8	95/02/17
*JUL	Julian (year, day of year 1 - 365)	yy/ddd	/ - . , &	6	95/048
*ISO	International Standards Organization	ccyy-mm-dd	- (fixed)	10	1995-02-17
*USA	IBM's USA Standard	mm/dd/ccyy	/ (fixed)	10	02/17/1995
*EUR	IBM's European Standard	dd.mm.ccyy	. (fixed)	10	17.02.1995
*JIS	Japanese Industrial Standard	ccyy-mm-dd	- (fixed)	10	1995-02-17

Any of the formats listed in Table C.1 can be specified for a date field in a database file. When DATFMT(*JOB) is specified, the date format is based on the DATFMT of the OS/400 job that is running when the database file is created.

The date format represents how the date is presented to the user. The length of a date field includes the date separator and is 6, 8, or 10 characters in length. The *date separator* is used to edit the date value. The formats *MDY, *DMY, *YMD, and *JUL support the five separators listed in Table C.1. The slash ('/') is the default separator for these date formats. The date formats *ISO, *USA, *EUR, and *JIS have a *fixed separator*. Therefore, the DATSEP keyword is not valid for date fields of this format.

Date Separator Keyword

To specify a separator other than the default separator, use the DATSEP keyword. The DATSEP keyword accepts one parameter, as follows:

```
DATSEP( *JOB | 'date separator' )
```

The date separator parameter is a quoted character and is used to edit a date field where the format is *MDY, *YMD, *DMY, or *JUL. The valid date separator symbols include:

- / (the slash)
- - (the minus)
- . (the period)
- , (the comma)
- & (the ampersand, for blank)

Optionally, DATSEP(*JOB) can be specified to indicate that the separator is based on the DATSEP value of the OS/400 job that is running when the database file is created.

The date format, including the date separator, is known as the *external format*. This format is used by all system interfaces to display and manipulate date values. In fact, the length of the field in the database is based on date format and not the internal format. The *internal format* is the format in which a date value is stored within the database file object. This internal format is not accessible through any high-level system interfaces. SQL, Query Manager, and all high-level languages such as RPG work only with the external format of date fields.

DATABASE TIME FORMAT AND SEPARATOR (Edit Character)

To specify the format for a time field, use the DDS TIMFMT keyword, as follows:

```
TIMFMT( *JOB | *HMS | *ISO | *USA | *EUR | *JIS )
```

The DDS TIMFMT keyword accepts the time format codes specified in Table C.2.

Table C.2: Time Formatting Codes					
Time Format	Description	Output Format	Separator	Length	Sample
*JOB	Job attribute	compile-time			
*HMS	Hours, Minutes, Seconds	hh:mm:ss	: . , &	8	15:30:00
*ISO	International Standards Organization	hh.mm.ss	. (fixed)	8	15:30:00
*USA	IBM's USA Standard	hh:mm am hh:mm pm	: (fixed)	8	3:30 PM
*EUR	IBM's European Standard	hh.mm.ss	. (fixed)	8	15:30:00
*JIS	Japanese Industrial Standard	hh:mm:ss	: (fixed)	8	15:30:00

The time format represents how the time is presented to the user. Time fields include a *time separator*. All time formats are eight characters in length.

To specify a separator other than the default separator, use the DDS keyword TIMSEP. The TIMSEP keyword accepts one parameter in the following format:

```
TIMSEP( *JOB | 'time separator' )
```

The time separator parameter is a quoted character and is used to edit a time field where the format is *HMS. Any symbol listed under the column heading "Separator" in Table C.2 can be specified. For example, TIMSEP('.') causes the period to be used as the separator. Optionally, TIMSEP(*JOB) can be specified to indicate that the separator is based on the TIMSEP value of the OS/400 job that is running when the database file is created.

The TIMSEP keyword is valid only for time fields where the format is *HMS. The TIMSEP keyword cannot be specified for time formats other than *HMS.

Timestamp Format

The format of timestamp fields is fixed. It is a single-format data type that optionally includes microseconds. The format of the timestamp data type follows:

```
CCYY-MM-DD-HH.MN.SS.MMMMMM
```

When specifying a timestamp value, the microseconds part is optional. If microseconds aren't specified, they are automatically set to .000000 by the operation accessing the timestamp. The other parts of the timestamp value are required. The following example is a valid timestamp value as used in RPG III programs:

```
'1995-06-21-15.00.00.000000'
```

Note that the lowest valid timestamp value is as follows:

```
'0001-01-01-00.00.00.000000
```

> **NOTE:** There is no way to retrieve microseconds within RPG IV. Currently, the TIME operation code retrieves, at best, milliseconds.

SPECIAL DATES AND TIMES VALUES

The value represented by the RPG IV *LOVAL and *HIVAL figurative constants corresponds directly to the type of field with which they are used. For date fields, January 1, 0001 is considered *LOVAL and December 31, 9999 is considered *HIVAL. Figure C.2 shows the *LOVAL and *HIVAL representations for DATE, TIME, and TIMESTAMP fields. Figure C.3 contains the *LOVAL representation for all available date formats.

Data Type	*LOVAL	*HIVAL
DATE	D'0001-01-01'	D'9999-12-31'
TIME	T'00:00:00'	T'24:00:00'
TIMESTAMP	0001-01-01-00.00.00.000000	9999-12-31-24.00.00.000000

Figure D.3: *LOVAL and *HIVAL for date and time fields.

The *LOVAL for the TIME data type is interesting. The value T'24:00:00' represents midnight. This is a valid time using the 24-hour military time format and represents the *HIVAL value. However, the value T'00:00:00' is a fictitious time. Most digital timers, however, use T'24:00:00' to display the instant of midnight. When incrementing, they go from T'23:59:59' to T'24:00:00' followed by T'00:00:01'. See Table C.3.

This problem is amplified when the *USA time format is used. Under *USA time, T'00:00 am' is used for *LOVAL, and T'12:00 AM' is used for *HIVAL. Because there is no such thing as 12:00 A.M., it's difficult to work with these values.

Display File Support for Date Variables

The primary OS/400 user interface language, DDS supports date, time, and timestamp variables presented to the user. The data-type used to indicate a date value is "L", a time value is "T," and a timestamp value is "Z."

When a date, time, or timestamp value (herein subsequently and collectively referred to as date) is added to a device file, the operating system manages how the date is displayed or printed.

When using date fields in a display file, the date follows the same restrictions and requirements as database date fields. The DATFMT and DATSEP keywords are also used similar to database date fields.

Table C.3: Lowest Value for Date Fields in RPG IV		
Date Format	Lowest Date Value	
	Masked	Raw
*MDY	D'01/01/40'	010140
*YMD	D'40/01/01'	400101
*DMY	D'01/01/40'	010140
*JUL	D'40/001'	40001
*ISO	D'0001-01-01'	00010101
*USA	D'01/01/0001'	01010001
*EUR	D'01.01.0001'	01010001
*JIS	D'0001-01-01'	00010101

When entering a date value into a workstation device file, the end-user is allowed to enter the date with or without the separators. When a date value is displayed, it includes the separator specified by the DATSEP or TIMSEP keywords.

There is one additional DDS keyword called MAPVAL (Map Date/Time Value). This keyword allows non-date values to be translated into valid date values. For example, if the end-user enters blanks into a date field on the workstation, those blanks can be automatically translated to valid date value. The MAPVAL keyword syntax is as follows:

```
mapval( (program-value1  output-value1 ) (program-value2 output-value2)…)
```

The program-value*n* is the from value. It is the value that is sent from or received into the program. The output-value*n* is the to value. It is the value that is written to the workstation or print device. The program-value and the output-value must contain valid date or time values. These values must be in the format specified by the DATFMT or TIMFMT keywords.

The MAPVAL keyword acts like a translation table. When an output operation to the device is performed, the MAPVAL list is searched for a value that matches that of the output field. If a match is not detected, the field's value is sent to the output device unchanged. If a match is detected, the field's value is translated to the output-value by searching the MAPVAL list for the first program-value that matches the value in the date field. Then, the corresponding output-value is sent to the device.

Appendix D

SOURCE CODE LISTINGS

The ZTOOLS source (pronounced "Zee Tools") contains useful subprocedures that can be included in any RPG IV release 2 (or later) program. The prototypes for the ZTOOLS procedures are listed on the following pages. Compile the ZTOOLS file as a module and then include that module on the CRTPGM when compiling an application. To download the latest source for these and other routines, go to the RPG IV Web site at http://www.rpgiv.com and click on the Downloads link.

ZINCLUDE PROTOTYPES

```
      /*************************************************************/
      /* Cozzi RPGIV Includes |  (c) 1996 by Robert Cozzi, Jr.      |
      /* ————————           All rights reserved.      |
      /* —————————————————-
      /* PC Filename(zINCLUDE.RG4) AS/400 Filename(ZINCLUDE) TYPE(RPGLE)
      /* This source file contains example source code for the RPGIV
      /* language for your consideration.
      /*
      /* These examples are provided "as is" without warranty of
      /* any kind. If you choose to use these examples, you do so
      /* at your own risk. Further, you agree to hold the author of
      /* these examples, the copyright holder, its agents and suppliers
      /* harmless for any results from the use or misuse of these
      /* enhancements. No warranty is expressed or implied and
      /* none is given.
      /*************************************************************/**
      ** Procedure interface for the get DayOfWeek function
      **     Format:  day-of-week = DAYOFWEEK( ISO-DATE )
      **     Input: A valid date in *ISO format
      **     Return value: -1 if an error occurred
      **
      **                   1=Sunday, 2=Monday, 3=Tuesday 4=Wednesday
      **                   5=Thursday, 6=Friday, 7=Saturday
      **
      **      See also:  WeekDay — Returns day of week in text format
      **
.....D*ame+++++++++++EUDS.......Length+TDc.Functions+++++++++++++++++++++++++++++
 D DayOfWeek       PR            10I 0
 D InDate                          D   CONST DATFMT(*ISO)
```

Figure D.1: ZINCLUDE prototypes for ZTOOLS (part 1 of 2).

```
/**************************************************************/
**
** Procedure interface for the get WeekDay (text) function
**     Format:  day-of-week = WeekDay( ISO-DATE )
**     Input: A valid date in *ISO format
**     Return value: Character string representing the day of
**                   the week:
**                   Sunday, Monday, Tuesday Wednesday
**                   Thursday, Friday, Saturday
**
**      See also:  DayOfWeek — Returns day of week as a numeral
**
D WeekDay          PR              10A
D  InDate                           D   CONST DATFMT(*ISO)


/**************************************************************/
**
** Procedure interface for the RUN function
**     Format:  Runcmd( 'cmd-string' : len of cmd-string : [graphic] )
**     Input: Any system command
**            Length of the system command
**            Optional: Double-byte character support parameter
**
D Runcmd           PR                      ExtPgm('QCMDEXC')
D  cmdstr                        3000A     Const Options(*VarSize)
D  cmdlen                        15P 5     Const
D  cmdDbcs                         3A      Const Options(*NOPASS)

/**************************************************************/
**
** Procedure interface for the TOUPPER function
**     Format:  upper-case-value = ToUpper( const 'char-string' )
**
**      Input: Character value to be converted
**
**      Output: The upper-case equivalent of the input value
**
.....D*ame++++++++++EUDS.......Length+TDc.Functions+++++++++++++++++++++++++++
D ToUpper          PR              1024A
D  tu_input                        1024A   CONST

/**************************************************************/
**
** Procedure interface for the NUMTOCHAR function
**     Format:  character-value = NumToChar( const numeric-value )
**
**      Input: Numeric value to be convert (no decimal positions)
**
**      Output: The return value is the character string form
**
D NumToChar        PI              32A
D  NumInput                        30P 0 CONST
```

Figure D.1: ZINCLUDE prototypes for ZTOOLS (part 2 of 2).

DAY OF WEEK ORDINAL

```
/****************************************************************/
/* Cozzi RPGIV Includes |  (c) 1996 by Robert Cozzi, Jr.
/* ──────────────
/* PC Filename(zTOOLS.RG4) AS/400 Filename(ZTOOLS) TYPE(RPGLE)
/* This source file contains enhancements to the RPGIV language.
/* These enhancements are provided as is without warrenty of
/* any kind. If you choose to use these enhancements, you do so
/* at your own risk. Further, you agree to hold the author of
/* these enhancements, the copyright holder, and its agents,
/* harmless for any results from the use or misuse of these
/* enhancements. No warranty is expressed or implied and
/* none is given.
/****************************************************************/
0001 H NOMAIN DATFMT(*ISO)
0002  /COPY ZINCLUDE

     ** Return the day of the week ordinal

.....PProcName+++++++..B...................Functions++++++++++++++++++++++++++++
0003 P DayOfWeek      B               EXPORT

.....DName++++++++++EUDS.......Length+TDc.Functions++++++++++++++++++++++++++++
0004 D DayOfWeek      PI            10I 0
0005 D  InDate                       D   CONST DATFMT(*ISO)

       ** BASEDATE is the day the calendar changed.
0006 D BaseDate       S             D   INZ(D'1582-10-14')
0007 D                                   STATIC
0008 D nDayOfWeek     S            10I 0 STATIC
0009 D nDays          S            10I 0

.....CSRnØ1Factor1+++++++OpCode(ex)Factor2+++++++Result++++++++Len++DcHiLoEq....
0010 C                 TEST                    InputDate               73

0011 C                 If        *IN73
0012 C                 Return    -1
0013 C                 Endif
0014 C       InDate    SubDur    BaseDate      nDays:*Days
0015 C                 CALLB     'CEEDYWK'                             73
0016 C                 Parm                    nDays
0017 C                 Parm                    nDayofWeek
0018 C                 return    nDayOfWeek

.....PProcName+++++++..B...................Functions++++++++++++++++++++++++++++
0019 P DayOfWeek      E
```

Figure D.2: ZTOOLS example procedures: Day of Week Ordinal.

Day of Week Text

```
          ** Return the day of the week as a string

.....PProcName+++++++..B.................Functions++++++++++++++++++++++++++++++
0020 P WeekDay        B                 EXPORT

.....DName++++++++++++EUDS.......Length+TDc.Functions++++++++++++++++++++++++++++++
0021 D WeekDay        PI              32A
0022 D  InputDate                      D   CONST DATFMT(*ISO)
0023 D Days           DS
0024 D  Sunday                        10A   Inz('Sunday')
0025 D  Monday                        10A   Inz('Monday')
0026 D  Tuesday                       10A   Inz('Tuesday')
0027 D  Wednesday                     10A   Inz('Wednesday')
0028 D  Thursday                      10A   Inz('Thursday')
0029 D  Friday                        10A   Inz('Friday')
0030 D  Saturday                      10A   Inz('Saturday')
0031 D  Day                           10A   Dim(7) Overlay(Days)

.....CSRn01Factor1+++++++OpCode(ex)Factor2+++++++Result++++++++Len++DcHiLoEq....
0032 C                    TEST(E)                 InputDate
0033 C                    If         %ERROR
0034 C                    Return     'Invalid Date'
0035 C                    Endif
          ** Note: Date validation is done her to avoid -1 return value
          **      by the DAYOFWEEK function.
0036 C                    return     Day(DayOfWeek(InputDate))

.....PProcName+++++++..B.................Functions++++++++++++++++++++++++++++++
0037 P WeekDay        E
```

Figure D.3: ZTOOLS example procedures: Day of Week Text.

RETURN AS UPPERCASE STRING

```
** Return the input string as an uppercase string

.....PProcName+++++++..B.................Functions++++++++++++++++++++++++++++
0038 P ToUpper           B                EXPORT

.....DName++++++++++++EUDS.......Length+TDc.Functions++++++++++++++++++++++++++
0039 D ToUpper           PI             1024A
0040 D   InputStg                       1024A   Const Varying

0041 D RtnValue          S                      LIKE(InputStg)

0042 D lower             C                      Const('abcdefghijklmnopqrstuvwxyz')
0043 D upper             C                      Const('ABCDEFGHIJKLMNOPQRSTUVWXYZ')

.....CSRn01Factor1+++++++OpCode(ex)Factor2+++++++Result++++++++Len++DcHiLoEq....
0044 C        lower:UPPER   XLATE     INPUTSTG      RTNVALUE
0045 C                      Return    RtvValue

.....PProcName+++++++..B.................Functions++++++++++++++++++++++++++++
0046 P ToUpper           E

.....PProcName+++++++..B.................Functions++++++++++++++++++++++++++++
0047 P ToLower           B                EXPORT

.....DName++++++++++++EUDS.......Length+TDc.Functions++++++++++++++++++++++++++
0048 D ToLower           PI             1024A
0049 D   InputStg                       1024A   Const Varying

0050 D RtnValue          S                      LIKE(InputStg)

0051 D lower             C                      Const('abcdefghijklmnopqrstuvwxyz')
0052 D upper             C                      Const('ABCDEFGHIJKLMNOPQRSTUVWXYZ')

.....CSRn01Factor1+++++++OpCode(ex)Factor2+++++++Result++++++++Len++DcHiLoEq....
0053 C        UPPER:lower   XLATE     INPUTSTG      RTNVALUE
0054 C                      Return    RtvValue
0055 P ToLower           E
```

Figure D.4: ZTOOLS example procedures: Return as Upper Case String.

CONVERT TO UPPERCASE

```
        ** Convert input string to uppercase

.....PProcName+++++++..B...................Functions++++++++++++++++++++++++++++
0056 P MakeUpper       B                    EXPORT

        ** Convert the input string (parameter 1) to upper case

.....DName++++++++++++EUDS.......Length+TDc.Functions++++++++++++++++++++++++++++
0057 D MakeUpper       PI                    OPDESC
0058 D  InputStg                    4096A    OPTIONS(*VARSIZE)

0059 D  WorkVar        S                     LIKE(InputStg)

0060 D lower           C                     Const('abcdefghijklmnopqrstuvwxyz')
0061 D UPPER           C                     Const('ABCDEFGHIJKLMNOPQRSTUVWXYZ')

0062 D descType        S            10I 0
0063 D dataType        S            10I 0
0064 D descInf1        S            10I 0
0065 D descInf2        S            10I 0
0066 D strlen          S            10I 0

.....C*Rn01Factor1+++++++OpCode(ex)Factor2+++++++Result++++++++Len++DcHiLoEq....
0068 C                  CALLP       CEEDOD(1 : descType : datatype :
0069 C                                     descInf1 : descInf2 : strlen)

0070 C                  Eval        workvar = %subst(InputStg : 1 : strlen)
0071 C       lower:UPPER xLate       workvar       workval
0072 C                  Return      RtvValue
0073 C                  Eval        %subst(InputStg : 1 : strlen) = workvar
0074 C                  return

.....P*rocName+++++++..B...................Functions++++++++++++++++++++++++++++
0075 P MakeUpper       E
```

Figure D.5: ZTOOLS example procedures: Convert to Uppercase.

RETURN LENGTH OF INPUT STRING

```
       ** Return the length of the input string to the caller

.....PProcedure++++++..B.................Functions++++++++++++++++++++++++++++++
0076 P Strlen          B                   EXPORT

.....DName+++++++++++EUDS.......Length+TDc.Functions++++++++++++++++++++++++++++++
0077 D Strlen          PI              10I 0
0078 D  InputStr                     4096A  CONST
0079 D nPos            S               10I 0
0080 D CheckStr        S                +1   LIKE(InputStr)

.....CSRn01Factor1+++++++OpCode(ex)Factor2+++++++Result++++++++Len++DcHiLoEq....
0081 C                   MoveL   InputStr      CheckStr
0082 C         ' '       CheckR  CheckStr      nPos
0083 C                   Return  nPos - 1

.....PProcName+++++++..B.................Functions++++++++++++++++++++++++++++++
0084 P StrLen          E
```

Figure D.6: ZTOOLS example procedures: Return Length of Input String.

In-Line ILE Procedures

There are several application program interfaces (APIs) that are supported in RPG IV. Several of these APIs are provided through the ILE that runs on the IBM AS/400 system. Specifically, there are two APIs that provide a way to access the Operand Descriptions (OPDESC) that are passed to subprocedures.

These APIs are known as *in-line procedures*. These are considered "in-line" because the RPG IV compiler actually copies the code for these procedures into the host RPG IV program. In other words, there isn't actually a CALL to the APIs at runtime, and the instructions performed by these APIs are embedded in the program calling the APIs.

The two APIs used in this book, CEEGSI and CEEDOD are prototyped in Figures D.7 and D.8. They are prototyped for documentation purposes and to simply provide access to the APIs themselves.

```
/****************************************************************/
/* Cozzi RPGIV Includes |  (c) 1996 by Robert Cozzi, Jr.       |
/* _____         All rights reserved.            |
/* _____-
/* PC Filename(zINLINE.RG4) AS/400 Filename(ZSYSINLINE) TYPE(RPGLE)
/* This source file contains example source code for the RPGIV
/* language for your consideration.
/*
/* These examples are provided "as is" without warranty of
/* any kind. If you choose to use these examples, you do so
/* at your own risk. Further, you agree to hold the author of
/* these examples, the copyright holder, its agents and suppliers
/* harmless for any results from the use or misuse of these
/* examples. No warranty is expressed or implied and
/* none is given.
/****************************************************************/
 ************************************************
 **   ILE In-line Procedure                  **
 **   CEEGSI - Get String Information         **
 ************************************************

.....DName+++++++++++EUDS.......Length+TDc.Functions++++++++++++++++++++++++++
     D GetStgInfo      PR                  ExtProc('CEEGSI')
     D  ParmPos                    10I 0
     D  s_datatype                 10I 0
     D  s_curlen                   10I 0
     D  s_maxlen                   10I 0
     D  s_errors                   12A   OPTIONS(*OMIT)
```

Figure D.7: Prototype for CEEGSI (Get String Information).

588

```
/***************************************************************/
** Procedure interface for the CEEDOD in-line function
**    Format:  GetOpDesc( parm-pos : desc-type : data-type :
**                        desc-inf1 : desc-inf2 : data-length )
**    Input: Relative parameter number
**    Output: desc-type -
**            data-type -
**                      1 = Invalid or unknown data type
**                      2 = Character data
**                      3 = Null terminated character string
**                      4 = Pascal-style character string
**                          Bytes 1 - 2 UINT(2) with data length
**                          Bytes 3 to ... data
**                      5 = Pascal-style chracter string
**                          Bytes 1 - 4 UINT(4) with data length
**                          Bytes 5 to ... data
**                      6 = Bit string
**                      7 = Bit string
**                          Bytes 1 - 2 UINT(2) with number of bits
**                          Bytes 3 to ... bit string
**                      8 = Bit string
**                          Bytes 1 - 4 UINT(4) with number of bits
**                          Bytes 5 to ... bit string
**                      9 = DBCS character data
**                     10 = DBCS character string with null termination
**                     11 = DBCS character data
**                          Bytes 1 - 2 UINT(2) with the data's length
**                          Bytes 3 to ... DBCS data
**                     12 = DBCS character data
**                          Bytes 1 - 4 UINT(4) with the data's length

**                          Bytes 5 to ... DBCS data
**            desc-inf1 -
**            desc-inf2 -
**            data-length =  Number of bytes of data passed to
**                           this parameter.

.....DName++++++++++EUDS.......Length+TDc.Functions++++++++++++++++++++++++++++
     D GetOpDesc       PR                  ExtProc('CEEDOD')
     D  ParmPos                      10I 0 Const
     D  o_desctype                   10I 0
     D  o_datatype                   10I 0
     D  o_descinf1                   10I 0
     D  o_descinf2                   10I 0
     D  o_fieldlen                   10I 0
     D  o_errors                     12A   OPTIONS(*OMIT)
```

Figure D.8: Prototype for CEEDOD (Get Operation Descriptor).

ADDITIONAL SOURCE LISTINGS

The source-file listings shown in Figures D.9 and D.10 are referenced throughout this book.

```
.....DName++++++++++++EUDS.......Length+TDc.Functions+++++++++++++++++++++++++++++
         D F1              C                   Const(X'31')
         D F2              C                   Const(X'32')
         D F3              C                   Const(X'33')
         D F4              C                   Const(X'34')
         D F5              C                   Const(X'35')
         D F6              C                   Const(X'36')
         D F7              C                   Const(X'37')
         D F8              C                   Const(X'38')
         D F8              C                   Const(X'39')
         D F10             C                   Const(X'3A')
         D F11             C                   Const(X'3B')
         D F12             C                   Const(X'3C')
         D F13             C                   Const(X'B1')
         D F14             C                   Const(X'B2')
         D F15             C                   Const(X'B3')
         D F16             C                   Const(X'B4')
         D F17             C                   Const(X'B5')
         D F18             C                   Const(X'B6')
         D F19             C                   Const(X'B7')
         D F20             C                   Const(X'B8')
         D F21             C                   Const(X'B9')
         D F22             C                   Const(X'BA')
         D F23             C                   Const(X'BB')
         D F24             C                   Const(X'BC')
         D ENTER           C                   Const(X'F1')
         D HELP            C                   Const(X'F3')
         D ROLLDOWN        C                   Const(X'F4')
         D ROLLUP          C                   Const(X'F5')
         D PRINT           C                   Const(X'F6')
```

Figure D.9: Function key attention identification bytes.

```
.....DName++++++++++++EUDSFrom+++To+++++TDc.Fnctions++++++++++++++++++++++++++++++
         D PSDS            SDS
         D  PGMNAM             *PROC
         D  PARMS              *PARMS
         D  MSGID                 40     46
         D  MSGTXT                91    170
         D  JOBNAM               244    253
         D  USRPRF               254    263
         D  JOBNBR               264    269  0
```

Figure D.10: Program status data structure.

Index

Note: Boldface numbers indicate illustrations.